Please remember that this is a library book,
and that it belongs only temporarily to each
person who uses it. Be considerate. Do
not write in this, or any, library book.

Contemporary Theories
and
Systems in Psychology

Under the Editorship of Gardner Murphy

HARPER & ROW, PUBLISHERS, NEW YORK AND EVANSTON

Contemporary Theories

and

Systems in Psychology

BENJAMIN B. WOLMAN

Queens College

To my wife Roma and my daughter Danielle

Contents

PREFACE   ix

PART I   *Conditioning, Behaviorism, and Purposivism*

CHAPTER 1   *The Great Beginnings*   3

1. PSYCHOPHYSICAL PARALLELISM AND INTROSPECTIONISM   3
2. FUNCTIONALISM   21
3. EDWARD L. THORNDIKE: CONNECTIONISM   32

CHAPTER 2   *Conditioned Reflexes*   42

1. THE OBJECTIVE STUDY OF THE HIGHER NERVOUS PROCESSES   42
2. CONDITIONING   48
3. THEORY OF PERSONALITY   57
4. CONCLUDING REMARKS ON PAVLOV   62
5. VLADIMIR M. BEKHTEREV: REFLEXOLOGY   64
6. UNDER THE BANNER OF MARX AND PAVLOV   67

CHAPTER 3   *Behaviorism and Reductionism*   76

1. JOHN B. WATSON: PSYCHOLOGY AS THE SCIENCE OF BEHAVIOR   76
2. THE EARLY BEHAVIORISTS   85
3. KARL S. LASHLEY: BRAIN MECHANISMS   88
4. DONALD O. HEBB: ORGANIZATION OF BEHAVIOR   93

CHAPTER 4   *Neo-Behaviorism and Learning Theory*   98

1. EDWIN R. GUTHRIE: LEARNING BY CONTIGUITY   98
2. CLARK L. HULL: DEDUCTIVE BEHAVIORISM   105
3. B. F. SKINNER: INDUCTIVE BEHAVIORISM   125
4. EDWARD C. TOLMAN: PURPOSIVE BEHAVIORISM   140
5. GREGORY RAZRAN: EVOLUTIONARY LEVELS OF LEARNING   156
6. LEARNING THEORY INFLUENCED BY PSYCHOANALYSIS   165
7. SOME PROBLEMS IN THE THEORY OF LEARNING   173

CHAPTER 5   *Hormic and Holistic Theories*   177

1. WILLIAM MC DOUGALL: HORMIC PSYCHOLOGY   177
2. KURT GOLDSTEIN: HOLISTIC SYSTEM   184
3. JACOB R. KANTOR: ORGANISMIC PSYCHOLOGY   191

Summary of Part I   194

PART II *Psychoanalysis and Related Systems*

CHAPTER 6 *Psychoanalysis* 199

1. METHODOLOGY 199
2. POSTULATES 204
3. THE UNCONSCIOUS 212
4. THEORY OF INSTINCTS: EROS AND THANATOS 222
5. DEVELOPMENTAL STAGES 230
6. THEORY OF PERSONALITY 241
7. SOCIETY AND CULTURE 266
8. PSYCHOANALYSIS AS A PHILOSOPHY OF LIFE 273
9. CONCLUDING REMARKS ON PSYCHOANALYSIS 277

CHAPTER 7 *Individual and Analytic Psychologies* 283

1. ALFRED ADLER: INDIVIDUAL PSYCHOLOGY 283
2. CARL GUSTAV JUNG: ANALYTIC PSYCHOLOGY 298

CHAPTER 8 *New Theories in Psychoanalysis* 318

1. PSYCHOANALYSIS MODIFIED BY CLINICAL EXPERIENCE 318
2. OTTO RANK: THEORY OF WILL 319
3. FURTHER DEVELOPMENTS IN PSYCHOANALYSIS 326
4. PSYCHOANALYSIS AND STUDIES OF CULTURE 330
5. PSYCHOANALYSIS AND EXPERIMENTAL PSYCHOLOGY 337

CHAPTER 9 *Away from Freud: The Sociological School* 344

1. NEW WAYS IN PSYCHOANALYSIS 344
2. KAREN HORNEY: PSYCHOANALYSIS WITHOUT LIBIDO 346
3. ERICH FROMM: HISTORICAL AND ETHICAL PSYCHOANALYSIS 355
4. HARRY S. SULLIVAN: A THEORY OF INTERPERSONAL RELATIONS 368

Summary of Part II 385

PART III *Understanding, Gestalt, and Field Psychologies*

CHAPTER 10 *Phenomenology and Understanding Psychology* 391

1. KANT'S HERITAGE 391
2. PHENOMENOLOGY 397
3. WILHELM DILTHEY: THE UNDERSTANDING PSYCHOLOGY 399

CHAPTER 11 *Personalistic Psychology* 407

1. EDWARD SPRANGER: PSYCHOLOGY OF PERSONALITY 407
2. WILLIAM STERN: PERSONS VS. THINGS 410
3. GORDON W. ALLPORT: PERSONALITY TRAITS 417

CHAPTER 12 *Gestalt Psychology* 422

1. OPPOSITION TO ASSOCIATIONISM 422
2. GESTALT: THEORETICAL FOUNDATIONS 429
3. GESTALT: PERCEPTION, LEARNING, AND THINKING 435

CHAPTER 13 *Field Theory* 443

1. FIELD THEORY VS. CLASS THEORY 443
2. LEWIN'S MATHEMATICAL CONCEPTS 450
3. LEWIN'S LOGICAL CONSTRUCTS 456
4. LOCOMOTION: THEORY OF BEHAVIOR 462
5. THEORY OF PERSONALITY 470
6. GROUP DYNAMICS 475
7. FIELD THEORY AS AN EXPERIMENT IN THEORY CONSTRUCTION 481

Summary of Part III 491

PART IV *Psychology and the Scientific Method*

CHAPTER 14 *The Scientific Method* 497

1. FIRST PRINCIPLES 497
2. COLLECTION OF DATA 503
3. INTERPRETATION OF DATA AND THEORY CONSTRUCTION 516
4. THE LANGUAGE OF SCIENCES 527

CHAPTER 15 *Some Crucial Questions and Tentative Answers* 530

1. THE PROBLEM OF REDUCTIONISM 530
2. LUST FOR LIFE 535
3. BEYOND PLEASURE 546
4. PERSONALITY: A BIOSOCIAL APPROACH 548
5. CONVERGENCIES AND DIVERGENCIES 549

Summary of Part IV 552

BIBLIOGRAPHY 557

INDEX OF NAMES 601

INDEX OF SUBJECTS 607

Preface

        The objective of the present volume is to give a comprehensive picture of the contemporary psychological theory. The emphasis is on a general psychological theory, and this is why the contributions of Piaget, Rorschach, Terman, and many other great psychologists have been omitted. Moreover, Thorndike's contribution to educational psychology and Freud's studies in psychotherapeutic techniques had to be left out also. Priority was given to methodological problems such as concept formation, relationship to other sciences, methods of research, and interpretation of empirical data.

The entire volume is divided into four parts. The first three deal with the theories, grouped in accordance with the principle of "common roots." The first part includes all theories that started with the orientation toward natural sciences. Pavlov and Watson are the leading exponents of this trend. The second part deals with psychoanalytic theories. The third part discusses all the theories that have been influenced by Kant, Windelband, Husserl, Dilthey, and the cultural sciences.

The last part, Part IV, devoted to the scientific method, is the exposé of my own "philosophy" of psychology. It is divided into a discussion of methodological problems (Chapter 14) and into a series of theoretical proposals (Chapter 15).

The various theories are presented, whenever possible, in a chronological order of their appearance, but the logical order of presentation has been given priority over the chronological one. Since this volume is written primarily for the American universities, special attention has been given to American psychology.

It would have been rather easy to present all the theories in the same logical order, e.g., what each of them has to say on a series of questions prepared by the author of the book; this would result in a greater uniformity of presentation but it would not do justice to the respective theorists. Each theorist developed his theory on certain assumptions and in a certain logical order, and there could be no justification for forcing all theories into a uniform frame of reference, foreign to the philosophy of the men who developed them.

Each of the four parts of this book is followed by a summary which highlights the main problems discussed in the respective parts. Each summary gives a bird's-eye view on the issues under consideration and may serve as an introductory statement of these issues.

In a book of this type some repetitions have been inevitable. They have been kept at a reasonable minimum dictated by pedagogic considerations.

In presenting the ideas and theories of the various psychological theorists, I tried to be as objective as possible. Hence extensive quotations were introduced in support of the descriptive parts and sometimes even instead of them. Thus the reader has first-hand contact with the creative work of the theorists. New and deviant theories received more attention than faithful elaborations of the works of the masters. E.g., the rebellious Rank received several pages whereas the scholarly and orthodox psycho-analyst Fenichel did not.

A mere presentation would, however, not do justice to the purpose of this book. Critical comments and evaluations were part of the thinking and working through of the ideas of others. Moreover, the selection of authors, the assignment of space, the order, the emphasis on some of their works—all this was inevitably influenced by my preferences. An absolute impartiality could be accomplished only at the price of lack of analytic understanding. The way out was to be as impartial as possible while presenting the views of the various authors and then to make my own opinions explicit, which I did in my remarks at the end of each presentation.

For the idea of this book and the initiative to write it, for the friendly encouragement and competent advice during the work, I am immensely indebted to the editor of this series, Gardner Murphy. It took six years to implement the idea. Hundreds of volumes and thousands of journal articles in seven languages have been read, scrutinized, abstracted, and elaborated. Quotations have been made, whenever available, from existing English sources or translations. An extensive bibliography, covering almost the entire relevant literature, has been prepared for each chapter or even for a part of it. Letters have been written to several authors for the sake of clarifying their ideas, but the presentation of their theories is my own responsibility. I am grateful for the advice of my distinguished colleagues, among them K. Goldstein, O. Klineberg, G. Razran, B. F. Skinner, and R. L. Thorndike, some of whom read parts of this book.

In this work, as in any other creative work, there has been 1 percent of inspiration and 99 percent of perspiration. The perspiration has been mine, but the inspiration I owe to my wife. To her and to our daughter I dedicate this volume.

BENJAMIN B. WOLMAN

New York
February, 1960

PART I

Conditioning, Behaviorism, and Purposivism

CHAPTER 1

The Great Beginnings

1. PSYCHOPHYSICAL PARALLELISM AND INTROSPECTIONISM

The Common Roots

Contemporary psychological theory is far from uniform. Psychologists are divided to a greater extent than are physicists or biologists. Psychological systems differ in methods of research, in the selection of problems to be studied, and in conclusions arrived at. When psychologists, like all other scientists, form theories or general and comprehensive systems of interpretation of their empirical findings, the differences among them are quite apparent.

In the second and third decade of our century these differences reached a climax. Psychological theory looked like a huge field covered by several independent groups, some fighting one another, some oblivious of the existence of others. It seemed that there was no room for a psychology; instead, several psychologies, independently pursuing their own causes, working their way through with minimum or no cooperation with each other occupied the stage.[1]

Contemporary psychology witnesses the encouraging phenomenon of *rapprochement* between the respective schools. We are still miles away from a generally accepted psychological theory and still divided into groups of disciples of Adler, Freud, Goldstein, Jung, Hull, Köhler, Lewin, Pavlov, Skinner, Tolman, and others. However, an ever growing desire to learn from one another is predominant today, especially in the American psychology. There is a rapidly growing body of empirical evidence, both experimental and clinical, and an increasing desire to stick to it. Men belonging to various schools of thought have learned to respect the contributions made by their adversaries. There is an eager exchange of information concerning the empirical data and their theoretical in-

---

[1] Cf. Edna Heidbreder, *Seven Psychologies*, Century, 1933; C. Murchison (ed.), *Psychologies of 1925*, Clark University, 1925; C. Murchison (ed.), *Psychologies of 1930*, Clark University, 1930; Robert S. Woodworth, *Contemporary Schools of Psychology*, Ronald, 1931.

terpretation. Psychologists today show more willingness to test hypotheses developed independently by the various theorists, and a growing inclination to borrow concepts from one another.

In such an atmosphere the study of similarities and differences between the various systems seems to be both timely and useful. Before one introduces new hypotheses or proposes new syntheses, one should take a good look at what has been made available by scores of workers. A thorough examination of the contemporary psychological systems, which do not yet form a unified psychological theory, may be of great help to all interested in the future research and theory formation in psychology.

Presentation of the existing differences and the potential similarities may proceed in either of two directions. One may start from the *common roofs;* we do not have as yet a common roof for all the interpretations of empirical data in psychology, but there are, probably, several common roofs or similarities in the results independently obtained by research workers. Needless to say, there are still deep differences between the various systems. The last part of this book is devoted to a discussion of some of these potential common roofs or similar solutions of a given problem, but it would be rather precocious to present the contemporary psychological theory in a continuum of uniformities or similarities.

Thus, the present status of psychological theory seems to warrant grouping the respective systems according to their *common roots,* or similarities in the problems posed by the various theorists. Even when the suggested solutions are different (consider Hull and Skinner, Horney and Sullivan, Stern and Lewin), the respective groups of systems represent communities of problems, similarities in areas under consideration, and proximities in methodology. Apparently, these communities depend upon their historical background and the intellectual heritage presented to them by their respective father systems.

Accordingly, some consideration must be given to the fact that at the crossroads of the centuries the foundations were laid for the contemporary psychological theory. Thorndike published *Animal Intelligence* in 1898; Pavlov's theory of conditioning came four years later; McDougall's theory was published first in 1908; Wertheimer's famous experiment was conducted in 1912; Freud's *Interpretation of Dreams* appeared in 1900.

The present volume does not deal with history of psychology and we shall not describe in detail the events leading to the origin of the great systems.[2] We shall sketch them briefly, just to "set the stage" for the

---

[2] The reader is referred to the following excellent studies in history of psychology: Edwin C. Boring, *A History of Experimental Psychology* (2nd ed.), Appleton, 1950; J. C. Flugel, *A Hundred Years of Psychology* (2nd ed.), Duckworth, 1951; Gardner Murphy, *An Historical Introduction to Modern Psychology* (rev. ed.), Harcourt, Brace, 1950.

twentieth-century psychological theory which is the subject matter of this book.

Away from Metaphysics

The second part of the nineteenth century brought spectacular achievements in the natural sciences. Great empirical discoveries were followed by daring theories and supported by an unprecedented development of precise tools and methods of research. Chemistry and physics, biology, and especially its two branches, physiology and neurology, far outdistanced everything that men had known previously. The glorious march of science enhanced the general belief in the ultimate and not too distant solution of the eternal problems of man and universe.

The sweeping victories of the empirical sciences considerably influenced the thoughts of those research workers who unsuccessfully tried to unveil the mysteries of the human soul. Psychology was generally considered a branch of philosophy. For centuries philosophers strove to understand human deeds and thoughts and to disentangle the body-soul dichotomy.

In the early decades of the nineteenth century these efforts came to a deadlock. Psychologists felt that nothing new could be added without a radical change in the frame of reference. Psychology was a branch of philosophy, and a part in that division of philosophy that was called metaphysics. Logic dealt with the rules of reasoning, epistemology with problems of cognition, and metaphysics analyzed the existing universe. Problems of matter and spirit were in the realm of metaphysics. Psychology, often called "mental philosophy," was a legitimate province of metaphysical speculations.

Yet metaphysics could not offer a solution to the psychological problems. The only tool applied by metaphysics was speculation, and the only proof offered was either a superficial observation of some selected phenomena or reasoning not supported by empirical data. No wonder psychological theories were produced in considerable numbers and differed from each other as much as their underlying metaphysical systems did. There was no way to prove which of these theories told the truth, nor was there any method available that could disprove them.

From this point of view, the history of psychology until the latter part of the nineteenth century was rather a history of intuition, reflections, some arbitrary decisions, and just plain guesswork. Even great philosophers were unprepared to deal with psychological problems scientifically and they often made arbitrary statements concerning the nature of soul, emotions, and reasoning. The leading mental philosophy was the theory of "mental faculties," which distinguished the respective "powers" or "faculties" such as will power, reason, memory, and emotion. Actually nothing was explained or predicted by a mere conversion of verb into noun. The classification of functions by forces that supposedly perform them failed to bring home any explanation of the discussed processes and did not help to predict them.

Some philosophers tried to relate psychology to what was known about the physical world. These materialistic interpretations followed, as a rule, in the footsteps of their contemporary science in the belief that the universe is built of little indivisible parts—atoms.

Atoms can be combined to form larger bodies. By analogy, mental processes could be interpreted by combinations or *associations* of ideas. British philosophers, starting with John Locke and David Hume, emphasized the importance of sensory perceptions and associations. David Hartley in 1749, in his *Observations of Man, His Frame, His Duty, and His Expectations,* which was a fundamental work in associationism, developed a psychological theory largely influenced by Newton's system. Hartley believed that physical and mental processes are united in the functions of the sensory appartus. The muscular motions, sensations, and ideas can become associated in such a manner that the repetition of one of them will evoke the repetition of the other. James Mill in 1829 elaborated further the theory of associationism by temporal contiguity. Ideas of objects are reproduced the way the objects have been perceived. The later British associationists A. Bain and J. S. Mill introduced, besides contiguity in time, association by similarity, difference, etc.

Johann Friedrich Herbart: Metaphysics and Associations

The last great system of metaphysical psychology was produced by Johann Friedrich Herbart. Herbart maintained that his system was based on "metaphysics, empiricism and mathematics."[3] Herbart stood at the crossroads between the British and French philosophy of empiricism and the German idealism. His empiricism was a sort of armchair striving toward empiricism rather than a truly empirical research system. Actually no empirical studies were conducted by Herbart, and his entire system was based on sheer speculation.[4]

Herbart's metaphysics was materialistic. He considered the soul one of the indivisible units of the physical world (*das Reale*, "the real"). This unit, like all other physical bodies, acted somehow in accordance with the laws of Newton's physics. Action called for reaction and nature resisted destruction. The soul responded to external stimuli by defensive responses which, "for the lack of better terminology," Herbart called perceptions. These perceptory responses of the *Reale* (or soul) to ex-

---

[3] Johann F. Herbart, *Psychologie als Wissenschaft,* Unger, 1824–25.
[4] Benjamin B. Wolman, "Johann Friedrich Herbart," *Hachinuch Quarterly* (Hebrew), 1942, **15**, 1–23.

ternal stimuli are the self-preservatory defenses of the soul (*Selbster-haltungen*).

The quality of the responses depends on stimuli as well as on the nature of the human soul. All responses, i.e., perceptions, are forces. These forces can be measured, and Herbart developed a mathematical system for their measurement.

The soul is a unit of matter and its activities are units of force, said Herbart. His psychology closely corresponded to physics and dealt with matter and energy. Forces can be combined and divided, directed in the same or opposite direction, mutually related, or mutually excluded. These forces are *perceptions,* and Herbart's dynamics dealt with the struggle of perceptions for a place in human consciousness. The repressed forces are drowned in the unconscious; they strive toward the surface and sometimes attain it.

This mechanistic-associationistic system of forces was developed independently of any physiological consideration. If Herbart's system was reductionistic, it was a reductionism to physics. Organic sensations such as hunger and thirst are represented by the *Gemeingefühl*, which is the general feeling or self-perception of the organism. Moods are the product of these organic sensations.

Herbart's theory of learning combined the concept of physical forces with associationism. Herbart believed in the "apperceptive mass" or some superfactor in soul that accepted new perceptions and assimilated and combined them with the old ones. The apperceptive mass is the totality of conscious perceptions that controls the activity of the soul.

Herbart's system of metaphysical psychology was the last great one. Any new metaphysics could have produced a corresponding new system in psychology, but no proof could have been offered by Herbart or by anyone else. Psychologists had to make a crucial decision: either to detach psychology from metaphysics and follow in the footsteps of the rapidly progressing empirical sciences or to doom their own efforts to eternal sterility.

The choice was readily made.

The Impact of Physiology

Some scientific discoveries may not have a permanent value and may not be able to survive criticism, but they are to be considered from a historical point of view as necessary stages in the development of human thought. Actually each step forward is a product both of the ingenuity of an individual mind and of the state of minds in a given culture at a given time. One may dare to say that Einstein's theory of relativity is a product of this genius' insight and of all the research that had been done by his predecessors and made available to him.

Research workers live at a certain time and within a certain space and they create something out of something else. Even creative minds need knowledge and stimulation, and both are offered to them by past and contemporary generations.

The new era in psychology started with influences that came from without. Physics and biology were the sciences that stimulated the shift from speculative to empirical and scientific psychology.

The great discoveries in physiology and Darwin's theory of evolution broke ground for new scientific psychology. Physiology studied human and animal organisms and analyzed the functions of the nervous system. These studies were par excellence empirical and dealt with problems of sensation and perception. Both the method and the problem were challenges to psychology.

In 1830 Charles Bell published a book on the *Nervous System of the Human Body.* Bell had proved in 1811 that the ventral roots of the spinal cord are composed of motor nerves only, while the sensory nerve fibers compose the dorsal roots and the spinal ganglia. Actually the distinction between motor and sensory functions had been made much earlier, but Bell (and simultaneously and independently François Magendie) discovered that these functions are performed by different nerve fibers. This discovery later enabled psychologists to present mental life as a stimulus-response relationship. Moreover, Bell and Magendie showed that conduction in a nerve fiber goes one way only, the stimulus always being conducted from the sensory organ to the center of the nervous system and never in the opposite direction. The response continues from the center to the muscle, never from the muscle to the center. This Bell-Magendie "law of forward conduction" paved the way for the later concept of the *reflex* as a one-way action of the organism.

Bell's theory was taken up and developed by Johannes Müller and Ernst Heinrich Weber. Müller conducted a series of experiments on frogs that permitted the division of neural activity of a reflex into three stages, namely, (1) centripetal conduction, (2) connections within the center, and (3) response going from the center to the proper muscles.

Johannes Müller followed in the footsteps of Bell and concluded, logically, that since perception depends on sensory nerves the content of perception cannot depend on stimulus only but is colored by the nature of the sensory nerve and its ending (the sensory organ). This led to the law of "specific energies of sensory nerves," stating that "external agencies give rise to no kind of sensation which cannot also be produced by internal causes exciting changes in the condition of our nerves." For example, sensations of vision are "perceived independently of all external exciting causes. . . . The excited condition of the nerve is manifested, even while the eyes are closed, by the appearance of light or luminous flashes which are merely sensations of the nerve, and not owing to the presence of any matter of light, and consequently are not capable of illuminating any surrounding objects." The same external stimulus may give rise to different sensations in the various senses. "The mechanical influence of a blow, concussion, or pressure excites, for example, in the eye, the sensation of light and colours."[5]

A sensory nerve may fail to respond to certain kinds of stimuli, either because the nerve is irresponsive to them (such as ear to light), or because of insufficient stimulation. Whenever a sensory nerve responds to a stimulus, it is always the same sort of response. Eyes can never hear; they always see.

Müller was much concerned with measurement of the speed of nerve conduction; this problem gave rise later to the study of reaction time. Müller believed that nerve conduction was very rapid and could not see how such velocity could be measured in living organisms.

While Müller in Germany was concentrating on the sensory nerves, Pierre Flourens in France was doing experimental work on the brain. He extirpated various parts of the brains of pigeons and carefully observed the psychological impact of the extirpation. Flourens' studies led to later discoveries of localization of brain functions. On the other hand, Flourens' work encouraged a reductionist type of psychology. Flourens found that cerebral lobes perform the functions of perceiving, understanding, memorizing, and willing and that the cerebellum coordinates movements. Psychologists could feel now that the relationship between memory, understanding, etc., and the functions of the nervous system was firmly established. The next step was to conclude that psychology and physiology were mutually related and complementary disciplines, and that psychology might become a truly scientific branch of human knowledge.

Psychophysical Parallelism

Weber's findings have proved that discrimination of weight is finer when weight is perceived by several senses. The old division into five senses was to be replaced by a newer concept of a larger number of senses. In Weber's experiments the problem was whether differences in weight could be determined better by the subjects if they were instructed to lift the weights instead of just holding them. Obviously in lifting the weights the muscular sense was added to the senses that perceive weight.

The result was affirmative: the more senses used, the more precise sensation. Besides this main result, a highly significant discovery was made in the experiment, namely, that the discrimination of change in weight was not simply related to the increase in weight. Weber found that the ability to discriminate small differences in a stimulus depends

---

[5] Johannes Müller, *Handbook of Physiology* (W. Baly, trans.), (1st ed.), 1838–42.

not on the intensity of the stimulus alone but on a certain ratio between the difference and the standard weight used in the experiment.[6]

This important discovery led to the formulation by Fechner of the so-called *Weber's law*. Weber's study was a milestone in the experimental research on sensation and it encouraged more general concepts regarding the nature of perception.

In 1860 Gustav Theodor Fechner published a volume entitled *Elements of Psychophysics*.[7] Fechner believed that he had found the bridge connecting physical and mental phenomena. All stimuli belong to the physical world; all sensations belong to the mental. A definite relation between mental and physical was discovered by Fechner and presented in a mathematical formula. Thus the process of sensation became the cornerstone of the new scientific approach.

Fechner's method was experimental; his data were quantitative; the mathematical relations between physical stimuli and mental sensations were clearly stated. As stimuli increase in geometrical progression, sensations increase in arithmetical progression. This was the generalization of Weber's findings which became known as Weber's law.

Fechner also elaborated upon the concept of threshold. The *initial threshold* was the minimal intensity of a stimulus necessary for the stimulus to be perceived. The *differential threshold* was the minimum of increase or decrease in intensity of the stimulus necessary for the perception of these decreases or increases.

Besides his careful studies concerning thresholds, which are an important contribution to physiology and psychology, Fechner developed three psychophysical methods: (1) the method of *limits*, in which the stimuli in an experiment are ordered either in increasing or in decreasing intensity; (2) the method of *production*, in which the subject controls the stimuli according to the experimenter's instructions; (3) the *constant* method, in which stimuli act upon the subject in an irregular order.

The impact of Fechner's work was tremendous. His study of the sensory processes became the generally accepted frame of reference in psychology for at least half a century. Even Fechner's critics, says William James, "should always feel bound, after smiting his theories hip and thigh and leaving not a stick of them standing, to wind up by saying that nevertheless to him belongs the imperishable glory, of first formulating them and thereby turning psychology into an *exact science*."[8]

James felt that Fechner's method was arid and futile, but one should not forget that Fechner introduced a quantitative method into the study of sensation and developed a system of experimentation in psychology.

---

[6] Ernst Heinrich Weber, *De Tactu: Annotationes Anatomicae and Physiologicae*, 1834.

[7] Gustav Theodor Fechner, *Elemente der Psychophysik*, 1860.

[8] William James, *Principles of Psychology*, Holt, 1890, Vol. I, p. 549.

Another outstanding scientist, Hermann von Helmholtz, studied the speed of neural conduction in both motor and sensory nerves. He found that the speed of conduction in the motor nerve was thirty meters per second. Although his estimate was much below today's estimate, his experiments gave impetus to the very popular studies of "reaction time." Of even greater importance for the growing psychological science was his monumental work in vision and hearing. Helmholtz applied Müller's law of specific energies and developed a thoroughly experimental method for the study of sensory reactions.[9]

All the aforementioned studies had been done by physiologists. It was quite natural that since these studies dealt with sensation and perception they attracted psychologists. Psychologists were seeking a way to escape from metaphysics, speculation, and philosophy and hopefully looked toward physiology to provide the very much needed guidance in a scientific method of inquiry.

Wilhelm Wundt: "Scientific Psychology"

Ground was broken for an experimental psychology, but many were still doubtful whether the old "mental philosophy" could be converted into a "pure science." Obviously, physiologists did a good job with sensation and nerves; apparently, these issues were on the border of psychology. Yet many problems, such as soul-body dichotomy, mental faculties, and introspection, were unresolved. The road leading from a scientific and experimental physiology toward the promising scientific and experimental psychology was blocked by too many barriers.

It took a great deal of courage to establish in 1879, in Leipzig, the first psychological laboratory. A man was needed who was well versed in contemporary psychology, philosophy, and physiology and capable of combining all three. Wundt was the man. "The new discipline," he stated in his preface to the first edition of *Principles of Physiological Psychology* in 1873, "rests upon anatomical and physiological foundations." Psychology was to become an experimental science that dealt with measurable stimuli and responses.

Could psychology become an experimental science? This was just what Wundt undertook to establish. But first he had to get rid of the nonscientific past and sever the relationship between the young and growing "scientific psychology" and the metaphysical "mental philosophy." The problems, inherited from the past, that confronted him, were soul, mental faculties, and introspection.

The first two had to be discarded. The last had to be manipulated somehow so as to make it acceptable to the scientific psychology.

Wundt took a new road. He postulated that the subject matter of

[9] Hermann von Helmholtz, *Handbuch der Physiologischen Optik,* 1856–66.

psychology was experience, and psychology was an *Erfahrungswissen-schaft* ("science based on experience"). This, indeed, was a great de-cision, which enabled him to evade the never ending discussions of the nature of the immortal soul and its relationship to the perishable body. Psychology simply does not deal with this issue, said Wundt.

According to Wundt, the subject matter of psychology is the experience itself, the immediate experience. This experience has two sides. On the one hand, it is the immediate experience of the experiencing person.[10] On the other hand, the experiencing person is a living organism that responds to external stimuli. Sensations are the elements of immediate experience. But sensations are aroused when a sensory organ is stimu-lated and sensory neurons conduct the excitations to the centers of the nervous system. Excitations of neurons and sensations are parallel phenomena.

The method appropriate for psychological study must combine (1) physiological type of experimentation, (2) self-observation of the ex-periencing subject, and (3) analysis of cultural products of human minds.

Self-observation or introspection as it was applied by earlier psy-chologists could hardly yield any scientific data. Wundt was convinced that "the endeavor to observe oneself must inevitably introduce changes into the course of mental events—changes which could not have occurred without it, and whose usual consequence is that the very process which was to have been observed disappears from consciousness." Therefore, he suggested combining introspection with experimentation, because psychological experiment "creates external conditions that look towards the production of a determinate mental process at a given moment. In the second place, it makes the observer so far master of the general situation, that the state of consciousness accompanying this process remains approximately unchanged. The great importance of the ex-perimental method, therefore, lies . . . also and essentially in the further fact that it makes observation itself possible for us."[11]

Wundt recognized the limits of the experimental method. In his day experimentation could be applied to certain processes but not to all of them. Thus he cautioned (1892) that in every department of investiga-tion the experimental method takes on a special character, according to the nature of the fact investigated. In psychology only those mental phenomena which are directly accessible to physical influences, not the totality of psychological phenomena, can be made the subject matter of experiment.

---

[10] Brentano took up the matter and suggested a sharp distinction between the "act" and the "content" of experience (see Chap. 10).

[11] Wilhelm Wundt, *Principles of Physiological Psychology* (5th ed., translated), Macmillan, 1910, author's preface.

This remark clearly indicates that scientific and experimenta psychology had to be limited to a fraction of the total area. The higher mental processes, said Wundt, cannot be studied by the experimental method. They can be studied indirectly by investigation of their products. These products are language, customs, beliefs, tradition, social institutions—i.e., the totality of human culture. Wundt suggested three research methods in psychology: introspection, experiment, and interpretation of historical achievements. By combining all three methods, psychology could achieve its objectives and cover the entire area of research.

Mind, said Wundt, is not an object (like soul); it is a process; it is something that goes on and of which we are aware. Mind is the conscious process that takes place in accordance with laws of causation.

The elements of this conscious process are ideas, feelings, and impulses. The first come from outside, the second and third from the organism itself. Ideas are composed of sensations. Sensations can be distinguished according to their quality and intensity. They are conducted by afferent nerves. Each sensation is followed by a muscular movement controlled by an efferent nerve. Association is a connection between sensation and movement and not, as in the old associationism, a connection between ideas.

Feelings do not come from any sense organ. They can be divided into pleasant or unpleasant, tense or relaxed, excited or depressed. Feeling is the "mark of reaction of apperception upon sensory content; feeling is active."

Volition can hardly be distinguished from feeling: Will is some sort of feeling, namely, a decision or resolution feeling, that leads to overt action. Volition is the very essence of life; it represents the needs of the organism and its tendency to purposive behavior.

Wundt maintained that psychology studies the processes of sensation, volition, and feeling. The unity of all these processes is called consciousness. The processes take place, change, and pass away in one's consciousness. What one can observe is the momentary state of consciousness or the "actuality" of it.

The unifying factor in mental processes is *apperception*. Apperception means assimilation, inclusion of new sensations, and their synthesis in the totality of consciousness. Feeling is the reaction of apperception to new sensory content. Volition is the active response. Apperception is the focal point of consciousness.

Obviously the content of Wundt's findings could not match his scientific strivings. Wundt's psychology was a combination of quite a few scientific data based on physiology with some general impressions gained from daily observations. His system leaned heavily upon the metaphysics of Kant, Herbart, and Schopenhauer. Despite Wundt's endeavor to be thoroughly empirical, neither the introspectionist method nor the amount of empirical data permitted fruitful generalizations at this stage of the development of psychological research.

Edward Bradford Titchener: Structuralism

The man who developed and systematized the "scientific" psychology established by Wundt was his pupil Titchener at Cornell University. Titchener was perhaps more Wundtian than Wundt himself. He felt that psychology, like any other science, dealt with experience. The subject matter of psychology was a certain kind of experience: experience in relation to organism, in contradistinction to the biological experience of organism in relation to environment.

Psychology is "experience dependent on an experiencing person" in contradistinction to other sciences, which are independent of experiencing persons. The temperature in this room is 85° whether one experiences heat or not. If one feels uncomfortable, this feeling is experienced by and is dependent on the experiencing individual, Titchener said.

The method of psychology, as of any other natural science, is observation. But in psychology observation is directed by the experiencing subject to his own experiences—it is *introspection.* Yet no interpretation of psychological experience is possible without physiology. The nervous system offers the final answers to the puzzles of introspection, but the nervous system is not a part of psychology; it is physiology. Physiology is the science to which psychological data have to be related for causal explanation. Thus Titchener made clear his stand on the issue of psychophysical parallelism.

Psychology deals with mind as the total sum "of mental processes occurring in the lifetime of the individual," and consciousness is defined by Titchener as the sum of mental processes occurring "at any given present time." The basic units of consciousness are sensations, images, and affections. Sensations are the elements of perception, images are the elements of ideas, and affections are the elements of emotions. The first two elements can be classified according to four attributes: quality, intensity, duration, and clearness. Affections can be classified on the basis of the first three attributes only because they have no clearness. Titchener did not like Wundt's concept of apperception. It seemed to him unempirical to assume the existence of an interpreting function such as apperception. Instead he emphasized the "attention" which adds clarity to functions.

Titchener distinguished between description and explanation in psychology. Description is given by answering the questions What? and How? The first deals with facts and the second with combinations of facts and their interrelationships.

The explanation of psychological processes (the question Why?) requires investigation into the functions of the nervous system. Titchener can be considered a radical reductionist. Psychological phenomena can be described in mentalistic terms derived from self-observation, but ultimately they have to be related to physiological factors.

According to Titchener, "The primary aim of the experimental psychologist has been to analyze the structure of mind to ravel out the elemental processes from the tangle of consciousness. . . ." Psychology is morphological in its character. "I do not think that anyone who has followed the course of the experimental method, in its application to the higher processes and states of mind, can doubt that the main interest throughout has lain in morphological analysis, rather than in ascertainment of function. . . . The experimental psychology arose by way of reaction against the faculty psychology of the last century. This was a metaphysical, not a scientific, psychology. There is in reality, a great difference between, say, memory regarded as a function of the psychophysical organism and memory regarded as a faculty of the substantial mind."[12] Titchener did not exclude the study of functions; he only stressed that structure is prior to function, and unless the structure of mind is revealed, none of its functions can be understood.

Titchener was a rigorous research worker and adhered strictly to the rules of scientific inquiry within the area determined by Wundt and by himself. Since psychology is the science of consciousness, the main method of study is rigorous introspection conducted by especially trained subjects.

Concluding Remarks on Wundt and Titchener

Despite all criticisms, Wundt's and Titchener's work must be regarded as important scientific systems in psychology. The subject matter was well defined; it was the human consciousness. The research methods were empirical, namely, observation, experiment, and measurement. Since consciousness was best perceived by someone whose consciousness was observed, obviously the best method was self-observation or introspection. Surely this was, at that time, the best solution for psychology. Neither speculative philosophy nor objective physiology could have offered a better solution. Because of introspection, psychology could have joined the respectable family of sciences and yet retained its specific characteristics resulting from the subject matter—mind or consciousness. Never does the topic of a scientific inquiry determine whether the inquiry is scientific or not. In any case, why should science withdraw from dealing with a certain topic? The *method* of study, not the area, determines whether a given inquiry is scientific or not.

[12] Edward Bradford Titchener, "The Postulates of a Structural Psychology," *Philosophical Review,* 1898, **7,** 449–465.

To Wundt and Titchener the subject matter of psychology was the experience of the experiencing person. This was, for all purposes, as legitimate a topic for study as any other. This issue, said the introspectionists, eluded external observation, and the best research method was that of self-observation. In order to make this observation more dependable, a special type of well-trained subjects was used in Leipzig and Cornell psychological laboratories.

Here some objections can be raised. Is introspection the best research method available? Does introspection provide for scientific study of this experience, called "inner" by Sully, "immediate" by Wundt, or "dependent on the experiencing person" by Titchener? Does consciousness cover the entire field of interest to psychologists, and if so, does introspection fully cover this field?

Animal psychologists covered their field without introspection. Child psychologists criticized introspection on several counts. First, it had definite limitations, imposed by the selection of subjects, who had to be well trained and carefully chosen. At best, introspective psychology was the psychology of a certain type of individuals and of only those aspects of their mentality that were open to introspection. Finally, there was practically no way to prove the validity and reliability of introspective findings.

Moreover, introspectionist psychology tended to strengthen a dualistic approach to human problems. Muscles, bones, blood, circulation, perspiration, and digestion belonged to the physical world; memory, learning, emotions, and reasoning belonged to the mental world. No one could actually build a bridge between these two worlds. Descartes assumed that animals were machines, automats, with no mentality whatsoever. Human bodies, to be sure, do not differ from animal bodies; the only difficulty was that it was impossible to reduce human emotions and reasoning to some sort of physiology. Descartes arbitrarily assigned the seat of the human soul to the pineal gland.

Introspectionism was not in a position to offer any better solution to the body-soul dichotomy. Of course, consciousness was a better term than soul; it contained a promise for an empirical approach. Titchener presented the issue clearly and forcefully; the Why? question in psychology had to be related to physiology. Unfortunately, it was not easy to find the way from consciousness to the nervous system. Physiology did not know the answer at that time, nor does it today.

The Challenge to Introspectionism

Several factors prepared the ground for the new psychological systems, which have expanded the area of psychological inquiry far beyond the limits of "what is being given in the inner experience." The most outstanding factors were mental tests, animal psychology, and psychiatry.

Binet's and Simon's tests have been a major development in the method of psychological research. Binet and Simon dealt with highly complicated processes of reasoning, comparing, and problem solving, brought together under the name of intelligence. The idea of mental tests, originally published in 1905 in Paris, was accepted, modified, restructured, and developed by several outstanding psychologists such as Spearman and Burt in Great Britain, Stern and Meumann in Germany, Kuhlman, Thorndike, Terman, and Yerkes in the United States.

In the United States the mental measurement movement gained momentum in army testing in 1917, in the Stanford Revision of Binet's tests in 1916 and later 1937, and in several widely used mental scales.

Mental measurements do not require introspection, yet the higher mental functions are being measured in a manner that enables one to predict future behavior and achievements. Although the theoretical discussion concerning the nature of intelligence still goes on, there can be little doubt of the diagnostic and prognostic value of mental tests in educational, clinical, and industrial psychology. Moreover, intelligence tests served as ample evidence that highly important mental processes evade introspection and the best way of getting some insight into their nature is to put them to test. The "atmosphere" of mental tests was entirely different from the one prevailing in the laboratories of Wundt and Titchener. While Binet dealt with a problem of a school system which had to be solved, while Yerkes faced a huge "human engineering" problem for the armed forces of the United States, Wundt's and Titchener's experiments were remote from life, and as arid as they were scientifically rigorous.

The second challenge to the introspectionist psychology came from animal psychology. Charles Darwin's study on the *Expression of the Emotions in Man and Animals* (1872) contained many truthful although not too precise observations. Darwin ascribed to animals emotional reactions similar to human feelings, and often used anthropomorphic expressions in talking about animals. Despite their shortcomings, Darwin's observations suggest in an irresistible way that there is quite a similarity between animal and human behavior and human psychology can gain much by the study of animal behavior.

The introspectionists imposed on themselves the limitations of self-observed phenomena. The vigorous pursuit of animal studies broke down the artificial barriers between laboratory subjects capable of introspection and other men and animals. The "new" psychology was sometimes careless about detail and eager to apply unproved analogy; it often oversimplified the issues under consideration. For instance, Loeb's concept of tropism was eagerly introduced into psychology, while it still remains to be proved whether a scientific law derived from the study of the lower biological species can be applied to the interpretation of life processes in the higher organisms. Lloyd Morgan's *principle of parsimony* enchanted psychologists. It reads: "In no case may we interpret an action as the outcome of a higher psychical faculty, if it can be interpreted as the outcome of the exercise of one which stands lower in the psychological scale."[13] This principle, far from being proved, strongly influenced the thoughts of psychologists in the direction of a non-introspectionistic and reductionistic psychology.

Another challenge to introspectionism came from psychiatric sources. Charcot, Liebault, Janet, and others (Chap. 6) have proved beyond doubt that people may love and hate, remember and desire, without being aware of what is going on in their minds. A psychology which deals only with conscious phenomena fails to encompass the totality of mental processes. Moreover, a psychology limited to conscious processes is doomed to fail even in its limited area, because unconscious factors seem to determine the conscious ones. The studies of suggestion and hypnosis, the analysis of what is going on below the conscious surface, and later on the Breuer-Freud studies (see Chap. 6) of unconscious motivation have shown that a psychology limited to the study of "what is being given in the inner experience" is hardly capable of interpretation and prediction of human behavior.

The accusation of aridity and futility in psychological inquiry, despite its scientific strictness, came from several sources. Some psychologists sadly admitted that psychology will never be able to interpret problems of human life. Obviously the highly scientific laboratory in the style of Wundt or Titchener could hardly be of any help in the understanding of human interaction, of social relations and institutions, of cultural problems, and of historical events. No wonder the philosopher-psychologist Wundt had to make a compromise and to find room for a non-laboratory psychology. The founder of the first psychological laboratory openly admitted that the great problems of social psychology and culture could not be dealt with by his introspecto-experimental method.

The introspectionist psychology was forced by its own limitations to give way to an entirely different conception of what psychology was and how it should go about its business. The introspectionists used to view the surface of the human volcano and avoid the study of the hidden forces. They observed carefully the smoke of a fire, described and measured its direction and size, but avoided the fire itself.

First Solution: Conditioning, Behaviorism, and Purposivism

There were three ways out of the impasse. The first, initiated by functionalism, opened new vistas for psychology by the study of totality

[13] C. Lloyd Morgan, *An Introduction to Comparative Psychology*, W. Scott, 1894, p. 53.

of actions. Instead of the small fraction of phenomena observed by introspection, the theories of conditioning and behaviorism encompassed the entire behavior. In their effort to be rigorously scientific they had to expel introspection and introduce objective observation as practiced in physics and chemistry. Once psychologists embarked on a policy of radical empiricism, no room was left for the concept of consciousness. The introspectionists' slogan "What is being given in the *inner* experience" was translated into the behavioristic slogan "What is being given in the *outer* experience." Outer experience, overt behavior, stimulus and response, action and reaction—these were the new areas of psychology. Strangely enough, this new psychology did not include the old area but denied its existence. The continuity of psychological research was seriously impeded, and many interesting and insightful ideas of the past were lost in the rapidly growing research into overt behavior, patterned on the models applied in the natural sciences.

The new research was directed toward physiology of motor and glandular processes. It was highly reductionist and biologically minded.

Several possibilities opened up. One of them was functionalism, which considered psychological phenomena as biological tools in adjustment processes. Another was a physiological reductionism suggested by Pavlov and related systems. Another was a highly mechanistic interpretation of human life based on conditioning and physiology suggested by Watson. Still another was the purposive, biologically oriented behaviorism of McDougall. Then came Guthrie, Hull, Skinner, Tolman, Razran, and others in a series of efforts to select or to combine various interpretations of conditioning. All these diverse systems started from the rejection of structuralism on the grounds of opposition to consciousness and introspection. All of them applied some sort of reductionism and all went far from the narrow path of introspection toward the study of the total human behavior.

The Second Solution: Psychoanalysis and Related Systems

The second solution was offered by Freud and his associates. While the behavioristic school broadened the horizon by including the totality of overt behavior and the *Kultur* school included social and cultural factors, psychoanalysis attacked the problem from the point of view of causation. Freud posed the questions: What is going on below the surface? Why do people act the way they act? Behaviorism introduced a precise method of observation of overt behavior. The "understanding" psychology introduced historical and culture background and made it possible to see human behavior in perspective. Freud introduced the dynamic point of view inasmuch as "dynamics" indicates causation.

Psychoanalysis broke away from both organic psychiatry and reductionistic experimental psychology. It was a daring enterprise that violated the principles of academic psychology and psychiatry. Psychoanalysis started from the irrational elements in human behavior, such as dreams and psychopathological symptoms, and developed into an all-embracing theory of human nature. It penetrated into the unknown, into what is not given in introspection, into the unconscious, deep-lying forces. Self-observation became an outdated and inefficient method in view of the discovered mechanisms of rationalization, denial, reaction formation, and projection.

In interpreting human behavior psychoanalysis went farther than the two other schools. As in any other theory, controversies and schism were unavoidable. Jung and Adler were the early deviants from Freudism, and scores of psychoanalysts interpreted human nature in a manner quite different from the one proposed by Freud. Recently more emphasis has been put on environmental factors, and the great students of the social and cultural issues, Kardiner, Horney, and Sullivan, developed their own frame of reference based on the Freudian concepts of unconscious motivation.

Third Solution; Understanding, Gestalt, and Topological Psychologies

The third way out was indicated by followers of Immanuel Kant. W. Windelband, E. Husserl, and especially Wilhelm Dilthey attacked the Wundt-Titchener type of psychology from a standpoint diametrically opposed to that of behaviorism. What was going on in the psychological laboratory was merely a "description" of certain phenomena, but never an "understanding" of them (see Chap. 10). Dilthey distinguished between humanities (*Geisteswissenschaften*) and natural sciences (*Naturwissenschaften*). While the latter apply mathematics the first apply psychology. At that time Windelband emphasized that the natural sciences were *nomothetic* or law seeking whereas the cultural sciences dealt with individual and unrepeatable *idiophenomena*. Dilthey went farther and emphasized that psychology cares for the individual; its main objective is not to describe or analyze but to "understand" (*verstehen*) him.

Actually Dilthey took up the problem as it was posed by Wundt. Wundt did not believe that involved mental processes could be studied by the experimental method. The lower mental processes, according to Wundt, can be studied by experiments that follow strictly the pattern set by physiological experiments; but no higher mental processes can be studied in the same way; Wundt called Külpe's experiments in thinking "mock experiments." History of civilization or of social institutions, law, religion, and the arts are areas in which a study of the higher mental processes can be successful.

Dilthey felt that psychology should be the method of cultural sciences, as mathematics is the method of natural sciences. It was a challenging idea, but at that time psychology was not ready to play this distinguished role. History, anthropology, and sociology did not wait. E. Spranger reversed the order and developed psychological concepts derived from social and cultural sciences. His psychological types are some sort of "reductionism" to the study of social institutions.

The dichotomy between natural and cultural sciences continued to perplex psychologists. W. Stern tried to resolve it in his treatise on person versus object, *Person und Sache* (Chap. 11). The gestalt psychologists tried to solve the problem by ascribing *Gestalt* to the physical world (Chap. 12). Lewin's field theory was a "working through" of Windelband's theory of idiophenomena (Chap. 13).

These are the three main sources of contemporary psychology: Pavlov, Freud, and neo-Kantianism. In planning this book we grouped the various systems around their common roots in one of the three great "father" systems of contemporary psychology. It may be rather difficult to find substantial similarities in conclusions reached by the respective systems grouped together. But the problems dealt with by them are rooted in one of the three father systems, and the present book was divided accordingly.

We shall start with the first group of systems. The functionalists and E. L. Thorndike are the forerunners of this group.

2. FUNCTIONALISM

Under the Aegis of Biology

Under the impact of Charles Darwin some psychologists turned to biology. Biology seemed to be better prepared than any other science to resolve psychological problems. Biologists have regarded humans as living organisms that struggle for survival, adjust to environment, and crave satisfaction. Hardly any other idea could lead to more fruitful studies in psychology. Psychology followed in the footsteps of biology and grasped the significance of mental functions as related to the totality of the functions of life.

The biologically oriented workers introduced the problems of heredity and environment, of adjustment to life and fight for survival. Living organisms display certain flexibility; they may change, develop, and learn. How do they learn? Are the acquired changes inherited, as Lamarck suggested? Biologists are split on this issue. Should these changes be interpreted by a purely mechanistic causation and the "survival of the fittest," as Darwin and Huxley saw it? Or is there perhaps some general aim and purpose in life, as Driesch explained?

Whether psychologists sided with Lamarck or Darwin, Spencer or Weismann, Driesch or Huxley, whether they accepted a mechanistic or a vitalistic point of view, these have been relevant problems that led to the development of the respective psychological systems. Almost all psychologists became increasingly aware of the vitality of this research area. Human psychology became an indispensable area in the study of the human species. Anatomy and physiology analyzed the human organism in its details. Psychology dealt with human life in its totality; it became par excellence a molar and functionalistic science.

The shift to general biology represents the second great revolution in the short history of psychology. At the first revolution psychology broke away from philosophy and, owing to the support received from physiology and neurology, became a respectable, though a bit arid, empirical science. Now, the great ideas of evolution, adjustment, learning, instincts, fight for survival, recapitulation, heredity, etc., opened new horizons for psychology.

The Forerunners of Functionalism

Darwin, Spencer, and Galton introduced the biological principles of evolution and adjustment into psychology. In 1855 Spencer published his *Principles of Psychology.* Evolution is a change "from indefinite, coherent homogeneity to a definite, coherent heterogeneity through continuous integrations and differentiations," says Spencer. These changes are functions of a continuous process of *adjustment* to external conditions. Each animal responds in a certain way to his environment; the higher the place of a species in the ladder of evolution, the more complex and differentiated are its responses. The simplest reactions are unflexible and represent a gross adjustment to environment. These are the *reflexes.* Higher animals have *instincts,* which are "compound reflex actions."

The higher the species, the more complex and more flexible is its behavior. The higher functions evolve from the lower ones in the process of adjustment. Mental activities are part of this process and thus are biologically useful. Spencer says that the more useful a function is, the more pleasant it is. The useful functions, even if acquired in one's life span, are transmitted by heredity to later generations.

Spencer's theory is associationism. "The persistence of the connection between states of consciousness is proportionate to the persistence of the connection between the agencies to which they answer." It is, however, an associationism rooted in biology and laws of heredity.

In his emphasis on pleasure in adjustment Spencer is, in a way, a forerunner of Sigmund Freud.

Charles Darwin's *Origin of Species* was published in 1859 and his *Expressions of the Emotions in Man and Animals* in 1872. Darwin maintained that life is struggle for existence. Better-equipped individuals have more chance for survival and for reproduction. Human behavior is *goal directed*. Those who adjust better to outer conditions have better chances for survival. Psychology has to study the ways of human adjustment. Emotions are biologically useful functions, and their overt expression serves a definite purpose. For example, showing of teeth in anger indicates the power of the teeth and readiness to fight; crying is calling for help; etc. All mental activities should be interpreted as adjustive functions of the organism.

Francis Galton studied differences in men and related them to hereditary factors. His studies on *Hereditary Genius* appeared in 1869. Galton applied statistical method to genetics, and his studies of individual differences led to the development of *mental tests* and methods of *correlation* between mental traits. Galton was interested in the improvement of the human race. His utilitarian point of view in scientific inquiry has had considerable influence upon psychologists in pointing to the applicability of psychological inquiry to the betterment of human life.

William James: Functionalism and Pragmatism

The man who grasped the significance of the biological-utilitarian approach to psychology and posed to psychology the question: What for? was William James.

James was a psychologist, biologist, expert in anatomy and physiology, and above all philosopher. His psychological theory cannot be properly understood unless it is viewed in the larger context of his philosophical system. His credo was: "My thinking is first and last and always for the sake of my doing."[14]

One aspect of James' philosophy was of notable importance for psychological theory. Virtually all contemporary psychologists strive toward a monistic interpretation of the human organism and behavior and face the difficult problem of reductionism. James was par excellence a non-reductionist. He was a *radical empiricist* and recognized the multiplicity and diversity of the universe. He saw no way to reconcile the empirically perceived diversity; to him reality was both unity and diversity. Therefore, although "no mental modification ever occurs which is not accompanied or followed by bodily damage,"[15] both mental and somatic processes are two respective sides of life.

Life is a process of adjustment. All we do, we do in the direction of better adjustment. It should be clear that "the distribution of consciousness shows it to be exactly such as we might expect in an organ added for the sake of steering a nervous system grown too complex to regulate

[14] James, *op. cit.*, Vol. II, p. 333.
[15] *Ibid.*, Vol. I, p. 5.

itself," said James. Consciousness represents the experiences, or the "phenomena" of mental life, while the organism and particularly the nervous system are the "conditions" of the mental life.

Consciousness is a product of evolution. It has "been evolved, like all other functions, for a use—it is to the highest degree improbable *a priori* that it should have no use." This use can be seen in various ways.

As a radical empiricist James challenged the unity of personality He believed that each individual has more than one "self." The material self is the totality of all material possessions, including one's own body, property, money, etc. Elation and depression are the emotional responses to the respective increase or decrease of possessions. The social self depends on identification with various social groups such as family, occupation companions, etc. Rise and decline in social status causes the same shift in emotions as rise and decline of the material self. The spiritual self includes all mental dispositions together; it is a sort of continuity of the various activities performed by an individual. The spiritual self is the center of action and adjustment.

No one is a homogeneous personality. "With most objects of desire," says James, "physical nature restricts our choice to but one of many represented goods, and even so it is here. I am often confronted by the necessity of standing by one of my empirical selves and relinquishing the next. . . . To make any of them actual, the rest must more or less be suppressed. So the seeker of his truest, strongest, deepest self must review the list carefully, and pick out the one on which to stake his salvation. All other selves thereupon become unreal, but the fortunes of this self are real."[16]

James was fully aware of the complexity of the problem. He knew the problems of abnormal psychology and was well acquainted with the research work of French psychiatry. There are unconscious states, split consciousness, amnesias, and morbid changes in personality. Thus James could not agree to Wundt's or Titchener's concepts; consciousness is, James said, a stream of thought, a changing continuum, a unity in diversity, and nothing else.

Irrational elements pervade our life. Even reasoning serves action, and actions are determined by needs, ends, and purposes. The way in which concepts are formed depends upon the conceiving person, and the "whole function of conceiving, of fixing, of holding fast to meanings has no significance apart from the fact that the conceiver is a creature with partial purposes and private ends."[17]

It is quite understandable that James was much concerned with learn-

[16] *Ibid.*, p. 309.
[17] *Ibid.*, p. 482.

ing, emotions, and motivation and paid considerable attention to the acquisition of habits. Habits are acquired by association. Contiguity is the basic law of association, defined by James as follows: "When two elementary brain-processes have been active together or in immediate succession, one of them, on reoccurring, tends to propagate its excitement into the other."[18] James' theory of learning did not deviate from the pattern established by the associationists. His associationism was mechanistic and non-introspectionistic and led to behaviorism.

James' theory of memory rejected the "faculty psychology" notion that memory is a mental faculty or power. He proved by experiments that memory cannot be improved by practice; practice may improve the retention of the practiced material only. The implication was that the idea of a memorizing power could not be accepted.

James introduced a systematic and classified list of instincts. He strove to find in the biological theory of evolution the answer to the dynamics of human nature. Instincts are inherited, common to a given species, usually useful and pleasant patterns of behavior. They are the ways of behavior. "Every creature likes its own ways, and takes to following them as a matter of course. . . . It is not for the sake of their utility that they are followed, but because at the moment of following them we feel that that is the only appropriate and natural thing to do."[19] Again James emphasized usefulness and pleasure as motives of behavior.

James' theory of emotions was a logical outcome of his evolutionistic-biological approach. It is the well-known James-Lange conception of emotions as a function of bodily changes, mainly physiological changes in muscles and viscera. "We feel sorry because we cry, angry because we strike, afraid because we tremble, and not that we cry, strike, or tremble because we are sorry, angry, or fearful, as the case may be. Without the bodily states following on the perception, the latter would be purely cognitive in form, pale, colorless, destitute of emotional warmth."[20]

It is hard to say whether James developed a new psychological theory. His original contribution, the theory of emotions, aroused much controversy and has been largely disproved by later studies. The greatness of James does not lie in this or any other particular research. He influenced psychology by his new and fresh approach to the problem, by his philosophical idea of pragmatism and his perception of psychological function as a part in the process of adjustment. What for? was the question he asked. And even if he himself could not furnish the answer, he guided psychologists in posing this fruitful question.

[18] *Ibid.*, p. 566.
[19] *Ibid.*, Vol. II, p. 386.
[20] *Ibid.*, p. 450.

John Dewey: Functionalism and Instrumentalism

It is often said that functionalism came to life with the publication of John Dewey's paper on the "Reflex Arc Concept" in 1896. In this paper Dewey said: "The older dualism between sensation and idea is repeated in the current dualism of peripheral and central structures and functions; the older dualism of body and soul finds a distinct echo in the current dualism of stimulus and response." Dewey complained about the "rigid distinctions" between sensations, thoughts, and acts and continued as follows: The reflex arc idea "leaves us with a disjointed psychology," which deals with sensation or peripheral stimulus, idea or central process, and motor response or act, as "three disconnected existences, having to be somehow adjusted to each other, whether through the intervention of an extra-experimental soul, or by mechanical push and pull."[21]

According to Dewey, one may distinguish between stimulus and response, but the distinction must be functional, not existential. This distinction is made for the convenience of research and should not lead to a misconception of reality. There is but one *process of adjustment* of the organism to the environment, and in this purposeful process stimuli and responses are a chain of deeds and not separate entities.

It would be rather difficult to understand Dewey's contribution to the psychological theory without paying due attention to his philosophical inquiries. In fact, Dewey's philosophical studies reached greater prominence and had more influence than his psychological studies.

Dewey was one of the leading American pragmatists; he could agree with Peirce and James that action precedes knowledge. Life is action. And what is the role of thinking?

Here comes Dewey's *instrumentalism*. People think in order to live. Thinking is an instrumentality which is used by man "in adjusting himself to the practical situations of life." Knowledge results from human effort to survive. Knowledge is a weapon in the fight for survival or a tool in the effort for adjustment. The business of knowledge is to help men to clarify their ideas in regard to nature, society, and ethics. "The prime function of philosophy is that of rationalizing the possibilities of experience, especially collective human experience."[22]

Dewey was mainly a social philosopher concerned with the well-being of men and their physical, social, and moral adjustment. Man was the center of Dewey's philosophy. Man and his adjustment to life, or "man's traffic with nature," was the main problem in his philosophy and psychology.

Life is learning, Dewey said, and this idea influenced the studies of

[21] John Dewey, "The Reflex Arc Concept in Psychology," *Psychological Review*, 1896, 3, 357–370.
[22] John Dewey, *Reconstruction in Philosophy*, Holt, 1922, p. 122.

Thorndike, Watson, and all the neo-behaviorists. The problem of learning was considered by Dewey to be the focal issue in psychology. "The child learns," he wrote, "to avoid the shock of unpleasant disagreement, to find the easy way out, to appear to conform to customs which are wholly mysterious to him in order to get his own way, that is to display some natural impulse without exciting the unfavorable notice of those in authority."[23]

What is innate is impulse. Dewey rejected the theory of specific and schematized instincts. He suggested instead that "impulses are highly flexible starting points for activities which are diversified according to the ways in which they are used. Any impulse may become organized into almost any disposition according to the way it interacts with surroundings. Fear may become abject cowardice, prudent caution, reverence for superiors or respect for equals. . . . The actual outcome depends upon how the impulse of fear is interwoven with other impulses. This depends in turn upon the outlets and inhibitions supplied by the social environment."[24]

Impulses may find direct, blind, unintelligent, and infantile outlets. They may be modified by learning, i.e., changed by interaction with environment. These modified impulses are called by Dewey "sublimated," which corresponds, although not too closely, to what was called "sublimation" by Freud (cf. Chaps. 4 and 6). In Dewey's terminology sublimation means something like social adjustment through learning. For example, anger may be converted into "an abiding conviction of social injustice to be remedied, and furnish the dynamic to carry the conviction into execution."

The mechanisms that control the interaction between organism and environment are habits. Habits, Dewey said, "assimilate objective energies, and eventuate in command of environment."[25] The impulses carry the energy or "dynamic" and, when they are incorporated in dispositions, they "furnish the dynamic."

Habits are complex and flexible mechanisms of behavior. Dewey distinguished between "routine" habits and "intelligent" habits. Routine habits offer satisfactory adjustment to more or less static environment. When environment is changing, a more flexible adjustment is necessary. Intelligence is the flexible habit that guides the organism in a better adjustment to a changing situation.

The most important function of intelligence is "reflective thought." "The function of reflective thought is to transform a situation in which there is experienced obscurity, doubt, conflict, disturbance of some sort, into a situation that is clear, coherent, settled, harmonious. . . . When

[23] John Dewey, *Human Nature and Conduct*, Holt, 1922, p. 98.
[24] *Ibid.*, p. 95.
[25] *Ibid.*, p. 15.

a situation arises containing a difficulty or perplexity, the person who finds himself in it may take one of a number of courses. . . . He may face the situation. In this case, he begins to reflect."[26]

Dewey distinguished several stages in the process of thinking as follows:

1. Suggestions, in which the mind leaps forward to a possible solution.
2. Intellectualization of the difficulty into a problem.
3. Hypothesis, the use of one idea after another as a leading idea.
4. Reasoning, the mental elaboration of the idea or supposition.
5. Verification or experimental corroboration obtained by testing the hypothesis.

As said before, Dewey's influence in psychology is more related to his broadly conceived philosophy than to his specific contributions to psychological research. First, his concept of instrumentalism paved the road for the functionalist approach to and purposivistic conception of psychology. Then, the emphasis on adjustment and learning led to a series of fruitful investigations in several laboratories. Dewey was opposed to the structuralists' "anatomy of mind" and introduced the molar point of view. And last, Dewey's theory of scientific inquiry stimulated the minds of Hull, Tolman, and scores of other research workers in psychology. It is worth while to mention that Dewey was in favor of operationism (Chap. 4) and, in a way, prepared the ground for this method of investigation.

Angell, Carr, and Robinson

The most outspoken exponent of functionalism was James Rowland Angell. Angell forcefully emphasized the evolutionary aspects in psychology. Human mind, he said, grows and develops, as centuries go by, in the continuous effort of better adjustment to environment. Angell regarded sensations, emotions, and acts of will as expressions of adaptation of the organism to its environment. To him functionalism was a turning point rather in the interests than in methods: He believed that the fundamental psychological method is introspection, but we are able to supplement introspection by immediate objective observation of other individuals.[27]

This shift in interests had a tremendous impact upon the future development of psychological theory. Instead of dealing with mental structures, functionalism considered human life an integral part of the biological processes of change and adjustment. Angell wrote: "We shall

[26] John Dewey, *How We Think*, Heath, 1933, p. 100.
[27] James R. Angell, *Psychology, An Introductory Study of the Structure and Function of Human Consciousness*, Holt, 1904, p. 4.

adopt the biological point of view. . . . We shall regard all the operations of consciousness—all our sensations, all our emotions, and all our
acts of will—as so many expressions of organic adaptations to our environment, an environment which we must remember is social as well
as physical. . . ."[28]

Angell said that the structuralists dealt with the "what" psychology,
while the functionalists dealt with the "how" and "why" psychology.
Psychological functions are "accommodary" or adjustment services. Very
little can be gained by the study of mental elements; in order to understand human life one has to consider the totality of the organism. A molar
and not a molecular approach is needed in psychology. It is not the elements of consciousness that should serve as the topic for psychological
inquiry but the functions of the mind as a mediator between organism
and environment.

Since adjustment is the main problem of functionalism Angell and
the other functionalists have attached great importance to the process of
modification of behavior. This led to an increased interest in habit
formation and learning theory, which became the main concern of Carr,
Robinson, Melton, McGeoch, and all other functionalists.

Harvey A. Carr believed that functionalism is a continuation and modification of associationism and that adaptation to the environment is the
main idea of functionalism. In the adaptive process motives act upon
the organism; there is always a sensory situation and a response to the
stimulus. Response is the activity that leads to a change in the entire
situation in the direction of satisfaction of the motive. Once the motive
is satisfied, the organism does not react to it any longer. The object by
which the motive is satisfied, e.g., food in experiments with hungry
animals, is called an incentive. A motive represents a genuine need; the
satisfaction of a motive is necessary for the survival and the well-being
of the organism. When the adaptive act is completed the action of the
motivating stimulus is terminated and the goal of the response accomplished.

Together with Edward S. Robinson, Carr introduced a series of new
laws of association. Carr believed that his functionalism represented a
new, quantitative, and experimental development of the associationist
psychology. In his textbook Carr emphasized the adaptive nature of
human behavior.[29] Every organism needs food, but food is not always
easily available and the organism must actively seek it. Some organisms—
infants, for example—are unable to satisfy their own needs. Sometimes
conflicting needs arise and a solution to the conflict has to be found.
The process of adjustment is a problem-solving process in which the

---

[28] *Ibid.*, p. 7.
[29] Harvey A. Carr, *Psychology, A Study of Mental Activity*, Longmans, Green,
1925.

organism must find its way in accordance with its own needs, its responsive equipment, and the environment.

Carr's ideas have been continued by Edward S. Robinson. Instead of stimulus and response Robinson suggested the terms of "instigating" and "instigated" actions. Among the instigating actions are sensory processes and sensations, perceptions, and ideational processes. The instigated processes include glandular secretion, perceptions, ideas, feelings, and muscular movements.

Robinson distinguished between laws of learning, called laws of "associative formation," and laws of recall and recognition, called laws of "associative revival." He believed that the strength "of any associative connection is a function of the conditions of contiguity, frequency, vividness, and so on, obtaining at the time the association was formed."[30]

Robinson introduced several new laws of association. He believed that association takes place in accordance with the laws of contiguity, assimilation, frequency, intensity, duration, context, acquaintance, composition, and individual differences. "It is my conviction that the facility of associative fixation is a function of all the factors enumerated. Probably several specific relationships are involved for each named factor and almost certainly there are other factors that have not been included in this list. But, if the assumption that these factors are important determiners of association be correct, then there are 'laws' of these factors whether our knowledge of them is definite or not."[31]

Robinson's associationism is not associationism in the traditional connotation of this term. For a functionalist the functions of motivation, adaptation to the environment, and motor activities are the main vehicles of human behavior, but associations are the main method by which the human mind learns and adapts.

Robert Sessions Woodworth: Dynamic Psychology

A. A. Roback in his biography of James[32] and later in his *History of American Psychology*[33] has said that in 1908 James wrote with a pencil on page 58 of Titchener's *Lectures on the Elementary Psychology of Feeling and Attention:* "shows how different the dynamic point of view is from the structural." Roback remarks that though Dewey used the word "dynamic" as early as 1884, this term was not much in use in 1908.

James' and Dewey's theories invited the term "dynamic." If "dynamic" is related to change and interprets the causal factors in change, functionalism is undoubtedly a theory of dynamics. If structuralism could be

---

[30] Edward S. Robinson, *Association Theory Today*, Appleton-Century, 1932, p. 66.
[31] *Ibid.*, p. 124.
[32] A. A. Roback, *William James: His Marginalia, Personality and Contribution,* Science and Art, 1942, p. 55.
[33] A. A. Roback, *History of American Psychology*, Library Publishers, 1953, p. 146.

compared to mental anatomy or histology, which dealt with the "elements" of mind and consciousness, functionalism could be compared to physiology.

Woodworth's dynamic psychology was, in a way, an outcome and continuation of the teachings of James and Dewey. The main question to be resolved by psychology was not what humans and animals feel and do, but *why* they feel and act in a certain way. Why, the physicist would ask, do trains move? And his answer points to the *dynamic* factor, the electricity. Analogously, psychology cannot be confined to the observation of behavior but must deal with the dynamics or causation of behavior. The stimulus-response chain does not answer the question. A very important link is missing, and Woodworth undertook to consider it. It was the living organism that had to be interpolated between the stimulus and the response. The stimulus stimulates the organism, which responds to the stimulus in accordance with its inner drives. Food stimulates the organism, provided the organism is hungry. Each organism has native capacities to do things in a certain way. The stimulus-response relation is the *mechanism* of behavior, but the driving power behind it is the *drive* that activates the mechanism.

Woodworth preferred the idea of general motivation as opposed to the idea of special instincts proposed by McDougall. Even more was Woodworth opposed to McDougall's conception of teleological motivation (Chap. 5). "The question is, whether the mechanisms for the thousand and one things which the human individual has the capacity to do are themselves wholly passive, requiring the drive of these few instincts, or whether each such mechanism can be directly aroused and continue in action without assistance from hunger, sex, self-assertion, curiosity."[34]

A mechanism may act as a drive if it facilitates and reinforces another mechanism. Acquired habits may act as driving forces or drives which may lead to new actions.

Woodworth was opposed both to Titchener's conception that psychology has to study mainly sensations and perceptions and to Watson's denunciation of introspection and limiting psychology to the study of motor and glandular behavior. Woodworth felt, as did all other functionalists, that psychology should embrace both behavior and consciousness in "an unbroken series of events." The S-R chain was modified by Woodworth into an S-O-R chain, O standing for the structures and functions of the organism. Psychology and physiology do not study two parallel processes, but one and the same "real process," and the motivating drives can be organic, such as hunger or fatigue, or not organic, such as self-assertion or curiosity.

Woodworth's dynamic psychology introduced an important emphasis

[34] Robert S. Woodworth, *Dynamic Psychology*, Columbia University, 1917, p. 67.

upon motivation and came quite close to the Würzburg school (Chap. 12) in its efforts to find out the driving forces behind human actions.

In a way, Woodworth's motivation theory was a forerunner to Tolman's "intervening variable" (Chap. 4). To the observable stimulus and response factors Woodworth added the drives that act as motivating forces within the organism and together with the stimuli represent the totality of factors that cause action.

Concluding Remarks on Functionalism

Titchener said that structural psychology dealt with facts "as they are" while functional psychology dealt with "what it is for." The purposivism of the functionalists was considered by Titchener a serious deviation from the scientific method. He believed that the business of science was to investigate things as they were without asking questions of aim or purpose. Titchener's criticism is probably only partially justified because some facts cannot be understood without the "what for" question. To this category belong all facts or activities which are goal directed. If a child raises a hand to pick up a piece of candy or to hit a playmate, a purely factual description of hand movements will miss the most relevant issue in this purposeful act.

Moreover, structuralism did not deal with all facts but mainly with those which could be perceived in introspection. Structuralism confined itself to a very precise study of a fraction of what should be regarded as the legitimate area of psychological research.

Functionalism prepared the ground for behaviorism and conditioning. Though the early functionalists preferred introspection, all of them admitted that the processes of adjustment could be observed from without and not necessarily by introspection. Learning and habit formed the main issue in adjustment, and this is precisely why Angell and all other functionalists attached so much importance to these processes.

On the other hand, functionalism led to purposivism; not only the behavioristic-mechanistic system of Watson but the purposive-hormic psychology of McDougall originates in functionalism. The "what for" question posed by the functionalists was taken up and answered by McDougall.[35]

3. EDWARD L. THORNDIKE: CONNECTIONISM

Historical Roots

Associationism has a long history, starting with the Aristotelian laws of association, the laws of similarity, difference, contiguity in time, and

[35] Cf. F. V. Smith, *Explanation of Human Behavior,* Constable, 1951, chap. 6.

contiguity in space. The English associationists in modern times based their theory mainly on contiguity in time.

David Hartley in *Observations on Man*, published in 1749, regarded simple sensations as elements of mental life closely interrelated with the sensory apparatus and therefore dependent upon somatic processes. Alexander Bain developed further the neurological theory of associations. He said: "As the brain advances in size and in complication, there is an advance not merely in those lower functions called Reflex and Automatic, but of the higher functions named intelligence, emotion and will. . . . With development of the brain proceeds, *pari passu*, development of the mind."[36]

Bain did not deal with associations in mentalistic terms. Being Darwin's and Spencer's contemporary and follower, he applied the mechanistic theory of evolution to psychology. He believed that the evolution of mind is a result of the development of the nervous tissues and their connections. The more complex these connections, the more complex the mental processes developed.

Associationism was the leading idea in the psychology of the nineteenth century. Herbart's metaphysico-mathematical system of psychology was permeated with associationism. The first truly experimental study of memory by Ebbinghaus in 1885 was based on associationism. Even Freud's theory is based on assumptions rooted in associationism (cf. Chap. 6).

Associationism took a new turn in our century. It was taken up by two great investigators, Thorndike in the United States and Pavlov in Russia, and elevated into a series of theoretical concepts by scores of research workers.

Neurons

Edward Lee Thorndike accepted Bain's ideas as a starting point for his own research. Thorndike put these ideas to a test and developed a full-fledged psychological theory which combines functionalism with associationism.

The foundations of this theory were physiological and reductionist. Thorndike firmly believed, at least at the earlier stage of his studies, that psychological findings should and can be related to the nervous system. The nervous cells, the neurons, offer the solution to the enigma of human behavior. Sensory processes depend on *afferent* neurons, which carry the impulses received by the sensory organs to the spinal cord or brain, and on *efferent* neurons, which work from the nervous centers to muscles, glands, etc. The neurons have extensions—dendrites—which contact the

[36] Alexander Bain, *The Emotions and the Will* (4th ed.), Longmans, Green, 1899, p. 47.

axons of other cells. Through the connections or synapses between the neurons a neural current is conducted. "The essence of my account of the physiological mechanism of learning," said Thorndike, "may be stated as follows. . . . The connections formed between situation and response are represented by connections between neurones and neurones whereby the disturbance, or neural current, arising in the former is conducted to the latter across their synapses. The strength or weakness of the connection means the greater or less likelihood that the same current will be conducted from the former to the latter rather than to some other place. The strength or weakness of the connection is a condition of the synapse."[37]

Thorndike's multivolumed work was based on the assumption that the connections between nerves determine the flow of neural current, which controls all psychological functions. Thus far Thorndike was an associationist. But he was James' pupil too. Life meant to Thorndike adjustment, and adjustment takes place through learning. He believed, with all other functionalists, that learning was the main issue in psychology, and his belief was shared by all who were influenced by James' pragmatism and Dewey's instrumentalism, including Watson, Hull, Tolman, Skinner, and others.

Learning

Years ahead of Pavlov and Watson, Thorndike developed a theory of behavior based upon studies of learning. He considered learning a trial-and-error process, and he called it later a *selecting* and *connecting* process.

One of Thorndike's best-known experiments is with a cat confined in a puzzle box. The cat was hungry, and food was outside. The box or cage was closed, and a concealed mechanism operated by a latch could open the door. The hungry cat bit, clawed, jumped, pushed, and dashed till the door opened. On succeeding trials the number of unsuccessful efforts declined slowly and irregularly. Finally the cat had "learned" how to operate the latch and to get the food outside the box.

Careful analysis of this and similar experiments disclosed the nature of the learning process. A satiated cat would not try to gain access to the food outside and apparently would not learn. Hunger or some other motive was necessary for learning.

The theoretical explanation of learning was based on neural connections between stimulus and response. Some connections were strengthened, some weakened. After a great number of trials to get out of confinement, and after some successful efforts, all the nonsuccessful

[37] Edward L. Thorndike, *Educational Psychology*, Teachers College, Columbia University, 1913–14, Vol. I, p. 227.

impulses will be *stamped out* and the particular impulse leading to the successful act will be *stamped in* by resulting satisfaction. After many trials the cat will, when put into the box, immediately claw the button or loop in a definite way, said Thorndike.

At this point Thorndike departed from a purely physiological interpretation of associations. His insistence on pleasure as the determinant in learning opened a discussion which is still very much alive among the various psychological schools. The radical behaviorist-type theories, such as Watson's, Guthrie's and others, reject the terms of "satisfaction" and "annoyance" and stick to "contiguity of stimulus and response," while Hull and others accept Thorndike's theory of reward.

Thorndike followed in the footsteps of James, who wrote: "If pleasure and pain have no efficacy, one does not see why the most noxious acts, such as burking might not give thrills of delight, and the most necessary ones, such as breathing cause agony."[38]

This principle of *usefulness of pleasure* was common to the entire group of biologically minded thinkers such as Spencer, James, Dewey, McDougall, and others. On the other hand, Thorndike's neo-association-ism was influenced by the earlier associationists, especially by Bain's pleasure-and-pain theory of association. Watson hoped to develop a psychological theory without recourse to subjectively perceived emotions. Thorndike felt that this was impossible, and that even in the most "objective" studies of animal psychology the postulate of pleasure is an indispensable one.

Thorndike emphasized this postulate over and over again. "Of several responses made to the same situation, those which are accompanied or closely followed by satisfaction to the animal will, other things being equal, be more firmly connected with the situation, so that when it recurs, they will be more likely to recur; those which are accompanied or closely followed by discomfort to the animal will, other things being equal, have their connection with the situation weakened so that, when it recurs, they will be less likely to occur. The greater the satisfaction or discomfort the greater the strengthening or weakening of the bond."[39]

Sheer practice is not conducive to learning, Thorndike asserted, and rejected the notion that frequency is one of the main laws of association. "Practice without zeal—without equal comfort at success and failure—does *not* make perfect, and the nervous system grows *away* from the modes in which it is *exercised with resulting discomfort*. When the law of effect is omitted—when habit-formation is reduced to the supposed effect of mere repetition—two results are almost certain. By the resulting theory little in human behavior can be explained by the law of habit; and by the

[38] James, *op. cit.*, p. 143.
[39] Edward L. Thorndike, *Animal Intelligence: Experimental Studies*, Macmillan, 1911, p. 244.

resulting practice, unproductive or extremely wasteful forms of drill are encouraged."[40]

The main law of learning was the law of effect. Successful steps in learning were rewarded, unsuccessful eliminated. Pleasure or satisfaction will ultimately determine which responses will be learned.

Thorndike tried to avoid mentalistic terms and used a definition of pleasure worded in "objective" terms, as follows: "By a satisfying state of affairs is meant one which the animal does nothing to avoid, often doing things which maintain or renew it. By an annoying state of affairs is meant one which the animal does nothing to preserve, often doing things which put an end to it."[41] Thorndike believed that this definition put his theory in the realm of "objective psychology." Satisfaction and annoyance, as defined by Thorndike, were not mentalistic terms but empirical concepts derived from careful examination of animals' overt behavior.

Laws of Learning

In addition to the law of effect Thorndike formulated other laws of learning, all of them corollaries of the law of effect. He criticized the associationist notion of the law of exercise but accepted this law as a subsidiary of the law of effect. He wrote: "When a modifiable connection is made between a situation and a response, that connection's strength is, other things being equal, increased." This is the law of use. Its counterpart is the law of disuse, which reads: "When a modifiable connection is not made between a situation and a response during a length of time, that connection's strength is decreased."[42] The laws of use and disuse form together the *law of exercise*.

The *law of readiness* dealt with motivation for learning. It reads: "When any conduction unit is in readiness to conduct, for it to do so is satisfying. When any conduction unit is not in readiness to conduct, for it to conduct is annoying."

In addition to the three laws of effect, readiness, and exercise Thorndike suggested five subordinate laws. The *law of multiple response* was related to learning by "trial and error." A new situation may lead to several responses till, after some experimentation, the right response brings the solution. Inability to make varied responses may prevent learning.

The *law of set* indicated that learning depends upon the learner's previous experiences and dispositions. Not every individual will reset in the same way to a given learning situation. Much depends on his "set,"

[40] Thorndike, *Educational Psychology,* Vol. II, *The Psychology of Learning,* p. 22.
[41] *Ibid.,* p. 2.
[42] *Ibid.*

or the "condition of man," and not only upon "the nature of the situation."

The *law of associative shifting* stated that it is quite easy to get "*any response of which a learner is capable associated with any situation to which he is sensitive.*"[43] This law corresponds to Pavlov's conditioning, and Thorndike gradually attached more and more importance to it.

The *law of assimilation* or analogy states that "to any situation, man responds as he would to some situation like it, or like some element of it. In default of any bonds with it itself, bonds that he has acquired with situations resembling it, act."[44] This law is, in a way, the law of similarity of the early associationists.

The *law of prepotency of elements* indicated the selectivity in learning. The learner may select the important elements from a situation instead of responding in an unselected way, at random, to a given situation. This law can be considered a bridge between Thorndike's concepts of learning and the gestalt concept. Actually, in later years, Thorndike came even closer to the gestalt point of view.

Besides these laws of learning Thorndike was much interested in the problem of *transfer of training*. Faithful to his connectionism, he stated that "a change in one function alters any other only in so far as the two functions have as factors identical elements."[45]

The Revision

Thorndike's main laws of learning in 1913 were the laws of effect, of readiness, and of exercise and five minor laws. In 1929, as a result of his studies in human learning, he modified the basic laws and added six new laws.

A major revision in Thorndike's system was the rejection of the law of exercise. Experiments were made on blindfolded subjects who were instructed to draw several times a line of a certain length. Despite numerous repetitions, no improvement was noticed. However, when the subjects were told whether they did it right or wrong, a considerable improvement took place. In another study Thorndike found that, although there is a slight improvement due to repetition of connections, the improvement due to reward is six times stronger.

In another experiment Thorndike asked the subjects to write down some nonsense words which were read to them. The spelling of these words was open to several possibilities. Each sound was repeated in the list of the nonsense words forty-nine times, and it was easy to find out whether the subjects tended to stamp in the sounds as a result of contiguity and frequency. For instance, a sound like the short *o* in the word

[43] *Ibid.*, p. 15.
[44] *Ibid.*, p. 28.
[45] *Ibid.*, p. 358.

for was repeated over and over again. In fact, almost all subjects wrote the short *o* as the vowel *o*. When the short *o* sound had been used ten times, it had been written down as the vowel *o* 8.37 times on the average. However, there was no significant increase in the use of the vowel *o* by the subjects; the third trial of ten gave the score of 8.61 and the fourth 8.06. Similar results have been received with the sounds *a* and *s* which have showed no increase in preferred spelling despite contiguity and frequency.

In still another experiment Thorndike proved that punishment (an annoyer) does not weaken the punished connection. He said: "There is no evidence that it takes away strength from the physiological basis of the connection in any way comparable to the way in which a satisfying after-effect adds strength to it."

The revision of Thorndike's theory brought it closer to its functionalistic origin. Trial and error played a lesser role in this new theory. A living organism is "set" on a certain activity and rewards have "confirming influence" upon association. The strengthening of responses by reward was now considered to be a product of the "direct confirmatory relation." This reaction is relatively independent of the affective strength of the satisfier; it is a function of drives or "overhead control in the brain." Thus Thorndike's theory in its new version was a radical reductionist edition of functionalism. Men and animals act in accordance with their drives. "Their behavior is purposive, and directed by biological causation."[46]

Further studies led Thorndike to the conclusion that this "confirmatory relation" is probably "set up and controlled by large fractions of the 'higher' levels of the cortex, often by what corresponds to the general 'set' and purpose of the animal at the time."[47]

The shift from a *molecular-physiological* approach to a *molar* one with a functionalist and biological flavor was even more pronounced in Thorndike's later work. "The strengthening by satisfying consequences may have a biological causation. . . ." The over-all control "should be able to react to a certain stimulus by a reinforcement of whatever connection has most recently been active, and . . . the stimulus that sets off this 'confirming reaction' should be satisfying to the over all control."[48]

Thorndike was for years criticized by gestalt psychologists. Finally, he yielded on some points. First, the "confirming reaction" was in itself a concession to gestalt. Instead of separate neurons Thorndike introduced a sort of general cortex activity—"overhead control in the brain." This activity was supposed to be relatively independent of the affective value of the stimulus. Obviously it was a function of the brain itself—and this

[46] Edward L. Thorndike, *The Fundamentals of Learning*, Teachers College, 1932, p. 312.
[47] Edward L. Thorndike, *An Experimental Study of Rewards*, Teachers College, 1933, p. 67.
[48] Edward L. Thorndike, *Man and His Works*, Harvard University, 1943, p. 33.

interpretation brought Thorndike quite close to the gestalt psychology (Chap. 12).

Another concession in the direction of gestalt was the *law of belongingness*. In one experiment three thousand attempts were made to draw with closed eyes a line four inches long. No significant improvement was achieved toward the end of the experiment, and no learning took place despite the repetitions.

Thorndike found that mere repetition of stimuli in temporal contiguity does not lead to learning. He administered a group test in which ten sentences were read loudly ten times. The first and second words of each sentence were the name and surname of a person. The sequence of the last word in a sentence and the first word of the following sentence had the same frequency as the first and second words of each sentence. However, the subject usually recalled the second word after being given the first one but could not recall the first word of a sentence when given the last word of the preceding sentence. Thorndike concluded that repetition of items in temporal contiguity is not too conducive to learning, unless some other factors are involved. In the reported experiment it was the belonging to a sentence and belonging to a name which produced results in learning.[49]

In fact, the principle of learning by trial and error discards learning by repetitions, since futile and inefficient steps made by the animal are not being learned despite repetition and only those leading to the goal are learned.

Additional modification in Thorndike's theory was brought about by his experiments on the "spread of effect."[50] Subjects were asked to respond with numbers from one to ten to some words pronounced as stimuli by the experimenter. The responses were interpreted loudly by the experimenter as being either right or wrong. Since the number of words used by the experimenter as stimuli was very large, it was practically impossible for the subjects to recall on further trials what they had actually said and how their statements were evaluated by the experimenter. After several trials Thorndike found that the responses called "right" (the "rewarded" responses) occurred much more frequently than the others. Moreover, all responses which were given in proximity to a rewarded one were better recalled than the others. This phenomenon was called by Thorndike the "spread of effect." Obviously these findings supported Thorndike's law of effect.

Intelligence

The idea of connectionism influenced Thorndike's work in other areas too. Most workers promoted the theory of intelligence conceived as a

[49] Edward L. Thorndike, *Human Learning*, Appleton-Century, 1931, pp. 8 ff.
[50] Thorndike, *Experimental Study of Rewards*.

general mental ability of comprehension, adaptation, and problem solving. Spearman suggested the distinction between general intelligence (G) and specific abilities (S), and Stern defined intelligence as "a general mental adaptability to new problems and conditions of life."

Thorndike rejected the idea of an over-all mental capacity. "The mind is really but the sum total of an individual's feelings and acts, of the connections between outside events and his responses thereto, and of the possibilities of having such feelings, acts and connections."[51] He proposed a quantity or synthesis theory. Intelligence, according to him, depended upon the "number of connections" in one's brain.

From a purely empirical point of view one could distinguish three types of intelligence. *Abstract* intelligence dealt with symbols, words, and concepts. *Social* intelligence had to do with human relations and represented the sum of leadership, tactfulness, and other social abilities. *Mechanical* intelligence was related to objects, tools, and machinery. The latter was the sum of manipulatory abilities with regard to physical objects.

Thorndike was opposed to Binet's tests because they were developed on the assumption of a general mental ability. Thorndike's tests, known as the Intellect CAVD (completion, arithmetic reasoning, vocabulary, directions), had a different rationale. There were four separate tests that were believed to measure four relatively independent abilities empirically recognized as representing abstract intelligence.

Thorndike emphasized hereditary factors in all kinds of intelligence. I.e., some people have, notwithstanding environmental influences, more nerve connections and are more intelligent.

Concluding Remarks on Thorndike

Forty years after Thorndike's *Animal Intelligence* was published, Tolman wrote: "The psychology of animal learning—not to mention that of child learning—has been and still is primarily a matter of agreeing or disagreeing with Thorndike, or trying in minor ways to improve upon him. Gestalt psychologists, conditioned-reflex psychologists, sign-Gestalt psychologists—all of us in America seem to have taken Thorndike, overtly or covertly, as our starting point."[52]

But even this statement does not contain the entire truth. Although Thorndike's efforts to synthesize objectivism and pleasure principle, reductionism and mentalism could not lead to the establishment of a consistent theory, it had provoked the thoughts of a whole generation.

Thorndike can be criticized on several points. First, there are many

---

[51] Thorndike, *Educational Psychology*, Vol. II, p. 367.
[52] Edward C. Tolman, "The Determiners of Behavior at a Choice Point," *Psychological Review*, 1938, **45**, 1–41.

good reasons to distinguish between *antecedent* motivation and *subsequent* gratification. Undoubtedly both are closely related, yet they are not identical. Seward's experiment can be used here for explanation of the differences between these two issues. Seward divided the rats used in his experiment into two groups. Both groups had to press a bar in order to reach food; however, the first group was not given food, whereas the rats in the second group were promptly rewarded as soon as they pressed the bar. The rats who had been rewarded learned more and better (motivation and gratification), but the not rewarded rats learned too (motivation only). The ratio in the number of responses per animal per trial in all three days of experiment was 41.7 to 33.3.[53]

Thorndike was often criticized on the ground that his law of *effect* is actually a law of *affect*. He tried to escape this accusation by introducing the term "O.K. reaction" as an effect of satisfiers. It is an "unknown reaction of neurones which is aroused by the satisfier and which strengthens connections on which it impinges." It strengthens connections whether they are pleasant and useful or wrong and useless.

Thorndike's law of effect has been open to criticism especially in relation to its supposedly retroactive influence. Since the effect comes after a given response how can it possibly influence it and stamp it in? Thorndike's solution to this problem seems to be satisfactory. He assumed that the physiological connections do not disappear immediately after the response has occurred. They function simultaneously with the effect and can be influenced by it.

The weakest point in Thorndike's theory seems to be his stanch reductionism. No evidence was offered in support of the theory of brain connections. All further studies done by several workers discarded the idea of brain connections as proposed by Thorndike.

What was stimulating in Thorndike's studies was his theory of learning, which is even today very much alive. The issue of reward still divides workers in this field into contiguity and reward theorists of learning.

But, in the development of psychological theory, physiological reductionism and mentalistic pleasure principle could not be so easily combined. Some psychologists rejected mentalism; some rejected reductionism. Still others strove to attain a synthesis on a higher level of theory construction. Thorndike stood in the middle between the "old" and the "new" psychology. Perhaps more than anyone else, he paved the way for new psychological systems, but he himself did not enter the door which he helped to keep open.

---

[53] J. P. Seward, "An Experimental Study of Guthrie's Theory of Reinforcement," *Journal of Experimental Psychology*, 1942, **30**, 247–256.

CHAPTER 2

Conditioned Reflexes

1. THE OBJECTIVE STUDY OF THE HIGHER NERVOUS PROCESSES

Pavlov's Postulates and Principles

None of the three "fathers" of contemporary psychology considered psychology his occupation. Freud was a practicing physician, Dilthey a philosopher, and Pavlov a pharmacologist and physiologist.

Ivan Petrovitch Pavlov never believed in a successful psychology. Although he did not suggest substituting physiology for psychology, he doubted whether psychology could ever develop into an independent discipline capable of an objective and truly scientific research. He strongly recommended that psychologists relate their concepts to physiology; while physiology is building the "foundations," psychology is expected to build the "superstructure." However, since physiological concepts are "necessarily spatial" and psychology deals with "subjective states," Pavlov felt that the position of psychology as a science was "completely hopeless."[1]

For most of his life, Pavlov avoided mentalistic terms. He pursued his research in an empirical, inductive, and experimental way, as if humans were higher animals and nothing else. He repeatedly emphasized that his study was "absolutely excluding psychological conceptions,"[2] and his study of the activity of the central nervous systems "has to do always with only objective facts—facts existing in time and space."[3]

A few principles, consistently applied by Pavlov, were repeatedly and emphatically stated, but no effort was made to prove them. These principles formed the very foundation of Pavlov's scientific outlook and an indispensable part of his philosophy as a natural scientist. He accepted them somewhat dogmatically with a certain degree of the optimistic naïveté of the nineteenth-century materialistic philosophers.

Pavlov believed wholeheartedly and enthusiastically in the *monistic and materialistic* philosophy. He believed that humans are a part of

[1] Ivan P. Pavlov, *Lectures on Conditioned Reflexes*, Liveright, 1928, p. 219.
[2] *Ibid.*, p. 214.
[3] *Ibid.*, p. 192.

nature, nature being interpreted as the sum of matter and energy. Whatever goes on in human life is going on in the nervous tissues and in the glands of inner secretion. Pavlov did not bother to take up the argument for or against introspection as other contemporary psychologists did. Therefore he easily avoided the pitfalls of behaviorism with its efforts to relate the covert behavior to unperceivable motions of muscles or glands.

Pavlov's way was clear, simple, and safe. He did not deny psychology; he simply did not care much for it. He often admitted that the processes going on in human nature were physicochemical processes, which could be "subjectively" interpreted, but he did not attach much value to these subjective, nonscientific comments. In this attitude he resembled Marx's materialistic philosophy but ascribed even less importance to psychology than Marx did (cf. section 6 of this chapter), for Pavlov's monism was a mechanistic and not a dialectic one.[4]

Pavlov applied the same mechanistic philosophy to the problems of causation. He subscribed to the theory of *mechanistic determinism* and professed a rigid, unviolable, necessary, and inflexible causation in animal and human behavior.

The third principle was a sort of *energetism*. Whatever goes on in the nervous system is a dynamic balance of energy with the processes of acquisition, discharge, stimulation, inhibition, irradiation, and concentration of energy. He wrote: "Let us take a certain reflex, i.e., there is excitation of a certain point in the central nervous system. If at the same time another reflex is evoked, another point in the central nervous system is stimulated, and the first reflex becomes weaker and may disappear. One may suppose that the exercise of the second reflex withdraws a certain amount of energy into its own centre at the expense of the energy of the first reflex centre; consequently less energy remains in the first reflex centre and its manifestation is weaker, or, if the diversion of energy is considerable, entirely absent. Other explanations can be given, but this one can not be gainsaid, as it corresponds well to the actual facts."[5] Obviously, all behavior was interpreted by Pavlov as a flow of energy regulated by a few relatively simple laws. The greater the energy of the stimulus, the stronger is its effect; the more energy-charged a nervous center is, the more powerful its reaction to the stimuli.

The fourth principle, the principle of *equilibrium*, corresponds to and resembles Cannon's *homeostasis* and Freud's *constancy* principles. Pavlov

[4] Pavlov himself was definitely opposed to Marxism, and especially to its social philosophy. He believed that Marxism "is sheer dogmatism" (see footnote 42 in this chapter). But Pavlov's ideas on the relationship between psychology and physiology suggest there is room for a bridge between Marxism (especially in Lenin's interpretation) and Pavlov. This bridge Soviet psychologists have been building (see section 6 of this chapter). Though Pavlov never accepted Marxism, the Soviet psychologists accepted Pavlov.

[5] Pavlov, *op. cit.*, p. 185.

wrote: "As a part of nature every animal organism represents a very complicated and closed system, the internal forces of which, at every given moment, as long as it exists as such, are in equilibrium with the external forces of its environment. The more complex the organism, the more delicate and manifold are its elements of equilibration. . . . All life, from that of the simplest to the most complex organism, including man [is] a long series of more and more complicated *equilibrations* with the outer world."[6] And further on he stated: Through the two main activities of the nervous system, the analysis of the external stimuli (perception) and creating of new temporary connections between these stimuli and the functions of the organism (conditioning), "a complete equilibrium of the systems of energy and matter constituting the animal organism with the systems of energy and matter of the environment" is established.[7]

The Analyzers

Pavlov suggested a modification of the theory of brain function. It has been generally accepted that the central nervous apparatus consists of the centripetal-sensory part and the centrifugal-motor part. Pavlov believed that all achievements and perfections in the nervous activity are located in the receptor cells and all the "extraordinary intricacies" of function and the "complicated perfections" of the apparatus are situated in the centripetal part of the central nervous system, not in the centrifugal part.

According to Pavlov, the reflex-arc has to be divided into three parts. The first is called *analyzer;* it begins in every "natural peripheral end" of the centripetal nerve and ends in the receptor cells of the central organ. The term "analyzer" is derived from the fact that the receptor cells decompose the external stimuli. The second part of the arc is the *connection* or lock between the receptors and effectors. The third part of the reflex-arc is the *effector* or the working part.

In 1910 Pavlov wrote that "the brain represents chiefly and probably exclusively (the last provisionally) the central end of the analyzers" or the "receptor centers," i.e., the brain endings of analyzers; the motor region should be considered as a receptor center with "special relation to movement."[8]

Pavlov postulated distinct *physiological centers* such as the food center, defensive center, cold and heat centers, motor center, etc. Each center represents a projection of the peripheral receiving apparatus and re-

[6] *Ibid.,* p. 129.
[7] *Ibid.,* p. 242.
[8] *Ibid.,* pp. 117–118.

sponds in a specific way to stimulation. This response is the unconditioned or innate reflex.

When several centers are stimulated, "the direction of stimulation is conditioned by the relative strength of the interacting centers. The food center is obviously a powerful physiological center; it is the protector of the individual's existence. It is evident that in comparison with the food center, the defense center is of less importance. . . . During the struggle for food the different parts of the body are not specially defended; among animals there are fierce tussles and fights for food in which occur wounds and serious injuries."[9]

The relative strengths of the centers depend on the amount of energy at their disposal. Provided the respective centers are "fully charged," some of them have more, some less intense reflexes. However, a weak center with a heavy charge may produce a stronger response and inhibit a strong center having a small charge.

Excitation and Inhibition

"Nervous activity consists in general of the phenomena of excitation and inhibition. . . . I shall not commit a great error if I liken these two phenomena to positive and negative electricity," wrote Pavlov.[10] As said before, the nervous centers are "charged" with energy. If a certain center is stronger, the energy from the weaker centers passes over to this stronger center and the previously active center becomes entirely quiescent.

This conduction of energy from one center to another is called by Pavlov excitation; accordingly, the center which attracted energy becomes "excited." Three laws govern the processes of excitation. The first is the spread or *irradiation* of the stimulation in the cerebrum. A stimulation in a certain group of nervous cells irradiates over large parts of the cerebrum, and the excitation started in a certain cortical point spreads in a wave into surrounding areas. The second law is the law of *concentration* of excitation. The wave of irradiated excitation goes back to the starting point. Pavlov's idea of equilibrium is well represented by the third law, the law of *induction*. The term "induction" was borrowed from Sherrington. Concentration of both excitation and inhibition is effected by the reciprocal induction; once an area is stimulated and irradiates, the neighboring areas develop inhibition and force concentration of the stimulated area. This phenomenon is called positive induction. Once an area is inhibited and the inhibition irradiates, the neighboring areas develop stimulation and force concentration of

[9] *Ibid.*, p. 188.
[10] *Ibid.*, p. 156.

inhibition. This is negative induction. In both cases "for the formation of the isolated foci of stimulation and inhibition in the cortex there is necessary, first of all, the presence of the corresponding stimuli; but once these foci have been formed, induction appears in the role of supporting mechanism for their maintenance and stability."[11]

Apparently the same three laws of irradiation, concentration, and induction apply to the second function of the central nervous system, *inhibition.* Pavlov remarked that "the cortical cells under the influence of the conditioned stimulus always tend to pass, though sometimes very slowly, into a state of inhibition."[12] The process of inhibition can be started by an internal or by an external agent. If during activity of one center another center is stimulated, an immediate diminution or even a complete cessation of action of the first center may follow. This is the case of external inhibition.

Internal inhibition is "the reverse side of excitation" and always follows excitation, in accordance with the law of reciprocal induction. What inhibition really is, Pavlov could not tell. "We must admit," he wrote in 1912, "that at the present time we know altogether nothing of the real nature of internal inhibition." However, his studies strongly indicate that both processes are processes in which some energy is being used, and probably both derive their energies from the same source. In another volume Pavlov discussed in more detail the pathological states of mind. He observed that the decline of inhibitory processes is related to a decline of the general irritability of the brain which seems to indicate a general decline of vitality.[13] The extreme difficulty of establishing a conditioned response to food and a metronome in an old dog seems to indicate a lower irritability of the nervous centers. The same old dog had great difficulty in the process of differentiation, which obviously depended upon the process of inhibition.

Pavlov related excitation and inhibition to anatomic factors. He hypothesized that the cortical cells of the cerebrum contain some sort of "excitatory substances." Each individual is born with a "store of excitatory substances" in his cortical cells. Some individuals are poorly endowed with these substances or lose part of them during their life span, and their cortical cells tend to pass easily into the inhibitory stage. All cortical cells are very sensitive and destructible; they develop a special process of inhibition when threatened by a functional destruction or depletion of their excitatory substances. Thus inhibition is "conserving and economic," reduces the functional destruction of cells, and accelerates the restoration of expended excitatory substances.

[11] *Ibid.*, p. 324.
[12] Ivan P. Pavlov, *Conditioned Reflexes,* Oxford, 1927, p. 391.
[13] Ivan P. Pavlov, *Activity of the Cerebral Hemispheres* (Russian), Leningrad, 1926.

Conduction and Connection

The main function of the nervous system is *reflex*. A reflex is usually started by an external agent's producing stimulation in the *receptor*, which is, as said before, the ending of a centripetal, afferent nerve. When this stimulation is *conducted* along the path of the centripetal, afferent nerve to the central part of the nervous system, and then to the efferent or centrifugal nerve, a reaction takes place. Under certain circumstances a given stimulus provokes a definite, always the same, reaction. As a rule, the reflex follows the same nervous path. "A reflex is the mechanism of a definite connection by means of the nervous system between the phenomena of the external world and the corresponding definite reactions of the organism."[14]

The nervous system is not only a conducting but a *connecting* system also. Modification in the circumstances under which the stimulus is applied may lead to the formation of *new* connections. As a result of these new connections a new functional union is formed in the path in which the excitatory process moves and a new reaction takes place. Under certain conditions, the usual stimulus-reflex path can be modified and a new, not innate but acquired, reflex can be established. This reflex is created, Pavlov hypothesized, by "intercellular membrane, if it exists," or by "fine ramifications between the neurons."[15] The site of this coupling is probably the synapses of the neurons, especially in the cortex of the cerebrum.

In Pavlov's experiments the reaction was intended to be kept constant (salivation), while the stimulus was manipulated (food, metronome, whistle, light, etc.). This is the classic conditioning research as distinct from another type of research, later developed by Pavlov and several American research workers, in which the reactions of the animal were manipulated.

In 1922 Pavlov concluded that conditioned reflexes could be formed in the motor region, and that the motor region, like the eye or ear, had a *receptor* function. Accordingly, the entire cortex "is only a receptor apparatus which in various ways analyzes and synthesizes the incoming stimulations. These stimulations reach the purely effective apparatus by means of descending connecting fibres."[16] The motor region in the hemispheres is a receptor of the whole movement apparatus spread over the entire organism.

Several experiments with auditory and visual stimuli in which the temporal and occipital parts of the hemisphere were removed led Pavlov

[14] Pavlov, *Lectures on Conditioned Reflexes*, p. 361.
[15] Ivan P. Pavlov, *Experimental Psychology and Other Essays*, Philosophical Library, 1957, chap. 9.
[16] Pavlov, *Lectures on Conditioned Reflexes*, p. 301.

to repudiate the theory of a narrow localization of centers of perception. He believed that "each *peripheral receiving apparatus* (the 'sense' organ) has in the cortex a *special central territory,* its own *terminus,* which represents its exact *projection in the brain.* Here, owing to the special construction of this area (probably the more condensed distribution of cells, the more numerous connections between them, and the absence of cells with other functions) can be effected highly complicated stimulations (the highest syntheses), also their differentiation (the highest analyses). However, the given receptor elements *transcend this central area,* extending out over a great distance, probably throughout the entire cortex, but the farther they are from their center, the more unfavorably they are disposed (in regard to their function). In consequence of this, the stimulations become more elementary, and the analyses less refined."[17]

This broadly conceived theory of brain localization permitted Pavlov to accept the idea of the compensating ability of the organism. In his experiments with partial destruction of various regions of the cortex he had several opportunities to observe how the remaining parts of the cerebral hemispheres take over the functions of the missing parts.

These are the physiological foundations of Pavlov's contribution to psychology.

2. CONDITIONING

The Unconditioned Reflexes

The basic element of interaction between the organism and the environment is called reflex. "Definite, constant, and inborn reactions of the higher animals to certain influences of the external world, reactions taking place through the agency of the nervous system, have for a long time been the object of strict physiological investigation, and have been named reflexes."[18]

These reactions are permanent and unchangeable. They are specific; i.e., a certain external stimulus acting upon a peripheral ending of a centripetal nerve becomes transformed into a nervous process, reaches a certain center in the nervous system, and excites its activity.

The reflex is positive when the stimulus calls for a process of excitation, and negative when a process of inhibition is started. Some positive reflexes, such as food, sex, etc., reflexes, provoke movement *toward* the stimulating object, whereas others provoke movement *away from* or *against* harming and destructive stimuli.

Pavlov saw no reason to distinguish between reflex and instinct. Both were considered by him innate patterns of behavior, the instincts repre-

---

[17] *Ibid.,* p. 302.
[18] *Ibid.,* p. 214.

senting, as a rule, more complex reflexes or a chain of them. Pavlov believed that one particular instinct or reflex is of fundamental importance, all other reflexes being its derivatives. All life is nothing but the "realization of one purpose, viz., the preservation of life itself, the tireless labor of which may be called the general *instinct of life*. This general instinct or reflex consists of a number of separate ones. The majority of these reflexes are positive movement reflexes toward the conditions favorable for life, reflexes whose object is to seize and appropriate such conditions for the given organism, grasping and catching reflexes." The chief grasping reflex is the food reflex, or grasping for material necessary for "completing of our vital chemical processes."[19]

In all the various actions of the instinct or reflex of life there is a certain rhythm; one desires food, becomes satiated, and is abstinent from food for a while till a new desire appears. The same holds true for collecting of objects, for sex, etc. Pavlov wrote: "The reflex of purpose is of great and vital importance, it is the fundamental form of the life energy. Life is beautiful and strong only to him who during his whole existence strives toward the always desirable but ever inaccessible goal, or who passes from one purpose to another with equal ardor."[20] People may collect comforts of life, knowledge, discoveries, or even most trivial things. But as soon as the reflex of purpose becomes inhibited people may even commit suicide.

Pavlov distinguished several innate or unconditioned reflexes, all of them derived from the reflex of life and each of them connected with a definite sensory mechanism or analyzer and a center in the nervous system. He distinguished between food stimulations which call out the reaction of salivation and electric current stimulations which call out the defense reaction. Destructive stimuli or, according to the "psychological terminology," pain stimuli provoke the defense reflex. Food calls for a positive reaction—grasping of the substance and eating it.

Pavlov believed that the strongest reflex was the food reflex. When the dog eats, the food center is in a state of excitation; since this is a very strong center, according to "the law of conflict of centers" all other centers will be in a state of decreased irritability and stimulation of them will have little effect.

As mentioned before, Pavlov's experiments indicated that the defense reflex of skin is second in importance to the food reflex. An animal exposed simultaneously to an electric current acting upon his skin and to a food stimulus will respond not with defense but with food reaction. However, if the destructive stimulus is directed to the bones, the center for destructive stimulation of bones appears to be stronger than the food center.

[19] *Ibid.*, p. 277.
[20] *Ibid.*, p. 279.

Pavlov distinguished a great number of reflexes, among them the thermic ones. There is an easy irradiation between the cold and warm centers which seems to indicate that these two centers are closely interrelated. Among other reflexes Pavlov mentioned the reflexes of sex, of freedom, of curiosity, etc., but more detailed analysis of this part of his work will be offered in connection with his theory of personality.

The "Temporary" Reflexes

Pavlov stated that reflex, being "a constant connection between certain phenomena and the action of certain organs," is a function of the lower part of the central nervous system, while formation of new and temporary connections is the main function of the higher parts of the central nervous system. The former connections are called "unconditioned reflexes" and the temporary connections are called "conditioned reflexes."

A conditioned reflex is formed in the presence of certain conditions. Whenever some indifferent stimulus synchronizes with a stimulus producing a definite unconditioned reflex, then, after a certain number of such coincidences, the formerly indifferent stimulus administered alone calls out the same reflex as the active stimulus which it previously accompanied.

Pavlov most often used two unconditioned stimuli, the food stimulus, which produced a positive reflex, and acid, which produced a negative one. In several carefully planned experiments the salivary secretion was conditioned to metronome beats, to the sight of geometrical figures and letters, to cutaneous stimulus, and to odor of camphor.

And here is how a conditioned reflex is born: When an object is placed in the mouth of the dog, some of its properties excite the simple reflex apparatus of the salivary glands; for the production of the conditioned reflex that action must synchronize with the action of other properties of the same object influencing other receptive regions of the body. Just as the stimulant effects, owing to certain properties of an object placed in the mouth (unconditioned reflex), may coincide with a number of stimuli arising from other objects, so all these manifold stimuli may by frequent repetition be turned into conditioned stimuli for the salivary glands.

In most of Pavlov's experiments the duct of the parotid gland in the dog was diverted by a small surgical operation. The saliva then flowed through an opening in the dog's cheek into a small glass funnel. A tuning fork was sounded, and eight seconds later meat powder was given to the dog. After ten times of presenting the food and the sound, some slight salivation came after the sound, and after thirty tests the saliva appeared in greater quantities (sixty drops).

Pavlov believed that conditioning takes place in the cerebral cortex.

In several experiments in which both hemispheres were removed no conditioning took place. But in later experiments by Pavlov and his associates auditory salivary conditioned reflexes were reestablished after the removal of both temporal lobes. Several other experiments have proved that conditioning in decorticated dogs is possible but it is "primitive and diffuse."[21]

Pavlov manipulated the temporal relationships between the unconditioned and conditioned stimuli. In most experiments the conditioned stimulus was administered a part of a second up to five seconds *prior* to the unconditioned stimulus and continued *simultaneously*. In this type of experiment the conditioned response followed immediately. In some other experiments the conditioned stimulus started much earlier, sometimes even a few minutes before the unconditioned stimulus, and continued until the latter's start. In such a case, provided a simultaneous conditioned response was already established, a *delayed conditioned response* took place.

In another series of experiments conditioned and unconditioned stimuli did not overlap but were separated by a time interval. As a rule, the longer the interval, the more difficult it was to condition, but always the conditioned stimulus was administered *before* the unconditioned stimulus.

Pavlov interpreted the nonsimultaneous conditioning by the assumption that some *trace* of the stimulus persisted in the organism after the conditioned stimulus was discontinued. When the conditioned stimulus was administered ahead of time, its trace persisted until the unconditioned stimulus was administered. Thus the traces of the conditioned stimulus and the unconditioned stimulus were simultaneous, and a reinforcement could take place in this *trace reflex*.

The already established conditioned responses can serve as unconditioned ones in further or "higher-order" conditioning. Once the sound of the metronome evoked salivation, a black square was held before the eyes of the dog for ten seconds and after an interval of fifteen seconds the metronome was sounded again for another thirty seconds. Now the metronome was used as an unconditioned stimulus and the black square as the conditioned one.

This higher-order conditioning brought less salivation, and a more powerful stimulus was necessary for its establishment. Pavlov's interpretation pointed to the fact that the new stimulus often acted as an additional inhibitor; thus a much more powerful original or unconditioned stimulus was necessary in order to produce a higher-order conditioned reflex.

The conditioned response is not to be considered identical with the

[21] Elmer Culler and Fred A. Mettler, "Conditioned Behavior in a Decorticate Dog," *Journal of Comparative Psychology*, 1934, **18**, 291–303.

unconditioned although they may be very much alike. In accordance with the division of the innate reflexes, also, the conditioned stimuli are divided into positive (i.e., provoking excitation) and negative (i.e., provoking inhibition). Obviously the conditioned stimuli are related, like the unconditioned ones, to the various functions of the organism such as food, sex, defense, and all are subordinated to the main instinct or reflex of purpose.

Generalization and Discrimination

A dog conditioned to secrete saliva in response to a metronome sounding 120 times per minute salivated in response to a quicker or to a slower sounding too. The conditioned stimulus became *generalized,* and the dog responded to a wider range of stimuli. Pavlov interpreted this phenomenon by irradiation. He quoted the study of the physiologists Fritsch and Hitzig, who proved that a contraction of a group of muscles might develop into tonic convulsions of the entire body, especially when the contraction was caused by a strong or continuous stimulation.

However, if in consecutive experiments with different metronome rates only one beating rate was reinforced by feeding, all other beating rates would gradually lose their effect and not produce any response. The dog became conditioned to a certain stimulus and *discriminated* between the various beating rates. A gradual bringing closer of the reinforced and nonreinforced stimuli indicated the *degree of discrimination.* Discrimination or differentiation was explained by the above-mentioned theory of concentration, which took place after irradiation, in accordance with the law of reciprocal induction.

In one experiment two spots on the dog's leg were chosen. Food was offered whenever one spot was lightly scratched and never when the other spot was scratched. The dog became conditioned to discriminate between the scratches in the two distant spots on his leg and reacted with salivation to one of them only. Gradually the nonreinforced spot was moved closer and closer to the reinforced one. When the two spots were very close to each other, the dog responded with salivation to each of them. No discrimination took place any more.

These processes of generalization and discrimination were described by Pavlov as follows: "If one chosen special agent is brought for the first time into connection with a definite physiological function, then the stimulation called out by this agent, coming to a certain point of the cortex, irradiates or spreads over the corresponding receptor centers; and thus not only the single point in the brain end of the given analyzer enters into the definite connection, but the whole analyzer or a greater part of it. And only later, owing to the opposition of the inhibitory process, does the field of influence of the stimulation become smaller until at last an isolated action is obtained."[22]

Reinforcement

In Pavlov's version there are two kinds of processes, conditioning proper and reinforcement of conditioning. As a rule, the unconditioned stimulus (food in dog's mouth) provokes the unconditioned response (salivation). The conditioned stimulus alone does not produce this response. However, when the conditioned stimulus is repeatedly presented with the unconditioned stimulus, the conditioned response is evoked. Pavlov originally assumed that the conditioned and unconditioned responses were identical, although the unconditioned response was considered innate and the conditioned acquired.

The focal point in Pavlov's theory is the concept of *reinforcement*. Reinforcement takes place whenever the conditioned stimulus is presented simultaneously or at least at an effective interval with the unconditioned stimulus. Repetition of reinforcement is necessary for establishment, strengthening, and continuation of conditioned responses.

Some psychologists believe that Pavlov's reinforcement was identical with Thorndike's "reward." Woodworth wrote: "It has become clear from all this work that Pavlov's 'reinforcement' and Thorndike's 'reward' are the same. They stand for the same positive factor in establishing an association."[23]

On a closer scrutiny of Pavlov's works we find it difficult to agree with Woodworth. Thorndike's explanation of reward was described before (Chap. 1) and it seems to have operated with an entirely different set of concepts and situations.

Pavlov has emphatically stated that the conditioned response must be started ahead of the unconditioned one. The conditioned stimulus must not coincide exactly with the unconditioned stimulus but must precede the latter by some seconds. Why?

The answer to this question can be easily inferred from the context of Pavlov's works. The inborn connections relate food to the food centers; thus food used as an (unconditioned) stimulus acts as a powerful agent on the food center and provokes salivation and a proper motor action. If simultaneously with this powerful stimulus a weak and neutral stimulus is administered, such as a metronome, whistle, or flashlight, it may have an immediate and partial inhibitory effect but cannot lead to a new excitation. However, if this neutral stimulus acts for a few

[22] Pavlov, *Lectures on Conditioned Reflexes*, p. 172.
[23] Robert S. Woodworth, *Contemporary Schools of Psychology*, rev. ed., Ronald, 1948, p. 66.

seconds prior to the powerful unconditioned stimulus, it will cause some degree of excitation. The unconditioned stimulus, starting shortly afterwards, causes a much greater excitation in a more powerful center, which takes over the energy from the former weak center. This flow of energy from one center to another creates new paths, new couplings, new connections, called conditioned reflexes. The stimulation which entered one center passed over to the stronger center in accordance with Pavlov's mechanistic theory.

Pavlov made it clear that the conditioned stimulus must be "weaker" than the unconditioned one; otherwise no conditioning will ever take place. "During the action of the unconditioned stimulus the positive conditioned stimulus loses its effectiveness, becomes inhibited."[24] When the dog had already started to eat, the metronome lost all its effect upon the dog's nervous system.

Pavlov said that one might substitute any accidental stimulus for food. Once it is presented simultaneously with food, it will call out the same motor and secretory reaction. However, this new signaling agent must be "to a certain extent indifferent, or at least not call out some other too strong reaction."[25]

Pavlov's theory is a theory of balance of energy regulated by induction, irradiation, and concentration, and the principle of mechanistic determinism. The "bigger" the cause, i.e., the stronger the load of energy, the more effect, i.e., the more conditioning. The stronger stimulus produces conditioning, while the weak one becomes inhibited. This reasoning has little in common with Thorndike's law of effect or with Hull's "need reduction" or any other sort of theory of reward.

Moreover, Thorndike's theory of learning was developed in the satisfaction-annoyance dimension, which Pavlov definitely evaded. Pavlov distinguished between food and destructive stimuli, usually referred to as pleasure and pain. However, these terms in Pavlov's context do not correspond to their use by Thorndike, or even Hull, Tolman, and Skinner (cf. Chap. 4). Pavlov conditioned the dogs to salivate when they were exposed to destructive electric stimulation (pain). Despite the damage to their skin, the dogs salivated in expectation of food, whereas no salivation was produced under a mild acid stimulation. Pavlov's solution of this puzzle does not correspond to the pleasure-pain dimension. His frame of reference was the relative strength or the *energetic load* of the stimulus and of the center of the respective analyzer. "If a strong electrical destruction of the skin, usually provoking a marked defensive reaction, is always accompanied by feeding, there can be elaborated without special difficulty the food reaction with the complete disap-

[24] Pavlov, *Lectures on Conditioned Reflexes*, p. 362.
[25] *Ibid.*, translator's note, p. 372.

pearance of the defensive [one]."[26] Stimulation passes over to the stronger
center. "You may cut, burn, or in any way destroy the skin, but instead
of the defense reaction you see only the signs of the food reflex, or
subjectively speaking, of a strong appetite."[27]

Pavlov remained faithful to his mechanistic theory of charges, discharges, and balances of energy. To him it was always the *rhythm of life,*
irradiation and concentration, excitation and inhibition, and the reciprocal induction—and nothing else.

Inhibition, Extinction, and Sleep

The question of motivation came again to the fore in the problem of
inhibition and extinction. In the old associationism the law of frequency
was the basic law. The ancient Romans used to say *Repetitio mater
studiorum est* ("Repetition is the mother of studies"), and for centuries
educators believed in the usefulness of repetition. Thorndike, even in
his revised theory, assigned a place of importance to the law of exercise.

Pavlov's experiments proved beyond doubt that the repetition of the
conditioned stimulus led to a gradual decline and extinction of the
conditioned response unless the conditioned stimulus was accompanied
by the unconditioned stimulus. Without this reinforcement extinction
always took place. Each unreinforced trial increased the extinction and,
the shorter the interval of time between the experiments, the faster the
extinction.

Pavlov distinguished between internal and external inhibition and
enumerated several kinds of internal inhibition. The first type of internal inhibition was called *extinction.* "If a well elaborated and stable
conditioned stimulus be repeatedly applied at short intervals alone,
without being followed by the unconditioned stimulus, then it begins
to decrease and gradually becomes inactive. This is not a complete
destruction of the conditioned reflex, but only a temporary suspension.
That it is so, is proved by the spontaneous restoration of the reflex after
an interval, unless during this time something acts unfavorably to its
restoration."[28]

Another kind of internal inhibition was *retardation.* When the unconditioned stimulus was applied three minutes after the beginning of the
conditioned one, the conditioned stimulus remained passive during the
beginning of this action and produced a conditioned response with a
delay.

Experiments with differentiation of stimuli explain the third type of

[26] *Ibid.,* p. 284.
[27] *Ibid.,* p. 228.
[28] *Ibid.,* p. 206.

inhibition. E.g., in experiments with differentiation of tones the neighboring, nonreinforced tones became inhibited, and the reinforced tone became conditioned. This was *differentiated inhibition.*

An addition of an indifferent stimulus to a well-established conditioned stimulus with reinforcement created the fourth type of inhibition, the so-called *conditioned inhibition.*

These four types of inhibition belong to the category of internal inhibition. An external inhibition takes place whenever a new agent acting upon the central nervous system struggles with other agents acting there already. Pavlov said: "Translating it into the language of neurology, we may say in the given case that a strongly excited point of the central nervous system decreases the irritability of all surrounding points."[29]

An inhibition may become *disinhibited* when an external stimulus acts upon an inhibited conditioned response and removes the inhibition. For example, when a moderate stimulus is introduced during the time of action of a delayed reflex, the new stimulus attracts the animal's attention and inhibits the inhibition, and saliva begins to flow immediately.

As said before, the laws of irradiation and concentration apply to both excitation and inhibition. This fact was demonstrated by Pavlov in experiments in which several conditioned stimuli were connected with one unconditioned stimulus. When the experimenter extinguished one of the conditioned stimuli, all the other conditioned stimuli became partially or fully extinguished. This was apparently a result of irradiation of the inhibition. After a while all the stimuli regained their power and only the one which was extinguished remained inactive. The inhibition receded and concentrated at its initial point in accordance with the law of concentration.

The most general inhibition is sleep. Sleep is a widely irradiated internal inhibition. Pavlov believed that sleep serves as a means toward the establishment of an equilibrium between the processes of destruction and restoration. Sleep is an innate, unconditioned reflex, but it may become conditioned.

The laws of sleep were formulated by Pavlov as follows: "A more or less enduring stimulation falling on a certain part of the hemispheres, whether or not it is of vital significance (and especially if it is without such significance), and no matter how strong it may be,—every such stimulation, if it is not accompanied by simultaneous stimulation of other points, or if it is not alternated with other stimulations, leads inevitably sooner or later to drowsiness and sleep. . . . Every monotonous and continuous stimulation leads to drowsiness and sleep."[30]

Any inhibition, said Pavlov, is a partial, localized, fragmentary sleep, confined within the boundaries of the opposite process of excitation. Sleep

[29] *Ibid.*, p. 215.
[30] *Ibid.*, p. 307.

is an inhibition spread over the entire cerebrum or a great part of it or even into the lower centers. When the inhibition spreads, sleep starts, but when the inhibition process is limited by oncoming stimuli, sleep disappears.

In collaboration with L. N. Voskresensky, Pavlov reported observation on the consecutive stages of sleep in dogs.[31] When the dog is awake, both secretory and motor reflexes are present. The dog responds to the conditioned stimulus with salivating and takes food as soon as it is offered. At the first phase of sleep the dog does not salivate but takes the food and eats it; the secretory reflex is inhibited. When the sleep becomes deeper, in the second phase, the dog salivates but does not take the food; now the motor reflex becomes inhibited and salivation disinhibited. In the third phase of sleep, in deep and complete sleep, both salivary and motor reflexes disappear.

Other experiments shed light on the nature of *suggestion* and *hypnosis*. At the transitory stage from the waking state toward sleep the dogs responded better to weak stimuli than to strong ones. This *paradoxical* phase of sleep corresponds to hypnotic sleep, in which the strong stimuli of the external world become weak and the weak stimulus, coming from the hypnotizer, becomes powerful.

3. THEORY OF PERSONALITY

"Lust for Life"

Pavlov was "deeply and irrevocably convinced," as stated in the Preface to his *Lectures,* that the physiological "objective" research would bring "the final triumph of the human mind over its uttermost and supreme problem—the knowledge of the mechanism and laws of human nature."[32]

Human nature, he believed, could be presented as a series of analyzing, conducting, connecting, and effecting functions of the nervous system, in accordance with the principles of determinism and equilibrium between organism and environment and interpreted as a chain of energetic processes. These energetic processes are excitation and inhibition, which follow the laws of induction, irradiation, and concentration.

Everything else is an application of and derivation from the aforementioned principles and laws. However, observing animal and human behavior, Pavlov was compelled to introduce some additional concepts which could not possibly be derived from his mechanistic theory.

The main reflex or instinct, said Pavlov, was the *instinct of life,* or the

[31] Pavlov, *Experimental Psychology and Other Essays,* p. 345 ff.
[32] Pavlov, *Lectures on Conditioned Reflexes,* p. 41.

reflex of purpose, the purpose being the preservation of life. Pavlov was never able to offer a physical or chemical or physiological interpretation of this statement, which could not be inferred from his system of postulates and laws. He observed, for example, that humans and animals collected objects. He concluded that this was an innate reflex or instinct, related to more a general instinct. The latter was the instinct of preservation of life or the instinct of purpose. This main reflex was not interpreted by Pavlov in terms of excitation, inhibition, irradiation, concentration, and induction. It stood on its own merits as an independent hypothesis, true or false, but not a mechanistic one. Once this main instinct or reflex was postulated, all the mechanistic rules could be applied to it.

All life, according to Pavlov, is realization of the main purpose, the preservation of life itself. The general instinct of life is composed of *positive-movement* reflexes toward conditions favorable for life and *negative-movement* reflexes guarding the organism against injury.

The positive-movement reflexes are grasping, catching, keeping, exploring, and acquiring. The food reflex is the main grasping reflex. "Every day we strive for certain substances necessary for us as a material for completing our vital chemical processes; we introduce this material into our bodies, become quiet for the time being, and strive again some hours later or next day to grasp a new portion of this material, *food*."[33] The other grasping reflexes, such as the exploratory reflex, originated from the food reflex and were probably transmitted by heredity. The same applies to the collecting reflex.

All reflexive action develops in a certain periodicity, order, and rhythm of "striving toward an object." Attainment of the object brings "a quickly developing calm and indifference." This peculiar "rhythm of life" is related to the law of reciprocal induction.

Fear and Aggression

Inasmuch as Pavlov tried to avoid "mentalistic" terms he had to face the fact that some dogs showed reactions strikingly similar to anger and fear in humans. Pavlov regarded the aggressive actions of the dogs as a "guarding" reflex. This is primarily an unconditioned reaction of the organism against injury. Some dogs showed much more hostility and aggressiveness than others.

The aggressiveness of the dogs could be increased by conditioning in three ways: first by putting the dog in a closed and isolated room; then by limiting the dog's freedom and tying him up in a harness; and last by the behavior of the experimenter. The more authoritative and dictatorial the experimenter, the more aggressive became the dog toward strangers. The more restrained and reserved the experimenter, the less

[33] *Ibid.*, p. 278.

aggressive the dog's behavior (cf. Kurt Lewin's "social climate," Chap. 13).

Pavlov distinguished passive-defensive (fear) reactions from active-defensive (anger) actions. He believed that dogs displaying a preference for passive-defensive reactions had a small reserve of excitatory substances or that these substances were extraordinarily destructible. Thus normal fear or pathological fears represent a case of predominance of inhibitory processes which indicate the weakness of the cortical cells.

Consciousness and Speech

One of the main difficulties of psychology, said Pavlov, was the fact that it did not deal with a continuous and unbroken series of phenomena, for the psychical life was composed in a checkered fashion of "conscious and unconscious elements."

Pavlov was not much concerned with the problem of consciousness. He believed that consciousness appears as a nervous activity of a certain part of the central hemispheres, possessing at the given moment under the present conditions a certain optimal (probably moderate) excitability; owing to this state new conditioned reflexes are easily formed and differentiation develops quickly and successfully. At the same time the other outlying parts function in a stereotyped manner because of their decreased irritability. The activity of these areas is subjectively described as unconscious, automatic.

In the waking state a certain part of the cerebral hemispheres is in the state of consciousness, which facilitates the optimum of conditioning and discrimination in perception. In sleep, in dreams, and in hypnosis the highest cortical functions are inhibited and the subcortical and the spinal cord centers remain active. These lower nervous centers are the seat of the unconditioned stimuli and of the basic instincts and emotions.

The conscious does not seem to be the monopoly of humans, but humans operate on a higher level of development and use symbols as representatives of reality in perception and conditioning.

The main difference between men and animals lies in speech. "In the animal reality is signalized almost exclusively by stimulations and by the traces they leave in the cerebral hemispheres. . . . This is the first system of signals common to man and animals. But speech constitutes a second signalling system of reality which is peculiarly ours, being the signal of the first signals."[34]

Experimental Neurosis and Mental Disorder

In some experiments with differentiation Pavlov gradually raised the pitch of the low tones making them more and more similar to the

[34] Pavlov, *Experimental Psychology and Other Essays*, p. 642.

high ones. At a certain point the difference became so small that the dog was unable to distinguish any more. In some cases the dog broke down and started to bark and bite, apparently exposed to conflicting stimuli of excitation and inhibition. This state was called by Pavlov "experimental neurosis." He described a similar case when a light circle used as a conditioned stimulus had to be distinguished from an ellipse. These two stimuli became undistinguishable when the semi-axes of the ellipse reached the ratio of 9:8. At that time, Pavlov reported, "the whole behavior of the animal underwent an abrupt change. The hitherto quiet dog began to squeal in its stand, kept wriggling about, tore off with its teeth the apparatus for mechanical stimulation of the skin. . . . On being taken into the experimental room the dog now barked violently. . . . In short it presented all the symptoms of a condition of acute neurosis."[35]

Some animals seem to succumb easily to stress while others show more resistance. Moreover, the different types of disorder developed under stress are related to the already existing differences in the behavior of animals. Some dogs easily form positive reflexes but it is difficult to produce in them inhibitory reflexes. The same dogs are characterized by the prevalence of excitatory reflexes and are usually very aggressive. When exposed to two opposite processes of excitation and inhibition in an experiment which called for differentiation that overtaxed their abilities, they broke down with a neurasthenia in which the inhibitory processes disappeared. Dogs which easily formed inhibitory reflexes were characterized by a quiet, timid, and submissive behavior. When exposed to the above-mentioned experiment, they faced a nervous breakdown of a hysterical type in which the inhibitory processes prevailed. The third type, the *central* or equilibrated, took strain well.

As a result of these observations Pavlov suggested a theory of personality types based on differences in behavior of the experimental animals, including their normal and disturbed behavior. In addition, Pavlov spent years in observing mental patients and developed a theory of types of nervous system which has been utilized in Soviet psychiatry.[36]

Temperaments: Types of Nervous Systems

Pavlov attempted to classify temperamental differences in relation to excitation and inhibition. His classification included the excitatory, the inhibitory, and the central or equilibrated type, which could be divided into quiet and lively types. Accordingly, Pavlov divided all his experimental dogs into four categories and believed that humans, too, could be classified in the same way. His division followed the four types sug-

[35] Pavlov, *Conditioned Reflexes*, p. 291.
[36] Joseph Wortis, *Soviet Psychiatry*, Williams & Wilkins, 1950.

gested in ancient times by Hippocrates, namely, choleric and melancholic, which were the two extreme types, and sanguinic and phlegmatic, which were the two equilibrated types.

The excitable dog, i.e., the *choleric*, responds quickly to positive stimuli, becomes easily conditioned, and is not easily inhibited. The choleric is "pugnacious, passionate, and easily and quickly irritated." The choleric type corresponds to neurasthenia.

The inhibitory type is the *melancholic*. To him "every event of life becomes an inhibitory agent; he believes in nothing, hopes for nothing, in everything he sees the dark side."[37] The melancholic type corresponds to the hysterical.

Between these two extreme and pathological types there are the two equilibrated or central or healthy types, the *phlegmatic* and the *sanguinic*. The phlegmatic is "self-contained and quiet; persistent and steadfast." The sanguinic is "energetic and very productive" but without constantly new stimulations gets bored and falls asleep easily.

Schizophrenia is, according to Pavlov, a severe hysteria. Pavlov believed that the inhibitory hysterical dogs "have very weak cortical cells easily passing over into various degrees of a chronic inhibitory condition" and "the basic features of human hysteria are also a weakness of the cortex." Schizophrenia is "an extreme weakness of the cortex, as a marked degree of hysteria. . . . In our inhibitory, hysterical dogs, by applying the functional difficulties presented by our experiments, we can make completely isolated pathologic points and foci in the cortex; in schizophrenia, in the same manner, under the influence of certain experiences of life, acting perhaps on the already organically pathological condition, gradually and constantly there appear a larger and larger number of such weak points and foci, and by degrees there occurs a breaking up of the cerebral cortex, a splitting up of its normally unified function."[38]

Cyclic psychosis represents an extreme case of neurasthenia. Neurasthenics have periods of intense activity and then times of deep depression with curtailment of their activities and abilities.

Temperaments are determined mainly by the properties of the hemispheres and of the subcortical centers. Obviously, temperaments depend upon innate qualities of the nervous cells. However, environmental influences may cause substantial modifications. Nature can be modified by nurture. Pavlov wrote: "As an animal from the time of its birth is subjected to the various effects produced by its environment . . . , the final nervous activity present in an animal is an alloy of the features peculiar to the type and of the changes wrought by the environment."[39]

[37] Pavlov, *Lectures on Conditioned Reflexes*, p. 377.
[38] *Ibid.*, p. 378.
[39] *Ibid.*, vol. II, 1941, p. 178.

4. CONCLUDING REMARKS ON PAVLOV

Pavlov's theory is basically a theory of the anatomy and physiology of the nervous centers. Applied to human behavior it represents a case in radical reductionism which relates psychological phenomena to a physiological theory. It is not surprising that psychologists became aware of the importance of this new theory; beginning with J. B. Watson, they incorporated Pavlov's method and findings in their respective systems. Pavlov's theory offered the missing link between human behavior and the nervous system. It was, undoubtedly, the best offer and psychologists accepted it wholeheartedly, very much to Pavlov's amazement.

However, very soon psychologists left the path paved by Pavlov. Since they were unable to prove or disprove the validity of the physiological interpretation, most of them dropped it. Hull, for example, did to Pavlov what Horney did to Freud: Horney continued psychoanalysis without libido;[40] Hull continued conditioning without the nervous system.

Although Watson accepted conditioning wholeheartedly, Pavlov could never have accepted behaviorism. Pavlov's intention was to study the nervous system, not to propose a psychological theory based upon his studies. He was opposed to the oversimplified application of his theory by Watson and his associates and criticized E. R. Guthrie as follows: "The psychologist takes conditioning as a principle of learning, and accepting the principle as not subject to further analysis, not requiring ultimate investigation, he endeavors to apply it to everything and to explain all the individual features of learning as one and the same process."[41] The physiologist, however, proceeds in the opposite direction. The physiologist is opposed to the deductive method applied by the psychologist. Pavlov criticized behaviorism for its indiscriminate putting together of psychology and physiology. He never denied the legitimate study of "subjective" phenomena and never identified the conscious with the nervous system. From that point of view he came, in a way, close to the Marxian philosophy (see section 6 in this chapter), which believed the human psyche to be a product of the physiological development and yet a separate, nonphysiological entity.

Pavlov's physiological theory was never fully proved, but it has been accepted on its face value by the official Soviet science. Thousands of experiments in conditioning have been conducted in the Soviet Union and all of them applied Pavlov's theory. "The technical quality of the experiments is of very high caliber," wrote a leading expert in con-

[40] Benjamin B. Wolman, "Psychoanalysis Without Libido," *American Journal for Psychotherapy*, 1954, 8, 21–31.

[41] Ivan P. Pavlov, "The Reply of a Physiologist to a Psychologist," *Psychological Review*, 1932, 39, 91–127.

ditioning and in Russian psychology.[42] Obviously experiments cannot "prove" a theory, and the same data can be interpreted in a different way. "It is unlikely," wrote Girden, "that learning, even of 'simple' conditioning, consists of synaptic switching of unit reflexes. The 'locus' of conditioning, as a consequence, can be expected to involve some integrating cerebral ('association') area outside of the specific pathways which mediate the conditioned and unconditioned stimuli and responses. . . . The association system may very well involve both cortical-subcortical recurrent pathways, or similar reverberatory circuits at either cerebral level alone. If these latter neurological mechanisms should be found to be essential in conditioning, the search for a *locus* is futile. The neurological correlate would be a pattern or circuit, rather than some change at a given synaptic center."[43]

This problem remains, at least for the time being, unsolved and rather controversial. The Russian research workers, although faithful to Pavlov, are aware of the problem. In the Soviet Five-Year Plan for Medicine, Section Six on Physiology and Pathology of Nervous Activity, they wrote: "Morphology has up to now not solved the problem of the method of approach to the study of finer connections, particularly of the synapses, and this significantly hampers research. . . . The synaptic apparatus was studied only with difficulty in the sphere of the spinal cord connections. So far as the structure of the synaptic connections in the subcortical and especially in the cortical formations is concerned, we have at the present time only isolated researches of exploratory character."[44]

Nor was the ages-old body-soul problem solved in Pavlov's laboratories. "I shall not touch on the problem," wrote Pavlov in 1913, "of how the brain substance creates subjective phenomena, etc." We can only endeavor to find out what sort of nervous processes go on in the hemispheres of the brain when we say we are "conscious" and speak of our "conscious" activity.

Thus the entire issue of reductionism stands as it did before Pavlov. Pavlov rejected the naïve and crude reductionism of Watson and Bekhterev, but in his own cautious reductionism he had to face unsurmountable difficulties which could not be brushed way by semantics. For the avoidance of mentalistic terms does not solve the problem. If one uses the term "defensive reaction" in order to avoid the subjective and mentalistic terms "fear" and "anger," he does not offer any interpretation of the phenomenon under consideration, nor does he solve any significant problem. When Pavlov said "life is beautiful and strong only to him who during his whole existence strives toward the always desirable

[42] Gregory Razran, "Soviet Psychology Since 1950," *Science*, 1957, **126**, 1100–1107.
[43] Edward Girden, "Some Neurological Correlates of Behavior," in H. Helson (ed.), *Theoretical Foundations of Psychology*, Van Nostrand, 1951, p. 121.
[44] Wortis, *op. cit.*, p. 247.

but ever inaccessible goal, or who passes from one purpose to another with equal ardor," this beautiful statement was as remote from physiology as Adler's *Geltungstrieb* or Lewin's level of aspiration or Freud's Eros.

In the last years of his life Pavlov was less rigid in his avoidance of mentalistic terms. He stated that there is no basic difference between his own conditioning and Thorndike's connectionism, although he would prefer to replace Thorndike's trial and error by a more objective term such as "chaotic reaction."[45] Moreover, he seems to have accepted the idea that conditioning and association are basically one and the same process. He wrote: "A conditioned connection is, apparently, what we call association by simultaneity. The generalization of a conditioned connection corresponds to what is called association by similarity."[46] And furthermore: "The temporary neural connection [the conditioned connection—B. W.] is the most universal physiological phenomenon in both the animal kingdom and in ourselves. At the same time it is a psychological phenomenon—that which psychologists call association, whether it be a combination of actions, impressions, letters, words, or thoughts."[47]

Yet the gap between physiology and psychology could not be closed even by Pavlov's theories. Pavlov pushed forward the frontiers of the scientific research, and his findings are a milestone in the study of human nature. The soma-psyche dichotomy, although still unresolved, came closer to some solution, and definite progress was made both in the method and in the results of research.

5. VLADIMIR M. BEKHTEREV: REFLEXOLOGY

Materialistic Monism

Vladimir M. Bekhterev was Pavlov's contemporary. Independently of Pavlov he developed a theory of conditioning and a psychological system based upon physiology. In 1904 he published a paper[48] and in 1907 a book under the programmatic heading *Objective Psychology*. Bekhterev believed that the future of psychology depended upon objective and external observation. His idea was to create a new and thoroughly scientific psychological system which would utilize physical and physiological data with the exclusion of mentalistic, subjective, and introspectionistic elements.

In order to develop such an objective and scientific psychology Bekhterev accepted the principle of mechanistic and *materialistic monism*.

[45] Pavlov, *Experimental Psychology and Other Essays*, pp. 578 ff.
[46] *Ibid.*, p. 261.
[47] *Ibid.*, p. 251.
[48] Vladimir M. Bekhterev, "The Objective Psychology and Its Subject Matter," *Vestnik Psikhologii* (Russian), 1904, pp. 660–666, 721–731.

This principle did not represent any innovation as far as the history of philosophy and psychology was concerned. The French Encyclopedists, Diderot, La Mettrie, Helvetius, d'Holbach, and others, had expressed similar materialistic ideas. Especially La Mettrie should be credited with the presentation of man as a part of material nature. Prior to Darwin, he had introduced the principle of continuity in the animal world and stressed the anatomic similarity between men and monkeys. Vogt, Büchner, and Moleschott were even more emphatic in saying that man "is what he eats," or that "nutrition determines human nature," or that "thought is secreted" by the brain.[49]

Bekhterev offered the most radical solution to the body-soul problem. Physical energy—this was his answer to the problem which perplexed the greatest minds of mankind. Bekhterev's materialistic solution encompassed both organic and inorganic nature and presented matter and psyche as phenomena of the same mechanical energy. Causation and motivation, learning and thinking became reduced to a mechanistic model of the human organism which resembled the mechanistic part of Descartes's theory. Bekhterev's all-encompassing energetic principle was even more general and elaborated than Herbart's mechanistic metaphysical psychology.[50]

Conditioning

But Bekhterev was not a metaphysician. He was an empirical scientist who, simultaneously with Pavlov, discovered conditioned reflexes. In a series of well-planned experiments conducted on humans and animals he administered an electric skin stimulus which produced a defensive reaction. Then a neutral stimulus was administered simultaneously with the electrical stimulus and the same motor response was evoked. Obviously the acquired response was a conditioned reflex, named by Bekhterev the "associate reflex."

Bekhterev conducted several ingenious experiments. In one famous experiment the "artificially associated respiratory motor reflex" was established. Whenever sudden cold is applied to the skin surface, an unconditioned breath-catching reflex occurs. In Bekhterev's experiments the breath-catching reflex became associated or conditioned to neutral stimuli in humans and in animals as well.

In another experiment Bekhterev elicited flexion of the leg as a conditioned response. When the leg was immobilized in such a manner that no flexion could take place, another limb responded to the stimulus with flexion. Obviously, *generalization* took place.

[49] S. A. Lange, *History of Materialism*, Harcourt, 1925.
[50] Benjamin B. Wolman, "Johann Friedrich Herbart," *Hachinuch Quarterly* (Hebrew), 1942, **15**, 1–23.

Bekhterev's experiments covered a great many areas of conditioning. In contradistinction to Pavlov's, Bekhterev's experiments are varied and include a great number of motor responses. J. B. Watson and other learning theorists applied many of Bekhterev's findings, and Bekhterev's impact upon the development of conditioning is second to Pavlov's.

Bekhterev believed that speech is a highly complicated symbolic reflex which grew from simple reflexes under the influence of experience and education,[51] and symbolic conditioning became incorporated in the studies of several Soviet studies (see next section). Bekhterev interpreted his empirical data in physiological terms. The cerebral processes are processes of excitation and inhibition of energy. The energy used in organic chemical processes expresses itself in two kinds of phenomena, *objective* and *subjective*. The subjective processes are those usually called psychological. They are, as a rule, accompanied by the decomposition of phosphorus, by an increase of bodily temperature, and by electrodynamic phenomena. Whenever albumen is created, whenever organic life exists, subjective processes take place. Thus Bekhterev ascribed subjective or psychological processes to all forms, levels, and species of living matter. He believed the conscious or consciousness to be one of the states of energy. The cerebral process, he wrote in his book *The Objective Psychology*, is at the same time "a physical process and a subjective process."[52] Consciousness is not a result, or a correlate, or a derivative of physiological process. It is a state of physical energy, related to central inhibition and resistance in the cortical physiological processes. All mental or subjective processes are secondary to physical ones; all physiological processes, even in the lowest biological species, are accompanied by corresponding subjective processes which actually form an inseparable part of the physiological processes. To put Bekhterev's ideas in simple terms one is tempted to say that the subjective processes form the other, and less important, side of the coin. They cannot be dealt with independently; they are secondary to physical processes.

All subjective processes are accompanied by a flow of energy in the nervous cells and tissues and, as said before, all objective processes are accompanied by subjective states. However, not all subjective states are conscious.

Concluding Remarks on Bekhterev

While Pavlov cautiously formulated his physiological theories and carefully avoided sweeping generalizations, Bekhterev was less modest

[51] Vladimir M. Bekhterev, *General Principles of Human Reflexology,* International Publishers, 1932, p. 216.

[52] Vladimir M. Bekhterev, *Objektive Psychologie—Reflexologie,* Taübner, 1913, p. 45.

and less cautious in his effort to build a bridge between physiology and psychology. One may say that Bekhterev's theory of energy ascribed mental functions to organic matter even in the lowest stages of evolution and reduced the higher mental processes to simple transformations of physical energy. Bekhterev assumed unity of physical and mental processes by raising the former and lowering the latter. The oversimplification of the problem did not help its solution, for mental functions are no better interpreted by substituting for them the physical term "energy." Energy in physics is just as logical a construct as libido in psychology; both can be operationally defined and both can be inferred from empirical data, but neither is an empirically observed fact. And on the other end of the bridge that Bekhterev believed he had built, primitive biological phenomena do not require any mentalistic interpretation whatsoever.

6. UNDER THE BANNER OF MARX AND PAVLOV

The Naïve Materialism

Russian psychologists tried very hard to combine the philosophy of Marx, Engels, and Lenin with the experimental studies of Pavlov and Bekhterev. For a while there was some confusion as to how Soviet psychology should actually develop. Two tendencies were apparent: one was represented by an extremely mechanistic approach in which physiology was expected to be substituted for psychology. This crude mechanistic-materialistic philosophy, mostly influenced by Bekhterev, led to the belief that "consciousness is a product of the inhibitions of the capitalistic system and will wither under socialism."[53] The tendency went as far as to the formation of groups under the leadership of a Soviet behaviorist, Yenchman. These clubs aimed at the "liquidation of the consciousness," which was "an illusory-deceptive product of the capitalist class system." Yenchman's club hoped that "through a correct socialist peripheral uninhibited living, consciousness could be more quickly liquidated."[54] Yenchman's ideas were apparently based on an oversimplification of Bekhterev's concept of consciousness.

In the early thirties most of the Soviet psychologists gave up the naïve materialism and tried to develop a psychological theory on the foundations of the dialectic materialism as expounded in the works of Marx, Engels, and Lenin. After 1931 a new era started in the history of psychology in Russia, which is, writes a reviewer, an era of a "genuine

[53] Razran, *op. cit.*, p. 1101.
[54] Gregory Razran, "A Note on London's Historical Survey of Psychology in the Soviet Union," *Psychological Bulletin*, 1950, 47, 146–149.

dialectical psychology, a *Soviet* psychology, based on dialectical materialism."[55]

The efforts of the Soviet psychologists to bring their studies in line with the official Marxist-Leninist dialectic materialism started in 1923 with Kornilov's "call to arms in behalf of a Marxist psychology frankly based on dialectical materialism."[56] This criticism was directed against Bekhterev's "vulgar materialistic mechanism," on the one hand, and all "idealistic" theories on the other.

Kornilov believed that Marxism considers psyche a property of most organized matter. The dialectic materialism does not reduce psychological processes to physiology; thus Kornilov proposed a theory of the reactions of the psyche to the material world. This theory of "reactology" is the study of human reactions to stimulations coming from without. Psyche and conscious were mere "subjective reflection" of what was going on in the nervous tissues.

Kornilov's theory was exposed to bitter criticism. The critics maintained that, while Kornilov's opposition to Bekhterev was justified, his "reactology" failed to represent faithfully the Marxian point of view. It seems therefore worth while to explain Marx's approach to psychology.

The Dialectic Materialism

R. S. Peters, who edited and abridged *Brett's History of Psychology*, explained the shift from biology toward the social sciences as follows: "Psychologists became increasingly aware that men were very different from animals not because they had a soul which animals did not have, but because they had a very complex social environment. They began to appreciate the large element of truth in Marx's saying that it is not the consciousness of man that determines his existence, but his social existence that determines his consciousness."[57]

However, Marx's influence upon psychology is much deeper than is stated by Peters, because Marx's theory emphasized the two-way process in the man-nature relationship. "Marx is never weary of repeating that the distinctive character of social development as opposed to natural processes of development lies in the fact that human consciousness is involved," and human beings "actively participate in making their own history."[58] Putting it in terms of the dialectical triad, the natural environment is the thesis, human needs and desires the antithesis, and the resulting human ideas and actions the synthesis. Moreover, in Marx's own

[55] Ivan D. London, "A Historical Survey of Psychology in the Soviet Union," *Psychological Bulletin*, 1949, 46, 241–277.
[56] K. N. Kornilov, "Psychology in the Light of Dialectic Materialism," in C. Murchison (ed.), *Psychologies of 1930*, Clark University, 1930, pp. 243–278.
[57] R. S. Peters (ed.), *Brett's History of Psychology*, Allen & Unwin, 1953, p. 702.
[58] Sidney Hook, *Toward the Understanding of Karl Marx*, Gollancz, 1933, p. 78.

words, "by acting on the external world and changing it, man changes his own nature."[59]

Karl Marx was critical of mechanistic-materialistic theories. He wrote in 1845 as follows: "The materialist doctrine that men are products of circumstances and upbringing and that, therefore, changed men are products of other circumstances and changed upbringing, forgets that circumstances are changed precisely by men and that the educator himself must be educated."[60] In other words, there is a bipolar process. "Men are producers of their concepts. . . . Consciousness can never be anything else than conscious existence. . . . It is not consciousness that determines life but life that determines consciousness."[61]

Thought and consciousness, wrote F. Engels in 1877, "are products of the human brain and the man himself is a product of nature. . . . The products of the human brain, being in the last analysis also products of nature, do not contradict the rest of nature but are in correspondence with it."[62]

Friedrich Engels, wrote Lenin, "constantly and exclusively speaks in his works of things and their mental images of reflections (*Gedanken, Abbilder*)" and "mind itself is only the highest product of matter."

According to Lenin, "Materialism in full agreement with natural science takes matter as the *prius*, regarding consciousness, reason and sensation as derivative, because in a well expressed form it is connected only with the higher forms of matter (organic matter)." For sensation "is connected with a particular kind of processes in matter organized in a particular way" and "there still remains so much to investigate, so much to find out about how matter, devoid of sensation, is related to matter which, though composed of the same atoms (or electrons), is yet endorsed with a definite faculty of sensation. Materialism, by putting clearly the problem, gives impetus to continual experimentation, thus making possible its solution."[63]

And this is precisely why Lenin as the head of the Soviet government was critical of Bekhterev and offered wholehearted support to Pavlov. While Bekhterev was obviously representative of a naïve materialism, Pavlov's theories were not identical with but more acceptable to Marxism. Pavlov dealt with nervous processes only but considered psychology the eventual function of higher organized organic matter.[64]

The correspondence between Lenin's and Pavlov's points of view

[59] Karl Marx, *Capital*, Vol. I, p. 198.
[60] Karl Marx, "Theses on Feuerbach," in Emile Burns (ed.), *A Handbook of Marxism*, Random, 1935, p. 229.
[61] Karl Marx, "German Ideology," in *ibid.*, pp. 212– 213.
[62] Friedrich Engels, "Anti-Dühring," in *ibid.*, p. 233.
[63] Vladimir I. Lenin, "Materialism and Empirico-criticism," in *ibid.*, pp. 636, 654.
[64] Strangely enough, Bekhterev tried very hard to adjust his theories to Marxism, while Pavlov was always independent and intransigent. After a prolonged period of trial and error Soviet psychologists adjusted their theories to Pavlov's findings.

becomes more evident from the following quotation from Lenin. "Engels opposed the 'vulgar' materialists, Vogt, Büchner and Moleschott because they assumed that thought is secreted by the brain as bile is secreted by the liver." "For every scientist . . . , as well as for every materialist, sensation is nothing but a direct connection of the mind with the external world; it is the transformation of energy of external excitation into a mental state."[65]

Natural science "holds that thought is the function of the brain, that perceptions, that is, the images of the external world, are effects of external objects on our sense organs. The materialistic elimination of the dualism of mind and body consists in this that the existence of the mind is shown to be dependent upon that of the body, in that mind is declared to be secondary, a function of the brain, or a reflection of the outer world."[66]

Psychology and Culture

In their effort to create a truly Marxist psychology, Vygotskii, Luria, Leontyev, and others developed a psychological system related to the history of culture.[67] Their approach resembled that of Spranger and Dilthey, but in the vein of the materialistic philosophy of history of Karl Marx. While the *Kulturwissenschaft* psychology (cf. Chaps. 10 and 11) developed in an atmosphere of the neo-Kantian philosophy with profound Hegelian influences, the Soviet "kulturpsychologists" tried to relate the development of the human psyche to consecutive socio-economic states of development. The history of mankind in its economic aspects was regarded by Luria, Leontyev, Vygotskii, and others as the frame of reference for psychology. The human mind was adapting itself to the economic development.

These studies utilized Marx's philosophy of history, the gestalt "sign" theory, and Pavlov's conditioning, with the emphasis put on the Marxian concept of the human psyche as a "superstructure" which reflects the more basic material and economic foundations of life and, in return, influences these foundations. To repeat Marx's rules in this issue: man is the product of the environment but he can change the environment.

However, even this approach did not satisfy the critics because the "cultural school" in the Soviet psychology apparently failed in the solution of the soma-psyche problem. The Soviet psychologists were called to pay more attention to physiology, for, as Chernakov explained, "The Marxist conception of the psyche starts with a recognition of the fact

[65] Lenin, *op. cit.*, pp. 643, 647.
[66] *Ibid.*, p. 657.
[67] A. R. Luria, "The Problem of the Cultural Behavior of the Child," *Journal of Genetic Psychology*, 1928, **35**, 493–506. L. S. Vygotskii, "Thought and Speech," *Psychiatry*, 1939, **2**, 29–54.

that the psyche or consciousness is a product of the brain and is a reflection of the outside world; which means that psychic phenomena are
derivative from, and dependent upon, physical reality, while the latter
is independent of the psyche and primary, because the outside world by
its very nature is material and develops according to laws governing
the movement of matter."[68]

This approach clearly indicated the direction in which the Soviet psychology had to go. Psyche is not a form of matter "but only a reflection
of matter," a reflection of objective reality, a reflection of the outside
world. But how could one develop a psychological theory within these
limits?

The only open avenue was to relate psychological data to physiological
findings, and to develop a psychology which could serve as a "superstructure" to physiology. Physiological foundations for such a psychology
were built by Sechenov and Pavlov. In this direction went the psychological inquiry in the U.S.S.R. as represented in the writings of Rubinstein and, in an even greater extent, in the studies of the last ten years.

S. L. Rubinstein: Toward a Synthesis

One of the outstanding theorists who tried to combine Pavlovianism
and Marxism with empirical studies in psychology was S. L. Rubinstein.
Rubinstein is undoubtedly the most independent and original among
the Soviet psychologists and for a while, he was the most accepted one.

Rubinstein distinguished two aspects in human personality: experience
and perception. The term "experience," which indicates the influence of
William Stern (cf. Chap. 11), represents the innermost and primary psychological fact. "The experiences of an individual comprise the subjective
part of his real life, the subjective aspect of the way-of-life of one's
personality."[69]

Experiences form the "dim background" out of which the consciousness
emerges. There is no clear dividing line between the dim experiences
and the conscious perception; drives and emotions "stem from a stimulation coming from the organism itself . . . drives reflect the organic
need and their source is somatic."[70]

The unconscious drives and feelings originate in the inner organs of
the body. "The nervous impulses which travel from the interoceptors to
the central nervous system do not arrive in the majority of cases to the
higher nervous centers in the cortex; thus they do not produce percep-

[68] E. T. Chernakov, "Protiv Idealisma Metafiziki v Psikhologii" ("Against Idealism
and Metaphysics in Psychology"), *Voprosy Filosofii*, 1948, No. 3, quoted after J.
Wortis, *op. cit.*, p. 261.

[69] S. L. Rubinstein, *Foundations of General Psychology* (Russian), Uchpedgiz,
1946, p. 7.

[70] *Ibid.*, p. 627.

tions, although they do modify the functional state of the nervous system, mainly its sensory organs."[71]

Once these unconscious drives and emotions which stem from the interoceptors of the inner organs become directed toward the external world, they become conscious. The conscious is what is related to the perception of objects. However, even the perception of objects is not entirely a "reflection of the outer world" but is colored by emotions which are an "immediate experience." Emotions do not represent the "content of the object" but the subjective "state of the individual" and his "attitude" to the object.[72]

"When an individual becomes aware of the object which serves for the gratification of the urge and which is the aim of the drive, . . . the drive necessarily turns into a desire. . . . This transformation . . . brings about a change in the inner nature of the drive. . . . The drive becomes conscious."[73] In other words, an object-directed drive is no longer unconscious; the perception of objects is the sign of the conscious.

In this manner Rubinstein tried to develop a psychological theory based on empirical data, faithful to Marx's distinction between "reality" and "consciousness" and closely related to Pavlov's physiological findings. Undoubtedly Rubinstein came quite close to the theoretical interpretations of human behavior as developed by European and American psychologists, yet remaining faithful to Marx and Pavlov. Some of his critics were dissatisfied with this *rapprochement.*

Chernakov criticized Rubinstein for a "compromise" with the Western psychology and Freudian influence.[74] The latter seems to be undeniable.

Back to Pavlov

In 1950 the joint meeting of the Soviet Academy of Sciences and the Soviet Academy of Medical Sciences decided to "reconstruct on the basis of Pavlov's teachings: physiology, psychology, pathology, psychiatry. . . ." Since then, as pointed out by G. Razran in an excellent analysis of the Soviet psychology, the entire field of psychological research in the Soviet Union has become subordinated to an orthodox Pavlovianism. "Like Marx, Engels, Lenin and (until recently) Stalin, Pavlov is now a Soviet classic, endowed with almost theologistic prescience of certainties and surely above criticism and impugnations—a doctrine which Pavlov himself, the thoroughgoing empiricist and anti-dogmatist, fought all his life and, indeed, considered ridiculous."[75]

[71] *Ibid.,* p. 199.
[72] *Ibid.,* p. 488.
[73] *Ibid.,* p. 628.
[74] *Op. cit.,* p. 267.
[75] Razran, "Soviet Psychology Since 1950," *Science,* 1957, **126**, 1100–1107.

The Russians felt that Pavlov and Marx could be reconciled. With the emphasis shifting to Pavlov, studies in conditioning moved into the foreground. But while in the United States conditioning developed mainly into a nonphysiological learning theory, in the U.S.S.R. the physiological elements in conditioning dominate the picture. Some highly specialized studies in conditioning of inner organs deserve to be mentioned.

These experiments dealing with the conditioning of inner organs serve as a bridge between the physiology of the inner organs and the psychology of the learning process. In a highly interesting experiment conducted by Balakschina and reported by Bykov, conditioned reflexes were formed in denervated kidneys and in kidneys with the hypophysis destroyed. When the kidneys were denervated and the hypophysis was destroyed, the conditioning took place. In such a case the kidneys function as a physical and not as a physiological apparatus.[76]

What makes the difference between a physical and a physiological apparatus? Bykov believes that irradiation and concentration of excitation and inhibition, and the positive and negative induction, will be understood with the progress of "the chemical dynamics of the mediating substances in the central nervous system." But this would mean not only that psychology could be replaced by physiology but that physiology could be replaced by chemistry. Is this bold reductionism possible today? Will it ever be possible? The statements expressed by Pavlov and his disciples are hopeful, and the future will show whether they were justified.

Bykov and his associates (W. N. Tschernigowski, G. P. Konradi, and others) have proved the existence of inner receptors in practically all inner organs and have utilized their discovery for a far-reaching research in interoceptory conditioning. They had to confront a problem which occupies one of the main positions in the American theory of learning (cf. Chap. 4), i.e., the problem of pleasure and pain in conditioning. Bykov remarked that "the absence of pain sensations does not necessarily mean the absence of other receptors," and it "has been definitely proved that some organs . . . are devoid of pain sensibility."[77] Bykov found that several organs have receptors and their functions could be conditioned, yet there is complete absence of any pain reaction. Among those organs are the *peritoneum viscerale,* the surface of the cerebral hemispheres, and probably some parts of the intestine.

The pain fibers terminate in the thalamus (the lateral dorsothalamic fasciculus). However, several experiments involving speech signals (Pavlov's "second order" conditioning) gave "convincing evidence of the role of the cerebral cortex in pain reception."[78] Some experiments were carried

---

[76] Konstantin M. Bykov, *The Cerebral Cortex and the Inner Organs* (W. H. Gantt, trans. and ed.), Chemical Publishing Co., 1957, pp. 36 ff.

[77] *Ibid.,* p. 279.

[78] *Ibid.,* p. 344.

out with anesthesia (novocain) of the stimulated area. The unconditioned stimuli gave no pain reaction (zero plethysmogram), but in combination with the conditioned stimuli a reaction was evoked, namely, a constriction and dilation of vessels. Moreover, Bykov reports experiments conducted by Pshonik which proved that "the cortex has the capacity for inhibiting or annulling pain by turning pain sensations into sub-dolorotic sensations."[79]

Bykov tried to prove that there is no reason to distinguish between the reactions to the impulses coming from without (*milieu extérieur*) and from within the organism (*milieu intérieur*). Both kinds of receptor conditioning can take place.

The main differences between interoceptors and exteroceptors was stated by Bykov as follows: First, in the great majority of cases the stimulation of the exteroceptors has been accompanied by a subjectively perceived sensation, while the stimulation of the interoceptors is either not perceived subjectively at all or at least not accompanied by definite and localized sensations. The stimulation of exteroceptors may lead to variant actions not determined by the nature of the stimulus or the stimulated organ. The stimulation of interoceptors leads to a reaction which may be complicated but is invariably determined by the nature of the stimulus and the stimulated organ.[80] Moreover, "impulses conveyed from visceral receptors should be characterized as subthreshold impulses as compared to those conveyed from exteroceptors."[81] They may cause "subconscious" sensations.

Bykov and his associates have conducted experiments in which the existence of interoceptors in the stomach was proved. At the time of pouring water into a dog's stomach, his hindfoot was exposed to an electric current which led to a reflex of bending of the leg. Thereafter, pouring water into the stomach led to the foot reaction, which became a conditioned reflex. Obviously the walls of the stomach contain some receptory apparatus (analyzer) which is capable of communicating with the cerebral centers. In several other experiments interoceptory conditioning was performed on kidneys, gall, and heart and even inner secretion was increased or decreased. The inner organs became conditioned to tactile, electric, chemical, vocal, and other stimuli.

Concluding Remarks on Soviet Psychology

With the growing emphasis on physiological factors and improved and more precise methods of study the Soviet psychologists were able to enter new areas of research such as speech, learning, perception, etc.[82]

[79] *Ibid.*, p. 341.
[80] *Ibid.*, p. 244.
[81] *Ibid.*, p. 277.
[82] Simon Brian (ed.), *Psychology in the Soviet Union*, Stanford University, 1957.

In contradistinction to the American psychologists, the Russians show conformity to one philosophy and they work within set limits of conceptualization centered around Marx and Pavlov, with Pavlov's influence dominating.

Within these limits they have achieved significant results in the direction of both interoceptive conditioning and "higher order" conditioning to words and symbols.[83] One wonders whether the results achieved are related to their philosophy or to a concentrated effort or to other factors. Whatever the reasons, the achievements in conditioning are considerable.

Soviet psychology tried very hard to move toward the hoped-for solution of the soma-psyche dichotomy. There is no doubt that significant progress was made as far as the physiological part is concerned; interoceptive conditioning offers new vistas in the study of unconscious processes and the pleasure-pain issue. But one cannot help wondering how much truth there is in what Pavlov said: that "the moment when the natural and inevitable joining and fusion of the psychological and physiological, of the subjective and the objective, will be accomplished is sure to come." Is this optimism justified? Is the answer near or at all possible? Are we coming close to crossing the soma-psyche bridge? Let us leave the discussion of this question to the last chapter of the book.

[83] A. R. Luria, *The Nature of Human Conflicts or Emotion, Conflict and Will,* Liveright, 1932.

CHAPTER 3

Behaviorism and Reductionism

1. JOHN B. WATSON: PSYCHOLOGY AS THE SCIENCE OF BEHAVIOR

Psychology Without Consciousness

The man who crossed the bridge and closed the gap between the study of animal behavior and the study of human behavior was John Broadus Watson. Watson combined into one system the philosophical pragmatism of James, the psychological functionalism of Dewey, the experimental method of animal psychology of Yerkes, and the conditioning of Pavlov and Bekhterev.

Watson's system is based upon *determinism, empiricism, reductionism,* and *environmentalism.* These four principles guided Watson's work and were incorporated with great consistency in his research. In Watson's own eyes his psychological system is such that "given the stimulus, psychology can predict what the response will be. Or, on the other hand, given the response, it can specify the nature of the effective stimulus."[1]

In accordance with radical empiricism Watson rejected anything that could not be observed from without. In his bias against unobserved phenomena, he outdistanced Pavlov, and in his zeal for a radical reductionism he was matched only by Bekhterev.

"I do not wish unduly to criticize psychology," said Watson in 1913. "It has failed signally, I believe, during the fifty-odd years of its existence as an experimental discipline, to make its place in the world as an undisputed natural science. . . . The time seems to have come when psychology must discard all reference to consciousness; when it need no longer delude itself into thinking that it is making mental states the object of observation. . . ."[2]

Instead, Watson proposes a psychology, "which I should attempt to build up that would take as a starting point, first, the observable facts

[1] John B. Watson, *Psychology from the Standpoint of a Behaviorist,* Lippincott, 1919, p. 10.
[2] John B. Watson, "Psychology as the Behaviorist Sees It," *Psychological Review,* 1913, **20,** 158–177.

that organisms, man and animal alike, do adjust themselves to their environment by means of hereditary and habit equipments. These adjustments may be very adequate or they may be so inadequate that the organism barely maintains its existence; secondly, that certain stimuli lead the organisms to make these responses. In a system of psychology completely worked out, given the stimuli the response can be predicted."[3]

Watson's psychology dealt with overt and observable behavior of the organism, its muscles, glands, and tissues. Watson hoped that all human behavior could be interpreted in physical-chemical terms. "Psychology, as the behaviorist views it, is a purely objective, experimental branch of natural science which needs introspection as little as do sciences of chemistry and physics. It is granted that the behavior of animals can be investigated without appeal to consciousness. . . . The position is taken here that the behavior of man and the behavior of animals must be considered on the same plane. . . .

"This suggested elimination of states of consciousness as proper objects of investigation in themselves will remove the barrier from psychology which exists between it and other sciences. The findings of psychology become the functional correlates of structure and lend themselves to explanation in physical-chemical terms."[4]

In his programmatic book Watson wrote as follows: "Psychology as a science of consciousness has no community of data. The reader will find no discussion of consciousness and no reference to such terms as sensation, perception, attention, image, will and the like. . . . I frankly do not know what they mean, nor do I believe that anyone can use them consistently."[5]

Nurture vs. Nature

Watson's idea underwent a definite evolution. Until 1915 there was no mention of conditioning. In 1915 in his presidential address to the American Psychological Association, he took up the matter of conditioned reflexes. In his book in 1919 conditioned reflexes became very prominent; in 1920 he reported conditioning of fears in humans.

In 1919 Watson still admitted the existence of innate instincts and emotions but limited them to very few relatively simple responses—fear, rage, and love. In 1925 he discarded completely the instinct theory. He was undoubtedly under the influence of Z. Y. Kuo (see Chap. 5, section 1), who believed that all human behavior is learned.

Watson took a radical environmentalistic stand in the nature-nurture

[3] *Ibid.*
[4] *Ibid.*
[5] Watson, *Psychology from the Standpoint of a Behaviorist*, p. xii.

controversy. He did not deny the fact that certain patterns of behavior
were innate but said they were very limited in number and rather
unimportant in comparison with the role of experience. "Give me a
dozen healthy infants, well formed," he declared, ". . . to bring them up
in and I'll guarantee you to take any one at random and train him to
become any type of specialist I might select—doctor, lawyer, artist, mer-
chant-chief and, yes, even beggar-man and thief, regardless of his
talents, penchants, tendencies, abilities, vocations, and race of his ancestors."[6] Yet Watson did not reject the concept of instinct. He believed
that instinct was "a hereditary pattern reaction, the separate elements
of which are movements principally of the striped muscles. It might
otherwise be expressed as a combination of explicit congenital responses
unfolding serially under appropriate stimulation." Instinct is a system
of inherited or unconditioned reflexes; instinctive activity is a complex
response of a series of reflexes to "sensory stimuli in contact with the
animal's body or at a distance in his environment."[7]

Theory of Learning

Watson was critical of Thorndike's annoyers and satisfiers, which had
the flavor of subjectively perceived emotions and introspection. Of all
the laws of association Watson preferred the laws of frequency and
recency. Most frequent and most recent acts were the successful ones;
in animal learning, the proper interpretation of learning was the one
offered by the laws of frequency and recency.

Bekhterev's and Pavlov's conditioning solved Watson's difficulties. Watson admitted that the term "habit formation," which he had been using
in his writings, was rather vague. The conditioned response offered a
better way of interpreting learning and could be "looked upon as the
unit of what we had been calling *habit*." And certainly, added Watson,
from that point on he gave the master his due credit.

Yet never was Watson's theory of conditioning an exact translation
and application of Pavlov's theory. Watson believed that the conditioned
stimulus was a "substitute" stimulus for the unconditioned one. Such
a statement was never made by Pavlov.

Experiments in conditioning in humans were first performed by Pavlov's disciple Krasnogorski. In the United States Florence Mateer published in 1918 a volume in which she reported her experiments in
conditioning in children. She used the method of placing a bandage
over the eyes of the child as conditioned stimulus before food was
placed in the child's mouth.[8]

   [6] John B. Watson, *Behaviorism,* Kegan Paul, 1925, p. 82.
   [7] *Ibid.,* p. 262.
   [8] Florence Mateer, *Child Behavior, a Critical and Experimental Study of Young
Children by the Method of Conditioned Reflexes,* Badger, 1918.

Conditioning or association by contiguity became incorporated in Watson's theory. Watson applied conditioning to most complex forms of learning. He considered trial-and-error learning a simple case in conditioning. Watson maintained that the right response was the most recent one and it occurred more frequently during the process of learning, since it appeared, at any rate, at least once on each trial. As said before, Watson incorporated Thorndike's sublaws of trial and error in his theory of learning while consistently rejecting Thorndike's law of effect.

Perception, Thought, and Speech

All human behavior was divided by Watson into *explicit* and *implicit*. Explicit behavior included all observable activities such as walking, talking, cutting wood, and smiling. Implicit behavior included the secretion of glands, some muscle contractions, and visceral and nerve functions.

Sensation and perception presented certain difficulties for behaviorism. Introspectionists tried to interpret these phenomena with the help of the descriptions given by the perceiving subject.

Behaviorists reject the notion of "sensation" because no one can observe another person's sensations. What can be observed is the response to a certain stimulus, be it visual, auditory, or olfactory. This is the method applied in animal psychology; the experimental animal responds to stimuli, and both stimulus and response are observable data.

In the controversy with the introspectionists Watson suggested the "verbal report" as the way out. Speech is an act of overt behavior just like any other act. It is a movement of lips and tongue, push of air, sound, etc. "Verbal report" is a sort of motor response to sensory stimuli. It should be considered at its face value like any other motor response. When the subject says, for example, "I do not see," he has said that he does not see. The verbal report "registers" the stimulus just as the thermometer registers the temperature.

Even the range of perception, from the red to the violet end of the spectrum, for instance, could be studied objectively, and Watson suggested the following procedure: By the use of any wave length and of an electric shock a conditioned reflex could be established. "We then increase the length of the wave rather sharply and, if the reflex appears, we again increase the wave length. We finally reach a point where the reflex breaks down, even when punishment is used to restore it. . . ." A similar procedure should be applied to the violet end. "In this way we determine the individual's range just as surely as if we had stimulated the subject with monochromatic lights varying in wave lengths and asked him if he saw them."[9] The verbal report of the subject

[9] Watson, *Psychology from the Standpoint of a Behaviorist,* p. 35.

saying "I do not see" can be, believed Watson, safely considered a part of the objective experimental procedure.

Watson went even farther in his reductionistic endeavor: Perception is a function of sensory nerves which "register" the stimuli and transmit them to the brain hemispheres. In accordance with the physiological theory of conditioning, the brain is not only a conducting but a connecting apparatus. The nervous impulses coming from the sensory receptors are transferred to the motor centers and lead to a motor reaction. Human behavior can be reduced to a sensory-central-motor chain of stimuli and responses. The same applies to the processes of memory. They are created by residues or afterimages of sensory stimulations combined with kinesthetic elements of the muscles of the mouth in implicit speech processes.

The child learns to speak through his own unlearned vocalization. Words are acquired by conditioning. The child learns speech and through speech establishes a firm contact with his environment.

At the beginning speech is overt behavior—"explicit," as Watson calls it. It is a sort of manipulation of the situation and environment by substituting words for overt manual movement. Not all movements are relegated to the larynx; shrugging of shoulders, nodding of head, frowning and grimaces, gestures and cries—all these are responses to a situation.

The most economic way of reaction is speech. Speech is thinking and thinking is speech. The overt expression of words, acquired by conditioning, becomes modified. As the child grows, he learns to avoid too much overt expression. He learns to speak subvocally, and no one can hear his voiceless speech. This voiceless speech, as well as vocal speech, is identical with thinking. The only difference between the two types of speech lies in the fact that the former is an implicit kind of behavior while the latter is explicit. Obviously neither kind of speech requires any "consciousness" or introspection.

As a rule, verbal-language reactions accompany manual and visceral ones. Man controls his behavior by verbalizing it; it is easier to manipulate and experiment with words than to manipulate objects.

Emotions

"An emotion," says Watson, "is a hereditary 'pattern-reaction' involving profound changes of the bodily mechanisms as a whole, but particularly of the visceral and glandular systems. By pattern-reaction we mean that the separate details of response appear with some constancy, with some regularity, and in approximately the same sequential order each time the exciting stimulus is prescribed."[10]

[10] *Ibid.*, p. 195.

Emotions stem from reflex activity in the erogenous zone. There are two kinds of this complex reflex activity called emotion. One leads toward movement; this is the *tumescence* reflex activity. The other type, the *detumescence* reflex, releases "the movements of avoidance."

Watson maintained that three innate emotions could be found in human infants: rage, fear, and love. These are the basic pattern-reactions which are inherited. Any other emotions or combinations of them are acquired by conditioning.

Watson produced what he believed to be empirical proof of the existence of these pattern-reactions in infants. "The *hampering of the infant's* movements is the factor which, apart from all training, brings out the movements characterized as rage. If the face or head is held, crying results, quickly followed by screaming. The body stiffens and fairly well-coordinated slashing or striking movements of the hands and arms result. The feet and legs are drawn up and down; the breath is held until the child's face is flushed."[11]

Fear is provoked in newborn infants by a violent noise or by a sudden removal of support. The reaction of love is produced by a gentle stroking of the genitalia.

Adult emotions are a product of the basic pattern-reactions but are largely modified by life experiences. "Apparently the hereditary pattern as a whole gets broken up. At any rate, it largely disappears (the parts never disappear), except under unusual conditions, and there can be noted only a reinforcement or inhibition of the habit and instinctive (exaggerated and depressed reflexes, for example) activities taking place at the moment." Especially "the implicit, mainly glandular and smooth muscular side of the pattern, remains. The emotionally exciting object releases important internal secretions which . . . reinforce or inhibit those actually in progress."[12]

All other emotions are derivations of the basic emotions developed by the means of conditioning. Shame is connected with punishment for masturbation. Jealousy arises as a response to interference with the innate emotional response of the erogenous zone. The affected individual experiences muscular tension and flushing of face, moves away from his spouse, withdraws or assaults.

Personality

Personality is the end-product of our habit systems. It is the sum of "the individual's total assets (actual and potential) and liabilities (actual and potential) on the reaction side."

Behaviorism regards personality as a totality of behavioral patterns.

---

[11] *Ibid.*, p. 200.
[12] *Ibid.*, pp. 197–198.

These patterns are quite consistent but not unchangeable. Some conditioned reflexes can become extinct or reinforced and new ones may become established. No individual remains himself all his life. Usually individuals do not change rapidly and one's personality undergoes slow and gradual modification. At any moment personality can be compared to "an assembled organic machine ready to run."

In the study of personality one has to consider the innate or unconditioned reflexes, the conditioned reflexes, and the physical and social environment and its influence upon personality development.

The task of psychologists is *to know in order to improve*. Human life, human relations, and societies are not unchangeable. Patterns of behavior can be conditioned and unconditioned, reinforced and extinguished. Psychology is an applied science and should be used for the betterment of men.[13]

It is up to men to make mankind happy and it is the task of the psychologist to be of help to mankind. Education which is nothing but conditioning is the powerful lever to be used by behavioristically oriented parents. "The universe will change if you bring up your children . . . in behavioristic freedom. . . . Will not these children in turn, with their better ways of living and thinking, replace us as society, and in turn bring up their children in a still more scientific way, until the world finally becomes a place fit for human habitation."[14]

Physiology or Psychology?

Watson believed that the motor pattern is a chain of movements; each movement arouses kinesthetic impulses which in turn produce the next movement. In his early studies on maze learning, he attributed the role of coordinating behavior to the kinesthetic processes. The latter offered Watson the necessary link between the observable stimulus and the observable response. Without them he was unable to explain what happens between stimulus and response. In the seventeenth century Descartes had perceived human behavior as a result of the motion of a fluid from the sense organs to the brain along the nerves and back from the brain to the nerve endings in the muscles. The brain (more precisely, the pineal gland) was regarded by Descartes as the seat of the nonmaterial soul, which controlled both perception and motility.

Apparently, a mechanistic and materialistic interpretation of human behavior must *reduce* psychology to a branch of physiology and actually deny the existence of anything outside the realm of anatomy and physiology. This was exactly what Bekhterev tried to do and Yenchman did.

Watson could not accept these naïve theories. He was determined to

[13] It is interesting to note that Alfred Adler expressed similar optimism (Chap. 7).
[14] Watson, *Behaviorism*.

apply the *methods* of the natural sciences but did not expect to attain satisfactory results by imitating their content. He did realize that between the two observable factors of stimulus and response something was going on which could not be overlooked or denied.

The solution of this problem offered by Watson was, in fact, an evasion, but this evasion was committed in the best tradition of Hume's empiricism. Watson simply refused to deal with unobservable data. Psychology deals with what *is* or *can be* observed. What is observed is the *explicit* behavior and what can be observed is the *implicit* behavior. Watson's psychology, named by him "the science of behavior," was closely related to and even overlapped physiology but it never was a physiology or a branch of it. "Behavior psychology" was not physiology for, as Watson put it, "nowhere in physiology do we get the organism, as it were, put back together again and tested in relation to its environment as a whole." Physiology deals with definite functions of the organism and "knows nothing of the total situations in the daily life of an individual that shape his action and conduct,"[15] while the psychologist deals with the relationship of the organism as a whole to its environment.

This molar-physiological approach seems to be of great significance in Watson's system. To Watson psychology is a natural science, a very close "scientific companion" of physiology, and the main difference between the two disciplines lies in the "grouping" of problems. While physiology deals with particulars, psychology, without neglecting "the functioning of these parts," is "intrinsically interested in what the whole animal will do from morning to night and from night to morning." Watson firmly points to the *molar* approach. "No matter what the human animal is doing, he does it as a whole." This physiological molar concept was the new point Watson endeavored to prove.

Concluding Remarks

An evasion of a problem does not equal its solution. Suppose all experimental subjects of the behaviorist react to stimuli and nothing else happens. The subjects do not "feel," "perceive," "think," "empathize," or do anything which looks or sounds like a "mentalism." All well and good, but how does the behaviorist know what is going on with his subjects? If he were what his subjects are, he would discharge visual or auditory responses, make verbal reports, and nothing else. How could the behaviorist interpret, reason, and develop any theory; how could he become convinced or believe in anything at all? "*L'homme machine*" of Descartes (with the exclusion of the soul) or La Mettrie (with some modifications) could not have developed any psychological

---

[15] Watson, *Psychology from the Standpoint of a Behaviorist*, p. 20.

theories, even mechanistic-materialistic ones. Obviously the behaviorist seems to consider himself an exception to the push-and-pull model of the behavioristic psychology.

Watson suggested eliminating from psychological investigation the "states of consciousness," because consciousness is the tool with which "all scientists work," and whether or not the tool is properly used at present by scientists is a "problem for philosophy and not for psychology."

But the "trouble with consciousness" started not because it had been included in some studies but because the entire field of inquiry was limited to consciously perceived phenomena, i.e., to the surface of a volcano or to the smoke of a great fire. Thorndike, Watson, and all animal psychologists widened the field in one direction, Freud in another. Once psychology included behavior which was not perceived by the subject (Freud) and which could be seen by others (Watson), there was no more need to expel consciousness. The consciousness or conscious is a legitimate though limited topic of psychological inquiry. Even the introspection method may be usefully applied in research with some degree of caution.

Watson was unable to keep his programmatic promise. He promised a psychology in which, given the stimulus, the response could be predicted and in which only observable data were included. But by introducing the "verbal report" Watson opened the door for introspectionism. The idea of the "verbal report" does not stand the test of logic. If a verbal report is good in the case of sensation, why is it no good in other cases? If it is a reliable and objective method, why behaviorism at all? Let subjects report verbally what they have seen by self-observation and the clock of psychology will be turned back to introspectionism.

It seems advisable to distinguish between the methodological approach of behaviorism and behaviorism as a theory of human behavior. The first insists on avoiding statements which cannot be proved by controlled experiments or observation. This kind of behaviorism must reject introspection, psychoanalysis, Rorschach, etc., as unscientific methods. The other kind of behaviorism has erected a mechanistic model of human beings with little credit to heredity and practically everything explained by conditioning.

One may accept the first sort of behaviorism without approving of the second. Watson tried to combine both and hence the apparent weakness of his system. Not all data are observable, and nonobservable data are not necessarily the same as observable ones. Any scientific inquiry comes to grips with nonobservable data; Watson and Bekhterev went about it in rather a crude and naïve way. Bekhterev lumped all nonobservable data together under the vague and pseudo-materialistic name of energy. Watson was less naïve and his term "implicit behavior" covers a great variety of phenomena. However, in his effort to reduce psychology to some sort of generalized physiology he reduced all unobservable data such as thinking, feeling, and perceiving to physiological facts of muscular tensions and glandular secretions which could not be observed but were believed to be observable in the future. One must ask at this point: What is the methodological advantage of shifting away from one kind of unobservable facts in an area under consideration to another unobservable group of facts without making sure that these two groups form a continuum? But Watson was not the first and maybe not the last to believe that inner secretion or electric waves are more self-explanatory than feelings or thinking and that physiological facts could be substituted for mental processes and everything would be explained in a scientifically satisfactory manner.

2. THE EARLY BEHAVIORISTS

Albert P. Weiss: Biosocial Behaviorism

The reductionistic aspect of behaviorism was vigorously defended by Albert P. Weiss. In 1925 Weiss published a volume entitled *A Theoretical Basis of Human Behavior*.[16] The conscious, mentalism, and introspection were banned from the realm of psychology. The entire functioning of the organism was interpreted in terms of physicochemical processes and interaction with the environment. Weiss propagated the most radical sort of reductionism. He believed that psychology could not deal with anything but the same elements of matter as physics did. The subject matter of any science is physical processes: psychology deals with those physical processes which take place in the nervous system. Protons and electrons are the elements of the physical world and there is no other world but the physical one.

Weiss emphasized the "biological and social components" of the behavioristic analysis. Through emphasis on social factors Weiss could draw a line between psychology and physiology. Both study physical phenomena in the nervous system, but psychology concentrates on the interaction between the organism and its environment. Such an approach, in the best tradition of behaviorism, kept psychology within the realm of the natural sciences and yet enabled it to analyze social and cultural problems. Whatever a man does, Weiss implied, is done in accordance with the laws of nature, and psychology is a branch of biology which, in turn, is a branch of physics. There are indeed no other bodies, no other events, no other entities but those which form the subject matter

[16] Albert P. Weiss., *A Theoretical Basis of Human Behavior* (2nd ed.), R. G. Adams. 1929.

of physics. However, the human organism is not only biological but social or, as Weiss put it, *biosocial,* and here new vistas open to the research worker.

Perhaps the newborn is a biological entity only, but as he grows and develops his behavior undergoes changes. One of the most important tasks of psychology is to study the impact of social forces upon human behavior. Human behavior is always biological and always social since other humans act as stimuli upon our organism. New responses to the new and changing social situation are the main topic of psychological inquiry. Child development and learning are the proper areas of study, which has to apply observation and experimentation patterned upon the natural sciences. Introspection, mentalistic terminology, the conscious, etc., will be of no avail in such an objective type of study as Weiss planned.

Weiss did not have the chance to implement his research program, which was both bold and consistent. His emphasis on interaction between the organism and its social environment was well accepted and several research workers continued what he initiated.

Edward B. Holt: Unorthodox Behaviorism

Watson and many other behaviorists expelled the conscious from the realm of science and tried to represent the human organism as a physiological apparatus and nothing more. The problem of the conscious was dealt with in a different manner by E. B. Holt. He did not discuss the term "consciousness" or "conscious." He suggested relating it to *epistemological realism,* which believes that objects are as perceived even when they are not perceived by us. The conscious would mean an adjustment of the sensorimotor apparatus to the perceived object; it is a sort of photographic lens which reflects the correct picture of the reflected object. In the controversy between epistemological criticism and realism, the former, starting with Kant, ascribed to perceived objects elements stemming from the perceiving subject. In contradistinction to this point of view the realists believe that we perceive the world correctly or almost correctly. At any rate, the nature of the world does not depend to any extent upon our perceptory apparatus. Holt, being a realist, logically concluded that the existence of the conscious was a function of the perceiving apparatus.

Watson's idea that thinking is merely a matter of language mechanisms was taken up by Holt. The passive language habits or the response to words is nothing but conditioning. Pavlov named it "second-order conditioning." Holt believed that words can "substitute" for the unconditioned stimulus in the same manner as conditioning was interpreted by Watson. In representing the problem of language as a higher-order conditioning Holt opened the way for future studies in verbal conditioning.

Holt's unorthodox behaviorism enabled him to take an attitude of keen interest in problems not directly related to the academic psychology and to utilize a great variety of sources outside his main field of endeavor.[17]

Holt, like Watson, rejected the idea of heredity as far as human behavior was concerned. He was convinced that even the unconditioned reflexes were acquired either in prenatal life or soon after birth.

Behavior patterns are acquired in two ways. The first way is learning. Learning may take place when the organism is exposed to either outer or inner motivation. Outer stimulation corresponds to what Pavlov and Watson studied in the experiments on conditioning when their subjects were confronted with stimuli coming from without. However, the inner needs or drives such as hunger, thirst, etc., may also force the organism to learn; "since their stimuli are contained within the organism, these cannot be avoided by ordinary avoidance response (locomotion, etc.) but will keep the organism restless until it acquires, by trial and error, very different and other intricate modes of response which will allay the internal stimulation."[18] Holt implied that learning may take place as a result of inner needs. In this way he paved the road for the future development of the learning theory by Hull (cf. Chap. 4) with the emphasis on drive reduction.

As mentioned before, Holt did not limit all human behavior to conditioning. He noticed that adults often preserve childish patterns of behavior although some of these patterns have never been reinforced. Such behavioral preferences established in childhood and persisting into the later years of life were called by Holt (after Janet) canalization. Gardner Murphy took up the idea of canalization and developed it into one of the main aspects of his theory of personality (cf. Chap. 15).

Walter S. Hunter: Anthroponomy

Hunter suggested substituting for the term "psychology" another name which would better represent the new science of human behavior. His choice was *anthroponomy,* in analogy to anatomy or astronomy, as a science of the laws (*nomos*) that govern human behavior. He wrote: "Psychology, unlike the other sciences, has not found it possible to continue with the subject matter bequeathed it by philosophy." "For good or ill the onward march of experiment, which no mere speculation and controversy can halt, has carried psychology along the way of the objective study of human behavior." "Psychology seems to describe

[17] Edward B. Holt, *The Freudian Wish and Its Place in Ethics,* Holt, 1915.
[18] Edward B. Holt, *Animal Drives and the Learning Process,* Holt, 1931, p. 125.

and explain, to predict and control, the extrinsic behavior of the organism to an external environment which is predominantly social."[19]

Hunter conducted experiments in *delayed responses* or *delayed reactions*. A light stimulus was directed toward the spot in which food was placed but the experimental animals were prevented from moving in the right direction. Then the stimulus was removed and after a lapse of time the animals were permitted to move freely. Hunter's dogs, rats, and racoons reacted successfully to the original stimulus despite the lapse of time. This reaction was named by Hunter the delayed reaction.

Hunter was the first to use the *temporal maze,* in which motor learning processes were studied. The temporal maze had no blind alleys. Hunter's temporal maze represented a continuous pathway in the shape of a rectangular number 8 with 8 square corners. His experimental animals acted in the maze as if they were avoiding repetition. Their choices seemed to be highly selective and not sheer trial and error.

Following the environmental orientation of behaviorism Hunter tried to substitute environment for the conscious. He believed that what comes from the outside and what we perceive is nothing but the outer world. Therefore, he concluded, "I wish to point out that the consciousness or experience for the psychologist is merely a name which he applies to what other people call environment."[20]

With this presentation Hunter was identifying the content of our perception with the function of perceiving. This naïve epistemological realism is characteristic of most of the early behaviorists. Hunter hoped to overcome the physical-mental dichotomy by overlooking the existence of mental factors, by replacing the fact that man perceives environment by the mere fact that environment is what is being perceived, and finally by confusing the perceiving subject with the perceived object. It was indeed a regression to pre-Kantian reasoning, common to Bekhterev, Watson, and many other naïve materialists.

3. KARL S. LASHLEY: BRAIN MECHANISMS

Support of Watson

Lashley is one of the leading authorities in the physiology of the nervous system, and his adherence to behaviorism has added prestige to Watson's method of interpretation. Lashley's studies stand on their

---

[19] Walter S. Hunter, "The Psychological Study of Behavior," *Psychological Review,* 1932, **39**, 1–24.

[20] Walter S. Hunter, "Anthroponomy and Psychology," in C. Murchison (ed.), *Psychologies of 1930,* Clark University, 1930, p. 283.

own merits; their implication for psychological theory parallels the studies of Pavlov, Bekhterev, and Bykov.

Lashley has been an outspoken follower of Watson. He wrote: "To me the essence of behaviorism is the belief that the study of man will reveal nothing except what is adequately describable in the concepts of mechanics and chemistry." And later: "The behaviorist denies sensations, images and all other phenomena which the subjectivist claims to find by introspection." Lashley was extremely critical of introspection, which is "an example of pathology of scientific method."[21]

Thus far Lashley offered an unconditional support to Watson. However, his own carefully planned experiments could not fit into Watson's theoretical framework. To begin with, Lashley, in contradistinction to Watson, did not accept uncritically Pavlov's theory of conditioning. In numerous and ingenious experiments he came often to conclusions not necessarily identical with those of Pavlov and he disagreed with Pavlov on the issue of generalization. Lashley believed that generalization does depend to a lesser degree upon the nature of the stimulus and to a much greater extent upon the nature of the organism. Furthermore, the gradient of habit strength is not a result of spread or generalization of "connections" but depends upon the stimulus threshold of the organism.[22]

The "Mass-Action"

As said before, behaviorism leaned heavily toward physiology. Watson saw the only difference between psychology and physiology in the psychological-molar versus physiological-molecular approach. Lashley's studies have shown the fruitfulness of the molar approach even in physiology.

In a series of experiments conducted by Lashley together with his former teacher, Shepherd I. Franz,[23] animals (cats and monkeys) were trained to escape from boxes similar to those used by E. L. Thorndike. After they had learned to escape, several parts of the cortex were cut away. Whenever the acquisition of the escape habit was recent, brain operations resulted in a complete loss of the acquired habit. However, whenever the habit was firmly established, the animals performed after the operation almost as well as before it. In other experiments the frontal lobes were severed and the animals learned without them as well as with them. Franz and Lashley summarized their conclusions as

[21] Karl S. Lashley, "The Behaviorist Interpretation of Conscious," *Psychological Review*, 1923, **30**, 237–272, 329–353.
[22] K. S. Lashley and M. Wade, "The Pavlovian Theory of Generalization," *Psychological Review*, 1946, **53**, 72–87.
[23] Shepherd I. Franz, *Nervous and Mental-Re-education*, Macmillan, 1923.

follows: "The experiments show that in the white rat the removal of large parts of the frontal portions of the brain does not greatly interfere with a learned reaction."[24]

In further experiments Lashley trained rats in the discrimination of light. After the rats had learned to discriminate brightness, Lashley operated on practically every part of the cortex, but in no case did the rats lose what they had learned prior to the surgical operations. Lashley was unable to prove that subcortical centers take over the function of the damaged cortical centers. The most justified conclusion was that the brain functions as a whole and the remaining parts of the brain take over the function of the damaged parts. Obviously these studies lend significant support to a holistic, molar point of view.

These and other experiments led Franz and Lashley to postulate two laws. The first was the law of *mass action*. Lashley was opposed to the theory of synapses within definite conduction units of the nervous system. Learning, he said, is not a product of the overcoming of synaptic resistances and establishing of new synaptic connections, as Sherrington[25] or Thorndike (cf. Chap. 1) implied. Lashley's experiment indicated that the retention of an established habit did not depend upon any specific synapses or any specific intercellular connections. "The rate of learning of the four mazes reported in this study is clearly a function of the total mass of tissue and the evidence presented indicates that retentiveness as such for these habits is conditioned in the same way." The amount, the mass of undestroyed tissues determines the degree of retentiveness irrespective of the area damage. Obviously this conclusion was not in accordance with the theory of localization. Furthermore, Lashley's experiments prove that the "visual discrimination habit which normally involves only the occipital cortex, is formed with equal facility in the absence of this area."[26]

Equipotentiality

Actually Lashley was not entirely opposed to the theory of localization. What his experiments proved was the importance of the amount of intact nervous tissue for the learning process and the ability of those intact remaining tissues to take over the functions of the destroyed tissues. This ability, named by Lashley *equipotentiality*, represents the second law in Lashley's theory, the first being *mass action*. In other words, the learning process is a process in which the entire *mass* of the

[24] Shepherd I. Franz and Karl S. Lashley, "The Retention of Habits by the Rat after Destruction of the Frontal Portion of the Cerebrum," *Psychology*, 1917, 1, 3–7, 13–18.

[25] C. S. Sherrington, *The Integrative Action of the Nervous System*, Scribner, 1906.

[26] Karl S. Lashley, *Brain Mechanisms and Intelligence: A Quantitative Study of Injuries to the Brain*, University of Chicago, 1929, pp. 128 ff.

nervous system participates and, if a part of the system is missing, the remaining parts are *equipotential* to carry on the activity which might be primarily a function of a certain area. Even when the visual area was removed and the rats lost the ability of pattern vision, they could still discriminate the intensity of light, avoid obstacles, follow the light signal, and obtain food.

Lashley's experimental studies in neurosurgery brought him close to the gestalt theory (cf. Chap. 12). Lashley found that relational properties do not depend upon the size, area of stimulus, etc.; square or rectangle is perceived as such under any circumstances.[27]

These and other studies brought Lashley to emphasize the gestalt ideas in perception and learning. Yet it would be rather difficult to include him with field theorists or gestaltists, for Lashley was highly critical of Köhler's field theory of excitation and never gave up his qualified but persistent adherence to Watson-Pavlov theories.[28]

Apparently Lashley was gradually putting more emphasis on "central" elements in the learning process; he did it much more than Hull, Tolman, or Skinner did. Even when Lashley concluded that only the "dominant" elements in stimuli become conditioned, he was still more in accord with Pavlov than with Köhler. Actually, Pavlov's studies imply that only the "stronger" stimulus will become conditioned, the term "stronger" being related either to the strength of the stimulus proper or to the strength of the stimulated center (cf. Chap. 2). The idea of set or selective conditioning was developed by G. Razran, who never was a gestaltist but always has been a brilliant and original interpreter of Pavlov (cf. Chap. 4). Selective conditioning is still conditioning and not gestalt.

Lashley emphasized the factor of *organization* in learning: In support of Krechevsky's theory,[29] which maintained that the rats do not act at random but are selective in their choice of clues, Lashley wrote: "The mechanism of nervous integration is such that when any complex of stimuli arouses nervous activity, that activity is immediately organized and certain elements or components become dominant for reaction while others become ineffective. In any trial of a training series, only those components of the stimulating situation which are dominant in the organization are associated. Other stimuli which excite the receptors are not associated because the animal is not set to react to them."[30]

---

[27] Karl S. Lashley, "The Problem of Cerebral Organization," in H. Klüver (ed.), *Visual Mechanisms*, Cattell, 1942, pp. 301–322.

[28] Cf. Ernest Hilgard, *Theories of Learning*, Appleton-Century-Crofts, 1948, pp. 296–297.

[29] I. Krechevsky, "A Study of the Continuity of the Problem-Solving Process," *Psychological Review*, 1938, **45**, 107–133.

[30] Karl S. Lashley, "An Examination of the 'Continuity Theory' as Applied to Discriminative Learning," *Journal of Genetic Psychology*, 1942, **26**, 241–265.

Reductionism

Thus Lashley can still be classified as a behaviorist, but not as an orthodox follower of Watson. Lashley explained his attitude as follows: "I
became glib in formulating all problems of psychology in terms of
stimulus-response and in explaining all things as conditioned reflexes. . . .
[However], the conditioned reflex turned out not to be a reflex, not the
simple basic key to the learning problem. . . . The nature of the stimulus
and of the response is intrinsically such as to preclude theory of simple
point-to-point connection in reflexes."[31]

Lashley was always consistent and persistent in his reductionism. In
1941 the great neurophysiologist Sherrington stated the pessimistic view
that brain and mind are still far apart and there is no way to bridge
the gap between the fact of brain and the experiences of mind. He
wrote: "The two for all I can do remain refractorily apart."[32]

Both Pavlov and Lashley expressed strong disapproval of this view.
Lashley wrote: "With this statement the greatest living neurophysiologist
despairs of finding a common ground between the sciences of the brain
and of the mind. He seems to have missed a solution of the problems by
no more than the turning of the page. In the same lectures he has faced
the problem of the nature of life and found that life is not a thing attached to this or that substance or chemical action, but is organized
activity, varying in character with complexity of structure and ranging
without discoverable discontinuity from the neatly crystalline simplicity
of the filterable virus to the elaborate organization of the mammalian
body. He has just missed seeing that mind also is not a thing attached
to life, a unique form of existence, but is a term including an indefinite
number of complex structures or relations."[33]

Concluding Remarks on Lashley and the Early Behaviorists

Lashley's theory represents a fruitful combination of a persistent
empiricism with a daring and consistent materialistic philosophy. Lashley
is undoubtedly the most scientific of the behaviorists and the best
equipped to handle the difficult problems created by the ardent reductionism of the behavioristic school.

Having conducted firsthand experimental studies in brain physiology,
Lashley is less prone to generalize than any other behaviorist. Some of
the early behaviorists oversimplified the problems instead of solving
them. They believed they could reduce human behavior to the overt
functions of the organism and its interaction with environment, and hoped

[31] Karl S. Lashley, "Cerebral Cortex versus Reflexology: A Reply to Professor
Hunter," *Journal of General Psychology*, 1931, **5**, 3–20.
[32] Charles S. Sherrington, *Man on His Nature*, Macmillan, 1941, p. 312.
[33] Karl S. Lashley, "Coalescence of Neurology and Psychology," *Proceedings of
the American Philosophical Society*, 1941, **84**, 461–470.

to be able to present psychology in physiological terms. Obviously they dealt with but a fraction of the phenomena, and even these phenomena were never put in physiological terms in a scientifically sound manner. No wonder that behaviorism in its orthodox form quickly lost ground.

Lashley was never an orthodox behaviorist. He deviated from Watson and Pavlov and came fairly close to Goldstein (cf. Chap. 5). In his later studies Lashley was no longer "glib"; he became a cautious, thorough, and persistent worker who tried very hard to find the continuity of organic life from "the neatly crystalline simplicity of the filterable virus to the elaborate organization of the mammalian body" and toward the human mind. Lashley never said that *"der Mensch ist was er isst"* ("Man is what he eats"). He is one of those great minds who believe in the soma-psyche continuity and who avoid sterile speculations, but whose empirical research brings more and more evidence of such a continuity. Whether this will be ultimately successful no one can predict.

4. DONALD O. HEBB: ORGANIZATION OF BEHAVIOR

Hebb's Position

It may seem unjustified to discuss the theory of D. O. Hebb in the same chapter with J. B. Watson and A. P. Weiss. It will probably seem less strange if our analysis of the writings of Hebb follows that of Lashley and both of them are included in the same chapter. As mentioned before, we follow in this book the principle of "common roots" rather than of "common roofs," and Hebb's original contribution to psychology shares its roots with the early behaviorists and their bold efforts to expel mentalism and to derive psychology from physiological data. There are deep differences between Hebb and Watson, yet both represent the same reductionism and empiricism, both emphasize the neurological aspects of psychology, and both pursue their studies in the spirit of associationism in contradistinction to gestalt and psychoanalysis.

Hebb's system is closely related and at the same time definitely opposed to Lashley's theory. Hebb emphasizes the local actions of cells and their more complex units and challenges Lashley's principle of equipotentiality. Hebb's writings display a certain effort to contradict both Lashley and Köhler. Hebb tried to develop a reductionistic system of psychology closely related to the observable data of neurology. However, instead of the synaptic connections between the neurons, he postulated organizational units allied to each other by synchronization of actions. Undoubtedly he is indebted to the gestalt theorists for his "organizational" deviation from associationism.

Assembly and Complex

Hebb's starting point is a group of sensory and motor neurons working together as a unit called an *assembly*. The cells which participate in an assembly are interconnected by several pathways and synapses. The discharge of energy ("firing") in these cells is coordinated and synchronized, so that they form a functional unit and act as a unit in the sensory and motor responses to oncoming stimuli.

Assemblies become formed by perceptual processes. If a person looks at an object, the cortical cells participating in this act become interconnected. They may be both afferent-sensory and efferent-motor cells, the latter directing the movement of eyes in the case of visual perception. In Hebb's words, "When an axon of cell A is near neough to excite a cell B and repeatedly or persistently takes part in firing it, some growth process or metabolic change takes place in one or both cells such that A's efficiency as one of the cells firing B is increased."[34]

The assembly of cortical neurons can undergo changes through either *fractionation* or *recruitment*. Fractionation takes place whenever some cells "fall out of line" and lose their synchronization with the assembly. Such a cell soon drops out. When neighboring cells join the assembly and become a part of it, recruitment takes place.

When our eye shifts from one item of an object to another, more assemblies are formed and these become interconnected. For instance, when we look at a triangle, we may first notice a definite part or angle. Several experiments with chimpanzees reared in darkness and with humans who see for the first time in their life after removal of a congenital cataract have shown that perception proceeds from parts to the whole. The human subjects noticed parts first and only after prolonged training could they grasp the figure. Hebb maintained that the perception of figures is not innate; it must be learned. Obviously his finding contradicts the findings of Köhler (cf. Chap. 12).

These associationistic ideas, which Hebb shared with Pavlov and Watson, in contradistinction to the gestalt, led him to postulate the *t* factor or the *superordinate system*. Whenever the separate assemblies become so well coordinated as to enable the individual to combine the respective elements perceived by him into a "distinctive whole," a *t* system of the assemblies has been formed. In looking at a triangle, our eye rests first on one of the *a* or *b* or *c* angles of the triangle. An assembly unit comes into being in our cortex. Then our eye shifts in the direction of the other two angles and two additional assembly units are formed. This shifting is reported as *phase sequence*. Any excitation "in one of the assemblies a, b, c and t is an unstable equilibrium which moves readily into another phase. The stability of a perception is not in

[34] Donald O. Hebb, *The Organization of Behavior*, Wiley, 1949, p. 62.

a single pattern of cerebral activity but in the tendency of the phases of an irregular cycle to recur at short intervals."[35]

Since the assemblies function almost simultaneously or at least are overlapping, their timing in the discharge of energy becomes synchronized and they form a *system* or a *complex* of assemblies. The superordinate *t* is defined by Hebb "as being whatever determinate, organized activity results from repeated activity in the earlier-developed or subordinate structures giving rise to it."[36] The *t* factor is instrumental in the formation of complexes.

Learning

Sometimes one assembly facilitates another and any *a* may facilitate a *b* or *c*. Attention is the "central facilitation" of perceptual activities or the tendency to form new complexes of assemblies.

Learning is a process in which *facilitations* are established in such a way that a certain neural unit, an assembly or a complex of cell assemblies, facilitates the oncoming of some other units. Once something has been learned, a given stimulus starts a series of well-established phase sequences. Once a definite cortical pattern has been established, on successive trials the same stimulus will set off the same phase sequences.

Simple relationships are as easily perceived by animals as by humans. In order to perceive more complex entities, the acquisition of the perception of a whole becomes important. Higher organisms are more capable of abstraction and generalization. Even if some elements of the totality are missing, they can still activate the *t* factor and perceive a triangle as a triangle despite the fact that the angles are not closed. This idea of perceiving of a whole or of a figure despite missing elements brings Hebb closer to the gestalt theory of *Prägnanz* (cf. Chap. 12) and K. Goldstein's figure-ground theory (cf. Chap. 5). However, one must admit that Hebb's theory stands on its own grounds in its original approach to learning, and the gestalt element in it is always secondary and never considered to be an innate feature of living organisms.

Motivation

In Hebb's theory motivation and emotionality are related to the phase sequences of assemblies of cells and complexes of assemblies. Motivation is related to the *persistence* in which phase sequences take place. Since mental integration is a question of timing, "metabolic changes, by altering time relations in neural firing, must tend to disrupt behavior. . . . If a metabolic change affects one cell much more than other cells in the system, it must drop out; if enough cells drop out, the assembly does not function. If, instead, all the cells in an assembly are affected to about

[35] *Ibid.*, p. 100.
[36] *Ibid.* p. 98.

the same extent, the system would continue to function; but the facilitation delivered to other assemblies might be modified in a way that would disturb, or redirect, the phase sequence (that is, the sequence of assembly actions)."[37]

This is Hebb's interpretation of "disturbance of behavior" resulting from the changes of blood content, such as take place in hunger or pain. Sleep is "the extreme case of a loss of motivation";[38] sleep is the opposite to motivation. Each phase sequence needs new content to maintain its organization and persistence. In order to maintain "motivation" or persistence in organization, new combinations of assemblies, new ideas, new perceptions must take place.

Pleasure is a transient state in which "a new synthesis in assembly action [is] being achieved." It is "a direct *growth* or *development* in cerebral organization."[39]

Hebb accepted Watson's theory of the three basic emotions, rage, fear, and love, with certain reservations, but he believed that learning took place even in these emotions. He believed that the sudden disruption of an established neural connection in the cortex causes fear. Animals and children fear the unknown and are frightened by a sudden change. "The immediate source of fear is a disruption of a coordination, principally acquired in the timing of cellular activities in the cerebrum. The disruption may be due to conflict, sensory deficit or constitutional change. With disruption there at once occur processes tending to restore the integration of cerebral activities; in fear these include either liminal or subliminal activation of processes determining avoidance. Optimally, avoidance tends toward completely averting the cerebral disruption, and at this stage avoidance without fear would be said to occur."[40]

Fear, like any other emotion, is actually a sort of neurological disturbance, said Hebb. It is a disruption of timing in the activity of neurons. This disruption may be caused either by a conflict in phase sequences or by a lack of sensory support for a given phase sequence, such as darkness, or by changes in metabolism.

Concluding Remarks

Hebb's system, briefly described here, is a product of a thoroughgoing investigation and bold speculation. The investigation is psychological; the speculation is neurological. Strangely enough, Hebb tried to subordinate his empirically sound observations of human behavior to a neurological model borrowed from modern physics. "What Hebb has done . . . is to apply some relatively recent notions from physics, notably

[37] *Ibid.*, p. 197.
[38] *Ibid.*, p. 223.
[39] *Ibid.*, p. 232.
[40] Donald O. Hebb, "On the Nature of Fear," *Psychological Review*, 1946, **53**, 259–276.

of reverberating circuits, to the nervous system and to test the fit for a number of psychological phenomena," writes Adams.[41] Adams suspects that this may be "good neurology," but he warns that "what appeared to some as an *extension* of psychological theory construction seems to be already becoming another strait-jacket."[42]

Actually what Hebb is doing is relating good empirical studies of human behavior (usually called psychology) to some fictitious model (never tested in the realm of physiology) of the actions of the nervous system. Of course, iron is stronger than wood, but who would substitute very thin pieces of iron for good solid lumber in building a house? With all respect to neurology (to a thoroughly empirical neurology), what's the good of relating observable psychological phenomena to imaginary physiological models?

Moreover, despite his great erudition and sophistication Hebb could not have avoided the pitfalls of radical reductionism. He used in his book phrases such as the following: "Pleasure is . . . fundamentally a directed *growth* or *development* in cerebral organization" (p. 232); "The factor of *interest* or *motivation* which is provisionally translated into the stability and persistence of the phase sequence" (p. 223); "The kind of activity *throughout the cerebrum* which we call consciousness . . ." (p. 219).

Actually it is not at all easy to translate motivation into a phase sequence of the synchrony in neural firings. These two languages do not convey the same things. It is Hebb's idea to relate phenomena reported in mentalistic terms, such as interest, motivation, etc., to phenomena reported in physiological terms, such as neurons, synapses, firing, etc. No useful purpose is served by saying that what has to be proved (and what no one has ever been able to prove) is that simple and self-evident. For no one has ever proved that any activity of the cerebrum *is* consciousness. By "calling" it consciousness no one could serve the cause of scientific progress nor could he solve any of the perennial problems of science.

Analogously, no "growth" of the cerebral organization *is* pleasure; and if it is, it has to be proved; if such a proof is possible at all, it should be offered.

From that point of view, the critical evaluation of Hebb's work must relate his method of reasoning to Watson's radical reductionism, with all credit given to Hebb for his originality and ingenuity in theory formation. As is the case with Lewin (cf. Chap. 13), Hebb's experiments stand on their own merits. Does his theory also? Let us leave the question open for future research and evidence.

[41] Donald K. Adams, "Learning and Explanation," in *Learning Theory, Personality Theory and Clinical Research. The Kentucky Symposium,* Wiley, 1954, p. 74.
[42] *Ibid.,* p. 75.

CHAPTER **4**

Neo-Behaviorism and Learning Theory

1. EDWIN R. GUTHRIE: LEARNING BY CONTIGUITY

Radical Empiricism

The most persistent advocate of conditioning is undoubtedly E. R. Guthrie. Guthrie considers association by contiguity in time, or "simultaneous conditioning," the most general law in psychology. "Stimuli acting at the time of a response tend on their recurrence to evoke that response," he says. Any other type of behavior can be derived from simultaneous conditioning. Especially the processes of learning represent the general law of simultaneous conditioning or association by contiguity in time of stimuli and responses. "The outstanding characteristics of learning which have been expressed in forms of frequency, intensity, irradiation, temporary extinction, conditioned inhibition, forgetting, forward and backward conditioning, and so on, are all derivable from this more general law," Guthrie believes.[1]

Guthrie was much aware of the importance of theory. He wrote: "It is theories that endure, not facts. Events are ephemeral and their descriptions also may be ephemeral. It is theory that lasts for years or for generations. It is theory rather than fact that leads to new controls over nature and events."[2]

The business of scientific inquiry is to "predict and control" the events of nature. The aim of scientific research is the discovery of scientific laws leading to the anticipation of natural events. The validity of scientific laws, including psychological laws, is "measured by their success in prediction."

Scientific laws deal with observable phenomena only. Guthrie's radical empiricism was uncompromising. "The laws of science describe the *observable* conditions under which certain classes of events take place."[3]

[1] Edwin R. Guthrie, "Pavlov's Theory of Conditioning," *Psychological Review*, 1934, **41**, 199–206.
[2] Edwin R. Guthrie, "Psychological Facts and Psychological Theory," *Psychological Bulletin*, 1946, **43**, 1–20.
[3] Edwin R. Guthrie, *The Psychology of Learning*, Harper, 1935, p. 187.

He rejected Thorndike's theory of synapses as an unnecessary and speculative assumption not supported by observable data. He was critical of
the gestalt "theory of the brain as a dynamic electrical field in which
any change in detail alters the whole pattern. The theory is quite safe,
of course, from experimental verification or disproof by any technique so
far developed and as an attempt to state the circumstances under which
action or learning occurs it is quite useless because it calls on unobservable determinants."[4]

Guthrie had definite ideas concerning theory formation in psychology.
Theories "enable men to confront new facts and deal with them successfully. Furthermore, theories are required to direct the search for
relevant facts. . . . It is theory rather than fact that leads to new controls over nature and events. From theory inferences can be made and
applications devised. Facts are likely to be local and temporary. Their
applications are limited. . . . Theory [must] be continuously produced
and continuously used to guide the collection of fact." However, as much
as facts have to be related to theory, theory must be related to facts.
Guthrie continued: "Facts may accumulate without theory; but they
will prove to be unstable and of little profit in the end. Theories may
flourish, if their basis lies not in scientific fact but in opinions and
presentations acceptable only to the members of a limited faction; but
they will be bad theories."[5]

Guthrie's methodological position is one of a radical empiricist reluctant
to delve into matters beyond our sensory perception. Apparently this
kind of empiricism does not conflict with reductionism inasmuch as
psychological data could be related to observable facts in any other
field of science. However, models or constructs are excluded from
Guthrie's theory; he prefers to stick to observable phenomena of behavior and hence his outspoken anti-reductionism. His anti-reductionism
does not reject physiology as such; it is merely opposed to relating
observable data in psychology to presumably interpretative theories
which deal with "invisible" elements of the nervous system and in the
cortex.

Learning

The organism responds to stimuli by contraction of muscles or secretion of glands. These responses are the basic elements of behavior. The
specific patterns of motor and glandular actions are called by Guthrie
movements. Pavlov's conditioning was mostly concerned with movements.

[4] *Ibid.*, p. 195.
[5] Guthrie, "Psychological Facts and Psychological Theory," *Psychological Bulletin,*
1946, **43**, 1–20.

Guthrie distinguishes between *acts* and movements. Any act is a movement but not vice versa. An act is a movement or a series of movements which brings end results. The achievement of the end result of an act is "dependent on the acquisition, through learning, of a specific stereotyped movement or set of movements for the accomplishment of the effect that defines the act."[6] Learning deals with movements, not with acts, and the association of stimuli and response movements is explained by contiguity. Thorndike's law of effect concerns acts and not movements. Thus, Guthrie concludes, Thorndike does not deal with the basic laws of learning.

Guthrie was highly consistent in rejecting the ideas of Thorndike. He explained his position as follows: "Our position is that what is associated is a stimulus and a response. It would perhaps be more exact to say that what is associated is some stimulation of sense organs and a corresponding muscular contraction or glandular secretion. By calling them associated we mean that the stimulation has become the occasion for the response because of a past association of the two."[7]

An ingenious experiment was designed by Guthrie and Horton in order to prove that learning is a process of association and of nothing else.[8] In the Guthrie-Horton experiment a cat had to learn how to get out of a box; a small pole in the midst of the cage floor was the release mechanism. Whenever the cat touched the pole, from whichever side and in whatever way, the door opened and the cat could escape and eat the food prepared outside the cage.

Guthrie's cat did not work as hard as Thorndike's cat did. The cat found the solution immediately. When put in the box again, he repeated his behavior. Whenever the cat acted the first time by pushing the pole with his back, the same kind of behavior was repeated again and again. If the cat escaped from the box by use of claws, the same action was repeated again and again. There have been very few deviations from this rule. Guthrie felt that he could safely state that what any animal would do at any moment was most securely based on a record of what he did the first time.

Guthrie believed that all principles of learning could be reduced to one, namely, to contiguity in time. He enumerated ten such principles, some of which we shall discuss. Guthrie hoped to prove that there is actually only one principle of learning. The first principle is conditioning itself, and Guthrie considered the possibility of reducing all other principles to this one. The second principle is the inhibitory

[6] Edwin R. Guthrie, "Personality in Terms of Associative Learning," in J. McV. Hunt (ed.), *Personality and the Behavior Disorders,* Ronald, 1944, Vol. I, p. 51.
[7] Edwin R. Guthrie, "Conditioning: A Theory of Learning in Terms of Stimulus, Response, and Association," in *The Forty-First Yearbook of the National Society for the Study of Education,* University of Chicago Press, 1942, p. 43.
[8] Edwin R. Guthrie and G. P. Horton, *Cats in a Puzzle Box,* Rinehart, 1946.

conditioning or conditioned inhibition; Guthrie believed that inhibitory conditioning is essentially the conditioning of inhibiting responses and behaves like any other conditioning. The third principle, of remote or delayed conditioning, deals with "delayed" or "trace" reflexes which in Guthrie's opinion are not direct conditioning at all. In these cases the conditioned stimulus precedes the unconditioned. Guthrie explained that a new stimulus which follows the stimulus for a particular act might easily be simultaneous with the proprioceptive stimulation involved in the act itself and hence become a conditioner of the act. Improvement as a result of practice is the fourth principle. Guthrie believed that conditioning should take place after a single trial. He wrote: "It is entirely possible that if Pavlov could have controlled all stimuli instead of a very few, conditioning would be definitely established with one trial instead of fifty or more."[9] The "strengthening" of a stimulus-response connection by repetition was regarded by Guthrie as a result "of the enlistment of increasing numbers of stimuli as conditioners, and not the result of the 'strengthening' of individual connections." Association, said Guthrie, could occur after one connection and last forever. Forgetting is not a matter of decay of old impressions and associations but a result of inhibition of old connections by new ones.

Guthrie had little difficulty in explaining forgetting, extinction, and unconditioning. He assumed that a stimulus pattern gains its full associative power on the occasion of its first pairing with a response. This statement corresponds to Thorndike's minor law of recency, but in Guthrie's theory it becomes the focal issue.

Guthrie explained extinction of a given conditioned response as an inhibition of this response by a new stimulus-response association. Any learned response will exist forever unless it is inhibited by a new response which is incompatible with the former one. A response is unlearned, not by extinction resulting from lack of reinforcement, but by inhibition. In Guthrie's theory there is no room for reinforcement.

Nevertheless, Guthrie agreed that repetition improves learning, because learning of a skill requires association of more than one activity. The more varied the stimuli, the more repetition is needed. This explains the fact that although an association between a single stimulus and a single response is established in a single coincidence, learning usually requires more than one trial. It is the complex structure of the stimulus that requires several trials till the response becomes associated with all the exteroceptive, proprioceptive, and interoceptive elements of the stimulus situation. A simple movement does not require repetitions, but a complex function composed of several movements will be learned

[9] Edwin R. Guthrie, "Conditioning as a Principle of Learning," *Psychological Review*, 1930, 37, 412–428.

through repetitions which enable all the separate movements to become associated.

The last response is usually the lasting response. Guthrie believed that the concepts of reward and punishment could be replaced by the principle of the last response. In a "reward" situation the last successful response either removes the animal from the learning situation or changes the situation to such an extent that no new associations related to the stimulus can be formed. These two facts can be readily explained. In a puzzle box success means escape from the box; in a maze situation success means feeding, which removes the drive-stimulus or at least reduces it substantially. In both cases new associations with the stimulus are rendered impossible. In other words, not the feelings caused by reward or punishment but the specific, overt actions caused by reward or punishment become conditioned and learned.

Motivation and Intentions

Little room was left in Guthrie's system for anything besides the overt stimulus and the overt response. The problem of motivation is rather circumvented by Guthrie. Hunger may become a factor in conditioning only through the act of eating. "The hunger dies when eating occurs. . . . [The] elements of the consummatory response tend to be present throughout a series of actions driven by a maintaining stimulus."[10] Hunger, food, etc., do not "reinforce" behavior; they simply introduce a new situation and in this way prevent unlearning. Obviously there is no room in Guthrie's theory for "annoyers" and "satisfiers" or for reinforcement interpreted as "need reduction."

Yet the idea of purposefulness or *intention* found its way to Guthrie's theory. Guthrie borrowed from Sherrington the idea of two consecutive steps, preparatory and consummatory.[11] But even the preparatory actions such as salivation in anticipation of food are conditioned. The *intention*, explains Guthrie, is "a body of maintaining stimuli which may or may not include sources of unrest like thirst or hunger but always includes action tendencies conditioned during a past experience . . . and in each case a readiness not only for the act but also for the previously rehearsed consequences of the act."[12]

However, Guthrie did not believe "that all stimulus-response associations are dependent on conditioning. Maturation of the nervous system appears to be the principal determiner of many classes of acts."[13] Guthrie admitted that certain differences in behavior are related to the differences

[10] Guthrie, *Psychology of Learning*, p. 152.
[11] Charles S. Sherrington, *The Integrative Action of the Nervous System*, Yale, 1906.
[12] Guthrie, *Psychology of Learning*, p. 205.
[13] *Ibid.*, p. 38.

between different biological species and gave ample consideration to the innate physiological factors. The internal stimuli stemming from glandular and muscular tensions are potent factors in conditioning; they are the "maintaining" stimuli.

Concluding Remarks

Guthrie's system has enchanted many psychologists by its simplicity and aversion to cumbersome theory building. The question is whether Guthrie's parsimonious approach has been fruitful in yielding the expected results in predictability. The main test of the system must be an experimental one.

In such a theory-testing experiment two groups of rats were used.[14] Both groups had to press a bar in order to get food. However, only the first group was permitted to eat the food; the second group was promptly removed without being able to have any food at all. Though both groups learned to press the bar, the rewarded group learned much better. Obviously Seward's experiment brings evidence contrary to Guthrie's assumptions; for both groups the stimulus situation was changed either by eating-reward or by removal, yet the rewarded rats showed far superior results as compared to the unrewarded. Seward believed that his experiments challenge the validity of Guthrie's propositions.

E. R. Hilgard in his excellent book on theories of learning quotes the experimental study of Sheffield and Roby[15] in which the non-nutritive taste of saccharin was used as a reward. Hilgard seems to believe "that the empirical support for Guthrie derives from the fact that the rat's behavior changes strikingly after the saccharin is ingested."[16]

However, the quoted experiment can only disprove the theory of need reduction of reinforcement; it cannot disprove, for example, Thorndike's law of effect or Pavlov's reinforcement by a stronger stimulus. Saccharin may be a "satisfier"; it may be a second-rank conditioned stimulus already associated with sugar. Thus the Sheffield and Roby experiment does not necessarily support Guthrie's theory of contiguity.

On the other hand, one must admit that Guthrie's theory covers at least a certain part of the empirical data and it stands very well the Thorndike law-of-effect criticism. For as several workers have proved, conditioning may take place without satisfiers or annoyers. Bykov's studies (cf. Chap. 2, section 6) are convincing on this point. Guthrie's

---

[14] John P. Seward, "An Experimental Study of Guthrie's Theory of Reinforcement," *Journal of Experimental Psychology*, 1942, **30**, 247–256.

[15] F. D. Sheffield and T. B. Roby, "Reward Value of a Non-Nutritive Sweet Taste," *Journal of Comparative and Physiological Psychology*, 1950, **47**, 349–354.

[16] Ernest R. Hilgard, *Theories of Learning* (2nd ed.), Appleton-Century-Crofts, 1956, p. 59.

studies show that there is no need for perceiving reinforcement as a
"reward," or "pleasure," or "need reduction." Moreover, conditioning
on the first contiguity and with a single contiguity is not an unusual
phenomenon.

As things stand now, one wonders whether Guthrie's theory is a
general theory of learning or is representative of a certain group of
phenomena. Obviously it cannot represent a general theory for it does
not answer the question *why* in certain experiments learning takes place
on the first contiguity and in others it does not.

Guthrie went very far in his generalizations. In his overzealous
empiricism he denied any reinforcement whatsoever. Reinforcement, as
formulated by Pavlov, is the key construct in the physiological theory
of conditioning. It represents the victory of a "stronger" stimulus, the
connotation of "stronger" being a given quantity of neurological energy.

Guthrie dropped the construct of reinforcement because he did not
care for any constructs at all. "Why does conditioning take place?" is
the question asked by the *theorists* of learning. Guthrie did not answer
this question. In his ardent empiricism, following in the footsteps of David
Hume,[17] he discarded the problem of causation. His theory follows
Hume in presenting learning not in a *propter quod* (because of which)
but in a *post quod* (after which) continuity. Thus one may wonder
whether Guthrie's theory explains anything at all. His system is a
description of *how* events take place without tackling the question of
why they happen. It is more presentation than explanation (cf. Chaps.
14 and 15).

A few years ago an effort was made to "formalize" Guthrie's theory.[18]
One cannot help wondering why Guthrie's clear and beautiful English
prose should have been translated into a series of less understandable
and less lucid, though very elaborate statements. As far as the content
of Guthrie's findings is concerned, no additional areas of study could be
included, nor could the causation problem be handled better. Even
after the remarkable work of formalization, Guthrie's system leaves
the causal questions unanswered.

Guthrie's radical empiricism deserves attention for its relentless
rejection of logical constructs, which are not derived from empirical
studies. One feels, however, that he went a bit too far and that his
rejection of any unobservable elements is more of a hindrance than a
help in theory construction. A theory cannot overlook the truth that
some facts are still (or will be forever?) not given in an empirical
observation and yet their impact on observed facts cannot be denied.

[17] David Hume, *A Treatise of Human Nature,* Clarendon, 1896, Vol. III.
[18] Virginia W. Voeks, "Formalization and Clarification of a Theory of Learning,"
Journal of Psychology, 1950, **30**, 341–362.

2. CLARK L. HULL: DEDUCTIVE BEHAVIORISM

The Hypothetico-Deductive Method

Clark L. Hull occupies a distinguished position in the contemporary psychological theory. No one else, perhaps with the exception of Kurt Lewin, was so keenly devoted to the problems of scientific methodology. Few psychologists have had such a mastery of mathematics and formal logic as Hull had. Hull applied the language of mathematics to psychological theory in a manner used by no other psychologist. Whatever exists, Hull believed, exists in a certain quantity; whatever relationships have to be discovered by science, they have to be presented by mathematical equations.

Hull discerned four methods leading to the discovery of scientific truth. The first method is simple, unplanned observation. The second is systematic, planned observation. The third is the experimental testing of some specific and mutually nonrelated hypotheses. The hypotheses come from intuition or observation and are scrutinized by a carefully planned experimentation.

All these methods have been quite fruitful, but Hull believed that the most fruitful one was the fourth method. It is a three-step method of research that applies a rigorous deduction from a priori set principles. First, a system of definitions has to be introduced. Then a series of highly conceptualized postulates (tentatively stated laws) is proposed. From these definitions and postulates a series of detailed theorems is rigorously deduced. The totality of definitions, postulates, and theorems form a systematic and integrated theory.

This theory should be tested by a carefully controlled experimentation. Any part of the theory which does not pass the experimental test has to be modified according to the experimental evidence.

Scientific theory constructed in such a manner represents a set of logical deductions from definite postulates of what should be observed under specified conditions. Any scientific theory should permit the observational determination of its truth or falsity.

Hull was not opposed to empirical generalizations and to the inductive method of research. He felt that the hypothetico-deductive method "reaches independently through a process of reasoning the same outcome with respect to (secondary) principles as is attained through the process of empirical generalizations."[19]

The advantage offered by a deductive method was apparent to Hull. Only mathematical and formal-logical statements have unlimited generality. If psychology, in accordance with the behavioristic program, in-

[19] Clark L. Hull, *Principles of Behavior,* Appleton-Century, 1943, p. 2.

tends to become an objective science patterned after other natural sciences, the deductive-mathematical method seems to be the most appropriate one.

In his preference for the hypothetico-deductive method Hull was influenced by *logical positivism* as promoted by the *Viennese circle* (cf. Chap. 14). The logical positivists or physicalists accepted David Hume's views on induction and causation and emphasized the importance of logical analysis. Moreover, some of them, such as R. Wittgenstein, R. Carnap, and others, saw the main test of philosophy in the clarification of language and development of a system of symbolic signs free from inner contradictions (the *immanent* truth). The more moderate M. Schlick insisted upon checking this system against a perceptible evidence (*transcendent* truth). The even more moderate French mathematician and philosopher H. Poincaré, the father of *conventionalism,* suggested that any system of postulates can be proposed, but it should be modified according to the results of empirical testing (cf. Chap. 14).

Hull was influenced by the moderate wing of logical positivism and by conventionalism. He attached great importance to formalization of scientific language and believed, as the physicalists did, that one may start from any set of postulates and axioms provided they are not mutually contradictory (the immanent truth). A theory, said Hull, "is a systematic deductive derivation of secondary principles of observable phenomena from a relatively small number of primary principles or postulates, much as the secondary principles or theorems of geometry are ultimately derived . . . from a few original definitions and primary principles called axioms."[20] And further on: "An observed event is said to be explained when the proposition expressing it had been logically derived from a set of definitions and postulates coupled with certain observed conditions antecedent to the event."[21] The postulates and axioms have to be checked against "observed conditions" in accordance with the principle of the transcendent truth (cf. Chap. 14).

Hull proposed four criteria for a scientific theory. The first concerns definitions and postulates. Definitions and postulates have to be (1) clearly defined, (2) mutually consistent, i.e., not contradicting each other, (3) formulated in such a manner as to permit deductions of theorems, and (4) as few as possible.

The second criterion concerns the implications and inferences to be deduced from the main definitions and postulates. All deductions have to be (1) clear, (2) exhibited, i.e., without tacit assumptions, and (3) detailed.

Hull's third and fourth criteria deal with the relationship between the theorems and experiments (the criteria of transcendent truth).

[20] *Ibid.*
[21] *Ibid.,* p. 5.

Theorems usually represent the anticipated outcome of experimental studies, which should verify the theorems. The third criterion proposed by Hull required that theorems should be closely related to empirical data; otherwise there is no way of checking them experimentally. "Metaphysics does not permit this continuous check on the validity of the deductions," but scientific data should be testable by experimentation.

The fourth criterion deals with the experimental proof of the theory.

Hull suggested a laissez-faire policy in regard to postulates. Only the law of inner consistency (the immanent truth) and the law of parsimony should be observed. If a set of postulates is really bad, said Hull, it will sooner or later come into conflict with results obtained by experiments and be modified or abandoned.

A theory constructed in such a manner must encounter a certain difficulty in its efforts to define precisely the terms to be used. However, since the "definition of a term always requires the use of one or more other terms, it follows that in any formal system there must be a number of terms which are not really defined at all. . . . Once an adequate set of such primitive concepts or undefined notions is available, the remaining critical terms employed in the system may presumably be defined with precision."[22] Obviously, the definitions dealing with "unobservables" must belong to the category of undefined notions or primitive concepts.

Even the most formalized system must apply non-formalized concepts, and even a mathematical system must use non-quantitative statements. "Since it appears probable that everything which exists at all in nature exists in some amount, it would seem that the ultimate form of all scientific postulates should be quantitative. Nevertheless it is a fact that many scientific principles, at least when first stated, are qualitative or, at most, only quasi-quantitative."[23]

Three steps lead to quantification. First, one variable has to be stated as a mathematical function of at least one other variable, usually in the form of an equation. Second, at least one factor in the equation, e.g., in the physical law of gravitation, the g, must be constant. Third, if measurement has to take place, a unit of measurement should be available.

In 1940 Hull presented his system in quasi-quantitative terms. In 1952 his system was almost entirely quantified.

The Biological Frame of Reference

Human behavior, according to Hull, is an interplay between organism and environment. In this interaction the stimulus is provided by the environment and the response is given by the organism. These two

[22] Clark L. Hull, "The Hypothetico-Deductive Method," in M. Marx (ed.), *Psychological Theory*, Macmillan, 1951, p. 220.
[23] *Ibid.*, p. 226.

facts are observable but the totality of the interaction must be viewed in some broader context which is not entirely an observable stimulus-response situation.

This broader frame of reference is the *biological adaptation* of the organism to the environment. The concept of adaptation in Hull's theory formation is "useful in making a preliminary survey in the search of postulates, but . . . once the postulates have been selected they must stand on their own feet . . . [and] must be able to yield deductions in agreement with observed detailed phenomena of behavior."[24]

Biological adaptation facilitates *survival of the organism.* Whenever the survival of the organism is not facilitated, the organism is in a state of *need.*

Hull defined need as a state of the organism in which a deviation of the organism from the optimum of biological conditions necessary for survival took place. When a need arises the organism acts and this action brings a reduction in the need. Any behavior is therefore (1) goal directed, and (2) this goal is the reduction of the need, which serves the promotion of optimal conditions for survival.

Drive (D) is a general condition of privation in the organism; it is "a common denominator of all primary motivations, whether due to food privation, water privation, thermal deviations from the optimum, tissue injury, the action of sex hormones, or other causes."[25]

Under the pressure of needs and drives the organism undertakes adaptive actions. The patterns of actions which lead to reduction of a need become predominant or reinforced. Apparently, this is exactly what Thorndike had in mind with "stamping in" in the law of effect (cf. Chap. 1, section 3).

A stimulus which leads to a need-reducing action may become associated with another, originally neutral, stimulus. This is conditioning as described by Pavlov. Hull believes that no conditioning will take place unless there is need reduction. Reinforcement is need reducing, and conditioning takes place only when there is reinforcement. In Hull's frame of reference "the conditioned reaction is a special case of the law of effect."

Reinforcement is explained by Hull as follows: "Whenever a reaction (R) takes place in temporal contiguity with an afferent receptor impulse ($\dot{s}$) resulting from the impact upon a receptor of a stimulus energy (S), and this conjunction is followed closely by the diminution in a need (and the associated diminution in the drive, D, and in the drive receptor discharge, s_D, there will result an increment, $\triangle$ ($\dot{s} \rightarrow$ R), in the tendency for that stimulus on subsequent occasions to evoke that reaction."[26]

[24] Hull, *Principles*, p. 66.
[25] *Ibid.*, p. 239.
[26] *Ibid.*, p. 71.

This tendency for a given stimulus to "evoke that reaction" on sub-sequent occasions is called *habit*. Habits are reinforced conditioned-response patterns; they are persistent patterns of behavior acquired by reinforcement. Once the reinforcing need is removed, habits may become inhibited, weakened, or extinguished. Habits are "set up by virtue of the law of reinforcement." Whenever habits do not lead to the biological adaptation of the organism and do not help survival they become subjects of the *experimental extinction* and gradually disappear.

Molar or Molecular

Most of Hull's explanations are stated in two languages, one of the empirical description and the other in neurophysiological terms. Stimulus (S) is defined by Hull in terms of physical energy such as mechanical pressure, sound, light, etc. When the organism is exposed to stimulus energy, an *afferent neural receptor* impulse (s) evokes a reaction (R). This process is described by Hull as follows: "When a stimulus (S) impinges on a suitable receptor organ, an afferent neural impulse (s) is generated and is propagated along connected fibrous branches of nerve cells in the general direction of the effector organs, via the brain. During the continued action of the stimulus energy (S), this afferent impulse (s), after a short latency, arises quickly to a maximum of intensity, following which it gradually falls to a relatively low value as a simple decay function of the maximum. After the termination of the action of the stimulus energy (S) on the receptor, the afferent impulse (s) continues its activity in the central nervous tissue for some seconds, gradually diminishing to zero as a simple decay function of its value at the time the stimulus energy (S) ceases to act."[27]

Hull's presentation relates behavior to nervous cells, brain, etc. Moreover, Hull seemed to believe that conditioning was influenced by chemical factors which he never explained. He believed that in final analysis all behavior could be reduced to physicochemical factors. He wrote: "It appears probable that when blood which contains certain chemical substances thrown into it as the result of states of need, or which lacks certain substances as the result of other states of need, bathes the neural structures which constitute the anatomical basis of habit ($_sH_R$), the conductivity of these structures is augmented through lowered resistance either in the central neural tissue or at the effector end of the connection, or both."[28]

In other words, conductivity is probably influenced by the chemistry of the blood. Hull could not go beyond this point because "neuro-anatomy and physiology have not yet developed to a point such that

[27] *Ibid.*, p. 47.
[28] *Ibid.*, p. 241.

they yield principles which may be employed as postulates in a system of behavior theory." Therefore, "any theory of behavior is at present, and must be for some time to come, a molar theory." Molar is opposed to molecular; "the latter would presumably deal with the action of the ultimate nerve cell, the protoplasmic molecules making up the neuron or perhaps the atoms constituting the molecule, or even the electrons, protons, neutrons, etc., constituting the atom. Thus the term *molar* as here used corresponds approximately to the term *macrocosmic,* or *coarse-grained.*"[29] The molar approach deals with the organism as a whole, the molecular with the detailed, fine, and exact elements of action of the nervous system. As said before, Hull preferred the molecular approach but, he stated, "Students of the social sciences are presented with the dilemma of waiting until the physico-chemical problems of neurophysiology have been adequately solved before beginning the elaboration of behavior theory. . . . There can be hardly any doubt that a theory of molar behavior founded upon an adequate knowledge of both molar and molecular principles would in general be more satisfactory than one founded upon molar considerations alone. . . . It is conceivable that the elaboration of a systematic science of behavior at a molar level may aid in the development of an adequate neuro-physiology and thus lead in the end to a truly molecular theory of behavior firmly based on physiology."[30]

It seems that Hull's approach could be defined as a "not-yet reductionism." Hull's main definitions and postulates are not firmly rooted in physiology or in any other science. His empirical and experimental data are neither physicochemical nor physiological nor neurological. His empirical data are derived from and defined in terms of overt behavior of the organism. The unobservable data, such as need, drive, etc., are defined in neurophysiological terms. Thus a certain ambiguity is noticeable in Hull's writings which stems probably from his hoped-for but not-yet-proved correspondence between behavioral and neurophysiological terms.

Hull's not-yet reductionism is not a matter of principle but is dictated by the lack of "an adequate neurophysiology." His heart was with the reductionism and, whenever it seemed possible, he introduced neurophysiological concepts. Moreover, his way of thinking was always influenced by his desire to use the physiological-molecular frame of reference. The fact remains that he operated with behavioral elements while having in mind the nervous system. Hull's frame of reference is one of interpreting behavior in terms of a living organism interacting with environment through the medium of the nervous system in accordance with the behavioristic tradition.

[29] Clark L. Hull, "The Problem of Intervening Variables in Molar Behavior Theory," *Psychological Review,* 1943, **50,** 273–291.

[30] Hull, *Principles,* p. 20.

Conditioning and Reinforcement

Hull's system underwent definite modifications from the programmatic paper published in 1935[31] through the comprehensive presentation in a series of papers and in the monumental *Principles of Behavior* (1943) toward its final revision in the *Essentials of Behavior* (1951) and in the posthumously published *A Behavior System* (1952). The main trend of modification was in the direction of a more rigorous formalization and quantification. Initially Hull worded his postulates in quasi-mathematical terms. Gradually, as experimental data permitted, the postulates were modified till Hull felt that he could incorporate in them the quantitative results of the experiments and formulate them as mathematical equations with the use of probability calculations.

Here we quote verbatim Hull's postulates and corollaries[32] with comments and interpretations whenever necessary.

POSTULATE I. UNLEARNED STIMULUS-RESPONSE CONNECTIONS ($_SU_R$)

Organisms at birth possess receptor-effector connections ($_SU_R$) which under combined stimulation (S) and drive (D) have the potentiality of evoking a hierarchy of responses that either individually or in combination are more likely to terminate a need than would be a random selection from the reactions resulting from other stimulus and drive combinations.

POSTULATE II. STIMULUS RECEPTION (S and s)

A. When a brief stimulus (S) impinges upon a suitable receptor there is initiated the recruitment phase of a self-propagating molar afferent trace impulse ($\dot{s}'$), the molar stimulus equivalent ($\dot{S}'$) of which rises as a power function of time (t) since the beginning of the stimulus, i.e.,

$$\dot{S}' = 465{,}190 \times t^{7.6936} + 1.0, \tag{1}$$

$\dot{S}'$ reaching its maximum (and termination) when t equals about .450″.

B. Following the maximum of the recruitment phase of the molar stimulus trace, there supervenes a more lengthy subsident phase (s'), the stimulus equivalent of which descends as a power function of time (t'), i.e.,

$$S' = 6.9310(t' + .01)^{-1.0796}, \tag{2}$$

where $t' = t - .450''$.

C. The intensity of the molar stimulus trace (s') is a logarithmic function of the molar stimulus equivalent of the trace, i.e.,

$$s' = \log S'. \tag{3}$$

[31] Clark L. Hull, "The Conflicting Psychologies of Learning—A Way Out," *Psychological Review*, 1935, 42, 491–516.
[32] All quotations taken from *A Behavior System*, Yale University Press, 1952, pp. 5–14.

POSTULATE III. PRIMARY REINFORCEMENT

Whenever an effector activity (R) is closely associated with a stimulus afferent impulse or trace (s) and the conjunction is closely associated with the rapid diminution in the motivational stimulus (S_D or s_G), there will result an increment (Δ) to a tendency for that stimulus to evoke that response.

Corollary i. Secondary Motivation

When neutral stimuli are repeatedly and consistently associated with the evocation of a primary or secondary drive and this drive stimulus undergoes an abrupt diminution, the hitherto neutral stimuli acquire the capacity to bring about the drive stimuli (S_D), which thereby become the condition (C_D) of a secondary drive or motivation.

Corollary ii. Secondary Reinforcement

A neutral receptor impulse which occurs repeatedly and consistently in close conjunction with a reinforcing state of affairs, whether primary or secondary, will itself acquire the power of acting as a reinforcing agent.

POSTULATE IV. THE LAW OF HABIT FORMATION ($_sH_R$)

If reinforcements follow each other at evenly distributed intervals, everything else constant, the resulting habit will increase in strength as a positive growth function of the number of trials according to the equation,

$$_sH_R = 1 - 10^{-.0305\dot{N}}, \tag{4}$$

where $\dot{N}$ is the total number of reinforcements from Z. Z is the absolute zero of the reaction potential.

The first three postulates represent in a final and quantified form Hull's main concepts. The organism functions under definite, innate needs and responds to stimuli in a manner in which the needs will be terminated. As experimental studies have shown, the most favorable interval between the conditioned stimulus and the unconditioned one was about .450 seconds, in which the maximum after-effect of the conditioned stimulus meets with the start of the unconditioned response.[33]

Hull's law of reinforcement as formulated in 1943 closely resembled Thorndike's law of effect: "Whenever a reaction takes place in temporal contiguity with an afferent receptor impulse resulting from the impact upon a receptor of stimulus energy, and this conjunction is followed closely by the diminution of a need (and the associated diminution in the drive and in the drive receptor discharge), there will result an

---

[33] Gregory A. Kimble, "Conditioning as a Function of the Time between Conditioned and Unconditioned Stimuli," *Journal of Experimental Psychology*, 1947, **37**, 1–15.

increment in the tendency for that stimulus on subsequent occasions to evoke that reaction. This is the 'law' of primary reinforcement."[34]

In its final formulation (in 1952, as quoted above in the third postulate), Hull preferred to use drive-stimulus (S_D) instead of drive proper (D). It seems that the drive-stimulus is more observable than the drive proper.

In a way Hull has reversed Pavlov's principles of conditioning. Things become conditioned, says Hull, because of reinforcement and not vice versa. A logical continuation of the third postulate is offered in the two corollaries. Once a certain stimulus has been associated with a certain drive, it becomes itself a (secondary) drive. For example, fear, curiosity, etc., can easily become drives once they become associated with hunger or pain or any other primary drive. Moreover, if this secondary drive causes a reduction in the intensity of the stimulus, it acts as a secondary reinforcement (Corollary ii). In Hull's words, "It follows that any stimulus consistently associated with a reinforcement situation will through that association acquire the power of evoking the conditioned inhibition, i.e., reduction in stimulus intensity, and so of itself producing the resulting reinforcement. Since this indirect power of reinforcement is acquired through learning, it is called *secondary reinforcement*."[35]

In contradistinction to Guthrie, Hull believed that the number of reinforcements strengthens the stimulus-response connection or the habit strength (Postulate IV). Habit strength, which is the persistence of the conditioning (the opposite to extinction), is a function of reinforcement.

Motivation, Inhibition, and Generalization

Let us start with Hull's fifth and sixth postulates:

POSTULATE V. PRIMARY MOTIVATION OR DRIVE (D)

A. Primary motivation (D), at least that resulting from food privation, consists of two multiplicative components: (1) the drive proper (D'), which is an increasing monotonic sigmoid function of h, the number of hours of food privation; and (2) a negative or inanition component (ϵ), which is a positively accelerated monotonic function of h decreasing from 1.0 to zero, i.e.,

$$D = D' \times \epsilon, \tag{5}$$

where

$$D' = 37.824 \times 10^{-27.496 \frac{1}{h}} + 4.001,$$

and

$$\epsilon = 1 - .00001045h^{2.486}.$$

B. The functional relationship of drive (D) to one drive condition (food privation) is: during the time from $h = 0$ to about $h = 3$, drive rises in a

[34] Hull, *Principles*, p. 71.
[35] Clark L. Hull, *Essentials of Behavior*, Yale, 1951, pp. 27–28.

linear manner until the function abruptly shifts to a near horizontal, then to a concave-upward course, gradually changing to a convex-upward course reaching a maximum of 12.3σ at about $h = 59$, after which it gradually falls to the reaction threshold ($_sL_R$) at around $h = 100$.

C. Each drive condition (C_D) generates a characteristic drive stimulus (S_D), which is a monotonic increasing function of this state.

D. At least some drive conditions tend partially to motivate into action habits, which have been set up on the basis of different drive conditions.

POSTULATE VI. STIMULUS-INTENSITY DYNAMISM (V)

Other things constant, the magnitude of the stimulus-intensity component (V) of reaction potential ($_sE_R$) is a monotonic increasing logarithmic function of S, i.e.,

$$V = 1 - 10^{-.44 \log S}. \tag{6}$$

POSTULATE VII. INCENTIVE MOTIVATION (K)

The incentive component (K) of reaction potential ($_sE_R$) is a negatively accelerated increasing monotonic function of the weight (w) of food or quantity of other incentive (K') given as reinforcement, i.e.,

$$K = 1 - 10^{-a\sqrt{w}}. \tag{7}$$

POSTULATE VIII. THE CONSTITUTION OF REACTION POTENTIAL ($_sE_R$)

The reaction potential ($_sE_R$) of a bit of learned behavior at any given stage of learning, where conditions are constant throughout learning and response-evocation, is determined (1) by the drive (D) operating during the learning process multiplied (2) by the dynamism of the signaling stimulus trace (V_1), (3) by the incentive reinforcement (K), and (4) by the habit strength ($_sH_R$), i.e.,

$$_sE_R = D \times V_1 \times K \times {_sH_R}. \tag{8}$$

Corollary iii. Delay in Reinforcement (J)

A. The greater the delay in reinforcement of a link within a given behavior chain, learning and response-evocation conditions remaining constant, the weaker will be the resulting learned reaction potential of the link in question to the stimulus traces present at the time.

B. The greater the delay in the receipt of the incentive by groups of learning subjects, learning and response-evocation conditions remaining constant, the weaker will be the resulting learned reaction potentials ($_sE_{R_d}$), the shape of the gradient as a function of the respective delays being roughly that of decay with the lower limit of the extended gradient passing beneath the reaction threshold, i.e.,

$$J = {}_sE_{R_d} = D \times V_2 \times K \times {}_sH_R \times 10^{-.15d} \times V_1, \tag{9}$$

where

$$d = \log S' \text{ of } V_1 - \log S' \text{ of } V_2.$$

Corollary iv. The Summation (+) of Habit Strengths

If two stimuli, S' and S, are reinforced separately to a response (R) by N' and N reinforcements respectively, and the ${}_{s'}H_R$ generalizes to S in the amount of ${}_sH'_R$, the summation (+) of the two habit strengths at S will be the same as would result from the equivalent number of reinforcements at S, i.e.,

$$_sH_R + {}_sH'_R = {}_sH_R + {}_sH'_R - {}_sH_R \times {}_sH'_R. \tag{10}$$

Corollary v. The Summation (+) of Reaction Potentials

If two stimuli, S' and S, are reinforced separately to a response (R) and ${}_{s'}H_R$ generalizes to S in the amount of ${}_sE'_R$, the two reaction potentials will summate at S as would the equivalent number of reinforcements in an original learning, i.e.,

$$_sE_R + {}_sE'_R = {}_sE_R + {}_sE'_R - \frac{{}_sE_R \times {}_sE'_R}{M}, \tag{11}$$

where M is the asymptote of ${}_sE_R$ by distributed trials.

Corollary vi. The Withdrawal (÷) of Habit Strength

If a smaller habit strength (${}_sH'_R$) is to be withdrawn (÷) from a larger habit strength (C), the result will be:

$$C \div {}_sH'_R = {}_sH_R = \frac{C - {}_sH'_R}{1 - {}_sH'_R}. \tag{12}$$

Corollary vii. The Withdrawal (÷) of Reaction Potential

If a smaller reaction potential (${}_s\underline{E}'_R$) is to be withdrawn (÷) from a larger reaction potential (C), the result will be:

$$C \div {}_s\underline{E}'_R = {}_sE_R = \frac{M(C - {}_s\underline{E}'_R)}{M - {}_s\underline{E}'_R}. \tag{13}$$

Corollary viii. The Problem of the Behavioral Summation (+) of Incentive Substances (K)

If two incentive substances, f and a, have $A\sqrt{w}$ and $B\sqrt{m}$ as the exponential components of their respective functional equations, the second substance will combine (+) with the first in the production of the total K according to the following equation:

$$K_{f+a} = 1 - 10^{-A\sqrt{w + m \times \frac{B_2}{A_2}}}. \tag{14}$$

POSTULATE IX. INHIBITORY POTENTIAL

A. Whenever a reaction (R) is evoked from an organism there is left an increment of primary negative drive (I_R) which inhibits to a degree according to its magnitude the reaction potential ($_sE_R$) to that response.

B. With the passage of time since its formation, I_R spontaneously dissipates approximately as a simple decay function of the time (t) elapsed, i.e.,

$$I'_R = I_R \times 10^{-.018t}. \tag{15}$$

C. If responses (R) occur in close succession without further reinforcement, the successive increments of inhibition (ΔI_R) to these responses summate to attain appreciable amounts of I_R. These also summate with $_sI_R$ to make up an inhibitory aggregate ($\dot{I}_R$), i.e.,

$$\dot{I}_R = I_R + {}_sI_R. \tag{16}$$

D. When experimental extinction occurs by massed practice, the $\dot{I}_R$ present at once after the successive reaction evocations is a positive growth function of the order of those responses ($\dot{n}$), i.e.,

$$\dot{I}_R = 1.84(1 - 10^{-.0434\dot{n}}). \tag{17}$$

E. For constant values of superthreshold reaction potential ($_sE_R$) set up by massed practice, the number of unreinforced responses (n) producible by massed extinction procedure is a linear decreasing function of the magnitude of the work (W) involved in operating the manipulanda, i.e.,

$$n = 3.25(1.1476 - .00984W). \tag{18}$$

Corollary ix. Conditioned Inhibition

Stimuli and stimulus traces closely associated with the cessation of a given activity, and in the presence of appreciable I_R from that response, become conditioned to this particular non-activity, yielding conditioned inhibition ($_sI_R$) which will oppose $_sE_R$'s involving that response, the amount of Δ_sI_R generated being an increasing function of the I_R present.

Corollary x. Inhibitory Potential ($\dot{I}_R$) as a Function of Work

For a constant value of n, the inhibitory potential ($\dot{I}_R$) generated by the total massed extinction of reaction potential set up by massed practice begins as a positively accelerated increasing function of the work (W) involved in operating the manipulandum, which gradually changes to a negative acceleration at around 80 grams, finally becoming asymptotic at around 110 grams.

Corollary xi. Inhibitory Potential ($\dot{I}_R$) as a Function of the Number of Responses

For a constant value of the work (W) involved in operating the manipulandum, the inhibitory potential ($\dot{I}_R$) generated by the total massed extinction of reaction potential set up by massed practice is a negatively accelerated increasing function of the total number of reactions (n) required.

POSTULATE X. STIMULUS GENERALIZATION
($_s\overline{H}_R$, $_s\underline{E}_R$, and $_sI_R$)

A. In the case of qualitative stimuli, S_1 and S_2, the effective habit strength ($_s\overline{H}_R$) generates a stimulus generalization gradient on the qualitative continuum from the simple learned attachment of S_1 to R:

$$_{s_2}\overline{H}_R = {}_{s_1}H_R \times 10^{-.0135d}, \tag{19}$$

where d represents the difference between S_1 and S_2 in j.n.d.,s, and

$$_{s_2}\underline{E}_R = D \times K \times V_2 \times {}_{s_2}\overline{H}_R, \tag{20}$$

and where $D \times K \times V_2$ is constant.

B. A stimulus intensity (S_1) generalizes to a second stimulus intensity (S_2) according to the equation

$$_{s_2}\overline{H}_R = {}_{s_1}H_R \times 10^{-bd} \times V_1, \tag{21}$$

where d represents the difference between S_1 and S_2 in log units and

$$_{s_2}\underline{E}_R = D \times K \times V_2 \times {}_{s_2}\overline{H}_R, \tag{22}$$

and where ($D \times K$) is constant and V_2 is the stimulus-intensity dynamism at S_2.

C. In the case of qualitative stimulus differences, ordinary conditioning and extinction spontaneously generate a gradient of inhibitory potential ($_sI_R$) which is a negative growth function of $_sI_R$ and d, i.e.,

$$_{s_2}I_R = {}_{s_1}I_R \times 10^{-ad}, \tag{23}$$

and in the case of stimulus-intensity differences,

$$_{s_2}I_R = {}_{s_1}I_R \times 10^{-bd} \times V_2. \tag{24}$$

Corollary xii. The Generalization of $_sH_R$ and $_sE_R$ on S_D as a Continuum

When a habit is set up in association with a given drive intensity (S_D) and its strength is tested under a different drive intensity, there will result a falling gradient of $_s\overline{H}_R$ and $_s\underline{E}_R$.

POSTULATE XI. AFFERENT STIMULUS INTERACTION

All afferent impulses (s's) active at any given instant mutually interact, converting each other into š's which differ qualitatively from the original s's so that a reaction potential ($_s E_R$) set up on the basis of one afferent impulse (s) will show a generalization fall to $_s E_R$ when the reaction (R) is evoked by the other afferent impulse (š), the amount of the change in the afferent impulses being shown by the number of j.n.d.'s separating the $_s E_R$'s involved according to the principle

$$d = \frac{\log \frac{_{s}E_R}{_{\check{s}}E_R}}{j}. \tag{25}$$

In Hull's theory motivation plays the most important role. There cannot be learning without reinforcement, and reinforcement brings a reduction of the drive or of drive-stimulus (S_D). Postulates V, VI, VII, and VIII represent the relationship between the strength of the drive and the resulting reaction potential ($_sE_R$). Obviously $_sE_R$ is a function of the drive (D) and of reinforcement or "habit strength" ($_sH_R$). In addition Hull introduced (in the eighth postulate) two variables, the dynamism of the signaling stimulus trace (V) and the incentive reinforcement (K). He arbitrarily assigned to each of them a decimal value, maximum of it 1.00, which was a way out of the difficult problem of measurement of D (cf. summary on Hull in this chapter). Drive is the main factor in conditioning; it provides primary and secondary reinforcement and facilitates the transformation of habit strength into reaction potential.

The problem of goal and teleology was one of the controversial issues between McDougall and Watson. Hull took a definite stand on this issue in the early stages of his work on theory formation[36] and included it in Corollary iiiB. The first type of time gradient is created by the rising and declining stimulus trace in conditioning of the classical type (Pavlov). The second type was geared to the operant conditioning (Skinner).

What happens when two stimuli become associated with the same response by independent, separate reinforcements? Hull's answer, given in Corollaries iv, v, vi, and vii, is represented in the form of mathematical equations which show that the sum obtained is less than the total of the two separate stimuli. Corollary viii gives the mathematical formula for summation of two incentive substances used in conditioning.

The problem of *inhibition* is handled by Hull (Postulate IX) in a manner entirely different from that of Pavlov. Hull distinguished between the *reactive inhibition* (I_R) and the *conditioned inhibition* ($_sI_R$). Inhibition is empirically observed as lessening or disappearing of the conditioned response. It is an *extinction* of the association between the conditioned stimulus and the conditioned response. Reactive inhibition is the reaction of the organism to effort; it is the aftereffect of a response caused by pain, fatigue, etc. The more of that reactive inhibition accumulated, the more likelihood for this inhibition to become conditioned ($_sI_R$). Both types of conditioning together form $_sI_R$, the *inhibitory potential* (Corollaries x and xi).

Postulates X and XI and Corollary xii remind one of Thorndike's spread of effect. The more similarity between the stimuli (in Thorndike's language, the more "identical elements"), the more chances for a substitution of one by the other. Hull's *gradient* of generalization (Postulate X) is actually a quantitative elaboration of the afore-mentioned principle of Thorndike.

[36] Clark L. Hull, "The Goal Gradient Hypothesis and Maze Learning," *Psychological Review*, 1932, 39, 25–43.

Postulate XI is an interesting application of the gradient of generalization which is represented by j, a constant determined by this gradient. In Hull's explanation, this equation defines the amount of reduction of the reaction potential ($_sE_R$) in a way which brought Hull quite close to the gestalt theory of perception (cf. Chap. 12).

Reaction Potential and Secondary Reinforcement

The remaining postulates and corollaries deal mainly with the oscillations of the reaction potential ($_sE_R$) and the secondary reinforcement. In 1939 Hull experimented with a trial-and-error type of learning, and his experimental data confirmed his theory of *alternation cycles*. In Thorndike's study of trial-and-error learning the incorrect answers were not eliminated at once but came back occasionally in the later trials. Hull was able to derive a probability equation of oscillations in behavior (Postulate XII), which was experimentally confirmed.[37]

POSTULATE XII. BEHAVIORAL OSCILLATION ($_sO_R$)

A. A reaction potential ($_sE_R$) oscillates from moment to moment, the distribution of behavioral oscillation ($_sO_R$) deviating slightly from the Gaussian probability form in being leptokurtic with β_2 at about 4.0; i.e., the distribution is represented by the equation

$$Y = Y_0 \frac{1}{\left(1 + \dfrac{X^2}{\alpha^2}\right)^m}.$$

B. The oscillation of $_sE_R$ begins with the dispersion of approximately zero at the absolute zero (Z) of $_sH_R$, this at first rising as a positive growth function of the number of subthreshold reinforcements to an unsteady maximum, after which it remains relatively constant though with increasing variability.

C. The oscillations of competing reaction potentials at any given instant are asynchronous.

Corollary xiii. Response Generalization

A. The contraction of each muscle involved in a habitual act varies its $_sE_R$ from instant to instant ($_sO_R$) about a central reinforced region of intensity which is approximately normal (leptokurtic) in distribution; this constitutes response-intensity generalization.

B. Where several muscles jointly contract to produce a given habitual act, the contraction of each muscle varies more or less ($_sO_R$) independently of the others, producing a qualitative deviation from the central tendency of the joint result of the muscular contractions originally reinforced; this constitutes qualitative response generalization.

[37] Clark L. Hull, "Simple Trial-and-Error Learning—An Empirical Investigation," *Journal of Comparative Psychology*, 1939, **27**, 233–258.

POSTULATE XIII. ABSOLUTE ZERO OF REACTION POTENTIAL (Z) AND THE REACTION THRESHOLD ($_sL_R$)

A. The reaction threshold ($_sL_R$) stands at an appreciable distance (B) above the absolute zero (Z) of reaction potential ($_sE_R$), i.e.,

$$_sL_R = Z + B. \tag{26}$$

B. No reaction evocation (R) will occur unless the momentary reaction potential at the time exceeds the reaction threshold, i.e., unless,

$$_s\tilde{E}_R > {_sL_R}. \tag{27}$$

Corollary xiv. The Competition of Incompatible Reaction Potentials ($_s\bar{E}_R$)

When the net reaction potentials ($_sE_R$) to two or more incompatible reactions (R) occur in an organism at the same instant, each in a magnitude greater than $_sL_R$, only that reaction whose momentary reaction potential ($_s\tilde{E}_R$) is greatest will be evoked.

POSTULATE XIV. REACTION POTENTIAL ($_sE_R$) AS A FUNCTION OF REACTION LATENCY ($_st_R$)

Reaction potential ($_sE_R$) is a negatively accelerated decreasing function of the median reaction latency ($_st_R$), i.e.,

$$_sE_R = 2.845(_st_R)^{-.483}. \tag{28}$$

POSTULATE XV. REACTION POTENTIAL ($_sE_R$) AS A FUNCTION OF REACTION AMPLITUDE (A)

Reaction potential ($_sE_R$) is an increasing linear function of the Tarchanoff galvanic skin reaction amplitude (A), i.e.,

$$_sE_R = .02492A. \tag{29}$$

POSTULATE XVI. COMPLETE EXPERIMENTAL EXTINCTION (n) AS A FUNCTION OF REACTION POTENTIAL ($_sE_R$)

A. The reaction potentials ($_sE_R$) acquired by massed reinforcements are a negatively accelerated monotonic increasing function of the median number of massed unreinforced reaction evocations (n) required to produce their experimental extinction, the work (W) involved in each operation of the manipulandum remaining constant, i.e.,

$$_sE_R = 4.0(1 - 10^{-.0110n}) + .46. \tag{30}$$

B. The reaction potentials ($_sE_R$) acquired by quasi-distributed reinforcements are a positively accelerated monotonic increasing function of the median number of massed unreinforced reaction evocations (n) required to produce their experimental extinction, the work (W) involved in each operation of the manipulandum remaining constant, i.e.,

$$_sE_R = .1225 \times 10^{.0647n} + 2.114. \tag{31}$$

POSTULATE XVII. INDIVIDUAL DIFFERENCES

The "constant" numerical values appearing in equations representing primary molar behavioral laws vary from species to species, from individual to individual, and from some physiological states to others in the same individual at different times, all quite apart from the factor of behavioral oscillation ($_sO_R$).

Corollary xv. Secondary Reinforcement by Fractional Antedating Goal Reaction ($r_G \rightarrow s_G$)

When a stimulus (S) or a stimulus trace (s) acts at the same time that a hitherto unrelated response (R) occurs and this coincidence is accompanied by an antedating goal reaction (r_G), the secondary reinforcing powers of the stimulus evoked by the latter (s_G) will reinforce S to R, giving rise to a new S $\rightarrow$ R dynamic connection.

Postulates XIII, XIV, XV, and XVI and Corollary xiv deal with the problem of the conditioned response or potential of reaction ($_sE_R$). Postulate XIII, which sounds like one of the axioms of Euclid, states the threshold of reaction must stand above the zero point of the potential of reaction. Obviously the higher the reaction potential, the more unreinforced evocations are necessary to produce experimental extinction. This mathematical relationship is formulated in the sixteenth postulate.

The seventeenth and last postulate deals with the problem of individual differences, a problem which could not be evaded by any psychological study. Pavlov (cf. Chap. 2, section 3) distinguished between various "temperaments." Hull was aware of the problem of individual differences but he did not go beyond the programmatic statement that individual differences "between species and species, individual and individual, and the same individual at different times" require proper consideration in psychological studies.

In the fifteenth and last corollary quoted, attention is again paid to the reinforcing power of an "antedating goal reaction." In the later chapters of the *Essentials of Behavior* Hull has added two corollaries. The sixteenth corollary explains generalization both in conditioning and in extinction in a case when "substantially the same muscles" are used in different negative or positive responses. The seventeenth corollary describes what happens when the anticipated goal reaction is frustrated. A frustrated anticipation may lead to increase in drive (D) and result in a higher reaction potential ($_sE_R$).

The seventeen postulates and seventeen corollaries are followed by 133 theorems in which the theoretical statements are formulated in a manner that permits "the observational determination" of truth or falsity of the theory. The method chosen by Hull for observational determination was laboratory experimentation.

Experimental Verification

All his life Hull was modifying his theory in an effort to keep it in accord with the experimental evidence. He was stating hypothetical postulates and putting them to an experimental test; obviously the experimental procedure was geared to the main goal of his research, which was to prove or to disprove or to adjust his hypotheses in accordance with the observational evidence. Some of these experiments, representative of Hull's method of theory construction, will be here briefly described.

In 1934 Hull tested the goal-gradient hypothesis.[38] In a specially constructed runway rats were trained to run to the food compartment. The experiment indicated "positive acceleration"; the closer to the goal, the faster was the running.

In the same vein several experiments were conducted by Hull and his associates. In 1947 Arnold trained rats in a special push-button apparatus with food reward.[39] Then the rats had to make a choice and press one out of four buttons. All four buttons started a car in motion but no food appeared; after all four buttons had been pressed, the food pellet appeared. No single push-button action was reinforced, but reinforcement was given to the entire series of four push-button actions.

Obviously at the start of the experiment with four buttons the rats had already had some $_sE_R$. The experimenter found an increase of speed in pushing buttons with a remarkable gain at the last button, the nearest to the reinforcement. In this case the results obtained by theoretical deductions and empirical experimentations were very close to each other, and Hull could rightly say that "This degree of agreement between experiment and theory is, perhaps, as close as may reasonably be expected in the present early stage of the science."[40]

Another experiment, reported by Hull in 1939, dealt with the fact observed by Thorndike, that the "stamped out" responses occasionally came again. In order to find out the quantitative relationship in the alternation of right and wrong answers Hull constructed a special box which was a modification of the Skinner box (cf. this chapter, section 3). The experimental animals, white rats, had to press either a horizontal or a vertical bar, both bars being reinforced in the earlier stages of the experiment. In the final stage of the experiment reward was offered to earlier reinforced and weaker vertical bar pressing. All experimental animals showed alternation cycles. Hull drew a curve in which this

---

[38] Clark L. Hull, "The Rat's Speed-of-Locomotion Gradient in Approach to Food," *Journal of Comparative Psychology,* 1934, **17,** 393–422.

[39] William J. Arnold, "Simple Reaction Chains and Their Integration. I. Homogeneous Chaining with Terminal Reinforcement," *Journal of Comparative and Physiological Psychology,* 1947, **40,** 349–363.

[40] Hull, *A Behavior System,* p. 165.

alternation was marked.[41] A strikingly similar curve was derived by him from his theoretical postulates. Again experiment and theory stated the same truth.

In 1937 Hovland carried out a series of experiments with human subjects on generalization. His studies led to quantitative statements related to the stimulus generalization of the galvanic skin reaction to excitation by auditory vibration.[42] The experiments yielded a "primary stimulus generalization gradient of extinction" fully corroborated by Hull's experimental and theoretical research.

Hull believed that 121 out of 178 theoretical statements included in the book *Behavior System* were experimentally tested, and 87 percent of them were substantially validated.

Concluding Remarks

The strength or weakness of Hull's system does not depend so much upon his being right or wrong on a certain issue. The focal problem is that of theory construction, to which we shall return in Chapter 14.

The hypothetico-deductive system in geometry was developed by Pieri. Critical of the intuitive factors in the classic geometry which uncritically assumed certain facts and relationships, Pieri tried to "objectify" geometry and develop a nonempirical branch of science based upon only two undefined and uncritical assumptions: point and motion. Anything else should be deduced by a rigid logical procedure.

It is still open to discussion whether Pieri's method is applicable to empirical sciences and if so, whether it is the best method for theory construction in psychology. Some critics of Hull seem to be enchanted by the indisputable thoroughness of his endeavor but feel that it would be rather too early to develop a hypothetico-deductive psychology.

It seems that some of the critics, as, for example, S. Koch in his highly sophisticated analysis of Hull's theory, fail to do justice to Hull. Koch's main effort was directed to a presentation of Hull's theory in an independent, dependent, and intervening variables continuum as suggested by E. Tolman. Although Hull accepted Tolman's idea, still Hull's theory was not constructed in such a continuum. Koch himself noticed that in Hull's *Principles of Behavior* "the terms 'independent variable' and 'dependent variable' are not explicitly used."[43] As Koch remarked, in Hull's theory only the independent and dependent variables are opera-

---

[41] Hull, "Simple Trial-and-Error Learning—An Empirical Investigation," *Journal of Comparative Psychology*, 1939, **27**, 233–258.

[42] C. I. Hovland, "The Generalization of Conditioned Responses," *Journal of General Psychology*, 1937, **17**, 125–148.

[43] Sigmund Koch, "Clark L. Hull," in W. K. Estes, S. Koch, K. MacCorquodale, P. E. Meehl, C. G. Mueller, Jr., W. N. Schoenfield, and W. S. Verplanck, *Modern Learning Theory*, Appleton-Century-Crofts, 1954, p. 26.

tionally defined, which is in accordance with Hull's policy of using operational terms on observable data only.

Hull's theory did not follow exactly the three-variable continuum. It comes much closer to some sort of applied geometry patterned after Pieri, in which the first part, the bulk of truthful statements, is axiomatically stated and everything else is derived by a logical inference from the postulates. The second, the applied part, is the testing of the system by experimentation and checking the a priori statements (postulates) against the a posteriori experimental results. Hull kept his promise of transcendent truth. As soon as the quantitative data obtained in experimentation became available, he transformed his postulates into quantitative statements.

However, on this point Hull is most open to criticism. Koch[44] brought sufficient proof that Hull's $_sE_R$ scale value differences were not "expressible on the same scale and in terms of the same unit." Moreover, Hull's "calibration" experiments did not fully justify the calibration. Koch maintains that Hull's quantified postulates are based on "remote inferences by *combining* arbitrary calculations," and he seems to have a point in his criticism.

One is tempted to say that Hull became, to a certain extent, a victim of his zest for mathematics. He knew mathematics and he loved it. Whenever the opportunity came, he quantified his statements, sometimes pursuing the issue *ad absurdum;* e.g., the seventh postulate of his general theory of behavior deals with the quantity of food necessary for conditioning in rats, and the thirteenth postulate represents the rat's reaction time as a general law of behavior. The generality of such statements has been repeatedly questioned by several critics

Hull's position on reductionism requires some clarification. His frame of reference was biological and he always related his theory to the living organism and the nervous system. Undoubtedly this simultaneous use of two languages, the language of observed psychological phenomena and the language of assumed physiological factors, is a source of ambiguity. Moreover, despite Hull's constant reference to neurophysiology, his theory does not make much use of physiological findings. Like most learning theorists, Hull did not include in his reasoning the physiological theory of conditioning offered by Pavlov (cf. Chap. 2). Nor did he develop his own physiological theory. Energy meant to Pavlov physical energy; excitation and inhibition are related by Pavlov to definite nervous substances; reinforcement was a product of greater *amount* of excitation; etc.

Hull always had the greatest admiration for physiology and an unlimited faith in it, but he did not *operate* with physiological terms. His love for physiology reminds us of Lewin's (cf. Chap. 13) love for

[44] *Ibid.,* p. 128.

mathematics. Neither of them fully utilized his much professed scientific preferences.

Hull's position could be described as a *proposed* but *not too well practiced reductionism*. One can easily read his works and understand well his theory in terms of the observable psychological data and the system of postulates from which the data are derived. Naturally, there is the broad frame of reference of the living organism and its physiological needs, but even the most radical anti-reductionist could not deny the fact that mental phenomena were somehow related to the living matter. As far as methodology of research is concerned, Hull's method, in contradistinction to Pavlov's, is non-reductionistic or, as we have named it above, *not-yet-reductionistic*.

Hull accepted the *molar* or *macrocosmic* or *coarse-grained* way of interpretation against his own convictions. He believed that ultimately a molecular theory based on a detailed knowledge of nerve cells could be developed. Until such time as anatomy and neurophysiology are sufficiently developed, "at the present, and for some time come," the theory of behavior must be molar. Again Hull expressed his preference for something which he was unable to implement.

In summary, one feels that probably Hull's contribution to psychological theory was much greater than Hull's own theory could be. Psychologists may accept or reject this or that part of Hull's theory or even reject it entirely. Yet there is a deep feeling of respect and admiration for the house that Hull built. His theory is entrenched with numerous and ingenious experiments conducted in most rigorous manner by himself and his brilliant friends, followers, and disciples, among them J. S. Brown, J. Dollard, C. I. Hovland, G. E. Kimble, N. E. Miller, H. O. Mowrer, K. W. Spence, H. G. Yamaguchi (to mention only a few), and some of them assumed themselves a leading position in the contemporary theory of learning. Hull's way of reasoning is impeccable, his explanations are lucid, and his constant double-check of theory against empirical evidence invites emulation. Some questions still remain open, among them the question of the generality of his statements and of the general validity of his quantifications and the most general problem of whether psychology should be studied in the manner in which Hull studied it.

3. B. F. SKINNER: INDUCTIVE BEHAVIORISM

Operationism

In one respect Skinner is diametrically opposed to Hull. Hull's main endeavor was to postulate a theory a priori and check the theorems against empirical evidence. Skinner avoided theory. He preferred to start from empirical data and gradually if at all, proceeded toward tentative generalization. Hull represents the *deductive* method in psychological research; Skinner represents the *inductive* method as it was introduced and developed by Francis Bacon, John Stuart Mill, and others (cf. Chap. 14).

Skinner's positivism is closely related to the positivism of Auguste Comte (cf. Chap. 14). Skinner insists upon dealing with observable behavior only and rejects any method of inquiry which is not based upon sensory observation or its application. The observed *data* have to be *identified* and stated in clear, unambiguous terms. The next step in research is to put the known facts into *classes* or categories and state *laws* representing their interrelations. Then comes the third and last step, development of high-order general *concepts*.

Skinner's system "confines itself to description rather than explanation. Its concepts are defined in terms of immediate observations and are not given local or physiological properties. A reflex is not an arc, a drive is not the state of a center, extinction is not the exhaustion of a physiological substance or state. Terms of this sort are used merely to bring together groups of observations, to state uniformities, and to express properties of behavior which transcend single instances. They are not hypotheses, in the sense of things to be proved or disproved, but convenient representations of things already known. As to hypotheses, the system does not require them—at least in the usual sense."[45]

The influence of Mach and the neo-positivists is apparent in Skinner's works. Psychology, as a scientific discipline, "must describe the event not only for itself but in its relation to other events"; and, in point of satisfaction, it must *explain*. These are essentially "identical activities," believes Skinner, and accepts "that more humble view of explanation and causation which seems to have been first suggested by Mach," in which "explanation is reduced to description and the notion of the function substituted for that of causation. The full description of an event is taken to include a description of its functional relationship with antecedent events."[46]

The scientist describes what he sees and as much as he can see and seeks functional relations between a given phenomenon and the antecedent and consecutive phenomena. This, Skinner believes, is the only and the total task of scientific inquiry.

Skinner believes that the "terms 'cause' and 'effect' are no longer widely used in science. . . . The terms which replace them, however, refer to the same factual core. A 'cause' becomes a 'change in an independent variable' and an 'effect' a 'change in a dependent variable.' The new

[45] B. F. Skinner, *The Behavior of Organisms*, Appleton-Century-Crofts, 1938, p. 44.
[46] B. F. Skinner, "The Concept of the Reflex in the Description of Behavior," *Journal of General Psychology*, 1931, **5**, 427–458.

terms do not suggest *how* a cause causes its effect; they merely assert that different events tend to occur together in a certain order."[47]

Skinner's philosophical convictions led him to reject the necessity of any postulates or any variables beyond observable data of the environment and the behavior of organisms. The external variable of which behavior is a function "provides for what may be called a causal or functional analysis. We undertake to predict and control the behavior of the individual organism. This is our 'dependent variable'—the effect for which we are to find the cause. Our 'independent variable'—the causes of behavior—are the external conditions of which behavior is a function."[48]

This attitude brought Skinner close to *operationism,* which is a current trend in the methodology of scientific inquiry. While we shall postpone the detailed and critical analysis of operationism to Chapter 14 of the present volume, a brief description of operationism might be helpful in understanding Skinner's position.

Operationism is a sort of radical empiricism which rejects any speculative approach to the scientific inquiry. As its name indicates, it emphasizes the necessity of keeping an open eye on the operations performed by the scientist. Operationism forces the scientist to abandon the position of naïve realism and to view critically his own research work. Moreover, operationism assumes that the only scientific statements are those which report the results of the scientific inquiry in terms of the deeds done by the research worker, i.e., the research operations.

To Skinner operationism is "the practice of talking about (1) one's observations, (2) the manipulative and calculational procedures involved in making them, (3) the logical and mathematical steps which intervene between earlier and later statements, and (4) *nothing else.*"[49]

The Problem of Reductionism

A small part of the environment or of the independent variables is enclosed within the organism. It is "private." A private event is distinguished by its limited accessibility for research and by nothing else. "We have no reason to suppose that the stimulating effect of an infected tooth is essentially different from that of, say, a hot stove," wrote Skinner.[50] In studying behavior we may have "to deal with the stimulation from a tooth as an inference rather than as a directly observable fact."

Skinner was fully aware of the body-mind problem. He wrote: "Modern science has attempted to put forth an ordered and integrated conception of nature. . . . The picture which emerges is almost always dualistic.

[47] B. F. Skinner, *Science and Human Behavior,* Macmillan, 1953, p. 23.
[48] *Ibid.,* p. 35.
[49] B. F. Skinner, "The Operational Analysis of Psychological Terms," *Psychological Review,* 1945, **52,** 270–277, 291–294.
[50] Skinner, *Science and Human Behavior,* p. 258.

The scientist humbly admits that he is describing only half the universe, and he defers to another world—a world of mind or consciousness—for which another mode of inquiry is assumed to be required. Such a point of view is by no means inevitable. . . . It obviously stands in the way of a unified account of nature. The contribution which a science of behavior can make in suggesting an alternative point of view is perhaps one of its most important achievements."

The traditional solution of the problem was based on the admission of certain "private events" into the body of scientific inquiry. "It is usually held that one does not see the physical world at all, but only a nonphysical copy of it called 'experience.' When the physical organism is in contact with reality, the experienced copy is called 'a sensation,' 'sense datum' or 'percept'; when there is not contact, it is called an 'image,' 'thought' or 'idea.' Sensations, images, and their congeries are characteristically regarded as psychic or mental events, occurring in a special world of 'consciousness' where, although they occupy no space, they can nevertheless often be seen."[51]

Skinner was strongly opposed to the use of terms which refer to "supposed nonphysical events," such as sensation, image, drive, habit, and instinct. If one assumes that there are such nonphysical events, these events are "private" and inaccessible to the public and to objective study.

Skinner's position can be defined as a methodological anti-reductionism. The task of the psychologist is to relate observable data of behavior to the environment in which it takes place. Skinner saw no reason to relate his data to data arrived at on another level of observation by other sciences. Although behavior is correlated to physiological factors, human behavior cannot be described in physiological terms or related to physical or chemical data. Skinner was opposed to explanations of observed facts of behavior "which appeal to events taking place somewhere else, at some other level of observation, described in different terms, and measured, if at all, in different dimensions."[52]

The only task of the scientific inquiry is to find out the relationship between the stimulus controlled by the experimenter and other experimental variables and the response of the experimental subject. What is considered today a "private" event inaccessible to scientific research will eventually, with the progress of research technique, become amplified and accessible to objective, public, and scientific study.

Reflexes

Psychology is the science of behavior. Behavior is defined by Skinner as "the movement of an organism or of its parts in a frame of reference

---

[51] *Ibid.*, p. 276.
[52] B. F. Skinner, "Are Theories of Learning Necessary?" *Psychological Review*, 1950, **57**, 193–216.

provided by the organism itself or by various external objects or fields of force. It is convenient to speak of this as the action of the organism upon the outside world, and it is often desirable to deal with an effect rather than with the movement itself, as in the case of the production of sounds."[53]

The simple unit of behavior is *reflex*. Skinner uses the term "reflex" in an unorthodox fashion. To him reflex is just any "observed correlation of stimulus and response." "The reflex as an analytical unit is actually obtained in *practice*. The unit is a fact, and its validity and the validity of the laws describing its changes do not depend upon the correctness of analytical assumptions or the possibility of a later synthesis of more complex behavior."[54]

In later writings Skinner preferred to identify the elements of a response instead of a response as a whole. He seemed to believe that each response consisted of smaller "atomic" units.

Behavior was related by Skinner to some general "biological advantage" which is not too precisely analyzed. Reflex responses are executed by the smooth muscles, such as the muscles in the walls of the blood vessels and the glands. Reflexes are "intimately concerned with the well-being of the organism. The process of digestion could not go on if certain secretions did not begin to flow when certain types of food entered the stomach. Reflex behavior which involves the external environment is important in the same way. If a dog's foot is injured when it steps on a sharp object, it is important that the leg should be flexed rapidly so that the foot is withdrawn. . . . Such biological advantages 'explain' reflexes in an evolutionary sense: individuals who are most likely to behave in these ways are presumably likely to survive and to pass on the adaptive characteristics to their offspring."[55]

Also the conditioned reflexes have "survival value" in helping the organism to modify its behavior and to adjust to changing conditions.

Since reflex is the basic unit of observable behavior, the scientific inquiry has to discover the natural laws governing the reflexes. Skinner distinguished between *static, dynamic,* and *interaction* laws.

THE LAWS OF BEHAVIOR

Static Laws

1. *The Law of Threshold.* The intensity of the stimulus must reach or exceed a certain critical value (called the threshold) in order to elicit a response.
2. *The Law of Latency.* An interval of time (called the latency) elapses between the beginning of the stimulus and the beginning of the response.
3. *The Law of Magnitude of the Response.* The magnitude of the response is a function of the intensity of the stimulus.

[53] Skinner, *Behavior of Organisms*, p. 4.
[54] *Ibid.*, p. 29.
[55] Skinner, *Science and Human Behavior*, p. 54.

4. *The Law of After-Discharge.* The response may persist for some time after the cessation of the stimulus.
5. *The Law of Temporal Summation.* Prolongation of a stimulus or repetitive presentation within certain limiting rates has the same effect as increasing the intensity.

Dynamic Laws

6. *The Law of the Refractory Phase.* Immediately after elicitation the strength of some reflexes exists at a low, perhaps zero, value. It returns to its former state during subsequent inactivity.
7. *The Law of Reflex Fatigue.* The strength of a reflex declines during repeated elicitation and returns to its former value during subsequent inactivity.
8. *The Law of Facilitation.* The strength of a reflex may be increased through presentation of a second stimulus which does not itself elicit the response.
9. *The Law of Inhibition.* The strength of a reflex may be decreased through presentation of a second stimulus which has no other relation to the effector involved.
10. *The Law of Conditioning of Type S.* The approximately simultaneous presentation of two stimuli, one of which (the "reinforcing" stimulus) belongs to a reflex existing at the moment at some strength, may produce an increase in the strength of a third reflex composed of the response of the reinforcing reflex and the other stimulus.
11. *The Law of Extinction of Type S.* If the reflex strengthened through conditioning of Type S is elicited without presentation of the reinforcing stimulus, its strength decreases.
12. *The Law of Conditioning of Type R.* If the occurrence of an operant is followed by presentation of a reinforcing stimulus, the strength is increased.
13. *The Law of Extinction of Type R.* If the occurrence of an operant already strengthened through conditioning is not followed by the reinforcing stimulus, the strength is decreased.

The Laws of Interaction

14. *The Law of Compatibility.* Two or more responses which do not overlap topographically may occur simultaneously without interference.
15. *The Law of Prepotency.* When two reflexes overlap topographically and the responses are incompatible, one response may occur to the exclusion of the other.
16. *The Law of Algebraic Summation.* The simultaneous elicitation of two responses utilizing the same effectors but in opposite directions produces a response the extent of which is an algebraic resultant.
17. *The Law of Blending.* Two responses showing some topographical overlap may be elicited together but in necessarily modified forms.
18. *The Law of Spatial Summation.* When two reflexes have the same form of response, the response to both stimuli in combination has a greater magnitude and a shorter latency.
19. *The Law of Chaining.* The response of one reflex may constitute or produce the eliciting or discriminative stimulus of another.
20. *The Law of Induction.* A dynamic change in the strength of a reflex may

be accompanied by a similar but not so extensive change in a related reflex, where the relation is due to the possession of common properties of stimulus or response.

21. *The Law of Extinction of Chained Reflexes.* In a chain of reflexes not ultimately reinforced only the members actually elicited undergo extinction.

22. *The Law of the Discrimination of the Stimulus in Type S.* A reflex strengthened by induction from the reinforcement of a reflex possessing a similar but not identical stimulus may be separately extinguished if the difference in stimuli is supraliminal for the organism.

23. *The Law of the Discrimination of the Stimulus in Type R.* The strength acquired by an operant through reinforcement is not independent of the stimuli affecting the organism at the moment, and two operants having the same form of response may be given widely different strengths through differential reinforcement with respect to such stimuli.

24. *The Law of the Operant Reserve.* The reinforcement of an operant creates a single reserve, the size of which is independent of the stimulating field but which is differentially accessible under different fields.[56]

Operant and Respondent Behavior

Whenever behavior is correlated to "specific eliciting stimuli" it is *respondent* behavior, and whenever no such stimuli are present it is called *operant* behavior. Any modification of the environment is called a stimulus, and a correlated part of the behavior a response. The observed relation between them is called reflex. A respondent reflex is regarded as a correlation of a stimulus and a response. The operant reflex is "a functional part of behavior"; it is spontaneous; it does not originate in the environment. "An operant behavior is an identifiable part of behavior of which it may be said, not that no stimulus can be found that will elicit it (there may be a respondent the response of which has the same topography), but that no correlated stimulus can be detected upon occasions when it is observed to occur."[57] Obviously the term "reflex" originally applied to respondent behavior only; however, Skinner believes an operant "may and usually does acquire a relation to prior stimulation."

There are two kinds of conditioning. Skinner says the S type of conditioning applies to respondent behavior and the R type is the conditioning of operant behavior. In Pavlov's experiments the reinforcer was paired with the stimulus. In Skinner's experiments the reinforcer is contingent upon the response. In Skinner's experiments with pigeons food is the reinforcer. Presenting food when the pigeon raises its head is reinforcement. "The change in frequency with which the head is lifted

---

[56] From *The Behavior of Organisms,* by B. F. Skinner, pp. 12–33, 105, 170, 228, and 229, Copyright, 1938, D. Appleton-Century Co., Inc. By permission of Appleton-Century-Crofts, Inc.

[57] *Ibid.,* p. 21.

. . . is the process of operant conditioning. . . . Through operant conditioning the environment builds the basic repertoire with which we
keep our balance, walk, play games, handle instruments and tools. . . ."
Operant reinforcement "improves the efficiency of behavior."[58]

Skinner revised Thorndike's *law of effect.* "Instead of saying that a
man behaves because of the consequences which *are* to follow his behavior, we simply say that he behaves because of the consequences which
have followed similar behavior in the past. This is, of course, the Law
of Effect or operant conditioning."[59]

The term "operant," wrote Skinner, emphasizes the fact that the behavior *operates* upon the environment to generate consequences. Whenever, in the standard lever-pressing experiment in the specially devised
box for experiments with rats (the Skinner box), the pellet of food was
produced in the presence of an additional stimulus (such as light or
sound) and was not produced without it, discriminatory conditioning took
place.

In operant conditioning the response comes first and then it becomes
reinforced. Not only may the stimulus be *discriminatory* but also the
response can be *differentiated.* In series of experiments with rats Skinner
successfully trained the experimental animals to act in different, new,
and never before practiced manners.

The Nature of Reinforcement

Thorndike believed that reinforcing stimuli were either pleasure or
pain producing. Hull substituted drive reduction for pain and pleasure.
Pavlov related reinforcement to the amount of energy discharged by the
stimulating factor. Skinner's non-reductionism prevented him from accepting Pavlov's interpretation, and the positivistic-inductive method
did not allow him to go beyond observable data. The observed data
merely witnessed to the fact that the more hungry the animal was, the
better was his response to the reinforcing stimuli of food; thus reduction
of deprivation was very often reinforcing. Skinner did not go beyond
this inductive statement and did not accept its generality or universality.
His experimental data show that conditioning might have taken place
without reduction of deprivation. Skinner is rather undecided as to what
really takes place in conditioning. Why does "reinforcement reinforce?
. . . The connection between reinforcement and satiation must be sought
in the process of evolution. We can scarcely overlook great biological
significance of the primary reinforcers. Food, water, and sexual contact,
as well as escape from injurious conditions are obviously connected with
the well-being of the organism. . . . It is tempting to suppose that other
forms of stimulation produced by behavior are similarly related to bio-

[58] *Ibid.,* p. 66.
[59] *Ibid.,* p. 87.

logically important events . . . A biological explanation of reinforcing power is perhaps as far as we can go in saying why an event is reinforcing. Such explanation is probably of little help in a functional analysis, for it does not provide us with any way of identifying a reinforcing stimulus as such before we have tested its reinforcing power upon a given organism."[60]

While Skinner felt unable to explain the nature of reinforcement, his experimental studies were a profound contribution toward the understanding of the problem. He could not find the answer to the problem of why reinforcement reinforced, but he offered a detailed and precise description of reinforcement.

In a series of ingeniously planned experiments with pigeons Skinner studied the *interval* and the *ratio* reinforcement; these two types of reinforcements are included in the category of intermittent reinforcements. In experiments related to the interval or periodic reinforcement, reinforcements were given at more or less fixed intervals, a definite number of times per hour. The results of this interval reinforcement have been rather stable and constant and highly resistant to extinction.

In experiments with the ratio reinforcement, the reinforcement was administered not at certain time intervals but after a certain number of responses. The less frequent the reinforcement, the quicker the response. The ratio of unreinforced responses to reinforced ones, called the *extinction ratio,* was in the interval reinforcement 20:1 and in the ratio reinforcement 200:1. The implications for education are quite obvious.

An originally neutral stimulus may become reinforcing through repeated association with a reinforcing stimulus. The neutral stimulus acquires "a reinforcing value of its own, and may be called a conditioned, secondary, or derived reinforcement. A secondary reinforcement may be extinguished when repeatedly applied to a response for which there is no ultimate primary reinforcement."[61]

Secondary reinforcements may become easily generalized. Whenever they become associated with several primary reinforcers, they may stimulate many various activities. Money, for instance, being associated with the acquisition of food, clothes, etc., is a good example of a secondary reinforcer which became quite generalized and stimulated a great number of activities.

When the operant behavior is not reinforced by delivery of food, the process of extinction starts. The total number of operant responses prior to complete extinction indicates the "reserve" of responses or *reflex reserve*—the number of responses which could be emitted without additional reinforcement.

[60] Skinner, *Science and Human Behavior,* pp. 81–84.
[61] Fred S. Keller and William N. Schoenfeld, *Principles of Psychology,* Appleton-Century-Crofts, 1950, p. 260.

The *reflex reserve* was originally defined by Skinner as the "*available activity,* which is exhausted during the process of repeated elicitation of which the strength of the reflex is at any moment a function." The reflex reserve indicates the spontaneous recovery from fatigue in respondent reflexes. In operant reflexes it is related to the "strength of reflex," which is proportional to the reserve. "All operations that involve elicitation affect the reserve directly, either to increase or to decrease it. Conditioning increases it; extinction and fatigue decrease it. . . . Facilitation and certain kinds of emotion increase the strength, while inhibition and certain kinds of emotion decrease it without modifying the reserve. The operations that control the drive also affect the proportionality factor. Without altering the total number of available responses, a change in drive may alter the rate of elicitation of an operant from a minimal to a maximal value."[62]

In his later writings Skinner apparently abandoned this concept. It became superfluous and in accordance with his philosophy of parsimonious induction he did not use it any more.

Drives

It has been quite easy to notice that the number of hours of food deprivation was related to reinforcement. In an experiment with eight rats Skinner found that the group of rats which suffered a severe food deprivation gave double the number of responses given by the group exposed to mild deprivation. However, deprivation was not correlated to extinction.

Deprivation can be measured; it is an operational term. The term "drive" is not. In his persistent avoidance of going beyond the empirical data, Skinner uses the term "drive" only as an abbreviated name for the operations by which the rate of responses could be measured. The term "drive," says Skinner, is "simply a convenient way of referring to the effects of deprivation and satiation and of other operations which alter the probability of behavior in more or less the same way. . . . There are many ways of changing the probability that an organism will eat; at the same time, a single kind of deprivation strengthens many kinds of behavior. The concept of hunger as a drive brings these various relations together in a single term. . . . A drive is a verbal device with which we account for a state of strength, and it cannot answer experimental questions. We cannot control the behavior of an organism by directly changing its hunger, its thirst, or its sex drive. In order to change these states indirectly, we must deal with the relevant variables of deprivation and satiation and must face all the complexity of these operations."[63]

[62] Skinner, *Behavior of Organisms,* pp. 26–27.
[63] Skinner, *Science and Human Behavior,* p. 144.

Thus, in the spirit of operationism, Skinner does not deal with drive as a cause of behavior; he prefers to discuss deprivation and satiation and to omit the term "drive." For instance, one could say that the eating of salty hors d'oeuvres makes a person thirsty and that thirst then drives him to drink. It is simpler, in both theory and practice, to restrict ourselves to the fact that consuming salty hors d'oeuvres leads to drinking.

When Skinner comes to the question how many drives there are, he asks instead in how many ways an organism could be deprived. The problem of satiation and deprivation should be dealt with in terms of the functional analysis and the question should read: How many kinds of behavior vary in strength independently of one another?

Apparently, reinforcement strengthens behavior in a given state of deprivation. The effect of deprivation can be experimentally tested.

Emotions

A similar operationistic attitude was taken by Skinner to the problems of emotionality. "The emotions are an excellent example of the fictional causes to which we commonly attribute behavior. We run away because of 'fear' and strike because of 'anger' etc.," ridicules Skinner.

Skinner sees in emotions "predispositions to act in certain ways. The 'angry' man shows an increased probability of striking, insulting, or otherwise inflicting injury. . . . The man 'in love' shows an increased tendency to aid, favor, be with. . . . The names of the so-called emotions serve to classify behavior with respect to various circumstances which affect its probability. . . ." Emotion can be defined as "a conceptual state, in which a special response is a function of circumstances in the history of the individual. . . . But so defined, an emotion, like a drive, is not to be identified with physiological or psychic conditions."[64]

In accordance with Skinner's theory of reinforcement, the emotional responses are reinforced by their consequences or feedback mechanism. Food is reinforcing to a hungry organism, and damage inflicted upon an opponent reinforces anger. Some emotional responses, as already observed by J. B. Watson, are not conditioned. An angry child may strike or bite without prior conditioning. Adults possess, as a rule, a "full fledged repertoire" of conditioned responses of angry behavior, verbal and otherwise.

Motivation (drives) and emotions overlap. An extreme deprivation is usually an emotional operation. The starving man is almost necessarily frustrated and afraid, and nostalgia includes both a drive and an emotion, says Skinner.

Emotions could be defined "as a particular class of strength or weakness in one or more responses induced by any one of a class of operations"

[64] *Ibid.,* pp. 162–163.

and should not be perceived as causes of behavior. The causes are the stimuli. The so-called emotions are indicators of probability of the strength of certain responses.

"As long as we conceive of the problem of emotion as one of inner states, we are not likely to advance a practical technology. The behavior observed during an emotion is not to be confused with emotion as a hypothetical 'state' any more than eating is to be confused with hunger. An angry man, like a hungry man, shows a disposition to act in a certain way. He may never act in that way, but we may nevertheless deal with the probability that he will do so. Just as we infer from a history of deprivation that a man is probably hungry even though he is unable to eat, so we infer that he is probably angry by showing that he generally behaves in an angry fashion upon similar occasions."[65]

Skinner consistently avoids the "mentalistic" terms "pleasure" and "displeasure." He prefers to discuss behavior in the dimension of *positive* vs. *negative* reinforcers. Positive reinforcers add something to the existing situation, e.g., food, water. Negative reinforcers remove something from a given situation, e.g., removal of an electric shock or of extreme heat. In experiments with both types of reinforcers the probability of response was increased.

One could translate Skinner's reasoning and say that the positive reinforcers procure pleasure and the negative reinforcers remove pain. But this translation is exactly what Skinner has avoided all his life. A positive reinforcer, he wrote, is any stimulus the presentation of which strengthens the behavior upon which it is made contingent. A negative reinforcer is any stimulus the withdrawal of which strengthens behavior.

An aversive stimulus can be withdrawn to reinforce behavior. In non-Skinnerian language the withdrawal of the stimulus reduces tension or reduces drive. In Skinner's operationistic description, it merely increases behavior or reinforces. For instance, shaming someone into an effort is a presentation of an aversive stimulus and withdrawal of it, if effort is made. Obviously, any stimulus which consistently precedes the aversive withdrawal of a positive reinforcer may come to act as a conditioned negative reinforcer.

Anxiety is a result of conditioning. Whenever "a stimulus characteristically *precedes* an aversive stimulus by an interval of time sufficiently great" certain *effects* or behavioral changes take place. These resulting changes are called anxiety. Any single aversive stimulus, such as the death of a friend, may be followed by the "feeling of doom," or similar anxiety states. Naturally, Skinner's term "anxiety" is not an "inner state" but "a set of emotional predispositions attributed to a special kind of circumstance."[66]

[65] *Ibid.*, p. 168.
[66] *Ibid.*, pp. 180–181.

Skinner offered a highly illuminating analysis of the psychology of punishment applied in an experimental study by W. K. Estes.[67] The positive reinforcers, in lay language, are rewards; the withdrawal of an aversive, negative reinforcer is a reward too. Punishment is an application of a negative stimulus or withdrawal of a positive one. Punishment stops a certain response by eliciting an incompatible response. When a child giggles in church, pinching the child will elicit pain and stop the giggling. A severe punishment may suppress, although not permanently, the occurrence of the punished behavior in the future. The third effect of punishment corresponds to what Freud called repression. Skinner, using terms of overt behavior, says that punishment may establish aversive conditions which are avoided by the organism.

The unfortunate by-products of punishment are reduction of efficiency of the punished organism, and generation of rage and fear. Instead of punishment, Skinner suggests extinction and positive conditioning of incompatible behavior.

Making Decisions

A functionally unified system of responses is often called *self*. However, this concept represents a presumably coherent system of responses and indicates some consistencies of behavior which can be doubted. Behavior is a function of environment, and "the pious churchgoer on Sunday may become an aggressive, unscrupulous businessman on Monday. He possesses two response systems appropriate to different sets of circumstances, and his inconsistency is no greater than that of the environment which takes him to church on Sunday and to work on Monday," wrote Skinner.[68] Decisions made by an individual are a function of environmental stimuli, just as any other responses are.

Skinner rejected the idea of an "inner self," will power, and any other constructs put between the independent and dependent variables. All areas of behavior, he believed, could and should be handled in the same manner of cautious, objective, and "public" observation.

In making decisions some variables are "private events" within the organism. Skinner saw in deciding a preliminary behavior responsible for the action decided upon and believed that even this complex problem could be handled without resolving to "inner factors."

The behavior of decision making helps one to escape from indecision. The oscillation between incomplete forms of response is time consuming and, therefore, aversive. The behavior which puts an end to this conflict by withdrawing the aversive stimulus is reinforcing. Socially administered reinforcement increases the probability of making decisions.

[67] William K. Estes, "An Experimental Study of Punishment," *Psychological Monographs*, 1944, **57**, No. 263.
[68] *Ibid.*, p. 286.

Thinking and problem solving can be defined as behavior "which, through the manipulation of variables, makes the appearance of a solution more probable. . . ." Whenever an organism is in a state of deprivation or aversive stimulation, one way out is to manipulate stimuli until those stimuli are hit upon which control the response which brings the solution to the problem. One increases the chances of a solution by looking over the problem carefully and arranging and rearranging all the relevant stimuli till the solution comes. Another method of problem solving consists of a review of tentative solutions.

Concluding Remarks

Skinner is the most persistent among psychologists in the application of an inductive empiricism. His method of rigorous observation and experimentation is, indeed, impressive. If a prize were offered for sober generalization and parsimonious use of concepts, it would be surely given to Skinner.

Skinner never accepted easy solutions offered by a shallow reductionism nor did he indulge in farfetched dualistic hypotheses. Whenever observations warranted it, new generalizations were introduced. Accordingly, Skinner introduced the concepts of operant behavior, of positive and negative conditioning, of intermittent reinforcement, etc. Whatever was said by Skinner, it was related to observed phenomena and their interrelationships.

And yet, what could one say if a chemist or a physicist confined his study to the observable data only? Did Einstein deal with an empirically perceptible fourth dimension? Did Mendelyeev observe all the chemical elements?

Skinner refused to deal with the crucial problem of motivation because "we cannot control the behavior of an organism by directly changing its hunger, its thirst, or its sex drive. In order to change these states indirectly, we must deal with the relevant variables of deprivation and satiation and must face all the complexity of these operations."[69]

Actually, we cannot control the behavior of human organisms even indirectly. No psychologist would try to produce experimentally sexual craving, or homosexuality, or the desire to rob or kill. The psychological laboratory works within a limited scope of experimentation. As far as human drives and emotions are concerned, the range of experimentation is very restricted.

Should this exclude human drives and emotions from the scope of psychological inquiry? If stars and moons do not fit laboratory work, should we change the subject matter or the method of scientific inquiry?

What was studied by Skinner was studied thoroughly and precisely.

[69] *Ibid.*, p. 144.

But what was omitted may represent some important problems of human behavior. Skinner says that "a child is made more likely to drink milk by restriction of his water intake." Any psychiatrist and child psychologist would contest this statement and present empirical evidence contrary to Skinner's, for human motivation is not a matter of supply and deprivation.

Skinner was strongly opposed to the "traditional pattern of looking for a course of human behavior inside the organism." He believed that this "pattern of an inner explanation of behavior is best exemplified by doctrines of animism. . . . The traditional procedure has been to invent an inner determiner, a 'demon,' 'spirit,' 'homunculus' or 'personality' capable of change of course or of origination of action."[70] Skinner seems to have taken a radical behavioristic stand, even more radical than J. B. Watson's.

Moreover, clinical and experimental studies of conversion hysterias, anorexias, and psychosomatic medicine cannot avoid this "inner" explanation so carefully avoided by Skinner.

Like many other scientists, Skinner tried to avoid the "bifurcation of nature into physical and psychic" by assuming that the organism "simply reacts" to environment. But it is not that simple. The reaction of the human organism to the environment is not the same as the reaction of amoebas. There must be some "inner causes." These may or may not be proved to be physiological, yet they cannot be dismissed. The business of science is to study *all* facts, even if they do not fit into some particular frame of reference.

However, it has to be said that what was observed by Skinner was observed very carefully, and a great part of the psychoanalytic findings fits well into his way of presentation. Skinner explained with great clarity the phenomena of repression, symbol, reaction formation, etc., without using Freud's "mechanisms." As a keen observer he could not have overlooked the contribution of another keen observer. What he resented was the freedom with which Freud introduced models between the independent and dependent observable variables.

The greatness of Skinner's system lies in his refusal to go beyond the question of why aversive stimuli are aversive and why positive stimuli are reinforcing. To go beyond it would mean to deal with the so-called "private events." And this is actually what Freud did. It was Freud's greatness that he had the courage to go beyond the observable data. One may say that both Skinner and Freud were looking on the same object: Skinner from outside, Freud from inside. Their findings cannot be mutually contradictory (cf. Chap. 6 on Freud and Chap. 14 on the scientific method), although they report on different sides of observed phenomena.

[70] B. F. Skinner, "Critique of Psychoanalytic Theory," in H. Feigl and M. Scriven (eds.), *Minnesota Studies in the Philosophy of Science*, University of Minnesota, Vol. 1, 1956, p. 79.

4. EDWARD C. TOLMAN: PURPOSIVE BEHAVIORISM

Is Tolman a Behaviorist?

K. W. Spence suggested dividing all theories of learning into two groups.[71] To the first, the stimulus-response (S-R) group, belong the theories of Thorndike, Hull, Guthrie, Miller, Dollard, and Spence. To the other, the stimulus-sign (S-S) group, belong Köhler, Koffka, Lewin, Tolman, Adams, and Zener. The stimulus-response group relies heavily on associationism, while the stimulus-sign group relates learning to the processes of perception.

Actually Tolman's system defies classification. Tolman has been no more influenced by Lewin than by Watson or Pavlov, no less by Freud than by McDougall or Woodworth. Tolman's system is unique in its deep consideration of the problems of theory construction and its emphasis on the need to develop a stimulus-response type of theory interpolated by theoretical interpretation of nonobservable factors. The authors of an excellent volume devoted to the scientific analysis of learning theories have been much influenced in their method of analysis by Tolman's methodology.[72] When Estes, Koch, and others critically reviewed the contemporary psychological theory, they related their findings to the triple factors of independent, dependent, and intervening variables as postulated by Tolman. Tolman's operationism, which insisted that psychological concepts be testable by "concrete repeatable observations," influenced an entire generation of psychologists, and Tolman's eclecticism invited a large number of intersystemic studies.

We have decided to include Tolman in this chapter of our book, which deals with neo-behaviorism, because of our principle of "common roots." We may doubt whether Tolman's system was a "genuine behaviorism," as Hilgard said,[73] but we have no doubts that Tolman's system was rooted in behaviorism. Tolman originally deviated from Watson on two issues, purposivism and molar behavior.

Tolman, like most contemporary neo-behaviorists, is a methodological non-reductionist. "Psychology, like physics, must take immediate experience for granted and then proceed to develop maps, rules and equations for finding one's way about. Physics develops one type of such a map and psychology another, and the two maps are ultimately to be fitted together

[71] Kenneth W. Spence, "Theoretical Interpretations of Learning," in S. S. Stevens (ed.), *Handbook of Experimental Psychology*, Wiley, 1951.

[72] W. K. Estes, S. Koch, K. MacCorquodale, P. E. Meehl, C. G. Mueller, Jr., W. N. Schoenfeld, and W. S. Verplanck, *Modern Learning Theory*, Appleton-Century-Crofts, 1954.

[73] Ernest R. Hilgard, *Theories of Learning* (2nd ed.), Appleton-Century-Crofts, 1956.

as to make complete prediction—complete finding of our way out—possible," wrote Tolman in 1936.[74]

The ultimate goal of science is the development of both psychological and physiological behaviorism. The facts and laws of physiology will presumably explain the facts and laws of psychology; however, "psychology cannot be explained by a physiology until one has a psychology to explain." Thus, psychology must use its own methods and tools and develop its own set of testable concepts, which should be eventually "fitted together." The observable acts of behavior are the legitimate subject matter of psychology in accordance with the behavioristic tradition.

Independent Variables

What can be observed and operationally assessed are the initiating causes of the behavior and the final resulting behavior itself. The initial causes of behavior consist of five *independent* variables, namely (1) the environmental stimuli (S), (2) physiological drive (P), (3) heredity (H), (4) previous training (T), and (5) maturity or age (A). Behavior (B) is a function (f) of S, P, H, T, A.

$$B = f_1(S, P, H, T, A)$$

The function (f_1) has to be broken down into a set of mental processes which will figure "in the guise of objectively definable *intervening variables.*"

The environmental stimulus (S) and the physiological drive (D) are the *releasing* variables. They "set behavior going." Heredity (H), previous training (T), and a given age or maturity (A) are *guiding* variables for they do not initiate behavior but determine to a great extent the final character of behavior which is initiated by S and P.

The stimulus (S) and the drive (D) can be observed and measured. The stimulation can be determined by the experimenter and easily described in operational terms. The physiological drive can be presented operationally and measured by the amount of deprivation in an experimental situation as it was by Warden's measurement of the time since the last feeding.[75]

The list of independent variables stated in *Purposive Behavior in Animals and Men* (1932) was revised in 1937 to include the following independent variables, divided into two groups. The first group includes the *individual difference* variables heredity (H), age (A), previous training (T), and some organic factors such as endocrine and vitamin conditions (E). The experimental independent variables include the *sum of*

[74] Edward C. Tolman, "The Intervening Variable," in M. H. Marx (ed.), *Psychological Theory,* Macmillan, 1951, p. 88.

[75] C. J. Warden, *Animal Motivation, Experimental Studies on the Albino Rat,* Columbia University, 1931.

preceding occasions (ΣOBO) on which a certain stimulus complex (O) was followed by a certain behavior (B) and this behavior was followed by another stimulus complex (O). The other independent variables are the *maintenance schedule* (M), meaning the state of the drive at a given time, the appropriateness of the *goal object* (G) which describes the incentive, the *stimuli* (S), the types of motor response required (R) by the experimenter in his experimental design, and finally the pattern of preceding and succeeding maze units (P) which represents the experimental tools and setup.[76]

Dependent Variables: Molar, Docile, and Purposeful Behavior

The dependent variables include the observable behavior of the organism. In maze experiments with rats Tolman proposed the *behavior ratio* as the measurable dependent variable. The behavior ratio is the frequency of the turns of the rat into the right alley divided by the total frequency of all right and wrong turns.

On the whole, behavior of organisms is active and selective. In Tolman's experiments the rat "often has to look actively for the significant stimuli in order to form his map and does not merely passively receive and reset to all the stimuli which are physically present."[77]

Although behavior is a stimulus-response affair, it is not a mechanistic S-R relationship. Tolman distinguishes two types of behavior. The first is simple reflex or tropism. The lower the organism, the more physiological its response. All behavior is "disturbance and quiescence," but only some of it is reflex; some is docile. The simple reflexes, like the spinal reflex, are molecular.

Docile or teachable behavior is *molar*. It is the function of the organism as a whole. Whenever the organism as a whole does something, such an action is goal directed and not a mechanistic stimulus-response connection.

Tolman's system deals with docile behavior. Docile behavior is *purposive* and *cognitive* and presents the problems of hierarchy of demands, sign-gestalt, readiness, and expectation. Docile behavior is molar; it does not break up into atomistic reflexes and it has a meaning. It is determined by the goal-directed perceptions of the totality of the situation, or the *sign-gestalt expectations.*

The sign-gestalt expectation, in simple language, represents a combination of perception and motivation. There are three "modes" of expectation, (1) perception, (2) memorization, and (3) inference, which could

[76] Edward C. Tolman, "The Determiners of Behavior at a Choice Point," *Psychological Review*, 1938, **45**, 1–41.
[77] Edward C. Tolman, *Purposive Behavior in Animals and Men*, Appleton-Century-Crofts, 1932, p. 201.

be translated as (1) cognition of the environment, (2) retention of perceived data, and (3) deriving of conclusions by inference in future and similar situations.

Tolman's main idea is that behavior is not a sequence of causes and effects but a chain of goals and actions leading toward the goal object. The experimental animals in Tolman's experiment do not follow Thorndike's trial and error nor Pavlov's or Skinner's conditioning. They have a "goal" and behave as if they were following some "signs" which made them "expect" to reach the goal. Perception and motivation are the main elements in Tolman's theory. The organism learns through the perception of the stimulus the sign which leads to a purposeful action of the organism. Thus the sign-gestalt expectation, which represents a combination of motivating and perceptory elements, must be considered the main concept in Tolman's theory.

Intervening Variables

Between the observable independent variables and the observable dependent variables Tolman postulates a set of inferred and non-observed factors.

The intervening variables are the determinants of behavior. They are divided into (1) immanent purposive and cognitive determinants, (2) capacities, and (3) behavior adjustments. They cannot be directly observed, but they can be inferred from behavior. "They are to behavior as electrons, curves, or whatever it may be, are to the happenings in inorganic matter."[78]

The original list of intervening variables (1937) included six factors coordinated to the independent variables. The intervening variable *observed* was correlated to the maintenance schedule; *appetite* to the appropriateness of goal object; *differentiation* to the types and modes of stimuli provided; *motor skill* to the types of motor responses required in the experiment; *hypotheses* to the cumulative nature and number of trials; *biases* to the pattern of preceding and succeeding maze units.

In 1952 Tolman revised his list of intervening variables and suggested the following three main variables: (1) the *need-systems*, which depend upon the physiological deprivation or drive situation at a given moment, (2) the *belief-value* motives, representing the degree of preferences of certain goal objects and their relative strength or "value" in gratification of needs or deprivation, (3) the *behavior-spaces*, a term obviously borrowed from K. Lewin (cf. Chap. 13). Behavior, says Tolman, takes place in the behavior-space, and the acting organism or the actor "moves" in the space. Some objects attract him—i.e., they have a positive *valence;*

[78] *Ibid.,* p. 414.

some repel him, for they have a negative valence. The term "valence" is used by Tolman in the framework of perception; some objects are *perceived* as to be sought or to be avoided.[79]

Motivation

"Behavior goes off, in the last analysis, by virtue only of certain final physiological quiescences, which are being sought, or of certain final physiological disturbances, which are being avoided. . . . Organisms are provided innately, at least vaguely, with sign-gestalt-readinesses as to how to get thus to and from, and also with the necessary accompanying demands to make them actually try thus to get to and from. Organisms are innately ready, provided they are also suffering at the moment from appropriate initiating organic states or excitements, to demand certain quiescences to-be-reached and certain disturbances to be avoided. And they expect that positive or negative commerces with the objects presented by stimuli will, or will not, get them to and from."[80]

Following in the footsteps of W. Craig[81] Tolman distinguishes appetites and aversions. The ultimate goal of appetites is the "state of physiological quiescence to be reached by commerce with the consummatory object." The ultimate goal of aversion is the state of physiological quiescence to be reached when the disturbing stimulus ceases to act upon the organism. Appetites and aversions are "states of agitation."

Tolman believes that the consummatory and avoidance responses of the organism are "usually docile and not wholly blind and reflex." The states of agitation or the "initiating organic states of excitement" are both purposive and cognitive.

An appetite or an aversion has three phases, as follows: (1) a *physiological state* metabolically determined, which gives rise to (2) a *demand* for action leading to a physiological quiescence and (3) a "sign-gestalt-readiness" as to the type of stimulus-object to be sought to achieve the demanded quiescence.

Appetites, such as hunger and sex, follow a metabolic cycle or rhythm. Aversions, such as fear or pugnacity, tend to be enduring and constant.

Following the example set by McDougall (cf. Chap. 5) Tolman set up a list of human appetites and aversions. Tolman distinguished six appetites: food-hunger, sex-hunger, excretion-hunger, specific contact-hunger, rest-hunger, and sensory-motor-hunger (aesthetic and play-hunger). The initiating physiological state of each appetite is the state of disequilib-

[79] Edward C. Tolman, "A Psychological Model," in T. Parsons and E. A. Shils (eds.), *Toward a General Theory of Action*, Harvard, 1952.

[80] From *Purposive Behavior in Animals and Men*, by Edward Chace Tolman, Copyright, 1932. The Century Co., p. 271.

[81] W. Craig, "Appetites and Aversions as Constituents of Instincts," *Biological Bulletin*, 1918, 34, 91–107.

rium in the organism. When this disequilibrium is in force, a demand is released for a state of physiological quiescence. The demand is accompanied by a sign-gestalt-readiness that the demanded quiescence lies in a certain means-end relation with a certain goal object. In the case of food-hunger the demand for alimentary satiation is accompanied by the sign-gestalt-readiness that certain types of food are the appropriate way of getting to satiation. In the case of contact-hunger the demand is for the quiescence of the physiological disequilibrium of bodily contacts such as thumb-sucking, bed-wetting, etc. Tolman was not sure whether these needs formed a part of sex-hunger as suggested by Freud (cf. Chap. 6) or were an independent appetite.

There are two aversions, said Tolman: fright and pugnacity. Fright is avoidance of injury and pugnacity is avoidance of interference. In fright the demand is to avoid the physiological disturbance of pain or injury and the sign-gestalt-readiness is that a certain fright-evoking object will lead to such pain or injury. In pugnacity the interference with one's activities is the physiological disturbance to be avoided.

As said before, the *motivators* of all behavior with the exception of "pure reflexes and tropisms" are the innate appetites and aversions. Appetites lead toward physiological quiescences, aversions lead away from physiological disturbances. In both cases the organism "is provided innately with certain more or less vague sign-gestalt-readinesses as to how to get thus to and from. In the case of an appetite he is provided innately with some vague sign-gestalt-readiness as to the type of consummatory object and consummatory response which will lead to the given quiescence—and also, it would seem, with some vague subordinate sign-gestalt-readiness as to how to explore in order to get the consummatory objects. That is, when the appropriate stimuli are provided he tends to 'perceive' the appropriate consummatory and subordinate objects and to respond more or less correctly to them."[82]

The appetites and aversions, called together *first-order drives,* are docile, i.e., capable of modification. In addition to these drives humans are motivated by *second-order drives,* such as curiosity, gregariousness, self-assertion, self-abasement, and imitativeness. The second-order drives are "in some measure due to their own innate initiating physiological states," so they are relatively independent of the first-order drives. However, being weaker than the first-order drives, the second-order drives usually become subordinate to the first-order drives.

At this point Tolman quoted Dunlap and Kempf. Dunlap related the dominance-submission pattern to disturbances in the tissues of the circulatory and respiratory systems.[83] Kempf developed a theory of drives, relating them to the viscera and skeletal muscles controlled by the

[82] Tolman, *Purposive Behavior*, p. 287.
[83] Knight Dunlap, *Elements of Scientific Psychology*, Mosby, 1922, pp. 324 ff.

autonomous nervous system.[84] Although, to quote Tolman, these are "arm-chair speculations," still, he believes, they perhaps do justify the notion that the second-order drives could have their own physiological initiating states plus their own definitive quiescences and disturbances.[85]

In the controversy between heredity and environment, or instincts and learning, Tolman took a moderate stand. He disagreed with the attacks on the theory of instincts, as follows: "Every response when it appears, represents a convergence between the effects of both inherited dispositions and past environmental media. Responses cannot, therefore, it is said, be subdivided into the two neat categories: instinct, or the primarily hereditarily induced, on the one hand, and habit, or the primarily environmentally induced, on the other. There can be no behavior purely dependent upon innate endowment and none purely dependent upon past training,"[86] and the first- and second-order drives, being innate, "qualify as instincts."

The second-order drives "seem to be aversions" for they "appear to be evoked primarily by external situations." They are not cyclical or spontaneously aroused, as are the appetites.

Some combinations of first- and second-order drives create *personality mechanisms*, such as phobias, compulsions, sex perversions, and the "somewhat less certain" psychoanalytically conceived processes of an Oedipus complex, transference, sublimation, compensation, and symbolisms. Tolman believed that all these personality mechanisms are modifications of sign-gestalt-expectations and readinesses released by the drives of the first and second order. The main mechanisms, he believed, are repression, fixation, and sign-magic.

Repression causes the repressed material to be insulated from new experiences. Once the repressed material is brought into the consciousness, its sign-gestalt sequences become exposed to new experiences and break up. Thus the phobia, which is a combination of fixation and repression, will be cured as soon as it is brought into the consciousness.

Theory of Learning

Tolman believed that the behavior of organisms is docile. With the exception of tropism and the simplest reflexes, all patterns of animal and human behavior can be modified by experience. Thus learning plays in Tolman's theory a prominent role.

There are three types of learning theory, said Tolman: the trial and error, conditioning, and gestalt. Tolman considered his own theory a subvariety of the gestalt.

[84] Edward J. Kempf, *The Autonomic Functions and Personality,* Nervous & Mental Disease Publishing Co., 1918.
[85] Tolman, *Purposive Behavior,* p. 293.
[86] *Ibid.,* p. 304.

According to Tolman, Pavlov's dog acquired "a sign-gestalt-expectation to the effect that 'waiting' in the presence of the sign-object, color or sound, would lead to the significate, food. . . . The response originally made the significate was also appropriate to the sign, as a temporal signal of this coming significate. . . . The response made after learning to the total sign-gestalt-expectation is the same as the response made before learning to the significate object by itself."[87]

Tolman was opposed to Thorndike's S-R connectionism. The experiments in latent learning, especially by H. C. Blodgett, contradict Thorndike's law of effect (cf. Chap. 1). In these experiments "the animal is presented initially with alternative response situations, under conditions of no reward or, at the most, of relatively slight reward for the one response as against the others. As the result, he acquires 'apparently only a very slight propensity to take what is later to be a correct route. Yet a very considerable 'latent learning' does take place—a learning which manifests itself as having taken place, the moment a real differential award is introduced."[88]

What actually takes place in the so-called trial-and-error learning is a refinement or building up of sign-gestalts. When the organism tries out both correct and incorrect responses, the respective consequences of these responses are discovered. Accordingly, the appropriately differentiated sign-gestalts were built or refined, said Tolman.

Learning, according to Tolman, is "an affair of sign-gestalt formation, refinement, selection and invention." The laws of learning should be divided into (1) capacity laws and (2) stimulus laws. The stimulus laws can be related either to the *material* of learning or to the manner of *presentation*.

The description of the laws of learning follows:[89]

CAPACITY LAWS (CONDITIONED REFLEX LEARNING)

The capacity laws are to be conceived in general as listing certain fundamental traits, capacities, aptitudes, the possession of which in the given individual or species will favor learning.

(a) Formal means-end-capacities (i.e., capacities for simple differentiation and prediction) are obviously essential even to such simple sign-gestalt formation as is involved in conditioned reflex learning. An animal must, then and there, be capable of differentiating the given sign, significate, and means-and-relation from others and of forming the connecting predictive relations. And the quicker and more facile he is at such differentiation and such prediction, the better he will be at such conditioned reflex learning.

(b) Dimensional means-end-capacities and discriminanda- and manipulanda-capacities. The animal must be capable also of achieving correct expecta-

---

[87] *Ibid.*, p. 331.
[88] *Ibid.*, p. 343.
[89] All quotations taken from Tolman's *Purposive Behavior*, pp. 374–388. Certain parts of Tolman's presentation have been omitted.

tions with respect to the specific sorts of dimensional material—space, time, gravitation, social relations, or what not—constituting the stuffs of the given sign, the given significate and the given means-end-relations. And the greater his capacities for such materials, again the better he will be at the given conditioned reflex learning.

(c) Retentivity. Finally, the animal must be capable of "retaining" these differentiations and predictions from trial to trial. And the better he is at retaining, the sooner he will thus learn.

Capacity Laws (Trial and Error Learning)

(d) Formal means-end-capacities, alternativeness, roundaboutness, final common pathness, etc. It seems quite obvious that, since trial and error learning is, as we have seen, not merely a discovery of what the individual paths lead to, but also an eventual selection among those paths, trial and error learning will be especially favored by the capacity for the more general field-relationships of alternativeness, roundaboutness, final common pathness, etc.

(e) Consciousness-ability plus ideation-ability. We are assuming that consciousness-ability, i.e., the capacity to run back and forth in a disinterested fashion over the elements of the field, and also ideation-ability, the capacity to "adjust" to such runnings-back-and-forth, are not involved to any appreciable extent in simple conditioned reflex learning. The animals that are conscious probably do not acquire conditional reflexes any more rapidly than the animals that are not thus conscious. (An interesting experiment to try in this connection would be to see whether simple conditioned reflexes could be acquired in sleeping conditions as readily as in waking ones.) We shall assume, however, that, when it comes to trial and error learning, this being conscious or this ideating is of very considerable advantage. The more the given animal, or species of animal, can "hold up" his practical behavior in order to reinforce by "actual" or "adjustmental" runnings-back-and-forth relative to the predictive and differentiative relations in the total field, the more rapidly, we must suppose, he will be able to build up a total field and the relations among the alternatives within such a field.

Capacity Laws (Inventive Learning)

(f) Creativity (creative instability). It seems obvious that a capacity to break out into new lines of behavior, ideationally or actually, will be fundamental for inventive learning. Two individuals of one and the same species may be exactly equal in formal and dimensional means-end-capacities, in consciousness-ability, ideation-ability, retentivity, etc., and yet the one is more inventive than the other. The less inventive will "understand" the matter, once it has been shown to him, with facility equal to that of the other. But he will be less likely to "hit upon" this matter initially and for himself. The more inventive will be better at inventive learning solely by virtue of being endowed with a larger dose of something to be called creativity, or perhaps even creative instability. This more inventive individual will be one who, for some reason, is especially prone to break out into new differentiations and predictions. He will break out, into responses which, as far as the given type of situation is concerned, have never occurred with him before. This inventive individual will be the one who is liable and "unstable." He will by virtue of some sort of internal breakdown, tend to do something "queer" and "foreign" in any given situation. He will have a large dose of creativity.

Stimulus Laws: Laws Relative to the Nature of the Material (Conditioned Reflex Learning)

Given the necessary formal dimensional means-end-capacities and discriminanda- and manipulanda-capacities and the necessary retentivity, then simple conditioned reflex learning consists, as we have declared, in the acquisition of single sign-gestalt-expectations and -readinesses. What now are the conditions in the "stimulus" material itself which will affect the formation and retention of such sign-gestalts? We seem to find three such conditions which we shall summarize under the heads of the Law of Togetherness and the Law of Fusibility and Other Gestalt-like Laws.

(m) The Law of Togetherness (i.e., of sign, significate, and means-end-relation) would state that in order that a specific sign-gestalt-expectation may be acquired readily, the parts of that gestalt, i.e., the specific sign, means-end-relation and significate, must be presented by the environment in some sort of a "togetherness" fashion which sets them off as a unit or "figure" from the total background of surrounding experience. Or, in other words, the given sign, means-end-relation and significate must vary together concomitantly, whatever the changes or lack of changes in the other surroundings. The dog will not learn to secrete saliva for the given color unless this color, together with the subsequent fact of its leading on to food, are actually placed by the experimental conditions into a single temporal "togetherness," which makes them stand out from all the million and one other concurrently bombarding stimuli. And the rat that learns to take the white side of the discrimination box as the sign for coming food, will not learn to do so unless again these parts—whiteness, entering, getting food—are, as such, placed "together" spatially, temporally and sequentially, or whatever it may be. This fact of the need of a "togetherness" for learning has indeed been prettily illustrated by Thorndike. He has called it the principle of "belongingness."

Or, in our own terms, it appeared that quite without any motivation on their part, the subjects did tend to connect the pairs into sign-gestalt wholes whereby the presentation of the first member of a pair did lead the subject then to expect the second member of that pair. Some sort of a "togetherness" of the members of a pair against the rest of the numbers and words as background caused them to form sign-gestalt wholes in which the first-coming word of each pair became the sign for the later-coming number of the same pair.

But indeed this fact of some sort of a "togetherness" as the essential condition for the formation of "organizations" (gestalts) is perhaps the main burden of the contributions of Gestalt Psychology to the problems of learning and memory. Köhler in particular seems to have emphasized this point.

(n) The Law of Fusibility.—The second gestalt law which seems to us to be involved even in Conditioned Reflex Learning—i.e., single sign-gestalt formation—we have designated as the Law of the Fusibility of sign, significate and signified means-end-relation. And what we mean by this law is that certain characters of signs, means-end-relations and significates will undoubtedly fuse together into single sign-gestalt wholes more readily than will others. It appears, in short, that there will be stronger dispositions toward gestalt-formation when the characters of the parts have certain relations to each other than when they have other relations. Some characters will organize themselves into gestalt wholes more readily than will others.

In the case of the conditioning of simple physiological reflexes this would mean, say, that certain types of to-be-conditioned stimuli, perhaps odors, should come to evoke salivary secretions, i.e., become a sign for coming food, more readily than will others. Whereas other types of stimuli—say, perhaps, noises—will more readily come to evoke avoidance responses. And, in the case of rats learning mazes, it would mean, perhaps, that it should take fewer trials to establish the running-on response to food than, say, to acquire the response of merely waiting in a detention-chamber for food or the like.

Again, however, it is to be noted that this law of the greater fusibility of some characters than others into single sign-gestalts is in a sense merely a further extension of the preceding law of "togetherness." The Law of Togetherness as worded above stated that some sort of temporal and spatial, or other, "togetherness" was essential to easy "gestalting," whereas this Law of Fusibility adds the further point that certain types of "qualitative togetherness" will also make for easier gestalting than will others.

(o) *Other gestalt-like Laws*. Finally, it may be pointed out that probably certain other gestalt-like laws ought to be included by us somewhere about here,—viz., laws concerning the career of the sign-gestalt-expectations in the course of forgetting. For the gestalt psychologists have brought it now to the attention of us all that the process of forgetting is not a simple one of mere weakening or dimming but is, rather, one tending to involve also actual changes and rearrangements in the qualities of the material which has been learned. Their doctrine is that, with the passage of time, the remembered material tends to be modified always in the direction of Prägnanz—that is, in the direction of "better," "clearer," "more stable," ("more pregnant") gestalts.

Laws Relative to the Nature of the Material (Trial and Error Learning)

Under this head there has been listed only one new law—

(p) *Interrelations among the spatial, temporal and other characters of the alternatives*. We present this as an additional law because, although this law has not yet, as far as we know, been demonstrated, it seems to us indubitable that the future must discover such a law. The field as a whole is a gestalt which grows out of the minor gestalts corresponding to the individual trials and errors. It seems probable, therefore, that there will be some especially gestalt-favoring relationships whereby such bigger wholes will most readily appear. Certain temporal, spatial, or qualitative interrelations between the alternatives will undoubtedly be more favorable to the building up of such total field-wholes, than will others.

Laws Relative to the Nature of the Material (Inventive Learning)

(q) We have designated it rather vaguely as the Law of Presentations and Characters favoring new closures and expansions of the field. Inventive learning differs from trial and error learning in that, whereas trial and error learning involves merely the building up of a total means-end-field out of alternative parts, all of which are actually experienced, inventive learning requires the extrapolation of such a field to parts never actually enjoyed. Such inventive learning will, therefore, be favored by whatever conditions, of content and the like, the gestalt psychology discovers as favorable to such extrapolations. There will, that is, no doubt be conditions in the placement—and order—and character-interrelations of the parts of the field, already given, which will be especially favorable to the invention of the required new parts. An instance of this would be the discovery by Köhler that in the case of the apes' learning to use a stick to rake in food, the solution came sooner when the stick lay on the ground near the food.

(u) [Frequency and recency are what] we designated as the correct use of the "law of exercise." For it is obvious that the more frequently and more recently the actual sequence of sign, means-end-relation and significate has been presented, the stronger, other things being equal, this resulting sign-gestalt will tend to be.

(v) Revival after Extinction, Primacy, Distributed Repetitions. Under this single, rather omnibus, heading, we have sought to gather together a variety of further conditions which, no doubt, still need more investigation but all of which have to do with the temporal relations of the presentation. It has been seen that the simple conditioned reflex, after it has been made to wane on a given day because of lack of confirmation, will nevertheless tend to revive on a subsequent day. And this, it seems, is closely related to the old doctrine of primacy, viz., the doctrine that those connections which are established early have an undue tendency to persist and revive. And again there is also the well-established orthodox finding that temporally spaced repetitions are better than temporally concentrated ones. We are concerned here, that is, with the various temporal conditions of presentation, and with the laws whereby some such temporal conditions are more favorable than others.

(w) Motivation (?). Next, as a third law under the head of conditioned reflex learning, we should suggest (with a question mark) the law of motivation. We should suggest, that is, that in so far as the significate is either a strongly to-be-got-to or a strongly to-be-got-from object, by virtue of a given appetite or aversion or by virtue of some established subordinate drive, that the formation of the given sign-gestalt-readiness and -expectation will tend to be facilitated. The evidence on this point is, however, by no means clear.

When we recall the latent learning experiments, we remember that they indicated that latent learning conditions (in which the food box was not strongly to-be-got-to) seemed, as far as pure learning was concerned, to lead to the requisite sign-gestalt-formations just as rapidly as and perhaps more rapidly than did the control conditions in which the rewards were always present.

It appears possible, therefore, that learning without any very obvious motivation can occur. But, on the other hand, it might also be contended that in such cases the learning would not have occurred, if it had not been for some "general" motivation of curiosity, or the like, which made all paths to some degree interesting. Obviously further experiments and further analysis are needed.

(x) Not "Effect" but "Emphasis." Finally, it now appears that, irrespective of whether or not the Law of Motivation holds, there is a Law of Emphasis which does hold. Any strongly inciting situation, good or bad, accompanying either the sign or the significate, or both, does tend to facilitate learning. Pleasant or repulsive odors, electric shocks and the like seem always to aid learning. And, further, it is to be noted that this seems to be all that we have left of the old, orthodox Law of Effect. The significate or the sign must, probably, have some "interest," positive or negative, to the animal (though perhaps not too much) if he is to respond to it and its relations at all. But it makes no difference whether this "interest" is due to its "goodness" or its "badness." In fact, if there be any differential effect at all, it may well be that the "bad," "unpleasant" consequences will "stamp in" the sign-gestalts leading to them more rapidly than "good" or "pleasant" consequences will stamp in the contrasted sign-gestalts.

LAWS RELATIVE TO THE MANNER OF PRESENTATION
(TRIAL AND ERROR LEARNING)

There is only one new law relative to the conditions of presentation which seems to appear when we pass from conditioned reflex learning to trial and error learning.

(y) It may be labeled the Law of Temporal Orders and Sequences in the presentation of the alternatives. There is perhaps as yet no very good experimental evidence as to this law. But it seems more than probable that, since, in trial and error learning, the animal has to build up a grasp of the interrelations in a total field, certain orders and successions in trying out these alternatives should be more helpful than others. If, for example, there are only two paths to be distinguished between, it may well be that alternate trying of the one and then the other may be less helpful in building up the total relationships than a concentrated bunch of takings of first the one path, followed by a concentrated bunch of takings of the second path. (Or it may be that just the reverse holds.) But in any case, it seems indubitable that there will be some law of this general sort, if we can but discover it.

LAWS RELATIVE TO THE MANNER OF PRESENTATION
(INVENTIVE LEARNING)

Finally, turning to inventive learning, we find but one more law. We have designated it:

(z) Temporal relations between the presentation of certain of the already given alternatives and the true solution. We have in mind here the undoubted fact that a final solution (i.e., the new sign-gestalt-readiness and -expectation) will be hit upon more successfully as a result of a recent dwelling upon certain of the other already given sign-gestalts than as a result of a recent dwelling upon others of them. We recall again in this connection the experiments of Brown and Whittell. It must be noted that these investigators found that the difficulty of any given multiple choice problem depended very much upon what problems had just preceded it.[90]

[90] From *Purposive Behavior in Animals and Men,* by Edward Chace Tolman. Copyright, 1932, The Century Co. By permission of Appleton-Century-Crofts, Inc.

Theory of Learning: Experiments and Modifications

In highly interesting experiments with chimpanzees the experimental animals acted as if they had the "expectancy" of the goal and made choices definitely leading to a rewarding achievement of the goal.[91] This *reward expectancy* represents one type of learning as seen by Tolman.

Learning is usually facilitated by hunger and food, i.e., by "drive and the possibility of its satisfaction." But learning itself, says Tolman, is the bringing together and organizing of perceptual experiences and nothing else. In several experiments inference or insight in rats was examined. A special maze was constructed in which three paths of different length led to the food box. In preliminary training, the shortest path, number one, was blocked and the rats developed preference for the use of the second shortest path, number two. The first two paths had a common segment. When this segment leading toward the food compartment was blocked, the rats chose the third path, which was the longest one and the least chosen in preliminary training. The rats behaved as if they were in possession of a *cognitive map*. This *place learning* was considered by Tolman indicative of the importance of cognitive processes in learning, in contradistinction to the mechanistic trial and error and to the conditioning theories.[92]

In experiments with *latent learning* the rats were allowed to run through the mazes without food. When, later on, the food reward was introduced, the rats who had had the chance to "explore" the maze learned much faster than those who had not. In an interesting experiment one food-rewarded group, one not rewarded group, one experimental group which was fed only once in the maze, and two control groups were employed; the experimental group was in the maze ten times, being fed there only once; when it was fed on the eleventh day, it matched in performance the group which was fed every day. Tolman's interpretation was that some "latent training" took place as a result of exploration without food reward.[93]

Tolman believed that learning depended primarily upon the expectancy of achievement and upon confirmation of the expectancy. The experimental animals seem to make predictions as to which step will lead to the expected solution. These predictions are usually in a considerable degree of agreement with the real probabilities.[94] On the basis of past

[91] John T. Cowles and Henry W. Nissen, "Reward Expectancy in Delayed Responses of Chimpanzees," *Journal of Comparative Psychology*, 1937, 24, 345–358.

[92] Edward C. Tolman and Charles H. Honzik, "'Insight' in Rats," *University of California Publications in Psychology*, 1930, 4, 215–232.

[93] Edward C. Tolman and C. M. Honzik, "Introduction and Removal of Reward and Maze Performance in Rats," *University of California Publications in Psychology*, 1930, 4, 257–275.

[94] Egon Brunswik, "Probability as a Determiner of Rat Behavior," *Journal of Experimental Psychology*, 1934, 25, 175–197.

experiences, the animal develops a *cognitive structure*. This cognitive structure (analogous to K. Lewin's field) is a system of hypotheses as to what are the best means leading toward the end.

Motivation, such as hunger or thirst, determines which parts of the situation will be *emphasized* and therefore included in the cognitive structure. Whenever the expectations are confirmed, learning takes place. Thus in Tolman's system emphasis replaced effect, and confirmation replaces reinforcement. In Tolman's system the confirmation of an expectancy by an experience corresponds to the role of reinforcing reward in Hull's system.

Tolman summarized his position as follows: "We shall designate the remembered food (or distant maze feature) as the signified-objects, or *significates*. Secondly, we shall designate the immediate maze features, the stimuli for which are now *re*-presented, as the sign-objects or *signs*. And finally, the direction-distance-relations involved in the manner in which, on previous occasions, the commerces with the signs led on to the commerce with significates, we shall designate as the signified means-end-relations. The process of learning any specific maze is thus the building up of, or rather a refinement of and correction in, the expectations of such specific (*sign, significate* and *signified means-end-relation*) wholes, or, as we may hereafter call them, sign-gestalts."[95]

In the revision of his theory of learning in 1949, Tolman distinguished six types of learning as follows:

1. *Cathexis* stands for connection or attachment of specific types of final positive goal objects or of final negative "disturbance objects" to basic drives (disturbance-object-negative goal). It is a connection between, e.g., a given type of food and the corresponding drive of hunger. "The learning of cathexis is the acquisition by the organism of positive dispositions *for* certain types of food, drink, sex-object, etc. or of negative dispositions *against* certain *types* of disturbance-object."[96]

2. *Equivalence belief* is a connection between "a positively cathected type of disturbance-object and a type of what may be called a sub-disturbance object."

3. *Field expectancy* takes place when one organism is repeatedly and successfully presented with a certain environmental setup. The organism tends usually to acquire such a "set" that "upon the apprehension of the first group of stimuli in the field, he becomes prepared for the further 'to come' groups of stimuli and also for some of the interconnections or field relationships between such groups of stimuli."

4. *Field-cognition modes,* so called by Tolman, are the new modes of

[95] Tolman, *Purposive Behavior,* pp. 135–136.
[96] Edward C. Tolman, "There Is More Than One Kind of Learning," *Psychological Review,* 1949, **56,** 144–155.

perceiving, remembering, and inferring which, in addition to new field expectations, are acquired in the course of usual learning experiments.

5. *Drive discrimination* is based on C. L. Hull's and R. W. Leeper's experiments, in which there is a definite relationship between the type of deprivation and the way the animals learn. In the reported experiments hunger-motivated rats responded in a different way from thirst-motivated rats.

6. *Motor patterns*, Tolman admits, are most simply conditioned by contiguity (as suggested by Guthrie).

Concluding Remarks

Tolman has combined Watsonian behaviorism and Pavlov's conditioning with Thorndike's law of effect and McDougall's purposivism and the gestalt theory of perception colored by Lewin's field theory. Tolman is in no opposition to Freud or, perhaps, to anyone at all.

However, Tolman's theory is not a mere conglomeration. It is a behaviorism as far as it insists upon the study of observable behavior. It is a gestalt in its learning theory. It is a purposivism in its general idea of behavior.

Tolman himself offered an interesting analysis of the affinities of his system of the purposive behaviorism to behaviorism, purposivism (the hormic psychology), and gestalt.[97] He accepts the definition of behavior as a "stimulus-response affair" but rejects Watson's way of interpreting behavior by a "premature neurologizing." Tolman considers behavior as a means-end relationship, i.e., purposive. However, he rejects McDougall's theory of instincts and "mentalism" and calls his own system "an objective, behavioristic purposivism." He relates his system to gestalt theory because he believes behavior is molar and meaningful. He disagrees with the gestalt theory on the issues of the psychophysical parallelism between psychological gestalt and neurological gestalt (the gestalt principle of isomorphism is discussed in Chap. 12). Moreover, Tolman does not confine his studies to gestalt only, and his theory is purposive in contradistinction to gestalt theory.

Tolman's theory raises two more penetrating questions in regard to theory construction in psychology. Why do the same (probably?) rats behave in different ways? Tolman's rats seem to show much more insight, goal expectancy, intelligence, and abilities than do Thorndike's or Skinner's animals.

And the second question is: Are Tolman's conclusions applicable to all organisms or only to those put to an experimental test? For example, Tolman's dove will not continue to avoid the loud sudden noise when it

[97] Tolman, *Purposive Behavior*, pp. 417 ff.

is "proved" to him that a "specific and particular loud noise threatens no final physiological disturbance."[98] How would Skinner's dove behave? Does the necessity of logical proof apply to Skinner's dove or does Skinner's dove only need "reinforcement"? How would a snake, a turtle, a snail react to the same situation? And how much of all that, if it is applicable to humans, is applicable, let us say, to an imbecile, a moron, an average or a gifted child? Tolman, being somewhat programmatic, left more questions than answers.

Yet credit has to be given to Tolman for his emphasis upon perception and motivation in learning. Whoever has taught school children or college students could not possibly deny it. Undoubtedly, as Tolman said, there is more than one kind of learning.

Tolman suggested that learning can take place on a lower and a higher level. Although his own studies were chiefly confined to the sign-gestalt learning, he considered the learning of simple motor patterns simple conditioning. Obviously, different animals can be conditioned by different methods. Moreover, the same animal can learn in different ways. But the solution of this problem was not offered by Tolman.

5. GREGORY RAZRAN: EVOLUTIONARY LEVELS OF LEARNING

The Evolutionary Approach

In the above mentioned study by K. W. Spence all contemporary learning theories have been grouped according to "necessary conditions," as follows: (1) reinforcement or law of effect theories, which include Thorndike and Hull; (2) theories that do not hold reinforcement to be necessary for learning—to this group belong Guthrie, Tolman, Lewin; (3) "To the third group belong two-factor theories which assume that there are two basically different learning processes, one governed by reinforcement and the other occurring independent of reinforcement."[99] To this group, Spence believes, belongs G. Razran.

Actually Razran's theory transgresses the borders of the two-factor theories. Razran has introduced a new way in the theory of learning which has opened new vistas in the psychological theory and offered a possibility of a *rapprochement* between Freud and Pavlov.

Razran's scientific equipment is enormous. Himself an experimentalist, Razran closely watched the solid 1500 experiments in conditioning in Russia and drew useful comparisons between the American and Russian research. Razran's erudition in his field led to objectivity and to a sense

[98] *Ibid.*, p. 273
[99] Kenneth W. Spence, "Theoretical Interpretations of Learning," in S. S. Stevens (ed.), *Handbook of Experimental Psychology*, Wiley, 1951, pp. 692 ff.

of proportion between the respective "schools" in psychology and enabled him to utilize the contributions of scholars using approaches different from his own.

Razran did not deny that there is room for cognition in *some* processes of learning, or that there is room for a Thorndike-type reward learning. But neither cognition nor reward nor contiguity is the only type of learning. It all depends on whom you condition and how.

Razran introduced the evolutionary point of view in the theory of learning. Conditioning of lower biological species such as paramecia,[100] or of decorticated and curarized animals,[101] or of visceral reflexes (cf. Chap. 2, section 6, studies reported by K. M. Bykov), clearly indicates that "primitive" conditioning depends directly on "some source of specific biological energy." Some conditioning requires verbalization and/or cognition, some does not. Some requires Thorndike's reward or Skinner's reinforcement, some does not.[102]

According to Razran, all three types of theories of learning, as represented by Pavlov, Thorndike-Skinner, and Tolman, contain a great deal of scientific truth. They should not be counterposed on one another. Actually each of them represents the process of learning on a certain level of the evolution of the organic world. The three ways of learning represent three consecutive stages in the evolution of organisms and their ever growing flexibility and adjustability to the environment.

On the lowest levels, as far as primitive organisms and viscera are concerned, the classic conditioning takes place. Responses are conditioned "when one of the responses is a response to a powerful biological need—hunger, thirst, sex, fear, damaging stimulus." The conditioning of the viscera is unconscious. It corresponds to Freud's id.

Thorndike's cats and Skinner's pigeons learned by reward, or "reinforcement" as conceived by Skinner. Razran does not see much difference between these two concepts. Tolman's experimental animals and Razran's subjects used perception in learning. This is the higher level of learning. It is "cognitive" learning. All three types of learning should be related in one all-embracing psychological system.

The Inductive Method

In the methodological controversy between facts (Skinner) and theory (Hull) Razran takes a moderate view. He believes, like Skinner, "that the primary task of the psychology of learning is to discover low-level

[100] S. Tchakhotine, "Réactions Conditionnés par Micro-puncture Ultra-Violette dans le Comportement d'une Cellule Isolée (*Paramecium caudatum*)," *Archives d'Institute Prophyl.*, 1938, **10**, 119–133.

[101] Edward Girden, "Conditioned Responses in Curarized Monkeys," *American Journal of Psychology*, 1947, **60**, 571–587.

[102] Gregory Razran, "Second Order Conditioning and Secondary Reinforcement," *Psychological Review*, 1955, **62**, 327–332.

(directly observable) facts and to array them into low-level functional relationships (parameters, laws) with a use of low-level concepts, and that this task may be—and often is—hampered and misled by 'transcendent' theories and concepts that are only loosely and fragmentarily anchored to empirical bases."[103] Hull accepted the facts of the classical conditioning and developed upon it an independent superstructure of his own theories on motivation and effect and mathematico-logical methodology. This is why Hull's "pillars-postulates need so much continual propping and are indeed in danger of crumbling altogether."

On the other hand, Razran is critical of Skinner's bias against theory. "Blunders in the history of science are not confined to unempirical rationalists and intuitionists. Mach, the chief theoretician of 'descriptionism' whom Skinner quotes and to whom he has been likened, opposed, as is well known, for descriptive reasons, the atomic theory of matter."[104]

What Razran proposes and practices in his experimental and theoretical work is a cautious inductive empiricism. Psychological research must start from the discovery of directly observable facts. These facts should be related to each other and presented in series of simple, low-level functional relationships, parameters, and laws. After this empirical systematization of an area of low-level facts has been achieved, 'theories are necessary,' primarily as aids in "search for high-level facts to 'explain' the lower-level ones."

This is the inductive method, which proceeds from facts to generalizations, concept formations, and theoretical structures based on firm empirical foundations. Razran wrote in a critical vein about the deductive method: "I am unfriendly towards the wholesale physics-like and engineering-like deductive conceptualization and mathematicalization that has gripped the American academic psychology in the last two decades or so. I don't think that what is good for physics is necessarily good for psychology. . . . Psychology is to me a top of a pyramid of sciences, and oversimplified mathematical models are in it no more justified—really less justified—than in physiology, pathology, biology, or biochemistry. I consider myself primarily an inductive theorist, this meaning that good theory must be preceded by a thorough empirical systematization. I am not an empty-organism positivist, liking as I do to anchor my concepts in the nervous system, and hoping that eventually the matter of psychological generalizations at neural levels will become not only an inferable but also an observable enterprise."[105]

[103] Gregory Razran, "The Dominance-Contiguity Theory of the Acquisition of Classical Conditioning," *Psychological Bulletin*, 1957, 54, 1–46.
[104] *Ibid.*, p. 14.
[105] Gregory Razran, "Levels of Learning," unpublished manuscript, 1958.

Man Is Not Only a Machine

Razran takes a definite stand on the issue of reductionism. He is definitely opposed to reducing psychology to geometry, to physics, to physiology, and to neurology. He does not subscribe to Pavlov's not parsimonious and not empirically tested specific neurological theories of induction, irradiation, concentration, and typology (cf. Chap. 2). Nonetheless, he believes Pavlov is basically right and classical conditioning is a good method of studying the activities of the cortex. The "neural view of conditioning as 'strong brain centers attracting weak ones' could obviously be regarded as a pictorial way of expressing a theory of neural dominance."[106]

Razran states that "whatever extra constructs the behaviorial psychology of learning may need, they must be grounded in and modeled after neural action rather than merely fashioned in the form of logical relations. True, the neural constructs have no predictive cash value . . . at the macrobehavioral level of conditioning proper, and are at present only promissory notes . . . at the microbehaviorial level of neural action. Yet—to continue the analogy—the debtor, the nervous system, is quite real, of known location and unquestioned solvency, and has paid off on a number of occasions. Hence, a formal neural systematization of classical CR acquisition (as a supplement to the behavioral systematization) would seem worth attempting."[107]

And this is exactly what Razran is trying to do in his experimental and theoretical works. Without giving up the behavioral systematization, he is trying, whenever possible, to relate behaviorial data to the "debtor," the nervous system. For, it is Razran's conviction, "Man is not a machine should mean that he is not only a machine, and not that he is never a machine and not even that he is not often a machine. A contrary view mistakes and mistates not only the evidence of the laboratory but also, I should say, the wisdom of the ages."[108]

The First Level: dg Learning

Learning is defined by Razran as a more or less permanent modification of one reaction by another. If the modifying action is designated by g or G (the capital letter indicating greater and the small letter lesser strength), then, in a simple case, g + d gives rise to a dg, dg indicating d modified by g. G imparts some of its characteristics to d.

This is what happened in Pavlov's conditioning when the reaction to

---

[106] Razran, "The Dominance-Contiguity Theory of the Acquisition of Classical Conditioning," *Psychological Bulletin*, 1957, 54, 1–46.

[107] *Ibid.*, p. 14.

[108] Razran, "Levels of Learning," p. 9.

the metronome assumed characteristics of reactions to food. The same applies to conditioning with infants. When an infant, nursed by a woman in a black robe, starts sucking movements at the sight of the robe, it is the dg type of learning.

In Pavlov's experiments the power of the conditioning stimulus and the power of the center determine the power of the conditioned response (cf. Chap. 2, remarks on reinforcement). The dG mechanism, says Razran, seems to be what Ukhtomski, the Russian neurophysiologist, called *dominance* or *prepotence*. The modification is caused by the action of a sheer neural strength with "no regard for reality and adaptiveness, no benefit of cognition, and little account of affectivity. . . ." Dominance is a principle of sheer "force," wrote Razran.[109]

This theory was introduced for the first time in 1930[110] and fully developed later on. Contiguity, wrote Razran, is a necessary but not a sufficient condition for the acquisition of conditioning. The amount of neural energy, the "strong get stronger," determines the process of conditioning.

The evidence for the dominance principle is drawn from three phases in conditioning which "seem to need specific translation into neural terms. First, there is the unmistakable finding that the lower limits of conditionability are considerability higher in the UR than in the CS continua, which, in conjunction with the fact that typical USs produce in general greater neural changes than CSs, clearly suggests the neural generalization that for conditioning to be effected the value of the US-initiated neural event must be considerably greater than that of the CS-initiated neural event, that is, the former must 'dominate' the latter. Second, . . . conditionability varies directly with the values of both the US-initiated and the CS-initiated neural events. Third, . . . beyond certain points the US- and the CS-initiated neural events interfere in some manner with each other and . . . by all signs this interference varies directly with the interfering variate and inversely with the interfered one."[111]

Razran himself stated that his theory is "most closely related to what may be found in the writings of Pavlov." Although Razran does not subscribe to Pavlov's theory of brain mechanisms such as excitation, inhibition, irradiation, etc., nor does he accept Pavlov's animal typology, Pavlov's system, states Razran, has "a very wide empirical base."

Contiguity is a necessary but not a sufficient condition for the acquisition of conditioning, says Razran. Moreover, "Guthrie's insistence that all CRs gain full associative strength in one trial appears to the writer

[109] *Ibid.*, p. 11.

[110] Gregory Razran, "Theory of Conditioning and Related Phenomena," *Psychological Review*, 1930, 37, 25–43.

[111] Razran, "The Dominance-Contiguity Theory of the Acquisition of Classical Conditioning," *Psychological Bulletin*, 1957, 54, 12.

also to have a philosophical rather than an empirical flavor. There is, of course, no denying that the classical conditioning of *some* reactions in higher animals and in men may be effected under some favorable conditions in one trial and that increments with repetition often stem merely from the enlistment of more 'conditioners'—or the involvement of more favorable conditions. But this is a far cry from any generalization that there is no efficacy difference in the very basic unit of learning between men and paramecia and among the vast hierarchy of responses of different levels in human beings and in higher animals."[112]

Razran is opposed to Hull's theory of learning for its "indiscriminate combining data from classical conditioning, operant conditioning, maze learning and even verbal learning." Hull's reinforcement "in the sense of drive reduction is neither a sufficient nor a necessary condition for classical conditioning, and motivation (drive strength) is only a general energizer or an indirect or more or less approximative UR *indicator* rather than a direct and independent CR *determiner*."[113]

Razran's review of 618 experiments with classical conditioning led him to reject the idea of food deprivation (usually equated with drive strength) as being of ubiquitous importance. "*Variations in US-magnitude* (or *US-intensity*) and in duration of food deprivation are *both* well reflected in the variations of UR-*magnitude*, and thus are of any specific value only *when information on the latter is not available*. Otherwise, they are operationally superfluous. What correlates with variations in CR-efficacy are variations in UR-magnitude, and it seems to matter little whether these magnitude variations are produced by differences in US-magnitudes, differences in the duration of food deprivation . . . or something else. Hence, a concept like drive strength is, as far as classical conditioning is concerned, of little heuristic and predictive value (the situation is quite different in operant conditioning). And if there is no value in drive strength, there is no meaning in drive reduction."[114]

The Second Level: dD Learning

The second "level" of learning takes place when g does not impart any of its characteristics to d, but strengthens d. The d becomes more frequent and more stable; the d becomes D. A good example is given in the dog's lifting the paw while receiving food and therefore lifting it quicker and better. Lifting of the paw did not take on the characteristics of eating but became stronger. In the classic conditioning the reaction to neutral stimuli became very much like the reaction to the meat powder, i.e., the d turned into dG. In second-level conditioning d

[112] *Ibid.*, p. 17.
[113] *Ibid.*, p. 10.
[114] *Ibid.*, p. 5.

did not change; flexion of a leg did not become similar to the food reaction. The d became stronger; it became dD.

This type of learning encompasses what Thorndike called "reward" and Skinner "reinforcement." It falls well in line with some post-Pavlovian experimentation in Soviet Russia, e.g., the experiments of Ivanov-Smolensky with children pressing rubber balls to obtain candies.

"The law of effect," maintains Razran, "is a special higher form of conditioning that may best be called qualitative conditioning, in which a quality, a detection, a tendency, an affect—a vector or a valence, if you prefer—is the chief conditioning datum. . . . This qualitative conditioning, unlike typical quantitative or mere linkage conditioning, operates only within a special group of responses and manifests a number of characteristics that are not predictable or derivable from facts of quantitative or mere linkage conditioning."[115]

Comparing the results obtained in Pavlov-type and Skinner-type conditioning, Razran noticed that the classical conditioning required the reinforcement-trial ratio of 1:3, while in Skinner-type experiments the ratio 1:50 was sufficient. In Pavlov's laboratories the extinction scores rarely exceeded a few dozen nonreinforced trials, while in Skinner-type experiments the scores run into hundreds or even thousands of trials. The great efficacy of the operant conditioning observed by Razran led him to the conclusion that Skinner-type conditioning is a different kind of learning. It is the second type, the dD type of learning, which "extracted from common sense reward, traditional hedonism, and Thorndike's law of effect goes in the current behavioristic literature . . . often under the name of instrumental or operant conditioning."[116]

This second type of learning does not extend to autonomic reactions. It is a more efficient but less universal type of learning. The strengthening of reaction by a reward given subsequently does not apply to primitive animals, decorticated animals, or to viscera. It seems that the second type of learning (dD) might be related to the pleasure-pain centers in the brain.

At a certain level of evolution, the organism "behaves and not only reacts, he influences the environment and not only is influenced by it." This kind of learning by reward, as studied by Thorndike and Skinner, "applies to the cat and organs which come in a direct contact with the environment. This kind of learning takes place whenever the man or the animal acts and influences the environment, i.e., in the external motor actions of animals and in motor-verbal actions of men. . . . This learning does not apply to the viscera nor does it apply to the animals in the

[115] Gregory Razran, "The Law of Effect or the Law of Qualitative Conditioning," *Psychological Review*, 1939, 46, 445–463.
[116] Gregory Razran, "Operant Vs. Classical Conditioning," *American Journal of Psychology*, 1955, 68, 489–490.

lower stages of evolution such as most of the invertebrates. This learning represents a higher level than conditioning. Experiments prove that this learning is more efficient, faster and more lasting than learning by conditioning."[117] This learning is called reward and punishment, or positive and negative reinforcement. From Razran's point of view there is not much difference between the two sets of terms.

The Third Level: M(dg) Learning

On the highest evolutionary level a new type of learning takes place. It is creative learning. "This learning is confined to our verbal-semantic or symbolic actions mainly. This is the learning of perception, reasoning and imagination. . . . One may call it also the intellectual learning," wrote Razran in 1957.[118]

The classical dg conditioning is the most universal, starting at the dawn of animal life. The second, the dD, level is less universal and more efficient. The third level, the M(dg), is least universal and most efficient. "A knowing subject may, on one hand, show complete unextinction, continue to give a conditioned reaction despite numerous non-reinforcements or he may, on the other hand, show immediate extinction and withhold a conditioned reaction despite hundreds of reinforcements. Cognition in the form of presumed M reactions enters the picture and begins taking control—at least part control," wrote Razran in 1958.[119]

Razran studied the influence of set and purpose in configural conditioning.[120] He administered the same conditioned stimuli to two groups of subjects. The conditioned stimuli were green and red lights. One of the groups had to solve a bolthead maze, while eating. The green light was a sign that they did the right thing in the maze problem; the red light signalized errors. The other group was just sitting and eating when lights were flashed.

Both groups were conditioned to the lights and both responded with salivary responses to single lights as well as to the composed pattern of lights. The group that had to solve the maze task responded better to the single lights, since the single lights guided them in their maze task. The other group, with no task assigned, responded better to the light pattern as a whole.

The experiments in configural conditioning served as evidence that sets and attitudes lead to more permanent learning in humans than sen-

[117] Gregory Razran, *The Psychology of Learning—Theory and Implications* (Hebrew), Teachers College (Boston), 1957, p. 14.

[118] *Ibid.*, p. 15.

[119] Razran, "Levels of Learning," p. 16.

[120] Gregory Razran, "Studies in Configural Conditioning. II. The Effect of Subjects' Attitudes and of Task Sets upon Configural Conditioning," *Journal of Experimental Psychology*, 1939, **24**, 95–105.

sory stimuli. In other experiments Razran conditioned the subjects to the sentence "Poverty is degrading" and received good transfer to the sentence representing a similar idea, "Wealth is uplifting," but not to the sentence "Poverty is not degrading." The element of cognition and meaning was decisive in this conditioning.[121]

Razran never accepted the gestalt theory in its orthodox form but he gives credit to Lashley and Tolman for the distinction of the cognitive or relational or semantic or conscious learning. A knowing subject may continue to give a conditioned reaction despite numerous nonreinforcements or may withhold a conditioned reaction despite hundreds of reinforcements.

In neurological terms, the dG learning is an opening of a new neural pathway. The dD learning is strengthening of a pathway. The M(dG) learning must be conceived as the opening of a new neural territory, the realm of meaning. It is the fastest, the most efficient, and the most lasting type of learning. As said before, it is the least universal.

All three types of learning "coexist" in humans and they often interact and conflict. Phylogenetic and ontogenetic studies show that the simple, classic, dG conditioning is the most universal phenomenon. It can be found in invertebrates, in infants, in decorticated animals, in various visceral organs.

In Razran's own experiments the human subjects always reacted in accordance with Pavlov's classic theory of conditioning, provided they had been uninformed about the aims and ideas of the experimenter. The "naïve" human subjects acted like Pavlov's dogs.

The dg learning brings about in man "significant changes in a wholly mechanical, machine-like, largely non-adaptive and, we may say, primordial biological way, an evolutionary continuation of the mesozoic era. . . . Pavlovian conditioning is at best adaptive in only an embryonic inchoate fashion. What adaptive sense is there in continuing to secrete saliva at the sound of a buzzer without food for 30 or 40 times and continuing to do so through spontaneous recovery for weeks or even months. The adaptive way would seem to be no food, no saliva . . . which is what happened on the third level. . . .

". . . Again there is the second evolutionary and more recent level of learning: . . . Man as a reward, pleasure, and pain sensitive organism. . . .

"And finally . . . the third and last type of learning, cognitive, volitional, semantic. . . . I have no objection to calling this learning rational, meaningful, logical. . . ."[122]

[121] Gregory Razran, "Conditioning and Perception," *Psychological Review*, 1955, **62**, 83–95.
[122] Razran, "Levels of Learning," p. 19.

Concluding Remarks

S. Freud, K. Bühler, and G. Razran emphasized the evolutionary point of view, but each did it in his own way. Razran's evolutionary levels are mainly phylogenetic with wide applications to ontogenesis, and they emphasize the adaptability of the organism to the environment.

Razran's evolutionism leads toward bridging the gap between experimental psychology and experimental physiology. Razran was too cautious to be carried into a shallow and not-too-empirical reductionism. Although a disciple of Pavlov, he did not accept uncritically all the physiological theories of Pavlov, nor did he ever substitute physiological models for psychological observations.

Moreover, by introducing the fruitful idea of evolutionary levels of learning Razran has offered a solution of the so-called contiguity vs. reinforcement controversy. Razran accepted both of them and assigned a place to each in his evolutionary ladder of levels of learning. With one stroke the controversy was removed, and the experimental data were put together in an orderly system of theoretical explanation.

On the top of the ladder Razran put cognitive learning. Now the S-S theories could find their place among the other learning theories and the road lay open for a general theory of learning.

Some questions, pointed or singled out by Razran, still await further empirical research and theoretical formulation. In Razran's theory the lowest, the dg, type of learning does not need reward. The second does. How about the third one? Furthermore, Freud apparently overlooked the mechanical, without pleasure, aspects of behavior (cf. Chaps. 6 and 15). But visceral learning, as emphasized by Razran, is unconscious and does not require reward. Razran believes in scientific convergencies and seems to expect Pavlov's and Freud's data to be utilized in an over-all system. Razran has indicated some possibilities but has not yet presented his findings in a fully developed theory.

While Razran's approach to the problem of reconciliation to psychoanalysis is a very cautious one, some of Hull's disciples have tried to incorporate psychoanalytic concepts directly in their theories.

6. LEARNING THEORY INFLUENCED BY PSYCHOANALYSIS

John Dollard and Neal E. Miller: Innate Drives

In his excellent volume Hilgard divided the present-day post-Hullian theorists of reinforcement into two groups, each of them subdivided as follows:[123]

[123] Ernest R. Hilgard, *Theories of Learning* (2nd ed.), Appleton-Century-Crofts, 1956, p. 422.

1. Single-factor theories
   a. Contiguity only (Sheffield, Seward)
   b. Drive reduction only (N. E. Miller)
2. Dual theories
   a. Drive reduction for instrumental acts only (Mowrer)
   b. Drive reduction for classical conditioning only (Spence)

We shall analyze one theory of each group, namely, the theories of
N. E. Miller and O. H. Mowrer. Our choice of Miller and Mowrer, as in
other cases throughout the present volume, was dictated by our preference for systems and theoretical formulations conceived in terms of
general psychology rather than for specific psychological problems.

Dollard and Miller can be classified as Hull's disciples although they
have introduced definite modification in Hull's theory of learning. Some
stimuli come from without, some from within the organism. Any stimulus
which is strong enough to cause a motor reaction is a *drive*. The motor
reaction aims at the reduction of the drive stimulus. Hunger, thirst, pain,
and sex are *primary drive stimuli* which elicit actions of the organism
leading toward the gratification or reduction of the drive stimulus. The
primary drives are, as a rule, closely related to the physiological processes
of the organism.

The neonate is endowed with primary drives which force him to act
but do not determine the course of his actions. The other factors which
influence the activities of the child are the specific reflexes, the initial
hierarchies of responses, and learning.

The specific reflexes are innate responses to certain stimuli. The initial
hierarchies of responses are innate also and indicate certain preferences of
reactions to stimuli. One child may cry, another may push away an unpleasant stimulus. The child's first response to any new stimulus is not
a matter of chance but a part of the child's natural endowment.

All the innate factors, the primary drives, the specific reflexes, and the
initial hierarchies, can be modified by experience. This modification of
behavior by experience is *learning*. All learning is association between
stimulus (cue) and response, and this association is named *habit*. Personality is a system of innate and acquired responses (habits). Since
habits can be formed, changed, and extinguished, personality is not
a rigid structure but a fluctuating system of innate and acquired behavioral patterns.

In contradistinction to many learning theorists Dollard and Miller
included in their theory the processes of natural growth and developmental stages as suggested by Sigmund Freud. Moreover, they incorporated in their research great portions of Freud's theory (cf. Chap. 6)
and believed that the infant's mind was unconscious. All drives, cues,
and responses are largely unconscious even in adults. "The child is

urgently, hopelessly, planlessly impelled, living by moments in eternal pain and then suddenly finding itself bathed in endless bliss. The young child . . . has just those symptoms that we recognize as psychosis in the adult. . . . Savage drives within the infant impel to action. . . . The higher mental processes (the Ego) cannot do their benign work of comforting, directing effort and binding the world into a planful sequence. . . . These are the tumultuous circumstances in which severe unconscious mental conflicts can be created."[124]

Behavior is related to five gradients. The gradient of *approach* indicates the increasing tendency to move toward the goal when one comes near to it; the nearer one is to the goal, the stronger the desire. Analogously, the gradient of *avoidance* indicates that the nearer the negative stimulus comes, the greater the tendency to avoid it. The third gradient indicates that avoidance is more powerful than approach. The fourth gradient indicates that the increase in drive-stimulus increases the strength of approach or avoidance. The fifth gradient states that in case of conflict the stronger response will win.

On these foundations of innate factors and developmental stages, much resembling the psychoanalytic propositions, Miller and Dollard built their theory of learning, leaning heavily on C. L. Hull's theory.

"Learning takes place according to definite psychological principles. . . . The learner must be driven to make the response and rewarded for having responded in the presence of the cue. This may be expressed in a homely way by saying that in order to learn one must want something, notice something, do something, and get something. Stated more exactly, these factors are drive, cue, response, and reward. These elements in the learning process have been carefully explored, and further complexities have been discovered. Learning theory has become a firmly knit body of principles which are useful in describing human behavior."[125]

This four-factor distinction does not deviate substantially from Hull's theory. As said before, any strong stimulus which elicits a motor reaction is named drive. The primary drives are rooted in the physiology of the living mother.

A cue is a stimulus which determines the nature of the response of the organism. The same stimulus may serve both as a drive and as a cue. Cues can be auditory, visual, olfactory, tactile, etc. A visual cue such as a blinding flash of light may elicit blinking of the eyes. An auditory cue may elicit a different reaction. Cues differ both in their quality (auditory, visual, etc.) and in their magnitude or intensity (strong, weak,

---

[124] John Dollard and Neal E. Miller, *Personality and Psychotherapy: An Analysis in Terms of Learning, Thinking and Culture*, McGraw-Hill, 1950, pp. 130–131.

[125] Neal E. Miller and John Dollard, *Social Learning and Imitation*, Yale, 1941, pp. 1–2.

etc.). The cues determine when and where the organism will respond as well as which response will be given.

The initial response to a certain cue is a result of the innate and initial hiearchy of responses which is found in every newborn organism. This hierarchy undergoes changes according to the individual's experiences. A given response may or may not be reinforced. Once it is reinforced a new *resultant* hierarchy of responses develops.

Reinforcement is the reduction of the intensity of the stimulus. Food introduced by mouth brings quicker results in learning than food introduced into the stomach fistula with the omission of the mouth. Mouth intake serves as a secondary reinforcement, but the fact that reduction of hunger is reinforcing is considered by Miller evidence of the stimulus-reduction theory of reinforcement as postulated by Hull.[126] Reward and reinforcement are identical in the theory of Dollard and Miller, but reward cannot take place without drive-stimuli. Rewards reduce the intensity or strength of drive-stimuli up to a point where further reduction becomes impossible. Thus reinforcement is always a stimulus drive reduction.

Nonreinforced responses are subject to extinction. A response repeated without reward becomes extinguished gradually, and spontaneous recoveries may take place. If not reinforced for a long period of time, the S-R bond, the habit, or the tendency to respond in a certain way will become completely extinguished.

Dollard and Miller related Thorndike's spread of effect to the *gradient of reinforcement*. Responses contiguous to the reward or in an immediate priority to it become stronger linked to the cue. The gradient of generalization relates to the gradation of cues in the degree of their similarity; the more similar the cues, the more chances for generalization in the responses.

At this point Dollard and Miller believed they had come close to psychoanalysis. Reinforcement, being a reduction in the drive-stimulus, corresponds to Freud's pleasure principle, and generalization corresponds to Freud's displacement. The latter statement underwent experimental testing.

In a series of experimental studies Dollard and Miller tested the hypothesis that the psychoanalytic concept of displacement can be presented as stimulus generalization. In one study they proved that frustrated individuals turn their aggression against inanimate nature or innocent individuals.[127] In other experiments Miller has shown the possibility of generalization from hunger stimuli to pain and fear, which, he believes,

[126] Neal E. Miller and M. L. Kessen, "Reward Effects of Food Via Stomach Fistula Compared with Those of Food Via Mouth," *Journal of Comparative and Physiological Psychology*, 1952, 45, 555–564.
[127] J. Dollard, L. W. Doob, N. E. Miller, O. H. Mowrer, R. R. Sears, C. S. Ford, C. I. Hovland, and R. T. Sollenberger, *Frustration and Aggression*, Yale, 1939.

corresponds to Freud's theory of interchangeability of drives.[128] The logic of this reasoning seems to be highly convincing.

One of the learned patterns of behavior is repression. (The term "repression" is used here in the same way Freud used it; cf. Chap. 6, section 6.) Repression is the response of "do-not-think about certain things." This response halts the reduction of fear in thinking about them; the repressing response is drive reducing and reinforced. Once more Freud's theory is believed to fit well in the framework of the theory of learning.

The secondary or learned drives, which "are acquired on the basis of the primary drives, represent elaborations of them, and serve as a façade behind which the functions of the underlying innate drives are hidden."[129] The basic mechanism of reinforcement (a reduction in strong stimulation) is the same for primary and learned rewards.

Consider fear. Fear is basically an innate or primary drive for it acts as a stimulus for action which brings a reduction in fear and is reinforcing. Fear could become a secondary drive when the fear responses were linked to cues which initially were not fear producing. Animals exposed to a shock in white compartments (clue) may later respond with fear reactions whenever put in these compartments, even without being exposed to shocks. Thus fear also can be a secondary or acquired drive.

Acquired drives may act as cues. Some responses are *cue producing* or leading to other responses. Language is a system of such cue-producing responses. Giving names to objects and to events is cue producing.

Words may be used as rewards, i.e., reinforcements. Verbal representations are helpful in reasoning. The immediate responses to the drive stimulus and cue must be inhibited or at least delayed. Only when a child has learned to speak and to think can he learn to wait and to "construct future in a controlled way." In reasoning we use symbols for testing the possible outcome of our actions, thus reducing the necessary amount of trial and error in learning. Reasoning helps in finding out the best way toward future action.

Language is a social product, and Miller and Dollard are much concerned with social factors in learning. It is not easy to predict a human's behavior without knowing his social environment. "Culture, as conceived by social scientists, is a statement of the design of the human maze, of the type of reward involved, and of what responses are to be rewarded. It is in this sense a recipe for learning."[130]

Miller and Dollard developed a theory of socialization of the child based on learning and imitation, in accordance with their theory of conditioning and reinforcement. There are three distinct elements in

[128] Neal E. Miller, "Theory and Experiment Relating Psychoanalytic Displacement to Stimulus Response Generalization," *Journal of Abnormal and Social Psychology*, 1948, **43**, 155–178.
[129] Dollard and Miller, *Personality and Psychotherapy*, p. 32.
[130] Miller and Dollard, *Social Learning and Imitation*, p. 5.

this process: (1) The infant is initially motivated by an internal *drive*. (2) The infant sees problems of behavior which serve as *cues* for imitation. (3) The infant acts and achieves, and is *rewarded* for his achievement. The reward is drive reducing and the acquired pattern of behavior is reinforced.

Dollard and Miller embarked upon a daring enterprise in psychological theory. Always keen experimentalists, they put psychoanalytic findings to work for learning theory. It would be rather too early to judge how successful the outcome was (cf. Chap. 8, section 5). However, no one can doubt that certain psychoanalytic concepts are testable and that learning theory may be enriched by the experiences of clinicians.

O. Hobart Mowrer: Two-Factor Learning Theory

Is all learning reinforced by drive reduction? Mowrer's starting point was the same as Miller's and Dollard's, but he soon modified his position and introduced the two-factor theory.

In his experimental studies in avoidance learning the reduction of fear was the reinforcing factor. Fear (or anxiety) stems from pain. Anxiety was the conditioned response, pain the unconditioned one. Avoidance learning was acquired by tension reduction. Mowrer explained his viewpoint as follows:

"There are clinical, experimental, logical, and common sense considerations which all suggest that there are two fundamentally different learning processes, which may be simply referred to as *solution learning* and *sign learning*. In the one case the subject acquires a tendency to action, an action which is the *solution* to some problem, be that problem either a primary drive or a secondary one. In the other case the organism acquires what may be most inclusively referred to as an *expectation, predisposition, belief* or *set*. . . . Solution learning is problem solving, drive reducing, pleasure giving; whereas sign learning, or conditioning, is often—perhaps always—problem making. In terms of the effector systems and neural tracts involved and the conditions under which they occur, these two forms of learning appear to be basically different."[131]

Sign learning corresponds to contiguity. In sign learning the autonomic nervous system participates. For instance, pain and fear are involuntary responses controlled by the autonomic nervous system. "Conditioning, it now appears, must be restricted to the process whereby emotions, meanings, attitudes, appetites, and cognitions are acquired, with 'solution learning' applying to all cases of overt instrumental habit formation."[132]

Mowrer's sign learning comes close to Guthrie's contiguity, and his

[131] O. Hobart Mowrer, *Learning Theory and Personality Dynamics*, Ronald, 1950, p. 5.
[132] O. Hobart Mowrer, "Two Factor Learning Theory: Summary and Comment," *Psychological Review*, 1951, **58**, 350–354.

solution learning corresponds to Skinner's instrumental learning. It deals with the skeletal responses largely under the control of the central nervous system. In solution learning the rewarding reinforcement is the decisive factor.

Mowrer tested several Freudian concepts in laboratory setting and seemed to have reversed Freud's position as far as the pleasure and reality principles were concerned. In Freud's theory the pleasure principle is the innate and primitive principle of immediate gratification while the reality principle involves postponement and modification in gratification acquired by experience (cf. Chap. 6). Mowrer relates the pleasure principle to the rewarding reinforcement in instrumental learning presumably controlled by the central nervous system. He relates the reality principle to Pavlov's classical conditioning, for in such conditioning the animal learns "not what is pleasurable and relieving, but what is actual, true, real."[133]

Mowrer developed his own theory of neurosis in contradistinction to Freud's. Freud, said Mowrer, made the assumption that parental punishments produce repressions. Freud's id corresponds to the primary drives, ego to the solution learning, and superego to social conditioning or sign learning. Expressing his own theory in Freudian terms, Mowrer said that "neurosis arises, not when an excessively severe superego develops and overpowers the ego, thus forcing a repudiation or repression of id forces, but rather when the ego, which is initially under the *complete* sway of the id, remains essentially id-dominated and directs repressive action *against the superego.* In terms of two-factor theory, this alternative view holds that the neurotic individual is one in whom the primary drives not only had but still have major control over the problem-solving processes and cause these to be directed toward the blocking, inhibition, or nullification of the secondary, acquired drives of guilt, obligation, and fear."[134] Repression is, Mowrer believes, the learning of how not to learn. Neurosis starts whenever the individual uses his problem-solving abilities to avoid new emotional learning or to paralyze existing emotional reactions.

Mowrer's two-factor theory takes into consideration the fact that some conditioning does not require reward and some does. This conviction Mowrer shares with G. Razran. However, while Razran places the three types of learning in an evolutionary order, Mowrer prefers to relate reward to pleasure and non-reward to higher processes. It seems that Mowrer was at this point misled by the ambiguity of Freud's pleasure principle (cf. Chap. 8, section 5).

Mowrer's theory is not a sheer compromise between Hull and Freud. Mowrer deviates from Hull as much as he deviates from Freud, and his

[133] Mowrer, *Learning Theory and Personality Dynamics*, p. 6.
[134] O. Hobart Mowrer, *Psychotherapy, Theory and Research*, Ronald, 1953, p. 145.

theoretical work while being far from completion, leads to the development of new conceptual tools and new ideas on human behavior.

Robert R. Sears: Dyadic Units

R. R. Sears has widened the horizons of learning theory both in the area of social psychology and in the direction of psychoanalysis. Sears participated in the frustration-aggression study with Miller, Dollard, Mowrer, and others. He accumulated a great deal of experimental evidence in support of the psychoanalytic propositions and wrote an excellent report on what was done in this field.[135] Some of his own experiments will be reported in Chapter 8, section 3.

As far as his own theoretical position is concerned, Sears tried to incorporate psychoanalytic and social psychological findings into the framework of a stimulus-response theory analogous to that of Miller and Dollard. The wealth of psychoanalytic observations was utilized by Sears, with a definite leaning toward Sullivan's theory of interpersonal relationships (cf. Chap. 9, section 4).

Most psychologists were concerned with what was going on with a single individual—with, that is, *monadic* units of behavior. Sears pointed to the fact that interpersonal behavior or *dyadic* units may be even more important. Consider an infant crying. The cries of the child are a cue stimulus for the mother. The mother picks up the child; this is her response to the stimulus. The infant smiles. The smiles of the infant reduce the mother's stimulus drive; it is drive reducing, or rewarding and therefore reinforcing. Mother's behavior can be understood in its totality only in interaction with the infant. The instrumental act of an individual, in this case the mother, is not a closed unit, for it includes interaction with environmental factors.

Sears presented his theory of interpersonal relations as follows:

"The behavior of each person is essential to the other's successful completion of his goal-directed sequence of action. The drives of each are satisfied only when the motivated actions of the other are carried through to completion. The nurturant mother is satisfied by the fully loved child's expression of satiety, and the child is satisfied by the expressions of nurturance given by his mother."[136]

Action does not go on in a vacuum. Each individual has certain potentialities or properties that determine what kind of behavior he will produce under any given set of circumstances. Personality is a description of those properties. A description of personality has to include reference

[135] Robert R. Sears, *Survey of Objective Studies of Psychoanalytic Concepts,* Social Science Research Council, Bulletin 51, 1943.
[136] Robert R. Sears, "Social Behavior and Personality Development," in T. Parsons and E. A. Shils (eds.), *Toward a General Theory of Action,* Harvard, 1952, p. 471.

to motivation, expectations, habit structure, and the individuals and actions in the person's environment.

Sears believes that personality factors are antecedents to individual and group behavior; on the other hand, personality development itself is a result of learning. Therefore there is a need for a theory "that has the following properties: its basic reference events must be *actions;* it must combine both *dyadic* and *monadic* events; it must account for both *ongoing action* and *learning;* it must provide a description of personality couched in terms of *potentiality for action;* and it must provide principles of personality development in terms of *changes in potentiality for action.*"[137]

Concluding Remarks on Dollard, Miller, Mowrer, and Sears

The studies of Dollard, Miller, Mowrer, and Sears have opened new avenues for cooperation between experimental and clinical psychology. Each of the two methods has its faults and virtues. The experimentalist conducts precise, controlled, and quantified studies, but the scope of his research is necessarily limited to issues which fit laboratory test.

From this point of view the above-mentioned workers introduced important innovations. Their research method has been strictly experimental and their experimental design beyond reproach. Their assumptions were rooted in the studies of Pavlov, Watson, and Hull. Yet they did not overlook the tremendous wealth of empirical (but not experimental) observations accumulated by Freud and related systems. Miller, Dollard, Mowrer, and Sears are not eclectics, and their acceptance or rejection of psychoanalytic propositions was dependent upon experimental testing. In fact, none of them has fully accepted or incorporated psychoanalytic theory. The frame of reference of all of them is the S-R bond, and all have selectively utilized certain psychoanalytic propositions. Mowrer went farthest in the effort to modify psychoanalysis to make it fit his two-factor learning theory.

7. SOME PROBLEMS IN THE THEORY OF LEARNING

Pavlov's Neurology Neglected

Pavlov's theory of conditioning was based on (1) observations of overt behavior of animals, (2) observations of overt behavior of animals combined with surgically induced variations in the nervous system, and (3) interpretation of behavior in terms of physiology of the nervous system.

[137] *Ibid.*, p. 477.

Right or wrong, this was a cautious and well-designed scientific procedure.

Now let us see what learning theories have done with Pavlov's conditioning. By all definitions, learning is a modification of behavior brought about by experience. Accordingly, conditioning represents either all learning or at least some category of learning.

The apparent weakness of psychology prior to the development of the theory of learning is probably related to its "static" nature and its efforts to perceive behavior in rigid terms of definite patterns. The theory of adjustment as promoted by the functionalists stimulated the search for determinants of adjustment. What makes organisms change?—that was the question which made history in psychology.

Two types of answers were given to this question, one by the giant of educational psychology, E. L. Thorndike, the other by the giant of physiology of the nervous system, I. P. Pavlov. Each proceeded in his own orbit; there was practically no clash between them, as there cannot be a clash of opinion between a scientist saying, "Mr. A is angry" and another saying, "Mr. A has an accelerated blood circulation." Since both of them were talking about something which took place at a certain time in a certain organism, it will be worth while to explore the relationship between the circulation of blood and the feeling of anger.

This exploration may proceed in more than one way and there is no reason to expect that ultimately one will prove that blood circulation *is* anger. What could be reasonably expected is that *some* relationship will be discovered indicative of *continuity* of the living matter in contradistinction to Descartes's radical dualism.

We have to admit that such a discovery has not yet taken place. No one has been able to find the method by which physiological data can be translated into psychological phenomena or vice versa. The creators of the great psychological systems, such as Pavlov's and Freud's, have been extremely cautious in this issue and avoided the pitfalls of an easy reductionism. Some workers, especially Watson and Bekhterev, denied the existence of the difficulty, assumed that psychology is a sort of physiology, and omitted the problem instead of facing it. At the other extreme, Dilthey and Spranger denied the existence of the difficulty, assumed that psychology dealt with the immaterial and nothing-to-do-with-living-matter cultural issues, and omitted the other part of the problem instead of facing it (cf. Chap. 10).

The learning theorists tried very hard to solve the problem. Being influenced by two sources of information, Thorndike and Pavlov, they have faced an almost unsurmountable task. Pavlov dealt with irradiation and concentration of energy in the cortical centers. Thorndike discussed the impact of annoyers and satisfiers. This is *not* the same. Thorndike's law of effect is related to Pavlov's reinforcement; probably they both

deal with similar or overlapping phenomena, but there is a great difference in the approach to the description. The same dollar bill will be
described differently by an economist, to whom it represents a financial
document, a chemist, to whom it represents a chemical composition of
a certain kind, and a painter, who will be attracted by the figures and
colors on the surface of the bill.

Learning theorists tried to move in both dimensions, which is undoubtedly a legitimate procedure. Errors have been made, such as making reinforcement and effect identical. But the difficulties in relating the
physiological terms of Pavlov to the psychological terms of Thorndike
led most learning theorists not only to give up neurological studies but
not to make any use of Pavlov's neurological theories. This happened
not because learning theorists did not care for physiology; on the contrary, even C. L. Hull constantly related his findings to the organism,
its drives, and its physiological needs. Hull's system sounds like a reductionistic system, but it is a strange type of reductionism, for the omission
of empirical neurological data is rather conspicuous.

Something similar happened to many learning theorists whether they
related their data to the living organism or not. Learning theorists took
Pavlov's findings and omitted Pavlov's neurology; thus they have applied
a *truncated theory of conditioning.* Undoubtedly Hull, Tolman, Skinner,
and others introduced precision and refinement and sophistication in the
study of conditioned reflexes. But the unrelatedness of their findings to
neurological data seems to call for additional and neurologically oriented
research. At this point it is good to mention Hebb's neurological speculations, and Razran's evolutionary levels.

Motivation

Another source of difficulties in present-day learning theory is related
to motivation. What makes a person learn?

One group of theories is represented by Pavlov and orthodox Pav-
lovians (cf. Chap. 2, section 1). It is characterized by a consistent
presentation of the problem in terms of nervous energy undergoing the
processes of excitation, inhibition, and induction. It is, in Razran's
definition, the principle of sheer force; the more energy, the more learning. Reinforcement, as presented by Pavlov, is not reward.

Another group of theories is represented by Guthrie and his followers.
However, contiguity, or pure associationism, as the only factor in conditioning has been widely contested.

The confusion of reinforcement with effect and drive reduction with
pleasure caused a great deal of superfluous controversy. After eliminating
the Pavlov-Ukhtomski-Bykov-Razran (on the lowest level only) term
"reinforcement" from further discussion, the controversy continues over

whether Hull's drive reduction and Thorndike's annoyers and satisfiers are one and the same thing. Obviously drive reduction is reduction of a drive, such as hunger, thirst, etc., whether it is pleasurable or not. Deprivation-action-satiation—this is Hull's frame of reference. Pleasure-displeasure, whether reducing or not reducing drives, is Thorndike's frame of reference. These two terms are not identical.

Sheffield and Roby[138] proved that the non-nutritive saccharin could be a reinforcing agent. This is very possible and it does not necessarily contradict Hull's theory. One may hypothetically state that learning may take place with and without pleasure, with and without drive reduction. Some conditioning, as the Russian workers have definitely proved, can take place without feelings of pleasure. Undoubtedly, as Razran explained it, this is true in regard to visceral conditioning.

Thorndike's annoyers and satisfiers and Skinner's type reinforcement probably apply to a certain category of learning, when pain and pleasure determine the amount of learning. Miller's and Kessen's experiments, in which learning was faster when food was given by mouth instead of directly to the stomach (cf. this chapter, section 6), do not refute Sheffield's data. In Miller's experiment reinforcement was given both ways, by drive reduction and by pleasure.

Ultimately one may feel that a promising solution was offered by Razran in his evolutionary levels. We are tempted here to suggest some modification: All learning is related to *neurological* factors, and there should be, in the future, a possibility of relating all, even the higher levels, of learning to neurological processes—autonomic, subcortical, or cortical (cf. Chap. 15, section 1).

As far as the *modes* of learning are concerned, we are inclined to believe that the problem is how to find the evolutionary ladder leading up from simple conditioning toward learning with perception.

But *motivation* is still another problem. One may observe that learning can take place on pre-hedonic, hedonic, and post-hedonic levels. More about this problem will be said in the last chapter of this book (Chap. 15, section 3).

---

[138] Frederick D. Sheffield and Thornton B. Roby, "Reward Value of a Non-Nutritive Sweet Taste," *Journal of Comparative Physiological Psychology*, 1950, **43**, 471–481.

CHAPTER 5

Hormic and Holistic Theories

1. WILLIAM McDOUGALL:
HORMIC PSYCHOLOGY

Vitalism

It may seem unjustified to include William McDougall in the part of our book which deals with behaviorism and conditioning. It seems to be even less justified to include K. Goldstein in the very same chapter. All his life McDougall was opposed to behaviorism, and Goldstein has little if anything in common with McDougall.

However, both theories are derivatives of functionalism and both have common roots with behaviorism. Functionalism dealt with psychological phenomena as functions of the living organism. The position taken by functionalism led to two kinds of interpretation. One was pursued by behaviorism. It was the method of objective study of behavioral phenomena considered as functions of the living organism. Behaviorism strongly endorsed the physiological point of view in a mechanistic deterministic manner.

Functionalism also opened the door to another type of interpretation. Living organisms are the subject matter of biology. While some biologists have accepted the mechanistic point of view, other biologists, called *vitalists,* have introduced the molar and telelogical point of view. Driesch, for example, has observed the ability of organisms to adjust to a changing environment and to regenerate lost parts. Thus the principle of *entelechy,* or of goal-directed behavior, gained strong support in natural science.[1]

McDougall went farther. He assumed that some purposive and hormic tendencies were characteristic of the inorganic world too; otherwise the continuity of evolution would be disrupted. Therefore he hypothetically postulated some "trace of mental nature" in the inorganic matter. McDougall clearly distinguished between inanimate nature and its inertia —locomotion being caused by external forces—and living matter, which

[1] Hans Driesch, *The Science and Philosophy of the Organism,* Gifford Lectures, Aberdeen, 1908.

"actively behaves." Psychology is the science of behavior and behavior is characterized by its termination when the goal is reached, in contradistinction to the inertia of inanimate nature. "The striving to achieve an end is, then, the mark of behavior; and behavior is the characteristic of living things."[2]

McDougall's theories were based on three main assumptions: (1) Behavior is purposive or hormic. (2) Each individual is endowed with certain purposeful behavioral tendencies called instincts or propensities. (3) The entire behavior is determined by instincts or their derivatives called sentiments or tastes.

As mentioned before, the holistic and purposivistic ideas of McDougall clashed with the mechanistic and deterministic behaviorism of Watson, yet both were the legitimate progeny of the psychological functionalism. McDougall was as much a disciple or follower of functionalism as Watson was; perhaps McDougall was more a functionalist than Watson was. The adversaries of functionalism accused functionalism of being purposivistic and therefore unscientific, just as the mechanistic school in biology was critical of vitalism. The giants of the theory of evolution such as Darwin, Galton, and Wallace were mechanistically minded. But Spencer's pleasure principle could be explained both in a mechanistic-causal and in a vitalistic-teleological manner.

Physiological Foundations

McDougall strove to combine a teleologic theory of evolution with a physicochemical frame of reference. Behavior is discharge of energy, McDougall said, and he formulated his thoughts in terms of a psychophysical reductionism. The basic energy is stored in the tissues in a chemical form and can be accumulated, discharged, and transformed into any other type of energy.

A certain type of this energy was called by McDougall "instinctive energy." Its task was to "liberate and direct" the stored or potential psychophysical energy. This instinctive energy enabled "conversion of potential energy stored in the tissues in a chemical form, into the free or active form, kinetic or electric or what not," McDougall explained.[3]

Patterns of behavior must be related to the psychophysical disposition. Any action is a discharge or redistribution of energy, action being a discharge and inhibition being a redistribution or "drainage" of energy. All behavior is a function of the nervous system. Just as the reflex action implies the presence in the nervous system of the reflex nervous arc, so the instinctive action also implies "some enduring nervous basis whose organization is inherited, an innate or inherited psycho-physical dispo-

[2] William McDougall, *Psychology, The Study of Behavior*, Holt, 1912, p. 20.
[3] William McDougall, *Introduction to Social Psychology* (23rd ed.), Methuen, 1936, p. 32.

sition which, anatomically regarded, probably has the form of a compound system of sensori-motor arcs," wrote McDougall.

Horme

The basic construct in McDougall's theory is *horme* or the urge to live, the desire to survive. All living organisms "behave," that is, act on purpose, and their main purpose is to survive. "The hormic theory holds," says McDougall, "that where there is life there is mind; and that if there has been any continuity of the organic from the inorganic, there must have been something of mind, some trace of mental nature and activity in the inorganic from which such emergence took place."[4] For acting on purpose is a sign of mind, be it even so primitive as in the protozoa.

Behavior is not always a product of external forces or a mere response to a stimulus. Certain activities start from within; they are spontaneous. Behavior is purposeful and serves adjustment to life and conservation of life, which is the main goal of all living organisms. Organic nature is endowed with the urge or propensity or instinct to live.

The general theory of horme leads to more specific postulates. The continuity of purposeful development is implemented by the heredity of certain dispositions which direct the behavior of the organism. These dispositions, called instincts, are inherited psychophysical dispositions which determine their possessor "to perceive or to pay attention to objects of a certain class, to experience an emotional excitement of a particular quality upon perceiving such an object, and to act in regard to it in a particular manner, or at least to experience an impulse to such action."[5]

Heredity

McDougall followed in the footsteps of Lamarck and assumed that acquired modes of behavior could be transmitted through genes to the next generation. This assumption is one of the fundamental principles of McDougall's theory. Unchangeable and inflexible instincts could hardly explain anything. Human behavior could not be interpreted unless learning was taken into consideration. But this was just what McDougall was opposed to. The only way out was to assume that acquired or learned patterns of behavior could be transmitted by heredity from one generation to another, in accordance with Lamarck's theory. McDougall trained twenty-three generations of rats in the following way. He placed the rats in a tank with two exits; whenever the rats tried to escape by the more illuminated exit, they received an electric shock. McDougall reported that the control group made 165 errors in learning how to escape by the

[4] *Ibid.*, p. 462.
[5] *Ibid.*, p. 25.

right exit and avoid the shock, while the twenty-third generation of the trained rats made only twenty-five errors.

These and other experiments which dealt with the heredity of acquired patterns of behavior stirred up a great controversy. As things stand now, it seems that heredity of acquired traits was never proved by McDougall or anyone else. Kuo proved on cats that environment and not heredity determines behavior.[6] Agar's experiments on rats have repeated Mc-Dougall's experiments with decisively negative results.[7]

Theory of Instincts

The best-known and most controversial issue in McDougall's theory was the instincts, defined by him as inherited psychophysical dispositions which determine the individual "to perceive or to pay attention to objects of a certain class, to experience an emotional excitement . . . and to act in regard to it in a particular manner."[8]

"It is not any one kind of movement that defines the instinct but the general tendency of using different and variously combined movements to bring about a result of a kind common to the species and of nature to contribute to the welfare of the individual," explained McDougall.[9]

The instincts were often described by McDougall as "release mechanisms or just easily exploding containers of energy." We might, he said, regard each instinct "as containing a store of potential energy which is liberated and directed into the appropriate channels when the instinct is excited, and which leaks or overflows in that restlessness which we have seen to be characteristic of *appetite*."[10]

McDougall was aware of the ambiguity of the instinct concept which represented both a releasing mechanism and a storage of energy. Therefore, on the same page he added that it would be perhaps better and more justified to postulate a general "store of energy" and regard the several instincts of an animal as somehow drawing upon a common store of reserve energy.

Instinct, says McDougall, is "a concrete fact of mental structure, which in the main we infer from the facts of behavior and of experience. . . ."[11] One has to distinguish between facts of "mental structure" and facts of "mental activity or functioning." The instinctual patterns of behavior were inherited or at least based on inherited predispositions. Instinctive action implies, says McDougall, "some enduring nervous basis whose

---

[6] Z. Y. Kuo, "The Fundamental Error of the Concept of Purpose and the Trial and Error Fallacy," *Psychological Review*, 1928, 35, 414–433.

[7] Quoted by F. V. Smith, *The Explanation of Human Behavior*, Constable, 1951, p. 115.

[8] McDougall, *Introduction to Social Psychology*, p. 25.

[9] *Ibid.*, p. 415.

[10] William McDougall, *Outline of Psychology*, Scribner, 1923, p. 107.

[11] *Ibid.*, p. 103.

organization is inherited, an innate or inherited psycho-physical disposition which, anatomically regarded, probably has the form of a compound system of sensori-motor arcs."[12]

The term "instinct" in McDougall's theory indicates three kinds of functions: perceptual, emotional, and motivational, or cognitive, affective, and conative.

The perceptual factors in instincts were emphasized in some of McDougall's later writings. "The instinct is not defined by the kind or kinds of bodily activity to which it impels the animal, but rather by the nature of the objects and situations which evoke it and, more especially, by the nature of the goal, the change in the situation, in the object or in the animal's relation to it, to which instinct impels."[13]

The central and main part of the instinct is the emotional part, such as tenderness in parenthood and feeling of fear in the escape instinct. This emotional part is inherited and cannot be modified by experience, whereas the sensory and motor parts of instincts can be changed by learning.

It has to be emphasized that McDougall's theory of instincts is not hedonistic, and the term "satisfaction of needs" does not correspond to, let us say, Freud's pleasure principle. "Each animal species is so constituted that it seeks or strives for certain natural goals, the attainment of which satisfies corresponding needs of the animal. Since these needs and the tendencies to satisfy them, to strive towards the corresponding goals (such as food, shelter and mate) are inborn and transmitted from generation to generation in all members of the species, they are properly called instinctive."[14] Then, "it is the teaching of this book that human behavior is built upon a basis of innate tendencies which are in all essentials very similar to the instinctive tendencies in animals."[15]

When McDougall substituted the term "propensity" for "instinct" he did it rather unwillingly under the pressure of criticism of his theory of instincts. Actually, the list of propensities as published by McDougall in *The Energies of Men* is, with minor exceptions, the same as that published formerly under the heading of instincts in *An Outline of Psychology* and in *An Introduction to Social Psychology*. McDougall explained that since the word "instinct" cannot be used without provoking controversy and needless difficulties, it is perhaps better to avoid it; and perhaps the best word to use here is the good old word 'propensity' . . . which is the name given in these pages (in accordance with an old usage) to any part of the innate constitution whose nature and function is to generate upon occasion an active tendency."[16]

[12] McDougall, *Introduction to Social Psychology*, p. 32.
[13] *Ibid.*, p. 417.
[14] William McDougall, *The Energies of Men* (2nd ed.), Methuen, 1933, p 26.
[15] *Ibid.*, p. 70.
[16] McDougall, *Outline of Psychology*, p. 110.

As mentioned before, the emotional part of instinctual behavior cannot be modified by experience or learning. The urge to eat, to fight, or to escape is inherited, but the way humans behave in seeking gratification for their instinctual desires is subject to change and can be learned and unlearned. For example, the instinct of pugnacity is an inherited pattern of behavior, "but its modes of expression have changed with the growth of civilization; as the development of law and custom discourages and renders unnecessary the bodily combat of individuals, this gives place to the collective combat of communities and to the more refined forms of combat within communities."[17]

Animal behavior is both instinctive and intelligent, said McDougall, and pointed to the possibilities of learning from experience. While every act of any animal is to some extent prescribed by the inherited constitution, that constitution itself provides the capacity for adaptation, for adaptive deviation from the pattern common to the species.

Classification of Instincts and Emotions

In 1908 McDougall described twelve instincts in humans, but in 1932 his list contained seventeen main instincts. The number of instincts and their classification was often a target for criticism, and McDougall's classification of instincts underwent, accordingly, several modifications until finally "seven primary instincts" became the core of his theory. The choice was based on the respective role played by each instinct in the life of the higher mammals and humans.

Each instinctive process, as mentioned before, is composed of three elements, the cognitive, the affective, and the conative. While the cognitive (afferent) and conative (efferent) depend upon experience, the affective element forms the central and invariable essence of the instinct. Each primary instinct is permanently accompanied by a primary emotion.

Here is the list of the seven basic instincts matched by the seven primary emotions:

Instinct	*Emotion*
Escape	Fear
Combat	Anger
Curiosity	Wonder
Repulsion	Disgust
Self-assertion	Elation, positive self-feeling
Self-abasement	Subjection, negative self-feeling
Parental	Tender Emotion

[17] McDougall, *Introduction to Social Psychology* (5th ed.), Methuen, 1912, p. 20.

Several other instincts were considered by McDougall to be of considerable importance: craving for food, mating, gregariousness, constructiveness, and acquisitiveness. The additional five instincts or propensities were sleeping, avoiding discomfort, migrating, crying, and laughing—altogether seventeen instincts. Besides these seventeen "propensities," McDougall mentioned the "desires" to sneeze, to cough, to catch breath, etc., none of them included in the list of instincts.

Several instincts related to the same object can become united into a *sentiment*. For example, the social behavior of humans and their involvement in groups and organizations is not a sole product of the instinct or propensity of gregariousness. The social sentiment may be a combination of love, tenderness, self-assertion, possessiveness, etc. The instincts are inherited, but their combinations, the sentiments, are derived from instincts under the influence of circumstances and experience.

Concluding Remarks

McDougall's critics have repeatedly pointed to his inability to provide adequate proof for his theories. Such failure cannot be excused in a scientific theory. McDougall failed to prove the theory of heredity of acquired patterns of behavior; his method of experimentation and the way in which he presented his data have often received sharp criticism. The idea of horme and purposive behavior was attacked not so much for its content as for the dogmatic way in which it was introduced. McDougall's reasoning was not too convincing in regard to his main hypothesis, and one could not help wondering whether this was the best way in which empirical data could be interpreted. When McDougall introduced his list of instincts his ideas were attacked on two points. Critics questioned the scientific usefulness of the concept of instinct and wondered whether the instincts do not lead into the pitfalls of the old faculty psychology: a man eats because he has the eating faculty, and fights because he possesses the faculty or instinct to fight. More criticism was aroused by the apparently arbitrary way in which the list of instincts could be compiled.

McDougall's method represents serious shortcomings in theory construction. His system presented insolvable difficulties for anyone who would try to test it. Writes one earnest critic: "In McDougall's system an innate neural organization is held to prescribe the form of perception or the significance which a given situation may have for the organism. The percept is then associated with a particular form of emotional excitement, which in turn is associated with a particular impulse to action, and this finally with the action which may persist until the condition of emotional dis-equilibrium and the experience of the associated impulses is alleviated. Neural organization, which would be difficult

to demonstrate, and felt impulses and emotional excitement, which a
difficult to describe and assess, both qualitatively and quantitatively, a
causally associated with observable activity."[18]

McDougall ascribed mind to nature, related neural processes to phys
cal ones, attached behavior to innate patterns—and all this with the ea
of a man who deals with simple, self-explanatory, and generally a
cepted principles. Unfortunately, this is not the case and most of M
Dougall's statements are concerned with highly complicated and mo
controversial issues.

Yet psychology has to give credit to McDougall for his searchir
spirit and for his daring effort to understand human behavior. His emph
sis on emotional and irrational elements in human behavior introduc
a refreshing breeze in psychological research. His idea of purposef
behavior was taken up by G. Allport and many outstanding behavioris
such as Hull and Tolman. Although not too many contemporary psychol
gists are McDougall's disciples, very many are indebted to him for t
wealth of ideas and problems that he has introduced into contempora
psychology.

2. KURT GOLDSTEIN: HOLISTIC SYSTEM

Holism

Goldstein believes that the only legitimate scientific procedure
gaining facts is the study of single phenomena or the "atomistic" meth
But, he said, the organism is not a sum of parts which could be studi
separately and then combined into a science of the whole organism.
clearly distinguished between physical and biological sciences. Both s
ences deal with symbols and signs that transcend the empirical facts.
physical science symbols may correspond to part processes and son
times operate with a system of fictitious science. This, Goldstein sa
is not permissible in biology, because "biological knowledge ne
a more complete image of an individual concrete character wh
must match as closely as possible the particulars from which we bu
it up. . . . In biology, symbols, theoretical representations, must
principle include quality and individuality in all their determinatic
Biological descriptions must exhibit a definite qualitative organizati
the symbol must have the characteristics of a Gestalt."[19]

Goldstein did not ascribe gestalt to inorganic nature. He found
"qualitative organization" in the living organism, which is a "who
This is why biological knowledge cannot be advanced by "add

[18] F. V. Smith, *The Explanation of Human Behavior*, Constable, 1951, p. 185
[19] Kurt Goldstein, *Human Nature in the Light of Psychopathology*, Harvard, 1
pp. 28–29.

more and more individual facts. The facts which are gradually included in the 'whole' as parts can never be evaluated merely quantitatively, in such a way that the more parts we are able to determine the firmer our knowledge becomes. In biology every fact always has a qualitative significance."[20]

With this statement Goldstein promoted a definite methodological position. Physical sciences operate with quantities; biological sciences, including psychology, operate with qualitative organizations. Accordingly, Goldstein does not make much use of statistics and prefers to concentrate on a detailed study of single cases.

As stated before, Goldstein is fully aware of the fact that the organism is composed of cells and tissues as a house is composed of bricks. Yet no architect would try to construct a house by adding a brick to a brick, and no psychologist should try to interpret the organism by adding a cell to a cell. The picture of the whole organism and its *Gestalt* should be interpreted in its totality, in a *holistic* manner.

Even from the methodological point of view the study of separate parts is inadvisable, because the separate, "isolated" parts of human behavior cannot be properly understood or perceived in perspective. Actually each single reflex, innate or conditioned, is a fraction of a totality of action and a partial expression of the functioning of the organism as a whole. To pay attention to a particular motion without considering the total situation may lead to an erroneous interpretation. "Only knowledge of the whole organism leads us to understand the various reactions we observe in isolated parts."[21]

Equalization of Energy

Goldstein's psychological theory is based on the principles of constancy equalization of energy. This principle corresponds to Cannon's homeostasis, Pavlov's equilibrium, and Freud's constancy principle. Goldstein assumes that whatever goes on in the human organism is an accumulation, distribution, and/or discharge of energy. Energy cannot perish, cannot be lost, cannot disappear. It is transformed and transmitted from one part of the organism to another or discharged when a state of hypertension is created.

As a rule, in a normal organism the amount of energy is fairly constant and evenly distributed, and a normal or *average* state of tension exists. Whenever this average state of tension is disturbed by inner or external stimuli, the organism tends to restore the balanced or average state. The actions of eating when hungry, escaping when frightened, fighting when assaulted are examples of this process of return to the average.

[20] *Ibid.*, p. 30.
[21] *Ibid.*, p. 123.

Goldstein calls this process the *equalization of energy*. In normal life excitation which has been changed by a stimulus returns after a period of time to its former state; that is, if no new stimulation occurs, it returns to a state of equilibrium.[22]

Goldstein's principle of equalization or constancy does not imply any release or removal of tension. "Freud," says Goldstein, "fails to do justice to the positive aspects of life. He fails to recognize that the basic phenomenon of life is an incessant process of coming to terms with the environment; he only sees escape and craving for release. He only knows the lust or release, not the pleasure of tension."[23]

Goldstein believes that living matter cannot be at complete rest. Life is constant tension, but this tension must be kept within certain limits. Equalization means the restoration of the "average" state of tension which usually is the optimal state of the organism. Equalization enables the organism to function in the most efficient way, for life is possible only within certain limits of stimulus; overstimulation and understimulation jeopardize the organism's chances for survival.

Equalization is established by an interaction between the organism and its environment. The organism responds to stimuli in a selective manner. When a noise is sounded, the ear responds to it. A stimulus which is beyond the capacities of the organism is not perceived by it. The organism simply "ignores" the stimulus and no equalization needed.

Some stimuli cannot be ignored; they are too powerful to be dismissed. The organism reacts to them with disorganization if no way of adjustment and equalization can be found. In such a case the organism feels a task beyond its capacity. Sometimes other parts of the organism take over and the excitation spreads over a large area. Sometimes the too powerful stimuli disrupt the functioning of the organism and create a state of shock which is experienced as anxiety.

Self-Actualization

The level of tension at which the organism is balanced varies from case to case. The perfect equalization would be the state of the organism in which its function can be performed most efficiently, most smoothly, and most economically. Goldstein emphasizes two vital functions of the organism, and the law of equalization applies to both of them.

These two main functions are the realization or *actualization* of self and the adjustment to or *coming to terms with the environment*. Both

[22] *Ibid.*, p. 14.
[23] Kurt Goldstein, *The Organism*, American Book, 1939, p. 333.

unctions serve survival; both offer the best possible chances for the rganism in its efforts to stay alive and to live at its best.

Human life has an implicit goal, a purpose, and a direction. It strives o completeness, to perfection, to full development. Goldstein's complete-ess or *becoming a whole* resembles the principle of *Prägnanz* of the estalt psychologists (cf. Chap. 12), but in Goldstein's theories the raving for completeness and the striving toward a full life are the main sue. On this point Goldstein comes quite close to McDougall's teleologi-al concepts of life; Goldstein's emphasis on zest for life and on the ffirmative, creative, assertive elements of human nature resemble Mc-)ougall's horme and Pavlov's instinct of life.

Striving toward completeness is the main motive of human nature. It is ie striving for *self-actualization*. "We assume only one drive, the drive f self-actualization, but are compelled to concede that under certain onditions the tendency to actualize one's potentiality is so strong that ie organism is governed by it."[24] In a normal organism "the tendency ›ward self-actualization is acting from within, and overcomes the dis-irbance arising from the clash with the world, not out of anxiety but out f the joy of conquest."[25]

Each organism has several potentialities for development and improve-ient. They are usually expressed in interests, preferences, and aptitudes. s a rule one likes best what one does best, for in doing things well one ıds his way toward completeness. "The organism has definite potenti-ities and because it has them it has the need to actualize or realize iem. The fulfillment of these needs represents the self-actualization of e organism," explained Goldstein.[26]

But no organism lives in a vacuum. One must consider the environ-ent to which it has to adjust or with which it must "come to terms."

oming to Terms with the Environment

As mentioned before (in the section on equalization), the organism acts to stimuli in a "selective" manner. The stimuli disturb the existing lance and the organism reacts to them in a manner which should re-tablish equilibrium.

This constant interaction between organism and environment requires ›m the organism a certain degree of flexibility. This is the ability "to me to terms with the environment." The organism must find the best ›ssible means of self-preservation and self-realization while facing the ›blems and challenges posed by the environment.

²⁴ Goldstein, *Human Nature*, p. 144.
²⁵ Goldstein, *The Organism*, p. 305.
²⁶ Goldstein, *Human Nature*, p. 146.

The functioning of the organism in relation to the environment can be flexible or unflexible or, in Goldstein's terminology, *abstract* or *concrete* respectively. If the organism accepts the environment as it is and passively adjusts to the given situation, it takes the *concrete* attitude. This lead to a rigid and unflexible type of behavior; the organism accepts the present, concrete situation and acts accordingly, without any effort to change the situation or modify its own methods of behavior. Concrete behavior is repetitious and constricted and lacks initiative. Abstract behavior is behavior in which the organism perceives the situation in its potentialities, adjusts to it accordingly, and modifies the environment or its own behavior or both.

Abstract behavior is "not determined directly and immediately by stimulus configuration but by the account of situation which the individual gives to himself. The performance is thus more a primary action than a mere reaction, and it is a totally different way of coming to term with the outside world. The individual has to consider the situation from various aspects, pick out the aspect which is essential, and act in a way appropriate to the whole situation."[27]

Normal behavior includes both concrete and abstract parts. In some situations we act in a concrete manner, without thinking or even realizing what we are doing. However, the general mental set of normal individuals is the "abstract attitude," that is, the ability to act actively, to have initiative, to consider the total situation, and to prepare themselves for activity.

Most cases reported by Goldstein in his classic study on brain injury have lost their ability for abstract behavior.[28] It seems though that those individuals function on their possible best—in a "concrete" manner.

Figure and Ground

Adjustment to the environment requires proper organization of the organism. It is the *figure-background* or foreground-background problem. "There is a continuous alteration as to which 'part' of the organism stands in the foreground. . . . The foreground is determined by the task which the organism has to fulfill at any given moment, i.e., by the situation in which the organism happens to find itself, and by the demands with which it has to cope. The tasks are determined by the 'nature' of the organism, its 'essence,' which is brought into actualization through environmental changes that act upon it."[29]

What is figure and what background is determined by the "task" which the organism has to fulfill at a given time. To a hungry person food is the figure and everything else is the background.

[27] *Ibid.*, p. 60.
[28] Kurt Goldstein, *After-Effects of Brain Injuries in War*, Grune & Stratton, 19
[29] Goldstein, *The Organism*, p. 111.

The ability of the organism for a holistic functioning and perceiving hings as figures in accordance with needs or tasks can be impaired in hildhood, especially when the child is exposed to excessive demands bove his capacities.[30]

rdered and Disordered Behavior

Goldstein distinguished two types of behavior. In situations of success person appears poised, calm, in good mood, and well adjusted. This /pe of behavior is called "ordered behavior." When a person fails in his isk and is unable to overcome his difficulties, his behavior becomes anx-)us, agitated, distressed, often frightened, and sometimes the entire rganism shows signs of disorder. Behavior in situations of failure was efined by Goldstein as "disordered or catastrophic behavior."[31] This pplies especially to abnormal individuals, but even normal individuals) through states of disorder and catastrophe.

Brain injury may incapacitate an individual's abstract behavior. How- /er, even the damaged organism tries to come to terms with the en- ironment. The undamaged parts of the brain take over the functions of ιe damaged parts and compensate for the loss. When a certain function seriously impaired, regression or *dedifferentiation* takes place; the ganism regresses to earlier, less differentiated patterns of behavior. ery often the organism develops "protective" mechanisms such as with- 'awal from a situation in which failure seems to be inevitable.[32]

Goldstein defined disease as "a shock to the existence of the individual .used by the disturbance of the well regulated functioning of the or- ınism by disease."[33] The goal of therapy is either to restore health or at ıst to enable the patient to exist despite his defects. Therefore simple mptoms have to be considered in their "functional significance" for the tal personality, for the *organism as a whole.*

Goldstein believes that the observation of sick individuals offers a :tter opportunity for understanding normal behavior than the observa- ›n of normal behavior itself. Pathological behavior is usually a simpli- d behavior and deficiencies of some kind reveal the interrelationships behavior. The sick organism tries to make some adjustment in order survive. These desperate efforts are easier to observe than are the ual adjustment processes in normal individuals.

[30] It is worth while to note that this writer has arrived at similar conclusions ng the Freudian frame of reference. See S. Arieti, G. Derner, K. Goldstein, Z. trowski, B. B. Wolman, "The Deterioration of the Ego in Schizophrenia," nposium, Eastern Psychological Association, 1958.
[31] Goldstein, *The Organism*, pp. 35 ff.
[32] See footnote 30.
[33] Goldstein, *Human Nature*, p. 6.

Concluding Remarks

Goldstein's approach is monistic and free of unnecessary models, whic
often complicate and obscure the picture. His theory is a good exampl
of a well-balanced empiricism which utilizes as few constructs as pos
sible. His distinction between the physical and biological sciences wit
the emphasis in psychology on the *case study* deserves the greatest a
tention by psychologists.

Goldstein shares simplicity and clarity of reasoning and cautious ecor
omy in introducing new concepts with Pavlov and Freud. The idea c
equilibrium is also common to all three of them. A keen observer lik
Goldstein cannot miss the apparent effort of living organisms to sta
alive. In this Goldstein meets again Freud's Eros and Pavlov's "instin
of life."

Goldstein's reservations as far as quantification and experimentatic
are concerned are moderate and realistic. He prefers to see the study
organisms in a natural environment. He does not dismiss experimen
but he prefers observation of the cases in a realistic life setting.

Goldstein deals with the organism as a whole and considers bo
physiological and psychological functions as functions of the same c
ganism. He does not put consciousness under the category of physiolog
but presents it as one of the functions of the organism. Thus he com
close to Pavlov's cautious approach in contradistinction to Watson's ar
Bekhterev's naïve and radical reductionism.

Goldstein's theories have been derived from his empirical studies
brain injuries, which brought him world fame, yet he is not a reductio
ist in the usual connotation of the word, as Watson, Bekhterev, Hull, ar
Hebb are. He does not try to force his psychological data into a stra
jacket of physiology although he is a leading authority in the field
neurology.

Dealing so much with injured organisms Goldstein became fully awa
of the two sides of their functioning, the physical and the mental. I
did not try to substitute one for the other. Neither did Pavlov or Freu
Pavlov used non-mentalistic terms but left the door open for a psych
ogy based upon (but not reduced to) physiology. Freud created a ps
chological system, but he was fully aware of the fact that mental li
while being a part of organic life, cannot be reduced to physiolog
Goldstein deals with the total organism and admits both approaches
the organism. Consciousness, he explains, is a person's awareness of
situation, of his own activity and purpose. It is a function of the organis
but it cannot be reduced to cerebral synapses. Goldstein's theory I
something of Spinoza's philosophy; there are two sides to the coin,
physical and mental. Both together form the whole organism.

3. JACOB R. KANTOR: ORGANISMIC PSYCHOLOGY

Interbehavior

J. R. Kantor is undoubtedly indebted to Adolf Meyer. Meyer introduced the idea of the mind-body unity and consideration of the human mind not as an independent "mind-stuff" but as a function or action of the higher organized living organisms. Psychology is a natural science like all other natural sciences and deals with the functions of the organism. Hence the name introduced by Meyer: psychobiology.[34]

These ideas were taken up by Kantor. Living organisms are not just objects or things. They live; they adjust to environment by interaction or *interbehavior*, which includes all actions of the organism, physical and mental alike.

The organism, stated Kantor, responds to stimuli and can store up energy. Its main actions serve the "maintenance of the individual." Psychological organisms are at the same time physical and biological objects. However, "psychology has its own subject-matter-specific interactions between organisms and stimulating objects."[35]

Kantor was opposed to the molecular approach in psychology. He believed that the organism is one psychological entity and acts always as a whole. The individual as a whole reacts to stimuli and interacts with the sources of stimulation. Therefore the study of the organism treated as an isolated entity may lead to many misconceptions. The organism functions not in a vacuum but in a definite environment, and the subject matter of psychology is the interbehavior of the organism with objects, events, and other organisms. The "field" of this interaction is the subject matter of psychological inquiry.

Kantor made a strong plea for a non-reductionistic psychology. "All sciences constitute investigative enterprises for the purpose of ascertaining the nature of specific events. . . . It is assumed that nature comprises intricate manifold of events—fields in which things (particles, waves, organisms, etc.) operate in certain ways and change under specific conditions. Each science including psychology isolates some phase of this manifold for its special object of study. The data and methods of psychology are therefore homogeneous with those of all other sciences. . . . All sciences are coordinate. . . . Psychology, then, does not require any specific neural or general biological guarantee for the reality of its data."[36]

---

[34] Adolf Meyer, *Common Sense Psychiatry*, McGraw-Hill, 1948.
[35] Jacob R. Kantor, *A Survey of the Science of Psychology*, Principia, 1933, p. vii.
[36] Jacob R. Kantor, "Interbehavioral Psychology," in M. H. Marx (ed.), *Psychological Theory*, Macmillan, 1951, pp. 318–319.

Psychology must develop its statements on two levels. The first level is the description of observable phenomena. Such a description is the result of "investigative contacts of the scientist with the events." The second level of the scientific inquiry is the interpretation of data. In the construction of interpretations the psychologist cannot incorporate anything which is "not derived from an original operation upon data. For example when a psychologist observes an organism discriminate a red from a green square, he cannot regard the color quality as a psychic or neural middle term between the stimulation—regarded as operation of light rays —and the response—considered as the operation of muscular processes . . . Constructions should not only be derived from and made applicable to original events, but also . . . whenever it is necessary to build upon prior constructions such building must be carefully controlled. . . What must be guarded against is building psychological construction out of prior biological (muscle action) and physical (energy) constructions as though these were preanalytic investigative events."[37]

This methodological anti-reductionism well reflects Kantor's position. Kantor does not deny the fact that mental processes are functions of the living matter. He is, however, strongly opposed to the idea that fictitious physiological models or constructs are any better than psychological ones. He is adamant in his opposition to the uncritical borrowing of concepts from foreign areas instead of developing them out of observable psychological data. Psychology, he believes, can function on its own merits just like any other empirical science and does not need any "support" from physiology.

As a matter of fact the physiological theories related to the functioning of the nervous system are biased and dualistic, and not prepared to offer sufficient explanation in their own realm. Kantor described in detail the physiological counterparts of psychology. In a volume published in 19 he exposed to a thorough and severe criticism several theories which tried to reduce psychology to physiological phenomena and localize mental functions in the cortex.[38] Kantor never denied the fact that mental functions are accompanied by physiological ones and he made a plea for "authentic" physiological psychology. Such a psychology will by no means represent the entire truth, for the subject matter of psychology is not the organism only but the "field" of "interbehavior" between organism and environment. Therefore the description of organic or physiological factors in psychology cannot replace the description of the psychological data. "The most elaborate description of such participating biological factors cannot cover the essential features of the psychological event

[37] *Ibid.*, pp. 320–321.
[38] Jacob R. Kantor, *Problems of Physiological Psychology*, Principia, 1947.

wrote Kantor.[39] However, an "authentic" physiological psychology could be very helpful.

Kantor's studies are a significant contribution in the methodology of psychological inquiry. His methodological anti-reductionistic point is well taken and clearly elaborated, and his theory of organism-environment interaction brings him close to K. Goldstein and K. Lewin.

[39] *Ibid.*, p. 337.

SUMMARY OF PART I

Part I includes various psychological theories brought together by their common start in the controversy over introspection. The first chapter sets the stage and describes the domineering trend of "structuralism" based on introspection. Both Wundt in Germany and Titchener in the United States have been experimental psychologists who, under the influence of the nineteenth-century physiologists, have introduced the experimental method into psychology.

Another group of psychologists, most of them in the United States, felt that the biological theory of evolution offers a more fruitful stimulation. James, Dewey, Angell, Woodworth, and others preferred to look on mental activities from the angle of adjustment to life. These psychologists, called functionalists, perceived consciousness not as a receptor-motor machine but as a weapon of the living organism in its fight for survival. This point of view, influenced by the American philosophy of *pragmatism,* undermined the status of consciousness as the only subject matter of psychology and challenged introspection as the main method in psychology.

The rapidly expanding animal psychology led to an ever increasing criticism of introspection. Thorndike's neo-associationism, called "connectionism," built a bridge leading from studies based on introspection to the new and objective psychology. Thorndike never burnt the bridge and his writings serve as a link between the "old" structuralism, functionalism, and associationism on one side and the "new" behaviorism and conditioning on the other. Whether the "new" was really new we shall see later.

The second chapter is devoted to I. P. Pavlov and his school. Starting with I. M. Sechenov, the Russian physiologists and neurophysiologists embarked upon the most fruitful research in the physiology of the nervous system and its relationship to behavior. Pavlov's main principles were monism, empiricism, conservation of energy, and determinism. Pavlov did not intend to develop psychological theory. He believed that a scientific psychology based upon physiology (but not reduced to it) still had to come. Meanwhile, the physiological foundations were laid by Pavlov.

194

Whatever is going on in overt behavior is related to connections in the nervous system and conduction of energy along the nerve paths. Some connections are innate, some acquired. The acquired ones are the conditioned reflexes, acquired in accordance with the dynamics of irradiation and concentration of energy.

A new world opened up to psychology, a world based on a definite theory relating observable behavioral data to a physiological theory well supported by experimentation.

Pavlov's contemporary, Bekhterev, discovered conditioning simultaneously with Pavlov and conducted ingenious experiments which led to the so-called instrumental conditioning. Bekhterev believed that physical and mental processes can be presented in one physical continuum of energy.

The Soviet psychologists, seeking guidance at the sources of Marxist philosophy, have been greatly influenced by the giants of neurophysiology, Pavlov and Bekhterev. In recent years the pendulum has swung in the direction of Pavlov, and the precision experiments in conditioning of covert behavior (interoceptive and proprioceptive) by Bykov and others are quite impressive. The Soviet psychology continues to lean heavily on both Marx's dialectic materialism and Pavlov's neurophysiology. These two theories are not irreconcilable, as the studies of Rubinstein, Luria, Smirnov, and others indicate.

The third chapter introduces behaviorism and a programmatic reductionism. A psychologist may or may not try to reduce psychology to physiology; this is merely one aspect of his theory. But some psychologists seem to believe that psychology must be reduced to physiology (Watson) or must not (Spranger). Then the issue becomes programmatic.

Independently of Pavlov and Bekhterev, some American psychologists were in search for a "scientific," objective psychology. This programmatic rebellion against introspection was introduced by J. B. Watson.

Watson incorporated conditioning in his theory. Psychology was to him either a science of behavior or not a science at all. According to Watson the only difference between physiology and psychology was that psychology dealt with the behavior of the "whole" organism. Apparently his point of view was molar. The early Watsonians, Weiss, Holt, Hunter, and Lashley, developed their own theories, perhaps with more sophistication in the body-mind problem. A new system of reductionistic psychology was developed by the neurophysiologist Lashley, introducing the principle of equipotentiality.

Hebb moved even farther away. A keen observer and experimentalist, he developed his own full-fledged neurological theory of behavior, opposed to Lashley's and emphasized the local actions of the nervous cells.

The fourth chapter is the longest chapter in the book. It is devoted to the neo-behaviorists and contemporary learning theorists. It starts with Guthrie's uncompromising theory of learning by mere contiguity in time supported by several carefully planned experiments.

The second section is devoted to the man who introduced the hypothetico-deductive method in the realm of psychology. C. L. Hull's method is an excellent example of theory construction in psychology. Hull utilized Pavlov's empirical findings on conditioning but replaced Pavlov's energetic principle of reinforcements by his own theory of drive reduction. Hull's theory is a result of deductive reasoning checked against rigorous experimentation.

The analysis of B. F. Skinner's works follows. Skinner's work is a case in radical empiricism, most carefully applied inductive method, and avoidance of theory. Skinner prefers description to explanation, observable data to postulates, mathematical functions to causality. He is an operationist. He introduced the distinction between the classical and instrumental conditioning based on modification of the method of experimentation.

The fourth section of this chapter is devoted to E. C. Tolman, the man who introduced the distinction between the independent, intervening, and dependent variables. Tolman's theory is still a branch of the tree that Watson planted, but it is indeed a very remote branch, much intertwined with the perception theory of the gestalt psychologists and purposivism.

A solution to the controversy between the various theories of learning was offered by G. Razran. Razran ordered the levels of learning to the evolutionary steps in the phylogenetic development. On the lowest level learning is performed by sheer neural strength. On the next higher level reward is the reinforcing factor. On the highest level cognitive learning takes place.

Dollard, Miller, Mowrer, Sears, and others introduced psychoanalytic concepts into the learning theory. All of them started with Pavlov and Hull but gradually modified their points of view and developed new and original theories.

In the last section of the chapter the author of the book points to the neglect of neurophysiological aspects of learning and to a certain confusion in the present-day theory of motivation in learning.

The fifth chapter is devoted to alternative solutions of the problem posed by the functionalists. Adjustment to life was interpreted by biologists both in mechanistic and in a vitalistic fashion. The same happened in psychology.

W. McDougall offered a theory of behavior dramatically opposed to Watson's. Watson's device was causation; McDougall's teleology. Watson emphasized environment; McDougall heredity. Watson believed in learning; McDougall instincts. McDougall's entire prolific work was an elaboration of his theory of instincts.

Yet both Watson and McDougall have "common roots" in James and Dewey and both deal with the role the mind plays in adjustment. Both lean heavily on physiology and both are mainly concerned with the overt behavior of organisms.

The other two purposivistic and holistic theories belong to K. Goldstein and J. R. Kantor. Goldstein's excellent studies in brain injury brought him world fame, and his thought-provoking theory of equalization of energy, self actualization, and adjustment to environment was based on painstaking observations. Kantor turned against reductionism and introduced the idea of interbehavior between the organism and the environment.

PART II

Psychoanalysis and Related Systems

CHAPTER 6

Psychoanalysis

1. METHODOLOGY

Sapere Aude

Psychoanalysis and related schools become a part of contemporary psychological theory after a long and complicated process of development. Psychoanalysis cannot be traced from the philosophical discussion about the human soul nor was it born in the atmosphere of the academic *Wissenschaft* of psychological laboratories. It took its start in medicine and it was, and partially is, a part of the medical discipline that grew exceedingly slowly in its endeavor to understand and treat mental disorder. While official medicine pursued rigorously the path of anatomy, histology, and physiology, rebellious psychoanalysis followed in the footsteps of "unscientific," "mentalistic," and "metaphysical" concepts repudiated by the official science, and studied the irrational and even metapsychological aspects of human life. Freud and his followers introduced into the area of irrationality the rational method of scientific inquiry and proved beyond doubt that being scientific is not identical with choosing a rational phenomenon but depends upon the method applied in the study of empirical phenomena irrespective of their being rational or irrational.

Originally Freud did not intend to create a full-fledged psychological theory, but finally he developed even more than a psychological system. All psychological theories started from a certain area, covered it thoroughly, and gradually expanded to the other fields. Pavlov studied conditioned reflexes. Watson applied conditioning to the study of several aspects of overt behavior. Skinner studied complicated learning problems. Goldstein started with brain injuries. Freud studied primarily mental disorder and went on to the analysis of the etiological factors. The etiological research shed light on child psychology and the laws of human growth and development. Then came a general theory of personality dynamics, then a study of human nature through the ages and a theory that dealt with the impact of society, culture, and religion on personality, till finally psychoanalysis, originally meant as a psychotherapeutic technique, became a great psychological theory encompassing almost every area of normal and abnormal personality and entering into the fields of sociology, anthropology, history, education, and the arts.

Rarely has any theory been exposed to so much bitter and sometimes unfair criticism as has psychoanalysis. In medical circles Freud was criticized for the neglect of organic factors. Academic psychologists criticized him for being unscientific; philosophers, for being unethical and degrading the dignity of men.[1] On one issue friends and foes had to agree: they could not help admiring the great moral courage of Freud, who dealt with the most controversial problems in a frank and forthright manner despite social pressures and taboos. Freud attacked the issues of love and hate, of sexuality and destructiveness, of life and death. He unmasked bigotry and hypocrisy and with unabated zeal penetrated the areas of mental health and illness, of an individual's growth and decline, of religion and crime, of creative arts and destructive wars. Nothing could stop him in the ardent pursuit of the truth; neither his personal biases nor even his own former statements were spared by his critical mind. He was anything but conservative or opportunistic; he had the courage to acknowledge his mistakes and to revise his theories drastically, even reverse them completely in some issues. He can serve as a noble example of scientific honesty that shuns compromise with the truth. Of Freud it can be said that he possessed the great virtue of a research worker: *Sapere Aude.*

His theories were taken up, accepted or criticized, by research workers and philosophers. Psychology and medicine, sociology and anthropology, history and philosophy, art and literature, political science and social and religious philosophy are indebted to the indefatigable and searching mind of Sigmund Freud.[2]

Empiricism

Freud was brought up in an atmosphere characterized by rapid progress in the natural sciences. He was born in 1856 and studied medicine. The natural sciences were celebrating, at that time, their great triumphs in several fields. The glorious progress of biology, physics, chemistry, anatomy, and physiology filled human hearts with the hope that the

[1] There have been several excellent presentations of Freud's work. Some authors (E. Jones, G. Murphy, R. S. Woodworth, and others) preferred to analyze Freud's work in a historical way, emphasizing the development of Freud's ideas. Many others (O. Fenichel, D. Rapaport, and others) chose the systematic way and organized Freud's theories around certain topics. This writer prefers to use the systematic way; accordingly, Freud's work is presented here in a new and systematized order, as seen by this writer.

[2] Cf. Sandor Lorand, *Psychoanalysis Today,* International Universities Press, 1950; Gardner Murphy, "The Current Impact of Freud Upon Psychology," *American Psychologist,* 1956, 11, 663–672.

riddles of the universe and of human nature would soon be solved, and the searching mind armed with adequate tools would soon penetrate the areas still belonging to philosophy or religion.

This optimistic outlook of the era of Darwin and Spencer enhanced Freud's preference for an empirical approach to psychology and instilled in him a strong dislike for any sort of speculation. Freud started by observing phenomena of overt human behavior in a clinical setting.

Originally he was more a neurologist than a psychiatrist, but at that time psychiatry was organically oriented. In 1885 Freud went to study in France with the great Charcot and was introduced to the enigmatic phenomena of suggestion, hypnosis, and hysteria. Back in Vienna, together with Breuer, he embarked upon the study of these phenomena, a study that bears witness to the empirical method employed by both of them.[3]

Freud's scientific method was a direct descendant of the British and French empiricism, represented by Francis Bacon's criticism of bias and "idols" and John Stuart Mill's "canons." In the best tradition of empirical inquiry Freud proceeded from observable phenomena to generalization and interpretation. He was not a naïve empiricist nor did he refrain from inquiry into unobservable phenomena. He developed far-reaching hypotheses that had to be verified by observation. Whenever his clinical observations did not corroborate his hypotheses or his hypotheses failed to interpret the empirical data, he changed his hypotheses accordingly.

Freud's method of investigation can be demonstrated in his approach to the study of dreams. He said: "If the dream is a somatic phenomenon it does not concern us; it can only be of interest to us on the hypothesis that it is a mental phenomenon. So we will assume that this hypothesis is true in order to see what happens if we do so. The results of our work will determine whether we may adhere to the assumption, and uphold it, in its turn, as an inference fairly drawn."[4] Freud believed that the objective of scientific inquiry is to understand the phenomena, to establish the connection between them, and to gain control over them. "Reality will always remain 'unknowable.' What scientific work elicits from our primary sense perceptions will consist of an insight into connections and interdependences which are present in the external world, which can somehow or other be reliably reproduced or reflected in the external world of our thoughts, and the knowledge of which enables us to 'understand' something in the external world, to foresee it and possibly to alter it. Our procedure in psychoanalysis is exactly similar."[5]

[3] Joseph Breuer and Sigmund Freud, "The Psychical Mechanism of Hysterical Phenomena," *Neurologisches Zentralblatt*, 1893; Joseph Breuer and Sigmund Freud, *Studies in Hysteria*, Vienna, 1895.

[4] Sigmund Freud, *A General Introduction to Psychoanalysis*, Perma Giants, 1949, p. 90.

[5] Sigmund Freud, *An Outline of Psychoanalysis*, Norton, 1949, p. 106.

The Scientific Truth

In the epistemological discussion concerning the terms of scientific evidence Freud was consistently a realist who believed in the transcendent truth, i.e., dependence of truth upon experience. Scientific thought, he said, endeavors "to eliminate personal factors and emotional influences, carefully examines the trustworthiness of the sense perceptions, manages to have new perceptions unobtainable by usual means, and isolates the determinants of these new experiences by purposely varied experimentation. Its aim is to arrive at correspondence with reality, that is to say, with what exists outside of us and independently of us. . . . This correspondence with the real external world we call truth. It is the aim of scientific work. . . ."[6]

This principle of correspondence with the external reality puts Freud in the camp of positivism as developed by Auguste Comte and against any sort of idealism as initiated by Immanuel Kant. Freud's empiricism is based on the assumption that scientific inquiry is based on sensory perception. Sensory perception itself, although it can be improved and should be improved by the microscope, telescope, etc., is a perception of the things that exist, independent of our perception.

There is not much in common between Freud's stern adherence to the principles of external truth (called the principle of *transcendent truth*, cf. Chap. 14) and the neo-positivists or logical positivists or physicalists, who emphasized the principles of *immanent truth*. Freud probably had them in mind when he called some of his contemporary philosophers nihilists and anarchists. "According to this anarchistic doctrine there is not such a thing as truth, no assured knowledge of the external world. . . . Ultimately we find only what we need to find, and see only what we desire to see. We can do nothing else. And since the criterion of truth, correspondence with an external world, disappears, it is absolutely immaterial what view we accept. All of them are equally true and false. And no one has a right to accuse any one else of error," Freud wrote about these philosophers.[7]

Theory Construction

Psychology, like any other empirical science, must go beyond the empirically observable data. A series of correct observations is a preliminary step in scientific inquiry, but science must go farther and discover the temporarily unobservable data and interpret all the data in some coherent system of relationships and interdependencies.

[6] Sigmund Freud, *New Introductory Lectures in Psychoanalysis*, Norton, n.d., p. 233.
[7] *Ibid.*, p. 240.

The study of these relationships as well as a tentative presentation of the facts that are temporarily not accessible to scientific inquiry forms a legitimate part of any theory formulation. Theory is, in an oversimplified statement, a series of hypotheses, postulates, models, etc., that connect the empirical data in such a system as permits understanding of their interrelationships and the prediction of future development.[8]

One can present psychoanalysis as a stimulus-response theory. The stimuli act upon the organism; then some action takes place. What goes on within the organism between the stimulus and the response forms the subject matter of psychoanalytic study. Freud developed a system of hypotheses or constructs that enables one, given the stimulus, to understand and to predict the response or, given the response, to state correctly what was the stimulus. Every practicing psychoanalyst applies these hypotheses. Once the patients tell him their life history (the stimulus or the independent variable), the psychoanalyst applies the psychoanalytic theory to the understanding of the patients' symptoms and in many cases he is able to predict them. Or vice versa: when the patients describe their symptoms, the psychoanalyst can to some extent visualize their life history as a stimulus that caused the symptoms (the response, or the dependent variable).

"We have adopted the hypothesis of a psychical apparatus, extended in space, appropriately constructed, developed by the exigencies of life, which gives rise to the phenomena of consciousness only at one particular point and under certain conditions," wrote Freud. "This hypothesis has put us in a position to establish psychology upon foundations similar to those of any other science, such as physics. In our science the problem is the same as in the others: behind the attributes (i.e., qualities) of the object under investigation which are directly given to our perception, we have to discover something which is more independent of the particular receptive capacities of our sense organs and which approximates more closely to what may be supposed to be the real state of things. There is no hope of our being able to reach the latter itself, since it is clear that everything new that we deduce must nevertheless be translated into the language of our perceptions, from which it is simply impossible for us to get ourselves free. But in this lies the nature and limitation of our science."[9]

These are the objective difficulties of theory construction in psychology. Freud could not believe that psychology could be presented as a series of mathematical equations (like physics or chemistry). The main difficulty in psychological theory remains the fact of the consciousness. But "conscious processes do not form unbroken series which are complete in

[8] Benjamin B. Wolman, "Historical Laws—Do They Exist?" *Proceedings of the Xth International Congress of Philosophy,* Amsterdam, 1948 (abstract).
[9] Freud, *Outline of Psychoanalysis,* p. 105.

themselves, so that there is no alternative to assuming that there are physical or somatic processes which accompany the mental ones and which must admittedly be more complete than the mental series, since some of them have conscious processes parallel to them but others have not." In addition, every science is "based upon observations and experiences arrived at through the medium of our psychical apparatus. But since *our* science has as its subject that apparatus itself, the analogy ends here. We make our observations through the medium of the same perceptual apparatus, precisely by the help of the breaks in the series of (conscious) mental events, since we fill in the omissions by plausible inferences and translate them into conscious material. In this way we construct, as it were, series of conscious events complementary to the unconscious mental processes. The relative certainty of our mental science rests upon the binding force of these inferences."[10]

Scientific laws are established by inference. The processes which psychology deals with "are in themselves just as unknowable as those dealt with by the other sciences, by chemistry or physics, for example; but it is possible to establish the laws which those processes obey and to follow over long and unbroken stretches their mutual relations and interdependences—in short, to gain what is known as an 'understanding' of the sphere of natural phenomena in question. This cannot be effected without forming fresh hypotheses and creating fresh concepts."[11] And this is exactly how Freud developed his theory.

2. POSTULATES

Causation

One can hardly understand Freud without being aware of the basic principles underlying his research. These principles cannot be directly proved by Freud or by anyone else. They do not emerge out of empirical research nor can they be represented as conclusions drawn from a successful experimentation. They have been assumed or postulated as guiding principles of research. Any new bit of factual data, any new experiment, any success in exploration strengthens the belief that these principles are useful for the furtherance of knowledge and represent a highly generalized truth.

The necessity to postulate principles applies not only to psychology but to practically all empirical sciences. Any empirical study that deals with some fraction of the world makes certain assumptions as to the nature of the world. Then, in accordance with the usual scientific pro-

[10] *Ibid.*, pp. 36–37.
[11] *Ibid.*, p. 36.

cedure, it tries to prove or, what is usually much more easily done, to disprove the postulated principles by data supporting or contradicting the assumptions.

Freud postulated some general principles such as causation, monism, mental energy, mental economy, the pleasure principle, and biogenetic evolution of the human mind. It is still doubtful whether any of these principles can be empirically proved today. Yet as long as no contradictory data are available and as long as empirical study brings in more and more data that fall in line with the postulated principles, these principles should be considered scientifically useful working hypotheses, and their value is being constantly increased by further research.

One of the principles is the principle of *causation*. Natural sciences, especially contemporary physics, struggle with the difficulties arising from a strict application of the causation principle.[12] No such difficulties have been encountered in any of the areas of scientific psychology. All students of psychology have to accept a more or less strict deterministic point of view. Freud accepted a most rigorous determinism that says, "no causes without effects, no effects without causes," and this is the most general research principle of psychoanalysis.

This determinism cannot be finally proved; it is only a principle that is being more and more corroborated by research. Once accepted or postulated, it forces the research worker to continuous efforts in finding causes and predicting results. Any success serves as evidence that one is on the right track and encourages further efforts that promise to bring additional proof. Lack of success indicates that one has to check and double-check his methods and look for additional data. This strict determinism helped Freud in the study of the most irrational areas of dreaming and symptom formation in neuroses. The principle "whatever is, has its causes" forced Freud to give up the theory of sex vs. ego instincts, to assume the existence of destructive instincts, and to be on constant guard in searching out minute details that might have been partial causes in the mental development and mental disorder.

The Problem of Reductionism

All his life Freud was faithful to the *monistic* philosophy and conception of unity of man and nature. His entire education was guided by the monistic and materialistic concepts of the human organism.

Freud was influenced by Charcot and his attention gradually shifted to psychogenic factors; yet never did he give up the search for organic equivalents of mental disturbance. It is not surprising that Freud's model of personality was influenced by physics, his theory of libido was modeled

[12] Benjamin B. Wolman, "Chance: A Philosophical Study," *Tarbitz, Hebrew University Quarterly* (Hebrew), 1937, **10**, 56–80.

after electrical concepts, and human actions were represented by him as discharges of energy.

In 1894 Freud wrote that it is "scarcely possible to avoid picturing these processes as being in the last resort of a chemical nature." He never gave up this belief; even when he introduced several non-reductionistic concepts, he kept referring to the future research which would probably close the gap between physicochemical and mental facts.

Among the first principles he postulated was the concept of energy. All mental activities and everything that psychology deals with are discharges of mental energy analogous to or some derivative of physicochemical energy. However, Freud did not try to close the gap between physical and mental processes by a simple reductionism that overlooked the differences between these two realms. He was very much against such a naïve reductionism.

In his last work, in which he aimed to bring together the doctrines of psychoanalysis and to state them, as it were, dogmatically—in the most concise form and in most positive terms—Freud wrote: "We know two things concerning what we call our psyche or mental life: firstly, its bodily organ and scene of action, the brain (or nervous system), and secondly, our acts of consciousness, which are immediate data and cannot be more fully explained by any kind of description. Everything that lies between these two terminal points is unknown to us and, so far as we are aware, there is no direct relation between them. If it existed, it would at the most afford an exact localization of the processes of consciousness and could give us no help toward understanding them."[13]

Freud never rejected the organic foundations of the mental life. Id, he said, contains "everything that is inherited, that is present at birth, that is fixed in constitution." But he never ran into a shallow reductionism. At best, he believed, one can assume, and never more than assume, that mental processes utilize some kind of energy that is at the disposal of the living organism. This energy is analogous to any other energy, and that is all we know. "We assume, as the other natural sciences have taught us to expect, that in mental life some kind of energy is at work; but we have no data which enable us to come nearer to a knowledge of it by analogy with other forms of energy."[14]

And this is how far Freud went in his reductionism. A consistent reductionism would lead to naïveté or to an arid although "highly scientific" tautology, and be of "no help toward understanding" of the mental phenomena.

Freud was a monist and never gave up the hope for a monistic interpretation that would combine both physical and mental processes. But, as things stand now, one has to reject reductionism for methodological

[13] Freud, *Outline of Psychoanalysis*, pp. 13–14.
[14] *Ibid.*, p. 44.

reasons and to develop some new hypothetical constructs independent of the physical sciences. This is what Freud actually did. He was fully aware of the fact that the new constructs were non-reductionistic and non-reducible to any of the constructs of physics or chemistry. He felt that the future might prove that some chemical substances were influencing the amount of energy and its distribution in the human mind. Such assumption would be today, to say the least, useless.

Today psychology must develop its own hypotheses and concepts.

The processes with which psychology is concerned "are in themselves just as unknowable as those dealt with by the other sciences, by chemistry or physics, for example; but it is possible to establish the laws which those processes obey and follow over long and unbroken stretches their mutual relations and interdepencences. . . . This cannot be effected without framing fresh hypotheses and creating fresh concepts. . . . We can claim for them the sense value as approximations as belongs to the corresponding intellectual scaffolding found in the other natural sciences, and we look forward to their being modified, corrected and more precisely determined as more experience is accumulated and sifted. So too it will be entirely in accordance with our expectations if the basic concepts and principles of the new science (instinct, nervous energy, etc.) remain for a considerable time no less indeterminate than those of the older sciences (force, mass attraction, etc.)."[15]

Fenichel, one of the leading thinkers in psychoanalysis, summarized as follows the scientific task of psychoanalysis:

"Scientific psychology explains mental phenomena as a result of interplay of primitive physical needs . . . and the influences of the environment on these needs. . . . Mental phenomena occur only in living organisms; mental phenomena are a special instance of life phenomena. The general laws that are valid for life phenomena are also valid for mental phenomena; special laws that are valid only for the level of mental phenomena must be added. . . . Scientific psychology investigates, as does any science, general *laws*. It is not satisfied with a mere description of individual psychic processes. . . . Its subject is not the individual but the comprehension of general laws governing mental functions."[16]

Mental Energy

Once the principle of monism is established and causation is accepted as a binding law, some dynamic factors producing change must be postulated. Another psychologist, Kurt Lewin (cf. Chap. 13) preferred to introduce the concept of forces. Freud, dealing with the organism as

[15] *Ibid.*, p. 36.
[16] Otto Fenichel, *The Psychoanalytic Theory of Neurosis,* Norton, 1945, p. 5.

a whole and considering mental phenomena a part of the functions of the living organism, found the concept of energy more useful and more in accordance with the monistic principle.

This postulate of mental energy enabled Freud to relate mental processes to the physicochemical.

The assumption is made that there is but one energy in nature and all the observable types of energy are variations or transformations of that basic energy, be it electrical or any other. If this is true in physics, it must be true in regard to chemistry, biology, and psychology. It does not mean that human thoughts *are* electrical processes, or that they can be reduced to quantities represented by amperes or watts or volts, or measured by encephalographs. Mental processes cannot be reduced to anything which is not mental. However, Freud believed, they somehow stem from the same physical source as anything else in the world. Mental energy is energy in the physical meaning of the word, i.e., probably something that can be transformed into another kind of energy analogous to the transformation of mechanical into thermic energy. Energy is not perishable; it can be accumulated, preserved, discharged, dissipated, blocked—but it cannot be annihilated. This postulate of preservation of mental energy, its transformability, its functioning in a close analogy to physical energy, is one of the guiding principles of psychoanalysis.

"Among the psychic functions there is something which should be differentiated (an amount of affect, a sum of excitation), something having all the attributes of a quantity—although we possess no means of measuring it—a something which is capable of increase, decrease, displacement and discharge, and which extends itself over the memory-traces of an idea like an electric charge over the surface of the body. We can apply this hypothesis . . . in the same sense as the physicist employs the conception of a fluid electric current."[17]

One may, therefore, postulate that psychic energy is not anything entirely new or different from other types of energy. Since electricity can be transformed into light or into thermic or dynamic energy, this serves as evidence for the physicist that the different types of energy are basically one energy only. It may also hold that psychic energy is a transformation of somatic energy. "The visceral excitation will then actually develop continuously, but only when it reaches a certain height will it be sufficient to overcome the resistance in the paths of conduction to the cerebral cortex and express itself as a psychical stimulus." And later: "Once it has reached the required level, the somatic sexual excitation is continuously transmuted into psychical excitation."[18]

[17] Sigmund Freud, *Collected Papers,* Hogarth, 1924, Vol. I, p. 75.
[18] *Ibid.,* pp. 97–98.

The Constancy Principle and Repetition Compulsion

One of the most important postulates of psychoanalysis is the principle of constancy. Whatever goes on in the human mind and whatever psychology deals with are related to energy. Energy is the explanatory principle behind all mental phenomena, and the distribution of energy is the second leading principle of Freud's theory.

Mental processes can be explained as follows: Any organism, inclusive of the human organism, is capable of responding or reacting to inner and outer stimuli. This capability of reaction to stimuli, or *irritability*, is a general feature of living, organic matter. When an organism is stimulated, a tension or disequilibrium takes place. Prior to the action of the stimuli one must postulate a state of equilibrium or, as Freud called it, Nirvana. Once the organism has been stimulated, the disequilibrium tends to terminate itself, and the organism tends to restore its former balance. This can be accomplished by discharge of energy. It is as if the mental apparatus tried to keep the quantity of excitation as low as possible or, at least, to keep it constant, and as if the increasing excitation were jeopardizing the existence of the organism. This tendency to restore equilibrium or homeostasis is called by Freud the *principle of constancy*.

Freud felt that heredity and embryology bear witness to the compulsion of organic life to repeat. Instincts express the conservative nature of the living substance. An instinct, Freud wrote, "is a compulsion inherent in organic life to restore an earlier stage of things which the living entity has been obliged to abandon under the pressure of external disturbing forces."[19]

Freud quoted Plato's theory of the origin of love that "traces the origin of an instinct to a need to restore an earlier state of things." In Plato's *Symposium* Aristophanes tells about primeval men who had two faces, four hands, four legs, and so on. Zeus cut them in two. But then Aristophanes tells, "the two parts of man, each desiring his other half, came together, and threw their arms about one another eager to grow into one."[20]

The same theory of the origin of love is found in the Indian *Upanishads*. The Atman was the only man. "But he felt no delight. Therefore a man who is lonely feels no delight. He wished for a second. He was so large as man and wife together. He then made this his Self to fall in two, and thence arose husband and wife. Therefore Yagnavalkya said: 'we two are thus (each of us) like half a shell!' Therefore the void which was there is filled by the wife."[21]

One may hypothetically assume that the living substance was torn

---

[19] Sigmund Freud, *Beyond the Pleasure Principle*, Liveright, 1950, p. 47.
[20] *Ibid.*, pp. 79–80.
[21] *Ibid.*, pp. 79–80.

apart into small particles "which have ever since endeavored to reunite through sexual instincts." If this were true, said Freud, then several biological processes could be interpreted by the tendency to restore an earlier state of things.

The principle of pleasure related to mental economy brings additional implications in two directions. Since the restoration of the former status is in itself pleasurable, then, by implication, the instinctual forces are bound to produce continuous repetitions of a disturbance until the balance is restored. When an individual suffers a traumatic experience and is unable to regain his prior balance, he will be prone to relive emotionally this unpleasant experience. This is what Freud called *repetition-compulsion.*

Freud and his followers have often noticed that an individual that suffered some highly unpleasant, damaging, or humiliating experience tended to act as if he were interested in repeating it, either by his overt behavior, leading to self-defeat, or in dreams. Usually the individual was unaware of this compulsion for repetition of tensions. However, once the tensions were resolved in the course of psychoanalytic therapy, they did not come back again.

The other implication deduced from the pleasure principle as a reduction of tension was the idea of Nirvana or of the perfect sleep. Once the tensions are removed, the infant falls asleep. Sleep is the escape from overstimulation and the perfect sleep is the perfect satisfaction.

But if this is the truth, death may be considered the perfect rest, balance, and happiness. This led Freud, as will be explained in the next section, to develop a theory of death instinct.

Principle of Economy

Energy is nonperishable. Various objects can be invested with it; it can be transformed; or it can be released or accumulated. Once some amount of energy is put into something, the latter becomes loaded or charged with mental energy as bodies become charged with electricity. This process of charging *ideas or objects* with mental energy was called by Freud *cathexis,* and objects or ideas invested with energy were cathected. Cathexis can be applied to external objects as well as to one's own organism.

Energy is transformable and displaceable. Mental processes are processes of *mental energy economics,* i.e., *quantitative* processes of investment, discharge, accumulation, transformation, etc., of mental energy. Some processes are more energy consuming, some less. Often an individual does not do anything and yet a great amount of energy is being consumed. When strong instinctual drives urge immediate discharge of energy, a great amount of energy is needed to prevent it. Individuals who have strong inner conflicts cannot be very efficient because too much of their energy is being tied up and they may feel very tired even if they do not do anything.

The mental economy depends on the strength of the stimuli, of the instinctual drives, and of the inhibitory forces. One may, in a simplified form, present human behavior as a series of reflex-arcs. A stimulus acts upon the organism causing a disequilibrium (perceived as a tension). Tension leads to an action, i.e., to a discharge of some amount of energy. The discharge of energy restores the equilibrium and is perceived as relief or relaxation.

However, this simple presentation does not contain the entire truth. Between the tension and discharge of energy something happens in the organism. Two contradictory types of forces step in, one type facilitating the discharge of energy which brings relief, the other preventing or postponing this discharge. The forces that urge and facilitate discharge are called by Freud *drives* or *instincts*. The instincts or instinctual drives press for discharge of energy, for lowering of the level of excitation and reduction of the tension in the organism. These forces help to restore the equilibrium. Since the tendency to keep equilibrium or homeostasis seems to be a general tendency of living matter, the instinctual drives must be basic, innate, and primary biological forces. The counterforces oppose the immediate discharge, ward it off, or repress it. These inhibitory forces stem originally from outside the organism but in the process of an individual's growth and development they become internalized. The neonate is endowed with instinctual forces that are the guardians of the mental equilibrium. The adult's mental mechanism is far more complicated. Between the stimulus and the response a complicated process of interaction between instinctual and inhibitory forces takes place.

Pleasure and Relief

The idea of pleasure and unpleasure as related to the mental economy of excitation was borrowed by Freud from Fechner, whom he quotes as follows: "In so far as conscious impulses always have some relation to pleasure or unpleasure, pleasure and unpleasure too can be regarded as having a psycho-physical relation to conditions of stability and instability. This provides a basis for a hypothesis . . . [that] every psycho-physical movement crossing the threshold of consciousness is attended by pleasure in proportion as, beyond a certain limit, it approximates to complete stability, and is attended by unpleasure in proportion as, beyond a certain limit, it deviates from complete stability; while between the two limits, which may be described as qualitative thresholds of pleasure and unpleasure, there is a certain margin of aesthetic indifference."[22]

Actually Freud inferred the ideas of constancy and economy from his observations on pleasure and unpleasure. From the logical point of view, the pleasure principle follows the principle of constancy. The mental apparatus endeavors to keep the quantity of excitation low, and any stimulus that increases the stimulation is felt as unpleasurable.

"We have decided," wrote Freud in 1920, "to relate pleasure and unpleasure to the quantity of excitation that is present in the mind but is not in any way 'bound'; and to relate them in such a manner that unpleasure corresponds to an *increase* in the quantity of excitation and pleasure to a *diminution*."[23] This is how pleasure and unpleasure are experienced by an infant. Any excessive stimulation coming from without, such as noise, light, etc., or from within, such as hunger, or pressure in bowels or bladder, is experienced as unpleasure. Once the excitation is removed the infant falls asleep in a feeling of happiness (bliss).

The stimulation of the organism by inner or external factors causes disbalance of energy or tension. Tension is experienced by humans as unpleasure, and, as said before, the instinctual forces press for an immediate discharge of energy so as to reestablish the equilibrium that existed prior to the disturbance. This discharge of energy brings relief and is experienced by the individual as pleasure or gratification of the instinctual demands. The perfect pleasure is the perfectly balanced state of the organism.

The sexual drives exemplify tension experienced as pleasure and discharge of energy as pleasure. The most profound feeling of gratification is associated with orgasm, which restores the equilibrium in the system. However, it is well known that sexual tension itself is often perceived as pleasurable. It is as if the expectation of relief is a pleasure in itself, and building up of this expectation by sexual foreplay is pleasant as a promise of the forthcoming complete gratification. It is the pleasure of a good appetite.[24]

3. THE UNCONSCIOUS

Mesmer and Hypnotism

For years psychology has been the science of the human conscious. Psychology dealt with conscious processes, defined by introspectionists as the processes observed by the experiencing individual or "given in his

[22] *Ibid.*, pp. 3–4.
[23] *Ibid.*, p. 2.
[24] Gardner Murphy, *Personality*, Harper, 1947; see chap. 5, on preparatory and consummatory responses, pp. 102 ff.

inner experience." Processes that the individual was aware of and nothing else were considered the legitimate area of psychology.

Several phenomena such as dreams, amnesias, hypnotism, etc., apparently belonging to the realm of psychology, were left out by psychology of the conscious. Yet it was rather arbitrary to dismiss the amazing mental phenomena of dreams, which captured the imagination of poets and prophets in ancient times. Far more difficult was it to overlook the strange lapses of memory that occurred in everyday life and in everyone's experience. Even more puzzling were the discontinuities in memory and the conscious caused by emotional disorders, known even in ancient times.

Ultimately psychology was forced to recognize suggestion and hypnosis as unusual but nevertheless true phenomena of the human mind. When Mesmer demonstrated his "animal magnetism" and "magnetic fluid," the official medical science censured him. A special committee appointed by the Académie des Sciences and the Faculty of Medicine in Paris concluded that since "the magnetic fluid could not be noticed by any of our senses therefore, such fluid does not exist."[25] Mesmer believed in a "magnetic fluid" that fills the universe, and the balance of this fluid in the human organism was believed to be a prerequisite for good health. The magnetizer could restore this equilibrium by touching the patients and thus magnetically controlling this fluid. A British surgeon, James Braid, rejected the idea of "magnetic fluid" but accepted the idea of influencing people's minds in a strange way which he named *hypnotism*. A French physician, A. Liebeault, published a book in 1864 about the influence of "moral factors" upon the human body and described his methods of treatment with the use of hypnotism. In 1882 the well-known neurologist Charcot presented at the Académie des Sciences a paper based on a comprehensive practice and research of neurological changes artificially induced in hysterical patients.

Freud came to grips with hysterical symptoms at Charcot's clinic at Salpêtrière in 1885. Charcot proved that hysterical symptoms can be produced and removed by hypnotic suggestion. Charcot himself interpreted hypnosis by a physiological theory which considered psychogenic disturbance a by-product of organic factors possibly related to heredity.

At the same time Pierre Janet in France developed a new theory of mental disorder. Although Janet insisted that mental disorder stems from degeneration, his theory was thoroughly psychogenic and dealt with nonorganic "automatism," named by Janet "unconscious."

In 1889 Freud attended Bernheim's experiments in hypnosis in Nancy. The hypnotized subject was made to experience several hallucinatory experiences. When he woke up, he maintained that he could not recall

[25] Gregory Zilboorg and George W. Henry, *A History of Medical Psychology*, Norton, 1941, p. 345.

anything. Bernheim urged the subject to recall what happened to him and assured him that he could recall everything. Surprisingly, the subject gradually recalled everything.

This experiment convinced Freud that an individual may not know that he knows. It was as if a part of mental life was concealed, not available to consciousness. Bernheim's studies finally did away with the common belief that humans are always aware of what they are doing and are always capable of making conscious decisions. The old-fashioned "faculty of will" was finally disposed of, and human beings were seen for what they really are: torn by emotions, often perceiving reality erroneously, sometimes hallucinating, and occasionally being pushed by some "irresistible impulse."

The psychological conception of a man as a rational being controlled by an intellectual "will power" was at an end. The time came when human nature with its irrational elements, unconscious mental life, and highly complicated mental structure was open for research.

Joseph Breuer and the Cathartic Method

Prior to his study in Salpêtrière under Charcot, Freud had been under the influence of a distinguished Viennese neurologist, Joseph Breuer. Back from France, Freud cooperated with Breuer and together they cured patients by letting them recall past experiences under hypnosis. The reliving of a trauma was the cure of the neurosis.

"The fundamental fact was that the symptoms of hysterical patients are founded upon highly significant but forgotten scenes in their past lives (traumas); the therapy founded upon this consisted in causing them to remember and reproduce these scenes in a state of hypnosis (catharsis); and the fragment of theory inferred from this was that these symptoms represented an abnormal form of discharge for quantities of excitation which had not been disposed of otherwise (conversion)."[26]

In 1895 Breuer and Freud published a volume entitled *Studies in Hysteria*. These studies reported successful treatment of hysterical symptoms by a method called *catharsis*. The assumption was made that emotional conflicts may lead to a transfer of some quantity of energy together with its emotional content from the conscious part of our mind to the unconscious part. This is *repression*. By helping a patient to relive the conflict the therapists opened the way for discharge of the repressed energy with its emotional content, the mind was cleared (catharted) of the unconscious emotional load (often called *complex*), and the neurotic symptoms were removed.

The success of the cathartic method was regarded by Freud as evi-

[26] Freud, *Collected Papers*, Vol. I, p. 289.

dence of the existence of the unconscious. What was conscious became unconscious by repression and conscious again by catharsis. Freud said that he was accustomed to deal with the unconscious part of the mind as with "something actual and tangible." Some of the symptoms of obsessional neurotics give the impression even to the patients themselves of being "powerful visitors" from another world.

Obsessive symptoms, Freud said, indicate a sphere of mental activity "cut off from the rest of the world." This sphere is the unconscious. Neurotic symptoms are produced in the unconscious and as soon as they are made conscious, the symptoms must vanish. Breuer and Freud arrived at these conclusions in their clinical practice. They had actually removed neurotic symptoms by making their patients conscious of the unconscious meaning of the symptoms.

Conscious, Preconscious, and Unconscious

Freud's theory of the unconscious was derived from experiences in hypnotism and catharsis. The spectacular phenomenon of *amnesia* and the restoration of memory in therapy called for an assumption of a continuum in which memories, loss of memories, and regaining of memories could be represented. Freud believed that the more "obscure and inacessible" areas have to be studied by the "least rigid hypothesis." This was his methodological strategy. But he did not consider the unconscious a theory or an a priori postulate; the unconscious, he said, is "a stock taking of the facts of our observation."

Even perceptions and mobility are not necessarily conscious. One may perceive objects without being aware of doing so, as in hysterical blindness, and one may move around unconsciously, as in somnambulism.

The newborn infant probably has no conscious but is undoubtedly "sensitive," i.e., he perceives and reacts to pain and pleasure. These perceptions and reactions are believed to leave memory traces. The unconscious stores memories which are inaccessible in the waking state, e.g., the memories of early childhood experiences. Many childhood wishes are unrealizable and yet imperishable; many happenings are registered in the infant's mind and yet are uncommunicable. It is exceedingly difficult to study the deep and preverbal layers of the unconscious. What Freud actually did was make an indirect analysis of the unconscious; in this analysis the observable phenomena of dreams, free association, slips of the tongue, and symptoms of mental disorder were studied as representatives of the great mental province of the unconscious.

In accordance with the homeostatic principle Freud believed that the infant's mind avoids overstimulation by falling asleep. The infant wakes up only when the pressure of stimuli such as hunger, bowel or bladder discomforts, loud noise, etc., becomes unbearable. As soon as he can get rid of the stimulus, he sleeps or is half-awake.

Even when the infant is awake he hallucinates rather than perceives, dreams rather than sees. But the external stimuli do not permit the pleasure of sleep to be perpetuated. The tension-provoking stimuli force the infant to perceive them, to cope with them, and to try to master them. This is probably the origin of the conception of reality, and this is the way the conscious emerges out of the unconscious. Tension leads to the development of the conscious.

The development of the conscious depends on the infant's growing ability to utilize his memories. Then memories accumulate, as it were, on the "surface" of the unconscious, easily accessible, and easily becoming conscious. This part of the unconscious forms the *preconscious.*

Thus the unconscious is divided in two parts: the preconscious and the unconscious proper. Some unconscious processes can become conscious without any difficulty. They can be recalled and the individual can easily become aware of them. They resemble conveniently stored goods, easily accessible. What is conscious is actually conscious for a short while only, and can easily pass into the preconscious. On the other hand, the mental processes of the preconscious can become conscious "without any activity on our part."

The preconscious is what is unconscious at a given time but can easily become conscious; it is latent or temporarily unconscious. Slips of the tongue, forgetting of well-known names and places, errors, misplacement of objects, etc., belong to this category. In contradistinction to the preconscious layer, the deeper layers of the unconscious are less accessible and may never become conscious.

The individual is conscious or aware of a small fraction of his mental processes at a given time. Thus the conscious (or consciousness) must be a result of a selective process. The unconscious tends to become preconscious and eventually conscious, but only a part of it actually becomes conscious. Some impulses and perceptions may become preconscious or conscious for a while and then be thrown back to the unconscious. Originally Freud ascribed to conscious and unconscious dynamic properties, but finally he relegated all dynamics to instincts and the "mental agencies" of id, ego, and superego (see section 6 of this chapter). Thus the terms "conscious," "preconscious," and "unconscious" do not indicate any dynamic forces in personality but, as Freud finally concluded, the "mental provinces." They are topographic concepts indicating the "depth" of the mental processes and their relative distance from the surface. What the individual is aware of is conscious; what he is not aware of but may become so at any time is preconscious; what he cannot become aware of without definite effort or cannot become aware of at all is unconscious.

Repression and Resistance

Freud distinguished between conscious rejection of an impulse (sometimes called suppression) and repression. In suppression the energy put at the disposal of the impulse that is seeking to "convert itself into action" has been withdrawn. The impulse has no more energy attached to it; it becomes powerless and exists merely as a memory.

Repression is "a vehement effort" that has been exercised to prevent the mental process in question from penetrating into the conscious and as a result it has remained unconscious. Repression is an act by which either a mental act is prevented from entering into the preconscious and forced back into the unconscious or a mental system which belongs to the preconscious is thrown into the unconscious. Repression is a "topographic-dynamic" conception.

What has been repressed tends to find outlets for discharge. Freud was always consistent in regard to the energetic principle (cf. "Postulates," section 2 of this chapter). All mental processes are processes in which some energy is accumulated, stored, blocked, or discharged. Some forces, whether conscious or unconscious, prevent the discharge of energy. The very same repressing forces, called later "defense mechanisms," forever resist the discharge of repressed energy. A person undergoing psychoanalytic therapy usually unconsciously "resists" the efforts of the therapist aimed at the discharge of blocked energies and the removal of tension. *Resistance* is nothing but continuation of repression. It requires a special therapeutic skill to undo the resistance and to release the repressed energies.

Dream Interpretation

Dreams are the main area in which the unconscious manifests itself and is accessible to research. The interpretation of dreams was considered by Freud the strongest point in his studies. Dream is a part of sleep, and sleep is a temporary refusal to face the outside world. Freud believed that our relationship with the world which we entered so unwillingly seems to be endurable only with intermission; hence we withdraw again periodically into the condition prior to our entrance into the world; that is to say, into intra-uterine existence. At any rate, we try to bring about quite similar conditions—warmth, darkness, and absence of stimulus—characteristic of that state. Some of us still "roll ourselves tightly up into a ball resembling the intra-uterine position."

Sleep starts with the wish to withdraw from reality. With this relaxing withdrawal the individual regresses to more primitive modes of activity and the controlling forces of the conscious are more and more reduced. The floor, so to say, is open to the voice of the unconscious—to the dream.

Dreams are a reaction of the mind to external or internal stimuli that act upon the organism in sleep. In dreams the individual attributes objective reality to the imagery that forms the material of the dreams. "A dream, then, is a psychosis with all the absurdities, delusions and illusions of a psychosis," said Freud. It is a consciously willed, temporary withdrawal from the external world and a regression to the state of mind that preceded the development of the conscious.

Dreams represent demands or wishes stemming from the unconscious; these wishes are usually repressed demands for instinctual gratification. Often the demands arise in the preconscious and are residues of the day's activities in the waking state. These demands may be related to a decision that has to be made or to a conflict to be resolved. The dreams of one night usually represent together one context and mostly each dream is the precondition of the following one.

These unconscious or preconscious demands are pressures coming up against the conscious part of personality, which represses the unconscious wishes. Later on Freud introduced the division of personality into three parts, each of them being a separate mental agency: the *id, ego,* and *superego* (see section 6). The ego is the guardian of sleep, and all the pressures are pressures upon the ego. The sleeping ego, Freud said, is focused upon the wish to maintain sleep; it regards a demand as a disturbance and seeks to get rid of the disturbance. The ego achieves this "by what appears to be an act of compliance: it meets the demand with what is in the circumstances the innocent fulfillment of a wish and thus disposes of the demand. This replacement of a demand by the fulfillment of a wish remains the essential function of dream-work."[27]

The *dream-work* transforms the unconscious or preconscious wish, which is the *latent* dream thought, into what the dreamer perceives, that is, into *manifest dream content*. To use Freud's examples, if a doctor has to wake up in the morning to be in a hospital on time, which is a case of a preconscious wish, he may continue to sleep and to dream that he is already in the hospital as a patient who does not have to get up early in the morning. The latent dream material is the conflict about getting up. The sleeping ego protected the sleep by means of the dream-work, which transformed the wish into the manifest dream content of being already in the hospital as a patient, thus disposing of the conflict.

Dreams protect one's sleep. All dreams deal with wishes which for some reason cannot be accepted in the conscious and waking state. Every dream is an attempt "to put aside a disturbance of sleep by means of a wish-fulfillment." This wish-fulfillment of a repressed impulse is toned down because the path to motor discharge is closed in sleep. The repressed impulse that presses toward motor discharge has "to con-

[27] Freud, *Outline of Psychoanalysis,* p. 55.

tent itself with an hallucinatory satisfaction." The latent dream thoughts are therefore turned into a collection of sensory images and visual scenes.[28]

Not all dreams represent a simple wish or a wish-fulfillment. Many dreams are rather unpleasant and some of them are horror-stricken nightmares. All dreams represent rejected or repressed wishes but some of them carry a violent inner conflict. What represents a gratification for the unconscious id may be perceived as a threat to the preconscious or conscious ego. In anxiety dreams the latent dream material has undergone little change and the demands are too great to be warded off. Sometimes when the threat to the ego is very great, as it is in nightmares, the individual gives up sleep and returns to a waking state.

Dream-work results in *dream-distortions*. Dream-work, as said before, is a result of a compromise between the unconscious forces that press for a discharge of energy and the opposing forces of the ego, the *dream-censor*, which inhibits, restrains, and counteracts these pressures. The dream-censor is the same force that represses the unconscious wishes, keeps them repressed, and resists their expression in free associations necessary for dream interpretation in psychoanalytic therapy.

The interpretation of dreams is based on a deterministic assumption that everything has a cause and an effect. This strict determinism is conducive to a thorough investigation of the manifest content of the dream. The continuity of human mental life is established when one accepts the Freudian idea that the dream is an expression of unconscious material. Irrational and nonsensical as the dream may sound, it always represents some unconscious processes which the dreamer does not know he knows and thinks he does not.

Analysis of dreams enabled Freud to discover the laws that govern the "primary," unconscious processes and to find the differences between them and the "secondary," conscious processes. In the unconscious the thought elements that in a waking state are kept apart are combined or *condensated* into larger units. One thought element of the manifest dream may represent a cluster of unconscious and latent dream thoughts. Usually, as dream analysis proves, the brief manifest content of a dream or what the dreamer perceives is an *allusion* to a great amount of unconscious thoughts and wishes.

Another law governing the unconscious processes is *displacement*. In the waking state instinctual energies are invested or cathected in definite objects. In dreams those cathexes or mental energy loads are easily shifted from one object to another. Sometimes very significant latent dream elements are barely mentioned or only alluded to in the manifest dream content, while unimportant unconscious elements may be represented in the manifest dream in a very clear manner.

[28] Freud, *New Introductory Lectures in Psychoanalysis*, p. 32.

As dream analysis implies, the unconscious uses its own language. It is the grammarless language of illogic, where contradictory elements are applied, and compromise is reached between mutually exclusive statements. Yes and no, true and false, reality and imagination are brought together in utter disregard for inner consistency.

There is no logic in dreams. In the *secondary elaboration* nonrelated elements may be put together and represented as a whole. An idea may be represented by its opposite; the causal relationship may be replaced by a merely temporal sequence. What is impossible in waking life may become possible and come true in a dream.

Dreams apply symbols, usually pictorial. Some symbols are universal, such as a house, which symbolizes the human body. When it is smooth, it symbolizes a man. When there are balconies and ledges, it represents the feminine body. Parents appear in dreams as kings and queens, siblings as little animals or vermin. Birth is represented by water, death by a journey. Most symbols applied in dreams relate to sexual organs and functions. The female sexual symbols are pockets, flower pots and vases, receptacles, bags, purses, drawers, jars and boxes, doors and gates; rooms and stores symbolize the uterus; watches and clocks symbolize periodic processes and intervals; snails and mussels symbolize women; a diamond represents the open female genitals; buildings such as chapels and churches symbolize women; apples, peaches, oranges represent breasts. A landscape with rocks, woods, and water represents female organs.

A cloak and a hat symbolize a man. Sticks, keys, knives, poles, pencils, guns, snakes, trees, hammers symbolize the male sexual organ. A bridge represents the male organ that connects parents during sexual intercourse. In symbolic meaning a bridge may indicate birth or death, transitions from life to death or womb to birth. Airplanes and balloons symbolize erection. Machinery represents masculine organs. The number 3 represents penis and testicles.

A spider usually symbolizes the aggressive, phallic mother, and fear of a spider represents fear of incest and abhorrence of the female sexual organs.

Sliding and gliding usually represent masturbatory activities, as does pulling off branches. Climbing, riding, shooting, dancing, mounting stairs or a ladder, rhythmical and violent motions represent sexual intercourse. Falling out and extraction of teeth symbolizes castration as a punishment for masturbation.

All these symbols are used in folklore, mythology, manners and customs, fairy tales, and popular jokes. To be rescued from water, as told about Sargon, King of Akkad, and Moses, means to give birth.[29] Going away on a journey is in dreams a symbol of dying; figurative expressions are "the last journey," "passed away," "gone away," etc.

[29] Sigmund Freud, *Moses and Monotheism*, Knopf, 1939.

When a patient describes his dream, the psychoanalyst's efforts aim at discovering the latent dream thoughts. He asks the dreamer to free himself from the impression of the manifest dream, to switch his attention from the dream as a whole to individual parts of its content, and to tell unreservedly all that occurs to him in connection with these parts. This is the technique of "free associations" based on the assumption that, once the controlling mental apparatus is eliminated, the subject's hidden thoughts will appear in his associations in a flood of memories, ideas, questions, and arguments. The free associations are not exactly the latent dream thoughts; the latent thoughts are contained in the associations, but not completely contained. It is as if the associations themselves were selective; some of them flow easily, and sometimes the dreamer seems to be thwarted; often he goes a long way around toward the latent thoughts and sometimes he conceals his thoughts entirely. The forces of resistance may prevent the expression of the latent dream thoughts. Thus the interpretation of dreams requires considerable skill and resembles, in a way, the solving of a puzzle where the final solution is verified by the fact that all partial solutions fit well together.

Psychology of Error

The unconscious wish finds outlets in several ways besides dreams. Everyone commits errors in daily life. Some errors are annoying because they express the opposite to the conscious wish of the individual. One kind of error is slips of the tongue. Often we wish to say one thing and say something entirely different; for example, a soldier says to a friend, "I wish there were a thousand of our men *mortified* on that hill, Bill," instead of saying *fortified.* Or a woman complains that she has an "incurable *infernal* disease" instead of saying *internal* disease. Or a professor says in his introductory lecture, "I am not inclined (*geneigt* instead of *geeignet* = "fitted") to estimate the merits of my predecessor." Or the Speaker of a parliament opens a session with the words "Gentlemen, I declare a *quorum* present and herewith declare the session closed."[30] In all these cases the unconscious wish was expressed.

Another type of error is mislaying things, losing things, forgetting things and names, mistakes in writing, misreading and mishearing, and erroneously carried out actions. An individual takes the wrong train, or forgets his umbrella, or cannot recall the address of a person whom he has visited several times, or cannot find a book he received as a gift from his wife, etc. In practically all of these cases some hidden forces are acting. In a special treatise Freud analyzed the psychology of error and found the source of the errors in the conflict between unconscious wish and conscious censorship. Nothing ever happens by chance, and the

[30] Freud, *General Introduction to Psychoanalysis*, pp. 31 ff.

errors indicate the effort to block a wish which somehow succeeds in finding expression despite the repressing forces.[31]

The Unconscious and Symptom Formation

The maintenance of certain internal barriers or defenses is a *sine qua non* of normality. Lowering of these barriers with a consequent pressing forward of unconscious material takes place regularly in the state of sleep and thus brings about a necessary precondition for the formation of dreams, wrote Freud. In sleep all of us behave as if we were psychotics. But if in the waking state unconscious becomes conscious and the individual's way of thinking, speaking, and acting is seriously regressed and includes condensations, displacements, secondary elaborations, and other unconscious elements, he is apparently psychotic.

The study of symptom formation in mental disorder shed additional light on the nature of the unconscious. Neurotic symptom formation, said Freud, is a result of a compromise between the unconscious demands or impulses and the reality-oriented, conscious censorship. The symptom comes into being as a fulfillment of an unconscious wish, distorted by the forces that oppose the wish-fulfillment. Here is a significant difference between symptom formation and dream formation. "The preconscious purpose in dream-formation is merely to preserve sleep and to allow nothing that would disturb it to penetrate consciousness. It does not insist upon confronting the unconscious wish-impulse with a sharp prohibiting 'No, on the contrary.' It can be more tolerant because a sleeping person is in a less dangerous position; the condition of sleep is enough in itself to prevent the wish from being realized in actuality."[32]

What are the dynamic forces pressing for a discharge of energy and what are the repressing, barrier-creating factors—these questions have to be answered in connection with Freud's theory of instincts and personality structure.

4. THEORY OF INSTINCTS: EROS AND THANATOS

The Instincts

The ultimate cause of all activity is called by Freud *Trieb* or drive, usually translated in English as "instinct." The source of the instincts is the chemophysical state of the organism. In Freud's theory instincts represent the bridge between the physical and the mental worlds; while rooted in the human body, they are the forces that release mental energy.

---

[31] A. A. Brill (ed.), *The Basic Writings of Sigmund Freud*, Random, 1938, pp. 35 ff.

[32] Freud, *General Introduction to Psychoanalysis*, p. 315.

"The instincts are mythical beings superb in their indefiniteness. In our work we cannot for a moment overlook them, and yet we are never certain that we are seeing them clearly," wrote Freud in 1933.[33]

Instincts are psychological concomitants of biological processes. They are borderline concepts between the mental and the physical and represent the demand "made upon the mind in consequence of its connection with the body."

Instincts arise from sources of stimulation within the body. They operate as a constant force. A person can escape an external stimulation but he cannot escape the inner stimulation caused by instinctual forces. Instincts have a source, an object, and an aim. The source is some excitation within the body caused by deficiency (such as hunger) or any other disturbance of the inner balance. The aim of any instinctual activity is to remove the excitation and to restore the inner equilibrium by a discharge of energy. The instinctual activity can be pictured as "a certain sum of energy forcing its way in a certain direction."

The aim of the instinct is always the restoration of equilibrium, which is accomplished by somatic change and is perceived as satisfaction. This aim requires some object by which it can be satisfied. The object can be one's own body or an external object.

There is a great possibility of modification in instinctual aims and objects and of transformation, fusion, and substitution of instinctual gratifications. "The evidence of analytic experience," said Freud, "proves conclusively that instinctual impulses from one source can join on to instinctual impulses from another and share their further vicissitudes, and that in general the satisfaction of one instinct can be substituted for the satisfaction of another. . . . The relations of an instinct to its aim and to its object are also susceptible to alterations; both can be exchanged for others, but the relation to the object is the more easily loosened of the two."[34] In other words, the energy at the disposal of an instinct can be cathected in (invested in, attached to) a certain object and under certain circumstances removed from this object and invested in another one.

Sometimes the instinctual drive comes to a stop and renounces its full gratification. This takes place when the instinctual drive becomes too powerfully cathected in a certain object. For instance, affection represents a case of permanent object cathexis which expresses itself in a constant care for the subject without sexual gratification. This process of suspension of gratification was named by Freud *aim inhibition*.

Instincts are capable of another modification when the aim and object are changed in a manner that makes them socially valuable. This modification is *sublimation*. Freud believed that works of art represent the process of sublimation. The energies put originally at the disposal of

[33] Freud, *New Introductory Lectures in Psychoanalysis*, p. 131.
[34] *Ibid.*, p. 133.

instincts may be turned into creative art; in such a case both the aim and the object of the instinctual drive have been replaced by an entirely different aim and object.

The Sexual Instincts

All living organisms act in accordance with two purposes, self-preservation and the preservation of the species. Accordingly, Freud distinguished self-preservation or ego instincts and sexual instincts. These two instinctual forces are often in conflict with each other. The sexual instincts are more flexible than the self-preservation instincts; they can be held in suspense (aim-inhibited), sublimated, diverted into new channels, distorted, and perverted; their gratification can be denied or substituted for and their objects can be easily changed. Freud said: "The popular view distinguishes between hunger and love, seeing them as representatives of the instincts that aim at self-preservation and reproduction of the species respectively. In associating ourselves with this very evident distinction we postulate in psychoanalysis a similar one between the self-preservative or ego-instincts on the one hand and the sexual instincts on the other; the force by which the sexual instinct is represented in the mind we call 'libido'—sexual longing—and regard it as analogous to the force of hunger, or the will to power, and other such trends among the ego-tendencies." He added: "We have defined the concept of libido as a quantitatively variable force which could serve as a measure of processes and transformations occurring in the field of sexual excitation. We distinguish this libido in respect of its special origin from the energy which must be supposed to underlie mental processes in general, and we thus also attribute a qualitative character to it."[35]

Freud did not postulate a single urge that leads to fertilization and preservation of the species. He believed that there are a great number of relatively independent instincts that stem from various somatic sources. All of them strive toward gratification in their respective somatic zone or to *organ pleasure.* In the process of ontogenetic development some of them merge with the sexual instinct proper that originates in the genital organs; some of these instincts will be eventually repressed, some partially incorporated in the final organization of the adult sexual functions.

Freud distinguished between source, object, and aim in sexuality. The source is a stimulation arising in some part or zone of the organism. The parts of the body that are capable of reacting to sexual stimuli are called *erotogenic zones.* The main erotogenic zone is the genitals, but many other parts of the body such as mouth or anus may, in certain cases,

[35] James Strachey (ed.), *The Standard Edition of the Complete Psychological Works of Sigmund Freud,* Hogarth and the Institute of Psycho-Analysis, 1953, Vol. VII, p. 217.

serve as erotogenic zones in the pregenital phases of a child's development.

The usual *object* of sexual urge is a person of the opposite sex, but often, as in homosexuality, a person of the same sex or, as in masturbation, the individual himself is the sexual object.

Freud broadened the concept of sexuality to include perversions and infantile sexuality, which do not lead to the usual aim of sex—fertilization and reproduction. In fact, perversions were never excluded from the realm of sexuality. A perverse sexual relation usually ends with orgasm and ejaculation analogous to the normal sexual intercourse, which may lead, in addition to orgasm, to fertilization and reproduction. Sexual activities of persons considered to be normal include several elements which, if performed exclusively and in place of normal intercourse, would be considered perverse. Kissing, for example, is an indispensable part of the sexual foreplay in normal individuals, but actually kissing gives a pleasurable arousal by a contact of two oral zones. Undoubtedly the mouth is an erotogenic zone, i.e., an area capable of producing sexual excitation. Some individuals achieve orgasm by kissing or some modification of it such as "deep kissing" (introducing the tongue into the partner's mouth) or by oral-genital contacts. Whenever kissing is a part of the sexual foreplay which leads to the union of the genital organs, it is considered normal. Only when kissing takes the place of intercourse and excludes the union of genital organs does it become a perversion. Obviously normal and perverse sexuality have much in common. Freud believed that normal sexuality grew out of something very similar to perversions and developed through modification of some elements, discontinuation of other elements, and incorporation of some.

The same applies to any sexual deviations. Onlooking, gazing, touching of erotogenetic zones, etc., are generally accepted and widely practiced parts of the sexual foreplay. If these practices take the place of intercourse, and exclude the union of genitalia, the foreplay becomes a pervert voyeurism. Or fixation of erotic interest on an object of clothing, for example, instead of on the genital organs, is fetishism.

Perverse sexuality points to the fact that sexuality is not limited to reproduction or to the function of genital organs nor is it necessarily heterosexual. There are several possibilities in regard to the source, aim, and object in sex. The genital organs may be replaced by the other organs for the purpose of gratification, as in the normal kiss, or by perverse practices, or by conversion symptoms of hysteria.

Once Freud assumed that both normal and abnormal sexuality stem from the same source, he had to conclude that sexual deviations are some sort of retardation or thwarting of the sexual development. This was a far-reaching hypothesis. Comparative studies in biology and embryology led him to believe that Haeckel's biogenetic theory can be readily applied to the development of sex. "Ontogenesis is a repetition of phylogenesis," Haeckel said, and Freud, in his essays about sex, accepted this theory and assumed that the child's sexual development is a recapitulation of the main phases in the evolution of sex in organic nature.

The study of sexual perversions in adults and the biogenetic principles led to the study of infantile sexuality. "The child is psychologically father of the man," Freud said. Infantile sexuality contains all the potentialities for the future development, which may lead in any direction—either into a normal or into an abnormal sexuality. Normal development takes place when the source, the object, and the aim of sex are combined in a consistent effort of unification of genital organs of two persons of opposite sex. The normal sexual source is the genitals; the object, an adult person of the opposite sex; the aim, heterosexual intercourse. The normal individual passes through development stages and if, for some reason, he retains the characteristics of one of them (remains "fixated"), he is considered abnormal. What is normal in infancy is abnormal in adulthood. A sexually abnormal individual is a sexually retarded individual. The infant is "a polymorphous pervert" that may or may not eventually become a well-adjusted adult.

The Self-Preservation Instincts

The entire activity of men is, according to Freud, "bent upon *procuring pleasure and avoiding pain.*" This activity is controlled by the *pleasure principle.* "We may venture to say that pleasure is *in some way* connected with lessening, lowering, or extinguishing the amount of stimulation present in the mental apparatus; and that pain involves a heightening of the latter. Consideration of the most intense pleasure of which man is capable, the pleasure in the performance of the sexual act, leaves little doubt upon this point."[36]

Sexual instincts always follow the pleasure principle. Self-preservation instincts, sometimes called ego instincts, as a rule do the same. However, the task of avoiding pain forces them to postpone, or sometimes even renounce, pleasure. This ability to compromise with reality and to consider what could be done and what price has to be paid for pleasure is the *reality principle.* The reality principle is a modified pleasure principle; it approves of pleasure, but not at any price or at any time. The reality principle is striving for pleasure combined with avoidance of pain; it is the ability to sacrifice one kind of pleasure for another.

The consideration of circumstances apparently makes a great difference between the two groups of instincts. Through ego instincts we learn to comply with reality. Sex instincts are less concerned with reality. The reality principle usually gets an early hold on ego instincts; sexual in-

[36] Freud, *General Introduction to Psychoanalysis,* p. 311.

stincts are not so easily controlled and it takes years before they become at least partially subordinated to the reality principle.

The other difference between sex and self-preservation instincts relates to their flexibility. The self-preservation instincts have a limited flexibility. One cannot change the zones or indefinitely postpone the gratification of hunger or thirst nor is there any way to substantially change the objects that satisfy hunger or thirst; all the objects that satisfy the basic needs for air, food, and fluids must contain respectively oxygen, nutritional elements, and water. The sexual instincts can be modified in regard to zone, aim, and object, and they are open to a great number of deviations, perversions, substitutions, and conflicts. This latitude does not apply to the self-preservation instincts.

Narcissism

In 1914 Freud revised his theory of instincts. Originally he felt that the libido or love instincts have to be distinguished from the ego or self-preservation instincts. After several years of clinical experience he discovered that libido may be directed to oneself and not necessarily to external objects only. Love for oneself precedes love for others; the newborn is not capable of loving other people.

Infants learn to divert part of the love primarily cathected (invested) in themselves and to cathect it in their mothers. This self-love was called by Freud *narcissism* after the Greek legendary hero Narcissus, who fell in love with himself.

Narcissism or self-love is a never terminated phenomenon. It starts probably in prenatal life and accompanies us till the last day of life. At the earliest stage of life it is the only channel of libido cathexis; all the energies at the disposal of the love instincts are invested in oneself in a stage called by Freud *primary narcissism*. Later in life, in cases when the object love is being thwarted, the libido may turn back to one's own person and *secondary*, morbid narcissism may develop.

The discovery of the phenomenon of narcissism destroyed the barriers separating the libido from the ego instincts. The ego instincts had to be considered from now on as a special case of libido cathexis, namely, as an investment of libido in one's own person. Now Freud arrived at a monistic interpretation of instinctual life: there is but one instinctual force, the force of love, the libido.

The conflict that often takes place between the sex and self-preservation instincts could now be interpreted in a different way. It is narcissism versus object love. In well-adjusted individuals there is a balance of cathexis in oneself and in others which permits the individual to protect himself and to take care of those whom he loves. In some individuals this balance is disturbed; some develop secondary and morbid narcissism after they have been seriously thwarted in the development of object cathexis. Some are unable to take care of themselves owing to insufficient narcissism or abundant object cathexis.[37]

Freud united under the name "Eros" all the forces that serve pleasure and enhance the vital functions of the individual. Eros encompassed all sexual and egoistic drives, and libido became from now on the name for all the energies that are at the disposal of the Eros.

Thanatos

In 1920 Freud again revised his theory of instincts. He wrote about this revision as follows: "After long doubts and vacillations we have decided to assume the existence of only two basic instincts, *Eros* and the *destructive* instinct. . . . The aim of the first of these basic instincts is to establish ever greater unities and to preserve them, thus—in short, to bind together; the aim of the second, on the contrary, is to undo connections and so to destroy things. We may suppose that the final aim of the destructive instinct is to reduce living things to an inorganic state. For this reason we also call it the death instinct."[38]

This new hypothesis of separate aggressive and destructive instincts was derived mainly from the study of sadism and masochism. The sexual gratification of a sadist depends upon pain and suffering inflicted by him on his love object, and of a masochist on pain inflicted on him by his love object. It was exceedingly difficult to interpret sadism in terms of libido theory, and the existence of a masochistic wish to suffer formed a most serious challenge to the libido theory.

Freud had to look for additional factors, that make people wish to inflict or to accept pain. This factor could not be related to libido and Eros. The only possible solution was to assume another driving force or another instinctual power that leads men to cause pain to others in an object-directed situation or to inflict pain on themselves in a self-directed situation. Such an instinctual force could be held responsible for the desire to hurt, to humiliate, and to destroy. The existence of this force was sufficiently proved by daily experience and by the testimony of human history. Humans are born lovers and haters; as much as there is energy (libido) at the disposal of the love instinct, there is no less energy (called *mortido* by Federn) at the disposal of the aggressive instinct. The final aim of the love instinct is to create life and the final aim of the aggressive instinct is to destroy life and to go back to inorganic nature.

When aggressiveness against the outer world becomes thwarted and

[37] Cf. Paul Federn, *Ego-Psychology and the Psychoses,* Basic Books, 1952; Benjamin B. Wolman, "Explorations in Latent Schizophrenia," *American Journal of Psychotherapy,* 1957, 11, 560–588.

[38] Freud, *Outline of Psychoanalysis,* p. 20.

cannot find satisfaction, it may, in certain circumstances, turn inward. It may, said Freud, increase the amount of self-destructiveness. An impeded aggression entails most serious dangers; it seems that we have to destroy things and people in order not to destroy ourselves. In order to protect ourselves from the tendency toward self-destruction we must find some external channels for aggressiveness.

All instincts, as stated before, turn out to be directed toward the reinstatement of an earlier state of things. As soon as a given state of things is upset, an instinct arises to re-create it. This tendency was called by Freud *repetition-compulsion*. It may become even stronger than the pleasure principle and often overcomes it. Repetition-compulsion explains the tendency to reproduce in dreams unpleasant and often traumatic experiences.

Life developed from inorganic matter. Once life started, an instinct was born that aimed at reinstatement of the inorganic state and destruction of life. This is, according to Freud, the origin of the destructive instinct, whose final aim is death or the reestablishment of inanimate nature. Life and death are interwoven; construction and destruction are inseparable. No vital process can be free from the death instinct. The erotic instincts try "to collect living substance together into ever larger unities," and the death instincts act against this "and try to bring living matter back into inorganic condition. The cooperation and opposition of these two forces produce the phenomena of life to which death puts an end."[39]

This idea of interrelationship between life and death is not a new one. Freud mentioned in this context the influence of the philosopher Arthur Schopenhauer and the Indian Nirvana. Another philosopher and scientist, Herbert Spencer, elaborated the idea and postulated a continuum of consecutive development and decline, evolution and dissolution, accumulation and dissipation.[40]

In the life of an individual, Eros and Thanatos may combine their resources, but they often fight each other. Eating is a process of destruction with the purpose of incorporation, and the sexual act is aggression that aims at the "most intimate union." Most of the impulses of sexual life are rarely purely erotic; usually sexual impulses are a combination of erotic and destructive instinctual demands.

In extreme cases, when the destructive instincts become the stronger part in the fusion of the two kinds of instincts, sadism or masochism results. In sadism aggressive impulses thrust the sexual aims away and the aim of hurting the love object is substituted for the normal sexual aim. Sexual gratification becomes possible only if pain is inflicted upon the sexual object. In masochism the aggression is self-directed, and sexual

---

[39] Freud, *New Introductory Lectures on Psychoanalysis*, pp. 146–147.
[40] Herbert Spencer, *First Principles*, 1860–1862.

gratification depends upon pain and humiliation inflicted by the love object.

When an individual is overwhelmed by the forces of Thanatos directed to the outer world, he becomes hateful and destructive, spreading pain and death around. When these forces are directed to himself, suicidal attempts may take place.

5. DEVELOPMENTAL STAGES

The Neonate

To be born is a traumatic experience that disrupts the well-balanced life in the uterus. Birth as the first trauma is the prototype of all anxiety feelings in later life. The organism is flooded by stimuli, tensions come to a peak, and the helpless organism is exposed to the shock of being born.

After birth the newborn's mental apparatus is exposed to stimuli far beyond his capacity to handle. The natural tendency is therefore to restore the mental economy through a withdrawal from reality by falling asleep. Once the unpleasant tension such as hunger is removed, the infant falls asleep with a feeling of profound happiness and bliss. Only when stimulated by hunger or cold or some other discomfort is he awake.

The neonate is thoroughly narcissistic. In this stage of primary narcissism outer objects are barely noticed.

The gratification of the infant's needs comes immediately and he is unable to distinguish between wish and reality, self and the outer world. He may feel as "omnipotent" when his wish is gratified (after receiving food or after eliminations) as he felt miserable when the tension arose.

The earliest signs of the neonate's attitude to the outer world can be characterized as an objectless longing for something or some sort of unconscious craving for unification with the outer world. This foggy longing is called by Freud the *oceanic feeling*. It is as if the infant were longing to go back to the uterus or, even farther, to nonexistence. Eros and Thanatos are united in the striving toward the all-encompassing and soothing passivity which ultimately means death.

The first pleasure-giving objects the infant meets are the nipples of the mother's breast or the bottle. The first somatic zone that experiences the pleasurable sensation of sucking is his mouth. Thus the oral stage of his instinctual development starts immediately after birth.

The Oral Phase

The biogenetic principle is one of the main reasons for the assumption that the child's sexuality is polymorphously perverse and leads through developmental stages to the adult and normal sexuality. Additional reasons for this assumption are derived from clinical studies indicating that normal and perverse sexuality develop from the same source, infantile sexuality. Both normal and perverse sexuality aim at the same goal—orgasm. Both stem from the unorganized infantile sexuality where various wishes and desires exist independently. In adult sexuality one component becomes dominant and the entire sexual activity becomes concentrated in one area, other areas being excluded or relegated to secondary roles. In normal adults the genital zone is dominant, in perversions some other zone. In childhood all areas or any area may strive for its own pleasure. Some adults whose sexuality remains infantile remain polymorphously perverse.

The development of each individual depends upon (1) innate instinctual forces, (2) biologically determined developmental stages, and (3) environmental influences. Freud never underestimated the environmental factors. How quickly, how successfully, how completely the individual passes these stages, how much of them is carried over into his adult life, depends mainly upon the interaction of the child with his environment.

The earliest sexual life of an infant represents a series of independent activities of single-component impulses each seeking pleasure in a bodily organ, i.e., organ pleasure. These various organs are *erotogenic zones*. They serve as centers for sexual gratification in the pregenital stages of libido development, prior to the subordination of all the sexual component instincts under the primacy of the genital zone.

The infant's first sexual excitations are connected with the feeding process. As the infant falls asleep at the breast, completely satisfied, "it bears a look of perfect content which will come back again later in life after the experience of the sexual orgasm." The infant may continue to suck even if he does not take any food; he is sucking for the pleasure of sucking.

Sucking for nourishment is the "prototype of every later sexual satisfaction." The desire to suck includes the desire for the mother's breast, which is therefore the first *object* of sexual desire. Love is attached to hunger, and sucking brings gratification both of hunger and of love. At the beginning the child does not distinguish between the mother's breast and his own body. As he turns to sucking for pleasure, the breast is given up as a love object and is replaced by a part of his own body; he sucks his own thumb or tongue, and his own body is his love object.

Whether the child was breast-fed or bottle-fed, weaned early or late, he always longs for the mother's breast and the mother as a whole, and she stays in his memory as his first love object and prototype of all love relations, whether he is a boy or a girl.

At the oral phase of libido organization object love is ambivalent and contains both Eros and Thanatos. The longed-for object is assimilated by eating or swallowing and annihilated at the same time. The infant wishes to swallow what he loves and his love leads to swallowing, i.e., to destruction of love objects. It is a cannibalistic tendency; a cannibal, said Freud, has "a devouring affection" for his enemies and devours people of whom he is fond.

Once the milk is swallowed, the infant does not care for it any more. Once tension is removed, he falls asleep and discontinues the contact with the outer world. This is a primitive kind of love—a love for a while, a love that terminates itself immediately after gratification.

Some adults who did not outgrow the oral stage may retain these destructive elements in their love in adult life. They love their love objects inasmuch as they can exploit them and love only as long as the exploitation goes on.

One of the earliest emotional ties to the outer world is *primary identification*. It is the wish to be like the other person, and it antecedes a true *object relationship*, which is the wish to possess the other person. Identification is not necessarily love: "It can turn into an expression of tenderness as easily as into a wish for someone's removal."[41]

Identification is accomplished by *introjection*. At the oral stage the infant takes things into his mouth and incorporates whatever he loves. Once he incorporates the object, he may believe himself to be like the beloved object. Since to love something at this stage is identical with the wish to incorporate it or to introject it, the oral introjection is the means for primary identification.

Primary identification, which is a general phenomenon in earliest childhood, has to be distinguished from what Freud called *secondary identification*, which takes place in pathological cases at a later developmental stage. Sometimes a loss of love object causes desexualization of it and giving up of object cathexis; the mourner "introjects" his love object, and his object relationship gives way to a regression to identification with the lost love object.[42]

One of the brilliant associates of Freud, Karl Abraham, suggested dividing the oral phase into *oral-passive* and *oral-aggressive*.[43] The oral-passive phase extends over several months of the first year of life; toward the second (often well in the second) year of life the oral-aggressive phase of libido development takes place. The oral-passive or oral-dependent stage is characterized by pleasure derived from sucking. At this stage the infant may not be able to distinguish clearly between himself and the external world and perceives in the sucking a self-gratifying and a taken-for-granted experience.

[41] Sigmund Freud, *Group Psychology and the Analysis of the Ego*, Liveright, 1949, p. 61.
[42] Karl Abraham, *Selected Papers*, Basic Books, 1954, p. 433.
[43] *Ibid.*, pp. 393 ff.

The oral-aggressive phase usually coincides with teething. The infant becomes aware of the fact that the mother's breast is not a part of himself, i.e., it is not always available as he wishes it to be. He can no longer take the breast for granted. When frustrated he forces his way through, he grabs and bites, he tries to receive his oral gratification by acts of aggression.

Eros and Thanatos are combined in the entire oral stage in its cannibalistic tendencies of swallowing. However, at the oral-passive stage the infant is basically not aggressive and takes for granted the supply of milk. At the oral-aggressive stage aggressiveness is being utilized as a weapon in procuring gratification. The infant swallows as before, but in addition he may spit and bite, and these are definitely aggressive patterns of behavior.

The Anal Phase

The second stage of libido development was called by Freud *anal-sadistic*. In the second and often third year of life the child derives considerable pleasure from excretion and learns to increase the pleasure by retaining feces and stimulating the mucous membranes of the anus.

"Infants experience pleasure in the evacuation of urine and the content of bowels, and they very soon endeavor to contrive these actions so that the accompanying excitation of the membranes in these erotogenic zones may secure them the maximum possible gratification. . . . The outer world steps in as a hindrance at this point, as a hostile force opposed to the child's desire for pleasure. . . . He is not to pass his excretions whenever he likes but at times appointed by other people. . . . In this way he is first required to exchange pleasure for value in the eyes of others."[44]

The child values his feces as "part of his own body and is unwilling to part with them." He may offer resistance to the social pressures and feel that the feces are his property and no one may exercise control over them. He may act aggressively by elimination; libido and hate are combined in anal eroticism in the pleasure of defecating and the sadistic "getting rid" of feces. When the child resists bowel training and holds back feces, he expresses in another way his opposition to adults.

The anal stage is ridden with another ambivalence besides the expulsion-retention one. Masculinity and femininity are distinguished at this stage by activity and passivity respectively. Masculine impulses are *scoptophilia* (gazing), onlooking, curiosity, desire to manipulate and to master, which easily develops into cruelty and sadism. Active expulsion of feces is masculine. Feminine impulses represent a passive desire con-

[44] Freud, *General Introduction to Psychoanalysis*, p. 276.

nected with the anal and hollow erotogenic zone. The rectum can be easily stimulated by accepting a foreign body that enters it. The anal ambivalence of masculine-active expulsion and feminine-passive reception of a foreign body may lead to bisexual tendencies in later life.

The child's sexual interest is primarily diverted to the problem of birth, usually caused by the birth of a sibling. Many children believe that babies are born by bowel and are eliminated as a piece of feces. Children's fantasies develop around the mystery of birth. The mother's gain of weight in pregnancy is often interpreted by children as an oral intake analogous to food intake that will be terminated in anal elimination of the newborn baby.

Abraham suggested subdividing the anal stage into the anal-expulsive and the anal-retentive stage. In the early and expulsive phase the child does not care for the external object and enjoys the sadistic expulsion of feces. Folklore and slang bear witness to these anal-aggressive tendencies, that often are kept alive in teen-agers and adults.

At the late anal or anal-retentive stage the child may develop affection for the feces, which become his love object. He may try to keep and to preserve them. Feces are the first possession that the child parts with out of love for the person who cares for him. Feces are the prototype of a gift, and subsequently of gold and money. On the other hand, feces symbolize babies since most children believe that childbirth is a process similar to defecation. Often the penis is regarded by children as analogous to the column of feces that fills the mucous tube of the bowel. The anal-retentive phase is considered the source of tenderness. Freud accepted Abraham's suggestions on this point and elaborated on the concept of tenderness in contradistinction to the oral type of love.

Tenderness stems from the wish to keep and to preserve the object that gives gratification and to take care of it. Only very small babies do not care, and tend to destroy objects that give them pleasure.

As the child grows, he cares more for pleasurable objects and wishes them to stay and to continue to serve as a source of pleasure. This new attitude to objects starts with his consideration for breast or bottle. Then it grows into a consideration for his mother, whom he wishes to keep and preserve as a source for a future and continuous flow of gratification. Toward the end of the anal stage, as Abraham found, "retention pleasure" outweighs "elimination pleasure."

Later on, as the object cathexis grows, the child cares for his property and pets and handles them carefully and with tenderness. The sexual instinct becomes *aim-inhibited*. The wish to perpetuate the existence of the love object may take the place of the wish to possess it. In well-adjusted adults the wish to possess and the wish to preserve are merged in marriage.

The Urethral Phase

The urethral developmental stage is an introductory period to the phallic stage, when genital organs become the main avenue of libido gratification. In both male and female the urinary tracts are closely related to the genital tracts, and children's sexual fantasies often confuse urine with semen and sexuality with urination.

Urethral eroticism is mainly autoerotic, for one's own body becomes the love object. This eroticism turns toward other objects with fantasies about urinating on them or being urinated on by them.

Urethral eroticism in girls develops sometimes into a retentive pattern, but usually it is aimed at the expulsion of urine and at the pleasure derived from emptying the bladder. The urination itself may be active and aggressive such as urinating on someone. In boys it leads to normal and active genital eroticism. In girls it leads to a conflict about their sex role and later on becomes associated with penis envy. The passive nature of urination felt as "let it flow," or loss of control over the bladder leads in boys to confusion about their sex, and quite often one may find feminine tenderness in men who have been bed-wetters in their childhood.

Training for bladder control leads often to conflicts with parents. Lack or delay in assuming this control is often punished by parents in a manner that hurts the child's self-esteem and provokes feelings of *shame*. Bed-wetting children often develop *ambitious* strivings in the struggle against this shame.

The Phallic Phase and the Oedipus Complex

Usually around the age of four the child enters the phallic stage of his libidinal development. The name "phallic" is derived from *phallos*, which means penis in erection. At this age the pleasurable sensations in the genital organs procured by manual stimulation assume the dominant role. The libido is being "placed" now in the genital organs, but it takes time for all sexual excitement to become concentrated in the genitals and discharged by them.

The most important development that takes place at the phallic stage is the Oedipus complex. Greek mythology, and later the great Greek writer Sophocles, told the story of a young prince, Oedipus, who killed his father, married his mother, and became the king. Oedipus did not know that it was his father whom he had killed and his mother whom he had married. Greek mythology considered the deeds of Oedipus not as a result of his malevolence but as an inevitable fate. When Oedipus' crime was discovered, he repented it and punished himself by pulling out his eyes. This legendary story was regarded by Freud as a symbolic story of the prehistorical development of human society and in accordance with the biogenetic principle, reexperienced by children.

Something similar to the Oedipus drama, Freud said, happens to the four- or five-year-old boy. Often he desires to possess his mother physically "in the ways which he has derived from his observations and intuitive surmises of sexual life and tries to seduce her by showing her the male organ of which he is the proud owner." The boy tries to take over his father's place; he considers his father a competitor and develops ambivalent feelings toward him. Although he loves and admires his father, at the same time he hates him intensely and wishes to annihilate him.

At this stage the penis becomes a source of pleasurable sensations. In contradistinction to the urethral desire to be fondled, there is a definite need for active push and thrust with the penis. It becomes a most precious source of gratification and pride.

The mother usually notices the masturbatory activities of the little boy, forbids him to play with his penis, and may threaten that unless he stops masturbating she will take away his penis. Often she warns the boy that she may tell the father, and the father will cut the penis off.

The little boy is aware of his vulnerability and inferiority in relation to the father, whose penis is larger. He is afraid the father may punish and castrate him. If he has had a chance to notice the difference between male and female organs, the castration threat becomes something very realistic and shocking. He believes that all people have had a penis but in some cases it was cut off by the omnipotent father. This castration fear is much stronger than the oral fear of being eaten or the anal fear of losing the body content.

The castration fear forces the boy to abandon his incestuous wishes. He may give up masturbation altogether and develop a passive attitude of a nature ascribed by him to his mother. This passive attitude conceals his increased fear of and hatred for his father, which sometimes develops later on into a defiant attitude against all men in authority. Nor does the boy give up his affection for his mother, which often turns into a dependence relationship, into a need to be loved. This attitude, with its strong feminine components and partial identification with the mother, may lead to a submissive attitude toward women.

In some cases the love for the father is stronger, and the little boy represses his phallic strivings toward his mother. Instead he develops a passive, pregenital sexual desire for his father. This *negative Oedipus complex* may lead to homosexuality.

In girls the Oedipus complex proceeds in a reverse order. In boys it causes castration fears that lead to its resolution; in girls there are no castration fears. As soon as the little girl realizes the organ differences between the sexes, she develops the *penis envy* which leads to love for the father. This is the feminine Oedipus complex, called *Electra complex*.

Originally the little girl believes that everyone is built the way she is. But as soon as she discovers that some people have penises, she wishes to have one and it occurs to her that she had a penis but lost it. "She begins by making vain atempts to do the same as boys and later, with greater success, makes efforts to compensate herself for the defect— efforts which may lead in the end to a normal feminine attitude."[45] Often she masturbates, using the clitoris as a penis-substitute. If the little girl clings to her wish to have a penis, she may develop masculine tendencies and become domineering and aggressive, and sometimes a homosexual. However, things may develop in another direction. She may become hostile to her mother because her mother did not give her a penis or took it away from her and because the mother possesses the father. The girl's wish to annihilate her mother and to possess her father's penis is typical for the feminine Oedipus complex. Love to the mother turns into hate; she is no longer a love object, and the girl reacts to the loss of the love object by *identifying* herself with it. She wishes to take her mother's role and instead of having a penis desires to be given a baby, which is a penis substitute. Her role now becomes passive, receptive; the road is paved for normal feminine sexuality.

The sexuality of the girl at this stage is focused in the clitoris. Clitoral masturbation is typical for this age, and it is sometimes accompanied by masculine fantasies in which the clitoris plays the role of a penis. In the case of a negative Electra complex a girl may dream about taking the role of the father and inserting her clitoris into the mother's vagina and having a baby with her.

In normal cases the love for the father or positive Electra complex leads to giving up the wish for a penis, identification with the mother, acceptance of the feminine-receptive role, and wish to have (to "incorporate") a baby.

The differences between masculine and feminine traits are described by Freud as follows: "When you say 'masculine,' you mean as a rule 'active' and when you say 'feminine' you mean 'passive'. . . . The male sexual cell is active and mobile; it seeks out the female one, while the latter, the ovum, is stationary, and waits passively. This behavior of the elementary organisms of sex is more or less a model of the behavior of the individuals of each sex in sexual intercourse. The male pursues the female for the purpose of sexual union, seizes her and pushes his way into her."[46]

But, Freud remarked, in some animals the female is the stronger and more aggressive party. Even the function of care for the infant is not always feminine. The function of feeding, caring for, and protecting the infant usually performed by mothers is not a passive waiting.

[45] Freud, *Outline of Psychoanalysis*, p. 97.
[46] Freud, *New Introductory Lectures in Psychoanalysis*, p. 156.

The best method for studying the differences between the sexes is to observe the way in which men and women develop out of the bisexual disposition of infants. In the earliest stages little girls are more dependent and docile and learn earlier to control bowels and bladder. In the anal-sadistic stage girls are no less sadistic than boys. In the phallic phase girls behave as if they were little men, and all their masturbatory activities concentrate around the clitoris, which is a penis equivalent at this stage.

The boy does not have to change his love object, which is always the mother, nor the erotogenic zone, which is the penis. The girl, on the contrary, has to change both. To become a woman she has to substitute father for mother as a love object and vagina for clitoris as the erotogenic zone.

In the pre-Oedipal stage girls are attached to their mothers just as boys are, with all the ambivalent feelings of love and hate of the oral, anal, and phallic stages. The turning away from the mother in the post-Oedipal phases may develop into a bitter resentment against her. The main reason is that the girl holds her mother responsible for her lack of a penis.

The difficulties and hazards of the phallic phase in girls are summarized by Freud: "The discovery of her castration is a turning-point in the life of the girl. Three lines of development diverge from it; one leads to sexual inhibition or to neurosis, the second to a modification of character in the sense of masculinity complex, and the third to normal femininity. The little girl . . . finds her enjoyment of phallic sexuality spoilt by the influence of penis envy. . . . She gives up the masturbatory satisfaction which she obtained from her clitoris, repudiates her love towards her mother, and at the same time often represses a good deal of her sexual impulses in general."[47]

The Latency Phase

The intensity of these feelings and conflicts depends upon the quantitative relation between the conflicting forces and the amount of pressure exercised by them on the child's mind. The child is usually protected from external dangers by his parents, and the loss of parental love means the loss of security. This fear of loss of support combined with the castration fear, reinforced by primeval sources, forces the child to give up his Oedipal incestuous wishes. He "introjects" the parental prohibitions and usually identifies himself with the parent of the same sex. This identification with parental wishes and acceptance of parental standards leads to the establishment of conscience and superego (see section 6).

At the next developmental stage, called by Freud the *latency period*,

[47] *Ibid.*, p. 172.

the Oedipal incestuous and aggressive feelings are repressed and forgotten. Part of the instinctual forces is put behind the parental prohibitions and used as anti-instinctual forces. The "internalized" parental prohibitions, which form the superego, threaten the child with severe punishment and keep under severe control his repressed Oedipal cravings. The child has identified himself with the threatening parental figure, which is in normal cases the parent of the same sex. The sexual interest of the child subsides considerably, mainly through inhibitions and sublimations. His love for his parents becomes desexualized and aim-inhibited. Although the sexual-sensual elements are preserved in the unconscious, the sensual goals of his sexuality become inhibited and the child's feeling toward the parents are rather tender than passionate.

As a result of the inhibition of the Oedipal cravings children give up their interest in persons of the opposite sex. At the latency period, usually between six and eleven, boys play with boys, girls play with girls. The children tend to associate and identify with the parents, adults, and peers of the same sex, and develop interests that increase their identification with and feeling of belonging to their own sex.

Puberty

At the time of puberty the libido becomes finally detached from its former relation to parents. In order to become psychologically and socially adjusted the boy has to direct his libido away from his mother to an external love object, and resolve the conflict with his father. This development takes place, as a rule, in the teen age.

Physiological changes bring to full-scale development the sexual urge and lead to new interpersonal relationships. In the period of rapid physical growth and glandular changes the genitalia become the main erotogenic zone and the desire for heterosexual contacts becomes dominant. Identification with the proper sex was accomplished in the latency period; now the adolescent strives toward action patterned upon the actions of the parent of the same sex.

In most cases the sensual and the "tender" undercurrent of love unite at puberty. The adolescent learns to combine the uninhibited and bursting sensual urge with deeply inhibited feelings of care, tenderness, and consideration for his love object. He grows into adulthood and becomes gradually more ready for marriage.

Often the unification of these two elements does not take place or is retarded or partially unsuccessful. In such cases the adolescent and later on the adult keeps separate his tender feelings and admiration for women who do not arouse him sexually, and becomes aroused and potent with women for whom he has neither respect nor any tender feelings. The maturation is in such cases far from complete; the tender and aim-inhibited attachment to the mother, normal for the latency period, was not overcome in the teen age and continues to act as a disturbing factor in adulthood.

In some cases, when the unresolved Oedipus complex remains in a highly intense fixation, the adolescent instead of giving up the desire for his mother identifies himself with her. The renounced love object becomes introjected into the ego, and severe emotional disorder may develop.

Fixation and Regression

The development of libido is a biological process, and the consecutive stages represent some innate tendencies to proceed in accordance with the laws of development. The idea of developmental stages was borrowed by Freud from biology, and especially from Darwin and Haeckel. The concept of gradual development as a natural process was strongly supported later by independently conducted observations of children. Gesell in America and Piaget in Switzerland developed theories of child development independently of Freud.[48] Gesell has established the *structure-function* principle, which implies that a certain pattern of activity may not start till the organism is ready for it. Piaget went even farther in suggesting definite developmental stages, some of them strikingly similar to those proposed by Freud.

Some critics of Freud have accused him of being too "biological"-minded and not "sociological"-minded enough. However, biology has never overlooked environmental factors and ecological considerations. Nor was Freud blind to social influences on libido development. Biology is not the opposite of sociology, and environment seems to be the determining factor in variations in the development of species.

"Owing to the general tendency to variation in biological processes it must necessarily happen that not all these preparatory phases will be passed through and completely outgrown with the same degree of success; some parts of the function will be permanently arrested," wrote Freud. The usual course of development can be "disturbed and altered by current impressions from without."[49]

These variations in libido development are caused by environmental factors. Parts of the libido or of its component impulses sometimes become arrested at an early phase of development. This arrest was called by Freud *fixation*. The fact that some portions of the libido became fixated increases the danger that in a later stage when facing obstacles the libido may *regress* to those fixations.

[48] Arnold Gesell, "Maturation and the Patterning of Behavior," in C. Murchison (ed.), *Handbook of Child Psychology*, Clark University, 1933; Jean Piaget, *The Language and Thought of the Child*, Harcourt Brace, 1926; cf. other works of Piaget.

[49] Freud, *General Introduction to Psychoanalysis*, p. 297.

Actually libido development is never perfect and rarely proceeds smoothly from one stage to the next. Often fixations are formed; often regressions take place. While the main body of the libido progresses from one stage to another, some units of it may become fixated. If, owing to unfavorable circumstances, the fixations are substantial, the main body of the libido becomes weakened and less capable of overcoming the external obstacles in development. Neurotic disturbances result from regression to an early developmental stage of the libido.

There are two types of regressions of the libido. The first type takes place when the libido returns to its early love objects. Obviously this regression revives the incestuous wishes. The other type takes place when the entire libido falls back to an early developmental stage.

Frustration may cause regression. Sexual urge seems to be much more flexible than hunger or thirst, and there are many ways to endure sexual frustration. Libido can be displaced; its objects can be easily changed; if one component of sexuality is frustrated, another may be satisfied.

Another way of handling frustration is *sublimation.* Sublimation is a diversion of a part of the sexual energy into nonsexual activities. Freud ascribed creative art to sublimation of libidinal energies and putting them at the disposal of the creative talent.

It would be rather impossible to sublimate the total amount of libido and there are some definite limitations as to how much sexual deprivation one may take. The measure of unsatisfied libido that the average human being can take upon himself is limited, said Freud. Sublimation is not always possible, and it discharges only a part of the libidinal energies.

The danger of regression under stress depends upon the strength of fixation and on the amount and duration of stress to which one is exposed. The fixation of libido is the internal, predisposing factor, while frustration is the external, environmental, and experimental factor. The development of the libido with all its unavoidable fixations represents the *predisposing* factor. This is the *sexual constitution* of the individual. On the other hand, the events and frustrations experienced by the individual are a powerful factor in causation of regression and neurosis. The relative importance of constitution and constellation or of fixations and frustrations varies from case to case.

6. THEORY OF PERSONALITY

Constitution and Constellation

In 1921 Freud introduced a new model of personality structure based on economic, topographic, and dynamic considerations.[50] It dealt with the distribution, balance, and mutual interdependence of the two

[50] Sigmund Freud, *The Ego and the Id,* Hogarth, 1947.

instinctual forces, Eros and Thanatos, and the energies at their disposal, the libido and the destructive energy—or the economy of mind; it dealt with the three mental provinces, the unconscious, preconscious, and conscious—or the topography of the mind; and it dealt with the three mechanisms of personality, the id, the ego, and the superego—or the dynamics of the mind.

"The determining causes of all the varying forms of human mental life are to be found in the interplay between inherited dispositions and accidental experiences," wrote Freud.[51] One instinct may be "innately too strong or too weak," or one capacity may be "stunted or insufficiently developed in life." The totality of the innate elements forms the *constitution* of an individual.

On the other hand, each individual is exposed in his life span to external situations. The totality of those situations forms the *constellation*. Some constellations are more, some less favorable to the development of an individual, but one has to bear in mind that what the constitution of one individual can easily handle may prove an unmanageable task for another.

Among constitutional factors the somatic structure is the first thing to consider. For example, anatomical and physiological sexual differences are of great importance for the psychological development of men and women. The instinctual forces are another constitutional factor and they form a bridge between the physical and the mental apparatus.

Constitution includes not only what is given at birth but also the biologically determined developmental phases. These phases Freud related to the phylogenetic development. He assumed, in accordance with Haeckel's biogenetic principle, that the hereditary disposition enables the infant to grow into a civilized adult, and to pass through an immensely long stretch of human development "in an almost uncannily abbreviated form."

This growth is impossible without parental and other educational influences. Whether the child will pass safely through the developmental stages or remain fixated on one of them depends primarily upon his experiences and his interaction with the physical and social environment. Freud never proposed rigid and universal developmental phases. He suspected that in different cultures these phases must undergo far-reaching modifications. The growth of human personality depends on life experiences, which may or may not encourage inherited potentialities, may foster or prevent growth, may stimulate development or thwart and cripple it. Mental health and disease are only partially dependent upon innate constitution. The environment, the constellation, and not the constitution, usually has the final say about personality structure, whether normal or abnormal.

[51] Freud, *Outline of Psychoanalysis*, p. 81.

The Id

The new personality model introduced a division of personality into three parts, the id, the ego, and the superego. The neonate has id only; the ego and superego develop later in life. Whatever is inherited or fixed in the constitution, and above all the instincts, which originate in the somatic organization, finds its first mental expression in the id. The id is the link between somatic and mental processes; it is "somewhere in direct contact with somatic processes, and takes over from them instinctual needs and gives them mental expression, but we cannot say in what substratum this contact is made."[52]

The id expresses the true purpose of the individual organism's life, namely, the immediate satisfaction of its innate needs. No such purpose as that of keeping itself alive or of protecting itself from dangers by means of anxiety can be attributed to the id. The id knows no precautions to insure survival. In fact, an immediate and unconditioned gratification of instinctual demand, forcefully pursued by the id, may lead to dangerous clash with the external world and to death of the organism.

The entire mental energy is stored in the id. This energy is primarily put at the disposal of the organic instincts, which are composed of fusions of two primal forces, Eros and destructiveness. The only endeavor of all the instincts, related to the various somatic organs, is satisfaction or immediate discharge of energy to remove tension and bring relief. This is what Freud meant by the *Lustprinzip* (usually translated: the pleasure principle); it is the urge for an immediate discharge of energy that brings an immediate relief and pleasure.

The id is entirely unconscious and therefore, at the beginning of an individual's life, everything is unconscious. Owing to the influence of the external world, part of the unconscious material of the id develops into preconscious material and the ego emerges. Not all the preconscious material remains a permanent property of the ego; part of it is lost, part repressed. In adults, the id's unconscious material is composed both of the original, unaltered, and almost inaccessible unconscious nucleus and of a relatively younger and more easily accessible material that has been repressed by the ego and thrown back into the id.

The mental processes in the id, the so-called *primary processes*, are not subject to the laws of logic. They may or may not help the survival of the individual. The id is cut off from the external world but performs perceptory functions in its own interior. The very fact that the id is governed by the *pleasure principle* and acts always in the direction of procuring pleasure and avoiding unpleasure indicates that the id is capable of perception. The self-directed perceptions and coenesthetic feelings disclose the economy of inner tensions and the balance of the

[52] Freud, *New Introductory Lectures in Psychoanalysis,* p. 104.

mental apparatus. Whenever the economy or the equilibrium of the mental apparatus is disturbed, the instinctual forces react in the striving for immediate discharge of energy. As said before, the id blindly obeys the pleasure principle. It knows no values, no right or wrong, no moral standards, no considerations for other people. It is a "cauldron of seething excitement," Freud said. "Instinctual cathexes seeking discharge"—that is all the id contains. The id's energy is unbound, fluid, capable of quick discharge, easily condensated and displaced.

Id does not change. "Conative impulses which have never gotten beyond the id, and even impressions which have been pushed down into the id by repression, are virtually immortal and are preserved for whole decades as though they had only recently occurred."[53] The repressed remains unaltered by the passage of time. In dreams long-forgotten infancy memories come back, and in mental disorder early childhood experiences play a decisive role. All other "agencies of the mind" or mechanisms of personality such as ego and superego grew out of and became separated from the id. All are ruled by the same principles of economy and pleasure.

It remains certain, Freud wrote in the last summary of his theory, "that self-perceptions—coenesthetic feelings and feelings of pleasure-unpleasure —govern events in the id with despotic force. The id obeys the inexorable pleasure principle. But not the id alone. It seems as though the activity of the other agencies of the mind is able only to modify the pleasure principle but not to nullify it; and it remains a question of the greatest theoretical importance, and one that has not yet been answered, when and how it is ever possible for the pleasure principle to be overcome."[54]

The energies stored in the id are the unbound, undirected, and uncontrolled resources of an individual's vitality. The id leads the individual to the most irresponsible type of actions resembling those of a neonate. Imagine an adult-neonate with all the power and skill of an adult governed by a "cauldron of seething excitement" and one has a picture of a man ruled by the id.

When the other mental agencies, the ego and the superego, develop, their energies are borrowed or derived from the id. It has to be emphasized again that the only source of mental energies, both of Eros and Thanatos, is the id, and parts of its energies become vested in the higher mental agencies.

The Archaic Ego

The neonate is exposed to stimuli but is unable to perceive clearly what is going on, or to move voluntarily, or to master the excitations created by inner and outer stimuli. These three functions—perception,

---

[53] *Ibid,* p. 104.
[54] Freud, *Outline of Psychoanalysis,* p. 109.

voluntary motility, and control of tensions—will eventually become the functions of the emerging ego.

The newborn has no ego. He is exposed to excitations which he cannot master. He becomes somehow dimly aware of them and feels uncomfortable and unhappy. Hunger, thirst, cold, noise, and other tension-producing stimuli flood his mental apparatus and produce a state of anxiety.

The first mental tendency that develops in the infant is to get rid of the disturbing stimuli. The infant himself is unable to do so. He is helpless and cannot survive without being taken care of. Help comes from without, and the disturbing stimulus of hunger disappears with the satisfaction of hunger.

The neonate's mental apparatus, as seen by Freud, resembles a body floating in water. Its surface is exposed to the outer world and receives external stimuli and discharges motions. Originally, the entire apparatus is id. Under the influence of environmental forces, acting on the surface of the id, this surface undergoes substantial changes and gradually develops into a separate part of the mental apparatus called ego. It must be emphasized that the influence of the environment produces changes in the external part of the id. The unconscious material of the id becomes transformed into the preconscious ego, in which the primary mental processes give ground to the emerging secondary processes.

This infantile, "archaic" ego knows and loves only itself. It is narcissistic. At this stage of primary narcissism, the infantile ego is only dimly aware of the external world. The infant is wrapped up in himself and in his needs; when his needs are gratified and tension is removed, he falls asleep or drowses in a feeling of bliss and omnipotence.

The gratification of needs comes from outside. Hunger is satisfied by mother's milk. In this early stage the craving for an object and the craving for removal of unpleasant stimuli seem to be identical. The cessation of hunger tension restores the narcissistic state and feeling of omnipotence. The supply of food regulates the supply of self-esteem. The desire for milk and the gratification of this need regulate the infant's self-esteem, which is so significant for the future growth of his ego. The feeling of self-esteem and omnipotence is attained in a state of complete relaxation and satisfaction.

This leads to some sort of inner contradiction. When the infant is free from disturbing stimuli, he falls asleep. Then the stimuli come again: there is hunger, pressure in bowels and bladder, irritation of skin, and the infant craves objects. At the earliest stage of life, the infant craves reality and tries to get rid of it. "This is the point at which a contradiction of basic importance in human life arises, the contradiction between longing for complete relaxation and longing for objects (stimulus hunger)," said Fenichel, a leading psychoanalyst.[55]

[55] Fenichel, *Psychoanalytic Theory of Neurosis*, p. 35.

As years go by the child is forced to give up his narcissistic feeling of omnipotence and ascribes omnipotence to the outer world which satisfies his needs. The adults around him seem to have unlimited power and the child may hope to share this omnipotence by fantasies about incorporating them or being incorporated by them.

Love of oneself by incorporation or secondary narcissism expresses itself in longing for unification with the omnipotent adults or other external forces which are believed to be omnipotent. The infantile ego is unable to distinguish clearly between self and other objects, and narcissistic love and object love are not yet separated.

As the child grows, his ego becomes gradually more capable of protecting the organism against threats coming from within and without. In well-adjusted adults the ego is the main mental agency controlling behavior. The better developed and stronger the ego, the better balanced and more adjusted the individual is.

The Tasks of the Ego

The main task of the ego is self-preservation of the organism. It performs this task in regard to the external world by becoming "aware of the stimuli from without, by storing up experiences of them (in memory), by avoiding excessive stimuli (through flight), by dealing with moderate stimuli (through adaptation) and, finally, by learning to bring about appropriate modifications in the external world to its own advantage (through activity). In regard to internal events and in relation to the id, the ego performs its task by gaining control over the demands of the instincts, by deciding whether they shall be allowed to obtain satisfaction, by postponing that satisfaction to times and circumstances favorable in the external world or by suppressing their excitations completely. Its activities are governed by consideration of the tensions produced by stimuli present within it or introduced into it. The raising of these tensions is in general felt as *unpleasure* and their lowering as *pleasure*. . . . The ego pursues pleasure and seeks to avoid unpleasure. An increase in unpleasure which is expected and foreseen is met by a *signal of anxiety*."[56]

The ego is concerned with discovering the most favorable and least perilous method of obtaining satisfaction. In this endeavor the ego takes into consideration the external world. The ego, too, is ruled by the pleasure principle. But in contradistinction to the id, the ego is capable of calculating the *consequences* of its behavior. The id is blind and bound upon immediate gratification of the instinctual demands while the ego is capable of logical reasoning, of considering causal relations, and of learning by experience.

Owing to these intellectual activities (which will be explained later)

[56] Freud, *Outline of Psychoanalysis*, p. 15.

the ego applies a modified pleasure principle. Ego clings to the task of self-preservation and postpones or suppresses instinctual demands that threaten the existence of the organism. Ego does not object to the gratification instincts but it guards the existence of the organism, which is the prerequisite for any pleasurable experience. For the ego safety is prior to pleasure. To put it in other terms, the id does not care for life which does not offer pleasure, and the ego does not care for pleasure which jeopardizes life. The id clings to instinctual cravings notwithstanding future results; the ego clings to reality and pursues the cause of pleasure provided there is no danger in it. This modified and limited pursuit of pleasure was called by Freud *reality principle*.

The Functions of the Ego: Reality Testing

The ego is the part of the mind that adjusts the organism to the external world. Several functions are performed by the ego, and one of them is the contact with reality. The ego perceives inner and external stimuli, weighs the possibilities of successful (maximum pleasure and minimum displeasure) gratification of the instinctual impulses, and takes into consideration the totality of inner resources (abilities, etc.), the totality of circumstances. It can be compared to the driver of a car on a crowded road. The driver (1) perceives what is going on outside the car, (2) perceives (or knows) the resources of his car, i.e., power, size, weight, roadability, brakes, etc., (3) weighs the chances of swift moving along the road, considering the necessary adjustment of his own speed and maneuvering of the car in view of the external conditions (the road being wet, slippery, other cars moving, etc.) and the conditions of his own car, (4) exercises proper control of his own car, (5) moves on the road in the direction of his goal trying to make the best possible time and the safest and most economical ride. One has to add here that the task of the ego is complicated by the fact that the id is not an engine but a bursting volcano that cannot always be controlled and in the car, symbolizing the organism, there is a "back-seat driver," the superego.

As said before, the first and most important task of the emerging ego is the contact with the outer world, i.e., the perception of objects. The narcissistic perception of one's own body is the first step in this direction. The infant dimly perceives some tensions stemming from within as from "inside something." This leads to the formation of his own body image, which emerges out of pleasant and unpleasant sensations of his own body. The perception of one's body as a definite object is an important step forward in the direction of perception of the outer world.

At the beginning perceptory and motor functions are diffused and intertwined. The newborn organism is flooded by the stimuli and is unable to control them. The passive experiencing of excitation is gradually replaced by observation, retention of perception (memory), and motor responses. The growing ego becomes an organized entity with differentiated functions, one of them being protection against too many or too strong stimuli.

The ego endeavors to control the incoming stimuli. When this is impossible, it regresses into id by falling asleep or fainting. Regression is a result of failure to master reality; it is a sign that the ego is too weak and unable to protect the organism against painful stimulation.

The process of perception of external objects starts with the primary, archaic *identification* with the perceived objects. Several functions are included in this archaic identification performed by the emerging ego. The infant puts the perceived things into his mouth, introjecting his first love objects. The *oral introjection* of the object indicates that perceptory, motor, and emotional processes are at this stage still undifferentiated from each other. Identification involves imitation of the perceived objects; it is an effort to master the too intensive stimuli by adjusting one's body to them.

As said before, the vague conception of the outer world is accompanied by a feeling of omnipotence. Once perception improves, the child becomes aware of his limitation and realizes that satisfaction of his needs depends upon external factors.

The early perceptions are vague, inexact, and undifferentiated. Objects are perceived in a diffuse manner and often overlap each other. Sometimes external objects are perceived as parts of the body (introjection) or parts of the self are ascribed to the external world (projection). The child is prone to ascribe pleasant stimuli to his own body and unpleasant stimuli to the outer world. Objects are perceived in relationship to the child's needs. They are classified as "good" when pleasurable and as "bad" when threatening. It seems that the child perceives himself as the center of the universe with all other objects revolving around him.[57]

The "surface" part of the mental apparatus is the perceptual-conscious or *Pcpt-cs* system. This system "is directed on to the external world, it meditates perceptions of it, and in it is generated, while it is functioning, the phenomenon of consciousness. It is the sense organ of the whole apparatus, receptive not only of excitations from without but also of such as proceed from the interior of the mind."[58]

The mature ego has at its disposal this mental apparatus. The mature ego is capable of "reality testing," i.e., checking the content of its perceptions against the outer reality and eliminating in the picture of the external world any elements that may stem from the "inner sources of excitation." Reality testing takes place by performing an action related

---

[57] Piaget arrived at similar results using a different research method. See Jean Piaget, *Judgment and Reasoning in the Child,* Humanities Press, 1930, and other works.
[58] Freud, *New Introductory Lectures to Psychoanalysis,* p. 106.

to a perception. If the action, such as closing one's eyes in visual perception or putting cotton in the ears in auditory perception, etc., removes the perception, it is evidence that the perception comes from the outer world. If visual or auditory perception is not affected by the action, then its source must lie within the organism itself.

The Functions of the Ego: Speech and Reasoning

The ability to talk is of crucial importance in the development of the ego. The use of words permits a better communication with other people and a better reality testing. In very early childhood and in cases of severe mental deterioration, the individual applies his own autistic vocal expressions understandable to himself only while normal speech is a means of interpersonal communication.

Speaking enables the child to think. Undoubtedly, there is a preverbal way of thinking as there is a preverbal consciousness and a preverbal perception. However, logical thinking requires verbal symbols that could be applied in several forms of logical manipulation such as generalization, abstraction, etc.

The earliest way of thinking, the archaic thinking, tolerates contradictions, is ruled by emotions, and is controlled by wish and magic beliefs. It is unorganized; it puts together things that are unrelated to each other; it takes parts for wholes, similarities for identities, and it confuses self with the outer world. The archaic thinking operates with primitive symbols, pictures, distortions, and substitutive figures. The symbols are pictorial, visualizing definite objects rather than classes of objects.

When later in life the ego takes over control of the thinking process, the pictorial-symbolic, prelogical way of thinking is retained in dreams and other unconscious processes. In cases of severe mental disorder, the individual may regress to these primitive, prelogical forms of thinking and become disconnected from verbal expression. In psychoanalytic therapy, the unconscious material becomes verbalized and is thus moved from the unconscious to the conscious.

In the process of thinking the residues of past experiences, stored up in memory, are utilized. "Thinking is an experimental dealing with small quantities of energy, just as a general moves miniature figures about over a map before setting his troops in motion," said Freud.[59] The ego brings together, unifies and organizes the mental processes, eliminates contradictions and develops into a coherent and well-functioning unit that keeps an open eye on what is going on, checks and controls the correctness of perceptions, and steers the entire mental system, avoiding unnecessary risks. Instead of the infant's hallucinatory images a precise

[59] *Ibid.*, p. 124.

picture of reality is put at the disposal of the individual enabling him to adjust better and to be more successful in life.

Motor Control

The mastery of the environment is one of the main tasks of the ego. This can be accomplished by action, and the adult ego controls the motor apparatus. Simultaneously with the development of sensory apparatus and with an increasingly better use of it, the growing ego learns to master, i.e., to inhibit and regulate, the motor functions of the organism. Originally, stimuli provoked immediate and unorganized mass reaction of the organism. One of the earliest and most important functions of the ego is to "bind" the instinctual impulses and to convert their mobile cathectic energy into a predominantly quiescent, tonic cathexis.

The ego learns to postpone reaction and to abide by the *reality principle*. This principle was first mentioned by Freud in 1911.[60] As mentioned before, it is not contradictory to the pleasure principle; it is rather a development of the latter. The ego pursues pleasure as much as the id does but the ego is concerned with the avoidance of displeasure and preventing of disastrous consequences of a blind pursuit of pleasure. Ego seeks the best way to procure a maximum of pleasure with a minimum of unpleasure.

Before responding to a given stimulus the ego weighs the possible consequences of the action. It learns to control the functions of the body, to withstand some amount of tension, and to discharge the energy in a way that provides the best possible (i.e., the least risky) gratification of needs.

The three milestones in this direction are the acquisition of the ability to walk, to talk, and to control the bowel movements. The functions of walking and talking increase the contact with the external reality. By the process of walking the child can reach new objects, meet new people, and experience new situations. The narcissistic and self-centered world of an infant gives way to a new world of many objects and people; instead of a passive and hallucinatory imagination and expectation, the child moves around, becomes an active explorer of reality, and tries to master it. With the development of the speech function, the child exchanges communication with the outer world and rapidly enlarges his field of knowledge. He begins to anticipate the reactions of adults, and his growing ego learns to avoid unpleasurable experience stemming from the instinctual wishes.

The ego "controls the path of access to motility, but it interpolates between desire and action the procrastinating factor of thought, during which it makes use of the residue of experience stored up in memory.

[60] Freud, "Formulations Regarding the Two Principles in Mental Functioning," *Collected Papers*, Vol. IV.

In this way it dethrones the pleasure principle, which exerts undisputed sway over the processes in the id, and substitutes for it the reality principle, which promises greater security and greater success."[61] The ego carries out the intentions of the id but only under conditions that guarantee a successful fulfillment.

The Functions of the Ego: Control of Inner Tensions

In a normal and stable state of mind the frontiers of the ego are firmly safeguarded against the id by anti-cathexes or charges of energy that control impulses. The superego can hardly be distinguished from the ego for the cultural values of the well-balanced individual are in harmony with his perception of reality. The ego in harmony with the superego invests or cathects energy in warding off some instinctual demands that are socially undesirable or dangerous for the survival of the organism.

In sleep the ego withdraws its cathexes from the sensory organs and severs the contact with the external world. The withdrawal of inhibitory anti-cathexes, usually directed against the id, is harmless, since the ego controls the movements of the organism. In sleep the reduction or withdrawal of inhibitions allows the id considerable but harmless freedom; the wishes that are warded off in the waking state now "occupy the stage" and expose themselves in dreams. In some pathological cases, such as somnambulism, the motor apparatus performs unconscious actions which the individual is unaware of.

The neonate does not have the ability to control the impulse for immediate discharge of energy, and the archaic ego is unable to master excitation. The growing ego acquires the ability to tolerate greater amounts of excitation and to control the tendency for panic reactions by anti-cathexes.

This defense apparatus grows from several sources. The child, driven by the id's demand for immediate gratification, is often exposed to painful consequences stemming from his physical or social environment. "The burned child dreads fire," says the proverb. The social environment, parents and other persons, may inflict pain on the child and force him to consider the dangers resulting from his urge for immediate gratifications.

As soon as the memories are stored in the preconscious and become easily accessible to the conscious, the ego develops defense mechanisms, not directed against the instinctual demands, but aimed at controlling them. The stronger the ego, the higher the tolerance of strain, whether the strain is created by outside sources or by inner pressures.

When the organism is exposed to external danger, the ego reacts with

[61] Freud, *New Introductory Lectures in Psychoanalysis*, p. 106.

fear. When the inner pressure stemming from the unconscious threatens the ego, the feeling of *anxiety* serves as a signal of danger.

Anxiety

Originally Freud regarded anxiety as a result of thwarted sexual urge. Unsatisfied libido and undischarged excitation cause anxiety neurosis. It seemed, said Freud, as if the unsatisfied libido were directly transformed into anxiety.

In 1920 in a monograph entitled "The Problem of Anxiety" Freud developed a new theory of anxiety. It did not contradict the former theory but reduced it to a special case only. Anxiety, said Freud, stems from the infant's inability to master excitations. The infant's system is unavoidably exposed to powerful stimulations beyond his ability to cope with. These traumatic experiences create in the child the feeling of desperate helplessness. This is the painful, horrible feeling of *primary anxiety.* The first experience of this kind is the birth trauma, in which the main characteristics of anxiety such as the accelerated action of heart and lungs play a decisive role in the child's survival. Later in life separation from the mother is anxiety producing; in the phallic stage, castration fear; in the latency period, the fear of superego.

The state of painful helplessness or anxiety may be revived in later life under trying circumstances. The feeling of being helplessly flooded is one of the main symptoms in practically all neurotic disturbances and especially in a traumatic neurosis. Inability to control excitation, whether it stems from sexual or aggressive impulses, creates the state of anxiety, which is always experienced as inability to master excitation. By this interpretation the early theory of anxiety becomes a part of the later and more broadly conceived theory, which says that any anxiety can be traced back to situations of external danger. Sooner or later the ego realizes that the satisfaction of some instinctual demands may create one of the well-remembered danger situations. Then the ego must inhibit the instinctual wishes. A strong ego accomplishes this task easily; a weak ego has to invest more energies in counter-cathectic effort to ward off the repressed impulse.

Anxiety, said Freud, is an affective state characterized by a specific unpleasurable quality, by efferent or discharge phenomena, and by the perception of these. Anxiety is "a specific state of unpleasure accompanied by motor discharge along definite pathways."[62]

There are three types of anxiety-producing situations in childhood, but they can be reduced to one type. These are the situations of (1) being left alone, (2) being in the dark, and (3) finding a strange person

[62] Sigmund Freud, *The Problem of Anxiety,* Psychoanalytic Quarterly Press and W. W. Norton, 1936, p. 70.

in place of the mother. All these situations represent the feeling of loss of the loved person. Anxiety seems to be a reaction to the perception of absence of or separation from the loved object and is probably experienced by an infant in birth trauma, in the weaning from the mother's breast, and later on in castration fears. In all these situations, privation causes an increased tension and an economic disturbance demanding some action, some discharge of energy.

In Freud's words: "If the infant longs for the sight of the mother, it does so surely, only because it already knows from experience that she gratifies all its needs without delay. The situation which the infant appraises as 'danger' and against which it desires reassurance, is therefore, one of not being gratified, of an *increase of tension arising from non-gratification of its needs*—a situation against which it is powerless."[63]

Anxiety is a sign of the ego's weakness. When the ego is hard pressed by external reality, it develops "reality anxiety." When it is pressed by the superego, which creates a feeling of guilt and inferiority, the so-called "moral" anxiety appears. When the pressures of the id threaten to disrupt the ego, a "neurotic" anxiety develops.

Objective or reality anxiety is a reaction to external danger. It is a reaction to an anticipated threat. Anxiety-preparedness may develop in one of the two following manners: Either the old experience called anxiety development is reexperienced as a signal of danger and the individual faces the danger by a proper action of flight or fight, or the past danger is reexperienced in its totality with all its paralyzing effects leading to an utter failure in counteracting the present danger.

Neurotic anxiety is experienced in three ways. One is the anxiety neurosis, usually felt as some sort of general apprehensiveness, dreadful expectancy, and uneasiness. The anxiety neurosis is usually caused by undischarged excitation and the unsatisfied libido energy is transformed into anxiety.

The other type of neurotic anxiety takes place in hysteria and in some other severe neuroses. The ideas attached to libido become repressed and distorted, and the energy, whether libidinal or destructive, turns into anxiety.

The first neuroses of childhood are phobias. An internal danger or fear of one's own libido or death instinct becomes transformed into a fear of external dangers. It is as if the neurotic anxiety became externalized and perceived as objective anxiety or fear of an external threat. The neurotic transforms the fear of his own libido (or death instinct), from which there is no flight, into an external danger that can be supposedly warded off by obsessive behavior.

Moral anxiety is a reaction to pressure which is exercised by the superego. It is experienced as feelings of guilt or shame or a feeling of

[63] *Ibid.*, p. 76.

one's inferiority and inadequacy. The factual threat to an organism does not necessarily produce anxiety. Anxiety can be produced by an imaginary threat, by inner tension, or by any other factor that is experienced as a threat.

In final analysis, it is not the danger itself that causes anxiety; accordingly, the pleasure principle is not identical with self-preservation. Freud said: "What is it that is actually dangerous and actually feared in such a danger situation? It is clearly not the objective injury which need have absolutely no importance psychologically, but it is something which is set up in the mind by it. Birth, for example, our prototype for the state of anxiety can hardly in itself be regarded as an injury, although it may involve a risk of injury. The fundamental thing about birth, as about every danger situation, is that it evokes in mental experience a condition of tense excitation which is felt as pain and which cannot be mastered by discharge. . . . The operation of the pleasure principle does not guarantee us against objective injury but only against a particular injury to our mental economy. . . . The magnitude of the excitation turns an impression into a traumatic factor which paralyses the operation of the pleasure principle and gives significance to the danger situation."[64]

Defense Mechanisms

The term "defense mechanisms" was introduced by Freud in 1894 and was not used for some thirty years. This is the name for techniques by which the ego wards off the instinctual demands of the id or the pressures of the superego. With the exception of sublimation, all defense mechanisms indicate an inner conflict.

One of the most important defense mechanisms is *rationalization*. In its attempt to mediate between the id and reality, the ego is often forced to ascribe rationality to the irrational demands of the id, to display a "pretended regard" for reality and, with "diplomatic dishonesty," assume that the id accepts reality while it actually distorts it. Rationalization is basically a fallacious reasoning which serves to represent over-irrational motivation as if it were rational and, at the same time, to protect self-esteem. It is used as a covering up for mistakes, misjudgments, and failures and it tries to justify behavior by reasons that seem to be rational.

A more serious distortion of reality is the mechanism of *undoing*. The individual seems to believe that he can undo or nullify his former actions that make him feel guilty. Expiation, e.g., is a belief that one may nullify his former deeds; whenever this belief is applied in the struggle of ego, the mechanism of undoing is being used. It is a kind of magic, said Freud, to "blow away" not only the consequences of an event but the event itself.

One step further in moving away from reality is the mechanism of

[64] Freud, *New Introductory Lectures in Psychoanalysis*, pp. 130–131.

denial. When reality becomes too painful or too dangerous to cope with, the infantile ego withdraws from any contact with it and refuses to acknowledge its existence. Memory and perceptions prevent unlimited denial of reality, but in some pathological cases the hard-pressed ego gives up reality testing and applies the mechanism of negating the unpleasant experience.

Introjection was mentioned in our description of the oral phase of development. It is the desire to swallow the love object and it is the prototype of any object relations. It represents the primitive and ambivalent attitude in which love and destruction are combined in incorporation of the love object and in identification with him. When in later life the individual is unable to develop more mature object relationships, the hard-pressed ego may set primitive introjection as an instinctual aim and accept identification as the only possible object relationship.

The opposite to introjection is *projection,* just as the opposite to swallowing is spitting out. In the early stage of development the ego draws a line between "something to be swallowed," which is pleasurable and belongs to the ego, and "something to be spit out," which is unpleasurable and belongs to the outer world.

The defense mechanism of *isolation* is often used in compulsion neuroses. This defense mechanism separates an emotional content from the idea into which the emotion was cathected, thus separating two parts of the same experience. In cases of "split ego" or "dual personality" part of an experience is kept separate from the rest of one's ego; usually it is a very unpleasant part that cannot be accepted by the ego. Isolation consists of a "transposition" of a refractory period in which nothing more is allowed to happen—no perception is registered, no action performed. It usually takes place after an unpleasant experience. The ego, unable to face pain or humiliation, stops functioning for a while.

One of the most important defense mechanisms is *reaction formation.* It is related to repression. When a wish or desire is repressed, the ego tries to prevent its reappearing. One of the methods used is to keep down the repressed impulse by developing a wish opposite to the original and repressed one. An individual who hates his father and is very unhappy about it may develop a ritual of affection directed toward his father; an individual torn by an impulse toward dirt may develop by reaction formation compulsive cleanliness.

Regression is applied by the ego in its struggle against the demands of the libido, usually against the pressures caused by the Oedipus complex. In compulsion neurosis the genital organization proves to be too weak to face the conflict between Oedipus desires and castration fears. When the ego undertakes the measures of defense just referred to, the first result achieved is that the genital organization (of the phallic stage) is wholly or partially pushed back to the earlier anal-sadistic stage. Regression is always related to fixation and may be limited to the erotogenic zone (e.g., regression to oral wishes) or it may be an over-all regression to primary narcissism.

The successful and normal defenses against objectionable instinctual wishes are called *sublimation.* Sublimation is a cathexis of instinctual energy into a substitute aim or object or both and channeling of the instinctual demands into new and desexualized strivings.

Repression and Resistance

The unconscious exclusion from the consciousness of objectionable impulses is called repression. Objectionable wishes or ideas are usually removed from the conscious and forgotten; the ego "pushes them down" into the unconscious and acts as if they were now extinct.

Once the ego has repressed the instinctual impulses, it endeavors to keep them repressed forever. Whenever the repressed material comes close to the surface and tends to come back into the conscious, the ego's defense mechanisms push it down, back into the unconscious. It is kept repressed by powerful counter-cathexes stemming from the ego and preventing it from becoming conscious again. The same forces that cause repression keep the repressed material under close guard and resist its unearthing. This action of the ego is called *resistance.*

The repressed material remains in the unconscious. It may be very active there and find outlets in dreams, slips of the tongue, etc. Sometimes it creates neurotic tensions. In psychoanalytic therapy it is important to remove the inhibitions, to "unmask" the neurotic symptoms and dispose of the energy attached to the repressed instinctual demands. This "catharsis," which originally formed the main method of psychoanalytic therapy, meets the unconscious resistance of the patient; resistance is actually a continuation of repression.

The "Quality" of the Ego

In order to perform this vast variety of tasks—learning from experience, sizing up the present situation, foreseeing future consequences, and being capable of control, postponement, and suppression of the instinctual demands—the ego must be a highly complicated apparatus. It has to control the entire sensory apparatus of perception, it has to master the motor apparatus, and it has to be able to withstand pressures coming from within and without.

Most of the ego "has the quality" or belongs to the "mental province" of the preconscious. It has access to the conscious and it can easily become conscious without any effort. On the other hand, the ego is "linked" with verbal residues, and the "presence of speech gives a safe clue to the preconscious nature of a process."

A considerable part of the ego is unconscious, and notably that part which may be described as its nucleus or its original part. Freud wrote: "Conscious processes on the periphery of the ego and everything else in the ego unconscious—such would be the simplest state of affairs that we might picture." This is probably the situation in animals. In men internal processes in the ego may also acquire the quality of consciousness. This complication is produced by the "function of speed, which brings the material in the ego into a firm connection with the memory-traces of visual and more particularly of auditory perceptions." Ego can be stimulated from within even more than from without. Ideas and other intellectual processes may become conscious. The simple equation "perception = reality (external world)" cannot hold any longer, since perception may stem from within, from memories, and from inside of the body. At the early stages the ego confuses inner stimulation with stimuli coming from the external world. These confusions are called illusions and hallucinations, and they take place whenever the ego is not fully alert in early childhood and in adults in dreams and in psychotic states. Owing to reality testing the mature ego is able to distinguish between inner and outer stimulation, between memory traces associated with verbal residues and actual, external reality.

The ego borrows its energy from the id. The instinctual demands of the id lead to investment of parts of its energy in objects. This object cathexis enables the ego to draw some amounts of energy from the id by means of various devices, one of them being identification. By identifying itself with the cathected objects the ego "recommends itself to the id in the place of the object and seeks to attract the libido of the id on to itself. . . . In the course of a person's life the ego takes into itself a large number of such precipitates of former object-cathexes."[65]

The Superego

Freud said: "The picture of the ego which mediates between the id and the external world, which takes over the instinctual demands of the former in order to bring them to satisfaction, which perceives things in the latter and uses them as memories, which, intent upon its self-preservation, is on guard against excessive claims from both directions, and which is governed in all its decisions by the injunctions of a modified pleasure principle—this picture actually applies to the ego only up to the end of the first period of childhood, till about the age of five."[66]

The new mental agency, the superego, develops as a result of weakness of the infantile ego. At the anal stage the child faces conflict with parents in matters of toilet training. The fear of punishment and the need for

[65] *Ibid.*, p. 108.
[66] Freud, *Outline of Psychoanalysis*, p. 121.

affection and protection force him to accept the parental admonitions and to "internalize" them, i.e., to consider them his own. For example, the little child may develop a dislike for playing with feces because his parents dislike him to do this.

These internalized prohibitions and self-restraints are "forerunners of the superego." Obviously they are very weak and, when no one is looking, they are easily disregarded by the child. However, these "forerunners" contain the main elements of the future superego, namely, fear of punishment and conformity with parental demands.

The actual development of the superego takes place toward the end of the phallic period. The fear of punishing parents comes to its peak in the Oedipus complex. The little boy, shocked by castration fear, is forced to give up his mother as a love object. The little girl, under the threat of losing her mother's love, is forced to abandon the father as her love object. The frustrated child of either sex regresses from object relationship to identification by introjection. Introjection of the love object is a common phenomenon in the oral stage and apparently oral regression takes place in the formation of the superego.

The introjected parental figures are idealized and seem to be more powerful and more glorious than they might be in reality. In most cases the father's image plays a greater role in the child's superego, which usually encompasses the images of both parents. The superego is originally a new element added to and introjected into the ego and forms a part of the ego; it develops later into a separate mental agency, often opposed to the ego.

The superego represents the "voice of the parents" and their moral standards as perceived by the child. Thus the superego may be irrational and childish, imposing rigid restrictions which persist into adulthood without much consideration for the present situation. One of the elements of the superego is the ego-ideal. The ego-ideal stems from an expression of admiration for the parents, to whom the child ascribed perfection. It is the striving toward perfection and an effort to live up to the expectations of the parents. Freud described it as follows: "The ego-ideal comprises the sum of all limitations in which the ego has to acquiesce, and for that reason the abrogation of the ideal would necessarily be a magnificent festival for the ego, which might then once again feel satisfied with itself. There is always a feeling of triumph when something in the ego coincides with the ego-ideal. And the sense of guilt (as well as the sense of inferiority) can also be understood as an expression of tension between the ego and the ego-ideal."[67] Freud often used ego-ideal as equivalent to what he later called superego; in the later works, however, ego-ideal refers to a part of the superego which represents the strivings for perfection as an important function of the superego.

[67] Freud, *Group Psychology and the Analysis of the Ego,* pp. 105–106.

The energy used by the ego for its inhibiting and anti-instinctual functions is drawn from the id. Also the anti-instinctual forces of the superego are derivatives of the instinctual forces of the id. The superego is mostly unconscious and is composed of both instinctual forces, love and hate, often with hate predominating.

It is quite obvious that the child's aggressiveness against his parents cannot find satisfactory discharge. His love for his parents or the parental strictness or something else may thwart the discharge of aggressiveness. The superego becomes endowed with a great part of the child's aggressiveness originally directed against the parents, and now, in the superego, directed against the child's own ego.

The ego's attitude to the superego resembles the child's attitude toward his parents. The ego needs affection and forgiveness. Its self-esteem depends upon the approval of the superego. When the ego lives up to the expectation of the superego, the superego reacts with a feeling of joy and pride. When there is a conflict, the aggressive forces stored in the superego turn against the ego with accusations creating feelings of guilt and depression. Depression is self-directed aggression; it is the result of the ego's being torn down by the superego, in resemblance to parental criticism of the child's behavior.

In manic-depressive disorder the individual oscillates between the joy and happiness resulting from the all-approving superego and the tortures of guilt feeling and depression when the superego becomes sadistic. In manic-depressive disorder the superego "becomes over-severe, abuses, humiliates, and ill treats his unfortunate ego, threatens it with the severest punishments, reproaches it for long forgotten actions which were at the time regarded quite lightly, and behaves as though it had spent the whole interval in amassing complaints and was only waiting for its present increases in strength to bring them forward and to condemn the ego on their account. The superego has the ego at its mercy and applies the most severe moral standards to it; indeed it represents the whole demands of morality and we see all at once that our moral sense of guilt is the expression of the tension between the ego and superego."[68]

In latent schizophrenia the ego is at the mercy of a severe and demanding superego. The introjected parental images assume a despotic control over the entire mental apparatus till the hard-pressed ego may give up the struggle and submerge in the unconscious in a psychotic breakdown.[69]

In well-adjusted adults the superego plays the role of self-observer and represents conscience and moral standards; it is the social and moral frame of reference of the individual. The adult superego differs con-

[68] Freud, *New Introductory Lectures in Psychoanalysis*, pp. 87–88.
[69] Wolman, "Explorations in Latent Schizophrenia," *American Journal of Psychotherapy*, 1957, 11, 560–588.

siderably from the superego established at the end of the phallic period by means of identification with the parents. The parents' influence at that time includes "not merely the personalities of the parents themselves but also racial, national, and family traditions handed on through them as well as the demands of the immediate social *milieu* which they represent. In the same way, an individual's superego in the course of his development takes over contributions from later successors and substitutes of his parents, such as teachers, admired figures in public life, or high social ideals."[70] As the individual grows, his superego gradually draws away from the infantile images of the parents and becomes more impersonal, more related to the objective social and ethical standards to which he subscribes. In well-balanced adults there is no conflict between the moral standards of the society as represented by the superego and the realistic consideration of self-protection and survival as represented by the ego and the reality principle.

Metapsychology

The description of Freud's theory of personality cannot be completed without a few remarks about occult phenomena. Despite objection raised by friends and foes, despite the apparent danger of being ridiculed, Freud wrote: "We intend to treat these things in just the same way as we treat any other material for scientific investigation. First, we have to establish whether these processes really occur, and then, but only then, when there is no doubt as to their actuality, we can set about their explanation."[71]

Unfortunately, said Freud, there is no way to prove or to disprove tales of wonderful happenings and miracles in the past, and séances of occultists with their media remind one of "children's pranks or conjurors' tricks." This sad state of things should not deter scientists. All phenomena of the human mind should be open for scientific research irrespective of their rational or irrational character and disregarding the fact that non-scientists might have had erroneous ideas about these phenomena.

Freud believed that one occult phenomenon, telepathy, is more accessible to scientific inquiry than any other. Telepathy was defined as an alleged fact that an event which occurs at a specific time comes more or less simultaneously into the consciousness of a person who is spatially distant, without application of any of the known methods of communication. Then two persons must be mutually emotionally involved. Freud quoted a case of a middle-aged man who dreamt that his daughter gave birth to twins, and actually the twins were born.

A similar case is the thought transference of some fortunetellers, who

[70] Freud, *Outline of Psychoanalysis*, p. 17.
[71] Freud, *New Introductory Lectures in Psychoanalysis*, p. 48.

often express the secret wishes of their clients. The question is, how could the fortunetellers possibly know about the hidden thoughts of their clients? But there is no doubt that these individuals often express the wishes of their clients without having any known access to or source of information about their clients' thoughts.

Another instance of thought transference was brought out by Freud in connection with psychoanalytic treatment when one of his patients told him about foresight a few minutes after a Dr. Forsyth had called on Freud. These phenomena of thought transference between patient and therapist in situations when deep emotional involvement of transference has been established have been reported by several psychoanalysts.

The anticipation of future risks and dangers is another metapsychological problem. Freud has noticed that certain individuals seem to have access to their own unconscious and are somehow aware of their own unconscious feelings about themselves and about others. They display a considerable degree of foresight which cannot be explained in terms of objective perception and logical reasoning.

Psychoanalytic therapy is believed to increase one's ability to "see through himself" and to give him an access to mental phenomena which are usually repressed and inaccessible. Actually one of the main tools of psychoanalytic therapy is the ability of the therapist to feel or empathize or somehow perceive intuitively what is on the patient's mind.

Since these phenomena are not too accessible for scientific study, room is left for speculation. The knowledge of hidden thought has been often ascribed to magicians and mysticists, and it has been a widespread belief that the occult may shed light on what has been unknown. "It can easily be imagined," wrote Freud, "that certain practices of mystics may succeed in upsetting the normal relations between the different regions of mind, so that, for example, the perceptual system becomes able to grasp relations in the deeper layers of the ego and in the id which would otherwise be inaccessible to it. Whether such a procedure can put one in possession of ultimate truth, from which all good will flow, may be safely doubted. All the same, we must admit that the therapeutic efforts of psychoanalysis have chosen much the same method of approach."[72]

This part of personality, the unconscious thought and perception, remains the least known area and the least accessible problem for scientific inquiry. Prior to Freud, dreams and symptom formation in neurosis were overlooked by the scientific inquiry. But it would be entirely unjustified to neglect some areas of human life simply because they do not fit into some logical system. Whatever goes on in the human mind is a legitimate object of psychological research. Undoubtedly, the deeper the layer and the more obscure the symptom, the more caution is required. But no

[72] *Ibid.*, p. 111.

part of reality is unscientific, and all phenomena should be subject to a rigorous scientific inquiry (cf. Part IV).

Character and Characterology

In psychoanalytic literature the term "character" indicates the more permanent and consistent patterns of overt and covert behavior. Character represents the totality of ways in which the individual meets frustrations, faces hardships, forms ideas, and relates to other individuals. The character of a man is influenced by social factors. By stressing different values and applying different educational methods each society encourages different elements in the development of the individual.

Fenichel believes that the term "character" is almost identical with the term "ego." However, a closer scrutiny of Freud's writings shows that these are two different although closely related terms established on a different level of description. Ego is a "dynamic" term, i.e., part of the dynamic apparatus that contains, besides the ego, the superego and the id. The term "character" deals not with the mental apparatus but with the behavior of an individual and is related to the history of his libidinal development, his fixations and regressions, his defense mechanisms and adjustments, and the totality of interactions between him and his environment. Character is not a function of the ego, although it certainly overlaps the ego. It is not entirely as Fenichel says: "Character, as the habitual mode of bringing into harmony the tasks presented by inner demands and by the external world, is necessarily a function of the constant, organized, and integrating part of the personality which is the ego. The question of character would be thus the question of when and how the ego acquires the qualities by which it habitually adjusts itself to the demands of instinctual drives and of the external world, and later also of the superego."[73]

The psychoanalytic theory of character has been, to a certain extent, influenced by Dilthey and Spranger (cf. Chap. 11). Accordingly, character represents in psychoanalysis the quality, the "how" of personality. Each personality contains various elements, but how they all work together, how the individual functions in life, and in what way he differs from other individuals—these depend on his character.

In psychoanalytic theory the problem of interaction between the various mental forces and agencies is of primary importance. Character is determined mainly by the relative strength of the id, ego, and superego, which are in turn influenced by education and other environmental factors.

The ego can deal with the instinctual impulses either in a cathectic or in an anti-cathectic manner. In well-balanced individuals the instinctual

[73] Fenichel, *Psychoanalytic Theory of Neurosis*, p. 467.

demands find proper outlets, i.e., they are cathected. The instinctual energies are cathected in the natural functions of the organism and in the objects of these functions. This type of behavior or the *cathectic* character perpetuates the instinctual demands and finds avenues of gratification in which the demands of the id, the ego, the superego, and the external world are brought into harmony. The cathectic character type finds ways to handle those instinctual demands which jeopardize this harmony. Either they become "successfully repressed" or their energies are sublimated, i.e., directed into new and more acceptable channels. Usually it is the Oedipal situation that leads to sublimation; in favorable circumstances the child gives up the object and aim of his Oedipal wish, and the energies related to the wish are not blocked but cathected in a substitute aim and object. The libidinal energy continues to flow but becomes desexualized. Successful sublimation, which depends upon the strength of the ego and upon the chances of identification with the parents, helps the individual to function smoothly while the unacceptable instinctual aims and objects are given up. In children some sublimations can be noticed in games in which sexual and aggressive impulses are harmlessly acted out.

Not always is the ego capable of a cathected type of behavior, and often anti-cathectic, i.e., reactive or defensive, behavior develops. In the *reactive type* of character, the ego wards off the instinctual demands by counter-cathexis. This expenditure of energy obviously impoverishes the mental economy and reduces the individual's efficiency. There is a continuous need for repeated counter-cathexes to ward off the unacceptable impulses. Anxiety accompanies the conflict between the ego and the repressed impulses and limits the ability of the individual to obtain full satisfaction in life.

The main mechanisms used in the reactive character type are reaction formations and phobias. Both defense mechanisms develop into habitual behavior patterns or character traits. Some reactive character types seem to be frigid as if they had a "feeling phobia" or fear of letting themselves experience the usual human emotions. Some others seem to be "hyperemotional" as a reaction formation against emotions. Some develop reaction formations against reaction formations. The reactive character traits seem to be a kind of armor used by the ego in its struggle against both instincts and environment.[74]

Apparently character somehow depends on the individual's history of libidinal development. Accordingly, character types can be distinguished. Freud and Karl Abraham, one of the earliest and most capable associates of Freud, have suggested the following character types, related to the developmental stages and points of fixation.[75] Oral

[74] William Reich, *Character Analysis*, Orgone Institute, 1945.
[75] Karl Abraham, *Selected Papers on Psychoanalysis*, Hogarth, 1927.

fixation results in *oral character* traits. This fixation is a result of either an abundant or an insufficient oral satisfaction. In the first case, the individual may develop an overdependent but optimistic attitude; in the case of oral deprivation depressive and aggressive tendencies may develop. In both cases orally fixated individuals demand narcissistic supplies from without, are self-centered, and wish to be helped by others. The oral-erotic character types are compulsive eaters, drinkers, smokers, and talkers, unless these tendencies were hidden by reaction formations or successfully resolved by sublimations. All oral character types are selfish "takers," always "hungry" and acquisitive, and desirous of "swallowing" more food or more love objects or more knowledge, depending on the specific nature of reactions and sublimations of their oral cravings.

Abraham suggested distinguishing between the early oral or oral-passive and the late oral-sadistic or oral-aggressive phases. The oral-passive fixation relates to sucking in the first months of the child's life. The oral-passive character type is passive and overdependent. He is easily disappointed when his cravings are thwarted and he does not take frustrations too well. He seems to believe that the world owes him maternal support and affection, and in his optimistic moods he hopes to receive it. The oral-aggressive type is related to frustrations in nursing, to biting and chewing; he is usually sarcastic, pessimistic, and cannibalistic and he tends to destroy his love objects. He seems to believe that the world owes him support and affection, but he doubts whether he will get what he wants. He often alienates his friends and displays disagreeable and offensive behavior as if trying to force them to give him the love and affection that the world owes him.

The *anal-erotic* stage has been subdivided by Abraham into anal-expulsive and anal-retentive; in both substages the conflict around toilet training leads toward peculiar anal fixations.[76] Orderliness, parsimony, and obstinacy are the three main anal character traits. Training for cleanliness may lead to compulsive behavior in washing, cleaning, and keeping one's own body and possessions extremely neat. Parsimony develops usually in the anal-retentive stage. Parsimony is an expression of the tendency to retain what one possesses. Feces are the prototype of transferable possession and at the anal-retentive stage the child is prone to postpone elimination and to enjoy retention. Anal character types are often stingy and unwilling to part even with useless objects. Obstinacy characterizes the anal-sadistic period. It is the child's first rebellion against the mother. The child refuses to give her the feces or he expresses the wish to eliminate indiscriminately in disregard of her toilet-training demands.

[76] Sigmund Freud, "Character and Anal Eroticism," in *Collected Papers*, Vol. II, pp. 45–50.

The *urethral character* type is ambitious, impatient, and envious. It includes oral traits and a tendency toward passivity. The urethral personality types have usually been punished for *enuresis* by being put to shame. The bed-wetter would like to hide his deeds and to avoid shame; hence the "burning ambition" not to be shamed anymore by anyone and the feeling of envy toward anyone who has made his life a success and has not been humiliated. The urethral personality type lacks, however, the persistence necessary for being successful. He often expects, in an oral fashion, that some outside forces will help him to attain success and glory.

The *phallic character* type develops as a reaction formation to castration fear. Self-assuredness, boastfulness, and aggressiveness are the main phallic personality traits, combined with a narcissistic self-love, vanity, and sensitiveness. Exhibitionistic and overtly aggressive behavior is a reaction formation to castration fear. The ambivalent feelings of need and fear of love, of courage and timidity are symptomatic for the phallic character, who tries to overcompensate by aggressiveness and to cover up his inner fear of castration and doubts concerning his own masculinity. Overtly daring and boisterous behavior is the façade behind which timidity and anxiety are hidden.

In girls penis envy may be either resolved or sublimated, or it may lead to reactive character traits. Penis envy may be elaborated either into a wish-fulfillment and assumption of a masculine role or into a vindictive feminine type with a tendency toward being humiliated and toward humiliating men.

Normal adulthood is characterized by the *genital character*. The supremacy of the genital zone over other erotogenic areas, the subordination of all genital aims to the normal heterosexual urge, and the proper choice of a heterosexual love object are the main elements of the genital character.

In accordance with the economic principle sublimation is facilitated when great quantities of excitation are discharged. When too much instinctual energy is blocked, sublimation is almost impossible, and reaction formations usually take place. In the genital character sexual energy finds proper outlets; emotions are not warded off but used by the ego. Pregenital impulses are partly subordinated to the normal heterosexual function and serve as a forepleasure; they become partially sublimated. The ego becomes the master of the total mental apparatus. The diversified instinctual impulses become coordinated, the Oedipus complex is resolved, and harmony is established between id, ego, and superego. The more harmonious the character, the more normal and better adjusted the individual.

7. SOCIETY AND CULTURE

The Socialization of the Individual

Freud's starting point was the individual, always the individual. The neonate, Freud believed, is neither social nor antisocial. He is asocial or presocial. His first feelings and motions turn toward himself in a narcissistic love. Soon the child becomes aware of the presence of need-gratifying objects and persons and part of his libido becomes invested (cathected) in them.

Pleasure-procuring objects and persons facilitate the development of object love, which is the prototype of any social relationship. The development of the child depends on social forces; in unfavorable environmental circumstances, the development of object love and social relations may be impaired and severe narcissistic fixations may occur. In normal cases, the child develops primitive and ambivalent social feelings in the oral stage. The first object love is ambivalent. The child tends to swallow what he loves and to love what he swallows; love and hate are combined in "cannibalistic" feelings.

Incorporation and identification represent the early, archaic pattern of interpersonal relations. A new type of relation starts with the development of consideration of the loved object, which begins at the anal stage. The child begins to see the love object as an independent entity and not as something that has to be swallowed and incorporated or that may swallow and incorporate him. The sensual aim becomes inhibited, and the child seems to have given up the wish to possess the object. Instead he begins to care for the survival of the object in order to preserve it. This new feeling of "tenderness" starts usually at the anal stage, when, according to Karl Abraham, retention pleasure becomes stronger than elimination pleasure.

Tenderness and aim inhibition are fundamental factors in social relations in adulthood although some individuals never become fully capable of consideration of other persons and take their friends for granted and some others are unable to develop aim-inhibited and desexualized friendly attitudes. The normal adult, however, is capable of having consideration for other individuals ·and of developing aim-inhibited and friendly feelings toward them.

Aim-inhibited feelings enable individuals to relate to one another in a nonsexual manner. The child-parent relationship, after the resolution of the Oedipus complex, becomes aim-inhibited and tender. The same applies to the normal parent-child relationship. Aim-inhibited impulses are the main factor in friendship between individuals. Since these impulses, wrote Freud, "are not capable of really complete satisfaction, they are especially adapted to create permanent ties; while those instincts (drives) which are directly sexual incur a loss of energy each time they are satisfied and must wait to be renewed by a fresh accumulation of sexual libido, so that meanwhile the objects may have been changed. The inhibited instincts (drives) are capable of any degree of admixture with the uninhibited. . . . It is well known how easily erotic wish develops out of emotional relations of a friendly character, based upon appreciation and admiration."[77]

As mentioned before, the aim-inhibited feelings start at the anal stage, but they become more fully developed at the end of the phallic period. Individuals with powerful phallic fixations are boisterous and not too considerate of other persons. In order to become well adjusted and capable of sharing social norms and responsibilities, an individual has to renounce his parents as love objects and identify himself with their norms and standards.

No one is socially adjusted without a fully developed superego, which is the carrier of social norms and values within one's mental system. As explained before, the superego is born toward the end of the phallic stage as a result of the Oedipus conflict. The image of the beloved parent becomes internalized in the child's mind and forms the superego. Very often the beloved parents stand as a symbol of perfection and as a model to be imitated, thus facilitating an idealistic pattern of social behavior.

In some cases "the object serves as a substitute for some unattained ego ideal of our own. We love it on account of the perfections which we have striven to reach for our own ego, and which we should now like to procure in this roundabout way as a means of satisfying our narcissism. . . . The ego becomes more and more unassuming and modest, and the object more and more sublime and precious, until at last it gets possession of the entire self-love of the ego, whose self-sacrifice thus follows as a natural consequence. The object has, so to speak, consumed the ego. Traits of humility, of the limitation of narcissism, and of self-injury occur in every case of being in love; in the extreme case they are only intensified, and as a result of the withdrawal of the sensual claims they remain in solitary supremacy."[78]

This kind of attitude is not only aim-inhibited. The aim-inhibited object (or person) becomes a model for imitation, an image of perfection, and a symbol of a goal to be attained. Such an attitude is found in adult life in the admiration for heroes, in submissiveness to leaders, in readiness for self-sacrifice for a lofty ideal.

[77] Freud, *Group Psychology and the Analysis of the Ego*, p. 119.
[78] *Ibid.*, pp. 74–75.

The Origin of the Social Order

In 1912 Freud published a volume entitled *Totem and Tabu.* In this monograph he introduced a hypothesis concerning the primitive forms of human society. In accordance with Darwin, Freud suggested that the primitive society was a horde governed by a despotic male, the "father" who "owned" all females in the horde. The primal father prevented his sons from gratification of their sexual needs. After the father's death, the youngest son, the mother's favorite, became the father's successor as the head of the horde or tribe.

The beginning of totemism was traced from the rebellion of all males against the tyrant. The paternal horde was transformed into a brotherhood of sons who killed the father, cut his body in pieces, and decided that no one would take his place. In order to preserve the new social order and to prevent another tyranny, the brothers established totem prohibition. Apparently, they could not prevent each other from forming new families with the male as the head of the family. But now, instead of one large family with a tyrannical father, there were several families whose fathers had to come to terms with one another.

Prior to the killing of the father, the sons lived under a permanent castration threat. After he was killed, the castration threat became "internalized" in the form of guilt feelings. Rituals have to be related to the castration complex. Freud discusses this problem as follows: "Castration has a place, too, in the Oedipus legend, for the blinding with which Oedipus punished himself after the discovery of his crime is, by the evidence of dreams, a symbolic substitute for castration. The possibility cannot be excluded that a phylogenetic memory-trace may contribute to the extraordinarily terrifying effect of the threat—a memory-trace from prehistory of the human family, when the jealous father would actually rob his son of his genitals if the latter interfered with him in rivalry for a woman. The primeval custom of circumcision, another symbolic substitute for castration, is only intelligible if it is an expression of subjection to the father's will (compare the puberty rites of primitive people). No investigation has yet been made of the form taken by the events described above among races and in civilizations which do not suppress masturbation among children."[79]

To Freud culture meant restraint. Social order developed out of restrictions imposed upon the two driving forces: sex and destruction. Incest and murder were forbidden. The killed father became totem, and all females inside the tribe became taboo.

[79] Freud, *Outline of Psychoanalysis,* pp. 92–93, footnote.

The Origin of Leadership

Freud assumed definite analogies between ontogenesis and phylogenesis, and he traced the origin of any human group from the primal horde. Primitive men ascribed to their chieftain magic and uncanny power. They were afraid of their leader and believed that it was dangerous to contradict him or to disobey his orders, or sometimes even to look straight into his eyes.

The same type of relationship applies to hypnosis when the hypnotist takes over the father role and reactivates in the subject the archaic inheritance of subservience to the father, to whom the subject surrenders his own will. Some uncanny and coercive elements can be found in the relationship of group members to their leader. In the minds of the group members the leader takes over the role of their superego. Freud believed that "a group is a collection of individuals who have introduced the same person in their superego, and on the basis of this common factor have identified themselves with one another in their ego. This naturally only holds for groups who have a leader."[80] The group is patterned upon a family with the head as a father substitute and the group members united in their admiration for and obedience of the primal father. They are acting under the assumption of being equally loved by the powerful father. "The indestructible strength of the family as a natural group formation rests upon the fact that this necessary presupposition of the father's equal love can have a real application in the family,"[81] said Freud. Accordingly, the phenomena of transference and hypnosis are explained by the fact that the therapist is perceived by the patient as the loving and omnipotent father who takes over their superego and controls their behavior.

Freud was influenced by Le Bon's study of the crowd and accepted the idea that individuals believe in a group as if they were under the spell of a coercing force and not as separate and independent entities.[82] Le Bon introduced the concept of group spirit, which was not accepted by Freud. Instead Freud introduced the concepts of the primal father and of transference.

Two main features of collective behavior were singled out by Freud. The inhibition of intellectual functions, such as criticism, judgment, and logical reasoning, and intensification of emotions, both hate and destructiveness and love and devotion, are the outstanding characteristics of

[80] Freud, *New Introductory Lectures in Psychoanalysis,* p. 96.
[81] Freud, *Group Psychology and the Analysis of the Ego,* p. 95.
[82] Gustave Le Bon, *The Crowd: A Study of the Popular Mind,* Fisher & Unwin, 12th impression, 1920.

group behavior. These two symptoms are typical for the transference situation in psychoanalytic therapy. Once the patient sees in the therapist the parent substitute, his intellectual functions become partially inhibited and his emotions intensified. This regression facilitates the emotional re-education which is the aim of psychoanalytic therapy. Group behavior can be interpreted in a similar manner: in the transference relationship to the leader the members of a group admire him and obey his orders while their capacity for criticism is reduced and their emotionality increased.

The Price for Civilization

Society cannot permit full freedom of action for each individual because absolute freedom for one may mean slavery for others. Some curtailing of individual freedom and inhibition of instinctual wishes is necessary for the survival of the society. Social norms grew out of this necessity. It is quite easy, wrote Freud, for a barbarian "to be healthy: for a civilized man the task is a hard one. The desire for a powerful and uninhibited ego may seem to us intelligible, but, as it is shown by the times we live in, it is in the profoundest sense antagonistic to civilization. And since the demands of civilization are represented by family education, we must remember to find a place too in the etiology of the neuroses for this biological character of the human species—the prolonged period of its childhood dependence."[83] The long childhood of humans and the inability of the human child to face the exigencies of life call for protective and restrictive actions of the parent. The parental restraint of the child's freedom and the thwarting of his instinctual wishes must lead to an inner conflict in the child's mind.

At this point, Freud concluded: "We cannot escape the conclusion that neuroses could be avoided . . . if the child's sexual life were allowed free play, as happens among many primitive races." But, on the other hand, this early repression must effect one's readiness for cultural growth, because "The instinctual demands, being forced aside from direct satisfaction, are compelled to take new directions which lead to substitutive satisfaction . . . and may become desexualized." One may conclude "that much of our most highly valued cultural heritage has been acquired at the cost of sexuality and by the restriction of sexual motive forces."[84]

The restriction of the destructive instincts is even more important than the restriction of sex. No society could ever have survived without imposing definite prohibition of the use of force. Inner conflicts and fights could destroy the social organization and taboos have been imposed on the use of force within the boundaries of family and tribe. The

[83] Freud, *Outline of Psychoanalysis*, p. 85.
[84] *Ibid.*, p. 114.

thwarted aggressiveness becomes internalized and stored in the superego, where it may turn against one's own person in acts of self-destructiveness. Freud explained this danger as follows: "When the superego begins to be formed considerable amounts of the aggressive instinct become fixated within the ego and operate there in a self-destructive fashion. This is one of the dangers to health to which mankind becomes subject on the path to cultural development. The holding back of aggressiveness is in general unhealthy and leads to illness. A person in a fit of rage often demonstrates how the transition from restrained aggressiveness to self-destructiveness is effected, by turning his aggressiveness against himself. . . ."[85]

Religion

In his studies of sociology and anthropology Freud could hardly evade the problem of religious feelings. He even went so far as to publish a volume on the origin of Judaism and the monotheistic religions.[86] Since this monograph goes far beyond the scope of psychology, we shall not deal with it here but confine ourselves to presenting Freud's view on religion as a social-psychological phenomenon.

Freud regarded religious feeling as a craving for protection and power. In early narcissism the child has the feeling of omnipotence. Gradually he must give up this feeling and instead ascribe it to his parents, who, so he believes, are omnipotent. Unsatisfactory object relations and frustrations lead to a secondary narcissism, which is the need for regaining the feeling of omnipotence and the wish for a reunion with the omnipotent beings. This is, Freud says, the source of religious feelings. The powerless individual strives to attain power by introjecting the powerful figures or a part of them or being incorporated by them.

Religion is, in Freud's judgment, "an attempt to get control over the sensory world in which we are placed by means of the wish-world which we have developed inside us as a result of biological and psychological necessities. But it cannot achieve its end. Its doctrines carry with them the stamp of the times in which they originated, the ignorant childhood days of the human race. Its consolations desire no trust. Experience teaches us that the world is not a nursery."[87]

Any religious group is based on the "illusion"[88] that there is a head or spiritual being who loves all the members of his group with equal love. This head is the father surrogate for all the group members, who consider themselves brothers in their faith. Several religious rites imitate brotherhood and sisterhood, and gods are called by the name of father.

[85] *Ibid.*, p. 23.
[86] Freud, *Moses and Monotheism.*
[87] Freud, *New Introductory Lectures in Psychoanalysis*, p. 229.
[88] Sigmund Freud, *The Future of an Illusion*, Liveright, 1928.

Religious feelings contain the elements of regression to childhood and a wish to be taken care of by a loving parent or parent surrogate and to live in a childhood-paradise united with family members in the love and admiration for the protecting father.

People who do not belong to the community of believers, who do not love the head or the god and whom he does not love, stand outside this tie. "Therefore, a religion, even if it calls itself the religion of love, must be hard and unloving to those who do not belong to it. Fundamentally indeed every religion is in this same way a religion of love for all those whom it embraces; while cruelty and intolerance towards those who do not belong to it are natural to every religion." But their love within the group and hate to outsiders applies to any other group which is based on libidinal ties. In fact today religious groups represent less of love and hate, and more of inhibition of libido. "If today that intolerance no longer shows itself so violent and cruel as in former centuries," Freud said, "we can scarcely conclude that there has been a softening in human manners. The cause is rather to be found in the undeniable weakening of religious feelings and the libidinal ties which depend upon them. If another group tie takes the place of the religious one—and the socialistic tie seems to be succeeding in doing so—, then there will be the same intolerance towards outsiders as in the age of the Wars of Religion; and if differences between scientific opinions could ever attain a similar significance for groups, the same result would again be repeated with this new motivation."[89]

Religion, Freud said, satisfies man's desire for knowledge and competes with science. Religion assures men of protection in face of the dangers and mishaps of life and promises them a happy end to their misfortunes. No science can do that. Science tries to help people to avoid misery or to alleviate it, but no science can offer a panacea for all human discomforts. The third task of religion is to guide men by a system of directions and prohibitions. Science cannot do that either. The business of science is to discover facts and to find their interrelationships. Some recommendations for behavior can be deduced from scientific facts and theories but science cannot offer directions for behavior. Religion combines teaching of the origin and nature of the universe with ethical precepts, with assurances of protection and happiness as reward for fulfillment of these precepts.

Thus, Freud contended that "the religious man's picture of the creation of the universe is the same as his picture of his own creation." This is why the idea of cosmogony of the God-Creator-Father is combined with ethical commandments and promises of comfort and protection. The Father, the symbol of parenthood, is the creator of life, the source of ethical norms, and the punishing and protecting force.

[89] Freud, *Group Psychology and the Analysis of the Ego,* pp. 50–51.

8. PSYCHOANALYSIS AS A PHILOSOPHY OF LIFE

With the analysis of the role of civilization and religion psycho-analysis crossed the boundaries of the empirical sciences and entered the realm of speculation. This seems to be the logical and inevitable outcome of psychoanalytic inquiry. Once Freud embarked upon the study of the problems men face in life, he could hardly stop at the gates of problems hitherto considered the domain of philosophy. Psycho-analysis had to cross this border too.

Freud seemingly avoided ethical and philosophical problems but he could not evade them. He suggested that the psychoanalytic therapist remain neutral and noncommittal on ethical issues. It would not be proper for a psychoanalyst to impose his moral standards on his pa-tients or to offer them a definite set of values. Psychoanalytic therapy aims at helping the individual to overcome infantile fixations and regressions and to become a mature adult. Moralizing would not help.

Moreover, one of Freud's endeavors was to discover the truth about human beliefs and attitudes, and the moral foundations of human be-havior have been scrutinized by the psychoanalytic investigation. Freud rejected the idea of a superhuman origin of the moral conscience. He wrote: "The philosopher Kant once declared that nothing proved to him the greatness of God more convincingly than the starry heavens and the moral conscience within us. The stars are unquestionably superb but, where conscience is concerned, God has been guilty of an uneven and careless piece of work, for a great many men have only a limited share of it or scarcely enough to be worth mentioning."[90]

Morality starts in childhood as it develops as a part of personality development. Small children are notoriously amoral. The first source of their morality is an external power, the parental authority which inhibits their pleasure-seeking impulses. Parents influence their children by affec-tion and punishment; punishment acts in two ways—as a threat of pain and as loss of love. Fear of punishment and of loss of love and reward for compliance are the main sources of children's compliance with the moral demands of the parents. To be bad means to do things that annoy parents and invite their grief and to be good means to do things that win their approval.

This state of affairs is carried over by adult men into their religious beliefs. Men believe that there is a superior, father-like power that re-wards people for good behavior, punishes wickedness, and protects human life. This belief carries over the experiences of early life when, Freud says, each child is "brought up to know its social duties by means of a system of love-rewards and punishment, and in this way it is taught

[90] Freud, *New Introductory Lectures in Psychoanalysis*, p. 88.

that its security in life depends on its parents (and subsequently other people) loving it and being able to believe in its love for them."[91]

The same applies to the phylogenetic development. The primitive man was forced by society to restrain his pleasure-seeking impulses. The norms established by the society for the protection of its members became internalized in the minds of individuals. Conscience is basically the fear of society; it is the inner restraint of the individual who is "virtually an enemy of culture," which is imposed on him. Moral and cultural restraints stem from without and the majority of men obey the cultural prohibitions "only under the pressure of external force . . . as long as it is an object of fear. This also holds good for those so-called moral cultural demands."[92]

There is another source of moral behavior—love for the other person. "Love for oneself knows only one barrier—love for others, love for objects. . . . Love alone acts as the civilizing factor in the sense that it brings a change from egoism to altruism."[93] Once people share the satisfaction of their needs, the libido chooses them as its objects. Members of a group primarily established for narcissistic purposes begin to like each other and cathect libido in each other. This object cathexis necessarily limits the narcissistic love of oneself.

On this point Freud's conclusions are quite similar to those arrived at independently by Piaget in the study of the child's morality.

For a Scientific Weltanschauung

Freud was a stanch follower of empiricism and positivism. It was quite possible, he said, that at the time of the early animism men had more self-confidence than we have today; although the demons of animism were hostile to men, men had considerable self-confidence derived from magic practices. In their fight against the forces of nature they used magic, which is "the first forerunner of our modern technology." They believed in the omnipotence of their thoughts and ascribed magic power to the spoken word. It took quite a long time for men to learn to observe natural phenomena and interpret them with scientific caution. Scientific inquiry gradually replaced magic, empirical observation took the place of anthropomorphic images, and criticism and logic were introduced instead of the wishful thinking of the early ages. Science is never as certain as magic. Unfortunately, the philosophy of our times has still preserved "essential traits of animistic modes of thought such as the over-estimation of the magic of words and the belief that real processes in the external world follow the lines laid down by our thoughts. It is, to be sure, an

[91] *Ibid.*, p. 224.
[92] Freud, *Future of an Illusion*, p. 19.
[93] Freud, *Group Psychology and the Analysis of the Ego*, p. 57.

animism without magical practices," wrote Freud.[94] Apparently Freud was opposed to the idealistic German philosophy and especially to Kant and Hegel and rejected the idea that the universe is ruled by the laws of logic.

The only source of human knowledge is a verified observation of empirical data. The results of these observations can be "intellectually manipulated" and put together into a system of generalizations and laws that represent the results of empirical research.

"It is inadmissable to declare," said Freud, "that science is one field of human intellectual activity, and that religion and philosophy are others at least as valuable, and that science has no business to interfere with the other two, that they all have an equal claim to truth, and that everyone is free to choose when he shall draw his convictions and in what he shall place his belief. Truth cannot be tolerant and cannot admit compromise or limitations, and scientific research must adopt an uncompromisingly critical attitude towards any other power that seeks to usurp any part of its province."[95]

Interpretation of History

History has attracted the attention of several psychologists. One may consider historical events as adventures in human nature and apply psychology to the interpretation of history or utilize historical data for psychological studies.[96]

Freud felt that the economic factor cannot be the sole determinant in human societies. He criticized Karl Marx for overlooking cultural and psychological factors and said that Marxism in Russia had acquired "an almost uncanny resemblance to what it was opposing," i.e., to the Czarist autocracy. Freud would agree that economic factors play a considerable role in history, but human nature has always been the driving power in history.

In 1933 Freud wrote: "It is probable that the so-called materialistic conceptions of history err in that they underestimate this factor. They brush it aside with the remark that the 'ideologies' of mankind are nothing more than resultants of their economic situation at any given moment or superstructures built upon it. That is the truth, but very probably it is not the whole truth. Mankind never lives completely in the present; the ideologies of the superego perpetuate the past, the traditions of the race and the people, which yield but slowly to the influence of the present and to new developments, and, so long as they work through the super-

---

[94] Freud, *New Introductory Lectures in Psychoanalysis*, p. 226.

[95] *Ibid.*, p. 219.

[96] Wolman, "Historical Laws—Do They Exist?" *Proceedings of the Xth International Congress of Philosophy*, Amsterdam, 1948 (abstract).

ego, play an important part in man's life, quite independently of economic conditions."[97]

Freud offered a psychoanalytic interpretation of history. History is made by men. Men and their instincts, emotions, inhibitions, reaction formations, and sublimations determine the course of history. The two great instinctual forces, Eros and Thanatos, live forever. Men have always been lovers and haters and the power of hatred has never ceased to incite men to wars.

There are two sources of hostility. The one is the primary force of threats, of instinct of death and destruction, which may be directed either against self or against the other man. The other one is self-love or narcissism. Narcissism works for the self-assertion of the individual and, in group processes, for the aggressive attitudes of groups toward people who do not belong.

This is why, said Freud, "closely related races keep one another at arm's length. . . . We are no longer astonished that greater differences should lead to an almost insuperable repugnance. . . ." One could not be too optimistic about the future of mankind, nor expect some miraculous solution of human conflicts.

Freud was highly critical of interpretation of history by some sort of "obscure Hegelian philosophy." The truth is that man and his instinctual forces determine the course of historical events. Man and not *"der absolute Geist,"* men and not dialectics, men and not logical systems make history. Can men harness their instinctual forces and make them work for peace?

The future of mankind, said Freud, depends on "whether and to what extent the cultural process developed in it will succeed in mastering the arrangements of communal life caused by the human instinct of aggression and self-destruction. In this connection perhaps the phase through which we are passing at this moment deserves special interest. Men have brought their powers of subduing the forces of nature to such a pitch that by using them they could now very easily exterminate one another to the last man. They know this—hence arises a great part of their current unrest, their dejection, their mood of apprehension. And now it may be expected that the other of the two 'heavenly forces,' the eternal Eros, will put forth his strength so as to maintain himself alongside of his equally immortal adversary."[98] This task can be accomplished, if ever, by means of education.

Education

"One of the most important social tasks of education is to restrain, confine, and subject to an individual control (itself identical with the

[97] Freud, *New Introductory Lecture in Psychoanalysis,* pp. 95–96.
[98] Sigmund Freud, *Civilization and Its Discontents,* Hogarth, 1930.

demands of society) the sexual instinct when it breaks forth in the form of reproductive function. . . . Without this [restraint—B. W.] the instinct would break all bounds and the laboriously erected structure of civilization would be swept away," wrote Freud.[99] Later on, as he developed the theory of the death instinct, emphasis was put on the need to restrain both instincts, and especially the aggressive one.

Civilization is built up at the cost of aggressive and sexual impulses, which must be partly repressed and partly sublimated. Each society demands that individuals limit aggression and mitigate sex. No society can survive without inhibition of instincts. The child must be educated in a way that will enable him to live in a society.

Freud wrote: "The child has to learn to control its instincts. To grant it complete freedom, so that it obeys all its impulses without any restriction, is impossible. . . . The function of education, therefore, is to inhibit, forbid and suppress, and it has at all times carried out this function to admiration. But we have learned from analysis that it is the very suppression of instincts that involves the danger of neurotic illness. Education has therefore to stem its way between the Scylla of giving the instincts free play and the Charybdis of frustrating them. . . . If we can find an optimum of education which will carry out its task ideally, then we may hope to abolish one of the factors in the etiology of neurotic illness, viz. the influence of accidental infantile traumas."[100]

9. CONCLUDING REMARKS ON PSYCHOANALYSIS

The Areas Covered

Three periods in Freud's work can be distinguished. In the first stage Freud, as a practicing psychiatrist, was mostly interested in neurosis and other aberrations from the normal behavior. In the second stage, which started around 1900 and lasted until about 1920, Freud developed a highly complex psychological theory. Although this theory was derived from clinical experience, it eventually became a general theory of personality rather than a study of mental disorder. In the third stage, after 1920, while Freud kept modifying his clinical theories and techniques, his main interest shifted toward the most general and universal problems of humanity such as war and peace, civilization, religion, etc.[101]

It is, indeed, difficult to believe that all this was done by one man. Judged by the areas covered by research, by its dimensions and diversity, Freud's work is impressive and perhaps unique. It could not be expected,

---

[99] Freud, *General Introduction to Psychoanalysis*, p. 273.
[100] Freud, *New Introductory Lectures in Psychoanalysis*, p. 204.
[101] In 1914 Freud wrote: "Psychoanalysis has never claimed to provide a complete theory of human mentality as a whole." *Collected Papers*, Vol. I, p. 338.

however, that such a grandiose undertaking could represent a uniform and equal degree of accomplishment in all the various areas covered by Freud's searching and indefatigable mind. Although Freud was quite consistent in his method of theory construction, he treated some problems rather passim, and in some fields his conclusions seem not to be a necessary inference from empirical data.

Some Unresolved Problems

One of the areas insufficiently clarified by Freud is perception. Freud said that the ego controls the motor apparatus, and the images of the external world are communicated to the id by the perceptual system. But the nature of both the motor apparatus and the perceptual system requires further clarification. The relationship between them and the ego is still another unresolved problem.

Another problem related to perception is the question of the perceptory functions of the id. The id is supposed to be "blind" and incapable of perception. It might well be asked whether the neonate, whose mental apparatus consists of the id only, is capable of perceiving. It is worth while to mention here Sullivan's hypothesis (cf. Chap. 9) concerning the "modes" of perception. The neonate's perceptions are probably diffused and often hallucinatory but still there are some perceptions. It is an unresolved problem whether empathy, telepathy, and other unconscious processes are functions of the id or of the archaic ego and what they actually are.

There has been some research in which Freud's clinical findings have been related to experimental psychology and learning theory, but there is still the unresolved question of relationship between learning on one side and fixation, regression, repression, etc., on the other (cf. Chap. 8).

Environmental Factors

Some writers, such as Clara Thompson,[102] maintain that Freud turned away from environmental factors to organic constitution. Thompson explains that originally Freud related hysteria to a premature sexual experience. Later on he discovered that the stories of childhood seduction often were fantasies or wishes of the patients themselves.

Actually Freud never turned away from environmental forces. Constitution and constellation, nature and nurture always were considered by Freud the two indispensable factors working together in shaping human fate. The instinctual forces are inherited and the developmental phases are embedded in the life of human organisms. What will ultimately evolve in human life is determined by the forces of environment that facilitate or prevent frustrations, fixations, and regressions, that make

[102] Clara Thompson, *Psychoanalysis: Evolution and Development*, Hermitage, 1953.

out of the "polymorphous pervert" which the infant is a normal and well-adjusted individual or an adult pervert. Freud strongly emphasized the impact of environment upon mental health and disorder. The sociologically oriented schools of psychoanalysis have some important ideas and observations, but their criticism of Freud is not always justified (cf. Chap. 9).

The Principle of Constancy

Freud's constancy principle can serve as the broadest framework for any theory of motivation. It represents a tension-relief continuum wittingly or unwittingly accepted by practically all psychologists. Horney's "safety and satisfaction" theory can be viewed as an effort to emphasize the social influences (safety) in obtaining gratification, i.e., in restoring the equilibrium. Adler's theory of compensation is more broadly conceived and represents the same striving to restore the balance. Sullivan's theory can be seen, in this respect, as an elaboration of Adler-Horney concepts of environmental influences that either create euphoria (the Freudian "bliss") by approval, or arouse anxiety by disapproval. Actually all psychoanalytic schools represent variations of the "constancy-homeostasis" principle.

The non-psychoanalytic schools utilize the same principle. Pavlov's reinforcement and extinction fall well in line with it. Hull's need-reduction theory and Tolman's physiological quiescence are applications of the same law. Goldstein's theory is par excellence a theory of homeostatic functioning of the human organism. Lewin's tension-relief theory is another example of the same principle.

An additional methodological advantage in acceptance of the principle of constancy relates to its universality. It would be in accordance with the scientific tradition to assume that the human mind is a part of nature and the general laws of the universe apply also to that fraction of the universe which psychology deals with.

Criticism of the Pleasure Theory

The subjective experience of this equilibrium was named by Freud pleasure-unpleasure. This part of his theory is quite vulnerable but not because scientific psychology must reject any subjectivistic or mentalistic or introspectionistic data. It would be, so this writer believes, extravagant to throw away the introspectively perceived data in order to satisfy some arbitrarily set principles of "pure science." Psychology cannot afford to give up this treasury and be left with the limited material produced by the rigorous method of external observation and experimentation.

However, there are some important reasons for doubts concerning the pleasure theory. Pleasure is, by definition, a mental process preceived, sensed, or experienced by the organism. As long as the organism is some-how aware or dimly aware on the conscious, preconscious, or unconscious level, the pleasure is a process to be accounted for.

But what happens if the organism is completely unaware of it and if nothing of the kind can be registered by the organism itself or by any observer? In such a case the pleasure principle becomes a hypothesis that evades proof. No evidence of any sort can be brought to prove it nor can any logical inference be applied in support of it. Freud assumed, e.g., that the neonate reacts with pleasure or unpleasure to stimuli. This can be inferred from the bulk of psychoanalytic theory and practice and, to a certain extent, it has been empirically proved by J. B. Watson, W. Stern, C. Bühler, and others.

Can the same be proved in regard to the lower functions of the human organism? In the discussion between the classical and neo-conditionists, Thorndike, Hull, Tolman, and Skinner seem to be in a stronger position than Pavlov, Watson, and Guthrie.

However, studies of conditioning in visceral organs conducted recently in Russia seem not to indicate anything of the kind of reward or pleasure assumed in visceral conditioning (cf. Chap. 2) and they are quite con-vincing. In other words, one may hypothetically conclude that at a certain point of phylogenetic and probably ontogenetic development the feeling of pleasure makes its appearance.

There is no evidence for and there are good methodological reasons against a universality of the pleasure principle. Would anyone assume that fertilization of plants, which corresponds biologically to sexual inter-course in mammals, is accompanied by any kind of sensation of pleasure?

Apparently the hedonic principle can explain a part of human behavior, and certain phenomena require an interpretation on an *ante-hedonic* level. On the other hand, certain human actions are probably *post-hedonic*, such as those involving moral responsibility, feeling of duty, idealism, self-sacrifice, and all other deeds of men in which not one's own happiness but the happiness of his fellow man is the motivating force.[103]

Freud was aware of these types of object relationships and found in them aim inhibition, tenderness, and sublimation. No new principle was introduced by Freud at this point, although new phenomena were ob-served. Obviously the pleasure and reality principles cannot be used here.

Freud felt the necessity to go beyond the pleasure principle in relation-ship to repetition-compulsion, sadism and masochism, and suicide. How-ever, repetition-compulsion can be easily explained by the constancy principle, and the instinct of death can hardly explain idealism. When a mother gives away the last piece of bread to her hungry child or when she

---

[103] The writer's point of view is briefly presented in Chap. 15. More research is in progress and will be reported elsewhere.

runs into a fire to save her child, she does not do it for self-destructive purposes. Her only aim is to save the child and she is willing to risk pain and destruction. Neither pleasure nor reality principle nor death wish could be applied in this case. Analogously, when men sacrifice their lives for their religious or political convictions, when they fight for freedom and justice it is neither for pleasure nor out of self-hate. Some other, post-hedonic interpretation should be introduced.

The Death Instincts

Freud's theory of death instincts has stirred a great deal of controversy. Even the orthodox Freudian Fenichel has been critical of Freud and said that "the speculative basis is the conservative character of the instincts, as characterized by the constancy principle, namely the fact that instincts tend toward getting rid of tensions. But there is also a phenomenon that seems to run contrary to the constancy principle, namely a hunger for stimuli, seen mostly in the sexual instincts."[104]

Moreover, Fenichel said, the idea of a death instinct is "neither necessary nor useful" and there is no need to assume "two basically opposite kinds of instincts, the aim of one being relaxation and death, the aim of the other being a binding to higher units." "The thesis of an instinct source that makes the organism react to stimuli with drives toward 'instinct actions' which then change the source in an appropriate manner, cannot be applied to a death instinct."[105]

Several other hypotheses have been introduced and some of them will be discussed in the following chapters. One thing is certain: there is a great deal of aggressiveness and destructiveness in human behavior, and practically all mental disorder entails profound destructive tendencies.[106]

Freud's Method

One may find more shortcomings and more unresolved problems. Some of them have been taken up by Freud's disciples and resolved in a manner which would not have been approved by Freud. A great deal of criticism has come from experimental psychology.

Yet Freud's work is undoubtedly the single greatest contribution to psychology. While some investigators have limited the study to mental phenomena visible from within (introspectionists) and others to phenomena observable from without (behaviorists), Freud dealt with the totality of mental life including the most obscure and inaccessible regions of the mind. It seems that Freud, luckily for himself and for generations

---

[104] Fenichel, *Psychoanalytic Theory of Neurosis,* p. 58.

[105] *Ibid.,* p. 60.

[106] Benjamin B. Wolman, "Psychotherapy with Latent Schizophrenics," *American Journal of Psychotherapy,* 1959, 13, 343–359.

of psychologists, avoided the mistake of speedily erected rigid theoretical structures. Herbart (cf. Chap. 1) is the best example of such a hurry; having a few unproved observations Herbart developed a series of mathematical functions supposed to explain the most complex mental processes. It seems that some contemporary scientists, even men of such stature as Hull or Lewin, have tried to present the complexity of mental life in a series of rigid mathematical propositions.

Wasn't the unprecise, nonmathematical, nonexperimental, and nonrigorous Freud more sound, more scientific, more knowledge-producing, more promotive of scientific inquiry than anyone else? Freud's scientific policy was cautious approximation. In discussing, e.g., the problem of pleasure and unpleasure, he wrote in 1920: "This is the most obscure and inaccessible region of the mind, and, since we cannot avoid contact with it, the least rigid hypothesis, it seems to me, will be best."[107] And, inasmuch as any scientific inquiry strives toward quantification and experimental proof, Freud's cautious empiricism may prove to be the most rewarding method.

[107] Freud, *Beyond the Pleasure Principle*, p. 2.

CHAPTER 7

Individual and Analytic Psychologies

1. ALFRED ADLER: INDIVIDUAL PSYCHOLOGY

The Early Schism

Adler and Jung represent a schism in psychoanalysis as it was formulated before the outbreak of the First World War. While the main body of psychoanalytic theory continued to grow, the separate branches grew too. Today the common past forms the main link between the splinter groups of Adler and Jung and the main body of the psychoanalytic movement. Each theory went far in its own direction, and today there are deep differences among the three psychological theories. Though all three have common roots, they no longer form one body of data nor do they have much in common in their concepts and theory.

Yet it is rather difficult to understand Adler or Jung outside of the context of their rebellion against Freud. Most of Adler's and Jung's ideas are related to their controversy with Freud, as if they were repeatedly saying, "On this point I agreed with Freud and on that I disagreed."

In the years 1911–12 Freud's theory was formulated in terms of libido-sex and ego-self-preservation instincts. The theory of the death instinct, of the superego, and the further development of the theory of ego, anxiety, and defense mechanisms came later. Adler's rebellion started with the problem: What is the driving power in man? Is it the hedonistic libido? Or the self-preservation instinct? And in these crucial questions Adler's answer was entirely different from Freud's.

Adler was faithful to Freud in the emphasis on the role played by early childhood in personality development. Adler believed that all significant attitudes of a man could be traced back to early childhood and that the nursery years are the formative years for all man's future attitudes. Yet Adler rejected Freud's theory of developmental stages and did not approve of the universality of the Oedipus complex.

Adler owes to Freud the idea of unconscious motivation, dream interpretation, and symptom formation. However, Adler did not accept Freud's theory of "mind-topography."

The Impact of Kulturwissenschaft

Freud's theory was built on the foundations laid by the natural sciences, especially biology. Charles Darwin's theory of evolution and adjustment, Ernst Haeckel's principle of biogenetics, the theories of preservation of energy and homeostasis, and a strict determinism form the bases of psychoanalysis (cf. Chap. 6, section 1). Although Freud embarked upon a methodological non-reductionism and formulated a full-fledged psychogenic theory of mental disorder in contradistinction to neurological theories, he postulated that mental energy was a sort of unexplained derivative of the energy that activates all living substance.

Adler's rebellion was directed against the biologically oriented psychoanalysis and led in the direction of the *Kulturwissenschaft* (cf. Chap. 1, section 1, and Chap. 10, section 3). Freud considered men as a part of the animate nature and traced the instinctual forces from man's ancestors. The instincts, said Freud, were the bridge between physiology and psychology, and they are the driving power in men.

Adler leaned heavily on the *Kulturwissenschaft* and believed men were driven by "creative power." It was a purely human force, not derived from biological factors. Adler, like all "understanding" psychologists (cf. Chap. 10), believed in the uniqueness of human nature and in the uniqueness of each individual. In the division of the sciences into natural and cultural sciences, as proposed by Windelband (*ibid.*), Freud belongs to the first category, Adler to the second.

Each individual is a unique case, an idiophenomenon. Wrote Adler: "Types, similarities, and approximate likenesses are often either entities that owe their existence merely to the poverty of our language, which is incapable of giving simple expression to the nuances that are always present, or they are results of a statistical probability. The evidence of their existence should never be allowed to degenerate into the setting up of a fixed rule. Such evidence cannot bring us nearer to the understanding of the individual case. It can only be used to throw light on a field of vision in which the individual case in its uniqueness must be found."[1]

Adler took up the discussion of the problem as it was presented by Dilthey and Windelband.

The Creative Power

Each individual always manifests himself as unique, be it in thinking, feeling, speaking, or acting. Even when two individuals do the same thing, it is still not the same. Each is endowed with an individual

[1] Heinz L. and Rowena R. Ansbacher, *The Individual Psychology of Alfred Adler,* Basic Books, 1956, pp. 193–194.

creative power, considered by Adler a third factor besides heredity and environment, for the creative power combines the innate potentialities and environmental influences into a movement toward overcoming of obstacles in one's path of life.

Thus the decisive factor in one's life is his *law of movement.* Adler believed that the establishment of the law of movement was the greatest step in the development of his theory. It is the way the individual arrives at the solution of his problems. It is the manner in which he goes about overcoming the obstacles in his life. The law of movement is entirely individual and unique for each person. Each individual can be characterized and recognized by his law of movement.

The child is born with a free creative power. This innate power is exposed to influences stemming from the child's organism and his environment. As a result of the interaction between his free creative power and these factors, the child chooses a path in life and a style of life. The free creative power is no longer free; it becomes involved in the total structure of the individual personality. It is the main determinant of personality because it utilizes the individual's heredity and environment.

Purposivism Versus Causality

The first principle of the individual psychology is *teleology.* Adler rejected the deterministic and mechanistic causation of Freud and moved in the direction of finality. This approach is shared by McDougall, Goldstein, and Tolman.

Adler wrote: "All psychic activities are given a direction, a previously determined goal. . . . *Every psychic phenomenon, if it is to give us any understanding of a person, can only be grasped and understood if regarded as a preparation for some goal.*" Consider the case of poor memory. "After excluding the possibility of all organic causes, we would ask ourselves what the objective of this weakness of memory is? . . . We should then have unmasked this weakness of memory as tendencious and could understand its importance as a weapon against a contemplated undertaking. In every test of ability we should then expect to find the deficiency due to the secret life plan of an individual."[2]

The final goal alone is a sufficient explanatory principle for anything the individual does, strives, feels, and thinks.

Adler accepted the validity of causality in the natural sciences but believed that "In psychology we cannot speak of causality or determinism. . . . Even organ inferiorities are effective only to the extent that we wish. Man can raise these inferiorities to rank and dignity; he can make them a cause. A large number of people cannot resist the tendency to do

[2] Alfred Adler, *The Practice and Theory of Individual Psychology,* Routledge & Kegan Paul, 1929, pp. 4–5.

so. A child born with serious shortcomings is likely to take a timid, hostile attitude toward life, but this is not causally determined, for we know that the attitude can pass if we make things easier for him."[3]

Adler's teleology corresponds to a certain extent to Freud's theory of primary and secondary gains. In Freud's theory an individual may wish to get sick to avoid tension (primary gain) or to win social approval (secondary gain). Adler's teleological philosophy is borrowed from Vaihinger's ideas.[4] According to Vaihinger's idealistic positivism, man's life is guided by certain ideas or goals. Man acts upon these ideas "as if" they were true. These ideas are not necessarily true representatives of reality; they may be fictitious; yet they exercise an irresistible power over man's actions.

Man's actions, said Adler, are related to causes but they are dictated by goals. The history of mankind is not an account of causes and effects; it is a history of ideals, beliefs, and strivings. "The final goal alone can explain man's behavior," wrote Adler.

Goals may be conscious or unconscious. They are a teleological device of the "soul which seeks orientation." When an infant cries he cries not only because he is hungry but in order to get food or win sympathy.

Even dreams are subordinated to the general goal of life. "The dream strives to pave the way towards solving a problem by a metaphorical expression of it, by a comparison, an 'as if.' . . . In dreams we produce those pictures which will arouse the feelings and emotions which we need for our purposes, that is, for solving the problems confronting us at the time of the dream in accordance with the particular style of life which is ours."[5]

The Aggressive Drive

In the beginning Adler believed that the main driving force in men was the drive for self-assertion. In 1908 he wrote as follows: "From early childhood, we can say from the first day (first cry), we find a stand of the child toward the environment which cannot be called anything but hostile. If one looks for the cause of this position, one finds it determined by the difficulty of affording satisfaction for the organ. This circumstance as well as the further relationships of the hostile, belligerent position of the individual toward the environment indicate a drive toward fighting for satisfaction which I shall call 'aggressive drive.' . . . Fighting, wrestling, beating, biting, and cruelties show the aggression drive in its pure form. . . ."[6]

The aggression drive leads men into several occupational choices. "The

---

[3] Ansbacher, *op. cit.*, p. 91.
[4] Hans Vaihinger, *Philosophy of "As If,"* Harcourt, Brace, 1925.
[5] Ansbacher, *op. cit.*, p. 82.
[6] *Ibid.*, pp. 34–35.

occupations of judge, police officer, teacher, minister, physician, and many others are taken up by persons with a larger aggression drive and often show continuity with analogous children's games. . . . Whereas the aggression drive so often withdraws from our perception through turning against the self and through refinement and specialization, it becomes altogether a hidden-figure puzzle in the reversal into the antithesis of the aggression drive. Charity, sympathy, altruism and sensitive interest in misery represent new satisfactions on which the drive, which originally tended toward cruelty, feeds."[7]

When Adler introduced the aggressive drive in 1908, Freud objected to it. Twelve years later Freud himself introduced the theory of the instinct to death and destruction, but meanwhile Adler had reversed his position.

Adler was exposed to criticism for replacing Freud's libido theory by the aggressive drive. Gradually Adler relegated aggressiveness and antisocial strivings to the role of neurotic signs. The neurotic strives toward personal superiority while the normal individual strives toward the perfection which benefits all, wrote Adler in 1933.

Inferiority Complex

Adler's theory of aggressiveness was related to his studies in organ inferiority. The first issue under consideration was penis envy in women, as found by the classic psychoanalysis. Adler generalized his findings. Whenever an individual has an organ inferiority, be it in the sensory apparatus or the digestive or respiratory tract, there is a tendency to restore the equilibrium by compensatory action. The unsatisfied demands increase until the deficit is made up through growth of the inferior organ or of some other organ which may serve as a substitute. According to Adler, approximately 70 per cent of the students of painting have been found to suffer from some optical disorder. Many orators, such as Demosthenes and Demoulins, originally were stutterers, and many great musicians, such as Beethoven and Robert Franz, had ear afflictions.

These were Adler's ideas in 1908. Two years later Adler was already critical of Freud although he broke away one year later, in 1911. In a paper published in 1910, Adler wrote: "For children with inferior organs and glandular systems . . . their growth and functioning show deficiencies and that sickness and weakness are prominent especially in the beginning." "These objective phenomena frequently give rise to a subjective feeling of inferiority. . . ." "Such children are thus often placed in a role which appears to them unmanly. . . . The renunciation of masculinity, however, appears to the child as synonymous with femininity. . . . Any form of uninhibited aggression, activity, potency, power, and the traits of being brave, free, rich, aggressive, or sadistic

[7] *Ibid.*, p. 36.

can be considered as masculine. All inhibitions and deficiencies, as well as cowardliness, obedience, poverty and similar traits, can be considered feminine."[8]

Adler shifted from the innate aggressive drive to the drive of overcoming one's feeling of inferiority. Submission to inferiority is feminine, rebellion against it is masculine. This aggressive rebellion was called by Adler *der männliche Protest* ("masculine protest"), and from now on this term was substituted for the aggressive drives. The masculine protest was, according to Adler, a normal and general phenomenon of compensation. Overcompensation is pathological. When the individual fears defeat in a useful compensation, he may, in a neurosis, prefer a useless, antisocial compensation.

The more intense the deprivation, the stronger the urge for compensation. The entire life of the child, his dreams, wishes, and play are filled with his goal to be a man, to be big and strong.

Both concepts, the inferiority and the protest, underwent changes in Adler's writings. In 1933 Adler emphatically stated that "to be human means to feel inferior," for every child is inferior in the face of life and of adults. The weakness of the child, his ever present inferiority feeling became now the main problem in Adler's theory.

The masculine protest was gradually transformed into a general striving for adequacy (*Vollwertigkeit*), for meaning something in life (*Geltungstrieb*), for security. The child is born weak and within his first four or five years a goal is set. This goal is compensatory, and the striving toward it is a striving to "security, power, and perfection." It is no longer striving for sheer power but for *overcoming* the difficulties of life and of one's own inferiority feelings.

Thus compensation is no longer limited to any specific organic or social deficiency or inadequacy. We all, wrote Adler, strive to attain a goal which will make us feel strong, superior, perfect.

Striving for Superiority

Human volition is usually interpreted in two ways. The first is the pleasure-pain antinomy and the other the survival-death antinomy. Adler did not deny the importance of seeking pleasure but he denied that this is the guiding principle in human life.

Nor did Adler agree that self-preservation or preservation of the species is the main driving force in men. We act, he said, every minute in violation of these two principles. We may wish to die when in pain and give up the attainment of pleasure when we or our self-esteem are threatened. The overemphasis on either principle is neurotic. Some neurotics over-

[8] *Ibid.*, pp. 46–47.

value pleasure in their effort to compensate for their organ inferiority and some overvalue life in compensation for their fear of death. The main guiding principle is the advancement of self-esteem, the overcoming of inferiority feelings, the striving for superiority. Pleasure or displeasure are only ancillary rewards on this great road to the final goal of man.

This striving for superiority is innate. It is a basic urge in man, comparable to Freud's instinctual forces of Eros and Thanatos. It is primordial, inherent in our nature. It is the continuous effort toward a better adaptation between man and world.

Said Adler: "Whether a person desires to be an artist, the first in his profession, or a tyrant in his home, to hold converse with God or humiliate other people; whether he regards his suffering as the most important thing to which everyone must show obeisance, whether he is chasing after unattainable ideals or old deities, over-stepping all limits and norms, at every part of his life he is guided and spurred on by his longing for superiority, the thought of his godlikeness, the belief in his special magic power. In his love he desires to experience his power over his partner. In his purely optional choice of profession the goal . . . manifests itself in all sorts of exaggerated anticipations and fears."[9]

On this point Adler's thinking ran ahead of Freud's. As early as 1908 Adler emphasized the importance of aggressive impulses. However, while in Freud's writing aggressiveness was a function of the death instinct, in Adler's theory it is the most general human striving, "an intrinsic necessity of life itself. It is at the root of all solutions of life's problems and is manifested in the way in which we meet these problems. All our functions follow its direction. They strive for conquest, security, increase, either in the right or in the wrong direction. . . . Whatever premises all our philosophers and psychologists dream of—self-preservation, pleasure principle, equalization—all these are but vague representations, attempts to express the great upward drive."[10] This upward drive, which stems from the feeling of inferiority, is the cause of human culture and progress.

Sociability

Freud was always aware of the impact of environment upon personality structure. The instinctual innate forces and the developmental stages are significant factors, yet the final outcome depends a great deal upon the individual's interaction with his environment. All of us, said Freud, have innate impulses and all of us go through developmental stages. But fixa-

---

[9] Adler, *op. cit.*, p. 7.
[10] Alfred Adler, "Individual Psychology," in C. Murchison (ed.), *Psychologies of 1930*, Clark University, 1930, p. 398.

tions and regressions, formations and malformations of the ego and the superego depend upon our environment.

What could Adler add to this? Adler presented the issue in sharper lines, in a focal position, and in a different light. Freud perceived the individual as a separate entity and then exposed him to the restraining or encouraging social forces. Adler, on the contrary, emphasized that community precedes the individual life. Man has always been in a society, never outside of it. Adler saw in social life the basic fact, and not in the individual's socialization.

Sociability in men is a phylogenetic and ontogenetic necessity in men, a *conditio sine qua non*. Adler stated that "Darwin already pointed out that one never finds weak animals living alone. Man must be included among these, particularly because he is not strong enough to live alone. He has only little resistance against nature, he needs a larger amount of aids to live and preserve himself. . . . Man could maintain himself only when he placed himself under particularly favorable conditions. These, however, were afforded to him only by group life."[11]

This is the phylogenetic point of view. From the ontogenetic point of view the need for group life is no less imperative. Newborn children are weak and their weakness makes child care a necessity.

Adler believed that the social interest or social feeling of an individual is an evaluative attitude toward life (*Lebensform*). It is the ability to "see with the eyes of another person."

Social interest coincides, at least partially, with empathy, identification, understanding of the other man, which makes us capable of friendship, sympathy, and love. Identification is defined by Adler as the ability to understand the other person and to see with the other person's eyes.

This ability for cooperation with others, the social interest or sociability (*Gemeinschaftsgefühl*), is an innate potentiality. But in order to attain the high degree of cooperation necessary for survival, this innate potentiality must be developed far beyond its initial stage. Moreover, the desire for superiority must be coordinated with sociability and even subordinated to it.

Even in 1908 Adler emphasized the "need for affection" in infants. While Freud, starting from the individual, emphasized the individual's need to give love, Adler took up the other side of the problem, the need to receive love. On this point, Horney and Sullivan (Chap. 9, sections 2 and 4) are Adler's disciples. This need became incorporated in the later writings of Adler in the "social interest."

Adler was opposed to Freud's idea of primary narcissism. He said that "when other schools of psychology maintain that the child comes into the world a complete egoist with 'a drive for destruction' and no other intention than to foster himself cannibalistically on his mother, this is an

[11] Ansbacher, *op. cit.,* p. 129.

erroneous inference based on incomplete observation. . . . These schools overlook in the relationship the role of the mother who requires the co-operation of the child. The mother with her milk-filled breasts and all the other altered functions of her body . . . needs the child just as the child needs her."[12]

According to Freud, social development in childhood is a product of the biologically determined developmental stages and the interaction between the child and his environment. Adler discarded the developmental stages. The biological background of personality, heredity, physique, etc., played a secondary role in his theory. Although at the beginning Adler ascribed a great deal of importance to the innate "organic inferiority," later on he did not regard any inferiorities, organic or social, as determinants of behavior. They became incorporated in the over-all life plan of the individual.

According to Freud, social development is a function of libido development. Adler was opposed to this idea. He wrote that it would not be possible to maintain that every drive has a sexual component. Adler separated sociability and sexuality. The social interest or sociability is "an innate potentiality which has to be consciously developed."

Accordingly, Freud's ideas of socialization of the child through repression, reaction formation, aim inhibition, envy, and superego formation became superfluous in Adler's frame of reference. Humans are born with the "innate potentiality." The Oedipus complex, is, according to Adler, not a universal pattern of development but merely an error in the upbringing of children.

In opposition to Freud, Adler believed that the child's initial and innate impulses of affection were directed toward others and not toward himself. Freud believed the newborn child to be a narcissist; Adler believed that self-boundedness is an artifact imposed upon the child by his education and by the present state of our social structure. The creative power of the child is misled toward self-boundedness instead of being guided into the normal channels of cooperation with other individuals.

In normal development the striving for superiority is blended with the social interest. All the actions of the individual should be useful to the society. In pursuing his own end, the individual is interested in others.

Conscious and Unconscious

Conscious and unconscious are not two opposites. As soon as we understand the unconscious, it becomes conscious; wherever we fail to understand the conscious, it becomes unconscious.

Unconscious is that part of our conscious which we have not fully understood. We tend to put aside thoughts which stand in our way and

[12] *Ibid.,* p. 137.

accept those that help us. "All individuals consider for the most part only things which are useful for their view and attitude. In other words, that becomes conscious which advances us, and that remains unconscious which might disturb our argumentation."[13]

When the child is about five years old his attitude to his environment is already firmly established. His personality evolves around his goal, and he perceives the world in the perspective of his own strivings. "The child builds up his whole life, which we have called concretely style of life, at a time when he has neither adequate language nor adequate concepts. When he grows further . . . he grows in a movement which has never been formulated into words and therefore, unassailable to criticism, is also withdrawn from the criticism of experience. We cannot say that something has not been understood or that this is a repressed unconscious. Rather we must say that something has been withheld from the understanding," wrote Adler in 1929.[14]

Sullivan's concept of "selective inattention" (cf. Chap. 9, section 4) sounds pretty much like Adler's reasoning. The similarity is even more striking in the following passage: "Because the individual adopts a certain particular approach, a certain attitude, a certain relation toward the problems of the outside world . . . , anything that does not fit this early-adopted attitude is more or less excluded . . . and is interpreted in accordance with the individual's view of the world. The same thing happens with regard to the inseparably associated emotional factors and the attitudes growing out of them. We can observe in the whole life . . . the direction selected by the individual for his striving. What is left over after this process of elimination by the life style remains as a part of the mental life and operates "unconsciously". . . or "not understood."[15] Sullivan did not add much to it.

Style of Life and Personality Structure

One can present the essence of human personality as follows: Human beings are born weak; they face hardships and feel insecure. This feeling of inferiority stimulates them to movement and action aimed at overcoming it. Such persistent movement toward superiority is called the *style of life*.

All men strive toward superiority but each strives in a different way. No individual adjusts mechanically to his environment. The style of life is the expression of one's individuality, for each individual sees the goal of superiority in an individual, unique way.

[13] *Ibid.*, p. 233.
[14] Alfred Adler, *Problems of Neurosis: A Book of Case-Histories,* Kegan Paul, 1929, p. 152.
[15] *Ibid.*

The style of life controls the totality of the child's behavior. All aspects of life become coordinated and subordinated to this over-all plan. The style of life represents the unity of the personality expressed in all facets of the individual's life: in his conscious and unconscious, in his thinking and feeling, acting and resting, in sex and in social interest.

In the first four or five years of life the child absorbs the impact of his own body and environment. Then the creative activity or the style of life begins. In contradistinction to Freud, Adler assumed that the ego or the goal-directed creative power is formed after the first four or five years of life. Moreover, once the Adlerian ego or self or creative power of striving toward the goal is formed, the total personality is under its perfect control. The ego represents the unity of personality.

Thus, Adler definitely shifted the focus of psychological inquiry from id and superego toward ego. Anna Freud did the same but within the theoretical framework of psychoanalysis.[16] Freud himself accepted her ideas and incorporated them in his theory of personality. To Freud the ego was an outgrowth of the id and the superego was an outgrowth of the ego. Freud's concept of ego assumed continuity between the innate id and its outgrowths, the ego and superego. Adler's ego was the innate creative force, as soon as it became goal bound.

Adler compared heredity to a "supply of bricks" of various quality used by each individual in a different way in building his style of life. What matters most is not what one has inherited but *what one does* with what he has. Even art and genius are not undeserved gifts of nature or inheritance but the individual's own creation.

An analogous reasoning applies to the environment. Adler strongly emphasized environmental influences but rejected the idea of an environmentalistic determinism. We are neither machines nor dictaphones. No experience, not even a traumatic one, is a cause of a future success or failure in one's life. Men give meaning to situations in accordance with their goals and life styles. Happy or unhappy experiences influence one's life not by their happening but through the meaning one attaches to them. It is not the experiences that determine the individual's course of action but the conclusions he draws from them. His learning, remembering, and forgetting are selective, guided by the promise of success of his life style.

Besides the creative force there are two important determinants of personality, the social interest and the *degree of activity*. This term resembles Edward Spranger's (Chap. 11) *Kulturformen*, i.e., the individual's attitude to the problems of life, which are, according to Adler, always social in nature. Adler's "degree of activity" reminds one of similar ideas expressed at about the same time by K. Lewin (cf. Chap. 13). Adler wrote in 1937: "It would be a tempting task for a psychologist

[16] Anna Freud, *The Ego and the Mechanisms of Defense*, Hogarth, 1948.

to show graphically the extent and form of the individual life-space."[17] Adler's "degree of activity" is well represented by the actions of a boy who runs away from home or starts a fight on the street as compared to a boy who sits home and reads a book. K. Lewin's indebtedness to Adler is quite obvious.

The psychological life of a person is oriented toward the final act, like that of a character created by a good dramatist. "The fictional, abstract ideal is the point of origin for the formation and differentiation of the given psychological resources into preparatory attitudes, readinesses, and character traits. The individual then wears the character traits demanded by his fictional goal, just as the character mask (*persona*) of the ancient actor had to fit the finale of the tragedy." Moreover, the ego or self or creative force guides the individual toward the ideal of himself. "In every case the point of the self-ideal (*Persönlichkeitsideal*) posited beyond reality remains effective. This is evidenced by the direction of the attention, of the interests, and of the tendencies, all of which select according to points of view given in advance."[18]

Adler's self-ideal corresponds to Freud's ego-ideal and later superego, but it plays a less important role in Adler's personality structure as compared to Freud's fully developed personality model. The way the self-ideal was worded by Adler indicated his unwillingness to consider this "ideal" as a part of the mental apparatus. It rather indicates a striving than an accomplishment. No wonder Karen Horney is indebted to Adler in her concept of self-image (cf. Chap. 9, section 2).

In the striving toward the goal character traits and complexes are formed. "The character traits are . . . the outer forms of the movement line of a person. As such they convey to us an understanding of his attitude toward the environment, his fellow man, the community at large, and his life problems. They are phenomena which represent means for achieving self-assertion. They are devices which join to form a method of living."[19]

Character traits are acquired. Individuals seem to believe that they lead them toward their goals of superiority. For instance, envy or distrust, ambition or laziness is such a trait acquired by an individual in the hope that it will bring him closer to his goal.

Emotions are intensifications or accentuations of character traits; they are forms of psychological movement, limited in time. They are purposeful and they serve the purpose of improving the situation of an individual. Joy, anger, fear, sorrow lead to an intensified movement of the individual, who makes an effort to come closer to his goal.

Complexes characterize the individual as schemata or personality traits

[17] Ansbacher, *op. cit.*, p. 164.
[18] *Ibid.*, p. 94.
[19] *Ibid.*, p. 219.

do. The complex is a useful concept, helpful in explanation of the individual's attitude to the tasks presented by the environment. The individual moves toward his goal and in so doing faces tasks. Failures of movement represent the various forms of the inferiority complex. The compensation is the *superiority* complex. The *redeemer* complex represents the desire to save someone. The *proof* complex represents the fear of failure and the desire to be always right. The *predestination* complex expresses itself in the belief that whatever happens to the individual is inevitable.

This goal directedness applies to the human body also. The body has its own language, the *organ dialect*. Enuresis is an expression of hostility to parents or a means of attracting their attention. Insomnia is an expression of ambition. Organic disorders usually express the craving for power. Usually each emotion has its own somatic expression and is expressed in the organ dialect. The choice of the organ usually depends upon the individual's childhood experiences subordinated to his craving for overcoming his inferiority feeling. A healthy individual may desire to become sick if the illness could bring him more superiority than health does.

Adler believed that the style of life can exert a permanent influence on the somatic development of the individual. "A courageous individual will show the effects of his attitude in his physique."[20] Body and mind are parts of one whole and there is a constant reciprocal influence between the two.

Typology

Alfred Adler believed, in accordance with Windelband's theory of idiophenomena (cf. Chap. 10), that human beings cannot be divided into classes or types. Although the goal of superiority and success is universal, each individual's attitude toward his goal is unique, and success has a different meaning for each individual. Classification is necessarily an unfruitful method. Therefore, Adler said, his classification or typology is merely an educational device, introduced "for teaching purposes" only.

In 1927 Adler interpreted Hippocrates' four temperaments, the sanguine, choleric, melancholic, and phlegmatic. The sanguine type is the most healthy, believed Adler. Since the sanguine person was not subjected to severe deprivations and humiliations, he has little if any inferiority feeling. He is capable of striving toward superiority in a happy and friendly manner.

The choleric is tense and aggressive. His striving for superiority and power involves a great expenditure of energy. He goes about attaining his goal in a direct, aggressive manner. His social adjustment is rather poor.

[20] Alfred Adler, *What Life Should Mean to You*, Little, Brown, 1931, p. 40.

The melancholic is overwhelmed by his inferiority feeling to such an extent that he lacks initiative in overcoming his obstacles. He is worrisome and undecided and lacks self-confidence and courage to take risks. He is not antisocial but does not participate too much in social interaction.

The phlegmatic has lost contact with life. He is depressed, slow, sluggish, not impressed by anything, and unable to make an effort for improvement.

In 1935 Adler introduced his own typology,[21] utilizing his concepts of degree of activity and the social interest as the two guiding principles in the grouping of personality types.

The first type displays a great deal of activity in pursuing his goal but lacks social interest. His lack of consideration for others makes him act in an antisocial manner. He is the *dominant* or *ruling* type. This type corresponds, obviously, to Hippocrates' choleric type.

The second type is the *getting* type. He lacks both activity and social interest and expects others to take care of him. He himself lacks initiative and consideration for others. The similarity between the getting type and the phlegmatic type is quite apparent.

The third type is the *avoiding* one. Instead of struggling for success and superiority, he stands still undecided. Both his activity and his social interest are very small. The avoiding type resembles the melancholic.

The fourth type is the *socially useful* one. He is active but his activity is in harmony with the needs of others and beneficial to them. The useful type closely resembles the sanguinic.[22]

Concluding Remarks

Adler's revolt against Freud has more than one meaning. The place of psychology in the realm of science is one of the most important controversies. Should psychology use observation, measurement, experiment, and become one of the natural sciences or should it be classified among the humanities, like history, aesthetics, etc.? Adler was strongly impressed by E. Spranger's *Lebensformen* (Chap. 11, section 1). Adler rejected the materialistic concept of energy, as K. Lewin did later. Both of them operated with the concepts of space, movement, and goal, but Lewin went much farther in styling psychology (cf. Chap. 13).

Adler's theory is more optimistic than Freud's. Freud saw a man torn between the forces of life and love, Eros, and the forces of death and destruction, Thanatos. The road to a peaceful coexistence of men was

[21] Alfred Adler, "The Fundamental Views of Individual Psychology," *International Journal of Individual Psychology*, 1935, **1**, 5–8.

[22] It is worth while to mention that Pavlov believed that sanguinics and phlegmatics were the normal types (cf. Chap. 2, section 3).

undermined with the dynamite of hate. No wonder many abhor seeing men as Freud saw them.

Adler believed in innate *Gemeinschaftgefühl,* i.e., a general sociability. Moreover, this sociability can be taught, fostered, and improved. Adler, the humanist and humanitarian, could not help believing in men.

The most important thing, wrote Adler, was to understand the individual as a whole. The over-all goal permits one to understand the meaning of the various separate actions of an individual and to perceive them as parts of a whole.

The goal of superiority, said Adler, was the governing principle, the source of unity of personality. But is superiority the governing principle of mental life?

Adler was never too systematic, never too consistent a thinker. He went a long way from the aggressive drive and organ inferiority toward the creative power which, as a goal-bound force, becomes the leading factor, the ego, the self. His presentation left many questions open. What is this creative force? Why does it become goal directed? How does in involve heredity and environment? Why don't people become reconciled to their feeling of inferiority? Are all people striving to superiority?

Are all people so worried about their weakness in comparison to the universe that all their life is one continuous effort to overcome it, to become superior, and to gain self-esteem? How general is this rule? Do experimental and clinical studies bring evidence in support of the generality of inferiority feeling and the drive toward superiority?

Adler's holistic and purposivistic approach creates insurmountable difficulties. The goal of life is either immanent in each individual, or set by external forces, or chosen by the individual. Adler rejected the first choice, which inevitably leads to a deterministic heredity. He rejected the second choice, which would make a "dictaphone" out of a man. He repeatedly stated that man himself creates his life plan. But what shaped man's mind in such a way that he would make this or that choice?

It is, probably, the deterministic bias of the present writer that forces him to be critical of any indeterministic theory. The universe seems to function in a pretty organized and ordered manner, and the rejection of the causal principle seems to be against empirical evidence (cf. Chap. 14).

Adler's opposition to causation does not sound too convincing. He stated that "each individual acts and suffers in accordance with his peculiar teleology," which sounds rather deterministic. Or, in the same passage, he stated that the springs of this teleology "may be traced to his earliest childhood, and nearly always we find that they have been diverted into false channels by the pressure of the earliest situations in the child's life,"[23] which implies even more causation. When Adler said

[23] Ansbacher, *op. cit.,* p. 93.

that things could have taken another turn and therefore they were not causally determined, he probably committed a logical error. With additional causal factors the picture would change; changed causes create new effects. Furthermore, teleology does not exclude causation, for there are causes which lead men to set goals.

Adler's analysis of human nature contains many brilliant observations and suggestions and it has to be said that Adler's influence is much greater than is usually admitted. The entire neo-psychoanalytic school, including Horney, Fromm, and Sullivan, is no less neo-Adlerian than it is neo-Freudian. Adler's concepts of sociability, self-assertion, security, self, and creativeness permeated the theories of the neo-analysts.

Clara Thompson says about Adler that "he anticipated by several years a more general acceptance of several similar ideas. He was a pioneer in applying psychoanalysis to the total personality. . . . He was the first person to describe a part of the role of the Ego in producing neurosis and to show that the direction in which a person is going, that is, his goals, significantly contribute to his neurotic difficulties."[24]

Adler's emphasis on the conscious part of the personality, the ego, was exceedingly helpful in the development of the psychoanalytic theory proper. It was stimulating even outside the borders of the psychoanalytic schools and therapeutic clinics. In the words of Gardner Murphy, "the mass of data relative to the problems of the ego that has come to us from Adler and his school is tremendously rich; we shall remain forever indebted for the ruthlessness and simplicity with which such problems were described in an era when Adler was generally ridiculed by the analysts and ignored by 'hard-headed' medical men. Adler did as much as any individual to make clear that the ego's problems are as central as sex or any other problems . . . indeed that for most civilized men they are the most burning problems of all."[25]

2. CARL GUSTAV JUNG: ANALYTIC PSYCHOLOGY

Irrationality as a Method

Carl Gustav Jung was the first president of the International Psychoanalytic Association, founded by Freud in 1910, and continued in this position till 1914, when he resigned his presidency and withdrew his membership.

The break came soon after Alfred Adler broke away from Freud. Both

[24] Clara Thompson, *Psychoanalysis: Evolution and Development*, Hermitage, 1951, pp. 160–161.
[25] Gardner Murphy, *Personality: A Biosocial Approach to Origins and Structure*, Harper, 1947, p. 593.

Adler and Jung disagreed with psychoanalysis as it stood prior to the First World War. They rebelled against Freud's theory of libido in its sexual connotation. Later on Freud himself revised completely his theory of libido (cf. Chap 6, section 4), but Adler and Jung were already far from the original point of controversy and the gulf was never closed. The differences kept growing, and today Adler and Jung share with Freud only those concepts which were acceptable to them before they broke away.

Adler, as said in the previous section of this chapter, was more concerned with the conscious processes than Freud was. Adler's theory is to a great extent a theory of what Freud called the ego. Jung moved in the opposite direction. His main interest and his numerous works were related to the unconscious processes. Freud distinguished between the parts of the unconscious which were conscious and became repressed and the parts which had never been conscious. Jung's works deal mainly with the deepest layers of the human unconscious. Freud believed that in well-balanced individuals the rational ego exercised a reasonable degree of control over the id and superego. Jung advocated some sort of cooperation between the rational conscious and the irrational unconscious.

Apparently Jung not only followed Freud into the realm of the unconscious but became enchanted by it. The primitive beauty of the primary-primordial mental resources, studied by Jung in psychotherapeutic practice and in anthropological and cultural-historical research, was tempting indeed. Jung progressively ascribed to the unconscious more and more importance. Freud saw human nature in the perspective of unconscious, preconscious, and conscious, the conscious being the controlling force. Jung definitely rejected the rule of the conscious.

Apparently Jung disagreed with Freud on more issues. This disagreement was, first of all, a methodological one. Freud persistently applied scientific analysis to all "mental provinces," including the unconscious. A great deal of his work was devoted to the primary processes, but the method he used was always the rational method and empirical observation. It was always the conscious part of Freud's mind that analyzed dreams.

Jung, as said before, was deeply involved with the unconscious phenomena and bluntly refused to apply to them the method of scientific analysis. He insisted that we must make sure that "we do not foist conscious psychology upon the unconscious," for the unconscious cannot be represented in terms of thinking, reasoning, etc. Jung refused to accept the idea that the unconscious processes could be perceived by and represented in terms of the conscious mind.

In a sense, Jung violated the Freudian principle of reality testing by saying that the unconscious "affects us just as we affect it. In this sense the world of the unconscious is commensurate with the world of outer experience."[26]

The conscious or consciousness, says Jung, is "the most unfavorable object imaginable for psychology. The essence of consciousness is the process of adaptation which takes place in the most minute details. . . . The unconscious is generally diffused, which not only binds the individuals among themselves to the race but also unites them backwards with the peoples of the past . . . and is . . . the object of a true psychology."[27]

Freud was a determinist, Adler a purposivist. For a long time Jung seems to have accepted both principles. Human mind, he used to say, is guided by both, for it is, on the one hand, a "precipitate of the past," and, on the other hand, the psyche "creates its own future."

Jung's discussion of this problem was devoted less to the search for truth and more to the analysis of the possible implications of causation and teleology for human attitudes to life. Jung was not sure that either of them could be proved or disproved; he accepted somewhat the Kantian position and believed that both principles are rather methods of cognition than laws of nature. The acceptance of causation would, however, make men feel unhappy, pessimistic, and unable to undo their past, while purposivism leaves more freedom to the individual. Consequently, decided Jung, man lives by aims as well as by causes. Jung did not see any contradiction in these two principles. Moreover, while he was opposed to the deterministic causalism, he introduced a fatalistic predestination theory through the eternal factors of ancestral history, which influence the actions of each individual.

In 1955 Jung introduced the idea of synchronicity and interpreted the phenomena of clairvoyance, telepathy, etc., by this principle. An unconscious idea may appear simultaneously in the physical world of happenings and in the mind of the individual. None of these phenomena is either a cause or an affect.[28]

The Libido

In 1912 Jung published his ideas concerning libido. In a volume entitled *The Psychology of the Unconscious* he introduced the concept of primal libido, which indicated the totality of undifferentiated psychic energy, analogous to Henri Bergson's *élan vital*. According to Jung, libido is the general energy of life, the "energy of the processes of life." He used the term "libido" in another, more limited, connotation as

[26] Carl G. Jung, *Two Essays on Analytical Psychology*, Dodd, Mead, 1928, p. 198.
[27] Carl G. Jung, *The Psychology of the Unconscious*, Dodd, Mead, 1916, p. 199.
[28] Carl G. Jung, and W. Pauli, *The Interpretation of Nature and the Psyche*, Pantheon, 1955.

psychic energy, perceived as a part of the broader concept of vital energy.

Jung maintained that human behavior is dominated neither by the all-powerful sexual libido of Freud nor by the mastery drive of Adler. There is only "undifferentiated life energy," which expresses itself at one time in the pursuit of sensual pleasure and at another time in the striving for superiority, artistic creation, play, and other activities.

Mental energy or libido is used basically for self-preservation and preservation of the species. When these biological needs are satisfied, it is available for the pursuit of other goals, such as cultural, social, or creative needs of the individual.

Jung accepted the idea that mental energy is a continuation of physical energy and that each of the two types of energy could be transformed into the other. "Life takes place through the fact that it makes use of natural physical and chemical conditions as a means to its existence. The living body is a machine that converts the amounts of energy taken up into its equivalents in other dynamic manifestations. One cannot say the physical energy is converted into life, but only that the transformation is the expression of life." And further on: "All the means employed by an animal for the safeguarding and furthering of his existence, not to speak of the direct nourishment of his body, can be regarded as machines that make use of natural potential in order to produce work. . . . Similarly, human energy, as a natural product of differentiation, is a machine; first of all a technical one that uses natural conditions for the transformation of physical and chemical energy, but also a mental machine using mental conditions for the transformation of libido."[29]

In later writings Jung concluded that both material and psychic energy stem from a third, prematerial, "brute" element.

One of the main principles of Jung's theory is the *principle of opposites* or dialectics. Life is contruction and destruction, creation and decay, waking and sleeping. It is a cosmic principle, reminiscent of the tenets of the ancient Greek philosopher Heraclitus and the idealistic German philosopher Hegel. It is the dialectic law of development through opposites, through the swinging from one extreme to the other, from a thesis to its antithesis. After oscillations comes stability; the deeper was the conflict, the more profound the stability.

This law serves as the guiding principle of the human mind. "Everything human is relative, because everything depends on a condition of inner antithesis; for everything subsists as a phenomenon of energy. Energy depends necessarily on a pre-existing antithesis, without which there could be no energy. There must always be present height and depth, heat and cold, etc., in order that the proces of equalization—

[29] Carl G. Jung, *Contributions to Analytical Psychology*, Harcourt, Brace, 1928, p. 46.

which is energy—can take place. All life is energy, and therefore depends on forces held in opposition."[30]

The greater the conflict between the opposites, the more mental energy comes out of them. Discharge of energy is caused by the state of inner conflict within a given system. The distribution of mental energy follows the principles of equivalence and entropy. The principle of conservation of energy or *equivalence* states that energy removed from one area will appear in another. Jung's theory is a faithful exposition of this principle. His principle of *entropy* is borrowed from the second law of thermodynamics. If one part of the personality is charged with a heavy load of libido and another with a low load, libido will move from the former toward the latter.

The two main rules of libido movements are *progression* and *regression*. When the opposite forces within the system are balanced and the psyche is in a state of equilibrium, the libido moves smoothly, from the unconscious layers of personality toward the conscious in the process of progression. "During the progression of the libido the pairs of opposites are united in the coordinated flow of psychical processes. Their working together makes possible the balanced regularity of these processes, which, without this reciprocal action, would be one-sided and unbalanced." The individual whose libido is in state of progression experiences the feeling of pleasure, happiness, and well-being. Jung calls it the "vital feeling."

In some situations the progression of the libido is thwarted. Dammed up, its flow is stopped. The opposites united in the flowing libido fall apart. The inner conflict mounts, great amounts of energy are generated, and "the vital feeling that was present before disappears and in its place the psychic value of certain conscious contents increases in an unpleasant way; subjective contents and reactions press to the fore and the situation becomes full of affect and favorable for explosions."[31]

The Symbols

Psychic energy, the libido, can be utilized in more than one way. Freud saw the basic drive in sex. Jung saw it in self-preservation. Food intake, according to Jung, is the primary factor. The child enjoys sucking not because sucking is a presexual function but because it is necessary for self-preservation. The child's interest in the mother is not sexual but nutritional, as the mother is the child's provider.

Jung did not deny the analogy between the rhythmical movements in sucking and in intercourse. However, he drew a clear-cut line. Sucking as a food intake is the primary function, and here Jung was at great variance with Freud.

[30] Jung, *Two Essays on Analytical Psychology*, p. 78.
[31] Jung, *Contributions to Analytical Psychology*, p. 35.

Mental energy is primarily used for survival functions, but once biological needs are satisfied, the surplus libido is transformed into cultural and spiritual phenomena. "The psychological machine which transforms energy is the symbol." "Symbols are the manifestation and expression of the excess libido. At the same time they are transitions to new activities, which must be specifically characterized as cultural activities in contrast to the instinctive functions that run their course according to natural law."[32]

The symbol is a *libido analogue* or libido equivalent which transforms libido from its biological, physiological service of the organism into cultural activities.

Signs and words communicate what is already known. Symbols interpret the unknown. One may use the cross as a sign representing divine love, but "the interpretation of the Cross is Symbolic, which puts it above all imaginable explanations, regarding it as an expression of an unknown and yet incomprehensible fact of a mystical or transcendent, i.e., psychological character, which simply finds its most striking and appropriate character in the Eros."[33]

Symbols emerge in the unconscious part of the human psyche. They are formed spontaneously, never thought out consciously. They may come to the conscious by the force of intuition or revelation and, if accepted by the ego, may become a major guiding force in the individual's cultural activities and creativeness.

The Conscious

The psyche is composed of three parts, the conscious, the personal unconscious, and the collective unconscious. The conscious and the unconscious are opposites that balance each other in a *reciprocal relativity*. The tension between the conscious and unconscious parts of the mind sets free psychic energy.

In our times the conscious part of the personality has been unduly overstressed, says Jung. The conscious forms the upper floors of a skyscraper, while the unconscious forms its lower floors. Conscious without unconscious would be suspended in the air and dangerously detached from the basic unconscious elements of human personality. A nervous breakdown is inevitable in such a case.

The consciousness or the conscious plays in Jung's theory a secondary role as compared to the unconscious. The conscious is useful in adjustment to the environment. "The essence of consciousness is the process of adaptation which takes place in the most minute details. On the other hand, the unconscious is generally diffused, which not only binds the

[32] *Ibid.*, p. 53.
[33] Carl G. Jung, *Psychological Types*, Harcourt, Brace, 1923, p. 502.

individuals among themselves to the race but also unites them backwards with the peoples of the past and their psychology."[34]

The central part of the consciousness is endowed with a high degree of continuity and is called by Jung the *ego*. The ego represents the conscious and fairly consistent attitudes of the individual toward the outer world.

Dreams and the Personal Unconscious

The personal unconscious is the superficial layer of the unconscious. It encompasses all the forgotten memories, subliminal perceptions, and suppressed experiences. In addition, it contains "fantasies (including dreams) of a personal character, which go back unquestionably to personal experience, things forgotten or repressed."[35]

Dreams represent both the personal and the collective unconscious. Freud believed that dreams represent a repressed wish; Adler introduced the idea that dreams foreshadow our future actions. Jung accepted both interpretations, but apparently his favorite interpretation went even beyond Adler's theory and he often interpreted dreams as prophetic anticipations of the future.

Jung developed the method of study of the unconscious by free word association. His "discrete-stimulus" method consists of an analytical study of the significance of individual associations. He used a list of one hundred stimulus words chosen and arranged in such a manner as to stir the most common emotions.

The subject is told to respond to each word with the first word that comes to his mind. The examiner records the response as well as the time required for the response. If the stimulus word is not connected with an emotional complex in the individual, he will be able to respond quickly with some other word.

Certain types of responses were regarded by Jung as indicative that the stimulus had aroused an emotional response. Even normal persons in a test with one hundred words would show some emotional reactions, but too many unusual reactions indicate an unstable person. Further analysis of these unusual reactions may give an indication concerning the emotional complexes. The reactions that are supposed to be indicators of emotional tensions are as follows:

1. A *delayed reaction* to a stimulus word indicates that a complex has been touched. A person who is excited cannot think, not because he is incapable of thinking, but because the excitement interferes.

2. *Multiple responses*, i.e., responses which use many words, show the inability to control reaction. Some examples of this type of response are:

[34] Jung, *Psychology of the Unconscious,* p. 199.
[35] Carl G. Jung, and Carl Kerenyi, *Essays on a Science of Mythology,* Bollingen Series, XXII, Pantheon, 1949, p. 102.

STIMULUS WORD	RESPONSES
To quarrel	Angry—different things—I always quarrel
To marry	How can you marry?—reunion—union
To sin	This idea is quite strange to me—I do not recognize it

The subject responds quickly with a word, then he fears he may give the experimenter some clue to his excitement, so he attempts to cover his confusion with other responses; people often chatter when they are confused.

3. A *personal response* to an objective stimulus shows a tendency to extend the ego. The following illustrate personal responses:

STIMULUS WORD	RESPONSE
To dance	Love it
Luck	Don't believe in it
Money	Poor, wish I had some

4. *Repetition of the stimulus word* in the association experiment indicates that the word has struck some complex and that the repetition is a defense, a pause to regain poise before a response is made.

5. *Perseveration* means giving the same response to the most varied stimulus words. This indicates that there is a dominant complex which many irrelevant words set off. For example, in the list of one hundred words a patient gave the response *long* ten times to the stimulus word when it was not at all logically connected with the word. Investigation showed that the word *long* was related to her difficulty. She and her husband worked a *long* time to save money to build a home. When they began building after a *long* period of time, they lost their money. They would have to wait a *long* time before saving enough money. But she was getting old and it would not be *long* before she would be too old to enjoy a home.

6. When the stimulus word strikes a complex, the subject may defend himself by responding with a *superficial association;* the subject may name anything that happens to be in sight.

7. Probably as significant as any of the complex indicators is the *failure to respond* at all. When the patient waits a number of minutes and finally says that he cannot think of a thing, it is fairly good evidence that a definite emotional blocking has been encountered.

8. *Failure of reproduction* often shows emotional tension. It is useful to go through the entire list of one hundred words a second time in order to determine the number of responses that are different on the second trial. When a response is different, the indication is that an emotionally accentuated complex has been touched. A person very easily forgets what

he has said under an emotional stress and is even likely to contradict a statement so made. Jung stated that in his experience a normal person has no more than 20 per cent different responses on the reproduction test, while abnormal persons have from 20 to 40 per cent.

9. *Accessory emotional reactions*—stammering, blushing, clearing the throat, sighing, weeping, laughing, acting surprised—indicate that a complex has been touched off. The meaning of the particular emotion reaction is not usually apparent, however, and care should be exercised in drawing an inference from it.

Jung's method is used to throw light upon the nature and significance of the different unconscious complexes.

The Complexes

In Freud's theory and cathartic method there was room for a concept representing a load of energy attached to an unconscious wish. It was the *complex,* such as the Oedipus complex or the Electra complex.

Jung went farther in assigning independent, "autonomous life" to the complexes. The conflict between the conscious and unconscious parts of the psyche generates psychic energy; this energy cannot be set under the control of the consciousness, and units so loaded with mental energy thus start their independent life.

These units of energy, set free, attract ideational content and form independent entities or constellations or *complexes*. Complexes are *autonomous partial systems* in the human mind; they form split personalities within a given personality; they indicate the relatively independent inclinations within the same individual.

In dreams these separate inclinations appear in a disguise of characters. It is as if the dreamer were experiencing the various characters that exist in his mind beyond his control. These "psychic splits" are universal; each individual is composed of several relatively independent individualities. Only when these complexes get too far apart from each other and from the rest of psyche is mental health jeopardized. When a complex reactivates elements of the deepest layers of the unconscious, the archetypes, and takes over control of the personality, a psychosis has developed.

One of these complexes is *persona*. *Persona* is Latin for a "mask." Actors had to wear different masks for different plays; analogously, said Jung, each individual wears different masks playing different roles in relationship to different people. The same man is a son to his father, a husband to his wife, an employer to his employees, a father to his children. In each situation he puts on a different mask. He can never be the totality of all his conscious and unconscious forces, and in each situation another part of his personality comes to the fore. The various relationships elicit different responses, and the degree of consistency in the different masks of one person depends on the inner integration.

It is worth while to mention that Jung's persona resembles James' multiple selves and also G. H. Mead's social roles, J. L. Moreno's role playing, and H. S. Sullivan's self (cf. Chaps. 9 and 15). Jung's persona represents the conscious attitude of the individual, the mask that he wears when he faces others. It is balanced by the unconscious; whoever tries to be too moral experiences powerful pressures from the opposite unconscious forces. Whenever the persona moves too far from its unconscious foundations, the unconscious forces will burst out and overthrow it.

The persona represents the conscious attitudes of the individual toward the outer world. It must be, therefore, related to the ego. But the *ego* in Jung's theory is merely a certain "condition of consciousness." It is a "complex of representations which constitutes the centrum of any field of consciousness and appears to possess a very high degree of continuity and identity." Accordingly the ego forms the kernel of one's *persona*, which represents the attitudes of the individual toward the outer world. The strong, domineering qualities in the individual gather together into the conscious ego and the ego is drawn into the persona. In some cases the entire "conscious area as seen by others, i.e., the persona, becomes identical with the ego. This is the case with individuals whose entire life is guided by a certain focal idea or talent."[36]

The weak and least adapted tendencies also gather together to form an unconscious complex, the *shadow*. The shadow contains the urges and wishes which cannot be approved of by the conscious ego. It is a personality within a personality. The shadow represents the forbidden sexual and aggressive impulses; it forces the individual to irresponsible and dangerous actions; it embarrasses the ego by tactless and stupid blunders; it gives the individual unpleasant, often weird feelings. The shadow has its own psychic energy. If strong enough, it may pierce the conscious and take over control. In such a case a mental disorder develops.

One of the main tendencies of the shadow is projection. "We still attribute to the 'other fellow' all the evil and inferior qualities that we do not like to recognize in ourselves. That is why we have to criticize and attack him."[37]

The shadow is the opposite of the ego and usually functions on the level of the personal unconscious. The deeper the shadow penetrates into the unconscious, the more opposite it becomes to the ego. The ego of a man is represented in his persona as a male figure; his shadow takes on the female form, becomes the feminine component in his personality, his *anima*. All men have feminine elements in their psyche and all women

---

[36] Jung, *Psychological Types*, p. 564.
[37] Carl G. Jung, *Modern Man in Search of a Soul*, Harcourt, Brace, 1933, p. 163.

have masculine elements. The unconscious, the shadow, of a woman is represented, accordingly, by the male figure of *animus*.

The Collective Unconscious

Jung believed that acquired traits and cultural patterns are transmitted by heredity. In each individual, he wrote, there are hidden "the great 'primordial images,' those potentialities of human representations of things, as they have always been, inherited through the brain structures from one generation to the next." Jung did not deny that besides these collective deposits, which contain nothing specifically individual, the psyche may also inherit "memory acquisitions of a definite individual stamp."

These primordial images are called "archetypes." Jung was much influenced by the French social scientists Émile Durkheim and Lucien Lévy-Bruhl and was especially impressed by the idea of *l'esprit du corps* ("collective spirit"). This collective spirit must be unconscious and manifests itself through the individual mind.

The contents of the archetype nature are manifestations of the collective unconscious. "They do not refer to anything that is or has been conscious, but to something *essentially unconscious*. In the last analysis, therefore, it is *impossible* to say *what they refer to*. . . . The ultimate core of meaning may be circumscribed but not described. Even so, the bare circumscription denotes an essential step forward in our knowledge of the pre-conscious structure of the psyche, which was already in existence when there was as yet no unity of personality."[38]

The archetypes represent the memories of a race and are deep unconscious forces in the deep layers of the mentality of the members of a race. Since Jung believed in the heredity of acquired traits and culture patterns, he ascribed to certain races inherited patterns.[39] In German patients he observed archetypes stemming from the pre-Christian era; the symbol of the ancient German god Wotan which expresses violence and cruelty was found in the unconscious of German people.

In later writings Jung came out with the idea that the psychic did not develop out of organic matter but that there is a primal, cosmic, prematerial, prephysiological level. At this level the cosmic elements gradually developed into material and spiritual, biological and psychic elements. At this prematerial and prepsychological level autonomous functioning systems developed the archetypes.

The autonomous functioning systems are deeply seated in the human nature. They are never conscious. When the total mental structure breaks up, they "possess" the mind.

[38] Jung and Kerenyi, *Essays on a Science of Mythology*, p. 104.
[39] Jung has been often accused of a friendly attitude toward the racist philosophies of the Nazis.

In normal cases these systems are expressed by symbols. Symbols can move up to the conscious, carrying the elements of the archetypes and the collective unconscious, as expressed in mythology. Mythology contains the dreams of mankind. Jung called the collective symbols *motifs* and believed that the motifs were the links between the individual and the cosmos.

The archetypes form the core of autonomous partial systems, independent of consciousness. Once an archetype is stirred up, it develops into an autonomous partial system and takes "possession" of an individual; the individual is mentally sick. These autonomous systems are *demons* and overwhelm the mind with their irresistible power.

Archetypes play an important part in Jung's theory of personality. An archetype is a universal idea that makes up part of our collective unconscious. It is always an inherited idea.

God is an archetype. We do not know the ultimate derivation of this archetype any more than we know the origin of the psyche, which is our total personality. Men always worshiped the sun-god who gives warmth and light. Jung did not prove or disprove the existence of God; e.g., the archetype of the hero does not prove the actual existence of a hero. Jung believed that all religions are different methods of stating the same idea of God as a symbol of the psychic energy which carries a tremendous load of libido.

There are many archetypes, appearing under different names in the various mythologies; among them are the archetype of mother, the Old Wise Man, which personifies past experience, the birth archetype, etc.

One of the archetypes is the child hero. The child Moses is saved out of the waters of the Nile; the child Christ was hidden by Mary and Joseph. The child symbolizes the emergence of the self; the libido regresses into the unconscious, enters the womb (in a symbolic analogy to sex), and emerges again in childbirth. "The 'child' is born out of the womb of the unconscious, begotten out of the depths of human nature, or rather out of Living Nature herself. It is a personification of vital forces quite outside the limited range of our conscious mind; . . . a wholeness which embraces the very depth of Nature. It represents the strongest, most ineluctable urge in every human being, namely the urge to realize itself."[40]

The Self

Jung was indefatigable in the development of his theory, and his later writings add so much to his earlier works that one wonders whether his work could be presented as one logical system.

In two erudite volumes entitled *Aion* and *Psychologie und Alchemie*

---

[40] Jung and Kerenyi, *Essays on a Science of Mythology*, p. 123.

Jung apparently accepted the idea that alchemists knew more psychology than any psychologists could have known. Jung believed that the "base" and "noble" metals in alchemy stand for base and noble elements in the human mind, i.e., unconscious and conscious respectively. Just as the alchemists tried to transform the base metals into gold, the human psyche performs the *unifying function* of merging unconscious and conscious.

This unifying function is relegated in Jung's later works to the anima. In his former writing anima was just one of the complexes; now it became the symbol of the entire unconscious and of all archetypes.

Whenever the individual is capable of raising the unconscious, powerful, libido-loaded, miraculous, *mana*-like anima from the unconscious into the conscious, the total personality undergoes deep and profound changes. The anima, elevated from unconscious into conscious, loses its tremendous load of libido. It becomes depotentiated and loses the power of *possession*.

The mental energy released by the now conscious anima is free, unbound. It is a tremendous quantity of energy which is neither conscious nor unconscious. This libido becomes the central point of personality between the conscious and the unconscious and is called *self*. The self, said Jung in his *Two Essays*, "has come into being only very gradually and has become a part of our experience at the cost of great effort. Thus the self is also the goal of life."[41]

The conflicting elements of conscious and unconscious come to harmony in the self. This integration of personality through the emergence of self is found in the art and religion of several people, especially of the Far East. It is represented by the *Mandala* symbol, in the form of a square or a circle with a central point. Mandala, according to Jung, represents the reconciliation of opposites, the fusion of the conscious and the unconscious.

The various complexes and systems within the personality strive toward expansion and expression. If one of them attracts too much libido, the other centers will oppose it and stir inner conflict. In normal individuals proper outlets are provided for the various aspects of personality. The process by which development of the respective parts of the personality is facilitated is called *individuation*. The aim of individuation is "to free the self from the false wrappings of the Persona on one hand, and from the suggestive power of the unconscious image (i.e., the anima) on the other."[42]

This diversifying individuation is a step forward toward integration of the personality and development of the *self*. The *transcendent function*

[41] Jung, *Two Essays on Analytical Psychology*, p. 268.
[42] *Ibid.*, p. 185.

takes place by which the *already differentiated systems unite into one whole.*

"If we picture the conscious mind with the ego as its center, as being opposed to the unconscious, and if we now add to our mental picture the process of assimilating the unconscious, we can think of this assimilation as a kind of approximation of conscious and unconscious, where the center of the total personality no longer coincides with the ego, but with a point midway between the conscious and unconscious. This would be the point of a new equilibrium, a new centering of the total personality, a virtual center which, on account of its focal position between conscious and unconscious, ensures for the personality a new and more solid foundation."[43]

No individual is born with the self. The self gradually develops out of inner conflicts, in the years of trial and experience. Jung rejected Freud's theory of developmental stages but suggested dividing the span of human life as follows:

The first five years of life are the years of self-protection. The libido is invested in the growth and development of basic skills like walking, talking, etc., necessary for survival.

Around the age of five libido flows into the sexual values, reaches its peak around the teen age, and leads the individual in choosing a mate, forming a family, and establishing himself in his bread winning occupation. The individual is extraverted, vigorous, outgoing.

In the late thirties or early forties great changes take place. The individual turns gradually toward spiritual and philosophical values; he becomes introverted, and interested in religious, moral, and spiritual values.

Four Functions

Life energy may take the form of "rational" processes determined by what Jung called "objective values," that is, activities which may be verifiable in terms of logical analysis. Or it may take the form of "irrational" processes, determined chiefly by "accidental perceptions," chance, and more or less illogical associations. Both cases are manifestations of the movements of the libido.

The rational process, in turn, is divided into two fundamental functions: "thinking" and "feeling." In parallel fashion, the irrational is divided into "sensation" and "intuition." The former functions are dominated by reasoning and judgment, the latter by intensity of perceptions but not by rational judgment. Sensation is the first reaction of the individual to the outer world; then comes *thinking* or "interpretation of

[43] *Ibid.*, p. 219.

that which is perceived"; next comes *feeling* or "evaluation of the perceived object"; last comes *intuition* or the "immediate awareness of relationships." Furthermore, "sensation establishes what is actually given, thinking enables us to recognize its meaning, feeling tells of its value, and finally intuition points to the possibilities of the whence and whither that lie within the immediate facts. In this way we can orientate ourselves with respect to the immediate world as completely as when we locate a place geographically by latitude and longitude."[44]

Thinking and sensation are masculine personality traits, while intuition and feeling are feminine, but each individual is capable of all four functions. Usually one of them is *dominant* in a given individual. The dominant function is carried by a great load of the libido energy into the conscious part of his personality and eventually, through fusion with his ego, becomes the guiding principle in his life. The entire mental life of an individual revolves around the dominant function. For example, all men use feeling for setting up the evolution criteria, but the "feeling type" will relate his entire life to this function. The dominant function occupies the center of the conscious, and its opposite, in this case "thinking," becomes necessarily unconscious. Any function on the unconscious level is undifferentiated, merged with other functions, and diffused. When the function is carried by the libido from the unconscious into the conscious it becomes *differentiated,* i.e., purified, separated from the opposite function. Usually the function which guarantees the most success, a talent, becomes dominant and differentiated.

The opposite function loses its load of energy to the dominant function. If, as a result of the drain of energy by the dominant function, the opposite function becomes exceedingly impoverished, it goes deep down to the lowest levels of the unconscious, stirs the archetypes, and leads toward mental disorder. The autonomous partial systems will then take possession of the human mind.

Introversion and Extraversion

"When the orientation to the object and to objective facts is so predominant that the most frequent and essential decisions and actions are determined not by subjective values but by objective relations, one speaks of an extraverted attitude. When this is habitual, one speaks of an extraverted type. If a man so thinks, feels and acts, in a word, so *lives,* as to correspond *directly* with objective conditions and their claims, whether in a good sense or ill, he is extraverted.

"His entire consciousness looks outwards to the world, because the important and decisive determination always comes to him from without.

[44] Jung, *Modern Man in Search of a Soul,* p. 107.

But it comes to him from without only because that is where he expects it. . . ."[45]

In extraversion the libido moves toward the outer world. Accordingly, the extravert is guided by the impression the external world leaves upon him. All interests, values, and attitudes are directed toward his physical and social environment.

The introvert, on the contrary, "selects the subjective determinants as the decisive ones. This type is guided, therefore, by that factor of perception and cognition which represents the receiving subjective disposition to the sense stimulus. . . Whereas the extraverted type refers pre-eminently to that which reaches him from the object, the introvert principally relies upon that which the outer impression constellates in the subject."[46] Accordingly, the introvert is self-centered and much involved with his inner world.

Extraversion and introversion can be organized around one of the fourfold features: thinking, feeling, sensation, and intuition. A brief description of each type of individual follows.

1. Extraverted Thinking Type. Accepts the world from the senses and uses his sensory impressions as a basis for logical analysis and construction of his reality. He is concerned with facts and their classification.
2. Extraverted Feeling Type. Determined by the feeling for the external object. The individual tends to feel and act according to the demands and expectations of the situation; he is able to establish friendship with others.
3. Extraverted Sensation Type. Conditioned by and oriented to the sensory and/or concrete features of a given object; he is the "realist" and "materialist."
4. Extraverted Intuition Type. The external object does not so much control his perception or sensation as offer him a suggestion for elaborating the possibilities of the object at the moment as something to manipulate and control.
5. Introverted Thinking Type. Marked by ideational patterns which have been almost completely organized subjectively till they suit the individual (so that he tends to become indifferent). He may have some success in social contacts.
6. Introverted Feeling Type. Dominated also by the "subjective factor." This individual lives within his own internal world of emotions and feelings. He is the daydreamer or the silent person who is at peace with the world.

[45] Jung, *Psychological Types*, p. 417.
[46] *Ibid.*, p. 472.

7. Introverted Sensation Type. Though attending to the external world, his perceptions are dominated by his subjective internal state. The creative artist may have this kind of character make-up.
8. Introverted Intuition Type. Directs his attention to imagery. These images are clues to his activity. He lives within himself and may be the so-called dreamer, religious prophet, fanatical crank, or artist.

Jung stated that type differences can be modified, as when a natural-born introvert is forced by circumstances into extraversion, but he believed that such transpositions are rather superficial.

Between these two types lie most people, who display both extraversion and introversion. They are called *ambiverts*. According to Jung, the four functions of thinking, feeling, sensation, and intuition appear in all individuals, but one of these modes predominates. A particular person's response to the world and to himself might be said to be typically or characteristically in this or that modality, which does not imply an absence of the other features. Which of these extremes one should strive for is a question of norms and values. In our society, despite the culturally approved stimuli to become extraverted, we find a place for some introverts—though we are likely to consider them a bit "queer" or perhaps divergent from the "best" in our values; doubtless the majority of people fall into the middle range of so-called ambiverts.

History and Culture

The eternal archetypes appear in each epoch in a different disguise, but they are always the same primordial images of mankind. Men cannot rid themselves of these archetypes, which express themselves in each historical epoch in a different manner. Historical symbols "arise directly from dreams or at least are inspired by them," especially the deep, great dreams, in which the archetypical symbols appear again and again.

The archetypes may become conscious through symbolization. Then they are called *motifs*.

When the archetypes or motifs or autonomous systems penetrate the psyche of groups they cause psychic epidemics or mass psychoses. Mass psychoses revive the deep-rooted archetypes common to a given race and embedded in the unconscious layers of its members.

In support of this theory of the racial unconscious, Jung referred to delusions and hallucinations of the insane, dreams of normal people, and widespread belief in superstition and magical influences. During periods of mental illness, the thinking of modern man tends to be of a prelogical, primitive nature. During sleep, when the lower levels of consciousness are permitted greater expression, the contents of our dreams are not only unreal and illogical but resemble certain bizarre thoughts of primitive man. We converse with animals, fly through the air with ease, and destroy our enemies by a simple gesture. In spite of our present-day rationalism, most of us are inclined to relate our misfortunes to having seen a black cat cross our path. The content of dreams and hallucinations, said Jung, is the same for all members of a given race. So it must be inherited.

Mythology is the anamnesis of a cultural group, a race. It represents the collective memory of a racial and cultural group. Just as a dream relates to the individual's past, mythology relates to the early childhood of a race. The common archetypical elements incorporated in the culture developed by a race, e.g., the Etruscan, the German, etc., are called *demons*. The demons are archetypes, historical symbols which draw individuals together "as if by a magnetic force, and thus a mob is formed; and its leader will soon be found in the individual who has the least resistance, the least sense of responsibility. . . . He will thus let loose everything which is ready to break forth, and the mob will follow with the irresistible force of an avalanche."[47]

Religion starts as an autonomous system of an archetype nature. It binds people together in their unconscious. People "live" and experience their religious symbols. The main archetype of religion is God. This archetype symbolizes the life energy and, accordingly, a great amount of mental energy is invested in it.

Under normal conditioning the conscious and the unconscious, the ego and the shadow are in harmony. Neurosis is a dissociation of personality, a war between the conscious and the unconscious. Neurosis is a downward, regressive movement of the libido. If it goes very deep and stirs the autonomous forces in the unconscious, a psychosis may develop.

Religion, by harmonizing the various aspects of personality, is an important factor in mental health. Modern man is beset by conflicting values and is often unable to reconcile them. Religion represents the unconscious, archetypical elements in harmony with the conscious elements of personality and society.

Concluding Remarks

Of all psychoanalytic theories Jung's have been the most criticized. For example, in an illuminating and quite objective description of the history of psychoanalytic thought, Clara Thompson wrote about Jung that "his thinking becomes more mystical and he creates a conception of personality which sounds like a rigid obsessional system."[48]

But Jung's method is all but rigid. It seems to be rather inconsistent, often whimsical, and almost haphazard. Jung introduced concepts with an ease which defied any principle of parsimony. In the beginning the

[47] Carl G. Jung, *Essays on Contemporary Events,* Kegan Paul, 1947, p. xi.
[48] Clara Thompson, *Psychoanalysis: Evolution and Development,* Hermitage, 1957, p. 168.

ego was the focal point of the consciousness, but later it became a sort of satellite rotating around the self "very much as the earth rotates around the sun." The persona was originally a conscious complex, the anima an unconscious one. Later on, persona and anima stood for the two entire zones of the conscious and the unconscious respectively. Originally Jung postulated conscious and unconscious; later he introduced a twilight area, a sort of "demilitarized" zone between the two, where they merge in a rather unexplained way.

Jung originally accepted both causation and purposivism, but in 1955 he added a third category, of contemporariness of events which supposedly occur at the same time and yet are not causally interrelated.

Jung very often used inconsistent and circular definitions. "The psychological machine which transforms energy is the symbol," he wrote. And later on, "Symbols are the manifestations and expression of the excess libido."[49]

Or consider Jung's definition of the ego: "By ego I understand a complex of representations which constitutes the centrum of my field of consciousness and appears to possess a very high degree of continuity and identity." But, "by consciousness I understand the relatedness of psychic contents to the ego in so far as they are sensed as such by the ego."[50]

Jung's theory was often criticized for being exceedingly involved. In his defense one may say that simplicity does not necessarily correspond to empirical data nor does complexity necessarily contradict them. Although one may be amazed at each new "Copernican revolution" of the same author, this is still not a reason for refutation of his theories.

The criticism raised against Jung is mainly directed against his arbitrarily, almost dogmatically, set system, which was changed several times almost at will. Despite his tremendous erudition in anthropology and history of culture, Jung displayed great eagerness to accept analogies as scientific evidence. Consider his enthusiasm for alchemy. Alchemy merges elements, and the human mind merges elements; thus, Jung concluded, alchemy offers the key to psychology. Jung's inquiry into human behavior was guided by the acceptance of mystical beliefs and of what some humans had perceived at certain times as being the true picture of the universe.

Jung's greatness lies in the wealth of his studies in the history of mysticism and irrational thinking. His apparent weakness lies in his uncritical enthusiasm for his discoveries. Instead of applying the rational tools of scientific inquiry to the irrational phenomena of the human mind in its ontogenetic and phylogenetic development, Jung accepted these phenomena as scientific truth. One could say that Mandala, alchemy,

[49] Jung, *Contributions to Analytical Psychology*, pp. 50, 53.
[50] Jung, *Psychological Types*, pp. 540, 535.

and pictorial symbolism are products of the human mind; perhaps they represent how the primitive and regressed human mind pictures itself. A schizophrenic may say that his mind *is* a television set controlled by his relatives, whose minds are a sort of remote-control apparatus. The business of scientific inquiry is to find out what made the psychotic think that way or how much symbolic, archaic thought is involved in that presentation. There is no reason to dismiss the statements made by a morbid mind; but it is even less rational to accept them as scientific truth. Freud looked into mythology, analyzed it, and found in it the products of sick and primitive minds. Jung was enchanted by mythology and accepted it as an authentic photographic copy of the human mind. Freud found an analogy between the prelogical thinking of mythology, of psychopathology, and of infancy. Jung accepted the content of mythology as scientific evidence in psychology. Freud exploited myth for scientific purposes; Jung accepted myth as scientific evidence.

In this volume we have carefully avoided saying which theory is true and which false. Actually, no theory is true in the empirical sense (cf. Chap. 14). The aim of this book is analysis and criticism of the methods used by the various psychologists in ascertaining empirical data and their interpretation. And from this point of view, Jung represents a unique case in contemporary psychological theory, for he and only he accepted intuitive and irrational phenomena on their face value.

Yet Jung undoubtedly offered some valuable observation into the darkest spots of the human mind. His studies in mythology and in mental disorder, especially schizophrenia, contain a wealth of important data. Those acquainted with the way the schizophrenic mind works cannot deny that Jung came across very important archaic elements in the human mind, where psychological factors so easily produce physiological disturbances and vice versa.

Jung observed these phenomena and tried to report them. He reproduced them in the language of schizophrenic thought, using terms such as "possessed," "cosmic," "live symbols," "demons," etc. He took his findings literally—and left open the question whether his observations were correct and whether his intrepretations corresponded to scientific analysis.

CHAPTER 8

New Theories in Psychoanalysis

1. PSYCHOANALYSIS MODIFIED BY CLINICAL EXPERIENCE

Orthodox and Unorthodox

Adler's and Jung's opposition to Freud was a matter of theory and principle. Both Adler and Jung rejected the concepts of Eros and Thanatos, the theory of developmental stages, and the id, ego, and superego personality model.

When Adler and Jung left the ranks of the psychoanalytic movement, psychoanalysis became very much a "school" united in the acceptance of Freud's method and set of principles. Now the entire system as developed by Freud and his faithful disciples was put to a continuous clinical test. Freud's theory grew and developed in a clinical setting; it was primarily a system of hypotheses related to the growth, development, and malformations in the human personality. Armed with Freud's theoretical and technical principles, scores of psychoanalysts tried to help people. The task was a tremendous one. Psychoanalysis was considered the only method by which human problems could be solved. The clinic was the laboratory and success or failure in the practical task of curing mental patients was considered equivalent to an experimental verification of the theory.

The difficulties faced in the therapeutic efforts forced Freud to recast his theoretical assumptions. So did his associates. Growing numbers of practicing psychoanalysts joined the ranks of research workers. Each new "case" presented new problems; each unsuccessful therapy called for revision or at least checking of the underlying principles. The area covered by clinical research has been constantly growing, and the empirical data derived from the scrutiny of thousands of life histories have expanded rapidly.

The clinical and theoretical studies went in all directions. Freud did not intend to develop an all-encompassing psychological theory, but the logic of the psychoanalytic system forced his disciples to apply psycho-

318

analysis to practically all possible aspects of human life. As Gardner Murphy said, "the insights of Freud, with reference to human motivation, impulse control, reality testing, and much else besides, are among the most profound ever vouchsafed to an investigator."[1] Motivation, control of emotionality, and perception were the main areas in which new developments took place.

Freud himself was not always in favor of the new developments. Some of them (such as O. Rank's and W. Reich's theories) he overtly rejected. Even before his death in 1939 psychoanalytic theory had been developing and growing, partially on more or less orthodox Freudian and partially on non-orthodox lines. Fenichel, Jones, Glover, Anna Freud, Federn, Hartmann, Loewenstein, Kris, and scores of other prominent workers in this field have continued psychoanalytic research in accordance with the main ideas of Freud. Some other disciples of Freud introduced so many and far-reaching modifications that their theories could no longer be placed under the roof of Freud's theory. What they have in common with contemporary psychoanalysis is common roots only. In accordance with the policy of this book, priority will be given to the new and original theories.

2. OTTO RANK: THEORY OF WILL

The Birth Trauma

Among those who started as orthodox and faithful disciples but ended in open rebellion and defiance of the basic principles of Freud was Otto Rank. Rank regarded birth as the most traumatic event in human life and as the major source of an overwhelming anxiety. Any other anxiety in later life was presented by Rank as an outcome of the basic birth anxiety. Since birth is separation from the mother's body, any future separations would revive this anxiety.

The male's desire for intercourse was regarded by Rank as a craving for the mother's womb, but the sight of the birth-giving female organs was fear producing. The figure of the Sphinx in the Oedipus myth represents the mother symbol, the mother to whom the man strives and of whom he is afraid, afraid of being enclosed. The Oedipus complex, says Rank, is a repetition of the primal birth anxiety. "The hero, who is not swallowed by the Sphinx, is enabled, just through the overcoming of anxiety, to repeat the unconscious wish in the pleasurable form of sexual intercourse with the mother."[2]

Both male and female abhor female sexual organs as associated with

[1] Gardner Murphy, "The Current Impact of Freud upon Psychology," *American Psychologist*, 1956, **11**, 663–672.
[2] Otto Rank, *Trauma of Birth*, Harcourt, Brace, 1929, p. 145.

the birth trauma. If they are not able to overcome this fear, homosexual reactions develop. According to Rank all homosexuals reexperience the asexual yet libidinal mother-child, womb-embryo relationship. The masochist seeks to convert the pain of birth into a pleasure by fantasies of being bound and beaten. The sadist has the "unquenchable hatred" of one who has been expelled and he violently forces his way back. The exhibitionist wants to return to a "paradisical" state of nakedness.

Prior to birth the individual was a whole and united with his mother. He was "bound inseparably with a greater whole" and experienced the feeling of totality and wholeness.

In his postnatal life the individual has to accept himself as an independent, whole, and "real" entity. What he fears is the fear of life, the fear of becoming an individuality. This fear of *individualization* is the fear of being himself, of making himself different from others.

The striving for independence and the fear of it, the fear of growing and the fear of going back to the womb are, respectively, the fear of life and of death. "This ambivalent primal fear which expresses itself in the conflict between individuation and generation is derived on the one side from the experience of the individual as a part of the whole, which is then separated from it and obliged to live alone (birth) and on the other side from the final necessity of giving up the hard won wholeness of individuality through total loss in death."[3] Apparently E. Fromm is heavily indebted to Rank's idea of fear of living and being independent (cf. Chap. 9, section 3).

Theory of Impulses, Emotions, and Will

The neonate is endowed with innate *impulses* analogous to Freud's id. The infant reacts immediately to stimuli and each tension brings an immediate discharge of energy. These tension-discharge processes are experienced by the individual as pain and pleasure.

As soon as the infant faces external obstacles, his blocked impulses develop into *emotions*. Rank distinguished between uniting and separating emotions, in resemblance with Freud's two instinctual forces. The uniting emotions are love, tenderness, submissiveness, etc.; the separating emotions are rage, fear, hostility, etc. Love emotions are "yielding," hate emotions are "hardening" and "defensive."

The emotional life fully develops at a higher stage, when *will* develops. According to Rank there is a deep-seated conflict between individuality and belongingness, between separation and unity. An individual cannot become himself unless he is separated from his mother and later on in his life independent and "separated" from the *social* pressures of the group and the *biological* pressures of sexuality (perceived by Rank as

[3] Otto Rank, *Will Therapy and Truth and Reality*, Knopf, 1947, p. 134.

the force which promotes the race). The will arises as an inner, negative, opposing force against a compulsion.

Growth and individualization require separation. Rank distinguished three developmental stages. At the lowest stage the individual comes to terms with the social pressures coming from his parents and the sexual pressures coming from within.

At the second stage an inner conflict arises. The individual forms his own concepts and ideals. He may, consequently, continue and develop his own independent philosophy or end in self-criticism and guilt feelings.

At the third stage this problem is solved. The individual has embarked upon his own way of creativeness, and "its continuous rebuilding or building anew, has created an autonomous inner world, so different and so much its own, that it no longer represents merely a substitute for external reality (original morality) . . . so that the individual must seek satisfaction and release in the creation and projection of a world of his own. In a word, with this type, from all . . . is formed neither a compromise, nor merely a summation, but a newly created whole, the strong personality with its autonomous will, which represents the highest creation of the integration of will and spirit."[4]

Rank distinguished three stages in the development of will. The restraints and obstacles of life call forth the first reactions of the will, called the "counter-will," which is usually an expression of opposition to parental prohibitions.

The second phase of willing is attained when the child expresses the desire to do things or to possess what others do or possess. It is the *competitive* will.

The third stage, of *positive willing,* is attained when the individual sets his own standards.

In the development of his will the child comes up against parental prohibitions. "The child must learn to eat and to control the excretory functions, when the adult wishes, not when he wishes. This counter-will in relation to this is commonly designated as 'bad' and 'hateful,' but this means restricted and eventually punished. Very soon also the physical expressions of sexuality are drawn in . . . the tender expressions of love toward certain persons are permitted to the child, are good; the purely physical element of the will is evil, bad."[5]

Rank's idea of parental approval and disapproval leading to guilt feeling is borrowed from Freud. Sullivan took it over and made out of it one of the main pillars of his theory (cf. Chap. 9, section 4).

Rank distinguished three personality types depending on the three developmental stages. The average type is conforming and accepts the will of his environment as his own. The average man pretends, plays

[4] *Ibid.* p. 265.
[5] *Ibid.,* pp. 273–274.

a role, but he "plays only himself, that is, must pretend that he plays in order to justify his being." He lives in an illusion and ignorance about his own mental life.

The neurotic rebels against his society. He is a nonconformist. While he does not accept the collective will, he cannot live alone. He feels tense, inadequate, remote from others. He cannot accept society nor can he accept separation from it.

The individual who passes through all three stages is the creative artist. The personality of the creative artist is "neither a compromise, nor merely a summation, but a newly created whole, the strong personality with its autonomous will, which represents the highest creation of the integration of will and spirit," wrote Rank.[6]

The creative man can "create voluntarily from the impulsive elements." He can "develop his standards beyond the identifications of the superego morality to an ideal formation which consciously guides and rules this creative will in terms of the personality. The essential point in this process is the fact that he evolves his ego ideal from himself, not merely on the ground of given but also of self-chosen factors which he strives after consciously."[7]

Creativity enables the man to overcome the biological compulsion of the sexual instinct and the psychological compulsion to emotional surrender. Creativeness goes beyond empiricism. Rank wrote: "Truth is what I believe or affirm, doubt is denial or rejection." The creative consciousness or fantasy "is the most positive expression of the counter-will, which not only says I will not perceive what is but I will that it is otherwise, i.e., just as I want it. And this, only this, is truth."[8]

Theory of Society and Culture

Rank believed that the primal family was the group marriage and children belonged to the group of mothers. The role of father was insignificant. Then matriarchy developed.

"The institution of group marriage fortified the position of women. The gradual dominance of the mothers not only over the children of the clan but ultimately over the men, as borne out by the 'matriarchal organization,' was seemingly a slow process resisted by man who still defended his supernatural origin and survival."[9]

The ancient men distinguished between the mortal body and the immortal soul (shadow). Originally men believed in their own immortality, i.e., the immortality of the shadow. Man fears death and tries to deny his origin from the mother's womb. According to Rank, the father of

[6] *Ibid.,* p. 265.
[7] *Ibid.,* p. 216.
[8] *Ibid.,* p. 247.
[9] Otto Rank, *Beyond Psychology,* privately published, 1941, p. 122.

Oedipus, Laius represents the type of man who rejects sex. Laius wanted no successor; he wanted to be his own immortal successor. He wished no children and tried to preserve himself indefinitely.

Thus the Oedipus conflict represents the wish of the individual to be neither father nor son but a free, independent self. It is the struggle between the individual ego, which wants to be immortal, and the sexual ego of the race, which is opposed to immortality of the individual in favor of procreation of the species.

This struggle between the individual's fear of death and striving for immortality on the one hand and his sexual-racial striving on the other went through several stages. In the earliest religions, said Rank, men believed in the immortality of their own souls (shadows). Totemism put an end to this belief and introduced the idea of incarnation. The spirit of the dead enters the mother's womb and a new life starts; a continuity of life develops.

In the Oedipus myth, the individual tries to recapture heroic stature by accepting fatherhood instead of his own self-perpetuation. The matriarchal organization gives way to the patriarchal. Through incest, which is rebirth, the man accepts the father's role.

Rank recast Freud's version of the Oedipus myth. The sons desired to return to the mother's womb and killed their father. All of them "took possession sexually" (intercourse is a substitution for the return to the womb), but all could not "return to her." Only the youngest son "remains as it were permanently attached to her, because no one after him has occupied the place in the mother. . . . This superiority really consists in the fact that he comes last and, so to say, drives the others away. In this he is like the father, with whom he alone, and from the same motives, is able to identify himself."[10] After the father's death the mother is the leader of the family. Now the youngest son assumes leadership. He represents both mother and father and becomes himself "the strict, just," but no longer violent father. He must "again be set up as the 'barrier to incest' against the desire to return to the mother. . . . Anxiety of the mother is then transferred as respect to the king and to the inhibiting Ego (ideal) motives which he represents (justice, state, etc.)."[11] Crucifixion represents punishment for rebellion against the father, and resurrection the birth. Mary is the sublimated mother.

"Religion tends ultimately toward the creation of a succoring and protecting primal Being to whose bosom one can flee from all troubles and dangers and to whom one finally returns in a future life which is a faithful, although sublimated, image of the once lost Paradise."[12] The religious development runs parallel to the historical-sociological development. The

[10] Rank, *Trauma of Birth*, p. 113.
[11] *Ibid.*, p. 92.
[12] *Ibid.*, p. 117.

original god represents the primal father; his son rebelled against him and became god. "The historical importance of Christianity rests on the fact that it was the first to place the Son-God in the center without simultaneously attacking the original rights of the mother and the secondary rights of the father," wrote Rank.[13]

The idea of birth pervades all areas of human life and art. Creativeness is an act of birth. The artist creates in "maternal pangs of creation." Primitive art created first "a vessel for a receptacle and a protection in imitation of the womb."

In ancient Greece the artist "raised himself in identification with the mother to creator of men, in that he attempts in his works of art to detach himself gradually and under great resistance from the mother. . . . From this 'moment' of simultaneously longed-for and yet not wished-for freeing from the bestial womb, from this eternal sticking fast in birth, which the neurotic constantly experiences afresh, as anxiety of the primal situation, the Greek artist and with him the entire race found the way to idealization by preserving in solid stone this stormy movement, which the Medusa head has kept in all its terrifying significance."[14]

Rank applied his ideas to the history of culture and distinguished between mother and father types of culture. The ancient Egyptian culture was a mother type, composed of the *religious* factor appearing in a peculiar cult of the dead, which emphasized in the preservation of the body the idea of a further life in the womb. The Egyptian culture included the *artistic* factor, appearing in an exaggerated esteem of the animal body (animal cult), and then the *social* factor, appearing in a high valuation of woman.

In the historical development these "maternal" motifs became modified. The cult of the sun-father indicates that father elements gained ground. Rank wrote: "The development of sun worship always goes hand in hand with a decisive turning from mother-culture to father-culture, as is shown in the final identification of the new born king (*infant*) with the sun. This opposition to the dominance of the woman both in the social sphere (right of the father) and in the religious, continues . . . to Greece, where it leads by means of the entire repression of woman even from the erotic life, to the richest blossoming of the masculine civilization and to the artistic idealization corresponding to it."[15]

Concluding Remarks

"While at first I was completely under the influence of Freudian realism and tried to express my conception of the creative man, the artist, in the biological-mechanistic terms of Freud's natural science ideology,

[13] *Ibid.*, p. 129.
[14] *Ibid.*, p. 159.
[15] *Ibid.*, p. 153.

on the basis of my own experience I have since been enabled to formulate these common human problems in a common human language as well. 'The Trauma of Birth,' a book written in 1923, marks the decisive turning point in this development. There I compared to the creative drive of the individual as treated in '*Der Künstler*' the creation of the individual himself, not merely physically but also psychically in the sum of 'rebirth experience,' which I understood psychologically as the actual creative act of the human being. For in this act the psychic ego is born out of the biological corporeal ego and the human being becomes at once creator and creature or actually moves from creature to creator, in the ideal case, creator of himself, his own personality."[16]

And here is exactly the dividing line between empirical science and speculative systems. Freud's main postulate was determinism. Rank believed that something can be its own cause ("creator of himself"). Freud postulated three determinants of human personality: the inherited instinctual forces, the biologically determined developmental stages, and the environmental influences. Rank introduced instead the "creative will."

Freud *observed* love and hate and hypothesized two instinctual forces. Rank introduced the fear of female organs, which the neonate probably never saw.

Rank undoubtedly deserves much credit in the area of psychology applied to art and ethics. His creative type may correspond to the picture of some unusually gifted individuals. Rank said that all men fear female organs; it is probably true of some. Rank said all men wish to live forever and do not wish to have children, unless they go through "rebirth"; it may be true of some men.

Rank unduly stressed the role of woman and femininity, presenting man in a struggle for independence from the archefemale, the mother. On this point his theory resembles Adler's masculine protest.

In summarizing Rank's contribution, one may say that Rank, like Adler and Jung, developed his own theory out of Freud's conceptual system. For better or worse, Freud's system represents a close-knit structure capable of answering practically all questions on the level of intervening variable. Whenever one suggests modifications they must either (1) result from contradictory empirical data, (2) be necessary in order to accommodate additional empirical data, or (3) offer methodological advantages. Rank's modifications of psychoanalysis hardly meet any of these criteria.

[16] Rank, *Will Therapy and Truth and Reality*, p. 210.

3. FURTHER DEVELOPMENTS
IN PSYCHOANALYSIS

Melanie Klein

Melanie Klein, a leading British psychoanalyst of children, accepted Freud's theories but put great emphasis on the aggressive impulses and believed that the formation of the personality structure takes place in the first year of a child's life, in contradistinction to Freud's developmental schedule.

Klein emphasized the importance of the second part of the oral stage, the oral-aggressive or oral-sadistic. She presented the picture of "an infant from six to twelve months trying to destroy its mother by every method at the disposal of its sadistic tendencies—with its teeth, nails, and excreta and with the whole of its body, transformed in imagination into all kinds of dangerous weapons."[17]

The infant accepts objects by swallowing them or rejects them by spitting them out. Pleasure-producing objects are introjected. This oral sadism of an infant may become intensified by frustrations.

According to Klein, the aggressive impulse is originally directed to oneself. The mechanism of projection enables the child to ascribe his own hostile feelings to his parents. A *paranoid position* develops in which the infant acts out his hostile feelings toward his mother.

If the mother gratifies the child's instinctual needs, she helps him to overcome his aggressive impulses. Love and fear combined lead to the formation of the superego. Freud said that the superego develops in the phallic stage; Klein believed that one part of the id turns against the other and inhibits it and the earliest introjected objects form the core of the superego.

The fear of one's own destructive impulses leads to projection. Then the child fears the supposedly hostile mother and wishes to swallow her. A new crisis develops, called by Klein the *depressive position*. The infant comes to realize that his mother is both "good" and "bad." After introjection of his love object the infant must go through a mourning and depressive mood as described by Freud and Abraham. Klein believed that the infant internalizes the "good breast" and the "bad breast." All pleasure is attributed to the good breast, all frustration to the bad, persecuting breast. Oral frustration may elicit the Oedipus complex even at that early stage of human life. Moreover, Klein assumed that at that stage the ego already was able "to project, deflect and distribute desires and emotions, as well as guilt and the urge to make reparations on new objects and interests."[18]

[17] Melanie Klein, *The Psychoanalysis of Children* (2nd ed.), Hogarth, 1937, p. 187.
[18] *Ibid.*, p. 224.

The main area of disagreement between Klein and the other Freudians relates to the former's deviation from that part of Freud's theory which deals with the development of the mental apparatus of id, ego, and superego. It has been a highly controversial issue between Melanie Klein and Anna Freud, for Anna Freud's main contribution to the psychoanalytic theory was her volume on the defense mechanism of the ego.[19]

Apparently, Klein's interpretation of early childhood phenomena goes far beyond empirical evidence. It is, at the present level of evidence, rather difficult to ascribe to an infant awareness of sexuality and Oedipus complex. Moreover, Klein's clinical evidence stems from her work with older children; neither she nor anyone else actually observed the kind of behavior she ascribed to one-year-old infants. Klein's deviation from Freud is an interesting speculation rather than an observation and has to be viewed as such.

Sandor Ferenczi: A New Theory of Instincts

Ferenczi suggested four stages in the development of reality perception. In the prenatal stage all wishes of the child are gratified; this, therefore, is the stage of *unconditional omnipotence*. The neonate probably feels that all his wishes are satisfied; he has only to wish and the wish will be immediately fulfilled. This is *hallucination-magic omnipotence*. Day by day the child faces reality and there are some disappointments and frustrations. Gradually he learns to overcome them by crying and gestures, and *magic gestures omnipotence* develops. Later on the child believes in the *magic of thoughts and words*.[20]

Normally the child gives up the feeling of omnipotence. The stimuli coming from the outer world, which he cannot master, bring with them some limitation of the feeling of omnipotence. Gradually the idea of omnipotence is given up.

While these observations were accepted by the main psychoanalytic school, Ferenczi made another suggestion, this time diverging from Freud. He mentioned that the patient's attitude toward the analyst not only is a product of transference but reflects the *real* relationship that took place between the two persons. Thus the so-called "participation" technique developed.

Freud's therapeutic technique could not be discussed in this book, but it forms an integral part of the system. Transference meant to Freud cathexis of instinctual energy in a state of regression. The patient loves and hates his analyst as if he were a child and the analyst the parental figure. Any other interpretation of patient-analyst relationship is not merely a modification of the therapeutic technique but a serious devia-

[19] Anna Freud, *The Ego and the Mechanisms of Defense*, International Universities Press, 1946.
[20] Sandor Ferenczi, *Contributions to Psychoanalysis*, Badger, 1916.

tion from Freud's theory. Obviously, Rank's ideas about will therapy and Ferenczi's participation bring us close to Sullivan's theory.

Furthermore, Ferenczi deviated from Freud in the interpretation of sexual behavior. Freud clearly distinguished between the life and the death instincts. To Ferenczi, and after him French and Alexander, sexuality is the channel for all "free-floating pleasure tensions of all organs." Ferenczi distinguished between the "utility function" of each organ and its surplus energy, which is shifted to the genital organ for discharge. According to Ferenczi sexuality is merely a discharge of all those "accumulated amounts of unpleasure which, side-tracked during the utility functioning of the organs, were left undealt with, undisposed of." And "whenever an organ fails to indulge its pleasure tendencies directly but renounces these in favor of the organism as a whole, substances may be secreted from this organ or qualitative innervations be shifted to other organs and eventually to the genital, it being the task of the latter to equalize in the gratificatory act the free-floating pleasure tensions of all the organs." Therefore, "in ejaculation all those autonomic tendencies (tendency to get rid of a part of the body) are summated, the carrying out of which was neglected by utility functioning."[21]

Apparently Ferenczi distinguished between useful purposes on one side and useless sexuality on the other. All organs function in a useful way. Their surplus excitation, which cannot be put to any useful purpose, is discharged through sexuality.

Ferenczi's theory puts in place of Freud's theory of love and hate a theory of useful and free-floating discharge of energy. Pleasure that serves the needs of the organism is put on one side, and sexual pleasure, which is for its own sake, is put on the other. Furthermore, Ferenczi distinguished between two ways in which the organism satisfies its needs. The first way is the *autoplastic,* or the change of the organism itself. Both ontogenetic and phylogenetic development bear witness to adjustment through inner changes. Living organisms adjust to external temperature, to external threats to the supply of food, etc., by undergoing changes in their structure, color of skin, actions, etc. Certain organisms adjust in an *alloplastic* manner, i.e., they modify the environment, by digging holes, building houses, etc.

Apparently Ferenczi has many keen observations to offer. One may say that in certain situations sexual discharge alleviates a general tension in the organism. What this writer doubts is that Ferenczi's observations justify his generalizations.

The study of the psychoanalytic type of psychological theory is quite impressive for its wealth of data, but it is threatened by its not too rigorous application of the principles of scientific inquiry. This problem

[21] Sandor Ferenczi, *Thalassa: A Theory of Sexuality,* Psychoanalytic Quarterly Press, 1938.

will be discussed at length in Chapter 14 of this book, but it must be said here that the ease with which Freud's foes and friends introduce new concepts represents a violation of the principles of scientific caution and thoroughness. Freud himself was quite aware of this danger and was exceedingly cautious in building his personality model. But if Freud's scientific method is open to criticism, the methods of Adler, Jung, Rank, Ferenczi, Klein, Alexander, Horney, Sullivan, Fromm, and others seem to be even more vulnerable (cf. Chap. 14).

Franz Alexander: Vector Theory

F. Alexander deviated from Freud's theory in the direction of psychosomatics. Alexander wrote that somatic and psychological analyses of life are "two approaches to the same thing." Furthermore, "the functions of the mind are as truly biological as locomotion and breathing, and are adaptive mechanisms which sometime in the future will probably be described in terms of physics and chemistry."[22] Life is a continuous cycle of supply, retention, and output of energy. "From the point of view of energy, life can be viewed as a relationship between three vectors: (1) the intake of energy in the nutritive substances and oxygen; (2) their partial retention for use in growth; and (3) the expenditure of energy to maintain existence, its loss in waste, in heat, and in erotic playful activities."[23]

The upper part of the gastrointestinal tract is best suited to intake of energy. Accordingly, the *gastric* personality type is inclined to receive, to take in. The middle and the lower parts of the gastrointestinal tract are well suited to retention and elimination. The *constipation* personality type is inclined to retain, while the *colitis* type is prone to give or to eliminate.

Alexander rejected Freud's theory of Eros and Thanatos and substituted for it a "metabolic conception of life as a process consisting of continuous anabolic construction and katabolic disruption of the complex biomolecules."[24] Alexander saw no need to regard the disintegrating factor as a death instinct.

According to Alexander, sexuality forms a part of the discharge system. "Sexuality discharges any surplus excitation, regardless of its quality," wrote Alexander. "When the organism reaches the limits of its growth, it can no longer increase and must divide. Surplus organic matter which cannot be integrated in a single biological unit is eliminated and becomes a new organism. . . . Propagation results from surplus energy generated by growth. The psychological equivalent of propagation is love."[25] Ac-

[22] Franz Alexander, *Fundamentals of Psychoanalysis*, Norton, 1948, p. 35.
[23] *Ibid.*, p. 44.
[24] *Ibid.*, p. 64.
[25] *Ibid.*, p. 76.

cordingly, the incorporative tendency of hunger is not considered by Alexander an erotic phenomenon, but the surplus manifestation of thumb-sucking is regarded as an oral-erotic phenomenon. The influence of Jung and Ferenczi upon Alexander is quite apparent.

While leaning heavily toward the organic interpretation of mental phenomena, Alexander was fully aware of sociological factors in personality development. Personality, he wrote, is the result of both heredity and the specific family constellation and cultural environment.

4. PSYCHOANALYSIS AND STUDIES OF CULTURE

Polyculturalism

Sociological and anthropological considerations form the common denominator of the entire neo-psychoanalytic movement. Almost all neo-psychoanalysts shifted from the hereditarian point of view toward environmental aspects of personality, from the genetic factors toward situationism, and from the monocultural analysis of mankind toward poly-culturalism.

Freud himself envisaged the future interest in studies in comparative anthropology and paved the road for them in his volume on *Totem and Tabu*. The interest in cultural anthropology was quite profound among the early Freudians, and as early as 1909 Karl Abraham, Freud's most orthodox and perhaps most brilliant disciple, published a monograph devoted to anthropological studies.[26]

An important contribution toward the development of psychoanalytic anthropology is the field studies of B. Malinowski. While conducting his research independently of Freud, Malinowski offered a definite support to psychoanalysis. Malinowski studied the culture of the Trobriand Islanders. He found that their Oedipus complex differs from that found in patriarchal families. In the societies described by Freud, Abraham, and others the son desired the mother and considered the father his rival. In the Trobriand Islands the father, *tama*, yields his role to his brother-in-law, *kadaju*, the mother's brother. "As soon as the child begins to grow up and take an interest in things outside the affairs of the household and his immediate needs, certain complications arise and change the meaning of tama for him. He learns that he is not of the same clan as his tama, that his totemic appellation is different, and that it is identical with that of his mother. . . . Another man appears on the horizon and is called by the child kadaju (my mother's brother). . . . He also sees as he grows up that the mother's brother assumes a gradually

[26] Karl Abraham, *Dream and Myths*, Nervous and Mental Disease Monograph Series, No. 15, 1913.

increasing authority over him, requiring his services, helping him in some things, . . . while the father's authority and counsel become less and less important."[27]

Malinowski's studies provided an important support to Freud's theory and at the same time broadened the horizons of psychoanalysis. The empirical studies of primitive cultures corroborated the main concepts of the psychoanalytic theory, but they clearly indicated that Freud's developmental stages greatly depend upon cultural factors.

Now the question could be raised whether the developmental stages could be modified by one's life experiences within a given culture, as Freud believed, or were merely a product of cultural influences. As will be shown, there is no consensus of opinion on this issue.

The anthropologists M. Mead and Gregory Bateson are not psychoanalysts, but they have applied the psychoanalytic approach to the study of the Balinese culture. Bateson and Mead described a symbolic courtship dance which reflects the knowledge of the Balinese males that they will eventually "marry a woman whose attitude toward human relations will be exactly that of his mother." Apparently Freud's theory of the Oedipus complex received strong support in this study. Moreover, "There is a conflict which recurs in each generation in which parents try to force the children of brothers to marry each other; to stay within the family line and to worship the same ancestral gods while the young people themselves rebel and, if possible, marry strangers. Fathers and brothers may help a boy to carry off a girl who is not kin but no male relative of the girl herself can admit complicity in any such scheme. An abduction elopement is staged . . . dramatized in a frequent plot; that of the prince who attempts to abduct a beautiful girl but through accident gets instead the ugly sister," wrote Bateson and Mead.[28] Always the Balinese man marries a woman who resembles his domineering mother.

Wilhelm Reich: The Character

The man who broke ground for a sociocultural deviation from Freud was Wilhelm Reich. Reich won his fame by his studies on the neurotic "character" and "armor," with a definite sociological slant. He was more Freudian than Freud himself in regard to the importance of libido. To Reich sexual potency was a criterion of mental health, and sexuality was the main factor in personality structure.

Yet Reich paved the road for a definite deviation from Freud and, for a while, believed in a *rapprochement* between psychoanalysis and Marx-

[27] Bronislaw Malinowski, *The Sexual Life of Savages in North Western Melanesia*, Routledge, 1929, pp. 5-6.
[28] Gregory Bateson and Margaret Mead, *Balinese Character*, New York Academy of Science, Special Publication, Vol. 2, 1942, p. 36.

ism. Reich noticed that the development of personality types or characters depends upon the socioeconomic system. Thus one may consider
him the forerunner of Horney, Kardiner, and Fromm. "In connection
with the sociological function of character formation we must study the
fact that certain social orders go with certain average human structures,
or to put it differently, that every social order creates those character
forms which it needs for its preservation. In class society, the ruling class
secures its position with the aid of education and the institution of the
family, by making its ideologies the ruling ideologies of all members of
the society. But it is not merely a matter of imposing ideologies, attitudes
and concepts on the members of society. Rather it is a matter of a
deep-reaching process in each new generation, of the formation of a
psychic structure which corresponds to the existing social order in all
strata of the population," wrote Reich in 1933.[29] But the man who subordinated personality structure to the economic system was Abraham
Kardiner.

Kardiner and Linton: Economic Determinism

In accordance with Freud, Kardiner maintained that the individual's
attitudes, values, etc., called by him "projective system," are shaped in
early childhood. The child's early experience are his child-parent experiences. Hitherto, child-rearing practices play the decisive role in shaping
personality.[30]

Child-rearing practices are "culturally patterned." Parents apply educational methods formed in their environment which reflect the culture
of their environment. Hence the child-rearing methods used by members
of a given society "tend to be similar." This similarity in parent-child
relationship must influence the children and develop in them similar
"personality configurations." Personalities of individuals growing in different cultural settings must therefore differ one from another, while in
a given society its members share similar early experiences and develop
a similar personality type, called by A. Kardiner and R. Linton the *basic
personality type.*

A culture, said Kardiner, consists of an organized collective of humans,
who have fixed modes of thoughts and behavior commonly accepted by
them, such as traditions, religious practices and beliefs, means of earning
a livelihood, rules and laws, child-rearing methods, etc. These fixed
modes of thought and behavior are known as institutions. Deviation from
the common acceptance of these institutions creates disturbance in the
individual and in his group.

There are a great many cultures, all of which have institutions that

[29] Wilhelm Reich, *Character Analysis*, Orgone Institute, 1945, chap. 18 (first published in 1933).

[30] Abraham Kardiner, *The Individual and His Society*, Columbia University, 1939.

are unique. Yet all cultures have institutions that are similar to one another, for all these institutions attempt to satisfy definite needs of humans. For instance, the infant's need to be nursed and cared for by the mother is met by all cultures with some degree of uniformity, although the duration of such care varies and the technique of rearing children differs widely. The institution of marriage is universal, although the regulations as to whom and how one marries differ in different cultures.

Apparently the individual is creator, carrier, and perpetrator of all institutions. An individual in a culture learns about the institutions in his culture by means of contact with other individuals. Thus, Kardiner attempted to discover and analyze the effects of institutions upon individuals. How institutions satisfy or frustrate the basic human needs and how an individual adapts himself to these institutions was Kardiner's main concern.

One of the most useful and informative means of obtaining these data is to make systematic and detailed studies of the institutions of several different cultures.

These studies, in which the combined method of projective techniques and life histories was applied, led to a definite deviation from Freud. Although the starting point of Kardiner's studies was psychoanalysis, his conclusions are not psychoanalytic. Consider for example, the impact of social relations on personality structure. Among the Marquesans, the number of men is much greater than the number of women. This situation was conducive to a more favorable position of women, and accordingly led to a different development of the male and female personality types. The Oedipus complex, concluded Kardiner, cannot be universal, for in the Marquesan society the father is the protector and caretaker of children of both sexes. The rejecting mother is often regarded as a competitor who takes away the beloved father. Again, the Tanala of Madagascar respect their parents; their repression of hostility resembles the puritan. This is interpreted by Kardiner as a result of an early and strict sphincter control. Tanala babies are carried by their mothers without diapers and if they soil the mother's clothes they are punished. Thus they arrive at sphincter control at the age of six months. In a study of the people of Okinawa, Moloney found that their flexible, permissive, and affectionate infant-feeding methods result in a friendly, cheerful, and secure personality type.[31] Kardiner's conclusion was that personality structure depends upon environmental factors rather than upon developmental stages.

Oral mastery, wrote Kardiner, does not result from frustration of sucking needs. Finger-sucking and other oral manifestations are not found among the Marquesans despite the fact that they are usually weaned after a few weeks of sucking. Their mothers are anxious not to

[31] J. C. Moloney, *The Magic Cloak*, Montrose, 1949.

lose the beauty of their breasts by prolonged nursing of their babies. According to Kardiner, oral mastery seems to develop from *economic anxiety.* The child who fears famine and is not sure that he will be supported by his parents may develop oral patterns of behavior.

Thus, socioeconomic factors play quite a prominent role in Kardiner's theory. The idea of universality of the developmental stages is replaced by the idea of adjustment to the physical and social environment. As a leading psychoanalytic anthropologist, Geza Roheim, remarked, Kardiner oscillates between an economic and a psychological determinism.[32]

Actually Kardiner did not oscillate and his point of view was clearly explained. The sexual instinct in man, he wrote, has well-defined characteristics: (1) The satisfaction of the sexual craving can be deferred. (2) It can be vicariously gratified. (3) Its energy (according to Freud) can be deflected into channels other than sexual (by sublimation). However, the need for food cannot be substituted for; its satisfaction cannot be deferred very long; and it is not capable of the process of sublimation.

As Kardiner showed, *food anxiety* plays a leading role in many cultures, and a great many institutions or mores have been elaborated with regard to eating. These mores have influence on *what* kind of food is eaten in a culture, *when* it shall be eaten, and *how* it shall be eaten.

Food anxiety will materially influence the behavior of individuals in any society. The problem is further complicated by the fact that economic pressures are never found singly. That is, there is no guarantee that the same pressure will produce the same effects in different cultures. The reaction to food anxiety may have several elements. Rational efforts may be made to get food, food may be taken from some other person, or hallucinatory gratification of hunger may be obtained by fantasy or dreaming. Several other anxieties may appear, such as the fear of being eaten up.

In our culture there is no generalized food anxiety because the means of production and exchange are under complete control and are well distributed. The technique for procuring food is part of those social pursuits of the individual which we call "economic." The reaction to food anxiety in our culture is highly individualized because of the differentiation in economic pursuits.

In several cultures food anxiety is a definite problem. There was food anxiety among the Marquesans because the islands on which they lived are subject from time to time to droughts which lead to serious crop failures and shortages of drinking water. The rational methods for dealing with this food anxiety consisted of storing food in great communal pits and the entire yield of the first crop went into these pits. This kept

[32] Geza Roheim (ed.), *Psychoanalysis and The Social Sciences,* Vol. I, International Universities, 1947, p. 30.

the Marquesans well prepared for emergencies most of the time. Nevertheless, there is evidence of an exaggerated anxiety about food, according to the anthropologist Ralph Linton. There was, first of all, an overevaluation of eating itself. The emphasis fell on bulk and not on quality of food.

Cannibalism was an important evidence of this food anxiety. There was also a fear of being eaten, which was expressed in many ways and led to a great many different kinds of institutions, the purposes of which were to relieve this fear. It was fear of being eaten which undoubtedly increased the hostility between tribes and the practice of cannibalism.

Although there was eating of enemies because of revenge obligations, there was also plain meat-hunting of enemy tribes for food, especially at times of food shortage. Linton, who collected all this material during a stay of nearly one year in the Marquesas, from 1920 to 1921, states that there was another indication that cannibalism was not merely ceremonial or practiced for revenge obligations. The Marquesans ate everything from infants up. There was ordinarily no cannibalism within the tribe, although in time of extreme famine a priest might designate certain victims who would be killed and eaten.

Marquesan eating habits and everything associated with food showed the effects of the periodic food shortages and the tremendous value placed upon food. For instance, at the age of ten every child went through the ceremony of sanctifying his or her hands. After this, he could prepare food for himself and others. Food for men and for women was prepared separately and even cooked at different fires and in different utensils. There were a number of taboos on food. Certain foods could not be eaten by people in certain occupations. Food was one of the few things subject to theft, for members of the family would steal food from one another but nothing else.

It can be readily seen, therefore, that food scarcity in the Marquesans led to the development of hypochondriacal characteristics within the personality structures of the individuals in that culture.

The Tanala of Madagascar, under the system of dry rice cultivation, showed little evidence of food anxiety. Linton was in Madagascar in 1928 and made a study of these people. The country in which they live has an elevation of 300 or 400 feet. There are no navigable streams, but the country is well watered. Sufficient soil was available, although it was poor and required ten to fifteen years of fallowing. There was no incentive for any family to raise more than it needed in the way of crops, for crops could be neither sold nor hoarded.

The rice crop was stored by the family. Yet, although there was no famine, every household was equipped with a series of measures of various sizes used to apportion the daily rations to the family members.

The old crop always carried over until the time of the next harvest. Though the Tanala had neither ceremonial attitudes nor magic connected with food, there was a rice ceremony which consisted of a small family offering made to the ancestors at the time of harvest. Also, charms were kept in certain villages in the hope of preventing hailstorms and locusts from destroying the rice crops.

Eating habits were quite simple. One meal a day was served in the afternoon. The personal cleanliness of these people was noteworthy. They washed their hands and mouth before and after eating. Each individual had his own eating spoon. However, at meal time the father sat apart in an elevated position and was served separately. His food dish had to be elevated above that of the other members of the family. For this purpose elaborate stands of basketry were made. The oldest son, from the age of four onward, was also served separately. However, the mother and the other children ate from a common dish. Meat was rarely eaten. In fact, the dream of cutting meat was a bad omen indicating a funeral in the family. Milk was taken only when the cow had more than her calf could use. Even the manure of a cow was not employed in agriculture.

There was little evidence of food anxiety among the Tanala. Their confidence in their ability to control their food supply came mainly from the certainty of their social and organizational aspects. Each individual was so trained in his social role, as well as in techniques which required no special skill, that he was bound in a system of sanctions and punishments. The father and oldest son of a family exacted subsistence and prestige from the labor of the younger sons. The younger sons were a dependable factor in the system of production, and their diligence was guaranteed by the threat of invoking the disapproval of their father. The level of prestige, standing, and status for the younger sons depended on their competing with each other in winning the father's favor. Thus, there was almost complete immobility in status for the younger sons of a family. This created, obviously, tension between the younger brothers against each other and against the oldest son. However, not against the father, whose position was too strong for any open hostility. Thus only two attitudes toward the father were possible, hatred and submission. The hatred was easy to suppress in view of the father's ability to confer favors and the son's ability to collect them. Aggression would usually emerge only when the rewards for submission were withdrawn.

Kardiner's theory represents an application of Freud's principles leading to a definite deviation from Freud's conclusions. Kardiner is still Freudian as far as the personality structure of unconscious, conscious, and preconscious goes and partially so in regard to the mental apparatus. Freud's theory of libido underwent in Kardiner's studies most radical changes.

5. PSYCHOANALYSIS AND EXPERIMENTAL PSYCHOLOGY

Methodological Criticism

There is a great deal of difference between the "social climate" of the early splits in the psychoanalytic movement and the later ones. Adler and Jung emphasized the differences between their systems and Freud's. They did their utmost to point to their original contribution in psychology.

This tense atmosphere gradually cleared up. Horney, Kardiner, Sullivan, Fromm, and many others readily admit how much they owe to Freud. Perhaps the personal tensions disappeared. However, not only the personal relations but the entire climate of research changed. In times past almost every year saw a "new" theory thrown into the confused psychological crowd. Today psychologists are more modest than they used to be and a healthier atmosphere has developed. In view of the continuously growing mass of empirical data and the improving research conditions no one could dare to claim the monopoly of truth. Psychologists today are less split into "schools" and have learned to adapt various methods and facts endorsed by their opponents. There is a continuous increase in mutual influence and mutual learning between research workers. Instead of barriers between the various schools there is a growing interdependence, interaction, and mutual understanding and learning among them.

Another shift took place—in the ways of criticism. However psychologists may agree or disagree with Freud, the "style" of their criticism has changed. The earlier critics attacked psychoanalysis from the viewpoint of true-false. The modern critics rather evade the question of whether Freud was right or wrong. They ask instead *how* he arrived at his conclusions, what his *empirical data* were, and what *logical inferences* he applied in his system.

This *methodological criticism* does not accept or reject psychoanalysis. Various psychologists point to the obvious weaknesses and deficiencies of clinical studies. The very asset of psychotherapy, transference, is a liability in research. The clinician, especially the analyst, uses in therapy the most precious tool: his own personality. Often the final results of psychoanalytic therapy depend upon the personality of the analyst. It is therefore generally accepted that an individual who plans to analyze others should undergo psychoanalysis in order to gain the mastery over his own emotional biases. How perfect one can be is a question open to discussion.

Evidently the clinician can hardly claim methodological equality with the experimentalist. Experiments are conducted in such a way as to provide optimum conditions for the isolation or modification of experimental variables. Nothing of that kind is available in the clinical method. Neither Freud nor any other psychologist who studies human nature in clinical situations can modify the conditions of research. He has to study his patients as they come and sampling is not possible in psychoanalytic studies.

Some Experimental Studies

Apparently psychoanalysis cannot become an experimental science for we cannot experiment with human life and destiny and we do not induce experimental upheavals. But to discard psychoanalysis as a science on the ground that it does not admit of experimental proof is just as justified "as to discard astronomy. Experimentation with the heavenly bodies is after all exceedingly difficult," remarked Freud.[33] Freud himself, nevertheless, in 1932 reported several experiments that corroborated his hypotheses. Schrotter experimented with sexual symbols. He told a woman to dream about intercourse with her lady friend, and the hypnotized woman dreamt indeed about her friend who in the dream held a travelingbag with the inscription: "Ladies only." In 1924 Betlheim and Hartman experimented with patients suffering from Korsakoff's syndrome. The patients were told some sexual stories and reproduced them with distortions well known in Freud's studies of dream work, dream distortions, and symbols.

Actually, practically all projective techniques are experimental tools which utilize the psychoanalytic frame of reference to a lesser or a greater extent.[34]

Several experimental psychologists tried to put psychoanalytic findings to experimental test. In an excellent summary of the experimental work Sears wrote: "The psychoanalytic way of looking at man's motives, defense, and personality structure has been so invigorating to psychological thought that experimentalists have been reluctant to let it remain unincorporated in the general science of psychology." There are two main difficulties in incorporating psychoanalytic findings in the body of experimental psychology. "The subjective character of the [psychoanalytic—B. W.] system has proved a difficulty, however, since it does not permit of conventional scientific tests of proof and disproof. . . ." In addition to this methodological difficulty, "psychoanalysis deals heavily in the more

[33] Sigmund Freud, *New Introductory Lectures in Psychoanalysis,* Norton, 1933, p. 36.
[34] Zygmunt Piotrovski, *Perceptoanalysis,* Harper, 1957.

potent emotions and motives, and if society is put hard to it to control sex, aggression, anxiety, pride, idealism, and unreason, it is little wonder the experimentalist shies away from unleashing them in his laboratory."[35]

Among the most significant experimental studies in this area that we shall mention here were those related to the problems of fixation, frustration, regression, and aggression. Fixation could be partial, i.e., fixation of the libido cathexis on a certain object or fixation on a certain developmental stage. Fixations may be caused by insufficient or lacking gratification of the instinctual desire or by an abundant gratification.

No direct experimental confirmation was received, but some experiments seem to offer indirect support to Freud's theory of fixation. Youtz[36] trained rats to press a small brass bar which released a pellet of food. He let one group of rats practice it (with food gratification) ten times and another group forty times. Then he broke the circuit. The group of rats which had had forty gratifications was much more resistant to extinction than the group with ten gratifications. Apparently the more gratification, the stronger the tendency to become fixated.

When the individual becomes frustrated he tends to regress to the point of fixation. He relinquishes the adult pattern of behavior and regresses to childish patterns. Regression may also take place in abundant satiation, when more primitive behavior may become tempting for it resembles the early and more sheltered stages of the individual's life in infancy.

In an experiment by Hamilton and Krechevsky rats were trained in a T-maze to choose the shorter alley in their run for food. After they learned it, the sides in the maze were reversed. The rats regressed to original habits.[37]

A similar experiment in instrumental act regression was conducted by O'Kelly, who trained rats in a maze. When the learning pattern was well established, he reversed the direction of running. The rats learned the new way. Then the rats were given plenty of food and they regressed to the former pattern of behavior.[38]

Summarizing the above-mentioned and several other experimental studies Sears concluded that "both data and logic support Freud's statement that regression is a function of fixation—habit strength—but it is a function of frustration in a secondary way only, and what effect frustra-

[35] Robert R. Sears, "Experimental Analysis of Psychoanalytic Phenomena," in J. McV. Hunt, *Personality and the Behavior Disorders*, Ronald, 1944, p. 306.

[36] Richard P. Youtz, "Reinforcement, Extinction, and Spontaneous Recovery in a non-Pavlovian Reaction," *Journal of Experimental Psychology*, 1938, **22**, 305–318.

[37] J. A. Hamilton and I. Krechevsky, "Studies in the Effect of Shock on Behavior Plasticity in the Rat," *Journal of Comparative Psychology*, 1933, **16**, 237–253.

[38] Lawrence I. O'Kelly, "An Experimental Study of Regression: II. Some Motivational Determinants of Regression and Perseveration," *Journal of Comparative Psychology*, 1940, **30**, 55–95.

tion has is primarily in the direction of influencing the strength of instrumental act sequences."[39]

Another set of experiments dealt with the problem of aggression resulting from frustration. Dollard and his associates (cf. Chap. 4, section 6) conducted carefully planned experiments in which frustration led to aggression.

Very often aggression becomes displaced. Whenever the cause of frustration is powerful or inaccessible or invisible, a displaced aggression may take place. N. E. Miller in experimental studies exposed rats to electric shocks and taught them to fight each other. Whenever another rat was not available for a fight, the rats attacked another object. In Miller's words, "When the direct response to the original stimulus is prevented by the absence of that stimulus, displaced responses will occur to other similar stimuli and the strongest displaced response will occur to the most similar stimulus present."[40] As mentioned before (Chap. 4, section 6) Miller related displacement to stimulus generalization.

In carefully planned experimentation with humans Doob and Sears studied the relationship between overt aggression and the expected satisfaction in comparison to the expected pain resulting from punishment. The subjects marked on a four-point scale the expected satisfaction and eventual punishment anticipated for their aggressive actions. Whenever the anticipated satisfaction was greater, an overt aggression took place; whenever the expected punishment was greater, the subject preferred the non-overt, inhibited form of aggression.[41]

An ingenious experiment related to Freud's theory of repression was conducted by Sears. He gave his subjects a list of nonsense syllables and asked them to memorize the list. Then a card-sorting test with an inevitable failure was administered. Then again the subjects were presented with the task of learning a list of nonsense syllables. This time, as a result of repression caused by failure on the card-sorting test, the subjects failed to learn the syllables. Sears believes that the card-sorting task left uncompleted was a threat to self-esteem and acted as a repressing factor.[42]

Additional carefully designed experiments in the same area were conducted by Zeller. Zeller used learning of nonsense syllables as the main task, thus following in the footsteps of Sears. The failure experience was

[39] Sears, *op. cit.*, p. 313.

[40] Neal E. Miller, "Theory and Experiment Relating Psychoanalytic Displacement to Stimulus-Response Generalization," *Journal of Abnormal and Social Psychology*, 1948, 43, 155–178.

[41] L. W. Doob and Robert R. Sears, "Factors Determining Substitute Behavior and the Overt Expression of Aggression," *Journal of Abnormal and Social Psychology*, 1939, 34, 293–313.

[42] Robert R. Sears, "Initiation of the Repression Sequence by Experienced Failure," *Journal of Experimental Psychology*, 1937, 20, 570–580.

provided by an imitative tapping of Knox cubes. In Zeller's experiment the failure was inhibiting or "repressing" only when it was related to an earlier learned set of syllables. Zeller believes that his results corroborate Freud's theory of repression, but he does not exclude some other interpretation of the same results.[43]

A few experiments conducted by Kurt Lewin and his associates seem to corroborate Freud's theory. One is the famous Zeigarnik experiment (cf. Chap. 13). According to Freud, a traumatic experience stimulates the mind to such an extent that no assimilation or discharge is possible. The traumatic situation is kept in the mind very much alive, as though the person had not yet been able to deal adequately with the situation, as though the task were still actually before him unaccomplished. This unaccomplished task causes lasting disturbances in the distribution of the available energy in the mind, Freud said. Lewin's experiments confirmed this idea.

In another experiment Barker, Dembo, and Lewin observed that children frustrated by the removal of attractive toys regress to a less constructive level of play (cf. Chap. 13). Anna Freud criticized this experiment.[44] She could not see how the mild frustration caused by the removal of toys could be compared to the emotional upheavals which S. Freud had in mind.

Observations of Manifest Behavior

In a summary of scientific testings of psychoanalysis B. A. Farrell concludes that several psychoanalytic propositions have been confirmed to some extent, strongly or weakly.[45]

1. Infants obtain pleasure from oral stimulation—confirmed by Levy[46] and Halverson.[47]

2. Infants obtain pleasure from genital stimulation—confirmed by Levy,[48] Halverson,[49] and Sears.[50]

[43] Anchard F. Zeller "An Experimental Analogue of Repression: II. The Effect of Individual Failure and Success on Memory Measured by Relearning," *Journal of Experimental Psychology*, 1950, 40, 411–422, and Part III, *ibid.*, 1951, 42, 32–38.

[44] Anna Freud, "The Contribution of Psychoanalysis to Genetic Psychology," *American Journal of Orthopsychiatry*, 1951, 21, 476–497.

[45] Brian A. Farrell, "The Scientific Testing of Psychoanalytic Findings and Theory," in H. Brand, *The Study of Personality: A Book of Readings*, Wiley, 1954, p. 451.

[46] David M. Levy, "Finger Sucking and Accessory Movements in Early Infancy," *American Journal of Psychiatry*, 1928, 7, 881–918.

[47] H. M. Halverson, "Infant Sucking and Tensional Behavior," *Journal of Genetic Psychology*, 1938, 53, 365–430.

[48] Levy, *op. cit.*

[49] H. M. Halverson, "Genital and Sphincter Behavior of the Male Infant," *Journal of Genetic Psychology*, 1940, 56, 95–136.

[50] Sears, *Survey of Objective Studies of Psychoanalytic Concepts*, Social Science Research Council, 1943.

3. Manual masturbation is more frequent among preschool boys than girls—confirmed by Koch.[51]

4. Small children exhibit extensive pregenital play—confirmed by Isaacs.[52]

All the above-mentioned studies empirically tested psychoanalytic propositions. None of these studies is experimental, but all are careful observations of overt behavior. Although the experimental method offers a definite advantage in regard to variation and control of data, several empirical sciences, including biology and astronomy, widely use observation.

Furthermore, if an observation failed to corroborate Freud's hypothesis, it could not disprove it for the very simple season that a great part of Freud's finding is related to the unconscious and unobservable processes. Whenever an observation does corroborate the psychoanalytic propositions, it cannot still serve as a final evidence, for it is valid only within the scope of the made observation. However, the greater the number of precise, carefully planned, and objectively conducted observations, the stronger is the support lent to the theory. Most of the above-mentioned studies offer such support. But more discussion about observation as a scientific method will be forthcoming in Chapter 14.

Some Sources of Confusion

Additional difficulty has been created by Freud's terminology. Freud's pleasure and reality principles do not refer to pleasure as distinct from displeasure and pain, or reality as distinct from unreality and fantasy. Freud's pleasure principle (*Lustprinzip*) means the principle of immediate, urgent discharge of energy. His reality principle is related to the ability to postpone or modify the urge for an immediate discharge of energy. Id operates on the lust principle, ego on the reality principle; both id and ego seek pleasure, but the ego seeks pleasure without unpleasurable aftereffects. The id presses for an immediate discharge of energy which brings relief and pleasure; the ego is more selective (Chap. 6).

O. H. Mowrer was misled by this ambiguity and related the simple, classical conditioning to the reality principle. In Mowrer's belief simple conditioning is controlled by the autonomic nervous system (cf. Chap. 4, section 6). Mowrer believes that Pavlov's dogs learned "not what is pleasurable and relieving," but "what is actual, true, real," and related to the reality principle, while the higher type of cognitive learning controlled by the central nervous system is related to the pleasure principle

---

[51] H. L. Koch, "An Analysis of Certain Forms of So-Called 'Nervous Habits' in Young Children," *Journal of Genetic Psychology,* 1935, 46, 139–170.

[52] Suzanne Isaacs, *Social Development in Young Children,* Routledge, 1933.

because it is rewarded.[53] The erroneous translation of *lust* is generally accepted and yet quite misleading.

Hilgard disagrees with Mowrer and prefers "to assign reality regulated functions, ego functions, to the cognitive apparatus: to the central nervous system and its related structure." Yet Hilgard also has difficulties with the two Freudian principles.

The probable source of error lies in the confusion of the terms "need," "tension," "pleasure," "reality principle," "reality testing" and "perception of reality." All these terms are used by Freud in a specific connotation which adds difficulties for the experimentalists. In the words of Hilgard, corresponding to Freud's pleasure principle is "the *law of effect* or *reinforcement theory*. The broad conception, common to both psychoanalysis and learning theory, is that a need state is a state of high tension." Hilgard continued: "Conforming of behavior to reality . . . surely has some resemblance to the earliest ego functions. Learned discrimination always involves conflict, and the conflict is resolved through the weighing of the choices of reward and punishment. . . . Sometimes, when discrimination is difficult, the rat mobilizes his experience . . . by making short runs first to one side and then to the other before the animal is committed to a choice. This appears to be a kind of symbolic reality-testing, an analogue of ego-type behavior."[54]

Some psychologists did not draw a clear line between the reality principle, reality testing, and reality perception as Freud did (cf. Chap. 6). Actually, the pleasure principle, as said before, is not related to the law of effect. But pleasure is. All behavior, according to Freud, is inspired by avoidance of tension and seeking of pleasurable relief. The reality principle is a modification of the pleasure principle in the direction of avoidance of displeasure. Reality testing is the distinction between inner and outer stimuli; psychotics have lost it. What the rats probably do is perceive reality and avoid pain. How this is related to Freud's theory of personality could not be easily answered by experimentalists using rats for the study of psychoanalytic concepts.

No wonder some experimental studies missed the Freudian point altogether and some modified Freud at will to suit their preconceived ideas. Yet the efforts to relate psychoanalysis to academic psychology should be encouraged, and Hilgard's chapter on Freud is one of the best studies in this area.

[53] O. Hobart Mowrer, *Learning Theory and Personality Dynamics*, Ronald, 1950, pp. 6 ff.
[54] Ernest R. Hilgard, *Theories of Learning* (2nd ed.), Appleton-Century-Crofts, 1956, pp. 291–294, and the entire chap. 9.

CHAPTER 9

Away from Freud: The Sociological School

1. NEW WAYS IN PSYCHOANALYSIS

Culture vs. Nature

If someone had asked Freud about the nature of human culture, he would probably have answered as follows: Human nature is the basis of culture. Culture is the product of human nature, and psychology of the individual is the key that opens the door to the study of culture.

If someone should ask Fromm, Horney, or Sullivan what the nature of human nature is, they would probably answer: Culture is the determinant of personality. Human nature is a product of culture, and interpersonal relations are the key to the interpretation of the riddle of human nature.

These imaginary replies point to the far-reaching consequences of one's approach to the problem of personality and culture.

There is a growing mass of data concerning personality and culture, and psychologists, sociologists, and anthropologists cooperate more and more in cross-disciplinarian studies.[1] Yet it seems as though the issue of the causal relationship between personality and culture represents tremendous difficulties. In the previous chapter we discussed the problem presented in Linton's and Kardiner's studies: Is personality a product of culture or vice versa? Do institutionalized social mores shape one's personality, or do certain types of personality create certain cultures?

Neither Freud nor the neo-psychoanalysts brought a final and conclusive solution to this problem. It seems that the orthodox and the new psychoanalysis *postulated* a certain type of relationship, and did it in quite opposite directions. To Freud culture is a result of personality structure. Men are driven by their drives and desires, sometimes sublimated or modified. Their social life is directed by the very same forces; e.g., oral or anal problems may become problems of social behavior.

[1] Stansfeld S. Sargent and Marian Smith (eds.), *Personality and Culture,* Viking Fund, 1949.

344

Most neo-psychoanalysis (cf. Chap. 8), and especially the sociologically oriented Fromm, Horney, and Sullivan postulate that society is the first cause in psychology. This assumption carries them beyond the borders of psychoanalysis. According to them, social relations mold personality, and there is little, if any, influence of instinctual forces upon society and culture.[2] Kardiner, too, is a sociologically oriented psychoanalyst, but he tried to reconcile his findings with Freud's principles. Horney, Fromm, and Sullivan no longer try to reconcile. They have moved away decisively in the direction of new theoretical systems which have little to do with Freud's concepts. This is why they could not be included in the previous chapter, under "New Theories in Psychoanalysis." They have created new conceptual systems, which, though rooted in Freudianism, can hardly be called Freudian.

The Social Climate

It cannot be a matter of sheer coincidence that sociologically oriented psychoanalysis developed in the United States. Sociological, anthropological, and social-psychological studies in comparative cultures have been appearing in this country on an unprecedented scale. American scientists, whether influenced by Freud or not, discovered new research possibilities and new techniques for studying the various cultural patterns and group relations.

Many of these studies, conducted by Benedict, Linton, Kardiner, Mead, Erikson, *et al.*, did away with the narrowness of some earlier theories of culture. A student of comparative sociology cannot assume that his government, his religion, and his country's philosophy are the only possible cultural patterns. His horizons widen and his outlook becomes more relativistic. By virtue of comparison and criticism psychologists are far more realistic than they were a generation ago.

The United States, as a country of immigration and multiple racial and religious differences, invites that kind of approach and encourages comparative studies. Social psychology has developed here into a scientific system, and there is a tremendous amount of research going on both in the theory and in practical application of social psychology.

Many European scholars came to this country after the centers of free thought had been destroyed in their homelands. They found here an extremely stimulating social climate. Kurt Lewin, Karen Horney, Erich Fromm, and Max Wertheimer, to mention just a few, have developed their best ideas in this country. They have participated in the collective effort of American psychologists and social scientists and put forward a vigorous empirical study of human relations. Clinical methods have been

[2] Clara Thompson, *Psychoanalysis: Evolution and Development*, Hermitage, 1950.

checked against experimental methods;[3] human groups have been studied experimentally;[4] individual behavior has been related to social norms and roles.[5]

The merger of the continental and American spirits has proved of great value in furthering scientific research.

The Common Denominator

There are considerable differences between Horney, Fromm, and Sullivan, and even more between the former and the latter two. However, all three have so much in common that it is justifiable to refer to them collectively as the sociological school.

Horney, Fromm, and Sullivan have common roots in Freudianism, but they have even more in common in their deviations from Freud. All of them discard the biological foundations of psychoanalysis: All of them deny the Freudian theory of instincts and libido; all of them deny the energetic principle of psychoanalysis.

The entire sociological group represents the environmentalistic point of view. They minimize the importance of hereditary forces and, therefore, are more optimistic about human nature. Horney and Fromm, and, even more, Sullivan, believe that men can be changed, since man is a product of environmental factors.

The entire sociological school tries to apply only certain concepts of Freud's theory to the interpreting of human behavior in a changing environment. They often reject the very essential principles of Freud and introduce new and challenging hypotheses that need verification. They cannot be called a distinct, settled "school," since for the most part their theories are still being formulated, but they have undoubtedly found new ways in psychoanalysis which lead away from Freud.

2. KAREN HORNEY: PSYCHOANALYSIS WITHOUT LIBIDO

Horney as Freud's Disciple

In 1939, Karen Horney published her book *New Ways in Psychoanalysis*. A practicing psychoanalyst, she had conformed to classic psychoanalysis for many years. Her book was a revelation and a revolution, throwing overboard the most accepted principles of Freudianism. No wonder it caused a storm of protests and violent criticism.

[3] Robert R. Sears, *Experimental Studies in Psychoanalysis,* Social Science Research Council, 1943.
[4] Gardner Murphy, Theodore Newcomb, and Lois Murphy, *Experimental Social Psychology,* Harper, 1937.
[5] George Mead, *Mind, Self, and Society,* University of Chicago, 1934.

Yet Horney regards herself as a Freudian disciple and accepts unconditionally several principles of the classic psychoanalysis. She believes in
absolute *causality*. There is no room for coincidence in mental life; everything that happens has a cause and, in turn, produces effects. "I regard,"
says Horney, "as the most fundamental and most significant of Freud's
findings his doctrines that psychic processes are strictly determined."[6]

Horney accepts fully the principle of *unconscious motivation*. Unconscious motivation is one of the general postulates of psychoanalysis. It
has less to do with the scientific theories of personality; it is rather a
general methodological principle. Acceptance of this principle does not
prejudge the content of motives, nor does it bring evidence as to the
nature of the driving power in man. It is merely a way of interpreting
human behavior by assuming that a man's activities may be guided by
factors unknown to the man himself.

Horney goes one step farther. She admits that these unconscious factors are emotional. The hypothesis of the unconscious was introduced by
Herbart prior to Freud. However, Herbart was an associationist and paid
very little attention to emotions (cf. Chap. 1). Horney, following in the
footsteps of the Freudian theory, explains the *emotional content* of the
unconscious.

In the study of the dynamics of the unconscious Horney remains faithful to Freud. Unconscious desires may be repressed and they may re-
appear as a wishful content in dreams. The repressed desires are re-
activated in the process of analytical therapy; in this process the therapist
has to account for resistance and transference phenomena. The neo-
analytic therapy follows Freud's methods of free associations too.

Horney is a *non-reductionist* to a much higher degree than was Freud.
She praises Freud, for his theory has "encouraged the venture into a
psychological understanding of phenomena which hitherto had been
ascribed to organic stimuli."[7] But Freud's non-reductionism was methodological only; Freud explained that as things stand now, it is safer to
develop a non-reductionist type of theory. He did not prejudge the issue,
and expressed the hope for an eventual final victory of reductionism.
Horney holds against Freud "his tendency to regard psychic manifestations as the result of chemical-physiological forces." She seems to be
indisputably non-reductionist.

The Challenge to Freud

Horney challenges Freud on several issues. She does not admit that
personality development depends on instinctual and unchangeable forces.
She denies that sexuality is the omnipotent factor. She challenges the

[6] Karen Horney, *New Ways in Psychoanalysis*, Norton, 1939, p. 18.
[7] *Ibid.*, p. 22.

general validity of the Oedipus theory; she doubts whether the troubles of a neurotic result from repetitional patterns formed in childhood. "All these theories," she says, "are open to criticism and must be regarded rather as an historical burden which psychoanalysis carries than as its pivotal center."[8]

Yet Horney's statement arouses quite serious doubts, because discarding of the libido theory cannot mean anything but a *denial of the very essence of psychoanalysis.* According to Freud, libido is the core of personality, which develops into ego and superego. The libido theory is the frame of reference of the psychoanalytic interpretation of human behavior. Libido is one of the most important logical constructs in psychoanalysis, and most other constructs are derived from it.

It is not easy for Horney to deny libido and claim to be Freud's disciple. But it would be even more difficult to accept libido and reconcile it with the cultural orientation. This is what Kardiner tried to do. Horney goes one step farther: she regards human behavior as a product of cultural influences and not of instinctual forces. Fromm and Sullivan depart even further in a more decisive denial of libido. No wonder the orthodox analysts regard the entire "sociological school" as a denial of the first principles of psychoanalysis.

Horney was the first to shift the focal point in psychoanalytic personality study from within the person to without. Constellation is more important than constitution; environment is more relevant than heredity; present conflicts in a personality weigh more than childhood entanglements.

Horney cannot accept Freud's theory regarding developmental stages. She sees in Freud's doctrine "that the libido develops in certain stages presented by heredity, the oral, anal, phallic and genital stages," another sign of Freud's biological orientation, which is "also greatly responsible for the assumption that the Oedipus complex is a regular occurrence."[9]

As a matter of fact, any developmental theory must be based on hereditarian principles. This holds true in regard to Piaget's or Gesell's developmental stages. Environmentalists must reject any theory of fixed stages of development independent from environment. To the environmentalist child development depends upon culture and child-rearing practices, and development cannot be dictated by unchangeable rules. There is good evidence for great differences in child development in various cultures and subcultures, and to this evidence Horney refers.

Environmentalists are skeptical in regard to any instinct theory. Both basic instincts, the love and the death instinct, are denied by the entire sociological school of neo-psychoanalysis. Hatred and aggressiveness are

[8] *Ibid.,* p. 17.
[9] Karen Horney, *The Neurotic Personality of Our Time,* Norton, 1937, p. 39.

regarded as products of culture and not as innate forces. As a matter of fact, certain societies have more aggressiveness than others.

Eros, as an instinctual and inherited force, is rejected by Horney, but she does not reject love in interhuman relationship: in her writings love is more than active sexual urge. It is a *nonsexual and passive need to be accepted.* This interpretation means a dual shift from Freud's concepts: from sex to *social acceptance,* and from active need to love to *the need to be loved.*

Horney does not deny the pleasure principle, but she objects to regarding it as sexuality. The pleasure principle should be applied to any type of satisfaction, since there is no evidence that all kinds of satisfaction are derived from sex. The pleasure principle should not be identified with sex, and it is not the only principle in human behavior.

Horney does not reject the role of sex as one of the basic and innate needs. She objects to what she calls Freudian "generality" of the sexual drive. "The basic contention implicit in the libido theory though not explicitly stated is that all bodily sensations of a pleasurable nature, or strivings for them, are sexual in nature."[10] This is what she questions, and she regards the libido concept as "unproved." Sex is indeed one of the basic needs, but not the all-important one. In neurotics, sex is not the cause but the result of neurotic maladjustment, and one of its symptoms, says Horney.

All further development of the libido theory meets with Horney's disapproval. She sees no evidence for the theory that character traits are transformations of libido, no evidence that early childhood experiences will reoccur in psychoanalytic treatment; she also doubts whether there is enough proof for the theory of sublimation. Point after point she discards the principles of psychoanalysis.

Negation does not take one too far. Horney had to introduce her own theory of human behavior, and her theory is based on two principles: *safety and satisfaction.*

"Safety and Satisfaction"

"Man is ruled not by the pleasure principle alone but by two guiding principles: safety and satisfaction," says Horney. This statement is the motto of all her writings and the cornerstone of her theories. "People can renounce food, money, attention and affection so long as they are only renouncing satisfaction, but they cannot renounce these things if without them they would be or feel in danger of destitution or starvation or of being helplessly exposed to hostility, in other words, if they would loose their feeling of safety."[11]

[10] Horney, *New Ways,* p. 50.
[11] *Ibid.,* p. 73.

This is the core of Horney's theory. Each individual has certain fundamental needs, for food, rest, and sex, and these needs must be satisfied. They cannot be combined into one, e.g., sex, as Freud combined them. However, all these needs can be brought together under the common heading of seeking satisfaction, and they represent the principle of pleasure.

Despite the fact that food and sex are the primary needs, they are not the decisive factors in human behavior. "People can renounce these things," states Horney emphatically. They will do so if exposed to danger.

If this is the case, what is the decisive driving power? Horney would say: *the need for safety,* the need to be secure and free from fear.

Fear and safety, these are the two poles of the basic needs. Man needs safety and avoids fear. He cannot enjoy satisfaction of needs unless he feels safe. Fear is the greatest enemy of man's health and happiness, and search for safety is the guiding principle in human behavior.

Horney distinguishes between fear and anxiety. Fear is an emotional reaction to a real danger, while anxiety is a reaction to a situation perceived subjectively as dangerous. Lack of acceptance in childhood creates the basic anxiety. "According to this concept the child not only fears punishment or desertion because of forbidden drives, but he feels the environment as a menace to his entire development and to his not legitimate wishes and strivings."[12]

Lack of satisfaction produces anxiety, said Freud. Horney says: Lack of acceptance produces *basic anxiety.* Basic anxiety is not innate; it is a result of environmental factors. The rejected or unwanted child, or a child in a broken or hostile home feels that he is "being isolated and helpless in a potentially hostile world. A wide range of adverse factors can produce this insecurity in a child."[13] The driving force in man is postulated by Horney in a non-instinctual manner; fear and anxiety are basic emotions though the result of life experiences.

Here lies one of the fundamental differences between Freud's system and Horney's. Freud regarded love and hatred as basic emotions while anxiety is a secondary phenomenon produced by a thwarting of the basic desires. Fear is not innate; it develops as a result of coping with reality and must be related to the reality-oriented ego. The counterpart to love is hatred, and fear develops later on.

Horney regards anxiety as a basic feeling and a counterpart to love. People need to be accepted, and basic anxiety is a person's reaction to lack of acceptance.

[12] *Ibid.,* p. 75.
[13] Karen Horney, *Our Inner Conflicts,* Norton, 1945.

Theory of Personality

Horney's theory of personality stands somewhat between Freud's, Adler's, and Sullivan's. The first of the two basic factors, satisfaction, falls in line with Freud's theories and represents a new version of the Freudian pleasure principle. The more important factor, safety or security, is close to Adler's self-realization and compensation and is common to Horney and Sullivan.

Horney makes it clear that the need for safety is socially created. She thinks that "particular needs which are relevant to understanding the personality and its difficulties are not instinctual in character but are created by the entirety of conditions under which we live."[14] Since this is the case, personality traits must be a product of environmental forces.

Horney compares Freud's dynamic concepts of personality to conditioned reflexes and she finds Freud much superior to other students of personality. Especially valuable to Horney is Freud's assumption that human motivation and driving power is emotional and not rational. But to her, human emotions themselves are a result of environment, and first and foremost of early childhood experiences.

Horney admits after Freud that character as well as neurosis develops in early childhood, but she rejects the principle of repetition-compulsion. "We recognize," states Horney, "that the connection between later peculiarities and earlier experiences is more complicated than Freud assumed; there is no such thing as an isolated experience; but the entirety of infantile experiences combines to form a certain character structure, and it is this structure from which later difficulties emanate. . . . Thus the analysis of the actual character structure moves into the foreground of attention."[15]

Early childhood was regarded by Freud as the most important period in personality development. In the first five years of life the child passes through decisive developmental stages which shape his personality.

Horney agrees with Freud as to the importance of early childhood but disagrees on several fundamental issues. Freud assumed that every child passes through the oral, anal, and phallic stages. These stages are biogenic and universal. However, how the child passes through these stages depends upon environmental factors and of course differs from case to case, with the various possibilities of fixation, regression, etc.

Horney contends that the development of the child depends upon *how the child is treated*. There is no such thing as universal anal stage or universal Oedipus complex. The child may have an Oedipus complex or may develop anal inclinations, but this is a result of parental personal-

[14] Horney, *New Ways*, p. 78.
[15] *Ibid.*, p. 9.

ities and behavior. Nothing is universal, Horney would say, and everything depends on culture and environment.

The child's needs can be dealt with in a satisfactory way by the parents, who thus contribute to his mental health. His needs may, indeed, be thwarted and frustrated. He may be bullied about, severely punished, or even entirely rejected by his parents. He may perceive his home environment as "unfair, unjust, begrudging and merciless," and this will influence his actual behavior and future development as well.

Although Horney agrees with Freud as to the importance of early childhood, she is at variance with him in regard to the impact of unfortunate events that occur in early childhood. The ways the child reacts to his environment combine and interrelate and form the structure of his personality. This "character structure" tends to be quite consistent in a person's lifetime development, but not the isolated experiences per se.[16] This interpretation brings Horney quite close to Alfred Adler.

Horney admits more flexibility in adult personality than Freud did, and she is quite optimistic about the possibility of a change in personality in adult age. Her optimism originates in the denial of instinctual forces and in the belief in the general human tendency toward constructiveness. This optimistic belief in human nature, as compared to Freud's pessimism, is common to her and Fromm and, in a way, to Sullivan too.

Freud postulated, Horney says, that instinct can only be controlled, or at best sublimated. "My own belief," she explains, "is that man has the capacity as well as the desire to develop his potentialities and become a decent human being. I believe that man can change and go on changing as long as he lives."[17]

This is Horney's credo. No "death instinct" and no inherited Eros instinct: man depends upon environment. Society can and should be improved, and then men will be happier and healthier.

Once again, Horney comes close to Alfred Adler's optimistic theory of social change and change in human nature.

Theory of Neurosis

Since personality is perceived by Horney in an environmentalistic fashion, deviation from normal behavior must be interpreted on similar lines. Normalcy, according to her, is a term related to culture. "With us," she says, "a person would be neurotic or psychotic who talked by the hour with his deceased grandfather, whereas such communication with ancestors is a recognized pattern in some Indian tribes."[18]

The sociological school in psychoanalysis emphasizes that Freud did not pay enough attention to the differences in culture. Horney strongly

[16] Horney, *Neurotic Personality.*
[17] Horney, *Our Inner Conflicts,* p. 19.
[18] *Ibid.,* p. 15.

feels that neurosis is a result not of inner conflict between ego, id, and superego but of conflict between an individual and his environment. She shifts the focal point in a neurosis from within a person to without. However, in her last book she emphasizes the "central inner conflict" between the real potentialities of one's self and the gratification of one's imaginary self.[19]

Horney accuses our society of breeding neurosis. Neurosis is a result of insecurity, and it may develop in childhood as the boy or girl is deprived of acceptance. A society based upon competition contributes substantially to development of insecurity and is conducive to neurosis, "carrying the germs of destructive rivalry, disarrangement, suspicion, begrudging, envy into every human relationship."[20]

The neurotic person tends to move in one of three possible directions, called by Horney "neurotic trends." The first is moving toward people, the second against them, the third away from them. Overcompliance is a manifestation of neurotic behavior; a neurotic person cannot risk alienating people and he tries to gain their acceptance by complying with their desires. Another kind of neurotic behavior is hostility and aggressiveness. The third neurotic trend is seclusion and withdrawal; the neurotic person is unable to face people and tries to avoid them. The common denominator of all three "neurotic trends" is obviously social maladjustment.

However, since social maladjustment per se cannot fully explain the nature and origin of neurosis, there must be more specific factors related to it. Horney says that certain personality traits prevent successful adjustment. Neurosis is a "certain rigidity in reaction and discrepancy between potentialities and accomplishments." It is a psychic disturbance "brought about by fears and defenses against these fears, and by attempts to find compromise solutions for conflicting tendencies."[21] This disturbance develops usually in early childhood as a result of child-rearing practices.

The neurotic tries to deny his inner conflicts by creating an artificial and unrealistic image of himself.[22] He believes himself far superior to the man he really is. This "idealized image" has for him the value of reality, thus helping him avoid awareness of his inner conflicts. Instead of using his energies for self-realization he wastes them in "search for glory," i.e., in actualization of his idealized self. This is the "central inner conflict," as presented by Horney in her later writings.

Concluding Remarks

Horney's contribution to psychotherapeutic practice seems greater than her contribution to psychological theory, and various psychothera-

[19] Karen Horney, *Neurosis and Human Growth*, Norton, 1950.
[20] Horney, *Neurotic Personality*, p. 113.
[21] *Ibid.*, p. 28.
[22] Karen Horney, *Are You Considering Psychoanalysis?* Norton, 1946, p. 21.

peutic practices owe much to her daring. However, Horney's contribution to psychological theory is considerable. Using the frames of reference of the psychoanalytic school, one would say that she has *shifted the focus in the study of personality from id to ego*. Id, the basic part of personality in Freudian theory, has almost disappeared in Horney's studies. This is not merely a cancellation of the term "id"; people may construct scientific models on Freudian lines using different terminology, but this is not the case with Horney. She actually has introduced a new model of personality, leaving very little if anything to innate factors, and has strongly emphasized the acquired one. She regards fear and anxiety as the basic human emotions, while Freud saw them in love and hatred.

However, this difference is not so great as it appears on the surface. Both Freud and Horney regard human nature as a product of heredity and environment. Freud never belittled environmental influences; as a matter of fact, the way the child passes from one stage to the other, whether the child remains fixated or regresses, sublimates or establishes reaction formation, is a matter of environmental forces. The innate love and hatred are molded into various behavioral patterns by external influences, and by inner balance of forces established under the pressure of these influences. Fear is the guiding factor in ego; fear is "reality oriented" and is a product of coping with external factors. Freud said that fear is acquired through life experiences; Horney, too, emphasizes in a different way that fear is a product of experience; the burned child dreads fire, and a child who has experienced rejection will develop anxieties.

Horney's personality model is far inferior to Freud's in clarity, consistency, and elaboration. Freud's personality model is constructed with the precision of a mathematician and the refinement of a sculptor. It is difficult to reshape it. It is much simpler to reject it or accept it as it is than to remold or restructure it. Most of the efforts to correct Freud bear the stamp of awkwardness and usually are frowned on by orthodox psychoanalysts.

Yet many have accepted or rejected one or another part of Freud's theory, despite the danger that tampering with one of the pillars may damage the entire structure or erect a shaky building. And this is precisely why without challenging the importance or validity of Horney's findings one is confronted with so many unanswered questions. The reader of Freud may reject or accept Freud's principles; accepting them, he is compelled to admire the magnificent consistency of the entire structure and the wealth of the empirical material used for it. When reading Horney one may often admit that she is right but the entire system is often imperfect.

Additional criticism is invited by the combination of Horney's environmentalism with Freud's mechanism. One can readily understand unconsciousness, resistance, repression, dreams, etc., applying Freud's libido theory. Rejecting the libido theory, one finds these factors less easily explained.

Both Freud and Horney face complementary difficulties in explaining the nature of emotional disturbances. Horney may ask Freud why only in certain cases libido acts conversely. Freud, in turn, may ask Horney why environment influences only certain individuals and makes them neurotic. Probably a *full* consideration given both to constitution and to constellation would be the proper one. Perhaps William Stern's "convergism" may be helpful here (cf. Chap. 11).

Summarizing Horney's contribution to psychological theory, we find that she has paved a new road in psychoanalysis. She called her programmatic book *New Ways in Psychoanalysis,* but her own system is only one of the many possible ways. Her trail is not a well-established highway; too many questions are left open, and too little evidence has been accumulated.

One must, however, admit that Horney has opened new vistas in psychological research. Whether her statements are "true" or "wrong" has yet to be proved, but she has shown new horizons of environmentalistic approach in psychoanalysis which invite further research and seem to be promising.

3. ERICH FROMM: HISTORICAL AND ETHICAL PSYCHOANALYSIS

Philosophy of History

It was Sigmund Freud who introduced the laws of evolution of the psyche into contemporary psychology. Freud was convinced that many ancient and archaic patterns are carried over into the personality structure of modern man. This principle has been applied in two ways. First, each individual is supposed to "recapitulate" the development stages of mankind (the biogenetic principle); second, contemporary social institutions such as law, religion, and family have developed from primitive social forms, and they transmit the heritage of the past to the present generation.

Fromm shifted away from Freudian philosophy on several points. He discarded the biogenetic principle and attached more weight to the cultural heritage. In fact, he regards human behavior at *any* historical moment as a product of cultural influences at a given time. His main assumptions are as follows:

"Man's nature, his passions and anxieties are a cultural product; as a matter of fact, man himself is the most important creation and achievement of the continuous human effort, the record of which we call history."[23]

This is, indeed, a far-reaching statement. Most psychologists deal with human behavior in terms either of individually inherited traits or of the individual's life experiences, or both. The environmentalists are likely to emphasize one's life history, the field theorists the immediate situation.

Fromm introduced new areas of research into the study of human nature. Human history serves him as a huge laboratory in human nature, where various patterns of behavior are shaped and reshaped. History is both a source of factual data and a major case study which enables us to understand the impact of social factors on human life. Fromm is an environmentalist, but he has found in history the changing scenery of the life of mankind and an important field for psychological study.

Freud's philosophy of history was an addition to his psychological theory; Fromm's philosophy of history was the cornerstone of his psychological theory. The reason is apparent. Freud regarded history as man-made, while Fromm regarded man as history-made. One is tempted therefore to say that Fromm has done to Freud what Marx did to Hegel. Both Fromm and Marx applied the principles of their masters in a reverse direction. Marx transferred Hegel's idealism and spiritualism into materialism and economism. Fromm reversed the order of man in society; instead of regarding society as a result of man's instincts, he regarded man as a product of social influences.[24]

The focal point in this shift from orthodox psychoanalysis is described by Fromm as follows:

"The assumption underlying the orthodox Freudian approach was that social phenomena and cultural patterns are to be explained as direct outcomes of certain libidinal trends. Thus, for instance, capitalism was explained as a result of anal eroticism or was the result of the operation of the death instinct. The method used here was the explanation by analogy. One tried to discover analogies between cultural phenomena and neurotic symptoms of a patient and then proceeded to explain the cultural phenomenon as being 'caused' by the same libidinous factors by which the neurotic symptom had been explained.[25]

Culture, according to Fromm, cannot be deduced from and interpreted by a theory of innate instincts, such as love and hate. Societies are not shaped by libidinal forces, as Freud said, but by objective conditions embedded in geography, history, and economics.

[23] Erich Fromm, *Escape from Freedom*, Rinehart, 1941, p. 13.

[24] Fromm is more modest than Marx. Marx boastfully stated that Hegel's theory stood on its head; he, Marx, put it on its feet. Fromm remarked that people standing on the shoulders of a giant may believe themselves to be taller than the giant.

[25] Erich Fromm, "Psychoanalytic Characterology and Its Application to the Understanding of Culture," in S. S. Sargent and M. Smith (eds.), *Culture and Personality*, Viking Fund, 1949, pp. 2–3.

"Each society is structuralized and operates in certain ways which are necessitated by a number of objective conditions; such conditions are the methods of production and distribution which in turn depend on new material, industrial techniques, climate, etc., furthermore political and geographical factors and cultural traditions and influences to which society is exposed."[26]

Fromm has transferred the focal point from within the individual to the external "objective conditions." The behavior of individuals is shaped by their society, and the society is molded by "objective conditions."[27]

This is a serious deviation from Freud, and a major step forward in the direction of environmentalism and situationalism. This is what Fromm has in common with Kardiner.

Culture vs. Nature

Man is a living organism, and as such he has certain physiological needs. He differs from other organisms in at least two respects. First, he does not satisfy his needs in an animal-like manner, in contradistinction to all animals, which satisfy their needs in a uniform, fixed, and unchangeable pattern of behavior called *instinct*.

Fromm accepted the generality of physiological needs. He would not oppose the application of the term "instinct" to these needs. What he could not accept was the idea that all humans follow the same pattern of behavior in pursuing their goals. He rejected instincts as uniform patterns of behavior in man. The higher the species and the more developed the brain of an animal, the less complete and rigid were the animal's instincts. The emergence of man occurred when instinctual behavior reached its lowest point. Man does not follow the instinctual pattern; he learns from his environment, and his behavior is conditioned by culture.

In fact, Freud regarded the id-level behavior as independent of cultural influences, but no adult individual could live on that level. With the exception of severely disturbed individuals, all of us live in some kind of balance between the id, the ego, and the superego, and the two latter are products of cultural influences. Moreover, Freud assumed that the instinctual forces can be modified, sublimated, suppressed, or repressed, but never annihilated (cf. Chap. 6). Fromm denied their very existence in humans. According to him, only lower animals display full-fledged instinctual behavior, while higher animals use less instinct and more learning. Man learns and reasons and his behavior is flexible and adaptable.

Fromm pointed out another difference between man and animal. While all men have certain common physiological needs, they differ from each other in the socially created needs. "Although there are certain needs, such as hunger, thirst, sex, which are common to man, those drives which

[26] *Ibid.*, pp. 4–5.
[27] *Ibid.*, pp. 4 ff.

make for the *difference* in man's character, like love and hatred, lust for power and yearning for submission, enjoyment of sensuous pleasure and the fear of it, are all products of the social process. The most beautiful as well as the most ugly inclinations of men are not a part of a fixed and biologically given human nature, but result from the social process which creates men."[28]

Is man an exception to the laws of nature? Fromm answered this question paradoxically: yes and no. Man is "a part of nature"; no man can escape the physical laws of the universe and no man can change them. Man can never free himself from the "dichotomies of existence." He lives but he must die; he has many potentialities, but he cannot realize them in his short life; man is a part of society, but he does not live in harmony with it and he is always a separate entity. Man is aware of himself as being a separate entity; he reasons, he may conceive of and understand the order of the universe. Thus he realizes his "powerlessness and the limitations of his existence." He knows that there is no solution to the eternal dichotomies; that he is a part of nature yet "transcends the rest of nature."

Besides these "existential" dichotomies man faces historical dichotomies. The contradictions in the life of society and individuals are man-made and can be solved by man. The contradiction between the abundance in production and the human inability to enjoy it in peace and welfare is a historical dichotomy. It is not an eternal and insoluble contradition of mankind; men can solve this problem.

Existential dichotomies cannot be solved. Often people try to deny their existence by development of "ideologies." One of the possible ideologies is religion and the belief in an immortal soul. While Freud saw in religion a kind of neurosis, Fromm arrived at the conclusion that "a neurosis is to be explained as a particular form of religion differing mainly by its individual, non-patterned characteristics."[29]

Man may try to escape the dichotomies of his life and appease his mind by a restless activity in business or in an incessant pursuit of pleasure. He may give up his freedom and integrity in order to feel related to others, but he will never find peace and satisfaction in this way.

The only true way to cope with the existential dichotomies is for man to unfold his own powers; they will lead him to achieve happiness. This ability to live a productive life is embedded in human nature.

In contrast to animals, man's most compelling problems are not those of hunger or thirst or sex. Humans strive for power and love, and fight for religious or political ideals; they do not live "by bread alone."

The existential dichotomies compel man to seek to restore the unity between himself and nature. In the search for unity man needs orientation

---

[28] Fromm, *Escape from Freedom*, p. 12.
[29] Erich Fromm, *Man for Himself*, Rinehart, 1947, p. 49.

in and devotion to the world. He may develop various "frames of orientation and devotion," but he must have some aim. These frames of orientation and devotion correspond to what is called "ideals." Everyone must have some ideal, although the ideals may be different in different persons. Man can choose between being devoted "to reason and love and being devoted to the worship of power and destruction. All men are 'idealists' and are striving for something beyond the attainment of physical satisfaction. They differ in the kind of ideals they believe in."[30] Everyone needs ideals in which to believe, and everyone can make his own life meaningful through devotion to an aim.

Each person can find productive outlets for his energies, "unless he is mentally or emotionally crippled." Man's productiveness creates material things, works of art, and systems of thought, but "by far the most important object of productiveness is man himself."

Man's life is a continuous process of creation. Physical growth proceeds by itself, but "it requires productive activity to give life to the emotional and intellectual potentialities of man, to give birth to his self."[31]

Psyche Down the Ages

Animals are a part of and live in accordance with nature. Man's history started with the denial of identity with nature: though he was a part of nature, he was no longer identical with nature. "He changes his role toward nature from that of a purely passive adaptation to an active one: he produces. He invents tools and, while mastering nature, he separates himself—or rather his group—as not being identical with nature."[32]

As man moved away from nature, he became more aware of his unchangeable fate. He could not change the laws of nature and he felt helpless and alone. Animals did not face dichotomies of life; men did. Man realized that his ultimate end was death.

The primitive man tried to escape his fate. He developed myth and religion and identified himself fully with his group or clan. His group-belonging saved him from the feeling of being alone. The group decided how one should live; the group assigned each individual a definite place; the group was the source of security.

The beliefs of the group shared by all its members alleviated man's isolation in nature. The primitive religions tied man to nature; people worshiped sun and moon, land and sea, winds and fire, animals and plants. These "primary ties" served to strengthen man's security feeling and deny by imaginary and magic devices that man transcends nature.

This situation could not last forever. Man's critical mind prevented him from remaining subservient to a group. People criticized and revolted,

[30] *Ibid.*
[31] *Ibid.*, p. 91.
[32] Fromm, *Escape from Freedom*, p. 33.

reasoned and developed new concepts. The ties of an individual with his clan and through it with nature loosened. In man's primitive stage, "while being aware of himself as a separate entity, he felt also part of the world around him." Later on people revolted against being subjugated to their group and nature. They strove toward independence, toward freedom of reasoning and decision and free use of all their powers. This process "which we may call 'individuation' seems to have reached its peak in modern history in the centuries between the Reformation and the present."[33]

In Western civilization the Middle Ages represent, in Fromm's view, the era of social security, solidarity, and stability. There was not much personal freedom in that time, since everybody's place in the society was well defined by his class status in the feudal system. However, members of each class enjoyed the feeling of belonging and they felt secure in the frame of their social class.

The Renaissance, the Reformation, and Protestantism destroyed the medieval system. Man gained more freedom, but his position in the new social order was less stable. He could develop more initiative and more criticism but had lost the feeling of solidarity and was more and more alone. The Renaissance encouraged the development of a "passionate ego-centricity." Protestantism destroyed the identification with God through belonging to the Church. Man had to pray alone and alone face his responsibility toward the Lord.

The freedom gained by men in Western civilization is rather a "freedom from" than a "freedom to." Man is free; he is free *from* slavery; he developed his own personality, and his life is more individualized, yet he has less security than in medieval times. Today he does not belong anywhere, and he is often alone and insecure. He is free *from,* but is not free *to* live, to develop, to enjoy life. His happiness is always at stake, always dependent upon his being accepted by others.

No wonder many individuals are ready to give up their freedom in order to regain security. This is how Fromm explains the rise of totalitarian systems in contemporary society. Quite often, as a result of the lack of "freedom to" live a more happy and secure life, men try to escape their "freedom from." Since this freedom has not brought security and happiness, they readily give it up and escape from it into the totalitarian system.

This is, however, not the only escape mechanism. Fromm maintains that there are four mechanisms of escape: sadism, masochism, destructiveness, and automaton conformity. The sado-masochistic mechanisms mean basically the giving up of one's independence. In sadism one may try to "make others dependent on oneself and to have absolute and unrestricted power over them." Another type of sadist tends "to exploit them, to use

[33] *Ibid.,* p. 24.

them, to steal from them, to disembowel them." A third kind of sadistic tendency is the wish "to make others suffer or to see them suffer."[34] A masochist feels inferior and tends to submit his own personality to another person. In an extreme case a masochist is willing to suffer under the control of a strong person in order to escape his feeling of loneliness.

Destructiveness is another escape mechanism. "I can," says Fromm, "escape the feeling of my own powerlessness in comparison with the world outside of myself by destroying it. . . . The destruction of the world is the last, almost desperate attempt to save myself from being crushed by it."[35]

The last escape mechanism is *automaton conformity*. It is a full conformity to social norms, to the point of complete negation of anything that is original and independent. It is a blind acceptance of the social pattern, and readiness to obey the leader unconditionally.

Childhood

Fromm follows in Freud's footsteps and applies the biogenetic principle. Childhood development presents a pattern similar to that of the history of mankind. "A child is born when it is no longer one with its mother and becomes a biological entity separate from her. Yet, while this biological separation is the beginning of individual human existence, the child remains functionally one with its mother for a considerable period."[36]

As the child grows, he faces restraints and prohibitions imposed by his parents. Unless parental behavior is exceptionally improper, the child will become more and more independent as he grows. Gradually the ties connecting him with his parents become weaker, as he develops more awareness of his individuality. This process of development brings about dangers similar to those in the history of mankind, for a higher level of individualization is accompanied by a decline in security feeling. The little child does not have much freedom, but he is happy and secure in his dependence on his parents. Maturity means more independence, but it also means less security than in childhood. Children who have been reared by hostile or domineering parents will be less prepared to face the problems of maturity and they may feel powerless, forsaken, and isolated.

Many individuals develop "escape mechanisms" similar to those developed by mankind. Thus they become sadists, masochists, destructionists, or automaton-conformists; the pattern of their defense mechanism is a product not of heredity but of their experiences in childhood.

Not only the defense mechanism but the totality of the child's character is molded by his parents. Families usually serve as "psychological agents"

[34] *Ibid.*, p. 144.
[35] *Ibid.*, p. 179.
[36] *Ibid.*, p. 25.

of the society and transmit the cultural values of their nation and class to the children. The child's character is formed by social and cultural patterns as represented by the characters of his parents. This is why most members of a group share significant character traits, and these common traits are called by Fromm "the social character." The child's "individual character" is a product of the specific environmental influences exercised by his parents.

Fromm criticizes Freud's genetic interpretation of psychological types. Freud saw the origins of the oral or anal type, for example, in fixation on the oral or anal level. Fromm seeks the origin of the personality differences between individuals not in the developmental stages of libido but in their *environmental experiences.* How the parents treat their child—this will determine the child's personality.

If a person develops into the oral-dependent or the anal-obstinate type, it is not because of a fixation but a result of *child-rearing practices.* Child-rearing practices that influence "character formation" are not only the feeding of the child and teaching him to control his bowels but the *total sum* of *social relationships* at home. If the home situation encourages friendliness and acceptance, the child is likely to develop the receptive-dependent personality traits. His childhood experiences will teach him that he got the most out of complying with others in trying to please them. If, however, the child receives everything only after a quarrel, a fight, or a period of stubbornness, he will probably develop the oral-aggressive or, in Fromm's terminology, exploiting-sadistic character. The child who grows up in a home atmosphere of "grab it" will probably follow this pattern of behavior all his life. In a home where scarcity, distrust, and suspicion prevail, the child will learn to keep what he gets and not let people take away anything that belongs to him. This is the typical anal attitude or, in Fromm's division, the hoarding-remote character.

Theory of Personality

Fromm does not deny inherited or constitutional patterns. He calls them "temperament." Temperament is the *mode* of reaction, and is "constitutional and not changeable." Temperament is correlated to somatic processes and is inherited.

Character is formed in life experience through social influences. Character is the relatively permanent "form in which human energy is canalized in the process of assimilation and socialization."[37] Character is determined by the individual's physical constitution and temperament, which are innate, and the totality of social and cultural influences on him. "Character is the specific form in which human energy is shaped by the dynamic adaptation of human needs to the particular mode of existence in a given

[37] Fromm, *Man for Himself*, p. 59.

society. Character in turn determines the thinking, feeling and acting of individuals."[38] Two parts can be distinguished in a person's character. The first is the "individual character." This part of character indicates the differences among the members of the same cultural group. The individual character carries the innate factors of personality and the specific influences of a given home environment. The other part, the "social character," is shared by the majority of the members of the same culture. The social character in personality "has the function of molding human energy for the purpose of the functioning of a given society. The members of the society . . . have to behave in such a way as to be able to function in the sense required by society. It is the function of the social character to shape the energies of the members of society in such a way that their behavior is not left to conscious decisions whether or not to follow the social pattern but that people want to act as they have to act and at the same time find gratification in acting according to the requirements of the culture."[39]

Fromm's "social character," if translated into the terminology of the orthodox psychoanalysis, would fit best into superego, as the part of personality that identifies itself with cultural influences. The focal point has been shifted by Fromm from the libido to environment, from the individual person to society. Freud worked from personality to society; Fromm and Sullivan interpret personality as a product of society.

Another point of difference between Fromm and Freud requires clarification. Freud emphasized the attachment of fixated libido to the various somatic zones. The anal type, for example, is not only a person who keeps money or hoards other objects; he is stingy in relation to his feces, too. While money or various objects represent the sublimation of his fears, his elimination tract clings to the infantile pattern of behavior in delaying elimination, and in an obvious inclination toward constipation. The same holds true in regard to the oral character, who not only sublimates his oral tendencies but is actually an eager drinker and/or eater (cf. Chap. 6).

Fromm does not deny the fact that character traits are somehow related to somatic symptoms. But, he says, the causal order has to be reversed. A person is receptive-dependent not because he likes to drink, or because he lacked sucking in his first year of life. His craving for drinking is not the cause but a *symptom*, an expression of his character. His character has little if anything to do with his sucking urge. Character is a result of the total home situation. Friendly, cheerful, and permissive parents may encourage great intakes of food; unfriendly and meticulous ones may be very strict in toilet training. The decisive factor in the child's character development is not the libido experience but the total home atmosphere, which is conducive to the formation of a certain character type. It is

[38] Fromm, *Escape from Freedom*, p. 278.
[39] Fromm, "Psychoanalytic Characterology," in Sargent and Smith. *op. cit.*, p. 5.

proper to mention at this point that this interpretation is similar to Alfred Adler's theory of "style of life" (cf. Chap. 7).

Personality Types

There are, according to Fromm, two kinds of relatedness to the outside world: that of assimilation and that of socialization. Socialization deals with people, assimilation with things. Socialization can develop into symbiosis, withdrawal-destructiveness, or love.

Symbiotic relatedness is a social relation the basis of which is dependence on others. The person avoids being alone and tries to become a part of another person either by "swallowing" him (*sadism*) or by being "swallowed" (*masochism*).

Withdrawal and *destructiveness* represent the passive and active type of social attitude respectively. Certain individuals try to gain some sense of security through isolation. They either withdraw from any contact with other individuals or become aggressive and destructive, aiming at the annihilation of others.

The attitude of *love* is the "productive form of relatedness to others and to oneself." Love implies care, respect, and responsibility, and it is the wish for the well-being of the other person.

Assimilation is the way people acquire or assimilate things. Both assimilation and socialization are called by Fromm "orientations," and they form the "core of character." "Orientations" are not determined by heredity but are shaped by environmental influences.

There are several patterns of assimilation, and all but one of them are nonproductive. The *receptive* orientation in a person is expressed by expectancy of help from the outside. The receptive type is the receiver and not the giver in material processes, in love, or in intellectual functions. The *exploitative* type of person, like the receptive, believes that all good is outside his person. He does not, however, expect to receive from others; he takes by force or cunning.

The *hoarding* orientation leads to negativism, pedantic orderliness, and rigidity. The outside world is perceived by the hoarding type as a threat and he tends to be saving and possessive.

The *marketing* orientation has developed in the modern era, since people's success today depends on a "personal acceptance by those who need their services or who employ them." Success today depends mostly on "how well a person sells himself" and "whether he knows the right people." This situation is not conducive to a feeling of security, since a person's value depends less on his personal qualities, and more on his success in a competitive market. The self-marketing attitude makes a man play the role of: "I am as you desire me."

Fromm's fifth character type is the *productive* one. The productive character is a combination of the previous four characters but is guided in the direction of love of others and creativity. The main traits of the productive character are devotion to the well-being of his fellow man and productive activity. Even the antisocial traits of the former types, e.g., exploitation, turn into positive traits, e.g., having initiative or leadership qualities.

Fromm suggested the following chart in characterology:[40]

FROMM'S CHART OF ORIENTATIONS

Assimilation	*Socialization*	
I. Nonproductive orientation		
a. Receiving (accepting)	Masochistic (loyalty)	} Symbiosis
b. Exploiting (taking)	Sadistic (authority)	
c. Hoarding (preserving)	Destructive (assertiveness)	} Withdrawal
d. Marketing (exchanging)	Indifferent (fairness)	
II. Productive orientation		
Working	Loving, reasoning	

Fromm offers several other tables of combinations or "blends" of the various orientations and says that the configuration of these elements makes for an endless number of variations in personality.

Society and Ethics

Fromm feels that "the choice between life and death is the basic alternative of the ethics. It is the alternative between productiveness and destructiveness, between potency and impotency, between virtue and vice. For humanistic ethics all evil strivings are directed against life and all good serves the preservation and unfolding of life."[41]

In his studies Freud carefully avoided value judgments and he abstained from introducing moral attitudes in therapy. Fromm criticizes him and doubts whether any therapy is possible unless the therapist takes a stand on moral issues. Adjustment is adjustment to a definite society and to

[40] Fromm, *Man for Himself*, p. 111.
[41] *Ibid.*, p. 214.

definite social modes and ethics. Freud's abstention from taking a stand is a product of a certain era, namely, the era of laissez faire and liberalism.[42] Fromm maintains that value judgments of a person determine his actions, and neurosis itself is a symptom of moral failure; a neurotic is a person who failed to achieve maturity and personality intergration; virtue is proportioned to productiveness, and ethics is related to health and confirmation of life.

Fromm says that Freud accepted the "traditional doctrine of the evilness of human nature. Man, to him, is fundamentally antisocial. Society must domesticate him, must allow some direct satisfaction of biological—and hence ineradicable—drives; but for the most part society must refine and adroitly check man's basic impulses."[43]

Fromm is more optimistic. He believes in human "constructiveness" and inherent primary potentialities. He assumes that virtue, courage, honesty, and creativeness are attractive to everyone, and there is no need for additional incentives for morality since moral behavior is a reward in itself.

The failure of modern culture, says Fromm, lies not in the fact "that people are *too much concerned with their self-interest* but that they are *not concerned enough with the interest of their real self;* not in the fact that they are too selfish, but that they do not love themselves."[44] People too often develop "escape mechanisms" and do not pursue true self-realization.

People are influenced by the authoritarian ethics, which maintains that man is an evil being, and only by victory over himself can he become moral. The authoritative ethics is based on the patriarchal family. Fromm interprets the Oedipus complex not as an incestuous conflict but as "the rebellion of the son against the authority of the father in the patriarchal family."[45] Freud's superego represents the "authoritarian conscience," while Fromm calls for a free and harmonious development of all the potentialities latent in an individual.

Fromm makes a strong plea for a society in which human problems can be solved. In such a future society "man relates to man lovingly." Fromm suggests the formation of a sane society which gives man "the possibility of transcending nature by creating rather than by conformity, in which a system of orientation and devotion exists without man's needing to distort reality and to worship idols."[46]

[42] Erich Fromm, "Die gesellschaftliche Bedingtheit der psychoanalytischen Therapie," *Zeitschrift für Sozialforschung,* 1935.
[43] Fromm, *Escape from Freedom,* p. 10.
[44] Fromm, *Man for Himself,* p. 139.
[45] Quotation from P. Mullahy, *Oedipus—Myth and Complex,* Hermitage, 1948, p. 271.
[46] Erich Fromm, *The Sane Society,* Rinehart, 1955, p. 362.

Concluding Remarks

Fromm's contribution to psychological theory can be summarized in four points:

1. Use of history as a psychological research area.
2. Theory of character.
3. Ethical interpretation of psychological issues.
4. Sociological orientation in psychological studies.

Fromm's analysis of history represents a great challenge both to psychologists and to philosophers of history. He tries to interpret human nature in view of historical events and to draw far-reaching conclusions. However, his historical comments do not follow the available data. For example, his story of man's alleged loneliness and group formation does not correspond to any data; his picture of medieval life is highly idealized; he has omitted all the physical and mental hardships produced by despotism, fanaticism, religious persecutions, witch-hunts, superstitions, plagues, wars, and other disasters. The era of the Renaissance and Reformation is painted black in disregard of the positive and productive aspects of those times. Fromm's story of freedom and escape is an interesting one but contradicts all observable data in the history of the French and American Revolutions. In fact, it does not correspond to any known historical data.

Fromm's characterology invites additional criticism. It reminds one of Spranger's *Lebensformen* (see Chap. 11) or McDougall's emotions (see Chap. 5) with arbitrarily set classifications. Fromm admits that character is "usually a blend of all of these orientations in which one, however, is dominant."[47] But if each character is a "blend," with no possibility of finding out anything more precise about its composition, what scientific purpose is served by introduction of the "character orientations" hypothesis?

This criticism is aimed at the abundance of types and subtypes, but not against the hypothesis that personality traits are influenced by environmental factors. This hypothesis seems to be a fruitful one.

Fromm's philosophical and ethical system emphasizes the optimistic approach to human nature. Freud's theory of the death instinct and of the conflict between human nature and culture has been regarded by the neo-psychoanalysts as unduly pessimistic. Both Horney and Fromm reject the death-instinct theory and believe in the "productiveness" of human nature. However, Fromm's philosophy of life does not warrant this optimism. Man is doomed to an eternal conflict with nature; since he knows

[47] Fromm, *Man for Himself*, p. 61.

too much, he is unable to accept his fate naïvely. Every historical stage leaves him "discontented and perplexed"; there is never peace of mind, never harmony between man and universe, but only a continuous struggle and search for new solutions, none of them ever a final one. This is, to quote Fromm, man's tragic fate: "to be part of nature, and yet to transcend it."

Yet, and this is worth while mentioning, Fromm calls for creativeness and virtues. Though the discussion of Fromm's philosophy and ethics transcends the borders of a scientific study of true and false statements, it is good to point to this revolt of a psychologist against objective truth in favor of moral judgments. Thus Fromm's writings confront scientific truth-seekers with the human problem of right and wrong.

4. HARRY S. SULLIVAN: A THEORY OF INTERPERSONAL RELATIONS

New Conceptual Tools

Sullivan is perhaps the only neo-psychoanalyst who developed his own conceptual system in psychology. He deviated farther from Freud than any other psychoanalyst. He abandoned the Freudian frames of reference and discarded most of the basic concepts of psychoanalysis, such as libido, ego, superego, sex theory, and character formation. He did not apply even Freud's terminology, which is quite an important factor. He borrowed from Freud only some principles in human dynamics, such as unconscious motivation, defense mechanisms, and dream interpretation. Sullivan can hardly be regarded as Freud's disciple. He is rather a fairly independent theoretician of psychology whose thoughts have been considerably influenced by Freud.

One should not study Sullivan with Freud's theories as an introduction. It is much easier to interpret Sullivan's theories using Horney or even Fromm as a "bridge" between Freud and Sullivan.

Sullivan was influenced by both Adolph Meyer's biological method and George Mead's theory of social status and role, and in various points his study shows a considerable similarity to the field theory. The most sociological-minded neo-psychoanalyst, Sullivan combined operationism and environmentalism with a certain kind of reductionism. He introduced the term "experience" as Watson would say "behavior," Stern *"Erlebnis,"* or Kurt Lewin "locomotion." He distinguished clearly between "physical" and "cultural" phenomena; he dealt with bodily needs in a fairly consistent reductionist manner. One wonders how much of Descartes's dualism entered into Sullivan's system: Descartes was at a loss to find the necessary bridge between the body perceived as a machine and the psyche perceived as a spirit. Sullivan crossed a similar bridge quite easily; he assumed that the release of energy (energy perceived in physical terms) is always controlled by social relations. This combination of physicalism with sociology is, to say the least, quite interesting and may lead to further fruitful studies.

Sullivan's theories grew out of his psychiatric experience, mostly with psychotics. While Freud introduced into psychology the richness of motivational problems, Sullivan called for more attention to perception and social interrelationship.

Satisfaction

Sullivan accepts the principles of teleology in psychological studies, following Adler and the entire neo-psychoanalytic movement. He postulates two basic purposes in human activities, *satisfaction* and *security*. People pursue the goal of satisfaction by satisfying hunger, thirst, need for sleep and rest, sex, and need for close physical contact with other people. All other activities "which pertain more to the culture which has been imbedded in a particular individual than to organization of his tissues and glands, [are] apt to belong in this classification of the pursuit of security."[48]

Sullivan goes so far as to introduce an almost dualistic approach in psychology. Satisfaction is basically somatic—it is a function of cells and tissues, of muscles and bodily organs—while security is a cultural phenomenon.

Both the striped and the unstriped muscles serve one purpose: satisfaction. What we experience as thirst or hunger or as a desire for air or sex is a result of muscular contractions. Physiological tension "provokes" our pursuit of satisfaction, and satisfaction brings relaxation and relief of tension.

"Tonic changes in the unstriped, involuntary muscles of the viscera—the internal organs of the body—are, from birth onward, intimately related to the experiencing of desires, needs for satisfaction. Heightened tone of the stomach wall is called out by depletion of our chemical supplies. Throughout life the pursuit of satisfaction is physiologically provoked by increased tone in some unstriped muscles; and the securing of the satisfaction is a relaxation of this tone."[49]

The entire process of seeking satisfaction is interpreted in a reductionist manner. The organic state, such as a heightened tone of the stomach wall, causes us to experience a "desire." When satisfaction is secured, the muscles relax and our alertness is reduced. The organism tends to rest or

[48] Harry S. Sullivan, *Conceptions of Modern Psychiatry*, W. A. White Foundation, 1947, p. 6.
[49] *Ibid.*, p. 43.

sleep. The highest experienced tension is terror, the most profound satisfaction and relaxation is sleep.

This interpretation of human needs has little in common with Freud. It seems to be closer to some kind of organismic theory (see Kurt Goldstein, Chap. 5). Sullivan's theory invites comparison with Cannon's homeostatic system: *tension* and *relief* follow each other, especially since tension and relief are interpreted by Sullivan in purely physiological terms, as a contraction and relaxation of muscles. This physiological process is later modified by social influences. The child soon learns that on certain occasions the immediate relaxation of muscles meets with parental disapproval. Parental disapproval causes a feeling of discomfort. This *empathized discomfort* stems not from the organism but from *interpersonal relationships.* The discomfort is so strong that it destroys the original comfort of relaxation. For example, as soon as there is any tension in bladder or bowels, the proper muscles act immediately to bring relief. However, this automatic relaxation may invite parental hostility, which produces in the child a feeling of "empathized discomfort." This feeling will bring the child to learn "to suffer increasing tension in the bladder and rectum and to resist the automatic relaxation of the sphincter muscles concerned in retaining the urine and feces. Failures in this are often accompanied by empathized discomfort, and success is often the occasion of empathized comfort which is added to the satisfaction from relief of tension."[50]

The child learns how to adjust his behavior to his environment. This process of adjustment is a result of his striving toward security. His activities are influenced by what the environment has to offer him in terms of being accepted and loved by others. The attitude of others toward the child produces in him the feeling of security or insecurity.

Security

Early childhood plays a very important role in the development of a person's feeling of security. The infant feels somehow, by empathy, whether he is accepted or not by the people who take care of him. The accepted and loved child develops a feeling of well-being and happiness. It is the feeling of *euphoria.* The need for satisfaction and the need for security follow the same path. The same mother feeds and cuddles, the same feeding process serves satisfaction and security.

From the very first days of life, "the infant shows a curious relationship or connection with the significant adult, ordinarily the mother. If the mother . . . is seriously disturbed . . . around the time of feeding, then on that occasion there will be feeding difficulty or the infant will have indigestion."[51]

[50] *Ibid.,* p. 44.
[51] *Ibid.,* p. 7.

The child somehow "feels" the attitude of people toward himself. This ability to perceive other people's feelings is called empathy. Empathy is interpreted by Sullivan as a kind of "emotional contagion or communion" between the child and the adults who take care of him. It is strongest from the age of six months to that of twenty-five months. The child responds to the emotions of his mother or father or any other parental substitute. All these are "significant" adults in his life, and they produce in him an empathized comfort or discomfort, in accordance with their friendly or unfriendly attitude to him.

Sooner or later, parents or other significant adults impose rules and restrictions upon the child's way of procuring satisfaction. We have already mentioned toilet training; a similar process takes place in telling the child to eat in a civilized manner. Failure to comply with parental requests invites disapproval and destroys the child's feeling of euphoria and security and produces *anxiety*. The patterns of parental behavior are products of the prevailing culture. The child's "euphoria," as said before, results from being accepted by his parents and/or other significant persons in his environment. Since the parents represent the social norms of a certain culture, *the child's adjustment to parental instructions and admonitions is actually adjustment to a certain culture.*

As the child grows, parents, teachers, and other significant persons actively introduce more and more customs and norms of their culture in the child. Acting in accordance with these norms brings the feeling of belonging, of being accepted, of euphoria. Disregard of the social norms causes disapproval, and the child will feel rejected. This is how the inhibitory mechanism is established: the child avoids disapproval and tries to comply with the requirements of his culture by inhibiting his desire for an immediate relief of tensions.

Whenever the biological needs of an individual cannot be satisfied in a socially acceptable way, i.e., in the manner in which the individual was trained in childhood, he has a feeling of insecurity and uneasiness, i.e., anxiety. *Anxiety is always connected with an increased muscular tension.* Muscles ready for a socially unacceptable action become inhibited, since their activity is likely to invite disapproval. For instance, the inhibition of crying or screaming stimulates higher tension in throat muscles. Anxiety is a product of a conflict between the need for satisfaction and the need to follow the socially acceptable ways of procuring satisfaction.

Anxiety can be regarded as a socially produced muscular tension. It interferes with "any other tension with which it coincides."[52] Anxiety prevents satisfaction in hunger and sex, interferes with normal mental functioning, and impairs the ability to perceive and understand things. The highest level of anxiety, terror, brings on a breakdown of personality.

[52] Harry S. Sullivan, "The Meaning of Anxiety in Psychiatry and in Life," *Psychiatry*, 1948, **11**, 1–13.

Avoiding or relieving this socially created anxiety usually brings the pleasant feeling of self-esteem. The ability to attain satisfaction and security means "power." Self-respect is a result of success in obtaining satisfaction and security.

Tensions and Transformation of Energy

Experience means what is going on within a person. The term "experience" is used by Sullivan in an "energetic" manner. There are two kinds of experience. The first type is readiness or "potentiality" for action, which is called by Sullivan "tension." The action itself—the second kind of experience—is called by Sullivan "transformation of energy."

"Tension" and "transformation of energy" sound like physicalism or reductionism, and Sullivan states blatantly: "I use these two terms in exactly the same sense as I would in telling about physics." Sullivan seems to feel pretty strongly about this issue.

Tensions are of two kinds. First, there are tensions of *needs*. Needs are either *general* or *zonal*. The general needs are physiological requirements of man as a living organism—food, water, reproductive activity. The zonal needs develop as a result of interaction between the respective zones of our body and the environment, e.g., the oral zone, the genital, the manual, the visual, etc. "Zonal needs" correspond vaguely to Freud's genetic zones. Although some of the areas pointed out are identical, there is quite a difference in the role attached to them respectively by Freud and Sullivan. Freud perceived the bodily zones as representative of the phylogenetic evolution of mankind and interpreted their ontogenetic role on the lines of the biogenetic theory (cf. Chap. 6). Sullivan perceives the zones as a product of certain life experiences. They are *zones of interaction with the environment* and do not represent phylogenetic developmental stages.

The second kind of tensions are the *anxiety tensions*. As mentioned before, anxiety is first manifested in early infancy. "Very young infants show grossly identical patterns of behavior when they are subjected to 'frightening' situations and when they are in contact with the person who mothers them and *that person* is anxious, angry, or *otherwise disquieted*. Something which develops without a break into the tension state which we have discriminated on the basis of its specific difference from fear can be *induced* in the infant by *interpersonal influence*, in contrast to the evocation of primitive fear by sundry violent influences from 'outside' the infant's body. This *interpersonal induction* of anxiety, and the exclusively interpersonal origin of every instance of its manifestations is the unique characteristic of anxiety and of the congeries of more complex tensions in later life to which it contributes."[53]

[53] *Ibid.*

Modes of Experience

All human experience occurs in three "modes." The first is the proto-taxic; the earliest experiences in human life are prototaxic. The infant's experiences are undifferentiated, having no division into time units, since he has not yet developed the awareness of being a separate entity. The prototaxic mode is a series of "momentary states," mostly unformulable and therefore incommunicable. Events come and go, and the infant is unable to localize them in time or space. This experience is a sort of mass experi-ence, unorganized, dim, as if made out of one piece. Some such experi-ences may be mystical and of "cosmic identification." "The one relation-ship which certainly exists between items of experience in the prototaxic mode is succession, place in organismic or biological time."[54] As the child grows, he learns "that objects which our distance receptors, our eyes and ears, for example, encounter, are of a quite different order of relationship from things which our tactile or our gustatory receptors encounter."[55] The child learns to differentiate between respective parts of reality. *Parataxic* experience is prelogical, since the child is unable to relate things and events to each other or to understand the laws of nature. Things are per-ceived without logical course or order. Experiences "take on personal meaning" and become organized into "personifications of myself." The parataxic mode of experience remains in adults' life in dreams, when things come and go without being logically connected. In childhood most waking experiences are of this kind.[56]

Children's language is "autistic," i.e., centered around "myself." Every-thing is related to personal needs and experiences. Language is a system of symbolic signs, but children's symbols are a product of their personifi-cation of themselves and of attaching imaginary traits to other people; children's symbols are therefore subjective, personal, and often imaginary. Step by step the child learns to associate certain signs with the behavior of other people and to pay attention to their experiences too. Children's parataxic mode and autistic talk give way to the syntaxic mode and interpersonal language.

The syntaxic mode is related to perceiving other people and validating one's experience against the experience of others. One's observations and judgments are "consensually validated" with the perceptions and conclu-sions of others. Sullivan is aware of the fact that even checking one's experiences against those of others cannot serve as evidence of absolute truth. It means only some kind of agreement with significant persons and makes possible communication and adjustment in a given social environ-

[54] Harry S. Sullivan, "Multidisciplined Coordination of Interpersonal Data," in Sargent and Smith, *op. cit.*

[55] Sullivan, *Conceptions of Modern Psychiatry*, p. 16.

[56] This description invites comparison with Piaget's studies on children's reasoning and language.

ment and culture. Of course, syntaxic experiences depend on cultural settings. Tensions may occur in either parataxic or syntaxic modes. Any frustration in seeking to satisfy hunger, or sex, or the need for physical proximity may be experienced in the syntaxic mode, or in the unorganized and highly imaginary parataxic mode. *Anxiety is always perceived in the parataxic mode.*

Children, and sometimes adults, develop "parataxic distortions" when they resort to another person on the basis of a distorted identification. They may attach nonexistent traits to certain people or may even invent imaginary characters ("eidetic persons").

Conscious and Unconscious

Although Sullivan refrains from the use of Freudian terminology, he does not disregard the theoretical and clinical importance of the psychological concepts represented by it. A person, Sullivan states, may be "wittingly aware" of certain performances of his own, while other performances remained unnoticed, outside his awareness.

Sullivan offers an interpretation of these facts. In infancy everything ocurs in the prototaxic mode; through the process of empathy the infant feels the attitude of the significant people toward himself, but all his perceptions are diffuse and vague. Since their approval brings euphoria and their disapproval denies satisfaction and gives anxiety, the child learns to concentrate on the factors pertinent to the significant persons. This is the origin of his "conscious" self-dynamism, which is compared by Sullivan to a microscope. Self-dynamism "permits a minute focus on those performances of the child which are the cause of approbation and disapprobation, but very much like a microscope, it interferes with noticing the rest of the world. When you are staring through your microscope, you don't see very much other than that which comes through that channel. So with self-dynamism."[57]

Self-dynamism is conscious, while anything else is not. Everything outside self-dynamism is either *disassociated* or *selectively inattended*. The first term corresponds to Freud's unconscious, while the latter resembles the preconscious (see Chap. 6). Only those processes which are pertinent to relationships with significant people become included in self-dynamism and the person is "wittingly aware" of them. Tension and energy transformation may be a "felt or wittingly noted state of being" or not. Tension per se is potentiality for action; energy transformations are actions; both tensions and energy transformations may have "felt or representational components" or may "transpire without any witting awareness."[58]

[57] Sullivan, *Conceptions of Modern Psychiatry*, p. 23.

[58] Sullivan distinguished clearly between potentialities for action and awareness of these potentialities, while Kurt Lewin's "psychological field" represents both the objective potentialities and the situation as perceived by the individual (see Chap. 13).

Developmental Stages

Sullivan distinguishes six epochs in personality development. The first developmental stage is infancy, which starts at birth and continues until the maturation of the capacity for language. The newborn child strives for unrestricted satisfaction of his needs and unlimited expression of his power. Both tendencies meet with a certain type of response from the mother; she may approve or disapprove of the behavior of the child. Since it is up to her to satisfy him or to deny satisfaction, the infant learns to adjust himself to his mother at an early stage.

This process of adjustment takes place because of the child's ability to feel somehow his mother's state of mind. Empathy is the nonverbal way of communicating emotion. The mother's approval is conducive to a euphoric state in the child, while the mother's disapproval may produce anxiety.

Sooner or later the infant learns to relate his pleasant feeling of euphoria or the annoying feeling of anxiety to his own behavior. Some of his activities are somehow connected with euphoria while others cause anxiety. He learns to perceive the signs of approval or disapproval and to act accordingly. Furthermore, through this compliance he makes considerable progress in the process of acculturation. Cultural influences transmitted through the parents determine the future structure of the self.

The self or self-dynamism develops through the approval and disapproval of others. "Since the approbation of the important person is very valuable, since disapprobation denies satisfaction and gives anxiety, the self becomes extremely important. . . . It has a tendency to focus attention in performances with the significant other person which got approbation or disfavor. And that peculiarity, closely connected with anxiety, persists thenceforth through life. It comes about that the self, to which we refer when we say 'I,' is the only thing which has alertness, which notices what goes on, and needless to say, notices what goes on in its own field. The rest of the personality gets along outside awareness."[59]

The infant develops three types of personifications of himself. When his behavior is accepted and praised, he develops self-identification of approval: This is the "good-me." Mild anxiety is conducive to "bad-me" personification of self. Unusual feelings of horror or shock lead to the diffuse and never fully conscious states of "not-me."

In infancy the child begins to develop personification of other people too. The feeling of euphoria is conducive to a "good-mother" personification, while anxiety states bring "bad-mother" personifications. Out of the

[59] Sullivan, *Conceptions of Modern Psychiatry*, p. 23.

personifications of significant people grow and develop later *eidetic* people, i.e., imaginary persons.[60]

The second developmental stage is *childhood*. Sullivan sets the upper limit of this era in the "capacity for living with compeers"; the next era, the *juvenile*, will start with school attendance.

Childhood is the era of the most pervasive acculturation processes. The child learns toilet habits, eating habits, cleanliness, and most of the habitual ways of behavior regarded as proper by the society and represented by his parents.

The child learns how to restrain his drive for *power*. Many of his activities are frustrated or prohibited by his parents. Some of his unacceptable desires are *sublimated*. The anxiety-provoking tendencies are diverted into socially accepted channels; they are partially satisfied by fusion with socially desirable ways of behavior.

The unsatisfied and undischarged parts of the drive or impulse find outlet in dreams, daydreams, or regressions to the pre-sublimation situation. Regression usually represents unsatisfied parts of a drive but it is also regression in the person's total behavior.

Quite often the child's efforts to get approval meet with parental lack of patience, fatigue, or some other kind of rejecting behavior. This may lead to distortions of the reality of the child; the child who craves parental love and receives nothing but rejection may develop paranoid distortions. He may regard himself as lonely and rejected in a cold and hostile world.

The child may then try to alleviate his anxiety by producing anger. Outbursts of anger undoubtedly bring relief from frustration, as several studies have proved.[61] A frustrated person may feel better after releasing his anger on an innocent scapegoat.

Sullivan introduced at this point a theory of emotions which is at great variance with Freud's theory. Freud regarded love and hatred as innate emotions; fear was to come later, as a result of experience. Horney regarded acceptance and lack of it, anxiety, as the basic emotions. Sullivan saw in anger a substitute for anxiety; most individuals successfully conceal their anxieties even from themselves, and their anger often serves as an outlet and a cover for anxiety.

The *juvenile era* starts in our civilization with school age. "The child manifests a shift from contentment in an environment of totalitarian adults toward an environment of persons significantly *like* him. Along with this budding ability to play with other children, there goes a learning of those performances which we call competition and compromise."[62]

Meeting other children encourages interpersonal validation of percep-

[60] Sullivan borrowed the term "eidetic" from Jaensch. Sullivan's connotation of eidetic would mean imaginary; eidetic people would mean either invented persons or real persons with imaginary traits.
[61] John Dollard et al., *Frustration and Aggression*, Yale, 1939.
[62] Sullivan, *Conceptions of Modern Psychiatry*, p. 18.

tion and leads gradually to the syntaxic mode. The child learns to pay more attention to the opinions of other children; he tries to become *popular* and fears to be alone or, even worse, rejected by his group. The child's process of socialization leads toward the establishment of personal friendship with one or more children.

Preadolescence starts between the ages of eight and a half and twelve. It is characterized by the appearance of the capacity to love. Usually the attachment takes place within the same sex; it is "isophile." Sullivan does not regard this as "homosexuality." Homosexuality comes later, often as a product of failure in heterosexual overtures.

In the preadolescent era most people develop "consensual validation" by exchange of words and ideas with their friends. In this exchange the preadolescent learns to check his perceptions with those of others and yields some of his interests for the sake of his group.

The preadolescent era plays the decisive role in one's future social relationship. Social experiences in this age will determine future social adaptability. In contradistinction to Freudian views, Sullivan asserts that preadolescence determines one's automatic ease or unvarying stress in dealing with any significant number of one's own sex.

Adolescence is an era of *patterning of lustful behavior*. The genital zone comes to the fore. Sex is not the driving power in man, but it is nevertheless a powerful factor in human life. Impulses to genital behavior cannot be easily disassociated, and in some individuals they cannot be disassociated at all. Sex will, "again and again, at whatever great expense to security, whatever suffering from anxiety, manifest itself."[63]

Sex enjoys in Sullivan's theory a privileged position. Sex can defy even anxiety and any other tension. However, it cannot be fully satisfied unless intimacy is provided. The heterosexual experiences in this developmental stage determine one's future ease or difficulty in making a satisfactory sexual adjustment in adult life. Thus Sullivan has shifted the focal point of sexual and other interpersonal adjustment from early childhood to preadolescence and adolescence.

Personality

In discussing personality Sullivan comes close to the field-theoretical psychology (see Chap. 13). Each interpersonal situation influences the personalities of the participating individuals. The total personality includes all possible ways of reaction of a certain individual, but in the presence of various persons various patterns of behavior come to the fore. Which part of a personality will play the decisive role in a given situation is a product of this situation, i.e., of the interpersonal interaction that takes place.

[63] *Ibid.,* p. 31.

This presentation reflects, obviously, George Mead's theory of social roles, but even more Kurt Lewin's "life space" and field theory. A person may appear in different roles, or a person is a product of social interrelationship.

Sullivan does not believe that personality can be perceived or interpreted outside of the social context of interrelationship. "Personality can never be isolated from the complexity of interpersonal relations in which the person lives and has his being."[64] Personality is a product of interrelationship with other persons; therefore it can hardly be regarded as a separate entity. Moreover, personality per se eludes scientific investigation, since it cannot be perceived outside the interpersonal relationship.

"In the course of psychiatric inquiry one discovers that it is not a person as an *isolated and self-contained entity* that one is studying, or can study, but a situation, an interpersonal situation, composed of two or more people." The traits which characterize the interpersonal situations in which one is integrated describe what one is. "Personality is . . . a function of the kinds of interpersonal situations a person integrates with others, whether real persons or personifications," comments Mullahy on Sullivan's theory of personality.[65]

Sullivan presents personality in two modes: in a "private mode," which is incommunicable, and in which no personality can be studied, and as a "relatively enduring pattern of recurrent interpersonal situations." The latter really deserves the label of personality. This "enduring pattern" is personality as grasped by scientific tools.

The "enduring pattern of behavior" is the way a person uses his energies. Here the conception of *self-dynamism* or *self-system* or *self* enters the picture. Sullivan thinks about energy in physical terms; to him dynamism means a "relatively enduring configuration of energy."

This energy is released in interpersonal relations. Self-dynamism is therefore the only part of personality which is observable and can be scientifically studied.

The directions of use or release of energy are a product of two basic factors. The first is the child's need for satisfaction and security. The second is the influence of the significant persons on the child's behavior. In other words, the child strives to use his energy in order to obtain the satisfaction of his needs and the feeling of euphoria. His activities are determined by the approval or disapproval of significant people. He avoids their disapproval, which brings him anxiety, and tends to seek satisfaction and security in a way which procures social approval.

Actually self-dynamism or the self-system means *how a person behaves.*

[64] Harry S. Sullivan, "Sociopsychiatric Research: Its Implications for the Schizophrenia Problem and for Mental Hygiene," *American Journal of Psychiatry*, 1931, **10**, 77–91.

[65] Patrick Mullahy, "A Theory of Interpersonal Relations and the Evolution of Personality," in Sullivan, *Conceptions of Modern Psychiatry*, pp. 122–123.

It is somewhat similar to Adler's "style of life" or Freud's "character." According to Sullivan energy is universal, but the consistent patterns of use of energy are environmentally conditioned. Self-dynamism or the self is a result of "reflected appraisals," since the "child experiences himself and appraises himself in terms of what the parents and others close to him manifest."[66]

As a result of the social pressure exercised by the parents and other significant persons, only certain patterns of behavior become disassociated or "selectively inattended." The disassociated processes do not belong to self-dynamism and are excluded from awareness. The person does not recognize them as parts of himself; he will deny their existence and not be able to recall them. The disassociated processes may express themselves in dreams, daydreaming, unintentional activities, etc., and may be recalled in psychoanalytic therapy.

Certain tendencies are not entirely disassociated but are "selectively inattended." Selective inattention applies to activity patterns which are unimportant to the significant person and therefore do not call for his approval or disapproval. The approved tendencies form the self-dynamism; the disapproved ones are rejected. Those tendencies concerning which parents do not express any attitude, will remain unnoticed, dim, and neglected. And as a result of interpersonal situations a person can become aware of these tendencies and, eventually, admit them to his self-system.

Interpersonal Relations

Sullivan believes that interpersonal relations are the subject matter of the scientific study of personality. The kind of person one is can be inferred from his behavior in relationship to other persons. People cannot be studied per se, but only in a "situation" in which at least one real and one "eidetic" person participate. The eidetic persons are usually people whom one has actually met in the past and personified in an imaginative manner. A man and his real or imaginary partners form the "interpersonal situation."

This presentation invites comparison with field theory. Sullivan does not subscribe to Kurt Lewin's theory; cultural influences and past experiences as interpreted by Sullivan do not fit into Lewin's "field at a given time." Sullivan gives full consideration to the past, and genetic and developmental factors are of the utmost importance in his theory. But the interpersonal situation as described by him is a "field" (see Chap. 13).

Sullivan's presentation of interpersonal relations also resembles the field-theoretical approach in another aspect. In interpersonal relations

[66] Sullivan, *Conceptions of Modern Psychiatry*, p. 27.

as seen by Sullivan all but one person "may be more or less completely illusory." Social relations may develop between an individual and a number of "eidetic" or imaginary persons; even nonexisting persons may influence human behavior, because behavior is oriented toward situations as we perceive them.

Gestalt psychologists would say that reality as perceived by a person is his *psychological field* (Chap. 12). If this "reality" differs considerably from what other people perceive, then, according to Sullivan, the person perceiving unrealistically suffers from parataxic distortions. Mentally sick or disturbed persons distort reality badly and adjust their lives to nonexisting persons, or to persons whom they perceive in an unrealistic manner. Kurt Lewin (see Chap. 13) has distinguished various levels of reality in the psychological field, and Sullivan's modes correspond in a way to Lewin's system.

Sullivan shows a considerable bias against "individuality." "The individuality of a particular electron is of no concern to the physicist; the individuality of the biologist's dog is not apt to confuse his biology of the dog. It is quite otherwise, however, with the traditionally emphasized individuality of each of us, 'myself.' Here we have the very mother of illusions, the ever frequent source of preconceptions that invalidate almost all our efforts to understand other people."[67]

Sullivan's definition of personality as "the relatively enduring pattern of recurring interpersonal situations" must include cultural factors. The child perceives by empathy how his parents feel about his behavior; parental attitudes are a product of culture and reflect the socially accepted pattern; school and society, peers and adults, constantly represent social norms. No person can be fully understod unless the observer relates his behavior to the actual interpersonal situation and to relatively constant social influences.

Concluding Remarks

Watson's theory has been called "a psychology of everybody but me." Sullivan's theory can be defined as "a between-people psychology." While Watson denies the possibility of the psychological study of an individual by himself, Sullivan denies the possibility of the psychological study of an individual not interrelated with other individuals and states that this interrelationship can be studied.

One wonders whether Sullivan's approach represents methodological cautiousness or a statement about matters of fact. Does he propose an epistemological limitation, derived from Kant's idealism, that "things per

[67] Harry S. Sullivan, "Introduction to the Study of Interpersonal Relations," *Psychiatry*, 1938, 1, 121–134.

se" are inaccessible to our cognition? Or does he suggest a temporary methodological restriction, that the best and the safest way to procure truthful information about a person is to see him in interpersonal relations?

Fromm-Reichmann, using Sullivan's frame of reference, says that "emotional difficulties in living are difficulties in interpersonal relationships; and a person is not emotionally hampered, that is, he is mentally healthy to the extent to which he is able to be aware of, and therefore, to handle his interpersonal relationships."[68] One would like to determine whether difficulties in interpersonal relationships are a result of emotional difficulties and a symptom of them or, as Fromm-Reichmann says, represent the emotional difficulties themselves.

Sullivan answers this question in a quasi-operationist manner. He says: "I can say with Bridgman that I act in two modes—my public mode [in which] I feel my inviolable isolation from my fellows. The inimitable private escapes and will always escape the methods of science. The true or absolute individuality of a person is always beyond scientific grasp."[69]

This quasi-operationist statement invites clarification. Sullivan can hardly be regarded as a consistent operationist or a faithful student of neo-positivism. Although the "public me" can be subjected to a set of operations, one doubts whether "eidetic persons," "self-dynamism," "not-me," and other Sullivanian constructs fit into any operationism at all (cf. Chaps. 1, 3, and 4). Skinner defines operationism as follows: "Operationism may be defined as the practice of talking about (1) one's observations, (2) the manipulative and calculational procedures involved in making them, (3) the logical and mathematical steps which intervene between earlier and later statements, and (4) *nothing else*."[70]

If this is a correct definition, Sullivan's theory has little in common with operationism, and no operations can be formulated which will prove or disprove most of Sullivan's propositions. Still, Sullivan's propositions may be truthful or at least useful tools in scientific research, despite their non-operationist origin.

Another case of lack of clarity is Sullivan's term "tension." "Tensions may be considered to have two important aspects; that of tension as potentiality for action, for the transformation of energy; and that of a *felt* or wittingly noted state of being."[71] Tension *is* potentiality for action, and tension *may* have felt or representational components. The reader

[68] F. Fromm-Reichmann, *Principles of Intensive Psychotherapy*, University of Chicago, 1950, p. 14.
[69] Sullivan, *Conceptions of Modern Psychiatry*, Foreword to second printing, p. vii.
[70] B. F. Skinner, "The Operational Analysis of Psychological Terms," *Psychological Review*, 1946, **52**, 270–277, 291–294.
[71] Sullivan, "Multidisciplined Coordination of Interpersonal Data," in Sargent and Smith, *op. cit.*, p. 176.

may conclude that tensions per se are not identical with tensions as experienced or felt by a person. One cannot help wondering which kind of tension is the subject matter of psychology.

Sullivan's entire system is rather a *deductive* one. Sullivan *postulates* a dualism of physics (energy) and culture (interpersonal relations) as well as a dualism of heredity (satisfaction) and environment (euphoria), with emphasis on culture and environment. He does not reject innate factors. He admits them into his theory under the heading of "satisfaction." Satisfaction covers all somatic aspects of behavior which are not the product of human experience, or interpersonal relations. Little consideration is given in Sullivan's theory to this factor. One may say that to Sullivan, "given a biological substrate, the human is the product of interaction with other human beings."[72] However, innate factors need not be considered only in the case where all interpersonal differences are a product of social relations. This holds true only in regard to identical twins; any other case represents a combination of innate and acquired factors. No doubt Sullivan, in contradistinction to Freud, puts much more weight on the environmental factors, to the disparagement of innate ones.

Sullivan's self-dynamism or self-system invites comparison with Freud's ego and superego. Self-dynamism or self develops as a result of parental appraisal. The "self" is reality oriented, like the ego, and represents the culture, like the superego. Sullivan denies the instinctual origin of both and, in view of his clinical experience, sees no reason for the Freudian constructs. Instead he introduces his own self-dynamism, which simplifies the relationship between conscious and unconscious.

Sullivan offers an interesting interpretation of the origins of the unconscious: It is the relationship with other significant people that makes the child become aware or unaware of some of his performances. Additional interpretation of this issue is given by inference. Since certain activities of the child may be interrupted by an outburst of hunger or rage, and then picked up and overtly continued, one may infer about their *covert,* or unconscious, continuation while they are overtly interrupted.

Summarizing Sullivan's contribution to psychological research and theory one must admit that Sullivan did develop a full-fledged psychological system. He covered the areas of child psychology and normal and abnormal personality and offered quite important suggestions in social psychology. Man is a combination of nature and culture; he is both nature- and culture-made. The newborn child represents "nature," but as he grows his behavior is more and more shaped by culture. This approach is common to the entire sociological school in psychoanalysis, but only Sullivan offered a highly conceptual system of interpretation of human behavior and development.

[72] Thompson, *op. cit.,* p. 211.

Methodologically speaking, Sullivan's theory is a system of postulates that tries to replace the Freudian system. It has apparent advantages in its shift to culture and its vigorous presentation of the social aspects of human life. Many social scientists will be influenced by the analysis of interpersonal situations; Sullivan's method of study in these situations may lead to new and fruitful interpretation of group relations, as it has already brought a considerable change in the clinical patient-doctor setting.

Here, in our opinion, lies Sullivan's greatness. Men become themselves in relation to others. Growth, maturation, adjustment, disturbances, or sickness can be fully understood only in their social interrelationships.

Concluding Remarks on the Sociological School

It is not easy to change the architectonic structure of a castle. Freud was a master in the art of logical thinking and his system was a formidable structure erected by the human mind.

As long as one follows the line of Freud's reasoning and adds an empirical observation here or there or streamlines his conceptual framework, as K. Abraham, E. Jones, O. Fenichel, E. Glover, A. Freud, and scores of others have done, the entire building is well preserved and perhaps improved. But as soon as one rejects any of the fundamental concepts, the entire building crumbles.

Apparently Freud's theory cannot be edited at will or easily "corrected." Whoever undertakes the daring task of changing the basic structure must be prepared to erect an entirely new structure.

None of the sociologically oriented neo-psychoanalysts was sufficiently equipped to undertake this task. The weakest of all three was, obviously, Fromm, whose theories have the least sufficient empirical background. One can be enchanted by Fromm's ethical zeal, but no one can consider his conclusions part of an empirical system of science.

Horney's studies in the sociological causes of neurosis (*The Neurotic Personality of Our Time*) are an important contribution toward understanding the etiology of mental disorder. Yet Horney's work cannot, if only by the limitations of its scope, be considered a sufficient substitute for Freud's conceptual system, although Horney was, undoubtedly, a keen observer and a thorough thinker.

The best-developed system was offered by Sullivan. It is a full-fledged psychological system. However, parts of it are a mere translation of Freudian concepts; his field-theoretical concepts are methodologically vulnerable (cf. Chap. 13, "Concluding Remarks"). But his theory of personality and his observations related to perception are thought provoking. Sullivan's system is no longer Freudianism; it is, to a great extent, a new psychological theory which stands on its own merits.

In summary, one can say that Freud's theory can be accepted, rejected, or modified, like any other psychological theory. But whoever undertakes the task of remodeling psychoanalysis must come armed with an empirical evidence or a methodological consideration superior to that offered by Freud. Horney and Sullivan made important contributions, but their factual or methodological superiority to Freud is doubted.

SUMMARY OF PART II

There are three "fathers" of contemporary psychological theory: Pavlov, Freud, and to a certain extent, Dilthey. The second part of this book is devoted to Sigmund Freud and to all those who remained faithful to him or rebelled against him.

Freud was more of a "father" than Pavlov or Dilthey. He created the system, he developed, changed, readjusted, and presented it to the world as one of the most elaborate products of the human mind.

Freud's starting point was the natural sciences. He adhered strictly to the principles of determinism, materialistic monism, conservation of energy, and empiricism. In philosophy Freud was a positivist, a disciple of J. S. Mill, A. Comte, and H. Spencer, but he did not accept the radical philosophy of the neo-positivists. His theory was deeply rooted in the biological sciences and their methods of research.

Yet the biologically oriented Freud, the materialistic positivist Freud, did not hesitate to modify the traditional empiricism and materialism but developed the most speculative psychological system based on non-reductionism. Freud's point is well taken and well justified. For what is good in clinging to the naïve empirical observations and stubbornly maintaining that the sun is moving and the earth is not? Or what is good in professing that the nervous system offers all the answers to psychological problems while the question is all but solved?

Freud is an example of courage and tenacity in a relentless, unabated search for scientific truth. Whenever a link was missing between observable phenomena, Freud interpolated, always most economically, a speculative hypothesis. This hypothesis could not be directly proved, but its application in the interpretation of observable data and their prediction offered convincing support to Freud's concepts.

On the issue of reductionism Freud offered the best possible solution. While firmly adhering to the idea of a continuum of the organic world, Freud had to postulate that mental energy is a *derivative* of physical energy and yet cannot be perceived and studied in physical terms. It is different, and there is no use

385

in assuming that an encephalogram indicates more than it does, or that the study of glands of inner secretion can help to predict one's behavior.

Scientific honesty and cautiousness forced Freud to accept the principles of the methodological non-reductionism, for the only way one can study mental phenomena is to accept them as being different from physical phenomena—different and yet a part of the continuum of living matter, just as flowers are different from roots and yet form a part of the plant in a continuum of growth from root to flower.

Armed with these principles, Freud made the greatest discovery in psychology. He discovered the unconscious processes. He proved their existence through meticulous research of amnestic and hypnotic phenomena, through dream interpretation, through the study of the psychopathology of daily life, and through his work with mentally disturbed individuals.

Then he proceeded to develop his theory in three realms: the realm of the topography of the human mind (conscious, preconscious, and unconscious), the realm of the driving forces (the instinctual drives of life—Eros—and of death—Thanatos), and finally the mental apparatus (id, ego, and superego).

Freud believed that personality is an outcome of (1) the innate, instinctual forces deeply rooted in organic sources, (2) the biologically determined but modifiable-by-environment developmental stages (oral, anal, urethral, phallic, latency, genital), and (3) the interaction between the child and his parents.

Chapter 7 describes the theories of the two first dissidents, Alfred Adler and Carl Gustav Jung. Adler's rebellion against Freud is, primarily, a rebellion against Freud's biological foundations and deterministic philosophy. Adler introduced the humanistic point of view, borrowed from Dilthey and Windelband. In a long evolution of his thinking, he finally arrived at the idea that striving toward superiority and consideration for the fellow man (sociability) are the main driving forces in humans.

Adler's main consideration was the way man relates to men in a conscious way; thus practically all the neo-psychoanalysts, such as Horney, Sullivan, and Fromm, owe to Adler no less than they owe to Freud.

Jung's theory took an entirely different course of development. Jung's main concern was the unconscious phenomena, divided into the personal and collective unconscious. Jung offered a wealth of research material in the history of culture with special emphasis on religion, symbolic thinking, mysticism, and alchemy.

Chapter 8 is devoted to further studies in psychoanalysis. It starts with the theories of Otto Rank, who, like Adler, believed in the inner creativity of men and developed a highly speculative theory of man's fear of death and fear of life.

Melanie Klein, F. Alexander, S. Ferenczi, W. Reich, and others deviated from Freud to a lesser degree than Rank did. Yet their theories cannot be considered a continuation of Freud's work. They contain more deviation than continuation.

Sociological and anthropological studies, especially those by A. Kardiner and R. Linton, are discussed in the fourth section of this chapter. Apparently Kardiner shifted the focal point from the inner forces acting in the individual to the forces acting in the physical and social environment.

Another possible modification of Freud's theory came from the studies of experimental psychologists. Although, as R. R. Sears' summary and other studies indicate, psychoanalytic propositions were not directly proved or refuted by the experimental method, the combination of experimental psychology and clinical psychoanalysis is very promising.

Chapter 9 deals with those who definitely broke away from Freud, the sociologically oriented Horney, Fromm, and Sullivan. Horney's starting point was the distinction between the biological need for satisfaction and the social need of humans for safety, for being accepted by others. Man, said Horney, can renounce satisfaction sooner than safety. Thus the needs for social approval become the central point of Horney's theory. Adler's influence is quite prominent.

Horney's studies of child development led to a series of interesting observations. The rejected child develops "basic anxiety," while the accepted and protected child develops in a satisfactory manner.

E. Fromm's theory starts with a speculative assumption, very similar to Rank's, that there is a dichotomy between nature and culture. Men tried to overcome the dichotomy by the security of social groups; when this security was destroyed by the contemporary culture, men "escaped from freedom" into dictatorship. Fromm appeals to the "creative forces" in human nature.

The most thorough and scientific among the neo-psychoanalysts is H. S. Sullivan. Sullivan replaced Freud's system by his own, which is only partially a change in terminology. Sullivan's emphasis on the field concepts brings him closer to K. Lewin. Sullivan's interesting studies in the level of perceptions (prototaxic, parataxic, and syntaxic) derived from his studies in mental disorder enrich the psychological theory and open new research possibilities.

In summarizing the second part of this volume, the author feels that none of the followers or opponents of Freud was capable of suggesting a system of hypotheses methodologically superior to Freud's or better equipped with empirical evidence. The various theories taken up in this part legitimately discussed or criticized one or another of Freud's conclusions, but no one could offer a better system. Therefore, the author of the book feels that Freud's theory is far superior to any other offered in this part; and if anyone suggests changes, they must have a strong factual or methodological backing.

PART III

Understanding, Gestalt, and
Field Psychologies

CHAPTER 10

Phenomenology and Understanding Psychology

1. KANT'S HERITAGE

The Common Problems

For the third and last time in the present volume we have to go back to the "roots" of the contemporary psychological theory. This time we must go farther back, to the common philosophical foundations of the great variety of theories described in the third part of this volume including those of Spranger, Stern, Wertheimer, Lewin, and others.

All these systems, which today have very little in common with one another, have their common roots in the German idealistic philosophy of Immanuel Kant and his disciples. Even today they still struggle with psychological problems as posed by Kant and Wilhelm Dilthey. Neither Kant nor Dilthey is the "father" of this group of psychological theories in the way Pavlov and Freud are. Although Pavlov continued the works of the early associationists Hartley and Bain and physiologists Flourens and Sechenov, it was Pavlov who developed the theory of conditioning. And, although Freud was influenced by Darwin, Spencer, Janet, and Charcot, it was Freud who developed the system of unconscious motivation.

Nothing of that kind could be traced in the systems brought together under the name of understanding, gestalt, and field theories. Nor was there here a leader comparable in stature to Pavlov and Freud. However, let us keep in mind that the systems discussed in the first and second parts of this volume often had in common only the topics of controversial issues; they shared the problems but not necessarily the solutions of the problems.

This principle of common problems unites all the theories brought together in Part III. All of them have been influenced by the intellectual heritage left by I. Kant and faced the psychological problems as posed by W. Dilthey.

"Pure" Reason

Kant's main work, *Kritik der Reinen Vernunft* (*Critique of Pure Reason*), appeared in 1781. The second edition of this book (1787) opened with the following sentence: "There can be no doubt that all knowledge begins with experience."[1] But the meaning of this experience presented by Kant in the *Kritik* and in several other volumes became one of the most controversial issues in the intellectual history of mankind.

While scores of disciples and followers believe that Kant opened wide the way for a truly scientific inquiry, many doubt it. Kant's main idea was that the sensualists (Locke, Hume) are right in saying that knowledge comes from the sensory perception; but perception gives us the knowledge of things not as they really are in themselves (*Ding an sich*) but as they appear to us (phenomena). The things as they are, the *things-in-themselves*, exist, but we perceive them the way our mind is capable of perceiving them. Thus Kant created a sharp dichotomy between the perceiving or experiencing subject and the perceived object. Therefore, knowledge "starts with experience" but it does "not arise out of experience." Knowledge starts with perception, but we perceive only the perceivable phenomena in a fashion determined by our mind.

The problem of the nature of the world was shifted from the objective facts to the perceiving subject, to the human "transcendental" mind and its boundaries. The content of knowledge necessarily includes sensations coming from the objects—color, weight, sound, etc. But the mind is not a photographic camera; the mind *orders* its perceptions of objects in time and space. Time and space are not found in the objective world; they are not empirical qualities of objects; they are a priori given, independent of experience, inherent in the human mind and embedded in its nature. The mind perceives the objects in the dimensions of time and space because this is the only way the subject, the human mind, can perceive the objects. "Take away the thinking subject and the entire corporeal world will vanish, for it is nothing but the appearance in the sensibility of the subject," wrote Kant. The world as perceived is a product of two factors: the sensory perception of the object and the a priori forms of the mind.

Thus time and space are terms of the mind. They are the a priori, synthetic, general, universal terms of knowledge. They need no proof, for they are the prerequisite of any proof; without them any knowledge would be rendered impossible. They are the way in which the mind perceives the phenomena. In addition to time and space, Kant postulated several rational *categories* inherent in our minds, such as relation (e.g.,

---

[1] Immanuel Kant, *Critique of Pure Reason* (M. Müller, trans.), Macmillan, 1881.

causation), quantity, quality, and modality. They are not derived from experience; they are pure concepts, a priori forms of perception and reasoning.

Although Kant accepted the fact that part of our knowledge is supplied by sensory perception, it is an information not about the true state of things but only about their appearance (phenomena) perceived in the framework of the workings of our minds and shaped by our cognitive terms. The only science is mathematics, because it represents a series of synthetic, a priori, absolute, nonempirical judgments which need no further proof. According to Kant, the only true knowledge was the a priori knowledge of pure mathematics or its application in sciences. Any empirical science is a science of phenomena and not of the absolute truth.

Turning to psychology, Kant saw no reason to assume the existence of a soul. The empirical science of man as a part of nature is called *anthropology;* psychology is a part of it.[2] As an empirical or pragmatic science, psychology, deals with the outer manifestations or phenomena of the self. The "self" is the thing-in-itself, but psychology, like any other empirical science, is limited to what is observable in terms of time and space and in the framework of categories.

According to Kant, all psychological phenomena could be reduced to three classes, namely, knowing (the reason), feeling (the emotions), and willing (the will). In the faculty of knowing Kant distinguished the passive *sensation* and the active *understanding.* Sensation is merely a passive receptivity. Mere sensation is not knowledge. Sensory perception is a change in our consciousness caused by external stimuli. The mind receives sensations, intuitively perceives pure time and space independent of phenomena. Then the mind orders the sensory elements within the framework of time, space, and categories.

Kant distinguished between the useful aesthetic feelings and the pain and pleasure feelings which were regarded as obstacles to pure "reason."

Whatever is in human consciousness is a product of a "transcendental synthesis" created by the transcendental self, the mind, and perceived in accordance with the terms of time, space, and categories. Therefore, the subject matter of the empirical psychology, the empirical self, is just a phenomenon like all other phenomena. It can be studied by external and internal observations and the statements made about it depend upon the perceiving, transcendental mind.

This transcendental mind, which imposes its laws (time, space, etc.) on nature, cannot be a subject matter of empirical studies; it determines the truth of empirical studies by their conformity to the a priori forms of the transcendental mind. The subject matter of psychology is the mental phenomena but not the mind itself.

[2] Immanuel Kant, *Anthropologie in pragmatischen Hinsicht,* 1798.

Kant's Impact upon Psychology

The only logical conclusion that could be drawn from Kant's *Kritik* and his treatment of the subject was that there were two ways in which psychology could develop. The first was the safe way of a priori statements about "spirit" or "transcendental mind," or "subject," counterposed to anything else in the world. The mind is the focal point of the universe. It is the eye which views everything and the center of being. Indeed, this anti-Copernican revolution brought about by Kant made the cognizant mind and its axioms the only true, safe, absolute, undisputable source of truth. Armed with the forms of space and time and the categories of quantity, quality, relation, and modality, the "mind" or spirit shapes the image of the world. Arthur Schopenhauer drew the most consistent conclusion and in 1819 elaborated a theory of *solipsism* which reduced all existence to the will and idea of the perceiving subject.[3]

No empirical scientist could build on such a foundation. But Kant left open another alternative, the so-called empirical or pragmatic psychology which forms a part of anthropology or the science of man. This empirical psychology has nothing to do with the mind, which, as a thing-in-itself, is inaccessible to empirical studies. The empirical psychology must be confined to observations of phenomena, i.e., to what can be observed by the mind and modified by the mind in accordance with its cognitive terms. Accordingly, psychology can be either of two things: It can be an a priori absolute science about something which evades empirical cognition; apparently this something, the "subject," the "mind," is nothing but a cluster of logical concepts produced by Kant with no effort to check it against empirical data. The other alternative, the empirical one, reduces psychology to an observation of real happenings, but it is a peculiar kind of observation dependent upon Kant's transcendent's spirit or mind and its a priori set forms. It seems, therefore, that Kant's theory of the absolute mind was saying a lot about nothing, and his empirical psychology was saying nothing about something. In other words, Kant's study of the transcendental self was a system of statements not related to reality, and Kant's study of the empirical self said practically nothing about something which was a part of reality.

If Kant were right, no science would be possible, not even psychology. The only true science, as perceived by Kant, was mathematics. But Bertrand Russell has shown that mathematics is not a science at all. It does not contain any true or false statements. It is merely a system of symbols. Russell remarked that during the nineteenth century mathema-

[3] Arthur Schopenhauer, *The World as Will and Idea* (Haldane and Kemp, trans.), Scribner, 1923.

ticians destroyed Kant's theory.[4] Einstein's theory rendered Kant's concepts impossible.

Kant believed that he put an end to metaphysics. What he actually did was put an end to empirical and scientific inquiry. According to Kant, the human mind perceived not what is but what the mind itself ascribed to nature. The most consistent of Kant's disciples was undoubtedly Arthur Schopenhauer.

Kant's psychology is one more case in this antiscientific process. The true mind, the perceiving self who operates with time and space and categories, is unknowable. It is the phenomenological part of it, its external appearance, that psychologists are supposed to study.

The great historian of psychology G. S. Brett wrote as follows: "Many would regard the legacy of Kant as a disaster for psychology. It perpetuated the rigid distinction between the outer and the inner with its accompanying assumptions both that there is a radical difference between what we know of our own minds and what others know of them, and that overt behavior alone can be scientifically described. . . . It also led people to believe that they were not doing science unless they were using mathematics. We have, therefore, the tendency developing for psychologists to explore all methods of obtaining quantifiable 'data' often without any fruitful assumptions to test."[5]

Freud was never influenced by Kant. Pavlov was opposed to him. But Dilthey, Spranger, Stern, and the gestalt and the field theorists never disentangled themselves from Kant's influence.

The Neo-Kantians

In the second part of the nineteenth century the neo-Kantians modified Kant's theory. Faced with the new experimental psychology and empirical studies of human actions and mental processes, they reconsidered Kant's epistemological apriorism and his theory of the human mind. The revisions of his theory, and the struggle between the French and British empiricism against Kantian speculations, left its mark on the emerging psychological science.

Kant's contemporary and follower on the Königsberg chair of philosophy was Johann Friedrich Herbart (cf. Chap. 1, section 1). Herbart, in opposition to Kant, tried to develop a materialistic psychology. He believed that the soul was one of the units or cells (*das Reale*) of which the organism is composed and hoped to be able to study human mind in a mechanistic manner.

[4] Bertrand Russell, "Philosophy of the Twentieth Century," in D. D. Runes (ed.) *Twentieth Century Philosophy*, Philosophical Library, 1947, p. 245.
[5] G. S. Brett. *History of Psychology* (R. S. Peters, ed.) Allen & Unwin, 1951, p. 508.

Another way out was proposed by the physicist and philosopher Ernst Mach. Mach rejected the idea of the things-it-itself. The world is nothing but the sum of our sensations, which form the content of our consciousness. Our sensations are the only source of truth and the task of science is to study these sensations and put them in order. Mach actually "introjected" physics into psychology and made the perceiving mind the center of any scientific inquiry. In his *Analyse der Empfindungen,* published in 1886, he maintained that all that is, the entire world, consists of our sensations.

At the time when Wundt, Ebbinghaus, Meumann, and others tried to develop an experimental psychology, most neo-Kantians were grouped around the Marburg school led by Hermann Cohen, and later on by Paul Natorp and Ernst Cassirer. Kurt Lewin is mostly indebted to Cassirer. The Marburg philosophers went farther than Kant. According to them, science does not discover the truth but constructs it, and the object is not *gegeben* (given) but *aufgegeben* (assigned as a task), "not presented to us as a given fact but set before us as an 'endless task.' In fulfilling this task the mind is governed by formal principles . . . which determine the structure of all possible experience." Thus, "All possible concepts of objects are specifications of these universal *a priori* forms."[6]

The other neo-Kantian group was formed by the Baden school headed by Wilhelm Windelband and Heinrich Rickert. In accordance with the Kantian tradition, they assumed that our cognitive experience (pure reason), practical experience (morality), and aesthetic experience are governed by some a priori abstract principles called by the Baden school *values.*

Windelband and Rickert counterposed the cultural or historical sciences (*Kultur* or *Geschichtswissenschaften*) to the natural sciences. They preferred the name "cultural sciences" to the old usage of "humanities" (*Geisteswissenschaft*), for "humanities" included the eternal values of logic, ethics, and aesthetics, while the *Kulturwissenschaft,* so they believed, dealt with empirical and passing events and values.

Both *Naturwissenschaft* and *Kulturwissenschaft* are empirical sciences. They differ in methods of research. The natural sciences seek the principles and laws that govern the given subject matter. Natural sciences are *nomothetic,* i.e., they seek general laws. The natural sciences are not interested in the single case; they are concerned with the necessary occurrences, with the laws that govern the universe.

The historical or cultural sciences deal with the individual, the unrepeatable and unique case; e.g., it happened just once that Napoleon retreated from Moscow in 1812. This event was unique and unrepeatable; it was an *idiophenomenon.* Sciences dealing with idiophenomena do not

[6] H. A. Hodges, *The Philosophy of Wilhelm Dilthey,* Routledge & Kegan Paul, 1952, p. 27.

seek general laws; the idiographic sciences are concerned with values and not with natural causes.

According to Windelband, psychology as studied by Wundt, Ebbinghaus, and others was a nomothetic science. Rickert emphasized that the natural sciences deal with cause-and-effect relationship while the historical sciences relate their data to cultural values.

2. PHENOMENOLOGY

Franz Brentano: Act and Content

Against this background came Franz Brentano and his disciples Meinong and Husserl. In 1874 Brentano published his important volume entitled *Psychologie vom empirischen Standpunkte*. This book can be regarded as another effort to solve the problems posed by Immanuel Kant.

Brentano distinguished between perception and observation. Outer objects can be both perceived and observed, but mental experiences can be perceived only. Brentano suggested that feeling and willing be combined in one category and divided Kant's "knowing" into presentation and judgment.

Brentano introduced an important and far-reaching distinction in the analysis of mental processes. When we see something two things take place. First comes the *act* of seeing; then comes the seen object, or the *content* of seeing. All acts have an *intentio*, or intention, i.e., a relationship to the object which "intentionally nonexists" within the act. Mental acts depend on content (physical objects do not), and they always refer to something outside themselves.

Edmund Husserl: Phenomenology

In 1900–1901 Edmund Husserl's *Psychologische Untersuchungen* appeared. Husserl tried to disentangle Kant's heritage by what he called a phenomenological reduction. According to Husserl, everything can be doubted with the exception of the fact that we humans have experiences (*Erlebnisse*). Our experiences cannot be doubted, for all phenomena the sciences deal with depend upon being experienced by the human mind.

What is found in experience is a phenomenon. Husserl did not accept Kant's idea that the phenomenon is a mere appearance of the true object-in-itself, an appearance seen as the perceiving subject is capable of seeing it. Phenomenology is a science of subjective processes by which phenomena are presented. As such, it should serve as a prolegomenon to all other sciences.

Husserl accepted Brentano's theory of mental *acts* or experiences and the fact that they are always related (intended) to physical objects which are not a part of the act (they intentionally nonexist in the mental acts). This distinction between the act and its content influenced Külpe, Bühler, and the gestalt psychologists.

Phenomenology is a philosophical science prior to and entirely independent of psychology. It goes beyond the factual experiences and concentrates on the ideal, essential elements of experiences. In this aspect phenomenology is much like mathematics; it is the "science of pure possibilities." This science of pure possibilities, wrote Husserl, "must everywhere precede the science of real facts."[7] The phenomenology of knowledge is the prerequisite of any science.

Husserl accepted Brentano's idea of intentionality of mental acts. All mental processes are related to objects. All the objects of phenomenological inquiry are, therefore, intentional objects; this intentionality, as will be shown in Chap. 12, influenced Külpe, Bühler, and the gestalt psychologists.

Philosophy and logic should not be reduced to psychology. Phenomenology deals indeed with the same mental processes that are the subject matter of psychology. The difference lies in the approach and method. Phenomenology merely *describes* mental experiences and their objects in the way they appear, the way they are presented. Psychology *explains* mental experiences and looks for their causal interrelationships.

With this distinction, psychology became a science of mental acts (*Akte*) and the contents (*Inhalte*) of these acts. The human mind, called by Kant empirical self, became a part of the objective world. We believe in its existence the way we believe in the existence of the objective world.

As mentioned already, Husserl's reasoning influenced a great many psychologists. It was, so to speak, a way out of the difficulties created by Kant's distinction between the "true," abstract, a priori knowledge and the meager, "untrue," empirical knowleage of phenomena.

Obviously, Husserl did not go too far from Kant. He put some mental processes of "experiencing" ahead of what was being perceived instead of admitting that these experiences themselves were part of the universe. Phenomenology did not solve the Kantian difficulties; it alleviated them by not accepting Kant's idea that phenomena are merely appearances of the real world. To a great extent phenomenology preserved Kant's anti-Copernican revolution, which put the perceiving or experiencing subject in the center of the universe.

[7] Edmund Husserl, *Ideas: General Introduction to Pure Phenomenology*, 1931, Preface, p. 13.

3. WILHELM DILTHEY: THE UNDERSTANDING PSYCHOLOGY

Kant or Empiricism?

Dilthey's role in the history of modern psychological theory is not comparable to that of Ivan P. Pavlov or Sigmund Freud. Dilthey was less productive in the field of psychology proper and less prominent in his own psychological research; thus his historical role as a "father" of a school is less significant than that played by Pavlov or Freud. The theories described in the third part of the present volume start with Kant, Husserl, Dilthey. Some are a direct continuation of Dilthey's ideas; some deviate from him; some oppose him; but all of them discuss the problems posed by him.

Both Pavlov and Freud represent empiricism and materialism in psychology. Both came to psychology from the realm of the natural sciences. Both were influenced by the Anglo-French empiricism, materialism, and sensualism of Hume, Locke, Voltaire, J. S. Mill, A. Comte, Charles Darwin, and H. Spencer. Both were determinists and believed mental processes to be a part of and a derivative from biological processes. Pavlov concentrated on the physiological foundations; Freud dealt with mental processes and applied to them the principles of the methodological non-reductionism. (Cf. Chap. 6, section 1.) Both were influenced by the associationism of D. Hartley, J. S. Mill, and A. Bain.

Dilthey's approach was different, for his main effort was to bring psychology closer to history, ethics, literature, and the arts.

Kant's transcendentalism influenced Dilthey's reasoning to a great extent. Determinism and causation were reduced by Dilthey to the role of methods of perception. "When we place objects in the relations of cause and effect, the sensory impressions contain only the condition of regular succession, whereas the causal relation itself again arises through a synthesis which springs from within us," wrote Dilthey in 1894.[8]

In contradistinction to Kant, Dilthey believed that the perceiving and the perceived mind are one thing. What we perceive in external perception are mere phenomena and what we ascribe to them. The perception of ourselves is far superior, more objective, and more precise. Dilthey explained: "In contrast to external perception, inner perception rests upon an awareness (*Innewerden*), a lived experience (*Erleben*), it is immediately given. . . . No matter how the sensation of a violet color may have arisen, considered as an inner phenomenon it is something indivisible." The lived experience "has no resemblance to the processes of nature. Here we continually experience combinations and connections in

[8] Quoted from H. A. Hodges, *Wilhelm Dilthey, An Introduction,* Routledge & Kegan Paul, 1949, p. 133.

ourselves, while we have to read combination and connection into the sensory stimuli. . . . It is thus that we conceive the ideas of unity in plurality, of parts in a whole, of causal relations, and by means of these understand nature by applying these conceptions to it under definite conditions of regular coexistence or succession."[9] On this point Dilthey deviated from Kant.

Dilthey was opposed to Kant on the issue of epistemology. To Dilthey psychology, not philosophy, was the fundamental science (*grundlegende Wissenschaft*). Dilthey accepted the point of view of the British empiricists D. Hume and J. S. Mill, who believed that a scientific psychology should be the basis of sociology, law, ethics, education, and other human studies in analogy to the way in which mathematics was the basis of the natural sciences.

Moreover, Dilthey could not accept the Kantian idea that mind and body are constructs of the perceiving subject and his a priori set rational principles. Kant's psychology dealt with one of the phenomena and its validity depended upon epistemology. Dilthey's psychology dealt with the human mind and epistemology depended upon psychology in the study of reasoning. Epistemology or the theory of cognition, wrote Dilthey, is a "psychology in motion, namely a psychology which moves toward a certain goal."[10]

Psychology has to be used in human studies as mathematics is used in the study of nature.

Attitude to Husserl and Windelband

The physical world, said Dilthey in opposition to Kant, exists independently of our cognitive processes. The cognitive processes or consciousness can be considered apart from the world they perceive. Their functions, mental acts, cannot be doubted. Whether their content is true or false, there is no doubt that the mind does something, is conscious of something (act), and that it is conscious of some external object (content). Thus psychology as a study of mental acts and their contents is to be the basis for epistemology and not vice versa, as Husserl proposed.

Dilthey was even more opposed to the neo-Kantians both in Marburg and in Baden. He did not accept the idea of the a priori values. Values, he said, are merely an expression of emotional attitudes of humans. He rejected the idea of transcendental ethics. Human beings strive to protect and improve their lives.

Dilthey could not accept Windelband's division into the idiographic sciences of history and culture and the nomothetic sciences of nature. As Windelband himself remarked, the same subject matter could be studied from both points of view. Dilthey went farther and said that geography,

---

[9] *Ibid.*, pp. 13–14.
[10] Wilhelm Dilthey, *Einleitung in die Geisteswissenschaften,* 1883, p. 42.

astronomy, natural history, economics, comparative psychology, philology, and even history have both idiographic and nomothetic aspects. Instead Dilthey proposed distinguishing between natural sciences and humanities (*Geisteswissenschaften*). Human studies, which include the mind and its products, have a special interest in the individual case. Whenever we study the individual (psychology), or the arts, or history, it is always the study of our inner processes, while the natural sciences look on their subject matter from without.

Descriptive and Explanatory Psychologies

Dilthey broke away from Kant on many points, but the main difference lies in the realm of psychology. Dilthey agreed with Kant that knowledge of the objective world is not real: it is knowledge of phenomena only. But knowledge of our own mind is a true knowledge of the true mind, the genuine thing in itself. The difference lies in the kind of perception. The external world we observe; our inner mind we experience, we live through (*erlebt*).

Dilthey found good reason to criticize contemporary psychology as being unable to present human experiences in their entirety. Too often it has been said that Shakespeare's *Lear, Hamlet,* and *Macbeth* "contain more psychology than all the psychological textbooks together." Great writers do not deal with "sensory perceptions" or "thresholds," but they understand man "in his entire reality." Therefore, wrote Dilthey, "one wishes for a psychology which could catch in the net of its descriptions that which these poets and writers contain over and above present-day psychology; a psychology which could take the thoughts which Augustine, Pascal or Lichtenberg make so penetrating by one-sided brilliant illumination, and make them serviceable for human knowledge in a universally valid system."[11]

Nevertheless, Dilthey was not opposed to the experimental psychology of his time. He simply found it inadequate as far as the understanding of man goes.

In 1880 Dilthey was already aware of the limitations of psychology. While the British associationistic psychology was patterned after contemporary physics, psychology was still far from the precision of the mathematical inferences. Nor could experimental psychology cover the entire area of the human mind. Psychological laws, wrote Dilthey, "are pure laws of form; they deal with the formal side of human actions and dispositions; they do not deal with the content of the human mind."[12] If mathematics is the foundation for all natural sciences, psychology has to play an analogous role in human studies.

A new psychology is required as a foundation for epistemology and

[11] Hodges, *Wilhelm Dilthey, An Introduction*, p. 132.
[12] Wilhelm Dilthey, *Gesammelte Schriften*, Teubner, 1924. Vol. VI, p. 43.

other humanistic studies. Dilthey noticed the distinction between explanatory and descriptive studies. A descriptive science (*beschreibende*) deals with observable phenomena, classifies and systematizes them. The explanatory science (*erklärende*) goes beyond the observable data and develops a system of hypotheses.

In his *Einleitung in die Geisteswissenschaften* (1883), Dilthey explained that the contemporary experimental and physiologically oriented psychology applied the wrong method. Even natural scientists have found, under the influence of positivism, that science should be descriptive. Science should not go beyond observable data. Generalization is the only permissible way of conclusion from what was given in the empirical observations. Psychologists too readily assume physiological causes. Dilthey was critical of such an easy reductionism.

Experimental psychology deals with sensations and their associations and fails to see the man as he sees and feels himself. The higher mental processes are overlooked. Explanatory psychology is unable to see what poetry or autobiography or art or religion have seen. Art and literature cannot take the place of a scientific psychology, but explanatory psychology falls short of what it should be. There is no need for explanatory psychology, said Dilthey, and in 1894 explained his views as follows:

"We know natural objects from without through our senses. However we may break them up or divide them, we never reach their ultimate elements in this way. We supply such elements by an amplification of experience. Again, the senses, regarded from the point of view of their purely physiological function, never give us the unity of the object. This exists for us only through a synthesis of the sense-stimuli which arises from within. . . . How different is the way in which mental life is given to us! In contrast to external perception, inner perception rests upon an awareness (*Innewerden*), a lived experience (*Erleben*), it is immediately given. Here, in sensation or in the feeling of pleasure accompanying it, something simple and indivisible is given to us."[13]

The Understanding Psychology

This quotation is taken from Dilthey's programmatic work, published in 1894. It was after a long period of preparation and hesitation that Dilthey published the *Ideas Concerning a Descriptive and Analytical Psychology* (*Ideen über eine beschreibende und zergliedernde Psychologie*). The main argument was directed against interpreting psychology in terms of physics and chemistry that had been introduced by the British associationists. Perhaps the idea of atoms was a useful construct in physics, but the breaking up of our mental life into small units, called sensations, ideas, and feelings, has no justification whatsoever, he said.

[13] Hodges, *Wilhelm Dilthey, An Introduction*, p. 133.

Physics is an explanatory science which makes certain a priori assumptions because its elements are not given in empirical observation. The theoretical constructs of physics are a necessary way to introduce a system and unity where unity cannot be found.

There is no need for such an "explanatory" procedure in psychology. The human mind is a coherent unity and there is no logical reason for splitting it up (*zergliedern*) into hypothetical elements. A man is a wholeness, a unit, and not a conglomeration of atoms.

Psychological phenomena are not perceived from without; they are experienced (*erlebt*) from within. They represent not a series of separate phenomena but a stream of inner processes. "Only by abstraction do we isolate a function or a type of connection from a concrete system." The totality and continuity of mind is empirically given, and the division of the functions of the mind into elements is a product of logical abstractions, generalizations, and categorizations. "In lived experience the processes of the whole mind work together. . . . The particular process is carried in lived experience by the whole totality of mental life, and the systematic connections within it and between it and the whole life of the mind belong to immediate experience (*Erfahrung*)."[14]

In the *Ideas*, Dilthey definitely and finally rejected the idea of explanation and introduced the concept of understanding:

The main objective of natural sciences is to "explain" (*erklären*) what is going on, while the objective of psychology is to "understand" (*verstehen*). "In understanding we start from the system as a whole, which is given to us as a living reality (*der uns lebendig gegeben ist*), to make the particular intelligible to ourselves in terms of it. . . . The apprehension of the whole makes possible and determines the interpretation of the particular part."[15] Psychological research should not deal with physiological elements but be "fruitful for the understanding (*Verständnis*) of life."

The structural unity of the mind should be the main consideration of psychology. The man as a whole is its subject matter. Natural sciences explain nature in terms of causes and effects. Psychology sees the totality of life in the inner experience.

When Dilthey suggested that psychology cease to be an "explanatory" science and confine itself to "descriptive" studies, his views expressed an opposition to reductionism and to psychophysical parallelism. Physicists introduce models and theoretical constructs because their observations do not lead to a coherent system. Physicists are forced to go beyond the observed "descriptive" data and form "explanatory" models of atoms, and other scientific hypotheses.

Psychologists, starting with David Hume, developed analogous meth-

[14] *Ibid.*, p. 135.
[15] *Ibid.*, p. 136.

ods and introduced the idea of mental atoms such as sensations, perceptions, etc., bound together into larger units by association. There is, however, no need to imitate physics. Psychological data, as mentioned before,
are given in "inner perception" and form a coherent system. Thus, psychology analyzes life "as it is."

The atomistic, molecular, associationistic psychology failed to perceive man as a whole and to describe the higher mental processes, so
well described by poets and writers. The contemporary experimental
psychology, said Dilthey, "proved to be the indispensable instrument
. . . for the establishment of an accurate description of inner mental
processes like the limitation of consciousness, the rapidity of mental
processes, the factors involved in memory and in the sense of time. . . .
But to knowledge of laws in the inner domain of mind it simply has not
led."[16]

The Mental Structure

Psychology should pay more attention to the dynamic unity of the
human mind, i.e., to its *structure*. This structure is not static, for the
human mind grows, undergoes changes, and becomes more coherent.
The process of growth is highly individual and unique in each case.

Each man is a separate entity, yet men are similar. Their similarities
should be studied and their common traits and differences described.
Each individual is a representative of his time or culture or group.

The methods of psychological research differ greatly from those used
in the natural sciences. The natural sciences *explain* by means of purely
intellectual processes. Psychological research "grows out of lived experience itself." The psychological understanding "starts from the system
as a whole," is given to us "as a living reality." Spontaneous psychological thinking passes over into psychological investigation.

Dilthey further developed Brentano's and Husserl's distinction between mental acts and their contents. Our inner experiences are acts;
they are the facts of being aware of objects; the objects which we are
aware of are the content. Acts are always a matter of experience
(*Erlebnis*); their content is always a matter of presentation (*Vorstel-
lung*). Every lived experience has a content. The act is the fact of being
conscious of something; that of which we are conscious is the content.

In accordance with Kant, Dilthey divided all mental acts or attitudes
into cognition, affection, and volition. Cognitive acts can be subdivided
into perception, memory, judgment, etc. Affective acts can be divided into
pleasure, pain, fear, love, hate, etc. Volition acts can be divided into
wish, decision, obligation, etc.

In all three areas the act and the content should be distinguished.

[16] Quoted after Hodges, *The Philosophy of Wilhelm Dilthey*, p. 203.

Dilthey explained it as follows: "I perceive a color, pass a judgment of it, feel pleasure, and wish to produce it. The element of the content of perception goes through all the various phases of the act. Yet each phase may relate to different colors and also to other objects."[17]

The unity of life is teleological, wrote Dilthey. "Knowing is in the researcher a teleological system. . . . In this whole teleological system particular functions work together to produce states which somehow have in consciousness the character of values or ends."[18] All the cognitive, emotional, and creative factors combine in the preservation of the teleological unity of life. The purpose is the main factor, and the mind works in the direction of the determinate "mental attitudes" (*Anlagen*).

This new psychology should serve as a foundation for all human studies. Psychological analysis "illuminates" human relations. "Without reference to the mental system on which their relations are grounded, the human studies are an aggregate, a bundle, not a system."

All human studies require psychological knowledge, wrote Dilthey in the *Ideen.* "Any study of religion leads to the analysis of concepts such as feeling, will, dependence, freedom, motivation; all these concepts must be interpreted in a psychological context. . . . Jurisprudence is based on psychological foundations, to which the concepts of norm, law, and responsibility are related. . . . The political sciences which describe the organization of society find in any social relationship the psychological facts of sociability, social control and subordination. These relationships required a psychological interpretation. . . . All the cultural systems, the economic life, law, religion, art and science, the various forms of social organization such as the family, community, church and state, are products of the functions of the human mind and, in final analysis, they can be understood only in the terms of the mind."[19]

Concluding Remarks

Kant, Husserl, and Dilthey exposed a new page in the history of psychology. Kant's contribution to psychology was rather negative and may be considered a regression in comparison with the studies of the sensualists and associationism.

However, Kant's impact upon psychology has been quite significant, especially in those German psychologists who have been educated in the spirit of his epistemological idealism. Kant introduced a sharp distinction between the perceiving subject and the perceived objective world and put the center of weight into the subject. This is why the author of this book believes that Kant's revolution ran contrary to Copernicus.

[17] *Ibid.,* p. 38.
[18] *Ibid.,* p. 43.
[19] Dilthey, *Gesammelte Schriften,* Vol. V, pp. 147–148.

Copernicus dethroned man and earth; Kant went in the opposite direction.

Husserl's problem was how to save scientific inquiry from the inevitable solipsism. His solution offered definite advantages over Kant's. Husserl did not question the existence of the objective world or the truthfulness of our perceptions. The fact that we experience (*Erlebnis*) the world is the cornerstone of his philosophy.

Then came Dilthey, who suggested another way out of the situation. He could accept neither Kant's disrespect for empirical studies nor the positivistic approach of experimental psychology. Dilthey did not pave a new road for psychology; he only erected a new sign. Spranger, Stern, and the gestalt and field theories took his sign as their starting point.

Dilthey could never overcome Kant's influence. Being torn between apriorism and empiricism, he accepted empiricism, but not the kind of empiricism practiced in the natural sciences—the empiricism of observation and interpretation. Psychology and other "humanistic" sciences (*Geisteswissenschaften*) were supposed to be empirical up to a certain point. They should describe but not explain.

Dilthey's method may give the impression of being very empirical but it is not. Science cannot be a catalogue of observations (cf. Chap. 14). However, according to Dilthey, psychological data are so different from the data in any other science that there is no need and no use for interpretation. Kant's anti-Copernican revolution was continued by Dilthey, and the Kantian dichotomy between man and universe occupied a large place in the reasoning of Spranger, Stern, and others.

Dilthey did not solve Kant's problem, for Kant's problem was never a problem that any empirical scientist could solve. Kant's dichotomies do not exist in the realm of empirical studies (cf. Chap. 14). Therefore Dilthey's solution based on the assumption that we "understand" mental phenomena is merely a game of words.

Moreover, Dilthey preserved for the human mind the central position. Perceptions do not convey the entire truth; there is something coming from within—categories, or, as later postulated by Wertheimer, *Gestalt*. The human mind is goal-directed; hence Ach's *determinierende Tendenz*, in opposition to associationism (cf. Chap. 12). Each human being is unique, said Dilthey, and hence Spranger's typology, and Stern's and Allport's *unitas multiplex* (cf. Chap. 11), and Lewin's insistence on the uniqueness of the human situation at a given time (cf. Chap. 13).

No one, with the exception perhaps of E. Spranger, was Dilthey's disciple. But all the psychologists whose theories will be described in the Chapters 11, 12, and 13 are indebted to Dilthey and deal with the problems posed by his unsuccessful effort to overcome the Kantian impasse.

CHAPTER 11

Personalistic Psychology

1. EDWARD SPRANGER: PSYCHOLOGY OF PERSONALITY

The Mental Structures

The man who implemented Dilthey's ideas concerning psychology based upon understanding was Edward Spranger. Spranger wholeheartedly accepted Dilthey's distinction between the explanatory, analytic, atomistic psychology related to the sensory elements and their physiological foundations and the descriptive, understanding, molar psychology whose subject matter is the human mind and its total structure. Leaving the explanatory aspect out, Spranger devoted his studies to the understanding of the individual as a whole because the study of elements "destroys the meaningful totalities of life." Moreover, Spranger doubted whether an "objective" study was ever possible in psychology. Psychology as a *Geisteswissenschaft* depends upon the personal philosophies of the psychologists and the cultural influences upon their convictions.[1]

Brentano's intentionality and mental acts took a new shape in Spranger's theory. Dilthey, Spranger's master, said that psychology should rather describe than analyze; understand rather than interpret; deal with the totality of human actions rather than with their fragments; turn to the humanities rather than to natural science. Spranger unreservedly incorporated Dilthey's theory and combined it with Brentano's influences. Accordingly, his theory was a theory of mental acts, but these mental acts were closed and goal-directed entities.

Spranger utilized Dilthey's concept of mental structures and named his psychology a *Strukturpsychologie* in contradistinction to Wundt's and Ebbinghaus' "atomistic" and reductionistic psychologies. Spranger's emphasis upon the molar approach led him to seek total situations to which the total individual would relate himself. These situations were the cultural values found by Spranger in his society.

[1] Edward Spranger, "Der Sinn der Voraussetzungslosigkeit in den Geisteswissenschaften," *Preussische Akademie der Wissenschaften,* 1929.

Opposition to Reductionism

Each mental act has a goal and is directed to a certain aspect of cultural life. Culture, whether art or religion or science, is the sum of products of the human mind. The various cultural aspects of mental life represent a choice of goals. Human mind, so Dilthey said, is teleological; the various goals of human life have been developed in the history of mankind and experienced in the life of each individual.

History, and not laboratory, is the proper place for the study of the human mind. Laboratory studies grasp minute and meaningless details. The experimental psychology is forced to look beyond its empirical data and "interpret them by referring psychological phenomena to physiology." This method, contended Spranger, leads nowhere, and human life cannot be understood in physiological terms.

Up to now, wrote Spranger in 1924, "psychologists tried to interpret the mental changes in puberty by relating them to somatic changes. . . . Physiological statements do not help psychology even one step. . . ."[2]

Psychology has to say what man experiences, how he experiences it, and what his former life experiences are. Physiological interpretations lead nowhere.

Explanation is the proper method for the natural sciences. Their subject matter is perceived from without, and they must build a system of hypotheses to link the causes and effects of the observable phenomena.

Psychology, as well as other human sciences, does not need to be explanatory. Its subject matter, human experience, is experienced from within, by the experiencing subject. The proper method for psychology is, therefore, the method of *understanding*.

Understanding means to "grasp in a meaningful way the mental relationships which are perceived in an objectively valid cognition. We understand only meaningful structures. . . . [Understanding] always encompasses the meaning."[3] Meaning is a complexity which represents a total value. Fractions of a mental action as studied by the experimentalists are meaningless. A total act is meaningful and represents a certain value in accordance with the goal toward which it is directed.

A descriptive psychology is based on the reexperiencing of life experiences. The understanding psychology goes deeper; it does not depend on reexperiencing only but reexperiencing of the essential elements, the categories, the orders and relationship of the mind. The influence of Kant and of Husserl is quite obvious here. The descriptive psychology, believed Spranger, was the first step; then the understanding grasps the main features of the mental experiences in their relationship to the goal and the values of the individual.

[2] Edward Spranger, *Psychologie des Jugendalters,* Quelle & Meyer, 1925, p. 24.
[3] *Ibid.,* p. 3.

The Six Personality Types

Spranger distinguished six human goal-directed patterns related to six areas of culture, namely, scientific theory, aesthetics, economic life, religion, sociability, and power politics.[4]

No human being is entirely devoted to a single value or a single goal. Spranger suggested six "ideal" types. These do not represent any living human personalities; they represent rather six types of philosophies of life. According to Spranger, each individual pursues one of these six philosophies and can be approximately classified as one of the six types. Obviously, no individual can be classified as a "pure" type.

The *theoretical* type is the intellectual who tries to reason out his problems. Whatever he faces in life, his is always an inquisitive approach and a search for the rational and systematic. The theoretical character may be empirical or speculative, a scientist or a philosopher, but he is always concerned with the finding of the truth. He seeks to perceive the world as a systematic, logically ordered unity.

The *economic* type is mostly concerned with the practical aspects of life. His main goal is self-preservation and economic security. He judges everything from the point of view of practicability and usefulness. The economic man looks for material values, and material success is his idol. He considers science a servant and tool to be used toward economic achievements; education, he believes, should be geared toward the goal of a practical adjustment to life.

The *aesthetic* type is individualistic and much impressed by the beauty and harmony of the universe. The aesthetic character is mostly concerned with the diversity of things, with their charm and grace. He is less concerned with the truth than is the theoretical type and with the usefulness of things than is the economic type.

The *sociable or social* character is friendly, congenial, considerate, and compassionate. He loves his fellow man and is kind and charitable. Unselfishness characterizes his behavior; the desire to help people in his main goal. The sociable character is less concerned with truth and beauty. His main values are moral good and sympathy.

The *power-politics* character desires to control people. He strives to outdistance people and to subjugate them. His main goal is to gain control over others. His is much concerned with politics and methods of influencing and ruling. He relates to the world in terms of power, of overcoming obstacles, and of domination.

The *religious* type is a mystic who seeks unity between man and universe. His main consideration is inner truth and harmony. His approach to life is based on contemplation and search for eternal unity with the cosmos.

[4] Edward Spranger, *Types of Men*, Niemyer, 1928, p. 37 ff.

Concluding Remarks

Spranger's radical non-reductionism forced the naïve reductionists to revaluate their statements. Spranger's emphasis on relatedness of personality types to cultural areas has influenced many psychologists, including G. W. Allport, A. Adler, K. Horney, E. Fromm, K. Lewin and others.

The apparent weakness of Spranger's theory stems from the Kantian dichotomy of man versus nature. Dilthey's solution led psychology into acceptance of a non-objective and non-testable kind of theory construction. "Understanding" cannot be a scientific method if science is a system of propositions open to empirical test (cf. Chap. 14). Spranger's method excludes an objective test.

Spranger's system of values and personality types is arbitrarily set. His use of the term "value" is ambiguous. Value means something leading to a goal, i.e., a utilitarian evaluation judgment, describing the usefulness of a certain thing as a means toward a goal. Value can be used as a substitute for cultural achievement.[5] Either way, Spranger's choice of six values is arbitrary, uneconomic, and not representative of the total number of human goals, aims, and achievements.

2. WILLIAM STERN: PERSONS VS. THINGS

The Man of Synthesis

No one was better prepared than William Stern to mediate between the experimentalists on one side and the humanists on the other. Stern's broad humanistic education, his philosophical erudition, his talent for keen observation and precise experimentation combined with inclination to generalization and sophistication, and finally his industrious and indefatigable personality made him the man of synthesis. The synthesis Stern aimed at was not an eclecticism; it was a genuine effort to reconcile opposites and to overcome dichotomies such as body-soul, nature-culture, and associationism-wholism.

Stern's contribution to psychology is rich and varied. His role in the history of mental testing in Germany is comparable to Binet's in France, Burt's in England, and Terman's in the United States. Stern's productive work included child psychology, educational and clinical studies, and several other areas.

In the controversy between the natural and humanist scientists in German psychology Stern, being both an experimentalist and a humanist, as always sought a reasonable compromise. Accordingly he offered a

[5] Benjamin B. Wolman, "Scientific Study of Educational Aims," *Teachers College Record*, 1949, **50**, 471–481.

solution to the distinction between *idiographic* and *nomothetic* sciences and between the descriptive and the understanding psychologies.

According to Stern, science seeks laws. These represent an invariable relationship common to a class or category of objects which have some similarity to one another. Thus all sciences are nomothetic. However, the "individuality is the asymptote of the science that seeks laws" and could and should be included in scientific research.

The first step in scientific procedure is the acquisition of empirical data. "*Descriptive psychology* is primarily concerned with the *acquisition* of data. Its aim is to represent mental events by succinct statements intelligible to others."[6] Description can deal with single phenomena as they occur or with the essential core of them in the *phenomenological* description, as suggested by Husserl. The described empirical data must be classified. The division of mental phenomena into cognition, emotion, and volition was too rigid. Instead Stern suggested division into perception, memory, thought and imagination, volition, and feeling.

Mental phenomena are complex and should be analyzed. The search for the elements is a legitimate scientific procedure, but it is not true, wrote Stern, that mental phenomena are merely aggregates of elements. The "elementaristic" psychology, starting with Hume, saw in the individual a mechanical sum of elements. This is wrong, wrote Stern, "for neither simple elements nor purely mechanical structures are immediately given in our experience of mental activity. . . . The fundamental principle opposed to the concept of element throughout this new psychology is that of 'Wholeness.' . . . Anything mental either is itself a whole (i.e., a unity meaningful in itself that is more or less definitely bounded), or belongs to a whole. Wholeness does not exclude an internal multiplicity of constituent parts and members; these simply lose the character of independent elements capable of existing by and of themselves. Instead they become subordinate 'aspects' of the whole and may be understood only in their relation to the 'totality.' . . . The methodological requirement that *scientific psychology always preserve the correlation* between past and whole, salience and ground, *analysis and totality*, applies without exception."[7]

Being influenced by Dilthey, Stern suggested that psychologists apply both the methods of explanation and of understanding. Explanation is subordination of concrete data to abstract laws. The three most important categories of psychological explanation are the *causal*, the teleological, and the genetic. These three types of explanation answer respectively the questions Why? What for? and How did it take place?

"It is a fallacy to consider the understanding psychology as being the

[6] William Stern, *General Psychology from the Personalistic Standpoint*, Macmillan, 1938, p. 10.
[7] *Ibid.*, pp. 14–15.

opposite to and independent of psychology as a natural science. There
is but one united psychological discipline; it seeks to know its subject
matter both in its basic nature and the conceptual laws which explain
it, as well as a wholistic value-structures which have a unique significance," wrote Stern in 1924.[8]

Explanation deals with the lawfulness of relationships, and understanding with their meaningfulness. When we comprehend a person as
a whole, we understand him.

The distinction between the natural sciences and the humanities
(*Geisteswissenschaften*) introduced by Dilthey has become superfluous,
wrote Stern. The natural sciences more and more emphasized the "wholeness of the organism and the meaningfulness of all processes of life." On
the other hand, the human sciences have started to apply statistics and
other techniques borrowed from the natural sciences. The gulf is obviously closing and it is the task of psychology to unite both methods.
Stern's method combined explanation and understanding.

Stern advocated a variety of research methods and was critical of any
one-sided approach. The behaviorist "shuts himself off" from any introspectionistic data; the psychoanalytic fanatic from the conscious phenomena; the experimentalist from all nonexperimental data. In an
exclusive experimentalism psychology is a self-defeating device. The
more precise is the experiment, wrote Stern, "the more isolated and the
more fundamental the observed phenomenon, and the more constant
are the experimental conditions, the more it is artificial and remote from
the study of the individual."[9] Experimentation as an auxiliary technique
can be very useful.

But all other methods can be useful also. Psychological phenomena are
"immediately experienced." Accordingly, introspection can be a useful
method too. Since mental activity includes both the world of nature and
the world of culture, the methods of the natural and cultural sciences
should be combined in the psychological study.

Mind and Body

Stern faced the problems posed by Kant, but he solved them in a
non-Kantian manner. He distinguished between the essence or *substratum* of the mind and the *empirical facts* of the mind. This distinction
differs from Kant's thing-in-itself and phenomena.

The substratum of the mind, said Stern, "must be something *that has
existence going beyond or prior of the differentiation into the mental and
the physical,* thereby certifying the original unity of the individual."[10]

This unity is not found in the inorganic nature, which is composed of

[8] William Stern, *Wertphilosophie*, Barth, 1924, p. 380.
[9] William Stern, *Differentielle Psychologie* (3rd ed.), Barth, 1921, p. 34.
[10] Stern, *General Psychology*, p. 69.

things (*Sache*), but is typical of a person (*Person*). The person is "a living whole, individual, unique, striving toward goals, self-contained and yet open to the world around him; he is capable of having experience."[11]

Psychology is "the science of the person having experience or capable of having experience," experience being "identified and interpreted in terms of its matrix, the unitary, goal-directed person."[12] "Personality," said Stern, is a "neutral" term in so far as the body-mind problem is concerned. It incorporates both terms and presents the problem in a new light.

Psychophysics is the science of lawful relations between stimuli and sensations. Physiological psychology and especially Wundt enriched psychology by their studies of sensory perception and localization of the functions of the brain. Biological psychology introduced the ideas of evolution, heredity, environment, and adjustment. Dilthey's psychology of history introduced the understanding of the nature of the individual. Spranger's psychology of cultural forms represents six realms of value.

All these diversified areas of psychology should be merged into the study of the individual. "The individual is not partly body and partly mind, but a person with the capacity for experience. He is a portion of a world that, although bounded on the outside, nevertheless continually exchanges substance and function with all other portions of the world; this is his corporeality. And he also has the capacity to reflect himself and the world inwardly; this is his mentality. The life of the person includes *both;* accordingly, there is no experience and no capacity for experience that is not bound up with the physical aspect of life and with bodily functions."[13]

Stern was indebted to Goldstein and Lashley. The nervous system functions both in a specific and localized manner and as a totality; accordingly, psychology deals with both parts and totalities, with the physical and the mental aspects of life.

Three Modalities

Stern distinguished three modalities of life. The first is biological. On this level the individual's *vitality* is dominant. Growth and maturity and reproduction are the vital functions. The vital world of the individual is his *biosphere*.

The second modality is life experience (*Erlebnis*). Experience is "life under cleavage and tension." All experience is either *salient*, standing sharply in focus, or *embedded* within totality, i.e., in the background.

[11] *Ibid.*, p. 70.
[12] *Ibid.*, pp. vii–viii.
[13] *Ibid.*, p. 84.

Each experience contains some salience and some embedding, some focal and some marginal elements, in close analogy to the figure and ground concept (cf. Chap. 12, section 2).

Experience has objects, stated Stern, accepting Husserl's distinction between act and content. The individual experiences himself and others, and there is always cleavage between the person and the world. The mind is "everything about the person that is experience or that is essentially related to experience."[14]

The content of experience is called a mental *phenomenon*. The individual *has* experiences and *acts* through them. Having an experience is a mental state. Acts are produced by contents and processes of thought.

Some experiences are short-lived; some are lasting *dispositions*. Dispositions are the possibilities, abilities for future experiences. Character traits, temperaments, and mnemic abilities are dispositions.

The third level or modality of life is absent in plant and animals. It is purely human and represents cultural, social, moral, and religious values. The individual accepts the social norms and standards, the moral code and cultural values of his social environment. This process is called by Stern *introception*. It resembles Freud's concept of superego formed by introjection and identification.

Experience has an intermediate position between biological vitality and cultural *introception*.

The Main Areas of Psychology

The entire field of psychology has been divided by Stern into (1) sense perception, (2) memory and learning, (3) thought, intelligence, and imagination, (4) drives, instincts, and volition, and (5) affective life. Stern's theory, unlike Pavlov's or Freud's, is a *complete* psychological system. Seemingly no area has been left out.

Stern was opposed to Wundt and the "elementaristic" psychology. Stern remarked that the concept of gestalt was not discovered by the gestalt psychologists but by Ehrenfels, K. Bühler, Krueger, and himself.

We perceive a gestalt independently of any specific sensory stimulation, wrote Stern. But he did not accept the idea of gestalt's being a fundamental phenomenon. It is man who perceives the world in separate wholes. Man can arrange the ticks of his watch in a three-part or four-part rhythm, or combine dots. "No Gestalt without a Gestalter" (the man who forms a gestalt), wrote Stern.

Moreover, the figure-ground distinction of the gestaltists was to Stern a matter of degree of the *salient* and *embedded*. Gestalt is the most salient phenomenon of perception. The ground is the *Ungestalt*, the least clear and least important, the embedded part of perception.

[14] *Ibid.*, pp. 78–79.

Learning is the acquiring of knowledge through repeated presentations, wrote Stern. *Involuntary* learning could be ascribed to two causes. The first lies in the external stimulus and its constant repetition; the second cause is the susceptivity of the individual. Strong and repeated impressions, whether desired or not, conscious or not conscious, become mnemically effective, said Stern. Apparently Stern's point of view is distant from any reward theory (cf. Part I).

A good example of involuntary learning is the acquisition of knowledge by little children. The child, wrote Stern, "asks for little songs not to learn them but to hear them; but all the same, at last he learns them. . . . In his walk he stops at every shop-window and expects all its glories to be pointed out and explained to him, not that he may know them tomorrow or in a year's time, but now, at this moment; but he thus acquires lasting knowledge of the appearance, significance, and use of things. . . ."[15]

While involuntary learning depends upon repeated coincidence, voluntary learning depends upon the goal, the interest, and the intelligence of the learner.

Stern developed his own theory of thinking. Leaning on Husserl and Külpe, Stern distinguished between the act of thinking and the content of it. In accordance with Brentano and Husserl (cf. Chap. 10) Stern described thought as a process that "*intends* something that is not (an object, a class, a relation, a meaning, a solution)."[16]

In the realm of action and striving Stern proposed several levels. The first is the level of *reflexes* or rigid inherited responses. Reflexes can be acquired or conditioned. However, "it is paradoxical to attempt to make such a *deranged* reflex the prototype of all learning, animal and human alike, and the basis of the science of human nature."[17]

Drives represent a higher level. A drive is an innate disposition toward the implementation of a personal goal. Stern distinguished four classes of drives: (1) *self-preservation*, which includes defense, flight, and nutrition; (2) *self-development*, such as superiority, aggressiveness, and adornment; (3) *social* drives, i.e., racial, herd, protective, initiative, and combat drives. Humans are endowed also with (4) *human* drives, such as the craving toward intellectual, ideal, and cultural objectives.

The *needs* represent a higher level. Whenever impulse is restrained by inner or outer inhibitions, a need arises. Need is a state of tension, stated Stern. Kurt Lewin (cf. Chap. 13) apparently borrowed this concept from Stern.

Drives and needs designate purposive forces. Instinct is a drive "whose

---

[15] William Stern, *Psychology of Early Childhood Up to the Sixth Year of Age* (3rd ed.), Holt, 1930, p. 226.

[16] Stern, *General Psychology*, p. 275.

[17] *Ibid.*, p. 379.

direction points not only to the final end, but also to the means by which
this end is attained."

The highest level of striving is called by Stern *volition*. Volition is a
"conscious anticipation of end and means."

Each individual goes through consecutive stages of salience and embedding. The cognitive and acting functions of the individual tend to
become salient; the experiences of embedding are the feelings. Feelings
are formless (*Ungestalt*) and in the background.

All feelings can be divided into pleasant and painful. Another polarity
has been introduced: the *excitement* of feelings leads to an expansion
of energy, and *tranquility* to accumulation.

Character and Personality

In Stern's terminology character corresponds to personality. "It designates the make up that the person possesses in his *totality*, but considers
this totality from one definite standpoint only, that is the predisposition
to acts of *will*."[18]

Stern combined the influence of heredity and environment in the
theory of convergence. Personality is a product of the converging influences of both heredity and environment.

Personality is the meeting ground of physical and mental, heredity and
environment, salient and embedded, total and partial. It is a *unitas
multiplex*, a unity composed of elements.

Unitas multiplex contains more than mere empirical unity. The fact
that the same individual may experience conflicting wishes and still be
himself, still be a unity, indicates that unity is the prerequisite of any
inner conflict. Personality is the continuum of human life; it is the
perpetual and consistent whole which the individual is.

Yet each individual is composed of parts. Stern called the constant
and goal-directed parts of the activities of the person *traits*.

"The constancy of a trait is merely an ideal or limiting concept—and
for two reasons. One is that man is at no moment of his existence merely
an adaptive, self-preserving creature; always there is in his behavior
a spark of self-development and growth. For this reason his finished
traits are never quite finished. In addition, a trait is never entirely independent of the world outside, but stands in constant active relationship
to it. It indicates the way in which the person reacts to the world; but
never are the stimuli that provoke the reaction entirely the same, and
never therefore are the various expressions of one and the same trait
completely in agreement with one another. The trait is each time slightly
different because it confronts other determining conditions; and these

[18] *Ibid.*, p. 436.

conditions produce not only a special coloring in each act that a trait arouses, but also can influence the trait itself in a permanent way."[19]

Stern distinguished between the driving traits, called *Richtungsdispositionen,* and the instrumental traits, called *Rüstungsdispositionen.* "The two factors of *Richtung* and *Rüstung,* however, closely interwoven, have nonetheless a certain independence of one another, and the most varied relations to one another. We are therefore compelled to distinguish between those dispositions that have a prevailingly directional character from those that are principally an implemental character. The former are purposive, they have a 'tendency to,' the latter are capacities, and have a 'potency for.'"[20]

Concluding Remarks

William Stern was a remarkably productive man and his research covered many varied areas. He occupies an important position in contemporary philosophy and psychology as a leading theoretician of personalism. Stern was the Director of the Hamburg Psychological Institute from 1916 to 1933 and undoubtedly the most influential German psychologist at that time.

Stern's contribution to psychological theory is often underestimated. Stern was the man who pointed to the possibility of reconciliation of opposite viewpoints. Especially significant is his idea of parts and totalities in perception, which may lead to utilization of both the associationistic and the gestalt contributions to psychological theory.

Stern's immediate disciples are G. W. Allport and K. Lewin. Allport took over the personalistic content; Lewin took over the philosophical approach only.

3. GORDON W. ALLPORT: PERSONALITY TRAITS

Idiophenomena

The problem of nomothetic versus idiographic approach to research has been analyzed in America by two outstanding psychologists: Gordon W. Allport and Kurt Lewin. Though the answers given respectively by Allport and Lewin to Windelband's question are far apart, a considerable proximity between Allport and Lewin resulted from their dealing with the same problem and facing similar difficulties.

As said before, both Allport and Lewin owe many ideas to William Stern and may be considered the American representatives of the *personalistic* school of thought.

[19] Quoted after Gordon W. Allport, *Personality: A Psychological Interpretation,* Holt, 1937, p. 312.
[20] *Ibid.,* p. 323.

Allport admitted that within a given culture people tend to develop "roughly comparable" ways of behavior or "modes of adjustment." Yet any two individuals never behave the same way. Each represents a unique case and is an idiophenomenon. Human behavior is idiographic and yet lawful.

Behavior is a continuous flow of energy, each successive act representing a convergent mobilization of all energy available at the moment, said Allport. The drives, which use the "plastic and modifiable nervous system," provide energy for action.

Motivation

Allport combined the teleological approach with the idea of learning by experience. He defined drive as "a vital impulse which leads to the reduction of some segmental organic tension." It has its origin in an internal organic stimulus of peculiar persistence, growing characteristically stronger until the organism acts in such a way as to alleviate the accumulating tension. The tensions within the system are parts of the functioning of the organism.

Allport has been critical of the contemporary learning theory (cf. Part I) and yet influenced by it. He strongly emphasized learning by experience versus heredity. People develop similar patterns of behavior as a result of certain "constellations of emotion, habit and foresight, better called *sentiments* or *interests,* and regarded as acquired rather than innate." Learning serves as a way not merely of extending and modifying purposes but also of *creating* them. These purposes are shared by numerous individuals, owing to the fact that people who live "in a similar environment, influenced by a similar culture, *would* develop similar goals and employ similar modes of obtaining them." These modes of behavior, though acquired, become *functionally autonomous,* i.e., independent of the original instigating drive. Modes of behavior are purposeful. Once established, they persist without further stimulation.

The basic drive can be accounted a cause of an infant's behavior but not of an adult's. Adult behavior has to be explained as an elaborate process of learning and growth. This process intervenes between the organic wants of infancy and the cultural wants of adulthood, involving all manner of linguistic, imaginal, and rational factors that ultimately transform the segmental cravings of infancy into desires no longer having any functional connection with them, but holding in their own right an autonomous place in personal life. The development of adult goals and aims exemplifies Allport's idea of functional autonomy.

Allport suggested using the term "drive" instead of McDougall's "instinct" or "propensity." Drives are primarily viscerogenic states of excess or deficit stimulation. Besides the pressures that arise in body cavities, blood stream, and autonomic organs, one may include among drives the irritation of proprioceptors and sensitivity (with customary adient response to external stimulation), wrote Allport.

There is no need to invoke genetic factors to explain human behavior. The functional autonomy of motives and the principle of contemporaneity suffice to explain human motivation.

Personality Traits

Allport accepted Stern's idea that personality was *unitas multiplex* and tried to assess the basic factors of this *unitas*. The emphasis was put on acquired goal-directed factors. Allport calls these acquired determinants of human behavior *traits*. Traits are modes of adjustment noted in one's "neural dispositions of a complex order." They determine the selective perceptions of stimuli and the choice of responses to them; thus they show "motivational, inhibitory and selective effects upon the specific courses of conduct."

A trait is a combination of motives and habits; it is a neuropsychic system that determines to a great extent which stimuli will be perceived (selective perception) and what kind of response will be given (selective action).

"Each individual has a certain number of such mental structures which determine his behavior in a unique way. A trait is a generalized and focalized neuropsychic system (peculiar to the individual) with the capacity to render many stimuli functionally equivalent, and to initiate and guide consistent (equivalent) forms of adaptive and expressive behavior."[21]

Human behavior is determined by several factors. The totality of mutually interdependent traits has to be considered as the main and fairly consistent element in behavior. Traits, sentiments, and attitudes are the "dispositions" to behave in a certain way, dispositions embedded within one's personality. Behavior depends upon traits, and upon special qualities of stimulus and the temporary distribution of tensions within one's psychophysical system. Motives, says Allport, are "personalized systems of tensions in which the core of the impulse is not to be divorced from the images, idea of goal, past experience, capacities and style of conduct employed in obtaining the goal. The whole system is integral. If biological drive plays a part (thirst, hunger, sex) it does so, not as *the* motive but merely as an irritable state of bodily tissues set within an intricate and personalized psychophysical system."

Human behavior is determined by a totality of factors acting *at a given time*. Although adult behavior can be traced back to behavior in

---

[21] Gordon W. Allport, *Personality: A Psychological Interpretation*, Holt, 1937, p. 289.

infancy, the bond between infancy and adulthood is broken. The tie between past and present is "historical" and not "functional," says Allport, and we recall Lewin's similar statement.

The motivation for action may come from without (from external stimuli) or from within (from segmental organic tensions or from traits). Traits may act as motives whenever there is a tendency to exhibit a certain type of behavior. Each act of behavior is "a convergent mobilization of energy available at the moment." The best summary of the principle of functional autonomy was given in 1946: This principle means that "(1) motives are contemporary . . . (2) that the character of motives alters so radically from infancy to maturity that we may speak of adult motives as *supplanting* the motives of infancy."[22]

In addition to traits, Allport introduced the concept of attitude. Attitude, as a trait, is a predisposition to act in a certain way, but the attitude reflects the relationship between the person and an object. "Ordinarily *attitude* should be employed when the disposition is bound to an object of value, that is to say, when it is aroused by a well-defined class of stimuli, and when the individual feels toward these stimuli a definite attraction or repulsion."[23] Obviously, the attitudes represent a certain type of trait.

Personality Structure

Psychologically considered, personality is what a man really is and does. It is the dynamic organization within the individual of those psychophysical systems that determine his unique adjustments to his environment, wrote Allport. Psychophysical systems mean habits, attitudes, dispositions, etc., "which are neither exclusively mental nor exclusively neural. The organization entails the operation of both body and mind, inextricably fused into a personal unity."[24] Personality indicates the manner in which an individual adjusts to his physical and social environment.

Allport calls the emotional elements in personality which are related to heredity *temperament.* "Temperament refers to the individual's emotional nature including his susceptibility to emotional stimulation, his customary strength and speed of response, the quality of his prevailing mood, and all peculiarities of fluctuation and intensity in mood."[25]

The behavior of a neonate is determined by heredity, innate reflexes, and innate drives. But, in accordance with the law of functional autonomy, the child will become an entirely different person in adulthood.

[22] Gordon W. Allport, "Motivation in Personality; Reply to Mr. Bertocci," *Psychological Review*, 1940, 47, 533–554.
[23] Allport, *Personality*, p. 295.
[24] *Ibid.*, p. 48.
[25] *Ibid.*, p. 54.

The uniqueness of the individual, the individual as an idiophenomenon —this is what is meant by the term "personality." Allport (together with P. E. Vernon) elaborated a method of measuring personality, called "Study of Values,"[26] based on Spranger's typology. Thus Allport has shown that the idiographic approach does not prevent one from applying measurements. In later studies Allport developed additional concepts related to the personality structure.

"An Ego-Structure (Sentiment of Self-Regard) is quite sufficient to keep an individual on the move. It seems to me unnecessary to seek its dynamics as McDougall does it in the twin and abstract properties of self-assertion and submission."[27]

Allport's latest studies introduce the concept of "propriate motives," which keep the personality together. This idea of integration of personality structure has been a necessary supplement to the great variety of motives, traits, and attitudes.

Concluding Remarks

Allport's contribution to psychological theory has been criticized chiefly in regard to the concept of the functional autonomy. This concept implies discontinuity of development from childhood to adulthood, and normal and abnormal behavior. It may be doubted whether such a discontinuity can withstand the growing body of contrary evidence.

Moreover, Allport's fruitful studies seem to be rather hampered than helped by their perpetual reference to the idiographic versus nomothetic dichotomy. As will be shown in Chapter 14, the entire issue belongs to the category of nonexisting problems.

One has to give well-deserved credit to Allport's penetrating analysis of problems in theory of personality, and social and clinical psychology.

[26] Gordon W. Allport and P. E. Vernon, *A Study of Values*, Houghton Mifflin, 1931.
[27] Gordon W. Allport, "Geneticism versus Ego-Structure in Theories of Personality," *British Journal of Educational Psychology*, 1946, 16, 57–68.

CHAPTER **12**

Gestalt Psychology

1. OPPOSITION TO ASSOCIATIONISM

The Associationists

It has often been said that associationism and conditioning developed the theory of learning, psychoanalysis created the theory of motivation, and the gestalt and field theories revolutionized the theory of perception and thinking. Undoubtedly this statement contains a great deal of truth. The origin of the gestalt theory is connected with the difficulties encountered by the traditional associationism in regard to perception and thinking. The associationists believed that (1) perception is a copy of objects, or a "mental image" of what has been perceived, and (2) thinking is a mechanical combination of those images. Gestalt psychology challenged both parts of this belief.

In 1829 James Mill formulated the law of association: "Our ideas spring up or exist in the order in which the sensations existed of which they are copies."[1] John Stuart Mill emphasized the analogy between associationism in psychology and the combination of elements in chemistry. He wrote in 1869 as follows: "The laws of the phenomena of mind are sometimes analogous to mechanical, but sometimes also to chemical laws. . . . When impressions have been so often experienced in conjunction that each of them calls up readily and instantaneously the ideas of the whole group, those ideas sometimes *melt and coalesce* into one another, and appear not several ideas but one."[2]

In 1855 Alexander Bain published in England a volume entitled *The Senses and the Intellect.* In this volume Bain accepted the idea of an inherited, instinctual, "untaught ability," but the emphasis was on association by contiguity, similarity and dissimilarity, causation, and other factors.

[1] James Mill, *Analysis of the Phenomena of the Human Mind,* Baldwin, 1829, p. 56.
[2] John S. Mill, *Notes and Annotations on J. Mill, Analysis of the Phenomena of the Human Mind,* Longmans, Green, 1869.

J. Ward and G. F. Stout: The British Functionalism

While Wundt, Titchener, and Ebbinghaus and later Thorndike, Pavlov, and Watson accepted the associationist tradition with certain modifications, several British, French, and German psychologists rejected it.

In 1886 James Ward started a weighty argument against associationism. His main idea was continuity. If associationists or physiologically minded psychologists were right, there would be no continuity in the conscious life of the individual. Continuity of feeling, thinking, memorizing, and acting cannot be understood on the basis of a mental atomism and associationism, whether spiritual or material. According to Ward one must postulate the unity and continuity of self-knowledge, a continuum of being conscious.

This continuity of consciousness cannot be reduced to a spiritual or phenomenological category as in Kant's notion. Nor can it be represented as a series of physiological sensory perceptions. The totality of consciousness is a primary unity; it is the *subject*. The subject is not "a combination or recombination of various elementary units."[3] This totality, the subject, is a non-reductionistic concept.

Ward believed that the subject matter of psychology is the experience (*Erlebnis*) of the subject. All experiences can be divided into (1) *cognition,* which is a "non-voluntary attention" to changes in the sensory continuum, (2) *feeling,* which means being pleased or displeased by these changes, and (3) *conation,* which is a voluntary attention that produces changes in the motor continuum.

The "material" for experience is given from without, but the "synthesis" comes from within. The synthesis, said Ward, comes from the subject, who organizes the material into a certain order. The organizing principles of the mind are time, space, unity, identity, resemblance, difference, substance, causation, etc. Although these "organizing principles" follow closely Kant's categories, Ward did not accept them as transcendental a priori principles or properties of the subject; they are *modes* of the activity of the human mind which grow and develop in human life.

Ward's ideas of a psychology which need not be either physiology or epistemology, and his theory of organizing principles of the human mind, and finally his emphasis on continuity and attention prepared the ground for the gestalt psychology.

James Ward and George Frederick Stout introduced in Britain a new trend which came close to what has been known in the United States as functionalism. "The presented whole is for them simply the sum of its presented components," said Stout, criticizing the associationists.[4]

---

[3] James Ward, "Psychology," *Encyclopaedia Britannica* (9th ed.), 1886.
[4] George F. Stout, *Analytic Psychology,* 1902, Vol. II, p. 48.

Stout aimed at the development of a "pure" psychology, free of physiological explanations and reductionism. Influenced by Brentano, Stout distinguished between mental processes (act) and their content, sensory perception. He divided all mental processes into cognitive and conative and subdivided the conative processes into willing and feeling. Whenever the mental process was related to an object, it was a cognitive process. To have an attitude toward an object is conation, for we either want or don't want it. When our volition is hindered, we experience pain. Unimpeded volition and unhindered action are experienced as pleasure.

Alfred Binet: The French Functionalism

Several European psychologists asked the questions asked by the American functionalists: What is the *use* of memory, perception, thinking, etc.? Do psychological abilities and action contribute toward one's adjustment to life? How, and to what extent do they contribute?

The great enterprise of mental testing, started in France by Binet and Simon, in England by Cyril Burt, in Germany by William Stern, and in the United States by scores of psychologists, served as an example of how psychology could be applied to life. Binet's study of thinking proved that thinking was not a continuation of perception and could not be interpreted in terms of "perceptory elements" as suggested by the associationists.[5] The idea of molar versus molecular concepts was vigorously promoted.

Furthermore, Binet's studies attacked the question of the "mental images." To the early associationists the answer was obvious. Human mind perceives the images of objects, and thinking is a combination of these images.

French psychology was relatively free from speculative ideas. The impact of the empiricism of the great Encyclopedists and later the works of French positivism had a beneficial influence upon it. French psychologists distinguished themselves in several areas of experimental, clinical, physiological, social, and educational psychology. In 1870 Taine published his famous work on intelligence (*De l'Intelligence*) and Ribot presented the British associationistic psychology in a volume entitled *La Psychologie Anglaise Contemporaine*. In 1885 Ribot taught the first course in experimental psychology at the Sorbonne, and in 1889 Beaunis and Binet founded there the first psychological laboratory.

Ribot himself turned toward abnormal psychology and prepared the ground for the studies of Charcot, Janet, and Freud (cf. Chap. 6).

The cautious empiricism of the French psychology, so different from the German speculations, guarded the French psychologists against the

[5] Alfred Binet, *L'Étude Expérimentale de l'Intelligence*, Schleicher, 1910.

eagerness and ease with which the Germans indulged in producing new theories and systems. The empirically minded French-speaking psychologists—Ribot, Binet, Simon, Charcot, Janet, Claparède, Michotte, Pieron, Piaget, and many others—made valuable contributions to the development of psychology. Contemporary psychology is much indebted to Charcot and Janet for their studies in unconscious motivation, to Binet and Simon for mental testing, to Piaget for developmental psychology, and to Claparède, Michotte, Pieron, and others for excellent studies in practically every single area of psychological inquiry. The prevailing climate of the French psychology has been the functionalistic idea of usefulness and purpose.

Against this background came Binet's experimental study on thinking. Binet used his two daughters as subjects and combined experimentation with introspection. He found considerable differences in the way the two girls handled the problems presented to them. These differences could not be interpreted in an associationistic manner. Moreover, Binet came to the conclusion that their thinking was done without "images"; it was imageless, just *pensées* (thoughts).

Binet's anti-atomistic and "imageless" interpretation of the thought processes influenced a great many psychologists all over Europe. In Switzerland, the educational psychologist Edouard Claparède developed this utilitarian-functionalist point of view. He considered psychological phenomena from the point of view of "their function in life" or "their use."[6] In his studies on perception, Claparède accepted a point of view similar to the gestalt theory, yet eclectic and empirical.

In Belgium, A. Michotte proved that recall of material could not be interpreted by sheer contiguity. The element of organization was emphasized in Michotte's conclusions, which brought him close to the gestalt school. In Germany the Würzburg school (discussed in the next section), deviated from the Wundt-Titchener method of study and emphasized the mental set and task.[7]

All these studies led toward the formation of the gestalt theory.

The Würzburg School

Simultaneously with Binet, G. E. Müller in Germany conducted experimental studies in memory which challenged mechanistic associationism from another angle. Müller's subjects, like Michotte's subjects, used to "organize" the material. Moreover, Müller noticed, memory processes were influenced by what he called the preparatory set (*Anlage*). Obviously the set was not given from without.

---

[6] Edouard Claparède, "Autobiography," in C. Murchison (ed.), *History of Psychology in Autobiography*, Clark University, 1930.
[7] A. Michotte, *L'Apprentissage du Mouvement et l'Automatisme*, Louvain, 1928.

Müller's idea was utilized by Oswald Külpe and his associates in Würzburg. As early as 1893 Külpe showed that the reactions of subjects to the reaction-time experiments depend upon the preparation of the subjects and differ accordingly.[8] The element of motivation was introduced as an experimental variable. Moreover, in a later experiment (1904), Külpe's subjects could concentrate on the given task and describe the suggested figure without becoming aware of the other figures. Apparently these subjects responded to the "figure" and not to the ground.

In 1901 Orth and Mayer published an experimental study on classification. They came to the conclusion that the responses of their subjects depend upon a certain set, called by the experimenters *Bewusstseins-anlage* ("sets of the consciousness"), often colored by feelings. In other words, the responses are not mere products of the stimuli but also depend upon some factors within the mind of the subject, i.e., upon his mental set.

Besides several other papers published by Külpe and his associates, in 1905 the papers by Ach and Watt appeared. Both of them introduced the concept of task (*Aufgabe*). The term "task" closely corresponds to motivation as described in Külpe's experimental work.

In Watt's experiment[9] the "task" influenced the way his subjects reacted. When the subjects were asked to classify, they had hardly any mental images. When the same subjects were asked to name a part, 50 per cent of their responses indicated mental images. The speed and nature of the associative processes could be influenced by the task, concluded Watt.

Ach further developed and elaborated Watt's concepts. The presentation of the aim, the task, obviously influenced the performance of the experimental subjects, in addition to the stimulus. The content of the aim-presentation determined the responses of the subjects. The subjects not only saw a colored card (stimulus) but saw it colored in accordance with the instructions. These instructions, which influenced the responses to given stimuli, were called by Ach *determining tendencies*. Experiments with hypnotic suggestions proved that the responses to stimuli could be easily modified in accordance with the determining tendencies.

The study of the determining tendency led Ach to accept the idea of an abstract, imageless thinking. He presented his subjects with the letters *C S V S*, but in accordance with the *simultaneous determined abstraction* they perceived only the letter S. All other letters were left out in the perceptory processes.

The abstraction of one element out of many present elements can be

[8] Oswald Külpe, *Grundriss der Psychologie*, Kirzel, 1893, p. 422.
[9] The English abstract of Watt's experiments was published in 1905: H. J. Watt, "Experimental Contribution to a Theory of Thinking," *Journal of Anatomy and Physiology*, 1905–6, **40**, 257–266.

directed toward future reactions also; then it becomes the *successive determined abstraction.* Factors which do not stem from the stimulus and do not participate in association obviously influence the reaction. These factors, presented under the names "set" (*Einstellung*), "task," "aim," or "determining tendency," point to a new factor besides the stimulus-response, i.e., the reproductive tendency. The subjects showed a productive tendency, and not a mere repetition of acquired images.

Selz continued the work of Ach and Watt on imageless thought and determining tendency. Selz was more radical than Ach and Watt and rejected the idea that response was a product of both association (reproductive tendency) and task (determining tendency). He believed that stimulus and task together form a unity, a total *Aufgabe.* Hence he came to the idea of "productive thinking" in which "the actualization of mental operations or solution methods, that is to say . . . processes of a reproductive nature can give rise to productive mental work."[10] In productive thinking the task with all its determining tendencies initiated the mental operations which served as means toward the problem-solving goal.

Karl Bühler: The German Functionalism

Karl Bühler, who was Külpe's disciple and associate, can be classified as a functionalist because of his emphasis on wholistic processes of adjustment, purposiveness, and opposition to the molecular-atomistic approach.[11]

In 1907 Bühler published a study with the title "Facts and Problems in Relation to a Psychology of Thought Processes: I. On Thoughts." He was mostly concerned with the question of what one's actual experience of thinking is.

In analyzing the introspective reports of his distinguished subjects (Külpe and Dürr) Bühler concluded that sensory, reproductive elements did not play a significant role in thinking. The most important items of the thought processes are what the subjects describe as "awareness of," "consciousness that," or most frequently "thoughts," in the manner proposed by Binet.

Thought cannot be reduced to sensory processes or mental images. It is a mental process which leads toward the solution of a problem; it is goal directed; it has a task (*Aufgabe*) and it is creative.

Bühler distinguished three types of thought, namely consciousness of rule, consciousness of relation, and intention. The first type was found mostly in solving mathematical, logical, and grammatical problems. The

[10] Quoted after George Humphrey, *Thinking: An Introduction to Its Experimental Psychology,* Methuen, 1951, p. 139.
[11] Gardner Murphy pointed to the similarities between the findings of Binet and Bühler and those of Woodworth. See Gardner Murphy, *Historical Introduction to Modern Psychology* (rev. ed.), Harcourt, Brace, 1949, pp. 229–230.

second type was applied when several parts of thought had to be related as a consequence of each other or as an opposition to one another. The intention type of thought occurred when a total problem was reviewed briefly and a solution came as a logical outcome of this review.

More than anyone else in the Würzburg group, Bühler emphasized the goal-directedness of thinking in opposition to Wundt and associationism. Bühler distinguished between acts and contents of thinking, in accordance with Brentano, to whom all the Würzburg psychologists were indebted.

Bühler wrote about himself as follows: "I came into the field of psychology at the time when all psychological behavior was described in terms of sensory reactions and associations. I never could believe in that 'classical association' theory but felt thinking was more than this. . . .

"As far as *gestalt psychology* is concerned, I was probably the first to enter this field with actual experiments after Ehrenfels and his school developed the new concept theoretically. Recently I have again become interested in the gestalt principle from another angle. The book that I have just finished '*Das Gestalt Prinzip im Leben des Menschen und der Tiere*' (The Principle of Gestalt in the Life of Man and Animals) defends the thesis that only living beings perceive, develop, and create Gestalten."[12] At this point Bühler came closer to W. Stern than to Wertheimer.

Concluding Remarks

In 1907 W. Wundt published a paper containing a severe criticism of the Würzburg school and related studies. The Würzburg experiments, wrote Wundt, were "experiments without instruments"; their conditions were not varied; not the experimenter but the subject was the real observer in them; and even the self-observation of the subjects was more of a self-description. Wundt was especially critical of the supposed "creativeness" of thought introduced instead of the associationists' reproduction of sensory images.

Associationism rests upon the reputable assumption of reproductiveness of mental phenomena. What came from the stimulus can be preserved and reproduced. Any theory of creativeness faces the difficult test of bringing sufficient evidence against the simple and convincing logic of associationism.

Yet it is undeniable that the European functionalists and the Würzburg school had a point in their controversy with associationism. Their emphasis on wholism, purposivism, and meaningful behavior influenced McDougall, Goldstein, and Tolman and prepared the ground for the gestalt and field theories. Human behavior cannot be reduced to a chain of consecutive sensory elements, they said. Whether it could be presented

---

[12] Bühler in a letter to the author of this book.

as something entirely different—that was the problem to be handled by the gestalt and field theorists.

2. GESTALT: THEORETICAL FOUNDATIONS

Methodological Considerations

The impact of Kant, Mach, and Husserl upon the thinking of the gestalt psychologists was considerable. Köhler explained that the naïve experience consists, "first of all, of objects, their properties and changes, which appear to exist and to happen quite independently of us. So far as they are concerned, it does not seem to matter whether or not we see and feel and hear them. Under these circumstances, it was a great step when man began to ask questions about the nature of seeing, feeling and hearing. And it was a revolution when he found that colors, noises and smells, etc., were merely products of influences exerted on him by his surroundings. . . . The form, the weight and the movement of things had to be given the same interpretation as colors and sounds; they, too, depended upon the experiencing organism and were merely end results of complicated processes in its interior."[13]

Gestalt psychologists introduced the concept of "organization" between the "stimulus and response" of the behavioristic theory. The physical environment, believed the behaviorists, is perceived as a series of separate stimuli. Actually the environment cannot be identified with what the man *experiences* as his environment. Science must, therefore, "construct an objective and independent world of physical things, physical space, physical time and physical movement, and had to maintain that this world appears at no point in direct experience."[14] This applies to the human organism also. The human body is accessible to us only as a part of our sensory experience; but this sensory experience does not reflect several separate sensations. Between the stimulus and the response processes of organization take place which build the elements into a complex unit.

Köhler admitted the debt to Husserl and phenomenology. Köhler wrote about objects as "objects of experience," as they appear phenomenologically to the perceiving subject. Husserl's idea of the fundamental elements appealed to Köhler, who wrote: "The legitimate pursuit of gestalt psychology is the analysis of the essential elements that exist in organization. This analysis is definitely more valuable than the analysis of purely sensory local data. The sensory data do not appear as such to the observer."[15] In other words, the organized totalities and not the sensory elements are the truly perceived phenomena.

[13] Wolfgang Köhler, *Gestalt Psychology*, Liveright, 1947, pp. 5–6.
[14] *Ibid.*, p. 7.
[15] Wolfgang Köhler, *Psychologische Probleme*, Springer, 1933, p. 17.

Opposition to Quantification

Gestalt psychologists were always suspicious of what they considered to be a premature quantative program of the behavioristic psychologists. "We are still much too easily satisfied by our tests because, as quantitative procedures, they look so pleasantly scientific," remarked Köhler. Actually, the I.Q. scores may be a result of various components in varying proportions, such as intelligence, accuracy, ambition, fatigue, etc. Statistical studies do not measure; they merely count. Without qualitative analysis behavior psychology "will easily become as sterile as supposedly it is exact."

Gestalt psychologists could not believe in the usefulness of statistical computations for obvious reasons. Measurements are based on the assumption of commeasurability, and such an assumption was feasible for atomistic psychology. Gestalt psychologists found that the same number of the same elements could form various configurations and present various experiences. What's the good, e.g., of adding the number of dots if the same number of dots can form a circle, a square, a rectangle, or a triangle?

In addition, gestalt psychologists put forward weighty methodological considerations against what they considered to be premature measurements. Köhler wrote: "If we wish to imitate the physical sciences, we must not imitate them in their highly developed contemporary forms. Rather, we must imitate them in their historical youth, when their state of development was comparable to our own at the present time. Otherwise we should behave like boys who try to copy the imposing manners of full-grown men. . . . If we are to emulate the natural sciences, let us do it intelligently. . . . At present, and in the broader historical perspective, qualitative observation may often be more fruitful than premature measurements. . . . If organisms were more similar to the system which physics investigates, a great many methods of the physicists could be introduced in our science without much change. But in actual fact the similarity is not very great. . . . Actually, however, young psychology could not resist the temptation which arose from the brilliant achievements of contemporary sciences. Every now and then a wave of short-sighted imitation swept it off its feet. Fechner himself was the first to copy adult physics when psychology was hardly born. Apparently he was convinced that measuring as such would make a science out of psychology. . . . Today we can no longer doubt that thousands of quantitative psychophysical experiments were made almost in vain."[16]

[16] Köhler, *Gestalt Psychology*, pp. 42–44.

The Physical Gestalt

The gestaltists were influenced by Brentano and yet developed a fairly independent point of view. They distinguished between phenomenological and physical realities. The shapes and figures are established by the action of forces which tend toward equilibrium. The perceived figures are "experiences" of the perceiving subject. They are phenomenologically real.

But there is, besides phenomenology, a physical reality. This includes the nervous system and its interaction with the environment. These two parts of reality must be interlocked and ruled by the same set of logical principles, an idea named by the gestaltists the postulate of *isomorphism*. Its content is simple: all phenomenological experiences are a true representation of "a corresponding order" in their "underlying" content of physiological processes.

Order, regularity, gestalt, is the *universal* principle that binds psychology and physiology into one system. Gestalt psychologists had to seek this order, the gestalt, in nature or accept the idea that all gestalts were a priori ideas.

And, indeed, Köhler found gestalt factors in inanimate nature with all its laws of *Prägnanz*, closure, etc. Electrostatic changes, he wrote, tend toward such a distribution as to produce an equilibrium of forces over the surface of the conducting body. In a drop of oil surrounded by fluids the inner and external forces interact in such a way as to create a balanced, symmetrical, "good" gestalt. Köhler accepted Mach's hypothesis, which implied that macroscopic physical states develop in the direction of equilibrium, stability, regularity, and simplicity. Now psychology could be set on a firm footing. Gestalt existed both in mind and in nature (*Physikalische Gestalten*).

Neurological Theory

The same principles have been applied to the study of the nervous system. Gestalt psychologists have been critical of the neurological models hitherto developed. Mental events have usually been explained, said Köhler, in terms of either inherited machine or secondary acquired constraints. In the "machine" theory, he wrote, connections between cells in the brain and effector organs are of the same type as the connections between points of sense organs and those cells, in a stimulus-response pattern. Any "local sensory fact" is determined by its stimulus.

Against psychological "atomism" the gestalt introduced the theory of "functional wholes" based on dynamic distribution and organization, in an analogy with an electric circuit. The theory of electric circuit has been used by the gestalt psychologists in their studies of brain mechanism.

The brain activity is guided by the principle of equilibrium, or at least reduced tension. Whenever there is a gap in the current, tensions build up on both sides of the gap and the electric current tends to close the gap. Thus the principle of *closure* is one of the most important principles of both the physical and the phenomenological worlds.

Köhler assumed that in the cerebral cortex a chemical substance is produced depending upon the intensity of stimulation, and the figure-ground phenomenon should be interpreted by a high concentration of ions inside the figure in distinction from the low concentration in the ground, and corresponding concentration in the cortex. The cortex is a field, and in it, as in any other dynamic field, the process itself and its conditions should be considered.

"Two varieties of factors determine the course of physical processes. In the first category are forces at work in the physical process itself, they represent its dynamic aspect. In the second category are those factors of the systems concerned which may be regarded as constant conditions for the particular process taking place. In the case of electric current an example of such a factor would be the spatial arrangement or the topograph of the conducting materials. In physical systems such conditions can sometimes be dominating, sometimes relatively unimportant. The internal dynamics of the process involved in the electric current example would be decisive in determining its course. On the other hand in machines built by human beings the importance of topographical conditions is almost always so predominant that the role of dynamics is reduced to driving the process along pathways entirely determined by those conditions."[17]

A machine, explained Köhler, is limited in its scope of activity and determined by its own structure and by external forces. A dynamic field, which is best exemplified by an electric circuit, is regulated by its own forces. Obviously, its activity scope is definitely wider and the freedom of action much greater. The brain functions as a dynamic field, and its forces can be self-distributed and self-regulated, always in the direction of equilibrium.

Köhler and other gestaltists found the machine model for the human nervous system incompatible with experience. Köhler rejected the notion that a local stimulus followed a well-established path toward a definite locus in the brain and a local reaction was emitted. The sensory and motor systems are not two separate entities connected by the nervous pathways; they are parts of one, total system, contended Köhler. Physiological investigations, he pointed out, "leave no longer any doubt that in ganglionic tissues the functions of individual nerve cells are dynamically related."[18]

[17] Köhler, *Psychologische Probleme*, p. 84.
[18] Köhler, *Gestalt Psychology*, p. 126.

Isomorphism

Köhler's theory of isomorphism is based on the assumption of unity of the universe. The part-whole relationship, the tendency toward the restoration of equilibrium, the tendency to closure, symmetry, and regularity rule both physical and psychological phenomena. Köhler emphasized that the "specific arrangement" of the psychological experience is "an accurate reproduction" of the dynamic arrangement of "corresponding physiological brain processes."

The principle of isomorphism "covers practically the whole field of psychology," wrote Köhler. It says that the order in which psychological phenomena are experienced is "supposed to be a true representation of a corresponding order in the processes upon which experience depends." In other words, the "experienced order in time is always structurally identical with a functional order in the sequence of correlated brain processes."[19]

Two areas, then, the experiential and the physiological, are ruled by the same set of principles. They are two dynamic fields operated by the same devices and organized in the same way. Gestalt is both physical and mental; the law of *Prägnanz* applies both to the physical world and to how the individual experiences it. The psychological field has been often compared to a geographical map, and its neurological counterpart to a territory represented on the map.

Psychological Field

Since the functions of the brain represent a dynamic field, the overt behavior of humans is a dynamic field too. This is, as said before, the essence of the principle of isomorphism.

Koffka was the man who tried to develop a general field theory of behavior. The dynamic field of psychological experience is the individual and his environment, and their interaction within the field forms the content of behavior. This field is a field of forces which tend to establish the best possible balance, the most symmetrical, stable, and simple configuration. The laws of gestalt, and especially of *Prägnanz*, apply to this field.

Human actions are usually related to physical reality not as it is but as it appears to the perceiving subject. The environment as perceived together with the perceiving subject form the *psychological field*. Kurt Lewin (cf. Chap. 13) developed an entirely different concept of the psychological field.

[19] *Ibid.*, p. 62.

Koffka's psychological field, also called "behavioral environment," corresponds to the phenomenological environment. It can be best exemplified by a story told by Koffka in his main work:

"On a winter evening amidst a driving snowstorm a man on horseback arrived at an inn, happy to have reached a shelter after hours of riding over the wind-swept plain on which the blanket of snow covered all paths and landmarks. The landlord who came to the door viewed the stranger with surprise and asked him whence he came. The man pointed in the direction straight away from the inn, whereupon the landlord, in a tone of awe and wonder, said: 'Do you know that you have ridden across the Lake of Constance?' At which the rider dropped stone dead at his feet.

"In what environment, then, did the behavior of the stranger take place? The Lake of Constance. . . . And yet . . . there is a second sense to the word environment according to which our horseman did not ride across the lake at all, but across an ordinary snow-swept plain. His behavior was a riding over a plain, but not a riding over a lake."[20]

The idea of a psychological field isomorphic to the physical field enabled the gestalt psychologists to develop a theory of volition and emotions. Disequilibrium between organism and environment causes tensions and activates forces moving in the direction of restoration of balance. A hungry organism seeks food, an angry man starts a fight. Personality is often called *ego* by the gestaltists.

Dembo's studies on anger have been generalized by Koffka and developed into a gestaltist theory of emotions.[21] Each psychological field contains an important subfield, the personality or the ego. Emotions will arise, Koffka says, when an object with powerful positive valence appears in the field but the subject is barred from reaching it. The impenetrable barriers cause strong tension, involving the ego area, and explosive emotional behavior will follow.[22]

This approach to the problem enabled the gestalt psychologists to minimize the anamnestic factors and to emphasize the influence of the present environment. The present environment and the person are the two poles of a dynamic field with forces acting between them. The present action of the forces and their striving toward an equilibrium are the determinants of behavior.

Kurt Lewin went farther and developed a new theory based on the field concept. But let us continue with the analysis of the contribution of the gestalt theory to the problems of perception, learning, and thinking.

[20] Kurt Koffka, *Principles of Gestalt Psychology*, Harcourt, Brace, 1935, pp. 27–28.
[21] Tamara Dembo, "Der Ärger als dynamisches Problem," *Psychologische Forschung*, 1931, **15**, 1–144.
[22] Koffka, *op. cit.*, p. 408.

3. GESTALT: PERCEPTION, LEARNING, AND THINKING

The Phi Phenomenon

In 1890 Christian von Ehrenfels introduced the idea of gestalt, or form, shape, structure. He noticed that the same melody could be played on different notes, and the same notes, differently arranged, gave a different tune. Analogously, the same blocks could be arranged in various ways and create various structures. The blocks and the tones, believed Ehrenfels, were given in perception, while the shape and the total structure came from the mind of the observer. This conclusion was apparently influenced by Kant's distinction between phenomena and the a priori category of quality.

In 1912 in Berlin Max Wertheimer conducted a series of experiments on perception of motion, with the assistance of Kurt Koffka and Wolfgang Köhler. He started from a vertical line exposed twice, the second time a little to the right or left of the first exposure. When the time interval between the two exposures was one-fifteenth of a second, the experimental subject saw one line moving to the right or the left. The same experiment repeated with several variations always gave the impression of motion. Wertheimer's experiments were carefully planned and they unmistakably led to the following conclusion:

If two discrete and stationary lines are exposed a short distance from each other and in a close temporal succession, the observer will perceive them as a single line moving from the position of the first line to that of the second. This phenomenon of apparent movement was called by Wertheimer the *phi phenomenon*.[23]

Laws of Gestalt

Wertheimer went one step farther; he concluded that besides the single resting positions of the line there was an additional factor responsible for the perception of motion. This uniting factor, which combined the separate elements into one whole, he called *Gestalt* (form, shape). This name expressed the anti-atomistic and anti-associationistic convictions of Wertheimer and his emphasis on a molar approach to the problems of perception.

In further studies on perception Wertheimer analyzed in detail the principle of organization. Suppose we see some dots; the dots can be grouped in several ways, forming a triangle, a square, or a circle. It is

[23] Max Wertheimer, "Experimentelle Studien über das Sehen von Bewegungen," *Zeitschrift für Psychologie,* 1912, **61**, 161–265.

the form, the shape, the configuration in which the dots appear that determines our perception.

In less structured situations the perceiving individual groups the dots in accordance with one or more principles of organization. Wertheimer distinguished the principle of (1) *proximity* of the elements to one another, (2) *similarity*, (3) *closure* (if a figure is drawn with incomplete lines, the perceiver completes it in his own mind; a sketch of a house, a person, a tree, a church drawn with a few lines can be easily identified despite its incompleteness). In addition to the afore-mentioned factors, Wertheimer distinguished the factors of (4) continuity; (5) familiarity, and (6) set; the concept of set was borrowed from the Würzburg studies. Other gestalt psychologists have added scores of principles or laws of organization.

Gestalt psychologists distinguish "good" figures from "poor" figures. A good figure is a figure in which the parts and the whole are well harmonized, and the parts are well subordinated to the figure. Simplicity, clarity, symmetry, and harmony are signs of a "good" figure. The gestalt concept of equilibrium is expressed by the law of *Prägnanz*. The law of *Prägnanz* means that organization tends toward the greatest simplicity, i.e., toward the best possible gestalt. This goal-directed tendency (equilibrium being the goal) has often been considered the main law of gestalt.

In 1915 Edgar Rubin, a leading phenomenologist and a disciple of G. E. Müller and D. Katz, introduced the idea of *figure* and *ground*. Perception is selective and not all stimuli are perceived with the same clarity. The perceptory elements organized in a whole catch our attention and are perceived with great clarity; they form the figure, while anything else in our visual field forms the background.

The gestaltists adopted the figure-ground idea. The perceptory elements are organized as a whole, as the gestalt; they form the figure. The remaining elements of perception form the ground. The difference between figure and ground has been, as mentioned already, explained in neurological terms by W. Köhler.

The gestalt theory of perception has been summarized by Köhler as follows: "Our view will be that, instead of reacting to local stimuli by local and mutually independent events, the organism responds to the *pattern* of stimuli to which it is exposed; and that this answer is a unitary process, a functional whole, which gives in experience, a sensory scene rather than a mosaic of local sensations."[24]

Learning by Insight

Gestalt psychology introduced a new theory of learning associated with the name of Wolfgang Köhler and the term "insight" (*Einsicht*). Köhler's

[24] Köhler, *Gestalt Psychology*, p. 103.

experiment on chimpanzees in the Canary Islands, where he had spent several years during the First World War, was a challenge to both the trial-and-error and the conditioning theories of learning.

Köhler's chimpanzees did not try and err in Thorndike's fashion, nor did they become conditioned in Pavlov's style. They grasped the new situation; they displayed orientation in learning and a great deal of intelligence. They did not try blindly all the possible responses; their behavior showed that learning included a considerable amount of goal-directed activity.

Köhler's chimpanzees were put in a cage and a banana was placed at a distance from the cage. Strings, sticks, and boxes were used by the experimental animals to get the banana; they apparently somehow perceived the situation and displayed *insight* in solving the problem.[25]

Koffka concluded that all learning was perceptual reorganization. "What the animal has developed during its 'latent learning' is a trace of a maze; this trace, being in communication with the present activity, regulates it more or less as the perception of the maze world."[26]

Koffka applied the laws of perception to the learning theory. Instead of reward or reinforcement, he introduced the concept of goal. "So long as activity is incomplete, every new situation created by it is still to the animal a transitional situation; whereas when the animal has attained his goal, he has arrived at a situation which is to him an end-situation."[27]

As said before, the main factor in the gestalt theory of learning is *insight*. Since the individual and his environment form a psychological field, perception of the field and gradual restructuring of it is insight. A description of what takes place in insightful learning was given by Yerkes after a series of experiments with primates: "Insight, in different organisms, may reveal common characteristics. (1) Survey, inspection, or persistent examination of problematic situation. (2) Hesitation, pause, attitude of concentrated attention. (3) Trial of more or less adequate mode of response. (4) In case initial mode of response proves inadequate, trial of some other mode of response, the transition from the one method to the other being sharp and often sudden. (5) Persistent or frequently recurrent attention to the objective or goal and motivation thereby. (6) Appearance of critical point at which the organism suddenly, directly, and definitely performs the required adaptive act. (7) Ready repetition of adaptive response after once performed. (8) Notable ability to discover and attend to the essential aspect or relation in the problematic situation and to neglect, relatively, variations in non-essentials."[28]

[25] Wolfgang Köhler, *The Mentality of Apes*, Harcourt, Brace, 1925.
[26] Koffka, *op. cit.*, p. 588.
[27] Kurt Koffka, *The Growth of the Mind*, Kegan Paul, 1924, p. 102.
[28] Robert M. Yerkes, "The Mind of a Gorilla," *Genetic Psychology Monograph*, 1927, **2**, 156.

Learning and Perception

Since learning is interrelated with perception, the laws of perception apply to learning. Koffka carefully elaborated this interrelationship.

The most general principle of learning is *Prägnanz* or the goal-directed tendency to restore the equilibrium. Learning takes place when there is a tension or a disequilibrium of forces in the psychological field; the learning process removes the tension and is, therefore, guided by the principle of *Prägnanz*.

The additional laws of learning are (1) similarity, (2) proximity, (3) closure, and (4) good continuation. When an organism learns a certain material which contains similar and dissimilar elements, the similar ones are learned more readily than the dissimilar ones. This is the law of similarity.

The law of proximity in perception becomes a law of temporal contiguity in the learning theory. The elements are grouped together both by factors of physical proximity (to form a pattern in space) and by proximity in time (to form a temporal configuration such as a tune, a sentence, a story, or any other configuration of elements happening in a temporal proximity).

The law of closure reflects the idea of striving for completion. Koffka explained the law of closure as applied to learning as follows: "So long as activity is incomplete, every new situation created by it is still to the animal a transitional situation; whereas when the animal has attained his goal, he has arrived at a sitution which is to him an end situation."[29]

The law of good continuation implied that we tend to learn better those elements which show consistency in their configurations.

The gestalt psychologists seemed to indicate that learning is improvement in gestalt; the learned figures become more symmetric, better organized, in accordance with the law of *Prägnanz*. Or, in the more general terms of the psychological field, the field becomes restructured and becomes a better gestalt.

The problems of retention and recall presented considerable difficulties for the gestalt theory. Koffka and Köhler solved this problem of presenting learning processes as *cognitive fields*. Fields can be structured and restructured. Learning processes change the structures of the fields; accordingly, they leave *traces*. In each repetition the former trace system is modified by the new trace system.

In experimental studies by Wulf (1922), Gottschaldt (1926), and others the importance of memory by association was minimized, and changes in the structure of the cognitive field were emphasized. In Wulf's experiments each repetition brought an "improvement" in the perceived figures

[29] Koffka, *Growth of the Mind*, p. 102.

leading progressively toward a better gestalt. In Gottschaldt's experiment a picture of the capital letter E was presented a great many times; yet the subjects who saw E only once could distinguish the shape of E in a church window just as well as those who saw E a great many times. Apparently memory itself and association did not help learning in this case.

Several gestalt experiments indicated that three processes take place in learning. The first is *leveling* or changing in the direction of symmetry and good distribution. The second, *sharpening*, consists in the accentuation of the essential elements of a figure, which makes it easily distinguishable. The third process is related to the clarity and simplicity of the perceived figure and is called *normalizing*. Apparently all three processes correspond to the general law of *Prägnanz* or moving toward a "good" gestalt. It is the "productive," goal-directed insight versus the "reproductive" conditioning which has been emphasized in the gestalt theory of learning.

Productive Thinking

The gestalt theory of learning led to studies in "productive thinking." The ground was prepared by the Würzburg school (cf. section 1 in this chapter). Wertheimer undertook the study of productive thinking and problem solving using a great many subjects, from little children up to Albert Einstein.[30]

Wertheimer distinguished three types of processes. Type *a* processes are concerned with decisive issues pertaining to structural problems and include such operations as grouping, reorganization, and discovery of essential features. The best thinking is productive thinking. It relates the means to the tasks and goals, and to the total situation. Whenever an organism faces a problem, the tensions will lead to an activity called problem solving or productive thinking. Productive thinking is assured by type *a* processes and almost eliminated by type *y* processes. Type *y* thought processes are blind and result in premature conclusions, miscentering, or a restless pursuit of a hypothesis without a sense of direction and subject to the influence of external factors. This type corresponds to learning by drill, associations, conditioning, and blind trial and error. Type *b* processes are partially productive and partially mechanized.

Wertheimer implied that analysis is not altogether eliminated by the gestalt theory. Analysis is futile when it is only a mere division into parts. In combination or association, things cannot be thrown together or related at random with utter disregard of structural aspects and interrelations. This does not lead to problem solving.

Wertheimer believed that methods for the description and measurement

[30] Max Wertheimer, *Productive Thinking*, Harper, 1945.

of structures and whole-qualities can be developed. Productive thinking deals with whole-qualities and part-whole relationships rather than with analysis into particles and association of them. Productive thinking looks for the "structural truth" rather than for a piecemeal truth, said Wertheimer.

One of the most important ideas of Wertheimer's theory of productive thinking relates to *centering* and *recentering*. In centering, there is a change or transition from a subjectively or personally centered view to a detached view with an objective grasp of the whole situation and of structural and functional requirements. This operation makes for the dominance of the objective structural and functional requirements of the situation and for a neutralization of and interference with effects of one's personal experiences and beliefs. Recentering is the obtaining of a new and penetrating perspective. It provides a new angle from which to view the question of multiple interests and achievement of creative persons, and the ability of scientists and engineers trained in certain fields to function, after a brief interval of orientation, in other fields at high levels of productivity.

Wertheimer questioned the usefulness of repetition. He wrote: "Repetition is useful, but continuous use of mechanical repetition also has harmful effects. It is dangerous because it easily induces habits of sheer mechanical action, blindness, tendencies to perform slavishly instead of thinking, instead of facing a problem freely."[31]

Wertheimer denied any application of trial and error in thinking. Thinking is goal directed and insightful and creates new gestalts. It changes the structure of the perceptual field. Several experimental studies, conducted by Duncker, N. R. F. Maier, and others, utilized the gestalt frame of reference.

Apparently the gestalt theory of thinking went a long way beyond the studies of the Würzburg school. The Würzburg school, wrote M. R. Harrower, "brought to light facts for the explanation of which they needed a concept such as the determining tendency . . . regarded as a force which could be set against the associative bond and even measured quantitatively. . . . It was not until the work of Duncker and Maier, following the line of attack suggested by Wertheimer, that we get a recognition of the determining tendency as the vector or tension produced by the structural properties of the problem. From this new point of view . . . it is 'needed' by the phenomenal problem situation itself, not merely demanded by the instructions."[32]

The Würzburg school proposed the set and the goal. The gestaltists ascribed purposeful activity to nature and men, activity leading toward a perfect gestalt.

[31] *Ibid.*, p. 112.
[32] M. R. Harrower, quoted after G. Humphrey, *op. cit.*, p. 175.

Concluding Remarks

Gestalt was defined by Köhler in two ways. The first connotation is that of a property or quality of things such as squareness or symmetry of geometric figures, shape or form of objects. The other connotation is that of an individual and characteristic entity existing as something detached and *having* a shape or form as one of its attributes. Gestalt psychologists use the term "gestalt" in this second connotation.

Moreover, they seem to ascribe to this entity peculiar attributes. Obviously, these attributes can never be seen. They can be inferred or introduced as intervening variables for the sake of interpretation of observable facts.

And here comes the great question. Gestalt psychology started as a rebellion against the aridity of the molecular studies of Wundt and Titchener. There cannot be any doubt that gestalt psychology stimulated more research work in the field of perception than any other psychological school. There cannot be any doubt that there is, as Tolman said, more than one kind of learning. Or, as Razran suggested, the highest level of learning must be related to perception, understanding, and configuration. There is no doubt that the gestalt studies in neurophysiology, figural aftereffects, figure-ground, etc., are thought provoking. Gestalt psychology has influenced several areas in psychology, including studies in child, social, education, and clinical psychology, and its experimental work stands on its own merits. But all this granted, the main concept used by Wertheimer, Koffka, and Köhler seems to be the most vulnerable. Why attach such importance to a whole, a configuration, or a totality? Why ascribe to this concept a central position in psychological theory? To quote Woodworth, "Wertheimer's experiment on visual movement was certainly interesting and important, but we may query why it was regarded as important enough to inaugurate a new school of psychology. Well, it was a clear case of a whole which was not a mere sum of parts."[33]

And this is the problem. Is a whole a new entity, and can a psychological theory be based on such an assumption? An expert on perception, F. H. Allport challenges this assumption.

"We have no objective evidence that a whole is anything other than the parts, provided always that the parts are taken as they *exist and operate together*. A whole that is something more, or other than this, must remain an inference. It is perhaps an 'impelling' inference, derived from striking differences in the phenomenology when the parts act together as compared with the phenomenology when they act alone. But it is still an inference. In questioning it, we are in no sense denying that there is a perceived unique 'whole character' that appears when the parts exist and

[33] Robert S. Woodworth, *Contemporary Schools of Psychology* (rev. ed.), Ronald, 1948, p. 124.

operate together. We question only the assumption that this 'whole character' comes from something other than, or more than, this set of conditions, or that there is an 'independent' whole, or that the whole acts to control the parts."[34]

Is this inference "impelling"?

[34] Floyd H. Allport, *Theories of Perception and the Concept of Structure*, Wiley, 1955 p. 143.

CHAPTER 13

Field Theory

1. FIELD THEORY VS. CLASS THEORY

"More Physico-Mathematico"

Psychologists have always been enchanted by physics. The exactness and beauty of the physical experiments and the resulting mathematical formulas have seemed to psychologists the prototype of any scientific research. To be scientific has often been considered synonymous with imitation of the methods and manners of physical research.

It should not be regarded as a mere coincidence that Kurt Lewin, the outspoken representative of non-reductionism in psychology, was so much influenced by physical and mathematical concepts. He is, in fact, a radical non-reductionist and does his best to keep psychological research within the area of psychology. Obviously, this is not a gestalt psychology. Lewin avoids physiology; he never borrows from biology or invites physics or chemistry to solve difficult problems in human behavior. He is painstakingly cautious and consistent and avoids confusing endocrine glands with behavior, or brain tissues with abilities. His theories are strictly behavioral and deal with human beings and their activities.

Notwithstanding this stanch non-reductionism, Lewin is more drawn to physics than are many other psychologists. His main efforts seem to be aimed at the establishment of a full-fledged psychological theory with no reference to neurology, physiology, chemistry, or biology but on the pattern of the physical sciences—something like the theory of electromagnetism or the theory of light. What he borrows from physics is not its content or laws but its methodological foundations; he loves the cleanliness of mathematical equations and the beauty of geometrical presentation. This is why one would like to call Lewin's theory *psychologia more physico-mathematico.* . . . Lewin's field theory is a product of the prevailing field-theoretical tendencies in modern physics, as associationism in psychology was a product of the atomistic theories in physics.

Gardner Murphy regards modern physics as one of the "parents" of gestalt and of field theory. "The era of atomism," he says, "began to come to an end and particles began to be understood as aspects of field relationships. . . . It is within this frame of reference, notably the developments in physics, that one must understand the development of field theory in psychology. The movement began when modern physics invaded the Gestalt psychology."[1]

Modern physics, while being empirical and down to earth, has achieved astonishing results due to conceptualization. This is the path to be followed by psychology, says Kurt Lewin. "Investigators are coming to feel that a mere piling up of facts can only lead to a chaotic and unproductive situation. . . . Even from practical point of view the mere gathering of facts has very limited value. It cannot give an answer to the question that is most important for practical purposes—namely, what must one do to obtain a desired effect in given concrete cases? To answer this question it is necessary to have a theory, but a theory which is empirical and not speculative. This means that theory and facts must be closely related to each other."[2]

Theory has to "conceptually represent and derive psychological processes." It has to conceptualize the empirical data and go beyond the observed facts.

Theory Construction

How should this theory be constructed?

A theory is a system of concepts related to observable facts in such a way that the empirical facts may be derived from the concepts. A system of concepts forms a theory. The concepts fill the gap between one observable fact and another. Lewin quotes Tolman's statement that "behavior cannot be derived from behavior." One has to introduce "intervening concepts," or as Tolman calls them, "intervening variables."

These concepts should fit the logical structure of psychological phenomena. No science can be purely empirical; empirical laws are functional relationships of observable data, and they have to be related to dynamic laws which are functional relationships of concepts. A system of concepts and dynamic laws forms a theory, and a theory should be constructed in such a manner that the empirical data are the logical outcome of the concepts and laws.

Any scientific theory, says Lewin, has to apply two types of concepts. Those of the "first order" are mathematical. They must "represent the logical structure of empirical relationships." Thus, the selection of a proper mathematical system is of greatest importance in theory construction. It is

[1] Gardner Murphy, *Historical Introduction to Modern Psychology* (rev. ed.), Harcourt, Brace, 1949, p. 298.
[2] Kurt Lewin, *Principles of Topological Psychology*, McGraw-Hill, 1936, p. 4.

imperative to choose the mathematical concepts that will suit the nature of a given science and by "coordinating definitions" to establish the rules of their application. Lewin believes that psychology should apply geometrical concepts, and he has introduced the topological geometrical system into psychology. In fact, his psychological theory has been called "topological psychology."

Lewin realizes that the same mathematical concepts can be used to represent different facts. He suggests, therefore, distinguishing between the formal and mathematical properties of concepts and their psychological and real content. The mathematical concepts should be accompanied by a set of psychological concepts. These are the *dynamic concepts* of psychological theory. Each of them has to be defined in regard to its conceptual properties and its relation to empirical data and to the causal laws. Some of these concepts are derived directly from observable data like behavior, environment, etc. Others cannot be derived from empirical data. They have to be introduced as "intervening variables" which cannot be perceived by observation. These are the *"conditional-genetic concepts"* or *"constructs."* A construct is by definition "a dynamic fact which is determined indirectly as 'an intervening variable' by way of 'operational definition.'"[3] Constructs have to be clearly defined, and their existence can be proved or disproved by empirical operations; the definition of conceptual properties of a construct must be coordinated to certain mathematical concepts; then their operational definition indicates the possibility of empirical proof. Lewin's dynamic concepts fill the space of intervening variables wherever behavior takes place. Between the independent variable, which is in Lewin's theory the observable total situation, and the observable behavior Lewin puts in the logical construct, which explains the relationship between observable facts. This explanation is causal or dynamic. Instinct, libido, drive, association, intelligence, excitatory tendency, tension, force, conditioned reflex—all these terms indicate, not empirical facts, but "dynamic facts the existence of which can be proved only indirectly by means of certain manipulations." They are the *intervening concepts* or *dynamic constructs* that "have been unavoidable in any worth-while psychology. Why not then introduce these concepts in a deliberate and orderly fashion, rather than permit them to slip in secretly and uncontrolled by the back door?"[4] No psychological theory can be developed on a purely empirical level. Theory means interpretation, and interpretation is derivation of empirical facts from theoretical concepts.

These constructs have been introduced in various ways by the respective psychological theories. Lewin pays more attention than most psychologists to the technique of theory construction. He says: "Logical

[3] *Ibid.,* p. 213.
[4] Kurt Lewin, "The Conceptual Representation and the Measurement of Psychological Forces," *Contributions to Psychological Theory,* 1938, **1**, 12.

form and content are closely interwoven in any empirical science. Formalization should include the development of constructs every one of which is considered from the start both as a carrier of formal implication and as an adequate representation of empirical data. This implies that the operational and the conceptual definitions are not arbitrarily related but show an internal coherence (e.g., the possibility of coordinating psychological force operationally to locomotion and conceptually to a vector is mainly based on their common feature of directedness). It further implies that the various constructs should be built up in such a way as to be parts of one logically consistent and empirically adequate system."[5]

The system of constructs as a whole should be empirically testable. Both the conceptual and the coordinating definition of an individual construct is a question of agreement or convenience. *"Laws and definitions are a network of statements which only as a whole can be viewed as right or wrong."*[6] Whether they are right or wrong depends on their relationship to empirically established facts and laws.

Lewin maintains that in modern physics there is considerable liberty concerning a single concept or law, but the system of concepts cannot be established at will. The establishment of a system of concepts represents considerable difficulty. The logical mathematical properties of the concepts and their relation to empirical data cannot be established prior to some knowledge of the empirical data. In Lewin's words, they "should be determined in view of the laws and the empirical data involved." Empirical laws, based on well-proved empirical or experimental data, do not suffice for establishment of the dynamic or conceptual laws. "For, as long as the conceptual properties of the constructs implied in a law are not clearly determined, the law cannot be said to be either right or wrong, because it lacks definite meaning."[7] But the meaning or conceptual properties of the constructs should be determined in view of the laws and the empirical data involved. It is, in a way, a vicious circle.

Lewin was fully aware of these difficulties. He suggested that the first definitions be made in a "tentative manner" and gradually clarified with the inductive method of "abstract classification" or generalization. The constructs have to be introduced tentatively and gradually tested and, if necessary, modified. The *raison d'être* of the constructs depends ultimately on their fruitfulness in research. The conceptual properties of constructs have to be analyzed as to their convenience or necessity in the context of psychological research as a whole. They have to be a priori proposed, and clarified by "gradual approximation" in actual empirical research.

Lewin saw no need to coordinate psychological theory and physiological

[5] Kurt Lewin, *Field Theory in Social Science,* Harper, 1951, p. 24.
[6] Lewin, "The Conceptual Representation," *Contributions to Psychological Theory,* 1938, 1, 16.
[7] *Ibid.*

concepts. H. Feigl quotes Lewin's oral remark that "the time for neuro-physiological explanations would not come for a thousand years!"[8]

Lewin was aware of the difficulties faced by the gestalt-field theory. He saw no reason for coordinating physiological systems and psychological systems; he did not believe that psychology and physiology can be connected by the concept of isomorphism. His dynamic concepts deal with psychological and physiological factors not as two separate systems but as identical ones. They deal with behavior as a whole, as a function of a person and his environment, and thus avoid two terminologies, one of psychology and another of physiology. Lewin sees no methodological advantage in reductionism.

There are four kinds of functional interrelation between constructs (often called dynamic facts) and observable facts, says Lewin: (1) logical interdependence between the constructs, (2) empirical interdependence between the constructs, (3) measurement of the constructs by observable facts, and (d) functional interrelation between observable facts.

Conceptual interdependence operates when one construct can be logically derived from the other by logical inference. There is no need for empirical proof in such a case.

Empirical laws indicate functional interdependence between at least two different constructs established empirically, e.g., the empirical relationship between velocity and weight in physics, tension and forces of locomotion in psychology.

"The Individual Case"

The problem of idiophenomena, which attracted the attention of Windelband and Dilthey (see Chaps. 1 and 10) has been attacked again by Lewin. "Laws are nothing more than principles according to which the actual event may be derived from the dynamic factors of the concrete situation"; therefore "the application of the laws presupposes the comprehension of the individual cases."[9]

This is not what Windelband had in mind. He regarded each individual case as a faithful representative of the laws of nature; of course, this statement applies to natural sciences only. Certain phenomena do not fit into this category, namely, the events of history, psychology, and other *Kulturwissenschaften*. The reason for the distinction between natural and cultural sciences lies in the fact that natural sciences operate with phenomena representative of the general law, whereas cultural sciences

---

[8] Herbert Feigl, "Principles and Problems of Theory Construction in Psychology," in W. Dennis (ed.), *Current Trends in Psychological Theory*, University of Pittsburgh, 1951, p. 201.

[9] Lewin, *Principles of Topological Psychology*, p. 11.

deal with unrepeatable, unique, and unpredictable events called *idio-phenomena*. No laws can be applied to them.

William Stern (see Chap. 11) tried to solve this problem by ascribing a double role to human beings. The "thing" and the "person" are united in one organism. A "thing" can be interpreted by the laws of nature while a "person" should be interpreted by culture.

Kurt Lewin attacks this problem on a methodological level. "The determination of laws is therefore only one side of the task of explaining mental life. The other side, which is of equal importance and inseparably connected with the determination of the laws, involves the task of representing concrete situations in such a way that the actual event can be derived from them according to the principles which are given in the general laws." [10]

Lewin regards the law as a principle by which the event can be explained. One has to manipulate the concrete situation so as to be able to derive and single out fact from the total situation in accordance with the principle.

What is derivation or tracing back? It is, Lewin says, the progression from "phenotypical" to "conditional-genetic" or "genotypical" characteristics. Phenotypical characteristics are the observable features of an object or event in a given time and place. Conditional-genetic or genotypical facts are the intrinsic and conceptual properties. If one describes a situation by means of conditional-genetic factors, the flow of observable events can be derived from this description as its logical and unavoidable consequence. If a given empirical situation can be described in a conceptual manner, all the actual events can be derived. Thus "correct representation of what 'is' is at the same an explanation of what happens." [11]

"Galileo's Revolt against Aristotle"

Lewin ascribed the method of testing simultaneously with general laws and specific cases to the great physicist Galileo. Lewin distinguished three epochs in the development of psychology. The first was "speculative" or "Aristotelian," at which stage psychologists tried to discover the "essence" of things and the cause behind all occurrence. Then came "descriptive" psychology and a reaction against the speculative theories; at this epoch psychologists were found "to collect as many facts as possible and to describe them exactly." Psychologists were hostile to theories and preferred to classify phenomena by abstraction.

Lewin feels that the time is ripe for the third epoch, the "constructive" or "Galileian," which he introduces. The goal of constructive psychology

[10] *Ibid.*, p. 11.
[11] *Ibid.*, p. 83.

is "to discover laws" and "to predict individual cases." This constructive psychology aims at elimination of nonpsychological concepts; it is non-reductionist. In contradistinction to speculative psychology, which believed that the causes of human behavior lie in either past or future, "Galileian" psychology believes that facts are the causes of events. Lewin strongly emphasizes the "*totality of the contemporary situation*" as the full cause of behavior.[12]

The Aristotelian method in psychology should be discontinued. Psychologists should follow in the footsteps of the Galileian methods of research. In a special paper (included in the volume on *Personality*) Lewin discusses the difference between the two types of concept development in physics, and their implication for psychology. "For Aristotelian physics the membership of an object in a given class was of critical importance, because for Aristotle the class defined the essence or essential nature of the object and thus determined its behavior in both positive and negative respects."[13] The classes are abstractly defined as the "sum total of those characteristics which a group of objects have in common." Only things which occur always or at least frequently are lawful, while other phenomena are not. Galileian physics, says Lewin, has introduced the idea that the same law governs the entire physical world. Galileo and his followers have shifted the emphasis from the observable traits of a *phenotype* to the conditional-genetic concepts of a genotype.

Relation to the environment has replaced the Aristotelian "nature" of things, and the concrete situation has taken the place of the abstract average. The very same process is expected to take place in psychology. Child psychologists ask, e.g., the Aristotelian question: "Do all children do that, or is it at least *common?*" Lewin feels that each individual case is representative of the totality of laws whether it happens once or every day. There are no exceptions to laws, and the "complete representation of even one given situation would presuppose the solution of all psychological problems and knowledge of all psychological laws. For scientific research the difficulties begin as soon as one tries to represent a 'given' situation. A complete representation of one situation would mean that the whole task of psychology is completed. The representation can be made only step by step and its progress must be parallel to the investigation of the dynamic laws. The representation of a situation implies no less theory than the laws which it presupposes."[14]

Lewin's way of reasoning can be described in a somewhat simplified manner, as follows. The nature of psychological events is idiographic. Each given situation is unique, changing, and dependent on the totality

[12] *Ibid.*, pp. 6 ff.
[13] Kurt Lewin, *A Dynamic Theory of Personality*, McGraw-Hill, 1935, pp. 4 ff.
[14] Lewin, *Principles of Topological Psychology*, p. 82.

of interrelationships in a given unit of space and time. It is impossible to derive, interpret, or predict the behavior of an individual unless the totality of his interrelationship at a given moment is being considered. All kinds of generalizations and classifications are useless, since each person's behavior is not a function of his belonging to a certain category or class but results from the total situation at a given time.

Each situation can be represented in conceptual terms, i.e., in conditional-genetic concepts. A full representation of one situation requires the substitution of the empirical facts by dynamic concepts and laws. That kind of representation of a situation is in fact interpretation, since individual facts "flow" from the situation as its "purely logical consequences." Therefore "a correct representation of what 'is' is at the same time an explanation of what happens."

2. LEWIN'S MATHEMATICAL CONCEPTS

The Use of Mathematics

It is a legitimate procedure to arrange scientific propositions in mathematical equations. In fact, mathematics is the best way to present empirical data. The ancient Ionian philosophers tried to discover the unity of the universe despite its apparent diversity. They tried to reduce the various and multiple factors to one or a few "elements." Numbers are the unifying element in scientific discovery, and whenever qualities can be perceived as quantities, the process of scientific analysis is greatly advanced.

The discovery of a proper mathematical formula or operation is often a milestone in the progress of scientific research, yet not all empirical data fit into mathematics, perhaps owing to the inadequate development of empirical studies or the unfortunate choice of a mathematical system to represent these data.

Sometimes empirical research workers wonder whether they can find a mathematical system which will enable them to represent their data.

Mathematics, Russell says, is not a science. It is a system of symbols and nothing else. Whoever introduces or uses a system of symbols has to state clearly how they are to be used in order to represent data typified by them in a univocal way. Mathematics is a language, a highly developed and precise means for representation and communication of truth. Mathematics per se does not discover any truth at all and mathematical formulas are neither true nor false. They are truthful only in the connotation of the "immanent truth" (cf. Chaps. 14 and 15). They are consistent and exclude self-contradiction but they do not contribute new information (empirical) or new laws (theoretical). Scientists have to disclose facts and their interrelationships and may *represent* and *communicate* the discoveries of facts and relationship by using mathematical symbols. Undoubtedly the proper use of mathematics offers tremendous advantages in scientific studies, adds clarity and consistency, and is far superior to any nonmathematical formulation of scientific data and laws. Lewin feels that empirical facts have to be represented by mathematical concepts in "an absolutely binding way" in order to obtain the benefits of their application. Mathematical concepts are far better than any other concepts, says Lewin. They are "distinguished from other means of representation, such as ordinary speech, in that they belong to a system of concepts which are related to each other in a univocal way."[15] He seems to believe that this univocality can be attained by empirical sciences as a result of the application of mathematical concepts, and he suggests the application of mathematical concepts to empirical research, provided they "represent the logical structure of these empirical relationships adequately."[16] Thus Lewin's question is not "whether mathematics" but "which" mathematics will best suit the nature of psychological data.

Topological Concepts

Lewin feels that geometry offers certain advantages to a psychologist since all psychological schools use terms like approach, withdrawal, social position, change in position, belonging, distance, direction, area, etc.

All these concepts are spatial, i.e., geometrical. Geometry can be utilized in any empirical research provided the kind of geometry chosen fits the dynamic characteristics of the empirical data. Since the basic psychological relationship is that of person and environment, *space* is the proper concept to be applied to psychological data.

Psychological locomotion, like achieving a goal or acquiring a higher status, does not fit the Euclidean geometry which is usually applied by physics. People may "move" toward their goal while moving physically away from it. Therefore psychological processes cannot be "univocally coordinated" to the physical space.

There is one kind of space that fits psychology, says Lewin. This space, representing the part-whole or point-environment relationship, is the topological space. Topological geometry has been chosen by Lewin to serve psychological theory, because he believes that the person-environment relationship can be best presented in the topological space.

Topology is defined as "a part of geometry which investigates properties figures which remain unchanged under continuous transformation."[17]

---

[15] *Ibid.*, p. 78.
[16] *Ibid.*, p. 60.
[17] Von B. Kerékjártó, *Vorlesungen über Topologie*, Springer, 1923.

These properties are non-quantitative. They represent relations of parts of a certain area—like part-whole relationship, connection, position, etc. —which are so important in Lewin's psychological theory.

Topological relationships can be well illustrated by a bit of elastic rubber. Though the piece of rubber can be stretched out in various directions, the relative position of points on it remains unchanged in the topological frame of reference.[18]

Topological geometry is a nonmetrical part of mathematics. Neither magnitude nor direction is defined; thus distances and sizes are unimportant.

The following topological symbols are used by Lewin:

$+$ "The topological sum," e.g., $A + B = C$, means region C is the sum of regions A and B.

$\cdot$ "Intersection," e.g., $A \cdot B = 0$, means A and B have no common points.

$\supset$ "Includes," e.g., $A \supset B$, means region A includes region B.

$\subset$ "Is included," e.g., $K \subset L$, means region K is included in L.

The *sum* of A and B means all points are part of both A and B. If A is a part of B, then $A + B = B$. In this case A is part of B and we use the symbol $A \subset B$. By intersection of A and B is meant the totality of points which are part of both A and B.

A polygon or an ellipse or a circle represents the same spatial relation in topology: all of them are closed regions. The difference in form, size, or dimension is irrelevant. If all points of a region can be mutually connected by a path, which is entirely included in the region, this region is called a *connected* region. A *closed* region includes its boundary points. The boundary of a closed region is a *Jordan* type of curve. The shape of this curve is of no importance at all, but it has to be a closed curve which does not intersect itself. The Jordan curve which encloses a closed region serves as a boundary between the enclosed and surrounding regions.

A *path* is a part of a Jordan curve; it does not intersect itself; it connects points in a region. Lewin believes that a path can represent *locomotion*, which means psychological activity. A simply connected closed region offers the simplest case for presentation of psychological dynamics: it has a boundary and it permits "locomotion" along the paths connecting the various points within the region.

If two regions have no common points they are called *foreign*. In such a case, the intersection of these two regions is zero. $A \cdot B = 0$.

Boundaries or boundary zones of regions which offer resistance to psychological locomotion are called *barriers*. If the barriers are im-

[18] Lewin's theory has often been interpreted from his graphs, but graphs were merely a pedagogical device. Here Lewin's theory is presented without them.

penetrable, the space of free movement may be limited. The more *rigid* the barrier, the greater the forces necessary to overcome it. The more *permeable* a barrier is, the easier it is to perform locomotion through it.

Some regions are *elastic*, i.e., tend to return to their original state after a change has been induced. The smaller the force needed to produce a certain change, the more *fluid* the region.

Life Space

Having introduced some topological concepts Lewin has to prove that these concepts are good for representation and interpretation of empirical data in psychology. In order to do it, he has to manipulate psychological data and transfer them from their phenotypical status (as they are seen by most psychologists) to the genotypical status, which permits topological operations on the empirical data.

The totality of coexisting facts which are mutually interdependent has been defined by physicists as a field. *Psychological field* is a totality of coexisting and mutually interdependent psychological facts, Lewin says; the life space is a psychological field which includes the totality of facts determining behavior.

Empirical data prove that the behavior and even the development of an individual are functions of his personality and his environment at a given time. Personality and environment in their interrelationship are called *life space* by Lewin. One can state that $B = F (P, E) = F (LSp)$ behavior is a function of personality and environment, or a function of the life space. This function, F, is what is usually called a law. Psychology has to view the life space, including the person and his environment, as one field.

The psychological field has to be represented as it exists for a person, including both his physical setting and his needs, dreams, and desires. The boundaries of the field can be quasi-physical, i.e., derived from physics, or quasi-social, i.e., derived from social science, or quasi-conceptual, i.e., derived from logic. When physical obstacles mark the limits of a region, they are called quasi-physical. When social laws, restrictions, or mores prevent the crossing of the boundary of a region, they are called quasi-social barriers. If the barrier is an intellectual one it is called quasi-conceptual. All these barriers, insofar as they represent a handicap to psychological locomotion, are obviously psychological barriers.

The difference between the physical world and the psychological worlds (life spaces) is that the former is a dynamic closed unity, while the latter are unclosed unities. In physics all changes are produced within the same physical space, while in psychology changes may come from without, i.e., from outside the borders of the life space. Psychological events are usually determined by the life space, but certain facts coming from physical space outside the life space may influence human behavior. These facts, to speak topologically, come from the "foreign" hull.

These are the limitations to the life space: "If someone saws a board, his behavior is determined not only by his goal but also by the nature of the wood and properties of the saw." Thus Lewin defines the life space as a "dynamically not closed world."[19]

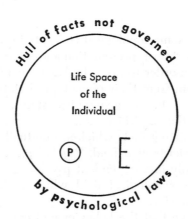

How can one determine which facts ought to be included in the life space? Lewin doubts whether consciousness can be used as the sole criterion for determining whether something belongs to a person's life space. He prefers to include "all real facts," and real to Lewin is "what has effects," whether a person is aware of them or not.

Physical or social facts are included in the life space "only to the extent and in the manner in which they affect the individual in his momentary state." Thus the life space is "the person and the psychological environment as it exists for him. We usually have this field in mind if we refer to needs, mood, goals, anxiety ideals," states Lewin in a paper published in 1943, and goes on: "The principle of representing within the life space all that affects behavior at that time, but nothing else, prevents the inclusion of physical food which is not perceived."[20]

A good definition of life space is offered by Cartwright in the Introduction to a posthumously published volume of Lewin's writings:

"The life space is defined so that at any given time it includes all facts that have existence and excludes those that do not have existence *for the individual or group under study.*

"In individual psychology, the environment and the person as con-

[19] Lewin, *Principles of Topological Psychology*, pp. 68 ff.
[20] Kurt Lewin, "Defining the 'Field at a Given Time,'" *Psychological Review*, 1943, **50**, 292–310.

sciously perceived by the person are ordinarily included in the life space. But, in addition, unconscious states are also included to the extent that by direct observation or inference the scientist can determine that they leave effects."[21]

Lewin "indicates that it is reasonably easy to decide to include within the life space, many things, such as needs, goals, cognitive structure, and the like and to exclude many others, such as physical and social events occurring at a remote distance and having no direct effect on the individual."[22]

Life Space and Topological Regions

Each part of the life space, says Lewin, has to be presented as a region. The term "region" can be used in two distinct ways, as "(1) Everything in which an object of the life space, for instance a person, has its place; in which it moves; through which it carries out locomotions. (2) Everything in which one can distinguish several positions or parts at the same time, or which is part of a more inclusive whole." The life space itself is a region, and a person within the life space is a region too. Obviously the region of a person is included in the region of the life space. The life space is not indefinitely divisible into smaller parts. The smallest region, which cannot be divided any more, is called "cell."

How can the positions of regions be determined? There are two ways. One can determine regions by *qualitative properties* of a person or of a group or by *locomotion or communication*. Lewin prefers the determination of regions by psychological locomotions.

The "space of free movement" includes all the regions to which a person has access from his present situation. The space of free movement is a connected region; there are no barriers within it.

There are two kinds of connection between regions: locomotion and communication. Locomotion must be presented as a path leading from one point to another. The connected region permits locomotion from each point within the region to any other point within it. The *mutual* positions of regions are determined by the paths along which locomotion takes place.

Actions are defined as psychological locomotions and should be presented as paths. Sometimes they can be represented as regions. For instance, a child who is playing with dolls and is called by the mother to go to bed has to change from the region of playing and to enter the region of sleeping.

If activity is a region, it is at the same time a medium, in contradistinction to a thing. Air is a medium for the flier. A medium is a region in which or through which locomotions can be carried out.

[21] Lewin, *Field Theory in Social Science*, Harper, 1951, pp. xi–xii.
[22] Lewin, *Principles of Topological Psychology*, pp. 93 ff.

A psychological goal is always a region a person would like to enter, or to assume a certain spatial position in relation to. Our activities are usually goal directed; they are paths leading from our present position toward the desired region.

A change in a person's position is represented as a locomotion from one region to another. Lewin reports, as an example, a study carried out in the nursery school of the College of Home Economics of Cornell University. The difficulty in feeding small children is handled by moving the child from regions of unpleasantness to a pleasant region. Lewin says that the adult tries to bring the child from one region to another. In the first regions the adult meets repulsive force. However, food is in the child's mouth; it will not be ejected. Lewin interprets this as follows: "As the child enters the region of 'real eating' his position and the direction of the field forces are entirely changed. When the child is in one of the preceding regions, for instance, when he holds the spoon halfway to his mouth, then a region of greater unpleasantness in which the adult tries to push him in, still lies ahead." When the child is once within this region of real eating, the region which lies ahead of him is more pleasant. Thus Lewin concludes: "The dynamic condition of a person depends in almost every respect directly on his position in a certain region."[23]

The Third Dimension

Lewin feels that most of his quasi-social and quasi-physical fields are satisfactorily represented in two dimensions. When he comes to represent imagination, hope, daydream, and similar phenomena, he feels compelled to introduce the third dimension, which will represent "degrees of reality." In order to indicate the level of reality in the life space, one must use the third dimension. The more unreal the level, the greater is its fluidity; i.e., its barriers offer less resistance, the boundaries of the part-regions can be easily shifted, and even the boundaries between person and environment are less clear. Usually, perception has the highest degree of reality, thinking has less reality, and daydreaming even less.

3. LEWIN'S LOGICAL CONSTRUCTS

Hodological Space

Topology cannot suffice for presentation of psychological data, though the part-whole relations and the concept of paths are of great help in presenting psychological data. However, topology does not deal with *direction* and *size*, which are indispensable concepts in psychology. The

[23] *Ibid.,* pp. 97–99.

topological structure of the life space determines which locomotions are possible at a given time, but what actually will happen cannot be predicted with the help of topological concepts only, because change cannot be derived by topology.

Lewin feels compelled to add the concept of "Hodological space" to his field theory. Direction in physics can be represented either as the *straight* line (in Euclidean space) or the *straightest* line (in Riemannian space). Lewin thinks that psychological direction is neither of these, and therefore a new type of space must be proposed which will suit the needs of psychological data.

This new space is called by Lewin the *hodological space*. In this space "the character of the distinguished path varies according to situation and direction in hodological space depends upon the properties of the field at large. . . . Hodological space distinguishes direction toward and direction from."[24]

Lewin is fully aware of the inadequacy of his definition. He says that the purpose of the hodological space "is to find a type of geometry which permits the use of the concept of direction in a manner which will correspond with the meaning that direction has in psychology."[25] Lewin hopes that axiomatization of this new geometry will be done later on by "a competent mathematician." Lewin does not question whether this new kind of spatial relationship can be constructed nor does he give any directions as to how to do it. He seems to believe in the omnipotence of mathematics and sincerely hopes that at some time his *ad hoc* proposed system will be elaborated and form a legitimate branch of mathematics. Meanwhile he proceeds with utilizing this new tool in the assessment of change, which is one of the most important processes in his psychology.

Psychological change, says Lewin, must have a direction. Behavior is change in a given situation. Behavior is locomotion in a certain direction, either toward an objective or away from it. Lewin assumes that human behavior is goal directed.

Topology does not deal with directions. Psychology does. This difficulty is dealt with by Lewin in a rather unexpected way. He invents a new kind of space, hodological space, in which directions do count. Psychologists may wonder about the ease with which this obstacle is overcome, and this ready solution may be frowned on by mathematicians. However, Lewin feels that now he can go on with his theory construction. He has a new geometry that fits psychological change and enables him to introduce the concept of direction into a certain kind of space. After solving the problem of direction in human behavior, he is ready to deal with the problem of size and measurement of locomotion.

[24] Lewin, "The Conceptual Representation and the Measurement of Psychological Forces," *Contributions to Psychological Theory*, 1938, **1**, 22–23.
[25] *Ibid.*, p. 23.

Force

According to Lewin all psychological theories may be considered to posit that human behavior is caused by directed entities. Call them propensities or libido, instinct or drive—you always have a directed entity as the cause of behavior.

Mathematicians distinguish scalars and vectors. Scalars are units of magnitude, while vectors represent both magnitude and directions. Physics operates with both types of unit, but locomotion and change always require vectors.

If anything happens, a change has taken place. Behavior is change. The cause of behavior is, as said before, a directed entity; it is a vector, a directed unit which has a certain magnitude and direction.

Lewin introduces the term "psychological force" as a construct and refers to what other psychologists call drive, excitatory tendency, libido, etc. Psychological force is a directed entity which has a certain magnitude analogous to that of physical force.

Galileo and Newton held that each body if left alone will move in a straight line with uniform and constant velocity; this is the law of inertia. Any change in the direction or velocity or both is a result of some force. Force is the cause of change.

Lewin considers any activity a change and ascribes it to a "psychological force." The term "force" is obviously borrowed from physics, but it is introduced into psychology and defined by Lewin independently from its physical connotation. Any "tendency to act in a certain direction" or any cause of activity is called force. Force has to have *direction*, magnitude, and point of application, and since then properties cannot be represented in the topological geometry, Lewin introduces them in the framework of his own hodological system.

The hodological system allows to be attached to the construct "force" the three above-mentioned conceptual properties: direction, magnitude, and point of application. The conceptual property of force is vector; its operational definition links it with psychological locomotion.

What kind of mathematical manipulation can be applied to force? Lewin feels that in some manner forces can be added, but he does not know how. "Can we speak of resultant [of forces—B. W.] if we do not know the laws which determine the direction and the strength of the resultant force of two given forces? Can we assume that the principle of parallelogram of forces which holds in physics holds in psychology too? . . . Everything seems to indicate that this principle does not hold in psychology. . . . Nevertheless, there seems to be a way in psychology to avoid the concept of resultants."[26] However, when several forces act on a

[26] *Ibid.*, pp. 83–84.

certain region, one must assume some kind of combination of them. A combination of forces acting at the same time at the same point is called *resultant force.* Though it is not known how to measure the resultant force, it can be safely assumed that locomotion takes place whenever the resultant force is greater than zero.

Forces can be measured indirectly, says Lewin, by relating them to observable facts. Measurement correlates the observable symptoms to dynamical facts (constructs). Constructs cannot be measured quantitatively because there is no measuring unit, no zero point, nor are equal units determined. But their symptoms satisfy the requirements for non-quantitative measurement.[27] Thus a rank-order measurement may be applied to measurement of forces. Whenever a person does something, his behavior is an effect of forces acting on him. Some of these forces are greater, some smaller, and the resultant behavior will indicate the rank-order quantity of forces.

Force Field

Forces act in a field, and a person's behavior in a given life space is a product of the resultant forces. A *force field* or field of force "indicates which force would exist at each point in the field if the individual involved were at that point."[28] A *conflict* refers to the overlapping of at least two force fields. *Frustration* has the same dimension as conflict. The distribution of forces away from one region is the force field of *aversion. Choice* means that a person is located between two positive or two negative mutually exclusive valences.

Forces acting in one's life space but originating in other persons and their wishes are called *induced* forces. In a group setting the leader induces forces into the life spaces of the individual members.

How far a force will influence behavior depends on the *potency* of the situation in which a person is involved. Potency of a region within the life space is the relative extent to which one is involved in a given area, when he is involved in more areas than one.

A goal has the conceptual dimension of a "force field"—that is, of a distribution of forces in space. Goal (or, in field-theoretical terminology, a positive valence) is a force field of a special structure, usually a force field where all forces point toward the same region.

Valence

If a region is attractive to a person, it has positive valence. Valence corresponds to a field of force which has the structure of a positive central

---

[27] *Ibid.,* p. 113.
[28] Kurt Lewin, "Constructs in Psychology and Psychological Ecology," *University of Iowa Studies in Child Welfare,* 1944, **20,** 1–29.

field, i.e., all forces in this field are directed in the direction of valence. If no other valences existed, the person would move in the direction of the positive valence from whatever position he was in.

Lewin defines valence in terms of forces acting on a person: "A region G which has a valence $(Va(G))$ is defined as a region within the life space of an individual P which attracts or repulses this individual." If $Va(G) > 0$, then $[f(P,G)] > 0$. Va is valence, G goal, fPG force from the person to the goal.

Valence is related to force but is not identical with it. "If the valence of a region decreases or increases because of a change of the intensity of the need the forces corresponding to the valence also will decrease or increase. However, the strength of the force fP,G does not depend only upon the strength of the valence, but besides, for instance, upon the relative position of P and G. By P's [person's—B. W.] coming closer to a goal, the force in the direction to the goal might increase."[29]

Forces directed toward a positive valence or away from a negative one are called driving forces; barriers are restraining forces.

Tension

Every construct in psychology needs a definition of its conceptual properties and a coordinating definition. Consider the concept "tension." Its conceptual properties are the following:

"It is a state of system S which tries to change itself in such a way that it becomes equal to the state of surrounding systems. It involves forces at the boundary of the system S in tension. . . . The tension in a system S has to be determined always relative to the tension of its neighboring systems." So much for conceptual properties; the coordinating definition of tension as related to psychology is as follows: "whenever a psychological need exists, a system in a state of tension exists within the individual."[30]

Psychologically speaking, tension is a state of disequilibrium between the individual and his environment. This objective state of disequilibrium or tension is perceived by the individual as a need.

This presentation of the problem of needs, which is actually the problem of motivation in human behavior, requires further consideration. Organisms tend to equilibrium, Lewin says, after Cannon and Goldstein (cf. Chap. 5). The principle of homeostasis is applied by Lewin to forces acting within a system and without it. It sounds in Lewin's theory somewhat behavioristic: whenever the balance is disturbed, the system tends to regain it.

However, Lewin cannot be satisfied with this objective law of homeostasis. The psychological field of an individual, in which all the forces act, cannot be void of subjectivistic perception. Tension as a lack of balance

[29] *Ibid.*, pp. 88, 89.
[30] *Ibid.*, p. 99.

between force fields is one side of the story, namely, the conceptual one. The other side is psychological reality as experienced by the individual; it is the "operational definition" of the very same process. In this definition tension is perceived by an individual as his need, like hunger, thirst, etc. Whenever a state of tension exists in the organism, a need is always perceived. Thus tension and need are not considered by Lewin as cause and effect but as two sides of the same process.

Needs are closely related to valences. Whenever the intensity of a need increases, the valence of objects or activities which may satisfy this need increases too. The hungrier one is, the higher the valence of food. And the hungrier one is, the easier to satisfy his hunger with poor food, because the valence of any kind of food is increased.

Causality

Lewin distinguishes two notions of causality. Causality may have a "historical-geographical" meaning in the case where all the relevant antecedent factors are taken into consideration. All the events that happened at a certain time and in a certain place belong to this category of causality. Lewin believes that in developmental psychology and in abnormal psychology the historical concept of causality may be applied.

He feels, however, that the "systematic" concept of causality is far more important. Effects are produced by concrete causes, i.e., by other events that *exist* at a certain moment. The question is, What kind of time relationship exists between the event or group of events called "cause" and the event or group of events called "effect"?

Aristotle distinguished between *causa finalis*, the aim or the future as a cause, and *causa efficiens*, the antecedent cause. Lewin feels that both definitions are wrong. Since neither past nor future exists at the present moment, they cannot have effects at the present.

Suppose, says Lewin, the foliage of a tree shelters me from the rain. The "systematic" causal explanation will be based on finding out the direction and velocity of falling drops, the position of leaves, my own position, etc. "In short," says Lewin, "one can represent the present situation and, by applying the laws of mechanics or other relevant laws, derive what event must occur in such a situation."[31] This systematic causality is in contradistinction to the causality which will tell the history of the tree, etc., and all other events which happened at a given time and in a given space.

Actually both ways can be applied in psychology. In psychological dynamics the systematic causality is far superior, says Lewin, because effects can be produced by contemporary events only. Lewin defines existence by its effects; what exists, he says, has effects, and an effect is an

[31] Lewin, *Principles of Topological Psychology*, p. 31.

outcome of what exists. Only the present exists, and behavior is an effect of coexisting, simultaneous factors.

"It has been accepted by most psychologists that the theological derivation of behavior from the future is not permissible. Field theory insists that the derivation of behavior from the past is not less metaphysical, because past events do not exist now and therefore cannot have effect now. The effect of the past on behavior can be only an indirect one, the past psychological field is one of the 'origins' of the present field and this in turn affects behavior."[32]

The study of life space requires "systematic" causation. Behavior of a person is a function of the person and of his environment. Lewin considers causality identical with mathematical function; he believes that behavior and person-environment are simultaneous facts, but he is aware that absolute contemporaneity is almost impossible. He is satisfied with a situation which remains "sufficiently constant" during the interval of time in question.

"Psychology has used diagnosis by *anamneses* rather excessively, particularly in classical psychoanalysis and other clinical approaches of personality. . . . Experimental psychology, on the whole, has shown a progressive trend toward testing the present situation. The method of determining the properties of a situation (S^t) by testing them at that time t avoids the uncertainties of historical conclusions. It does not follow, however, that this method eliminates considerations of time periods altogether. A 'situation at a given time' actually does not refer to a moment without time extension, but to a certain time-period."

"Field theory states that the change dx/dt at the time t depends only on the situation S^t at that time t." "The field-theoretical principle of contemporaneity in psychology then means that the behavior B at the time t is a function of the situation S at the time t only (S is meant to include both the person and his psychological environment), $B^t = F(S^t)$ and not, in addition, a function of past or future situations $S^t - n$ or $S^t + n$."[33]

4. LOCOMOTION: THEORY OF BEHAVIOR

Equilibrium

Behavior is change, says Lewin. What are the reasons for the change? Lewin assumes a state of equilibrium between person and environment. Should this equilibrium be disturbed, a *tension* arises which leads to locomotion that brings relief (restores the equilibrium).

[32] Kurt Lewin, "Field Theory of Learning," *Forty-First Yearbook of the National Society for the Study of Education,* 1942, **41** (Part II), 215–242.

[33] Lewin, Kurt, "Defining the 'Field at a Given Time,'" *Psychological Review,* 1943, **50,** 292–310.

Human behavior is a continuation of tensions, locomotions, and reliefs. Tension is "a state of a system of an individual" in relation to the tension of neighboring systems. Whenever there is a lack of equilibrium between two systems, a state of tension arises. A system in tension tends to change to become equal to the state of surrounding systems. The activity directed toward removal of tension and establishment of equilibrium is *locomotion*. Locomotion is a directed activity, and it aims at restoraton of the equilibrium.

The sequence tension-locomotion-equilibrium is equivalent to the sequence need-activity-relief. Whenever a psychological need is felt, there is a state of tension, and the individual acts in order to achieve relief. Failure or frustration causes additional tension; discharge of a system under tension corresponds to what other psychologists call satisfaction of a drive or of a motive. The satisfaction of the need corresponds to a release of the tension within the system.

An individual's behavior is a product of the situation, says Lewin. This statement can be qualified as a definite sort of environmentalism. Lewin has in mind the environment "at a given time" in contradistinction to other environmentalists, who are mainly concerned with the past influences of the environment on a person's behavior.

Since Lewin cares little about past influences and is concerned with the environment as it is in the present, his system should be called *situationism* rather than environmentalism. Behavior depends on the state of equilibrium or disequilibrium between the forces acting in the field. The kind of behavior one can expect from an individual depends mainly on the individual's situation. In different situations he will behave differently, responding to the structure of environment, to forces, and to valences.

Lewin says that there are two ways to explain behavior. Theories of the first type locate the forces for locomotion within a person; they correlate needs to tensions within his inner-personal regions. Freud's theory of libido falls into this category since it emphasizes the inner and instinctual forces.

Lewin considers this kind of theory fallacious, since forces for locomotion cannot be derived logically from tensions within the person. Wherever a positive or negative valence exists in the environment, there is a state of tension within the organism. Valence is only partially dependent on the state of the organism; e.g., the valence of food is related both to the degree of hunger and to the extent of its availability, which is independent of psychological factors. When food appears in the psychological field of a person whose system is in tension (of hunger), the food is a positive valence because it can reduce the tension. Thus the entire issue of motivation, and the problems of inner drives and outer incentives (cf. Chaps. 2, 3, and 4), has been restructured by Lewin. In his theory, behavior is a movement or locomotion which has a definite direction. This direction is either toward the objects and persons having positive valence or away from objects and persons having negative valence. Things have positive valence if they can remove a tension. Tension is a state of disequilibrium. Tensions arise within the organism; valences are in the environment.

Both are included in a dynamic field within which forces are acting on a person in the direction of the positive valence or away from the negative valence. As a result of the action of forces (which results from tensions and valences), a locomotion takes place. This locomotion reduces tension and brings relief. Locomotion is, topologically speaking, movement from one region to another in a given space. Psychologically speaking it is goal-directed behavior which results, according to Lewin, from the "totality of coexisting facts." J. F. Brown summarizes Lewin's theory of locomotion as follows: "Psychological activities may be ordered to *locomotions*. One individual in this sense has the character of a *thing*. The space through which the locomotion occurs has the properties of a *medium*. . . . Media have dynamic properties such as fluidity, permeability, cohesiveness and the like." All these terms can be operationally defined, says Brown. "*Fluidity* is defined as the ease of locomotion in the medium. *Degree of freedom* of social locomotion is the comparative number of directions in which social locomotion is possible. *Permeability* means the ease with which locomotions are executed through the barrier. And the forces activating all locomotions in the psychological field are to be ordered to the concept of vector. These vectors represent forces causing psychological locomotion."[34]

One can readily conclude that Lewin has shifted the force point of human dynamics from inner drives, impulses, libido, etc., toward the external factors of stimulation, incentive, and situation. Even tension within the organism cannot arise independently from environment. Man cannot be considered, according to Lewin, a separate entity; he is part of a dynamic field. Person and environment are bound together in a field and cannot be separated.

Tension Systems

An experimental study of behavior of individuals in a state of tension was conducted by Lewin's pupil, Miss Zeigarnik.[35] Zeigarnik found that uncompleted tasks are much better retained in memory than completed ones. Her findings support Lewin's hypothesis that attainment of a goal or successful locomotion in the direction of positive valence relieves tension, while an uncompleted task preserves the existing tension. Once a tension has been created by a task or goal, the organism is inclined to act in order

[34] J. F. Brown, "On the Use of Mathematics in Psychological Theory," *Psychometrika*, 1936, **1**, 7–15, 77–90.

[35] Bluma Zeigarnik, "Über das Behalten erledigter und unerledigter Handlungen," *Psychologische Forschung*, 1927, **9**, 1–85.

to remove the tension by a locomotion in the direction of the goal. As long as the goal is not attained, and the need is not satisfied, a force corresponding to the valence of the goal region exists and leads the individual to an action in that direction. And this is precisely why uncompleted tasks are kept very much alive in the individual's memory.

Zeigarnik's experiment was based on the following assumptions. First, the intention to reach a goal G corresponds to a tension t in a certain system S^c within the persons, so that $t\,(S^c) > 0$. Then, if the goal is achieved the tension is released: $t\,(S^G) = 0$, if $P \subset G$. An additional assumption was made, namely, that a need leads not only to an overt activity of locomotion toward the goal, but to thinking about the activity too. Using the topological presentation one may say that the force causing the tendency to locomotion in the direction of the goal $f_{P,G}$. acts both on the reality level of doing and on the unreality level of thinking.

Zeigarnik gave 18 to 22 tasks to 138 subjects. The subjects were permitted to complete some of their tasks and were prevented from completing others. If memory was correlated to satisfaction, the completed tasks should be retained longer. However, the experiment brings evidence to the contrary and challenges the Freudian assumption of forgetting of unpleasant experiences. Zeigarnik's subjects recalled much better the unfinished tasks, as compared to the satisfactorily completed tasks. The ratio of recalled unfinished tasks (RU) to recalled completed tasks (RC) was approximately 1:9. Apparently, says Lewin, the force acting upon a person who has not completed the task is greater than the force acting upon a person who has completed it. Thus, $f\,(PU) > f\,(PC)$.

A similar experiment was conducted by Ovsiankina.[36] She studied the frequency of resumption of interrupted activities. Her hypothesis was that once a quasi-need is induced, it tends toward discharge by activity. Ovsiankina gave her subjects various tasks to perform. Then she interrupted them and watched through a one-way screen what they were doing. About 80 per cent of the subjects resumed the task. The frequency of resumption indicated the existence of a system of tension which caused activity directed toward completion of the tasks.

Lissner gave his subjects a puzzle, a riddle, and a translation, then interrupted them at a certain point and gave some substitute activities. Some of the substitute activities were easier and some more difficult than the original tasks. The difficulty of a task has been measured by the amount of time needed for its completion. After completion of the substitute activities some subjects tended to resume the interrupted activity. The ratio of resumption was adversely proportional to the difficulty of the substitute task. Apparently the more difficult the substitute task, the greater was its substitute value, and the less the subjects felt the need to resume

[36] Maria Ovsiankina, "Die Wiederaufnahme unterbrochener Handlungen," *Psychologische Forschung*, 1928, 11, 302–379.

the original activity. The conclusion is that the difficult substitute task gave more chance to relieve the tension.[37]

Karsten's studies have tested the hypothesis that repetition may reduce the positive valence of certain activities and even change it into a negative one.[38] These experiments are of considerable importance in the theory of learning and challenge the law of frequency (cf. Chaps. 2, 3, and 4). Karsten ordered her subjects to make strokes in a certain rhythm till they refused to continue even if the experimenter urged them to do so. As the subjects showed that they had had enough, they were asked to make strokes in another rhythm until spontaneous cessation. Then the subjects were asked to continue to make strokes in another rhythm; this was continued till the subjects refused to make any strokes whatsoever. Each sort of rhythm was regarded by Karsten as a separate region. At the beginning the subjects were willing to enter the new region, which meant that the region had positive valence, but repetition changed the positive valence into a negative one. The "satiated" subjects refused to remain in that region. Thus, concludes Lewin, satiation leads to a change of positive valence into a negative one, and repetition may be of no help in learning or even give adverse results.

Barriers, Distances, and Valences

Dembo studied the problem of frustration and anger.[39] When a goal is unobtainable, a *barrier* is said to prevent the person from locomotion in the direction of the desired region. Dembo asked her subjects to throw rings over a bottle. The experimenter increased the difficulties by catching the rings, moving the bottles, etc. The subjects started to rethrow the rings and, when severely frustrated, placed the rings on the stick. Frustrated adults behaved "childishly," shifting from a realistic field to a nonrealistic one.

Usually barriers increase the valence of an object. Whenever the barriers are very difficult, they produce frustration, anger, and regression to a less realistic type of behavior.

As the distance between an object of a certain valence and a person increases, the force of the valence usually decreases. As the child comes closer to a toy, its valence increases. Fajans studied one- to six-year-old children. She put objects of great positive valence before them in distances varying from 8 to 100 centimeters. With increasing distance the positive valence of the objects tended to decrease, as witnessed by the

[37] K. Lissner, "Die Enspannung von Bedürfnissen durch Ersatzhandlungen," *Psychologische Forschung*, 1933, **18**, 218–250.

[38] Anitra Karsten, "Psychische Sättigung," *Psychologische Forschung*, 1928, **10**, 142–254.

[39] Tamara Dembo, "Der Ärger als dynamisches Problem," *Psychologische Forschung*, 1931, **15**, 1–144.

decrease of emotional tension in the infants. In older children things were more complicated, probably because they viewed the obstacle as dependent upon the will of the examiner.[40]

Level of Aspiration

How people evaluate their success and failure depends on previous experience and standards based on it. Hoppe[41] administered a certain task to 124 subjects. The task was performed in 88 seconds on the average. When Hoppe set the goal of performing the task at 120 seconds or more, his subjects refused to accept their achievements as success. Similarly, when he set the goal at 60 seconds or less and most of his subjects failed, the failure did not produce in them a feeling of having failed. Apparently they evaluated their own performance on a certain level of expected achievement. This expected level of future performance has been named by T. Dembo "level of aspiration." Hoppe's subjects experienced a feeling of success and failure when the goals ranged from 65 to 110 seconds. Obviously, this was the range of their level of aspiration.

In Lewin's theory the level of aspiration is related to the problems of the real or unreal psychological field. The degree of reality of a goal influences an individual's evaluation of his own achievement.

Most of the recent experiments on level of aspiration utilize the following technique. The subject is required to state quantitatively his expected achievement, mark on examination, adding, scoring, etc. Then the task is administered. The difference between the actual level of performance and the expected one is the "difference score." Gould[42] used six measures: synonyms, substitution of digits, speed in addition, steadiness, cancellation of letters, and sliding metal disks into a bull's-eye. The "scores of difference" between expected and actual behavior, which indicate that the level of aspiration varied, and their intercorrelations ranged from .04 to .44.

Frank[43] found that there are at least three factors involved in setting the level of aspiration: first, the need to keep the level of aspiration as high as possible; second, the need not to fail; third, the need to be realistic.

Several studies on the level of aspiration have indicated that the level depends on the potentialities of the individual (as perceived by him) and on environmental influences.

[40] Sara Fajans, "Erfolg, Ausdauer und Aktivität beim Säugling und Kleinkind," *Psychologische Forschung*, 1933, 17, 268–305.
[41] F. Hoppe, "Erfolg und Misserfolg," *Psychologische Forschung*, 1930, 14, 1–62.
[42] R. Gould, "An Experimental Analysis of 'Level of Aspiration,'" *Genetic Psychology Monographs*, 1939, 21, 1–115.
[43] T. D. Frank, "Recent Studies of the Level of Aspiration," *Psychological Bulletin*, 1941, 38, 218–226.

Perception and Memory

Perception and learning are as closely interrelated in Lewin's system as in the gestalt theory (see Chap. 12), though Lewin elaborated the issues less than the gestalt psychologists did.

Perception cannot be regarded as a source of energy, nor can perception serve as the driving power in human behavior, says Lewin. Perception of an object may *influence* behavior in the following manner. A newly perceived object may elicit a certain tension within the organism, either of attraction or of repulsion depending on whether the object represents a positive or a negative valence to the person. Consequently he may start locomotion toward the perceived object or away from it. Behavior has not been dynamically produced by perception (perception did not supply the energy), but nevertheless the direction of behavior was related to and guided by perception.

Perception plays a prominent role in one's psychological field. Whatever is perceived by an individual belongs to his psychological field. Lewin has made hardly any specific statement about memory, though Zeigarnik's experiment deals with this problem. As stated above, Zeigarnik's subjects had to perform some tasks, half of which they were permitted to complete and half of which were interrupted by the experimenter. Then the subjects were asked to recall their tasks. The ratio of recalled completed tasks to recalled incompleted tasks was 1:9. This has been explained as an indication of better memorizing of an interrupted task. The plausible interpretation offered by Lewin has related memory to a state of tension in the organism. Whatever has been completed does not give rise to tension and tends to be forgotten. The uncompleted tasks are related to tension (need to complete) and, therefore, they have been kept alive in the subjects' memory.

A critic of Lewin[44] has raised the question of why the completed tasks were recalled at all. If memory is related to tension, what kind of tension accompanies the completed tasks? An additional difficulty arises from Lewin's insistence on contemporary causation. How can past events influence one's behavior if they do not exist any more? Or, perhaps, should our memories be included in the field-at-a-given-time? Apparently Lewin did not elaborate sufficiently his point of view on the problem of memory, which poses considerable difficulties to a field theorist.

Learning

Lewin's theory of learning is at variance with the associationist or conditioning theories of learning. Lewin does not perceive learning as a

[44] Sylvia H. MacCall, "A Comparative Study of the Systems of Lewin and Koffka with Special Reference to Memory Phenomena," *Contributions to Psychological Theory*, Duke University, 1939, 2, No. 1.

stimulus-response process but as a process of *perceptual organization* or *reorganization*. Learning always involves insight, he says, and insight is a perceptual process. Thus Lewin, together with the gestalt psychologists, represents what Spence[45] calls the sign-significate theories of learning in contradistinction to the stimulus-response theories (cf. Chap. 15).

Lewin shares with the gestalt psychologists the idea that learning is basically perception and insight is a process of structuring or restructuring the perceived area. The structure of a region as perceived by an individual is the "cognitive structure." Learning is behavior, i.e., a locomotion from one region into another. When a person changes his position from one region to another, the structure of his life space undergoes a change. The same holds true of locomotion in learning. Learning and insight "can always be viewed as a change in the cognitive structure of the situation. It frequently includes differentiating and restructuring in the sense of separating certain regions which have been connected and connecting regions which have been separated."[46]

Thus perception is the main issue in Lewin's theory. One has to admit that gestalt and field theories have raised an important issue which has been either overlooked or at least insufficiently clarified by other theories of learning. What is the relation of learning to perception? Is any perception learning or any learning perception, as Lewin suggests? Obviously these problems are far from being solved (cf. Chap. 15).

Lewin distinguishes four types of learning: (1) learning as a change in knowledge, i.e., in the cognitive structure; (2) learning as a change in motivation, i.e., in valences and values; (3) learning as acquisition of skills by voluntary control of the body musculature; and (4) learning as a change in group belonging or ideology, i.e., learning as a process of acculturation.[47]

Learning as a change in knowledge is basically a process of differentiation of a formerly unstructured area. What has been unclear, diffuse, and unstructured becomes differentiated, specific, divided into subregions, and connected by paths.

Learning may involve another type of change in the cognitive structure, and not necessarily the "subdividing of regions into smaller units." Learning may take place through *any* change in the cognitive structure of the psychological field, such as connections and disconnections, differentiations and dedifferentiations. Any change in the meaning of a word or of a situation means learning; thus any perception or any change in perception is learning. During childhood time perspective undergoes considerable

[45] Kenneth W. Spence, "Theoretical Interpretations of Learning," in S. S. Stevens (ed.), *Handbook of Experimental Psychology*, Wiley, 1951.

[46] Kurt Lewin, "Behavior and Development as a Function of Total Situation," in L. Carmichael (ed.), *Manual of Child Psychology*, Wiley, 1946, p. 804.

[47] Kurt Lewin, "Field Theory of Learning," *Forty-First Yearbook of the National Society for the Study of Education*, 1942, 41 (Part II), 215-242.

change and becomes enlarged. The child learns to distinguish between reality and unreality levels of the life space (whereas the little child does not discern between daydreams and reality).

Lewin criticizes the use of repetition in learning. As Karsten proved, too many repetitions may lead to satiation, which may result in dedifferentiation of the field and unlearning. All changes in the cognitive structure are produced by forces, either acting in the field itself or resulting from the needs, valences, and hopes of the individual. All intellectual processes are influenced by the goals of a person; therefore repetition without a goal may lead to unlearning. Change in valences and attitudes is another kind of learning. The valence of an activity, says Lewin, depends partly on its meaning and therefore on the cognitive structure of the psychological field. Studies on food preferences have shown that dislike for a food can be easily changed by attaching a new meaning to it, e.g., by telling a story in which the disliked food is much liked by the hero of the story. Any change of motivation is a change either in the needs of a person or in the means of their satisfaction; obviously it is some sort of learning too.

Level of aspiration is an important factor in learning. Level of aspiration depends both on the potentialities of an individual and on the influences of the group to which he belongs. Too high or too low a level of aspiration discourages learning, but one can learn to set his level of aspiration properly.

Lewin distinguishes between "learning by force" and "learning democracy." Sometimes an individual is forced into a given situation, and then he may adjust himself. Learning by punishment is an enforced learning that narrows down the space of free movement and produces a sort of prison-like situation. In reward the individual is permitted more freedom than in punishment but all the ways to reward are blocked "save the disliked but requested activity." Learning by punishment always involves enforcement and "policing" to prevent the individual from avoiding punishment and to preclude his escape from the field.

5. THEORY OF PERSONALITY

Personality as a System of Regions

Personality can be represented as a region or a group of regions. It cannot be represented in the same way as the environment, because the environment is a medium through which locomotion takes place, while a person cannot serve as a medium through which or within which locomotion is carried out.

The various regions and boundaries within a person are "dynamically interdependent." This interdependence of regions means that the state of one region is influenced by the state of another. Speaking topologically, they are "connected" regions. However, there is no "locomotion" within a person but communication only, says Lewin.

In Lewin's theory, personality plays the role of a part of a field. Person and environment together form a field. What is the person? One part of this field, perhaps the central part of it, which does not serve for locomotion but may change its place as a whole.

Does this presentation satisfy the psychologist's need for explanation? Lewin believes so. He maintains that from this kind of conceptualization or representation of a personality as a region or a system of regions within a field, relevant acts can be predicted. Consider the difference between the outer, inner, and innermost regions within the personality; the Freudian problem of regression can be interpreted as dedifferentiation of the regions of personality. Though this method of interpretation ignores many problems, it should be considered an earnest effort made by Lewin to escape Stern's dualism of "person" and "thing" (cf. Chap. 11). Lewin's theory permits one to interpret personality as *"unitas multiplex,"* since personality can be represented either as one region or as a system of regions.

"It is always necessary," Lewin says, "to represent both person and environment in the life space. We also have mentioned that one has to distinguish within the person certain strata and regions. For certain problems, however, one can represent the person in a first approximation as a point, for the following reason: The person is a strongly unified whole. When we are not dealing with the dynamic differentiation of the person into past regions, we can consider the person as a single system and can represent it as an undifferentiated region or as a point in the sense explained above. One can use such a representation especially in cases that concern the locomotion of a person as a whole. For more exact representation one will always have to show the person as a differentiated region."[48]

Inner and Outer Regions

In the analysis of personality structure Lewin follows the gestalt pattern. The person is represented as a "connected region" (or system of regions) divided into part-regions and separated from the environment by a Jordan curve. Some of the regions are "inner," some are outer; the outer regions are motor-perceptual, analogous to the division suggested by Koffka (Chap. 12).

There are difficulties in distinguishing between the inner-personal system of regions and the motor-perceptual system, e.g., the understanding of speech may be considered as taking place in either zone. Additional

[48] Lewin, *Principles of Topological Psychology*, p. 113.

difficulties are encountered in distinguishing between the perceptual regions and the motor regions within the boundary zone, since, e.g., the eye serves both as a perception and as a motor (expression) region.

In the motor-perceptual boundary zone the more "peripheral" regions should be distinguished from the "central" ones. The motor system, says Lewin, can be "dynamically connected" to one inner zone only, serve only one inner region at a time. In other words, when personality is involved in a given activity, other activities are excluded. When one fights, for example, his entire personality is directed toward his motor activities, and any other motor activity must stop.[49]

The inner regions of personality can be divided into peripheral and central regions. The central regions have less communication with the environment. This distinction seems to result from Karsten's and Dembo's studies on satiation and anger. Karsten[50] proved that the more central the involved regions are, the more quickly they are satiated. Dembo[51] showed that the peripheral zones of personality respond more easily to anger-provoking stimuli because they are closer to the motor zone and the overt expression of anger comes readily. When the inner strata are touched they seldom respond with overt anger, since there is no direct connection between them and the motor zone.

In emotional tension people tend to impose on themselves more self-control, i.e., to strengthen the boundaries between the peripheral and motor regions in order to avoid an immediate outburst of emotions. The central regions tend to unite under emotional strain, which compresses the entire inner region and makes it less differentiated and the individual behaves in a less mature manner. People under great emotional tension regress and become more primitive. When the tension within the inner regions becomes unbearable, emotions may break through the barriers, sweep the motor regions, and cause overt and sometimes violent physical motion, says Lewin.

Lewin believes that his theory of emotion within the framework of topology enables one to solve most empirical problems. Emotions are tensions within the inner regions; control of emotions depends on the strength of interregional walls. All emotions are expressed by locomotion but not all emotions act in the same way. Joy, for instance, weakens the boundaries between the inner and the motor regions, thus facilitating an overt expression. Sorrow acts in the opposite direction. Powerful emotions destroy the inner boundaries, reduce the number of regions, and lead to dedifferentiation of the total personality system.

[49] This statement recalls Cannon's studies on emotions and Gardner Murphy's principle of dominance.
[50] Karsten, *op. cit.*
[51] Dembo, *op. cit.*

Personality Types

There are considerable differences in personality structure of various persons. A child's personality is less differentiated and less integrated than that of an adult.

Lewin does not advise comparison of the number of regions, because what may give the impression of being one homogeneous region may turn out, on closer analysis, to be more than one. The dynamic unity of a region does not prejudge the degree of differentiation.

The degree of "wholeness" in the child is greater than that in the adult. "A change of one part of the system in the child usually influences all other parts to a much greater extent than in the adult," says Lewin,[52] and the relative separateness of the regions is smaller in the child than in the adult. A person is "harmonious" if the various part-regions are balanced. If some regions are poorly connected or isolated, a person is mentally disturbed.

"The degree of primitiveness of behavior," says Lewin, "seems to be a good symptom of the degree of differentiation of a person. Also the achievement of a person in an intelligence test seems to depend above all on the degree of differentiation of the person, or at least on the differentiation of certain part regions."[53] Stress may bring dedifferentiation of the whole personality, thus lowering the mental level of behavior.

Certain regions within a person may play more important roles than others. They may shift in accordance with the pressure of environmental forces. Usually the new (young) regions are more flexible than the old ones and less resistant to change. Consistency in behavior depends on the older regions and their relative strength. Lewin distinguishes various types of personality which developed as a result of environmental influences, e.g., the German personality type is a "closed" type as compared to the American "open" type (see section 6 of this chapter).

Differentiation and Dedifferentiation

The life space of the neonate is an undifferentiated field. As the child grows his life space becomes more and more differentiated, for perception and learning areas hitherto inaccessible or unshaped become structuralized and differentiated. There is a differentiation of needs which can be represented as an increase in differentiation of inner regions. Development is differentiation of both inner and outer regions of personality and of the total life space as well.

The child's life space contains many inaccessible regions and the space

---

[52] Lewin, *Principles of Topological Psychology*, p. 183.
[53] Lewin, *Dynamic Theory of Personality*, p. 207.

of free movement is rather limited. As the child grows, more areas become accessible (e.g., play forbidden to little children is now permitted), but certain areas close down.

Lewin has proved experimentally that frustration leads to regression. A group of five children were carefully observed to determine their level of constructive playing with toys. The average mental age of the children was fifty-five months. Lewin, Barker, and Dembo let the children play with some toys and rated the level of constructiveness.[54] The use of a toy telephone for conversation apparently indicated a considerable degree of constructiveness. Then the children were shown very interesting new toys and were permitted to play with them for a brief time. After a few minutes the new toys were taken away. Undoubtedly the children felt badly frustrated. When brought back to the old toys, the children did not continue to play in a constructive manner in accordance with their mental age but regressed seventeen months on the average and struck the telephone, scribbled with the pencils, etc. Frustration, Lewin concludes, leads to regression. The differentiated regions of personality become dedifferentiated and less mature.

Personality and Environment

No student of personality has ever denied the importance of environment and the impact of changing situations. Surely personality undergoes changes, and various devices have been invented in order to account for both the continuity and the changeability of human nature. However, Lewin seems to deal with changeability only. "If the life space is a totality of possible events, then 'things' that enter the situation, especially the person himself and psychological 'objects,' have to be characterized by their relationship to possible events."[55]

Sociologically minded psychologists would say: a person is the product of environmental influences and of some hereditary factors. After the environmental forces have been active for a time, they have had some influence on the individual. When the individual comes to face a new situation, this new situation probably modifies, to a certain extent at least, his way of behaving. But there are already some established ways of behavior which may or may not be modified by the new situation. In Lewin's terminology this would mean that a "thing" entering the situation will behave in accordance with its own nature. Obviously this is a "class theory" statement which cannot be accepted by field theorists.

In Lewin's description the personality per se seems almost to disappear. The behavior of an individual is a product of interrelationships.

[54] Roger Barker, Tamara Dembo, and Kurt Lewin, "Frustration and Regression: an Experiment with Young Children," *University of Iowa Studies in Child Welfare,* 1941, 18, 1–314.

[55] Lewin, *Principles of Topological Psychology,* p. 16.

Various objects in one's psychological field invite him to do certain things or not to. However, these valences and their strength and distribution are "properties of the environment" and not of the person. A person's needs are "tensions" or disequilibrium between him and his environment.

Only overt and manifest behavior like locomotion or communication caused by attraction or repulsion seems to be considered by Lewin. The interplay between person and environment is the only way to study personality. The functions of the inner and outer layers of personality cannot be dealt with outside the context of the personality-environment field.[56]

6. GROUP DYNAMICS

Principle of Transfiguration

Lewin's studies in social psychology are usually referred to as "group dynamics." In this area Lewin has achieved most success and prominence. The outstanding feature of his social psychology is the application to group behavior of concepts borrowed from the psychology of the individual. Apparently Lewin does not subscribe to the concept of group mind, but he strives to introduce a substitute term for it. He feels pretty strongly that a group is a unit which has to be analyzed as a whole rather than as an aggregate of individuals.

Lewin applies the gestalt principle of transfiguration to the study of small groups. He says: "To the psychologist who has observed the historical development of the concept of 'whole' or Gestalt in psychology, most of the argumentation about the group mind sounds strangely familiar. It took psychology many steps before it discovered that a dynamic whole has properties which are different from the properties of their parts or from the sum of their parts." Therefore, "whatever has been of scientific value in the concept of group mind resolves itself into the concrete and familiar problems of dynamic wholes in sociology and social psychology."[57]

The individual and his environment form a psychological field. Similarly, the group and the environment of the group form a "social field." Lewin explains this as follows: "A basic tool for the analysis of group life is the representation of the group and its setting as 'a social field.' This means that the social happening is viewed as occurring in, and being the result of, the totality of coexisting social entities, such as groups, subgroups, members, barriers, channels of communication, etc. One of the fundamental characteristics of this field is the relative position of the

[56] It is worth while to compare Sullivan's theory (Chap. 9) to Lewin's. Sullivan seems to be influenced by Lewin.

[57] Lewin, *Field Theory in Social Science*, p. 146.

entities, which are parts of the field."[58] The structure, the possible loco-motions, and the distribution of forces within the field are the decisive factors in group behavior.

This analogy between group psychology and individual psychology is the first principle of Lewin's group dynamics. The mutual position of regions within a person's field and the forces acting there are the decisive factors in a person's behavior. The very same statement applies to group behavior provided the term "person" is replaced by the term "group."

The second outstanding feature of Lewin's approach to the study of groups is the issue of causation. Most psychologists trace behavior to factors in time and seek the causal antecedents to a given situation. What happened before is usually the cause of what happens afterwards. Lewin sticks consistently to his "systematic causation" in regard to group be-havior, too. He considers group behavior as a function of the total situa-tion. The social-field-at-a-given-time offers the entire interpretation of group behavior. Simultaneous interrelationships are causal relationships, and group behavior can be causally derived from the totality of coexist-ing factors, Lewin says.

The third principle in Lewin's theory of group behavior lies in the ap-plication of topological and vector concepts to the group in close analogy to the topological and vector psychology of the individual. Regions, boundaries, barriers, forces, valences, etc., are applied to groups with no reservation whatsoever.

Forces Within the Group

There has been some confusion in the definition of group. Group has been defined as a number of individuals who share some common traits, or have some common norms, or other similarities.

Lewin distinguishes between class and group. People who have the same or similar traits can be classified as belonging to the same category or class. Similarity in traits or even goals is not a prerequisite of a group.

Group are characterized by "dynamic interdependence" of their mem-bers. This means that the state and actions of each member depend on the state and actions of other members. A group can be best represented as a system of connected regions or as a differentiated region. A person's status within the group can be topologically represented as the position of his region as related to other regions (members) of the group. This dynamic interdependence of regions (members) within a group re-sembles the dynamic interdependence of the respective regions within a person.

Each group is exposed to cohesive and disruptive forces. The dis-

[58] *Ibid.*, p. 200.

ruptive forces may result from (1) too strong barriers between the members of the group that hamper communication within the group or (2) conflict of the individual's goals with those of the group.[59]

Each group is a field of forces. Individuals are attracted to or repelled from a group depending on the kind of valence the group represents to them. Interaction and communication within a group depend on the mutual position of its regions, which represent the respective group members, the barriers between the members, etc. The "we-feeling" of a group is represented as a force corresponding to the needs of the group as a whole. Cohesiveness of a group depends on the relationship between the forces that attract the members and the forces that repel or disrupt. If a group is in a position to satisfy the needs of its members, it has a positive valence, the term "valence" being used in the same connotation as in the psychology of an individual.

Morale of an individual and of a group depends on "time perspective." It is related to the hope that "sometime in the future the real situation will be changed so that it will equal my wishes." Hope means similarity between the level of expectation and the irreality level of wishes. "Tenacity in the face of adversity is the most unequivocal index of high morale. Group morale depends on 'time perspective,'" says Lewin.[60]

Social Climate, Leadership, and Group Decision

Lewin, Lippitt, and White[61] conducted experiments in "social climate." They established two children's clubs and induced in each of them a "social climate" of democracy and autocracy respectively. Later on they developed three "climates," namely, democracy, autocracy, and laissez-faireism.

Each group was composed of five children equated in regard to age, intelligence, and physical and socioeconomic status, with proper consideration given to balanced social relations within the groups. The behavior of each group was determined by specially trained leaders. The "democratic" leader cooperated with group members and encouraged group discussion and decision. The "autocratic" leader made all decisions himself and gave orders to group members. The laissez-faire leader remained passive, allowing the children to do whatever they pleased. The "social climate" of each group was actually created by its leader. In the

[59] John R. P. French, "The Disruption and Cohesion of Groups," *Journal of Abnormal and Social Psychology*, 1941, **36**, 361–377.

[60] Kurt Lewin, *Resolving Social Conflicts* (G. W. Lewin, ed.), Harper, 1948, p. 105.

[61] Ronald Lippitt, "An Experimental Study of the Effect of Democratic and Authoritarian Group Atmospheres," *Iowa University Studies in Child Welfare*, 1940, **16**, 44–195; Benjamin B. Wolman, "Education and Leadership," *Teachers College Record*, 1958, **59**, 465–473.

democratic group children were friendly to one another. The feeling of group belongingness was stronger in the democratic than in the autocratic club. The democratic group as a whole had greater potency, and children in that group were less aggressive toward each other. In the authoritarian group the children were rather aggressive; they attacked one child and this "scapegoat" had to leave the group. The laissez-faire social climate was introduced by a leader who let the children do whatever they pleased, himself offering very little encouragement and guidance. The cohesiveness of this group was quite low and its efficiency limited.

The main idea of the experiment was that group behavior depends on a social climate which can be artificially induced by the leader. The same idea has been applied by Lewin and his associates in several other settings.

Lewin also conducted experiments in group decision.[62] In one of them he tried to change deeply established food habits. Two methods were used: lecturing and group discussion. A follow-up study showed that only 3 per cent of the housewives participating in the lecture group shifted to the new kind of food as compared to 32 percent who changed food habits as a result of group discussion.

Similar results have been obtained with rural mothers in a maternity hospital. Twenty percent of the mothers who were approached individually by the nutritionist about the value of feeding their infants cod-liver oil followed the instruction, as a follow-up study two weeks later proved. The mothers who received the same information in a group, discussed it, and decided to follow it gave better results; 45 percent of them were feeding the infants cod-liver oil.

Lewin interpreted his findings with the help of two factors. First, group pressures do not permit easy change in habits. It is much easier to change a habit if the entire group participates. Second, group discussion activates the group members and more forces are made available for a change in behavior.

Intergroup Relations

Lewin applies topology to studies of intergroup relations and ethnic tensions and represents each group as a region. A minority group in a given country may live as a closed group or it may be scattered all over the country. In the first case minority group A corresponds to a connected limited region within enclosing region B. In the second case the scattered group is topologically a nonconnected region.[63]

[62] Kurt Lewin, "Group Decision and Social Change," in T. Newcomb and E. Hartley (eds.), *Readings in Social Psychology*, Holt, 1947.

[63] Kurt Lewin, "Psycho-Social Problems of a Minority Group," *Character and Personality*, 1935, 3, 175–187.

Lewin exemplifies his theory by the history of Jews. The ghettos formed a connected limited region within the enclosing region of the Gentile world. Jews came in contact with one another, without having "much contact with the rest of the population." The abolishment of ghettos necessarily changed the topological structure of the Jewish minority, making them a scattered group and a nonconnected region. Quite a bit of Jewish security feeling and cohesiveness was lost in the new situation.

Lewin distinguishes communication from locomotion. Locomotion must be represented as a path, while communication is considered a region or a part of it. Though communication between the various parts of the Jewish population was not impaired much, locomotion and interaction were hampered.

Minority groups enjoy less freedom of movement than the majority group. Several regions or areas of activity are restricted and barriers of prejudice and discrimination prevent free movement. Thus, minority groups suffering from restriction of their "space of free movement" may become aggressive. Similarly, this applies to children or adolescents whose space of free movement has been restricted by powerful adults.

Social relations are not stationary; Lewin calls them "quasi-stationary" processes. For example, a degree of discrimination against a minority group indicates the interaction between two parts of a population. Certain social forces move toward more discrimination, while other forces may oppose it. A change in the quasi-stationary equilibriums may mean a change from the present level to the desired one, and this is how research and action can be combined. Lewin has always stressed that action requires a sound theory for action, and theory should be applicable to action. Once the social psychologist understands the forces which cause intergroup tensions, he can by manipulating them alleviate the tension or even remove it. Lewin was very optimistic concerning the role social psychology might play in human relations.

Human attitudes and beliefs are a product of belonging to a group and sharing its social norms. These beliefs once established are quite consistent and it is almost impossible to influence an individual's mind unless a proper change in the social climate of his group takes place.

Therefore, the reeducation of a nation (Lewin meant the de-Nazification of Germany) requires deep changes in the social norms of the entire nation. "It is obviously hopeless to change the cultural patterns of millions of people by treating them individually," says Lewin. "Fortunately, the methods generally called 'group work' permit reaching whole groups of individuals at once and, at the same time, seem actually to be more efficient in bringing about deep changes than the individual approach is."[64] An individual is more likely to accept new norms and patterns of behavior if this change encompasses his group as a whole and the new

[64] Lewin, *Resolving Social Conflicts*, pp. 40–41.

values and patterns do not jeopardize his group belongingness. The experiments on group decision mentioned above fully corroborate this hypothesis of a change in beliefs produced by influencing an entire group, Lewin says.

Personality and Culture

Personality changes with the change of the position of regions and other interrelations within the life space. Life space includes person and environment, and social factors form a substantial part of the environment and of the total life space of a person.

An individual is exposed to pressures of external forces and inner tensions resulting from a disequilibrium between himself and his environment. The kind of tensions produced by forces stemming from the social environment are of utmost importance for the development of the personality. Too strong pressures, as stated above, may compress the regions of personality and reduce their number. The structure of one's life space is highly dependent on these social forces, and since different cultures activate different kinds of pressures, one should conclude that personality type depends on culture.

Child-rearing practices represent social forces that mold personality. Each stage in child development represents a restructuring of the life space. "The change from the group of children to that of the adults is a shift to a more or less unknown position. Psychologically, it is equivalent to entering an unknown region, comparable to coming into a new town," says Lewin.[65] The child's "space of free movement" can be represented as a topological region surrounded by inaccessible regions. The barriers are either the child's inability to enter these regions or the prohibitions from entering them imposed by parents.

Adolescents belong to an overlapping region of children and adults. They do not wish to belong to the children group, but they are not accepted in the adult groups. They are "marginal men" and, like all marginal men, are insecure, unstable, and hypersensitive.

The space of free movement allowed to a child varies from one culture to another. In pre-Nazi Germany this space was much narrower than it is in the United States. The differences in child-rearing methods have necessarily produced considerable differences in national characteristics. The German type of personality is more closed, less sociable, less inclined to informal and casual human relations than is the American personality type.

[65] Lewin, *Field Theory in Social Science*, p. 137.

7. FIELD THEORY AS AN EXPERIMENT IN THEORY CONSTRUCTION

The Issue of Conceptualization

Lewin's field theory requires additional study from the angle of theory construction. His theory is undoubtedly a major contribution to psychological thought and especially to its top-level theory construction. Lewin never tried to cover the entire field of psychological research, nor did he develop a full-fledged "system" like, e.g., Freud's. What he had in mind was a system of very general concepts from which the psychological empirical data could be derived by means of logical manipulation.

Undoubtedly this is a legitimate procedure, and Lewin's theory offers a challenging example of theory construction. His method is hypothetico-deductive, like Hull's (cf. Chap. 4), but it is different from Hull's in the fundamental principles of theory construction.

Lewin's method of theory construction can be summarized briefly as follows: Theory is a system of concepts. These concepts are not classificatory but constructive and represent psychological reality as it is, including each individual and specific case. Representation of reality is the task of scientific theory in psychology. Lewin did not escape the pitfalls of this reasoning. He was not aware of the fact that conceptualization means classification; any time Lewin or his disciples talk about regions or boundaries they do not talk about a given field but apply to a given situation some general concepts or categories. Lewin included a given situation in a *class* or category of similar situations to which it belongs. This procedure is contradictory to Lewin's bias against class theory, but any conceptualized system such as mathematics or syntax operates with generalized terms or concepts, and mathematics and syntax are class theories. Conceptualization means classification, since any concept is a logical procedure of giving a common *name* to one or more bodies, events, symbols, etc., by which any other body or symbol called by the same name is a member in the same class. Any object "belongs" to *several* classes owing to certain similarities or identical elements; classification may be more or less conducive to developing knowledge, but any system of knowledge starts with grouping similar objects into classes and creating general concepts.

This is the *nominalist* notion of concept. Surely Lewin and other contemporary psychologists would not subscribe to the *realist* notion of concepts, which attaches separate and independent existence to general concepts like the idea of speed, the idea of warmth, etc.—independently, that is, from all given and empirically perceived speeds, temperatures, etc. Speed and warmth are general concepts derived from phenomena grouped together under a common name. Obviously psychologists operate with concepts derived from empirical observations by the means of abstraction, generalization, and formation of *classes*. These concepts serve as the common names for all objects included in the class, and the various objects are *designates* of the common name or concept.

Lewin's conceptualization is self-contradictory. To be consistent, he should have denied the existence of any psychological laws at all, since each situation contains everything. Actually he generalizes, and puts similar situations like "punishment," "regression," "tension" under a common heading, whereas he should have discussed the punishment of a certain child, regression in a given personality, or tension in a particular organism.

Conceptualization is abstraction, generalization, and classification and nothing else. In the early stages of scientific development this was regarded as the scientific procedure. Surely it is one of the first steps of scientific inquiry, because scientic research tries to see the general despite the particular and to grasp the general law despite the unique cases (see Chap. 14).

Lewin opposes the Aristotelian notion of classification based on external appearance. In his paper on Aristotle, Lewin states that "these classifications lose their importance" and today we seek "to classify the whole field on the basis of other, essentially functional differences."[66] This is exactly what is taking place in all sciences, and Lewin is aware of it. Unfortunately in his later writings Lewin seems to have lost this conception and to have given up the idea of any classification at all.

The "revolt" against Aristotle is oversimplified by Lewin. Aristotle's concept formation was corrected by Galileo but not rejected. In the course of scientific inquiry more economic and more valuable classifications have been introduced. In botany, e.g., instead of division of plants into trees, bushes, and flowers, a division has been introduced based on genetic laws. The new division is not a denial of classification nor is it field-theoretical. It is simply more convenient methodologically because it enables us to discover some valid relationships between the objects of study and facilitates new and promising abstractions, generalizations, and classifications. No one can say that Aristotelian division was "false"; it was uneconomical because it left some gaps and overlaps and it was rather futile because it did not help to discover the relevant causal factors. This is why Aristotelian classifications have been abandoned and replaced by more scientific classifications. However, the most important Aristotelian contention, which says that no single object has any meaning whatsoever unless referred to "an abstract term applicable to other individuals," is still valid.[67]

The other pitfall in Lewin's method of theory construction is his belief

[66] Lewin, *Dynamic Theory of Personality*, p. 5.
[67] Cf. Morris R. Cohen, *Reason and Nature*, Harcourt, Brace, 1931, p. 13.

that presentation equals interpretation. Lewin has probably been misled by the shift in physics from the search for the "nature" of things to a more functional approach. Instead of seeking in vain for the "true nature" of fire, scientists know fairly well about the processes that take place within the observable phenomenon of fire.

Lewin interpreted this shift as if representation meant interpretation. Representation, like the shift from the phenotypes to the genotypes, may be a useful step in theory construction and sometimes it offers a better and more convenient setup for derivation of the causal relationship. However, presentation per se is never a theory; it is, if properly done, a step leading toward the theory but not the theory itself.

Field as a Construct in Psychology

"*The psychological field,*" explains J. F. Brown,[68] "is a *space* construct to which descriptions of psychological behavior may be ordered. Space is a *manifold* in which *positional relationships* may be expressed. In general the manifold may be *continuous* or *discrete,* and position may be defined in terms of *distance* and *direction* as in *Euclidean* space or only in terms of relation as in *topological* space." "In the language of constructs, there is a vector in the psychological field, activating the rat (man) towards the goal (cheese or the solution of the problem). Both the organism and goal are to be ordered to positions in the psychological field. . . . The value of this vector depends on its position in the field. . . . But the magnitude which must be assigned to position within the psychological field is non-metricized. *Point values in the psychological field are not yet metricized in character while those in physical fields are metricized.*"

"Not yet," says Brown. "Certainly at the present time," says Lewin, "there are no metrical determinations available concerning psychological life space. . . . not only the concept of distance but also that of direction goes beyond purely topological determinations. As a matter of fact the determination of directions in the psychological life space is as difficult as that of distance."

Is "field" a convenient construct in psychology? Lewin answers that psychological theory is a system of concepts which determine causal relationships. Causal relationships in human behavior must include both general laws and individual cases, and encompass both person and environment. Field theory and no other theory can meet these requirements.

Two problems are brought together here. Lewin could never rid himself of the dichotomy postulated by Windelband. Lewin never realized that all phenomena are idiophenomena and in spite of this, science deals

[68] Brown, "On the Use of Mathematics in Psychological Theory," *Psychometrika,* 1936, 1, 7–15, 77–90.

with abstraction and generalization; there is no need for special techniques to deal with special cases.

The second problem is personality versus environment. Undoubtedly one cannot give a full account of a person's behavior without considering environment. However, Lewin never brought any evidence to deny the fact that each individual has certain abilities and personality traits due to heredity and not to environment; and there is no reason not to deal with human behavior as the result of interaction between heredity and environment.

Lewin feels that the use of the field theory in psychology is justified by the nature of psychological phenomena and field phenomena. But how does Lewin know that this is precisely the nature of psychological happenings? His theory is a logical conclusion drawn from this assumption. Yet he has never brought any evidence to that effect and actually he begs the principle. Surely he could have made any hypothetical assumption, but this should have been made explicit. He could say, e.g., that psychological phenomena are idiophenomena. That kind of statement in an empirical science requires either empirical proof or methodological approval. Empirical proof could follow a pattern such as this: Suppose such-and-such is the nature of psychological phenomena; then come series of observations, experimentations, or other truth-discovering procedures; finally comes the conclusion that our hypothetical statement has been verified or at least strongly supported by our investigation and therefore may be accepted in our system. Unfortunately, Lewin assumes that on the basis of language usages like "approaching," "striving," etc., psychological phenomena are field-theoretical, and he concludes that field theory is best suited to deal with these phenomena.

Psychological field has already two connotations in the gestalt theory. One is the reality as perceived by the individual; the other is the brain and the environment, called sometimes the dynamic field and other times a psychological field. The first connotation is *perceptual* only, while the latter forms a part of the reductionist notion of mind (mind as a field) introduced by gestalt psychologists (see Chap. 12).

Kurt Lewin added his own interpretation. Psychological field means "a totality of coexisting facts." This is usually identified with life space, which means the total sum of possible activities of an individual. The two notions, though similar, are by no means identical. If psychological field is defined as a field which includes all facts that have effect upon an individual, there should be no objection to having such a term, but this term may prove of little use, for it may include practically everything.

The conception of a "psychological field at a given time" may lead to some difficulties, because a given time may be a small fraction of time. Lewin is aware of this danger of breaking behavior into microcosmic units, and he sets arbitrarily "sufficient units of time"; which is not too precise a statement. The criticism of Lewin's "historical approach" was raised by Gardner Murphy. "Let the time on the chronoscope gradually reduce to zero and try to imagine just what is 'going on' in the organism in zero duration. Indeed, the typical Lewinian experiments, . . . deal with transformations in time, as must all experiments on the functions of living individuals. Moreover, the difference between short time and long time durations can scarcely be elevated to a position of such tremendous importance."[69]

Lewin says that the level of aspiration is "influenced by the ability of the individual." But what exists before: abilities or the level of aspiration? Obviously the level of aspiration is a result in the measuring of "historical causality" so much disliked by Lewin. However, how can Lewin admit the term "ability"? How can ability be squeezed into life space or field-at-a-given-time?

At best, field theory can operate with momentary and overt actions in an ultra-behavioristic manner. Innate capacities or acquired abilities, drives and motivational patterns, all of which exist persistently and evidence themselves in the constancies of human behavior, cannot be reached by a field theory.

Lewin's Mathematics

Lewin tried to fit psychology into geometry. It was a difficult and ungrateful task. Human behavior does not fit into Euclidean geometry or the Riemannian system. Lewin tried topology; he did not know much about it and was aware that he was using not too convenient a tool, as he wrote: "The mathematical concepts allow us to distinguish only connected and nonconnected regions. In terms of topology there are no transitional cases. Dynamically, however, there are doubtless transitions between completely dependent and completely independent regions."[70] The main difficulties arise out of the difference between mathematical "boundary" and psychological "barrier." The issue of personality represented as a system of regions creates additional difficulties in topology. Are the various regions that form personality independent regions or the subparts of one region?

Lewin knew very well that often one had to make arbitrary decisions while trying to adjust psychological (dynamic) facts to mathematical concepts of the topological system. Moreover, one of the most important features in Lewin's psychology, the concept of direction, is left out by topology. "Although topological principles are necessary, in themselves, they are not sufficient to determine directions," Lewin wrote, and felt

[69] Gardner Murphy, *Historical Introduction to Modern Psychology* (rev. ed.), Harcourt, Brace, 1949, p. 305.
[70] Lewin, *Principles of Topological Psychology,* p. 173.

compelled to introduce a new mathematical system, "hodology." Lewin admitted that he was not a mathematician and did not "axiomatize" his geometry. He hoped, however, that this "could well be done later on by a more competent mathematician."

But this has not been done and perhaps cannot be done. At any rate, how can one "explain" psychological data by a vague and not elaborated proposal for a mathematical system? "The purpose of hodological space is to find," says Lewin, "a type of geometry which permits us to use the concept of direction in a manner which will correspond essentially with the meaning that direction has in psychology."

But the concept "direction" in psychology has to be interpreted or derived from mathematical constructs. These mathematical constructs have to be introduced as a part of a mathematical system. They cannot be found in any of the existing mathematical systems. Lewin knew that they had to be defined and axiomatized by a competent mathematician, and all this has not been done. In the meanwhile, he has developed a psychological system based on these nonexistent yet mathematical foundations.

Lewin may be considered a victim of his love for mathematics. His was a creative mind, unusually productive, ingenious, alert, and stimulating. His works contain virtually hundreds of daring and challenging ideas about relations between perception and motivation, regression and dedifferentiation, level of aspiration and satisfaction, group decision and change of social norms, etc. His experimental techniques are ingenious, thought provoking, and realistic, and pave the road for new research.

Yet one is tempted to raise the question: What is the relationship between the tremendous experimental work done by Lewin and his disciples and Lewin's theory? Most of Lewin's findings about level of aspiration, group dynamics, regression, recall in tension, satiation, etc., could be easily interpreted without topology.

In fact, topology has imposed heavy and unnecessary restrictions on Lewin's studies. Wherever he tried to force his findings into the narrow frames of topology, he did injustice to himself and impaired his own work. Neither Lewin nor his associates ever made any mathematical operations with the topological or hodological systems. At best, topological and vector symbols were used as a *means* of communication, and even this in some kind of private language which shortens good English words and makes them understandable to a limited number of interested followers. Lewin's mathematics is merely a system of symbols, not real mathematics, since there are no rules as to how these symbols can be manipulated in any of the arithmetic or algebraic operations. Lewin did not go beyond the stage of definitions and graphic presentation of his system and did not establish rules for mathematical operations with his symbols. Therefore, his mathematics can hardly be called mathematics at all.

At any rate, even the best-elaborated system of symbols such as a language or mathematics serves for the presentation and communication of truth; it does not discover any truth and cannot be regarded as a scientific theory.

Systematic Causality

Lewin has suggested the distinction between two types of causality, neither being causality in any of the accepted terms. Any definition of causality includes at least two phenomena, sequence in time, called by John Stuart Mill "the unconditional, unvariable antecedent," and result, the "invariable, certain and unconditional sequence." Spinoza has defined causality as follows: "*Ex data causa determinata necessario sequitur effectus, et contra si nulla detur determinata causa, impossibile est, ut effectus sequetur.*"[71] ("Effect follows a given determined cause; it is impossible for an effect to follow if there is no such a determined cause.")

In the long and eventful history of the concept of causality, it has been generally agreed that causality is some kind of temporal sequence. The controversial issue was whether causality involves anything else besides this sequence, and if it does, what does that additional factor involve? David Hume fought against causality because he felt that all we know is the temporal sequence only, and there is no reason or evidence to assume anything besides this sequence in time (*post hoc* but not *propter hoc*).

In modern physics the usability of causality has been challenged. In microcosmic physics the issue has been raised whether causality retains its usefulness in view of the quantum theory. In all the discussions centering around causality, causation is considered a peculiar type of sequence in time which may or may not enable us to make predictions.[72]

Lewin believed that representation of a given situation plus application of proper laws is "systematic causation" "which permits the derivation of next phenomena, while the historical causality gives an account of what happened but once."

No causal studies fit into Lewin's second category of just telling about the past, nor in the first category, which "refers to types and to laws in which there are no dates."

All causal studies deal with phenomena which have place and date, insofar as they deal with *individual causation*, which happened once,

---

[71] Benedictus Spinoza, *Ethica*, I, axiom 3.
[72] Cf. Benjamin B. Wolman, "Chance: A Philosophical Study," *Tarbitz, Hebrew University Quarterly* (Hebrew), 1938, **10**, 56–80.

or *types* or classes of objects or events if they deal with general laws of causation. Mr. A, e.g., had a breakdown because his life history was such and such, and he suffered from too great a conflict; this is individual causation. Many people have a breakdown when their life history is a given kind and the stress is too great; this is a law of general causation which deals with a class or type of people. What Lewin suggests as a "systematic" causality is not causation but interpretation, which may or may not be causal.

Explanation or derivation is not necessarily equivalent to causality. One can use for explanation the reverse causal relation, e.g., there were clouds because later there was rain. Raining is not the cause of the clouds, but it is a good logical explanation by *implication*. Explanation is not necessarily related to time, while causality is. Explanation may be teleological, may be based on classification too.

Similarly one has to reject the identification of mathematical function with causality. Function indicates that whenever *a* changes, *b* changes and vice versa. Obviously it holds true in causality, because any causal system can be represented as a mathematical function. But not the reverse. There are many mathematical functions which are not causal— e.g., two effects from the same cause, or two factors which stand to each other in no time relation.

Lewin insists that past events cannot be a cause of present ones because the past does not exist any more, and only what exists has effects. If Lewin is right, psychological life space may be a cause of behavior of an individual but it cannot be a result of anything else, because the life space is the totality of present factors (personality and environment). Lewin does not go to this extreme and he acknowledges historical causality. "Past events can only have a position in the historical causal chains whose interweavings create the present situation."[73] And yet (on the same page) Lewin says: "Past events cannot influence present events." The difference is in approach: in the "historical" causation they can influence events, in the systematic they cannot. One wonders why two contradictory notions of the same term were used, one of them generally accepted (historical causation) and the other contradicting the general notion as well as the first one used in the same theory. Lewin defines existence by causality and causality by existence, which sounds tautological.

Lewin used the following example: He would like to know whether the floor of his attic is strong enough to support a certain weight. He may, in this case, follow two procedures. The first would be an anamnesis, or a life history. This anamnesis has to test the properties of the attic in the past and, which is more difficult, to prove that nothing unknown happened to the attic. If he has done both, and, in the case of changes,

---

[73] Lewin, *Principles of Topological Psychology,* p. 35.

if he knows the nature of the changes, he may get a satisfactory test. But a much better method of testing the strength of the floor would be to test its present situation.

This example indicates a confusion between interpretation and causation. Causation can be used as interpretation but there are other methods of interpretation besides causality. What Lewin had in mind is a diagnosis without causal studies, which is often undertaken. A Rorschach or Stanford-Binet tests the present situation and is a quite reliable diagnostic tool. However, successful therapy requires more than an analysis of the "situation-at-a-given-time." The genetic and causal factors that lie in the past are needed for understanding of the situation-at-a-given-time and, needless to say, are extremely important for the proper therapeutic procedure. In fact, without full understanding of the *etiology*, any treatment is more guesswork than scientific procedure. Scientific inquiry is not only the description or analysis of the situation-at-a-given-time, as Lewin suggested, but the assessment of the *dynamic, causal* factors that precede and cause the given situation.

Here we come to the source of the main weakness of Lewin's theory. Lewin painstakingly developed a system of concepts and constructs and initiated a series of most ingenious and important experiments. Yet his theory falls short of dynamic interpretation of behavior inasmuch as it is a field theory. Why, e.g., do groups behave differently? Why do people have different potentialities? Lewin's answer: the total situation, merely repeats the questions but offers no answer. Lewin's "situation" or "field" includes cause and effect together and does not permit causal studies that distinguish clearly between cause and effect.

Concluding Remarks

The ingenious experiments of Lewin and his pupils and associates are an important contribution to psychological research. Studies of interrupted tasks, substitution, level of aspiration, regression as a result of frustration, and group dynamics represent a weighty addition to psychological data and thought. One may ask whether these and other findings could not be established without field theory and topological and hodological systems. Certainly one can accept the validity of the experiments and utilize their findings without accepting Lewin's mathematics. It is not too difficult to incorporate Lewin's experimental heritage in the great treasury of psychological research, without considering it the logical result of or derivation from Lewin's field theory. The findings stand on their own merits, and, as many friendly critics have pointed out, Lewin's experiments may outlive his general theory.

However, Lewin's theoretical work should not be underestimated. The idea of field theory can be utilized in furthering psychological research.

Several psychologists have faced the difficulty of the cause-goal di-chotomy, e.g., Freud and Adler, Watson and McDougall. Freud and Watson postulated deterministic causality, while Adler and McDougall sought the purpose of human behavior.

Kurt Lewin's solution to the problem is remarkable. In fact, this prob-lem is already solved by Lewin's definition of behavior as locomotion caused by forces. Psychological forces could be either scalars or vectors. Obviously they are vectors; they are directed entities. Thus Lewin com-bines in vector psychology both causal and purposive interpretation.

Lewin's emphasis on the interrelationship between intellectual proc-esses and goals has opened new vistas in psychological research. Lewin tied cognitive structure to valences, or perception to motivation. All intellectual processes are determined by purposes, said Lewin, and no research in perception can overlook this point (see Chap. 15).

The theory of learning is much indebted to Lewin. His incorporation of perceptual factors in learning and his explanation of the organization factor in perception seem to have permanent value in the theory of learning.

In group dynamics Lewin was a pioneer and inventor of new and realistic research techniques. His experiments with groups in action sug-gested new possibilities for experimental work in social psychology. His slogan of uniting research and action has been extremely rewarding. Actually Lewin has done most in spotting new areas of research and new possibilities. Perhaps this contribution is more important and more valid than his efforts to create a system of psychological laws. Some critics doubt whether Lewin defined any laws or developed a full-fledged theory. "Laws," said Spence, "are statements of relations between *independently defined variables.*" Lewin's formula $B = f (P, E)$, meaning behavior is a function of person and environment, seems to overlook the problems in-volved in the usual formula $R = f (S)$.

Spence concluded: "That this field approach to the problems of psychol-ogy has been fruitful and valuable is amply supported by the experi-mental contributions it has made, although in the writer's opinion, the theoretical superstructure has played a much less significant role than is sometimes credited to it."[74]

One is tempted to compare the role of Lewin in the history of modern psychology not to that of Galileo but to that of Heraclitus in ancient philosophy. The Ionian philosophers were concerned with the nature of things, while Heraclitus maintained that the only continuum is change. This is what Lewin tried to introduce into psychology: "The center of interest shifts from *objects to processes,* from state to change of state."

---

[74] K. W. Spence, "The Nature of Theory Construction in Contemporary Psychology," *Psychological Review,* 1944, **51**, 47–68.

SUMMARY OF PART III

All the psychological systems described in the third part of the present volume faced the problems posed by Kant, Husserl, and Dilthey.

Thing vs. person was the main problem discussed by W. Stern. Content vs. act was the problem of Brentano and of Husserl. Sensory atomism vs. organization was the problem of gestalt theory. Idiophenomena vs. generalizations intrigued Lewin.

Chapter 10 deals mainly with Kant, Husserl, and Dilthey. Immanuel Kant's transcendental idealism created a grave problem for any future scientific inquiry. Psychology had to become either an "empirical" description of "mental phenomena" whose true existence could not be proved or an a priori epistemology dealing with the "transcendental subject" whose existence could be doubted.

The neo-Kantians struggled with the problems created by Kant. But obviously there is no solution to nonexisting problems. The cleavage between the "perceiving subject" and everything else created insurmountable difficulties for those psychologists who were influenced by Kant's heritage.

Brentano's and Husserl's solution offered a definite advantage over Kant's. Husserl did not question the existence of the objective world or the truthfulness of our perceptions. Yet he left unexplained why the perceiving subject, who is just a little speck of dust in comparison to the universe, should become the center of the universe.

Then came Dilthey. Dilthey's contribution has been more of a sign on a road than a paving block. His psychology is more of a hint than a statement, more of an indication of scientific needs than their satisfaction. Dilthey suggested a way out. The natural sciences have to *explain* their phenomena using hypotheses; this does not apply to psychology, which has direct access to the mental processes which are experienced (*erlebt*). The proper method of psychology is to *describe* mental life in its totality and to *understand* its aim and meaning.

Spranger's theory of personality types, which was actually a theory of types of culture (*Lebensformen*), implemented Dilthey's program. Spranger did not seek causes and effects or build a scientific system of hypotheses. Instead he

491

suggested dividing humans into six types according to their preference for abstract truth (theoretical), material achievements (economic), mysticism (religious), beauty (aesthetic), sympathy for human beings (sociable), and power (political).

Chapter 11 describes the personalistic theories of E. Spranger, W. Stern, and G. W. Allport. As said before, Spranger was the only psychologist who fully implemented Dilthey's ideas of a descriptive and understanding psychology.

Stern's work was thorough and encompassing. Stern is one of the few psychologists who developed an all-embracing system. He hoped to reconcile the two methods distinguished by Dilthey. According to Stern, personality is *unitas multiplex*. As long as we deal with the elements of this unity, we may apply the explanatory method; wherever we deal with personality as a whole, we must describe and understand.

Allport continued Stern's work with the main emphasis on unity in complexity. He developed an original theory of "mental traits" and the idea of "functional autonomy."

The first section of Chapter 12 describes several theories opposed to associationism. Some of them, especially those of Ward, Binet, and Bühler, have often been called "the European functionalism." Their functionalism resembles the American functionalism in its criticism of the atomistic molecular approach and of associationism.

The opponents to the stimulus-response theories introduced the idea of task, imageless thought, and preparatory set. A group of experimental psychologists led by Külpe and the so-called Würzburg school went even farther in the rejection of the notion that mental life was a series of reactions to series of stimuli. Thought was their main area of interest in Würzburg, and according to their school of thought, thinking was guided by a "task" and "determining tendencies."

The main part of Chapter 12 is devoted to gestalt psychology and its three great creators, Wertheimer, Köhler, and Koffka. Gestalt psychology started as an opposition to atomism and associationism. The famous experiments on motion proved beyond doubt that a series of still positions could be perceived as one continuous motion.

Additional experimental studies led to the development of a new theory of perception and learning. The organism does not react with isolated responses to isolated stimuli, but it responds as a whole to complex patterns of stimulation. These patterns organize the parts into a whole, a shape, a figure, in German a *Gestalt*.

Accordingly, learning cannot be a process of association or conditioning. It is a perceptual process of orientation in the patterns of environment. *Insight* was the new term coined by the gestaltists, and it means grasping of the gestalt of the situation, orientation in the totality of relationship, and ability to act accordingly.

While Köhler studied learning, Wertheimer devoted a great deal of time to the problems of thinking. Again the organization, the grasp of the structure of the situation, the gestalt was found to be the main factor in creative thinking.

Where does the gestalt come from? Gestalt psychologists faced an alternative: either to accept Kant's categories or Dilthey's synthetic ability of the mind and ascribe the gestalt to the perceiving mind, or to ascribe the gestalt to nature. They took an anti-Kantian stand and looked for "physical gestalts" everywhere, in inanimate and living nature.

The best model for a physical gestalt was the electromagnetic field. The human brain is not a machine but is such a field, concluded the gestaltists. Thus the organism responds with a total organized pattern of reactions to the pattern of stimuli to which it is exposed.

The next step the gestaltist had to take was to coordinate the mental and the neurological processes. The concept of *isomorphism* was the solution. Brain and behavior are two dynamic fields; the psychological field represents the neurological field in the same way as a geographic map represents a region.

Chapter 13 analyzes the field theory. Kurt Lewin took over, almost literally, the idea of the psychological field, in which the individual and his present environment are the two poles. Being well educated in philosophy and always method-conscious, he proceeded to develop a system of hypothetical constructs. His studies represent a case in sophisticated theory construction, daring and ingenious, yet much open to empirical criticism.

Lewin was more influenced by the neo-Kantians Windelband and Cassirer than by any of the gestalt theorists. He looked for a scientific method capable of dealing with idiophenomena, and his solution was highly original.

Lewin invoked Galileo vs. Aristotle, Windelband vs. Comte, non-metricized topology vs. any other mathematics, contemporaneity vs. causation, physical models of vectors vs. biological motivation. His system was never completed, his mathematics never put to a test; his ingenious experiments discovered many significant solutions, yet never offered a complete picture of his theory.

Lewin's main contribution seems to lie rather in posing penetrating questions than in offering satisfactory solutions. But his philosophical analysis of psychology as a science, his belief that to describe means to interpret, is undoubtedly a great challenge to the methodology of scientific inquiry in psychology. Thus in the present volume, which emphasizes the theoretical and systematic approach to psychology, the chapter devoted to Lewin is one of the largest.

The problems raised by Kant, Windelband, and Dilthey have been answered in various ways. Spranger, Stern, the gestalt psychologists, and the field theory accepted the challenge of Dilthey, and the discussion of Dilthey's ideas and postulates forms the bulk of the above-mentioned theories. All of these dealt with problems posed by Dilthey, but each solved them in a different way. All have common roots and similar topics of discussion, but they differ in the answers they offer to the problems of *Kultur, Geist,* and *Naturwissenschaften.*

PART IV

Psychology and the Scientific Method

CHAPTER **14**

The Scientific Method

1. FIRST PRINCIPLES

Definition of Science

The term "science" denotes both a certain type of activity and the results of it. Often a distinction is made, and rightly so, between the "research" activity and the resulting "system," both legitimately described as "scientific."

Scientific research is a human activity aimed at the discovery of truth. A scientific system is a system of propositions or statements or sentences representing this truth.

Men can seek truth in various ways, but not all of them are scientific. If someone inquires about the price of a given car, he is obviously in search of the truth, yet neither the buyer nor the seller is a scientist. However, someone investigating the relationship between the national income and the prices of cars is probably engaged in a scientific research which may lead toward a series of statements which form a scientific system or a part of it.

The scientific search for truth, the research, and the resulting scientific system evidently deal with a certain kind of truth and seek it in a certain manner. Science has no monopoly of truth; most of the statements we make in our daily life are truthful, but only a few of them are scientific. Research does not deal with the obvious.

The following criteria for a definition of science, derived from what sciences are like, are empirical, not a priori; they seek the common elements in research and systems of physics, astronomy, biology, and other sciences.

1. Scientific statements express a *discovery of truth*. They contain the best available information about things and about what happens to them. They express the results of the search for truth.

Obviously, the definition of truth requires further clarification, which will be offered later on.

2. There is an *objective proof* or *evidence* for each scientific statement. Evidence is the mark that distinguishes between scientific and nonsci-

entific statements. Scientific research is, to a great extent, an effort to bring evidence for the scientific statements or propositions. This evidence is *objective,* i.e., independent of a given researcher; any other researcher should be able to verify, refute, or corroborate the statements. Scientific systems are not dogmatic; they are due to change with the progress of research.

3. Scientific statements are *general,* or as general as the research in a given field warrants. The general concepts are a product of abstraction and classification; science groups things and events, classifies them, and seeks the most general truthful information concerning them. The more advanced sciences operate with highly generalized and abstract statements.

4. Scientific statements are *systematic.* They are put in a certain order depending upon the objectives of the researchers, the nature of the subject matter, or the method of research. A mere collection of true statements does not form a science; a scientific system requires a certain order —e.g., premises, theorems, proof; or independent, dependent, intervening variables; or any other systematic arrangement.

5. Scientific statements go beyond the empirical data. They *interpret* the data and *infer* the relationships between the observable things and events. They seek the *relationships,* whether causal, teleological, formal-logical (implication, inference), mathematical (e.g., functions), or any other.

6. These relationships are presented as a system of *hypotheses,* which express the *laws of nature* or a part thereof in a given area of research. The laws of nature, such as gravitation, evolution, osmosis, etc., indicate the regularities of all happenings in the universe.

7. Scientific statements concerning present or past events lead to a correct *prediction* of future developments. The aim of scientific research is to discover the truth in order to predict future happenings. "*Savoir pour prévoir,*" said Auguste Comte, the father of positivism. Predictability is often used as a method of verification; when the scientist, knowing the present, correctly predicts the future, his knowledge of the present is confirmed.

8. Scientific statements are *applicable* to future research and to practical life. Applied sciences, technologies, and techniques rely on scientific inquiry and its results. Success in applied sciences, such as agriculture, medicine, and education, depends largely upon their scientific foundations.

9. All sciences deal with things and with what happens to them (events). Thus all sciences are *empirical.* The nonempirical systems, such as mathematics, logic, etc., are not sciences. They are methods of research or methods of presentation (languages).

Sciences can be divided at will (depending on the purpose of those who divide them) into physics, chemistry, biology, sociology, history, etc; or into social, biological, etc; or into sciences dealing with inanimate and animate nature.[1] Like any other classification (cf. this chapter, section 2), the classification of sciences should be useful (serving some purpose) and economical (able to find a place for each item without unnecessary overlapping). Some classifications are better than others. A. Comte suggested the classification of sciences in the order of decreasing abstraction; psychology was not included in his system.[2] Windelband and Dilthey (cf. Chap. 10) excluded cultural sciences and humanities from the realm of the natural sciences, which was neither useful nor economical (cf. section 2 of this chapter).

It has been proposed to include *all* sciences under the name of natural sciences, and to divide all sciences into *descriptive* and *praxiologic* sciences.[3] The descriptive sciences present their statements as true or false propositions; the praxiological sciences deal with statements related to what and how to do. Obviously the applied sciences are praxiologies; politics and ethics should be included among them.

Psychology is an empirical, descriptive science belonging to the group of biological sciences for it deals with living organisms. It deals with them from a very peculiar and highly *controversial* point of view. Obviously psychology has overlapping areas with physiology and sociology; its subject matter is behavior, or overt and covert behavior, or experiences of organisms. Whatever its limits are, it seeks the truth in accordance with the nine principles stated above.

Epistemological Problems

There are various methods of ascertaining the truth, starting with naïve realism and ending with critical idealism, or even solipsism, through various other solutions, including critical realism and pragmatism. Naïve realism assumes that our senses never err; Kant's critical idealism assumed that they never tell the truth.

Some philosophers believe that they can determine the criteria of truth. Kant's critical idealism and James' pragmatism have been discussed in the present volume.

An assumption is made here that the world exists independently of the "perceiving subject" or of anyone who "thinks," "doubts," or "experiments." It seems not too reasonable to assume that philosophers know more about the nature of the physical world than did Newton, or Ein-

---

[1] Carl G. Hempel, "The Logical Analysis of Psychology," in H. Feigl and W. Sellars, *Readings in Philosophical Analysis*, Appleton-Century-Crofts, 1949, p. 382.

[2] Auguste Comte, *Cours de Philosophie Positive*, (2nd ed.), Bailière et Fils, 1864.

[3] Benjamin B. Wolman, "Scientific Study of Educational Aims," *Teachers College Record*, 1949, **50**, 471–481.

stein, or Darwin.[4] Unless it is assumed that the world exists and man is a
part of it, any further reasoning seems illogical. Any discussion of one
biological species outside the context of nature is self-contradictory.

Whoever studies the nature of things and events must start with the
assumption that he studies something; otherwise he is wasting his time.
This assumption of the existence of the world independent of man's
knowledge of it is the assumption of *radical realism,* which believes
that the world does not start or end with one of its species, called *Homo
sapiens* or subject or mind or any other name. For if one doubts the
existence of the world, there cannot be any reason to assume the existence
of one species.

Man, like many other biological species, lives and acts or behaves.
One of his actions is directed to the search for truth or the knowledge
of things and events. James emphasized the usefulness of this action.
Suffice it to say that "scientific research" is part of this action, guided
by the principles described above. It is immaterial for our purposes to
discuss the usefulness of research; even useless research is research.

Once we assume that man is a part of an existing world, we may ask
how correct his perception is, and to what extent his propositions concerning the world or a part of it (be it ourselves) correspond to what
the world is.

Modern students of theory of cognition, the epistemologists, distinguish
two basic types of truth: *immanent* and *transcendent* truth. Immanent
truth is assured whenever a system of propositions is free from inner
contradictions. The geometrical system of Euclid represents such a
system of statements based on immanent truth.

Some of the neo-positivists of the Viennese circle (*Wiener Kreis*)
suggested relating any scientific inquiry to a system of logical propositions independent of empirical proof. Others, among them M. Schlick, in
addition to immanent truth, introduced the principle of transcendent
truth, i.e., free from any contradiction with empirical data obtained by
observation. The Warsaw logicians (*Szkola Warszawska*) insisted on
transcendent truth as the criterion for scientific inquiry.

Mathematicians may be satisfied with immanent truth. Any other
branch of human inquiry which deals with any part of reality, be it
physics or astronomy, history or psychology, must insist upon checking
its statements against reality as empirically perceived by our sensory
apparatus.

Obviously, an empirical science must accept the demands of the
epistemologic maximalism, as represented by Moritz Schlick and the
Warsaw School. The maximalists are not satisfied with the "inner consistency" of a system of propositions interpreted as a "lack of inner

---

[4] Benjamin B. Wolman, "Theory of History," *Philosophical Review,* 1949, **46,** 342–
351.

contradictions." The world is the world of things, and science is the cognition of them.

T. Kotarbinski, in his classic work on logic,[5] has coined the term *reism*, understood as a conviction that only physical bodies do exist. No one should attach the same type of existence to relationships, generalizations, and logical constructs. Logical constructs should be introduced as methodological help in interpretation of what happened to the bodies.

Let us follow in the footsteps of Bertrand Russell. There are two types of propositions, the analytic and the synthetic or descriptive. *Analytic* statements are definitions. Definitions are arbitrary logical constructions that may be set at will. A definition is absolute or necessary only inasmuch as those who apply it like to have it so. All mathematical propositions are actually symbolic definitions, freely constructed and operated according to the rules set by those who like to have those rules set. The Euclidean geometry is a system of symbolic operations based upon a set of arbitrarily set axiomatic statements. Once we accept some proposition, we may derive other propositions from it by manipulations performed according to arbitrarily set mathematical or logical rules. Having accepted a definition and determined the rules of the game, we may arrive at absolutely certain conclusions, such as, for instance, the formula that $(a+b)^2 = a^2 + 2ab + b^2$ or the Pythagorean law of a triangle: $a^2 = b^2 + c^2$.

Synthetic or *descriptive* propositions are statements about things and what is going on with them. These propositions result from our perception of nature and the interpretation of our perception. Obviously they are neither "necessary" nor certain nor absolute. Only formal-logical and mathematical statements, based upon arbitrary definitions and rules, are absolutely proved. No descriptive proposition has ever been absolutely proved. All descriptive and empirical sciences operate with synthetic propositions that are subject to change with the improvement of our perceptive tools and method and better understanding of the nature of things.[6]

Accepting Russell's explanations one may say that the progress of scientific research depends upon (1) improvement of our perceptual tools, by which we perceive things and events, and (2) improvement of our theoretical interpretation of the things and events.

Facts and Theories

Empirical sciences deal with their subject matter on two levels. First come the *data* as perceived by our senses with the help of the tools that make perception more testable, more accurate, and more precise. Then

---

[5] Tadeusz Kotarbinski, *Elementy Logiki, Teorji Poznania i Metodologii Nauk*, (Polish), Warszawa, 1929.

[6] Bertrand Russell, *Principles of Mathematics* (2nd ed.), Norton, 1938.

science has to *interpret* the data and, going beyond the empirical studies, to formulate a *theory*. A theory without facts is a useless speculation, said D. Hume. But data without a theory is not a science either, said Poincaré; they are merely catalogues or inventories of facts, not scientific systems.

A theory is a result of carefully amassed, scrutinized, and analyzed empirical data. A theory that contradicts these data is meaningless, say the epistemologic maximalists, who require that theory be free from inner contradictions (immanent truth) and free from contradicting reality (transcendent truth).

Since the time of the Ionian philosophers human minds have tried to penetrate behind the variety and diversity of observable facts and disclose the unifying factor or factors in what happens in nature. The Ionian philosophers believed that there were only a few "elements," which appeared in the empirical world as a variety of objects and bodies.

Modern scientists use better tools and are more critical, but the aim of scientific inquiry has not changed much. Facts are today better perceived and more carefully measured by precise tools, but the purpose of any scientific inquiry is to go beyond the observable data and to discover the *laws of nature*. A theory in present-day science tries to uncover and to present as precisely as possible the *regularities of the universe* in such a manner that each single body or event can be related, interpreted, and predicted by these laws of nature.

The same holds true for the science of human nature, psychology. Plato and Aristotle tried to interpret human behavior by postulating the immortal soul. In present-day psychological language, soul is a hypothetical construct that was used to interpret human behavior. Plato tried to go beyond the diversity of human types and to disclose the underlying and unifying factors. He believed that the human soul is composed of three strata: the vegetative, the appetitive, and the rational.

Kant distinguished reason, emotions, and will. And as one questions the need for hypothetical constructs, the question is whether these or any other interpretations help to interpret, relate, and predict the facts.

Present-day psychology does the same thing though in a highly skilled manner. Mere cognition of facts is of little scientific value. Scientific inquiry in psychology endeavors to discover the laws that govern its area of research.

As long as psychology belonged to the realm of armchair speculations, it was easy to form a system of arbitrarily set statements and call them a psychological theory. In the first two or three decades of our century it was comparatively easy to bring together a cluster of facts and to write down a great many far-fetched statements. Owing to the lack of factual data it was possible and perhaps advisable to fill the empirical gap by a sophisticated "system." Step by step the hypothetical systems were confronted with the growing body of empirical data accumulated by scores

of empirically minded workers. Today we sometimes hear voices warning against the overdoing of empirical research and insufficient work in
theory construction. Obviously psychology needs a balanced production
in both collection of data and their interpretation.

2. COLLECTION OF DATA

Observation

A systematic, planned activity of perception of things and events is
called observation. What does a psychologist do? He observes bodies
and events. If his subject matter is psychology of men, he observes
human organisms and what the organisms do.

Science may discover unity where simple, crude perception reports
variety, and disclose differences in complex things that seem to be uniform. Psychologists, like all other scientists, gradually improve their tools,
techniques, and methods and gain more precise knowledge of mental
processes.

The body-soul, physical-mental, organic-psychological issue does not
belong to methodology. In what way psychological processes differ from
other physical processes is not a question that can be answered in a
chapter on methodology. It is one of the issues all psychological theories
struggle with (cf. Chap. 15). One thing is obvious: psychological processes are processes of living matter.

Undoubtedly, there is a great deal of overlapping between psychological and physiological research. Suffice it to look into the studies of
Weber, Fechner, Wundt, Pavlov, Köhler, Lashley, Goldstein, Hebb, and
others; the overlapping is obvious since both psychology and physiology
deal with the functions of organisms.

Several psychological processes—pain and pleasure, for instance—can
be directly observed only by the individual in whom they take place.
Obviously, the truthfulness (validity) of results obtained by introspection
as a method of observation must be verified by other methods, because
introspection cannot be as objective as any other observational method.
Yet introspection produces a wealth of information about psychological
processes, and in some cases it is the main source of information. Introspection seems, therefore, to be inevitable in psychology. To give it up
would be equal to throwing away a precious tool because it is not
precise enough.

Psychologists cannot afford to reject any method that brings factual
information. The studies of Suzanne Isaacs and W. Stern in child psychology, of Charlotte Bühler and Stanley Hall in adolescence, of Ebbinghaus
and K. Lewin on retention, of Piaget and Gesell in development repre-

sent a great variety of research methods. All these studies, whether based on biography, systematic observations, questionnaires, interviews, or experimentation, exemplify the various approaches within the empirical method.

Some psychologists, in their effort to adhere to strict empiricism, seem to be more severe than physicists. The natural sciences go beyond observable data to develop hypotheses and theorems which contradict our daily observations. No one has ever "seen" that our earth is round and that it is rotating. Everyone can easily "see" the sun rising at dawn and setting at dusk. Several chemical elements have been discovered before they have been empirically observed. Einstein's theory of the fourth dimension contradicts our empirical sensory experiences.

Some psychologists insist upon a radical version of empiricism. The early behaviorists insisted upon the study of overt, manifest, observable phenomena.

Even today, some psychologists suggest staying away from unobservable phenomena; B. F. Skinner represents this point of view. Guthrie insists that "the laws of nature describe the *observable* conditions under which certain classes of events take place."[7]

No wonder several psychologists opposed Freud's theories and accused them of being nonempirical. But obviously a certain class of psychological facts is unobservable. Consider amnesia. When an individual forgets something and, influenced by hypnosis or psychoanalysis, recalls what he has forgotten, the entire process is inaccessible to any observation, from within or without. Yet the process of amnesia undoubtedly took place, for its end products were observable. The *inference* of their existence is a legitimate procedure of empirical sciences, which will be discussed in section 3 of the present chapter.

Operationism

One of the most radical methods of observation is called *operationism*. Operationism has been defined by E. C. Tolman as a science which "seeks to define its concepts in such a manner that they can be stated and tested in terms of concrete repeatable operations by independent observers."[8] In other words, operationism observes not only the object to be observed but also the operations performed by the observers in the process of observing objects.

P. W. Bridgman, the creator of empiricism, stated that "the original impetus toward the operational analysis in physics came from a consideration of Einstein's procedure in the theory of relativity. Einstein had

[7] Edwin R. Guthrie, *The Psychology of Learning,* Harper, 1935, p. 187.
[8] Edward C. Tolman, "Operational Behaviorism and Current Trends in Psychology," *Proceedings of the Twenty-fifth Anniversary Celebration of Inauguration of Graduate Studies,* University of Southern California, 1936.

realized that certain terms, like 'absolute length,' 'absolute duration,' 'absolute simultaneity' were devoid of empirical meaning because no observational or experimental procedures were or could be specified for their application. The operational criterion here serves to distinguish physics from metaphysics."[9]

As long as operationism points to the need for careful definitions and critical observation of the tools and operations performed by the observing scientist, it might be considered a useful brand of empiricism. However, there is nothing new in it. F. Bacon, D. Hume, J. S. Mill, C. S. Peirce, and others carefully elaborated the methodology of empirical studies and the principles of the inductive method.

But operationism says that if a question is to have a meaning it must be possible to find operations by which an answer may be given to it. And this is no longer empiricism. It is, once more, a return to the "perceiving subject."

The man who overdid in the observation of the observer was I. Kant. Kant "psychologized" the universe, so to say, and made man the center of the world. Kant's "perceiving subject" is not a real man, who is, indeed, but a speck of dust in the gigantic world. Kant's "subject" is a giant viewing the empirical world through the glasses of his a priori set categories. As mentioned in Chapter 10, A. Schopenhauer went one step farther and concluded that the subject creates the world at will.

When Bridgman turned the light on the operations performed by scientists, he could not predict that he would land on Schopenhauer's barren island of solipsism. But nothing else could have been expected. Once the center of scientific inquiry was moved from the objects of inquiry to the operations, machinations, speculations, and/or imaginations of the inquiring subject, all roads led to solipsism. This is the inevitable outcome of Kantianism, Machism, and operationism. P. W. Bridgman, being a consistent and daring thinker, stated bluntly what others have hidden under various excuses. If scientific inquiry depends upon the "operations" conducted by the researcher, the conclusion reached by Bridgman is perfectly logical: "In the last analysis science is only my private science,"[10] defined in terms of operations performed by "me." If all knowledge has to be presented in terms of the perceiving subject and his "operations," the perceiver and not the perceived objects becomes the center of the universe.

Psychologists were shocked by this development. A leading exponent of psychological theory, S. S. Stevens, tried to save operationism by introducing the concept of social agreement. It resembles Sullivan's consensual validation. But does it save operationism?

[9] Herbert Feigl, "Operationism and Scientific Method," *Psychological Review*, 1945, 52, 250–259.

[10] Peter W. Bridgman, *The Nature of Physical Theory*, Princeton University, 1936.

The defense of operationism by Stevens is an honest effort to preserve the objectivity of scientific inquiry. Stevens suggested following operational principles and he believed that they were "induced generalizations" and "verifiable."

"1. Science, as we find it, is a set of empirical propositions agreed upon by members of society. This agreement may be always in a state of flux, but persistent disagreement leads eventually to rejection. . . .

"2. Only those propositions based upon operations which are public and repeatable are admitted to the body of science."[11]

Stevens' rejection of solipsism is well taken, for science cannot be developed as a private world of a scientist. Thus Stevens saved the public character and objectivity of science. But not the operationism; operationism as a method which insists upon defining scientific statements in terms of the operations performed by scientists leads either to solipsism or to solipsism-in-groups, i.e., group folly. The fact that many people participate in the operations does not make them scientific or truthful. Consider witchcraft or superstitions, both "public and repeatable" and both unscientific and untrue.

Stevens believes that operationism discovers pseudo-problems, and a pseudo-problem is a proposition which cannot be put to experimental test.[12] When no operation can be formulated which either proves or disproves a proposition, the proposition represents a pseudo-problem. In Stevens' words, "A term or proposition has meaning (denotes something) if, and only if, the criteria of its applicability or truth consist of concrete operations which can be performed."[13]

Now, operationism becomes an epistemological theory which, as will be shown, can be easily refuted. The naïve realist says: "If I see it, it is. What cannot be seen does not exist and is therefore a pseudo-problem." The operationist says: "If I can do something with it, it is. I prove things by doing, by performing operations. If I cannot do anything with them, they are pseudo-problems." For example, a mute catatonic may have delusions. If they cannot be "operationally defined," they represent a pseudo-problem. Circulation of blood prior to the discovery of methods by which it could be observed was a pseudo-problem. Copernicus, Kepler, Newton, and Laplace are guilty of dealing with problems not necessarily operationally defined. The same holds true for Pavlov, Freud, Goldstein, Piaget, Rorschach, Binet, and many other great scientists and psychologists.

Furthermore, a question can be raised as to the validity of the operational method. What is the proof that the observations of the operationist

[11] S. S. Stevens, "Psychology and the Science of Science," *Psychological Bulletin,* 1939, **36**, 221–263.
[12] *Ibid.*
[13] S. S. Stevens, "The Operational Definition of Psychological Concepts," *Psychological Review,* 1935, **42**, 517–527.

made on his own concrete observations are more valid than any other non-operational observations? How can such a statement be verified? Operationally or otherwise? In what way can one "operationally" disprove superstition and witchcraft? Definite "concrete" operations have been performed and "proved." Moreover, if intelligence is what intelligence tests measure, no objective truth will ever be discovered. The Russian psychologists, for example, prefer not to use intelligence tests, yet they seem to make quite intelligent statements about intelligence. Since the producers of tests of intelligence may have their disagreements, a uniform definition of intelligence in terms of operations may be impossible. Thus operationism without Stevens' correction is a solipsistic denial of science, and with Stevens' social correction it does not offer any protection against "group solipsism" or errors committed by a group of research workers.

What is good in operationism has been said and practiced by all empiricists. But empiricists do not insist on narrowing their propositions to terms of operations performed by them. One must conclude, therefore, that the operationists overdid themselves in psychology. Even in physics a strict operational theory is practically impossible. An analysis of Divac's quantum theory has proved that even this theory "presupposes a particle analogy which is not directly given in experimental data" and therefore does not meet the rigorous requirements of operationism.[14]

Kant told philosophers to look on the looking eye. Bridgman called scientists to look on their hands and tools. Kant should be given credit for his criticism of the naïve realism in epistemology. Bridgman should be given credit for his criticism of the naïve realism in the methodology of sciences. But both Kant and Bridgman overdid their observations of the observer and attached too much importance to him, in view of the proportion between man and the entire universe, and rather naïvely believed that the observations of the actions of the observer are more truthful than the observations of all other things.

Classification

When the scientist perceives objects and events, he compares them, seeking similarities and differences. Trees growing in a park show similarities and differences; some of them have similar bark, leaves, and fruit, and the botanist groups them together as a "class" of, e.g., oak trees.

No two oak trees are identical; they differ in size, shape, number of branches and leaves. The scientist *abstracts* or overlooks the differences and groups objects together on the basis of at least one similarity. For

[14] Mary Hesse, "Operational Definition and Analogy in Physical Theories," *British Journal of Philosophy of Science*, 1952, 2, 282–294.

example, all objects made for sitting on, whether they are made of wood, aluminum, iron, or any other material, whether they are tall or short, old or new, are called chairs. One common denominator suffices for classification.

Objects can be classified in more than one way. The objects in a room can be divided on the basis of their shape, use, material, color, size, weight, age, price, human attachment to them, etc.

Classification can be done at will, but scientists usually abide by two rules. First, any classification must serve some *useful* purpose as far as scientific inquiry is concerned. The botanist sees no point in classifying trees into short, medium, and tall ones, but he finds it scientifically useful to distinguish oaks, pines, birches, etc. The reason for his preferences is obvious and simple and has nothing to do with the "essential" elements of the phenomenologists. A classification of trees according to height does not help in the discovery of the biological processes in trees, while the classification on genetic lines does. For a lumber-trade economic researcher the size of the trees may be important. In abnormal psychology the problem of classification of mental disorder is highly controversial and quite important, because it determines diagnosis and prognosis.[15]

The second rule of classification is *economy*. A certain object should not belong to two classes within the same system of classification or the classification is self-contradictory. If we classify as young anyone below fifty and as old anyone above forty, all people between forty and fifty belong to both classes.

Practically all typological efforts in psychology violate the principles of classification to a lesser or greater extent. On the Allport-Vernon scale everyone belongs to more than one Sprangerian type. There is no way of distinguishing between the introverts and extroverts of Jung; Kretschmer's and Sheldon's types badly overlap; in clinical experience individuals usually show Freudian fixations on more than one level; other typologies seem to be even less economic, and to promote science less.

Classification leads toward the formation of abstract concepts. The formation of classes and the formation of class concepts or conceptualization are functions of the human mind; there is nothing absolute or external about concepts. To quote William James, paper can be conceived as a "thin thing," or a "hydrocarbonaceous thing," or a surface for writing, and "whichever one of these aspects of its being I temporarily class it under, makes me unjust to the other aspects. But as I always am classing it under one aspect or another, I am always unjust, always partial, always exclusive. My excuse is necessity—the necessity which my finite and prac-

---

[15] Otto Fenichel, *The Psychoanalytic Theory of Neurosis*, Norton, 1945; Harry S. Sullivan, *The Interpersonal Theory of Psychiatry*, Norton, 1953; Benjamin B. Wolman, "The Continuum Hypothesis in Neurosis and Psychosis and the Classification of Mental Disorder," Eastern Psychological Association Symposium, April, 1959.

tical nature lays upon me. My thinking is first and last and always for the sake of my doing, and I can only do one thing at a time."[16]

Nothing is truly essential. Essential to what? It depends upon the purposes and ends of man; obviously the phenomenological distinction of essentials is arbitrarily set.

Generalization and the Problem of Idiophenomena

Once objects are classified on the basis of one common denominator, true statements can be made regarding a certain class of objects.

Such a statement concerning a class is called a *generalization*. It expresses a truth concerning a class, or group, or category of objects. It can be phrased: "some" members of a certain class or "all" members of a certain class are so and so. Sometimes psychologists do not pay enough attention to this distinction and confuse "some" with "all." In the "Conclusion" about each system discussed in the present book, the generality of the propositions of a given system has often been discussed. McDougall's pairing of instincts and emotions led to a question as to whether the respective feelings did always accompany a certain propensity. Many psychoanalytic and related propositions represent the type "often" instead of "always" it is so and so. The principle of reward in learning should, as Razran pointed out, be stated as a generalization applicable to a certain class of learning situations but not to all of them.

A considerable methodological difficulty has been created by Windelband's distinction between the nomothetic and the idiographic sciences. The unrepeatable, individual, unique phenomena evade generalization and are not subject to the laws of nature. Therefore, concluded Windelband, the individual and unrepeatable events are not the subject matter of natural sciences. Natural science deals with *generalia* such as water, rain, air, waves, iron, etc., but cannot deal with, e.g., the fact that Napoleon lost the battle of Waterloo or that John lost his memory as result of a shell shock.

The medieval discussion between "realism" and "nominalism" has been revived in the story of idiophenomena. The "realists" ascribed existence to water in general, iron in general, love in general, while the "nominalists" dealt with drops of water, pieces of iron, and men in love and believed that water, iron, and love in general are merely *names of classes* of objects and events.

The nominalist point of view, to which this writer subscribes, ascribes existence to things and events and to nothing else. Furthermore, it can be shown that each thing or event is an idiophenomenon. Not only the lost battle of Waterloo is a unique and unrepeatable phenomenon, but even the sunrise of that day, and the death of so many men, and

[16] William James, *The Principles of Psychology*, Holt, 1890, Vol. II, p. 333.

the water that flowed that day in the rivers of France, and the rain that fell on the plains, and the amount of electricity in the air at that time— all these were unrepeatable events. There is no such thing as water, iron, love in general. The subject matter of all sciences is idiophenomena.[17]

Yet sciences strive toward the most general truth. Science, explained H. Poincaré, does not pile up facts like bricks but connects them and builds houses on the basis of generalizations.[18] The scientist isolates elements (abstracts) and groups the idiophenomena on the basis of common elements. Each lion, each eucalyptus tree, each piece of iron, each somatic cell, each case of gravitation, each case of love, each mental breakdown is an idiophenomenon and yet they can be put together with other idiophenomena on the basis of at least one common trait. The scientific statements about each class can be worded in such a way as to express a general truth. Accordingly, each schizophrenic patient is definitely an idiophenomenon, for no other human being has suffered from exactly the same disorder and in exactly the same way. Yet all schizophrenic patients can be grouped together and valid statements can be made about their common hardships.[19]

In this discussion of idiophenomena it is worth while to quote the philosopher Morris Cohen: "That all existing beings, animate or inanimate, are individuals, no rationalists needs to deny. But that is in no way inconsistent with the fact pointed out by Aristotle that there is no knowledge or significant assertion with reference to any individual, except in terms of universals or abstractions. I may in a dumb way point to a single object or I may grasp it with my hand, but I cannot mean anything and I cannot even say 'this' about it without using an abstract term applicable to other individuals. If I use a proper name, it has the meaning only by convention which ultimately involves abstract terms."[20] Our language uses generalia, but generalia are mere names and nothing else.

All general concepts of psychology stem from classification and generalization. Each individual case can be fully interpreted by relating it to all the possible classes to which it belongs. The movement of a speck of dust cannot be described in terms of gravitation only; it proceeds according to the laws of nature, which include in this case gravitation, friction, movements of air, and many more. A scientist who took into consideration *all* the relevant laws could predict all the movements of the speck of dust flying in the air. For there cannot be any violation of the laws of nature.

[17] Benjamin B. Wolman, *Prolegomena to Sociology* (Hebrew), Kiryat Sefer, 1948.
[18] Henri Poincaré, *La Science et l'Hypothèse,* Flammarion, 1903.
[19] Benjamin B. Wolman, "Explorations in Latent Schizophrenia," *American Journal of Psychotherapy,* 1957, 11, 560–588.
[20] Morris R. Cohen, *Reason and Nature,* Harcourt, Brace, 1931, p. 13.

Such knowledge of a single fact is practically impossible. Usually scientists try to study their problems by reducing the number of variables and simplifying the process under consideration. This is a standard laboratory procedure—to look for "typical," "normal," "usual," "average" examples in which the individual peculiarities are kept at a minimum. Statistical methods are geared to this goal.

However, the higher and more complex the processes, the more dissimilarities are found. Two drops of water are not identical, but even less identical are two plants belonging to the same species, and even less are two humans. And that is one of the sources of objection to generalizations in psychology.

But dissimilarities do not prevent generalization. A combination of similar elements may lead to different total structures, and similar structures may be composed of different elements. In the pursuit of truth psychologists seek the different and the common, the individual and the general, to the molecular and to the molar. Each of them contains some truth: the case study and the statistical survey, the life history of an individual and the results of a nation-wide study of intelligence.

Quantification in Psychology

Quantification is indicative of a higher level of comparison, abstraction, and generalization, first, by counting with numbers. Counting indicates the degree of similarity between two aggregates such as the number of books on a shelf and the number of students in a class. Two aggregates may have one identical element, their number.

Counting is an abstraction, and a precise one. Quantification in the form of counting and, even more, measurement are very exact methods of comparison, abstraction, classification, and generalization. The use of quantification increases the precision in research methods and makes them more scientific.

Mathematics can be used in psychology in three ways: first, as counting and measurement on the level of collecting of empirical data; second, as a method of testing hypotheses in experimental and statistical studies (e.g., the hypotheses of Hull have been laboratory-tested in a quantitative manner; discussion concerning the etiology of mental disorder often utilizes statistical data as one of the best methods of evidence); third, as offering unusual advantage in precision of statements.

The syntactic (mathematical) statements, theorems, and equations "are absolutely true or absolutely false. They are true if they are consistent with the rules laid down for playing the game, they are false if they break the law. But these absolutely true statements say nothing at all, unfortunately, about objects or events, and they reveal no secrets of nature. It is by way of semantical rules that we tie the mathematical model to the empirical world," but it often fits as poorly "as a borrowed hat."[21]

These sound words of warning have been said in times when some psychologists tend to overdo measurements and others endeavor to introduce into psychology the methods of non-metricized mathematics.

J. F. Brown wrote that at the present time fundamental measurement is impossible in psychology and in social science: "Where fundamental measurement is not possible, simple assignation of number to the qualities of nature has advantages, but such assignations ought not to be honored with the title of measurement. For psychology such a service is performed by rating scales, Intelligence Quotients, and the common psychophysical methods. In general, sciences start with such numerical assignations and through a very complicated process reduce these to measurements."[22]

But it is practically obvious that there are several kinds of measurements possible in all sciences of behavior: How many are unemployed? How many marry, divorce, migrate? How often are crime, theft, violence, suicide committed How many vote? All this is measurement, namely, measurement by enumeration.

To quote Stevens again, any new number is admitted to the union of numbers "provided it obeys the old rules. It is analogous to the admission of a state to the union: the new state must agree to obey the federal laws. The laws of the number union have to do with addition, multiplication, substraction, and division, and the new numbers must behave themselves when these operations are applied."

How do Kurt Lewin's numbers "behave"?

They do not behave at all, because Lewin did not operate with them. He was a brilliant psychologist and an ingenious experimenter. He introduced a set of signs, calling them topology, hodology, field theory, and vector psychology. All these were signs, and signs invite the formal discipline of syntactics. Mathematics is one of these formal disciplines and, like any other formal discipline, it sets rigorous rules. Kurt Lewin did not violate these rules, but he has hardly added or developed any mathematical rules at all.

The Experimental Method

The most precise, planned, and controlled observation is experiment. Experiment is the most scientific research method. Only experiments make possible controlled observation, variation of factors, perfect quantifications, and rigorous, objective checking of hypotheses.[23]

[21] Stevens (ed.), *Handbook of Experimental Psychology*, Wiley, 1951, p. 3.
[22] J. F. Brown, *Psychology and the Social Order*, McGraw-Hill, 1936, p. 470.
[23] Cf. Oscar Kempthorne, *The Design and Analysis of Experiments*, Wiley, 1952.

The advantages offered by the experimental method should, however, not prevent us from looking into its shortcomings. The main weakness of the experiment as far as behavior of the organism is concerned lies in the fact that an experiment is an observation of an artificially determined pattern of behavior. Thorndike's experimental animals had virtually no choice but trial and error. Imagine an organism enclosed in a maze with high walls which would prevent him from any insight or oversight; he would be *forced* to try and to err. But give him low or transparent walls and he would probably find the solution with one glance as Köhler's chimpanzees did. A great part of the difference between the classic and the operant conditioning stems from the differences in the tools used, in the nature of the equipment, and in the experimental design.

The experimental method sets its own limits by setting the experimental situation. The greatness of experimentalism lies in its precision and control of variables, but the experimental set itself creates a new pattern of behavior. No biologist would limit his studies of animals to observations in a circus with specially trained animals; some psychologists would. Biologists prefer the *ecological* method, which is the study of the animal in its natural environment. One wonders how albino rats, pigeons, or cats would learn in situations which are different from a puzzle box, maze, or Skinner apparatus.

Even more spectacular are the differences between Thorndike and Guthrie. Both used a cat in a problem box with a release mechanism inside the box and food as incentive outside. Despite similar settings they arrived at different results. Thorndike's cat struggled against odds for quite a while, and only after a long series of trials and errors, learned to open the box. Thorndike explained the behavior of his cat as typical for all cats and perhaps all mammals, and saw in this behavior the clue to a general learning theory based on trial and error, illustrated on the learning curve, and the law of effect.

Guthrie's cat seemed to be bound to defeat all the opponents of the learning theories of his master. Guthrie's cat found the solution almost immediately. Then there was quite a lot of consistency and stereotypy in the following trials with a minimum of deviations from the established pattern.

Behavior is, for all practical purposes, an interaction between the organism and its environment. Obviously there is more than one way for such interaction to take place. And this is probably why experimental data have to be presented not as the total truth but as a limited truth. One may say that if a certain organism is enclosed in such and such apparatus (a definite type of environment) and exposed to such and such stimulus this will be the reaction. If the statement is backed up by a vigorous experimentation, it is a true statement insofar as it reports the behavior of a *certain* organism in a *certain* setting. It does not, however, cover what was not covered in the experiment, namely, any other situation in which the organism may respond to a given stimulus in a slightly or even substantially different way. Especially in experiments with the highest biological organisms, capable of a great variety of responses, caution should be advised.

Once we are reconciled to these limitations, we may and should admit that the experimental method is the most reliable method. Some suggestions, however, should be offered at this point. First, conclusions derived from experiments must be limited to what has been actually done in the experimental situation. Experiments should be designed to be as close as possible to realistic situations in which subjects face their usual environments. For example, formal intelligence testing of small children seems so remote from the child's usual interaction that one cannot be surprised at the unreliability of test results. And, as far as learning theory is concerned, there must be more than one kind of learning for the various species and more than one way of learning for each organism. Accordingly, a realistic setting for experimentation may offer certain advantages.

However, even a so-called realistic setting may be nevertheless misleading. A remarkable case is the experiment in "social climate" conducted by Lewin, Lippitt, and White (cf. Chap. 13). In this experiment three social climates were supposedly established by the experimenters, the autocratic, the democratic, and the laissez-faire, and far-reaching conclusions were drawn by the experimenters.

Actually leadership in all groups was autocratic, because all the leaders were appointed by the experimenter and not chosen by the children. In the so-called democratic group the leader was benevolent and, like a sort of liberal-minded despot, permitted the children to participate in group decisions. The children knew very well that he was their leader and they had no power to overthrow him. The true choice of a leader is the outstanding feature of democracy. Benevolent tyrants who listen to the needs and voices of their subjects are *not* representatives of a democratic system.

The second leader was a cold, ineffectual autocrat. Autocrats are not necessarily cold or unfriendly. At any rate, this was a poor type of leadership; in the assignment of duties and division of labor the leader overlooked the interests and inclinations of the group members. Not all autocratic leaders are poor judges of human nature.

The laissez-faire leader was not a leader at all. The children expected him to be one, i.e., to take initiative and to offer guidance. His passivity was a denial of leadership. Were he absent, the children would probably organize themselves better. In his presence they did not dare to do so, for they probably knew that he had the power of leadership but he did not exercise it.[24]

A criticism of the experimental method in psychology was offered by G. S. Klein.[25] Klein remarked that the appearance of *significant relations* was often prevented by the rigorous experimental procedure of keeping variables constant. Instead of grasping the process as a whole, the experimentalists often omit important factors by their tendency to eliminate and isolate experimental variables or to keep them constant.

However, this criticism cannot undermine the validity or reliability of experimental procedure. The criticism should be directed against oversimplification of mental processes and overgeneralization of conclusions. The experimental method is undoubtedly the most valid and reliable method in psychology.

Additional limitations of the experimental method in psychology stem from the fact that experiments cannot handle too well the patterns of covert behavior; overt, violent types of action do not fit into a laboratory setting. Nor can experimenters test the entire gamut of human drives and feelings.

This part of psychology is handled daily by the clinical psychologists. The clinicians deal with *all* phenomena of human nature, normal and abnormal, overt and covert, rational and irrational. The wealth of clinical material is overwhelming; child growth, perception and reasoning, learning and forgetting, love and hate, happiness and misery, physiology and psychosomatics are seen day by day in a great variety of situations.

The clinician sees his subjects in homes and schools, in hospitals and clinics. He interviews them and their families and reports on all that is going on in their minds and actions. Clinical studies broaden our knowledge of psychology; experimental studies make it more reliable.

The experimentalist studies but a part of human behavior but he studies it with great precision. The clinician studies the totality of human behavior. No wonder this wealth of clinical material is not too conducive to precision and can be easily misinterpreted. The scientifically minded clinician cannot help envying the experimentalist's precision. When the experimentalist says three and five equal eight, it is so. When the clinician says 3000 plus 5000 equals 8000 he is not sure he counted carefully; some errors are almost inevitable.

Thus observational and even more experimental studies aimed at the verification of clinical findings are exceedingly important for the future development of psychological theory. The results obtained by the two

[24] Benjamin B. Wolman, "Education and Leadership," *Teachers College Record*, 1958, **59**, 465–473.

[25] George S. Klein, "A Clinical Perspective for Personality Research," *Journal of Abnormal and Social Psychology*, 1949, **44**, 42–50.

methods independently of each other cannot be identical, but they should not be mutually exclusive.

3. INTERPRETATION OF DATA AND THEORY CONSTRUCTION

Induction and Deduction

Science is not a collection of facts, just as a house is not a pile of bricks, said the great French mathematician and philosopher H. Poincaré. How to build this house? Let us listen to a great American philosopher, E. Nagel: "While every experiment requires the use of principles of interpretation, the evidence for the truth of these principles comes ultimately through observation and experiment. . . . The propositions which science at any time certifies are either confirmed in all possible experiments, or are modified in accordance with the best available evidence. There is thus a continual appeal from facts to principles, and from principles to facts. . . . *In the order of the development of our knowledge,* therefore, theory and observation are of equal rank."[26]

Which should come first, observation of facts or their interpretation? The answer is obvious, and in the empirical sciences the method of choice is the *inductive* method. However, a deductive method may just as well be used in empirical sciences. Science may proceed from fact to interpretation, or a tentative interpretation may be tested by facts. Any scientific system must be composed of empirical data and their interpretation.

Edna Heidbreder wrote in 1933: "The simple truth is that psychology does not at present possess enough facts with which to test its systems. Its need of facts makes it disparage speculation, its lack of facts makes it resort to practice, and it does so at times with a bad conscience. . . ." But "scientific knowledge does not merely accumulate. . . ." Frequently "guesses on the basis of inadequate evidence have proved to be powerful and, in actual practice, indispensable tools, which science regularly employs."[27]

The tendency to develop deductive systems in psychology became prominent with C. L. Hull and K. Lewin. Many scholars seem to believe that this is the only or the best road for psychological theory. Feigl suggested defining "theory" as "a set of assumptions from which can be derived by purely logico-mathematical procedures, a larger set of empirical laws." The theory "furnishes an explanation of these empirical

[26] Ernest Nagel, *Logic Without Metaphysics*, Free Press, 1956, p. 152.
[27] Edna Heidbreder, *Seven Psychologies*, Appleton-Century, 1933, p. 15.

laws and unifies the originally heterogeneous areas of subject matter characterized by those empirical laws."[28]

But the most important problem is whether the statements called by Feigl "empirical laws" can pass the test of observation and experiment. If they do, their theoretical assumptions are still not proved, but they are not rejected, which is a satisfactory situation for any theory.

Moreover, it seems that Feigl's "levels" correspond specifically to a Hull type of theory. From a more general point of view, it seems advisable to distinguish between a hypothesis or hypothetical interpretation and a system of hypotheses, i.e., a theory.

Hypothesis

A hypothesis is a statement which is not yet proved to be true. The statement "two and two is four" is not a hypothesis. Nor is it a hypothesis that birds have two legs or that all humans are mortals. These are observed, well-known facts.

Hypothetical statements are used for information which we believe to be true. Scientists use hypothesis whenever they deal with unobservable bodies and events or unobservable relationships. Phlogiston was such a hypothesis; it proved to be wrong. The theories of airplanes, television, submarines used to be hypothetical hopes; now they are facts.

Some hypothetical statements have been proved. The prevention of poliomyelitis by the use of the Salk vaccine proved that the hypothesis concerning the nature of poliomyelitis was true. Empirical studies have shown that the hypothesis which related schizophrenia to tuberculosis was untrue. Watson's hypothesis of subvocal speech was never proved; nor was the "drive reduction" hypothesis. Goldstein's theory of compensation and Freud's hypothesis of the unconscious have a great body of supportive evidence.

The aim of scientific inquiry is to discover the truth. Sometimes it is useful to state the truth tentatively, as a hypothesis, even before all the evidence or even a part of the evidence has been produced. Let us call such a hypothesis a *postulate.* In the inductive method it is legitimate to draw a tentative conclusion from insufficient empirical data and then to test it against further data. In the deductive method it is legitimate to start from any tentative assumption and then to put it to an empirical test.

Hypotheses should be formed in such a way that they are a help and not a hindrance in the search for truth. Accordingly, the formation of hypotheses must follow certain rules.

[28] Herbert Feigl, "Principles and Problems of Theory Construction in Psychology," in W. Dennis (ed.), *Current Trends in Psychological Theory,* University of Pittsburgh, 1951, p. 182.

1. *Immanent truth.* Hypotheses may be true or false as their future testing will prove. They must, however, be free of inner contradiction; each hypothesis or each system of hypotheses should be developed in accordance with the principles of logical implication and inference. Obviously, the use of hypotheses must be persistent. Once a hypothesis has been stated it must be applied till further empirical research or other methodological considerations suggest its modification or abandonment. Careless use of hypotheses and their modification at will (cf. Jung, Rank, and others) is self-defeating.

2. *Testability.* A hypothesis should be open to proof or refutation by empirical test. The best test is a controlled experiment.

3. *Usefulness and parsimony.* New hypotheses have to be introduced only when the old ones fail to account for empirical data or some other methodological considerations. Hypotheses should be as sparse as possible, and as simple as possible.

4. *Anticipation.* Hypotheses should be geared to the goal of anticipation of future events. *"Savoir pour prévoir."*

5. *Wording.* The wording of a hypothesis must not be ambiguous.

Hypotheses, Constructs, and Intervening Variables

Some students of the scientific method in psychology seem to believe that there is only one way to form hypotheses, briefly explained as follows: Psychology as an empirical science must start from the observable interaction between the organism and its environment. This interaction is called behavior and is sometimes misrepresented as an equivalent of the subject matter of psychology, although even J. B. Watson had to admit that psychology must deal with phenomena which do not belong to the category of this overt interaction; thus Watson included *implicit* behavior in his studies.

But this has not been the end but the beginning of the difficulties. Behavior can be conveniently presented as a *stimulus-response continuum,* the stimulus standing for the totality of actions done by the environment and the response standing for whatever happened with the organism as a result of the stimulation. However, even a superficial observation shows that the response of the organism is *more* than a response to the stimulation: a hungry rat and a satiated one will respond differently to the sight of food. Credit has to be given to R. S. Woodworth for modifying the S-R formula into S-O-R, in which O stands for the organism, and it is understood that R is a result of what was produced by S and O together. Undoubtedly it was a substantial improvement in the presentation of psychological events.

Tolman refined Woodworth's proposition and presented the S-O-R formula in a continuum of experimental variables in which S is the indepent, R the dependent, O the intervening variable.

It must be said that this way of treating psychological data is by no means the only one. Lewin, Sullivan, and others would not distinguish between S and O. McDougall's propensity does not fit too well either. Wertheimer's gestalt is not an intervening variable. Tolman's intervening variable stands for a partial cause of the dependent variable; the other partial cause is the independent variable.

Obviously there are many types of hypothetical statements and not all of them can be presented as variables intervening between the independent and dependent variables. Consider Allport's trait, Freud's ego. Hull's drive, gestalt insight, Pavlov's irradiation, Lewin's field. All these are *logical constructs*.

MacCorquodale and Meehl suggested that the logical constructs are better elaborated, more meaningful elements than the intervening variables.[29]

This distinction between intervening variables and hypothetical constructs introduced by MacCorquodale and Meehl has been further elaborated by Feigl, who preferred to call the constructs *existential hypotheses*. These "fill out" the space assigned to intervening variables, as, e.g., the hypothetical constructs of the theory of genes "fill out" Mendel's conceptions of heredity, or the intervening variable of temperature is being identified with the existential hypothesis of micro-states of molecules. The existential hypotheses are introduced "on the basis of some new and heterogeneous area of evidence." "At the price of existential hypotheses we achieve a reduction (often a very considerable one) of the hitherto unreduced dispositional concepts or intervening variables."[30]

The scientific theory may introduce logical constructs at any level of explanation provided they are clearly defined and serve a useful purpose. Logical constructs may fill a gap in observation. Watson's subvocal speech, Allport's trait, Freud's unconscious are intended to report facts which cannot be directly observed. They cannot be presented as intervening variables.

"*Unconscious* has more and more been made to mean a mental province rather than a quality which mental things have," said Freud.[31] The unconscious as a "mental province" is a logical construct of mind. Most logical constructs are "methodological bridges" used for interpretation of behavior. Freud's model of personality is composed of several constructs: id, ego, and superego. These constructs are more complex. So is reinforce-

[29] K. MacCorquodale and Paul E. Meehl, "On a Distinction Between Hypothetical Constructs and Intervening Variables," *Psychological Review*, 1948, **55**, 95–107.

[30] Feigl, "Principles and Problems," in Dennis, *op. cit.*, pp. 194–195.

[31] Sigmund Freud, *New Introductory Lectures in Psychoanalysis*, Norton, 1933, p 102.

ment, intelligence, Oedipus complex, adjustment, learning, etc. All are logical constructs, or concepts useful in the search for truth.

As said before, in certain situations the experimental variables can be grouped as independent, dependent, and intervening variables. Logical constructs are often used as intervening variables.

Molar and Molecular Hypotheses

Psychologists have expressed their preference for the use of either molar or molecular hypotheses for the explanation of behavior. Associationists presumably preferred molecular hypotheses; contemporary psychologists seem to prefer molar.

Psychologists' molar concepts, according to Feigl, are a "close-to-life" empirical law. By analogy with physics, Feigl suggested switching from macro- to micro-explanations in psychology, because the molar type of analysis "yields at best a set of empirical laws, always of statistical character, often with only rather low degrees of correlation." Feigl thinks "that physics as well as psychology cannot get away from the mediaeval ideas of powers, capacities, or faculties as long as they remain on macro-level."

For instance, said Feigl, the "soporific power of opium" does not explain the empirical regularity, but it tells about each individual case. This type of explanation is a "low level explanation." A higher level explanation "would have to enter into the physiological-chemical effects of alkaloids upon the nervous system."[32]

The same can be said about psychology. There is an interesting parallel between the opposition of Mach and Ostwald to the atomic theory in chemistry and in physics and that of gestalt and field psychologists to "atomistic" explanations of behavior.

To Feigl all molar theories represent a rather low level of interpretation. A higher level will be approached with the introduction of micro-theories. Freud's or Lewin's models should be "appraised in terms of the isomorphism they attain with the corresponding structures and processes certified by the physiological approach."

Feigl seems to identify micro-theories with neurophysiology. The history of psychological thought bears no proof of his standpoint. A vitalist may be molar and neurophysiologically minded. Kurt Goldstein is a neurosurgeon and holistic and molar; gestalt has introduced the molar concept of magnetic field, which is based on neurophysiology.

Reductionism

It is a legitimate scientific procedure to relate less-known facts to better-known facts. This is the origin of reductionism in psychology.

[32] Feigl, "Principles and Problems," in Dennis, *op. cit.*, p. 191.

One of the leading representatives of reductionism in psychology, Carroll Pratt, would like psychology to "resolve itself" in a "basic" discipline like physiology. Only then will psychology become a truly scientific system.[33]

Pratt's idea is tempting, but let us consider it in a broader context and learn by comparison. Can biology resolve itself in physics? All living organisms are physical bodies. When a hungry animal goes a-hunting, the laws of gravitation, acceleration, thermodynamics, etc., are still binding, but they are not sufficient for the interpretation of animal behavior— or even of the behavior of a simple cell. For, although biology is rooted in physics and chemistry, it cannot be reduced or interpreted by them.

It seems that there is some confusion in the discussion of reductionism. Reductionism in *methods* should not be confused with the reductionism in *theory*. Methods of research can follow the path established in other, let us say more "basic," sciences, but the results of research formulated as psychological law may defy the laws of other sciences. Or, notwithstanding a non-reductionist method of research, psychologists may arrive at the formulation of psychological laws identical with the laws discovered in other sciences.

For example, Köhler's reductionism in psychological theory is not a product of a methodological reductionism. Gestalt psychologists have always been opposed to quantification and any other emulation of methods of physics, but they have presented the results of their research in terms of physical sciences—as forces, fields, isomorphism, etc. Freud developed his theory in psychogenic terms, but he believed that mental processes are derivatives of physical processes. Neither Köhler, nor Pavlov, nor Freud, nor Goldstein believed that *anger* is a secretion or a contraction of muscles.

Let us use the following example for a better explanation of the problem. One may push a stone in anger or grief, knowingly or unknowingly, in dream or in a waking state. All these are irrelevant factors for the interpretation of the stone's movements and the prediction of its behavior. The relevant factors are the amount of energy, the direction of the movement, the weight of the stone, friction, etc.

However, when one individual pushes another individual, all the aforementioned factors become secondary. Of course they do exist, but it is far more important to know the motives and perceptions of the pushing individual and the motives and perceptions of the pushed one. In order to interpret what happened and to predict what will happen next, an analysis of motivations and perceptions of the two persons is necessary. Men are not stones, and no behavioristic theories borrowed from physics would enable us to predict human behavior. A heartbeat is not fear, a swollen jaw is not toothache, birthgiving cramps are not labor pains,

[33] Carroll C. Pratt, *The Logic of Modern Psychology*, Macmillan, 1948.

alcohol in the stomach is not identical with a gay mood. It is important to see and to seek to interpret these relationships; the psychophysical parallelism, Pavlov's methodological dualism, Köhlers' isomorphism, Lashley's brain mechanisms, Goldstein's theory of organism, Freud's cautious restraint from physiology—all these are legitimate efforts to face the problem.

The problem remains unsolved. Psychology cannot be dissolved in physics or reduced to physiology because psychological phenomena deal with problems that do not exist in the other sciences. The two outstanding psychological issues, perception and motivation, are not existent in inanimate nature. Awareness of pain and pleasure, striving toward goals, and all conscious and unconscious activities are the subject matter of psychology only.

This is precisely why all efforts toward reductionism are doomed to fail, and methodological reductionism has even less chance than theoretical reductionism. Theoretical reductionism, which tries to derive psychological phenomena from physics, chemistry, and physiology, has at least good backing in empirical facts. Perhaps there is some kind of isotropism, or parallelism, or energetism; at any rate human beings are living organisms. Unfortunately we do not know today much more about it than was known at the time of Descartes. Naïve statements and sweeping generalizations were made then and are made today.

Methodological reductionism forces the issue. The presentation of human behavior as a series of physicochemical changes, tensions, reactions, or tropisms is rather inadequate and does not help much in the understanding and prediction of the higher mental processes. Nor does any kind of field theory operating with forces, vectors, etc.

We know today the weaknesses and shortcomings of the solutions proposed by Dilthey or Titchener, and we have made considerable progress thanks to Pavlov, Freud, and Hull, but the main issues are far from being solved. Psychological issues and problems can and should be attacked from various angles, but there is no escaping the fact that these problems are not found in physics, and no solution borrowed from that science can solve them.

Psychologists have to learn to face reality, psychological reality. Physicists too do not know the answers to some of their basic problems, but they do not try to borrow dubious answers from other sciences.

As said before, it is a legitimate procedure to relate less-known facts to better-known facts. If physiology, biology, neurology, etc., can help, let us make use of them. But to invite neurological speculations is even less justified than to use psychological ones. Speculations in psychology can perhaps be forgiven because so many psychological symptoms are unobservable. Neurology should be called in to increase the number of observed data and to reduce the area of speculative interpolations. But there is no reason to increase the vagueness of psychological theory and to add to psychological speculations neurological speculations. Physiological and neurological elements introduced into a psychological theory must belong to the category of observed phenomena; otherwise psychological theory does not need them. We already have too many constructs and inferential statements, and there is no need to add new ones borrowed from an area where external observation is the only legitimate scientific procedure.

The conclusion is that psychologists, like all other scientists, are entitled to and should be encouraged to borrow from other sciences, especially from the more "basic" sciences such as biology, physiology, and neurology. They should borrow the best-proved statements for support of their own findings and hypotheses. But, since these statements cannot take the place of psychological inquiry, the best policy is to be found in *methodological non-reductionism.* Psychology must go its own way irrespective of one's hopes or beliefs that ultimately everything stems from the organic (cf. Chap. 15, section 1).

Causation

After a painstaking search for facts and their grouping together in classes, the research worker is tempted to seek the interrelationships between the various factors. These interrelationships disclose *how* and *why* things happen; they are the milestones in scientific inquiry.

The relationships can be logical (inferences), mathematical (functions and correlations), teleological, and causal. It is our belief that only causation offers interpretation and makes possible prediction.

Let us start with discussion of the other types of relations. Logical inferences are made irrespective of physical reality; mathematicians operate very well with $\sqrt{-1}$ or i, which obviously is an unreal number. Inference is a formal logical procedure independent of the content of the propositions. This is obviously not what is sought by empirical scientists including psychologists.

Mathematical functions and correlations are often used in empirical studies. They may be related to causal relations in one of three possible ways: (1) the causal relations do not exist, and the only factual relationship between bodies and events is the mathematical function, (2) the functional and the causal relationships are one and the same thing, (3) the only relationship is the causal one, which can be expressed in terms of a mathematical function.

The second alternative can be easily discarded. Consider the functional (but not causal!) relationship between the sines of one angle in a triangle and the sines of the other angle. The last alternative seems to be acceptable. The first requires further clarification of the concept of causation.

The issue of teleology should be divided into two. As long as teleology is presented as the striving of the organism toward a goal (cf. K. Goldstein), it does not contradict causation, nor does it contradict empirical observation. The idea of a universal goal has practically no supportive evidence.

Actually, no scientific research is possible without some sort of causality. Scientific inquiry usually seeks the unknown factor x, as follows:

$$a+b = x, \qquad \text{ergo } x = a+b$$

or

$$a+x = b, \qquad \text{ergo } x = b - a.$$

In empirical sciences we may proceed from the known causes to the known laws toward unknown results. Very often we proceed from the known causes to the known results toward the discovery of unknown laws.

Even if one substitutes probability[34] for strict causality, probability in the natural sciences represents causal relations although inexactly defined. Without causation no statistical probability could exist beyond the point of sheer chance.

The opposition to the causal principle started with D. Hume, who wrote as follows: "We have no other notion of cause and effect, but that of certain objects, which have been always *conjoined* together, and which in all past instances have been found inseparable. We cannot penetrate into the reason of the conjunction. We only observe the thing itself, and always find that from constant conjunction the objects acquire an union in the imagination."[35]

Kelson thinks that the inclination to consider experience as a two-elements process, one of which is the cause and the other the effect, can be derived from the primitive tendency to consider all experience as an expression of divine laws in which offense and retribution are interpreted as cause and effect.[36]

Even if this were true, it would only point to the historical roots of the concept of causality and would not help in resolving the question of causal relationship in present-day science.

Auguste Comte went farther. *"Tous les bons esprits reconnaissent aujourd'hui que nos études réelles sont strictement circonscrites à l'analyse des phénomènes pour découvrir leurs lois effectives, c'est à dire leurs relations constantes de succession ou de similitude, et ne peuve nullement concerner leur nature intime, ni leur cause, ou première ou finale, ni leur mode essentiel de production. . . . Ainsi toute hypothèse qui franchit les*

[34] Hans Reichenbach, *The Theory of Probability* (2nd ed.), University of California, 1949.

[35] David Hume, *A Treatise of Human Nature* (T. H. Green and T. H. Grose, eds.), Longmans, Green, 1874, Part III, VI, p. 394.

[36] H. Kelson, "Causality and Retribution," *Philosophy of Science*, 1941, 8, 553-556.

limites de cete sphère positive ne peut aboutir qu'à engendrer des discussions interminables, en prétendant prononcer sur des questions nécessairement insoluble pour notre intelligence." (In abbreviation, our real studies are confined to the analysis of phenomena in order to discover their laws, i.e., their constant relationships of sequence or similarity, and we should not be concerned with their nature or cause.)[37]

Similar reservations concerning causation have been presented by W. Dingle: "All that observation tells us on this matter is that certain states of a physical system invariably succeed other states. We go beyond this at our peril. We have no right to say that there is some hidden element, some 'cause' in the first state which fashions the second; or, if we do say it, we must perpetually remind ourselves that it is merely a mode of expressing invariable sequence and nothing more. 'Cause' is like Newton's 'force,' a term used as a conventional means of describing phenomena, and if we give it a significance beyond that we will sooner or later meet our Einstein who will take it from us."[38]

In two studies devoted to the methodology of natural[39] and behavioral[40] sciences the following proposals have been made. The proposals represent *one* principle, for the behavioral sciences are a special case within the realm of the natural sciences. Causation is a *genetic sequence which comes with an ontological necessity.* The cause of an event is given by the answer to the question: *Why* did it happen? The cause of a body is given by the answer to the question: *What* did it come from? The effect *results* from the cause; it is its inevitable product. Why did this house fall? The *total cause* must include material, construction, erosion, climate, wear and tear, etc.

Causation is a peculiar type of necessary sequence. That $\sqrt{4}$ is ± 2 is a *logical* necessity, a sequence related to laws agreed upon in mathematics. That days follow nights is an *ontological* necessity, a sequence related to the laws of nature. But nights do not result in days; therefore this is not a causal sequence. Fertilization *results* in birth; a bullet in the head *results* in death; here the sequence is *genetic* and ontologically necessary and, according to our definition, *causal.* The striking of a match lights a fire; the ingestion of medicine kills germs; traumatic experiences lead to neurosis. All these cases are cases of partial causation. Complete causation, as pointed out before, must include the totality of causation factors.

It is proposed here to postulate that all that happens is a chain of causes and effects. This postulate of *determinism,* accepted by Pavlov, Freud, Goldstein, Lashley, and many others, cannot be directly proved.

[37] Comte, *op. cit.*, p. 229.

[38] William Dingle, *Science and Human Experience*, Williams & Norgate, 1931, p. 88.

[39] Benjamin B. Wolman, "Chance: A Philosophical Study," *Tarbitz, Hebrew University Quarterly* (Hebrew), 1938, 10, 56–80.

[40] Wolman, *Prolegomena to Sociology.*

It is being proved daily by all our observations, and to doubt it would mean to doubt any regularity in the universe.

Contemporary physics has in one area certain difficulties with causation. It is the quantum theory, in which the deterministic principle is not applicable. Yet physicists have not given up determinism in any other area of research. A leading physicist, M. Planck, stated that "physical science together with astronomy and chemistry and mineralogy are all based on the strict and universal validity of the principle of causality."[41]

Such a difficulty does not exist in psychology. A deviation from determinism in psychology would make things unexplainable.

Laws of Nature in Psychology

Laws of nature represent the permanent patterns of happenings. They express the regularity of the world. Sun and stars, plants and animals move in a certain and definite manner. Gravitation, electrolysis, splitting of atoms, growth of plants and animals—these are the eternal regularities, the laws of nature. Who knows the present facts and the laws of nature can predict the future facts. The ultimate goal of theory is their knowledge.

"A theory in present-day physics," wrote Spence, "is a system of highly abstract constructs used to integrate sets of empirical laws that without the theory would appear to be quite unrelated. Examples of such integrating devices are the electromagnetic theory of radiation and the kinetic theory of gases. In contrast, what passes for theory in the behavior sciences serves primarily as a device to aid in the formulation of descriptive laws. Theory in psychology, then, consists primarily in the introduction or postulation of hypothetical constructs to represent the unknown or uncontrolled factors in a situation under observation."[42]

Spence's judgment may sound a bit harsh. Psychology deals with more complex problems and has had less time to study them; undoubtedly psychology is methodologically less advanced than physics. However, psychology and physics and all other sciences introduce constructs in the process of theory formation. But ultimately any scientific system is a system of laws of nature. Their degree of abstraction must vary from science to science.

There is still a great deal of controversy among psychologists (cf. Chap. 15, section 5), but the growing body of empirical data leads inevitably to an ever increasing agreement in conclusions. Cannon, Pavlov, Köhler, Freud, and Goldstein talk about the same principle of equilibrium even when they use different terms. There is general agreement

[41] Hugo Bergmann, *Der Kampf um das Kausalitätsprinzip in der jüngsten Physik,* Barth, 1929; Max Planck, *Where Science Is Going,* Norton, 1932, p. 147.

[42] Kenneth Spence, "Theoretical Interpretations of Learning," in S. S. Stevens, *Handbook of Experimental Psychology,* Wiley, 1951, p. 690.

that the laws of preservation of energy apply to mental processes. S. Freud, J. Piaget, and A. Gesell introduced the laws of development.

The laws of nature in psychology are part of the laws of nature. They express the regularity of happenings in the area of nature studied by psychologists. Psychologists deal with highly complex processes, and the discovery of laws of nature in that area is not an easy task. No wonder there is still so much controversy.

Laws of nature in psychology either exist or do not exist. They cannot be invented. They must be discovered, proved, and put in words. Some philosophers seem to believe that the logic of science is merely the logical syntax of the language of science.[43] Obviously this is not true. The problem of language is legitimate but it is not the only or the main methodological problem.

4. THE LANGUAGE OF SCIENCES

The Problem of Communication

All scientific data have to be recorded and communicated. Science is a system of *statements*—a definite kind of statements (true, proved, systematic, general, etc.) made or *expressed* by a scientist and *communicated* to others. Scientific discoveries are not included in the body of science unless they are properly stated and communicated.

Scientists today do a painstaking job in presentation and communication. They like to say what they have to say in a clear, unambiguous manner. A special science of communication, a science of language, has been developed, mostly in two forms: the first is *syntax*, which deals with the conventional language and its proper use; the other is *mathematics* or the language of abstract symbols.

The tremendous growth of the *science of signs* may lead sometimes to an overenthusiastic distortion of the goals of scientific inquiry. The only goal of scientific inquiry is the search for truth; everything else is a means toward this goal.

One of these means is presentation and communication. Syntax and mathematics are indispensable tools of scientific research, but they are not the only ones nor can they take the place of empirical research.

Some philosophers seem to believe that these tools are the science proper.[44] They regard scientific systems as systems of signs, whereas scientific systems are systems of true statements about things. These systems can be ordered to or expressed in systems of signs. While the formal study of signs plays an important role in scientific theory, it is nothing

---

[43] Rudolf Carnap, *Philosophy and Logical Syntax*, Kegan Paul 1935.
[44] *Ibid.*

more than a study of the tools of presentation and communication. Poor systems of signs may unfavorably present the scientific system; a good, convenient, consistent system of signs may enhance the clarity and communicability of a scientific system. However, even the most formalized system of signs does not make a scientific system more scientific and more truthful.

The problems of presentation and communication of scientific data are more modest than the neo-positivists believe. Still they are of considerable importance for the development of scientific theories.

Systems of Signs

The choice of a system of signs in which to put the results of empirical research is a matter of methodological convenience, but it is not an entirely free choice. Deciding on a definite system of signs depends on a thorough examination of the facts concerned, the character of the scientific data, and the nature of a given system of signs. The character of the scientific data cannot be manipulated; nature does not care to please the scientist. Obviously the system of signs must be adjusted to a given research area and branch of science, but there are definite limitations to the manipulation of signs. No system of signs which is self-contradictory can be used for scientific inquiry. This basic law of immanent truth does not prescribe how a system of signs is composed or constructed, how flexible it is, or how useful it must be for future studies.

Careful studies are required in order to state the degree of adaptability of a certain system of signs to a certain area of scientific investigation. Quite often new systems of signs are invented and after careful scrutiny applied to a certain area of research.

Mathematicians do not care whether their statements do or do not represent any portion of reality. The role played by the sign i, which is $\sqrt{-1}$, is well known in the history of electricity. It is the task of the empirical scientist to find or to invent a system of signs in which scientific data can be presented.

Any system, even a system of signs, has its own logic. Without this it would be not a system but an aggregate. An empirical research worker must be aware of the rules underlying a given system of signs *before* he utilizes it for presentation and communication of his findings. Unless a given system of signs fully corresponds to the empirical data and enables free transition in both directions—from the observed facts to the conceptualized signs and vice versa—this system should not be accepted as the tool for presentation and communication. Sometimes a system of signs is unable to carry and transmit the content it is supposed to carry. Composers know that not every system of notes can transmit faithfully the content of their compositions, nor is every instrument capable of reproducing each musical composition. One cannot translate the works of masters like Dostoevski or Romain Rolland or Shakespeare into the language of a primitive tribe. But literary Russian, French, English, and many other languages can do a perfect job.

Language Problems in Psychology

Thus the "linguistic" decision of an empirical research worker may be quite important for the presentation of his findings and do justice or injustice to his entire work. Many research works suffer from unclear presentation. The terms used are often ambiguous or not well defined; the reasoning may not be too rigorous; the terms may be used loosely. Especially in psychology are the dangers great because the conventional languages are permeated with pictorial and nonprecise statements.

The history of human knowledge knows many never ending arguments resulting from verbal confusion and lack of clarity in definitions of terms applied. The use of mathematical symbols instead of the conventional language has often resulted in greater clarity and avoidance of pseudo problems.

Psychologists today successfully apply a great variety of mathematical devices, especially in the field of mental measurements.[45] It seems that the usual statistical methods are very well suited to handling most of the problems presented by laboratory work in perception, learning, and related areas.

Sometimes the difficulty arises from an improper choice of the system of signs. Herbart, for example, tried to order his metaphysical ideas to concepts of numbers. Obviously his data could not be measured, and Herbart's mathematics was neither mathematics nor psychology.[46]

Undoubtedly Kurt Lewin was much more cautious. Most of his definitions are clear and logical, his statements precise and well elaborated. Yet one cannot help feeling that Lewin was, in a way, a victim of his mathematical system. Once he decided to order psychology to the language of topological geometry, he had to adjust his empirical findings to the rules and laws of topology such as barriers and regions. After Lewin's untimely death his work in group dynamics was continued by his disciples, but there has been very little continuity in the use of his mathematical concepts and language.

Apparently topology imposed on Lewin additional difficulties in communicating his findings. Either topology is not suited to presentation of psychological data or Lewin failed to make proper use of it. In either case he was compelled to construct a kind of "one-man language," and this is exactly the opposite to what scientific language is meant for.

[45] Herold Gulliksen, *The Theory of Mental Testing*, Wiley, 1950.
[46] Benjamin B. Wolman, "Johann Friedrich Herbart," *Hachinuch Quarterly* (Hebrew), 1942, **15**, 1–23.

CHAPTER 15

Some Crucial Questions and Tentative Answers

1. THE PROBLEM OF REDUCTIONISM

The Dichotomy

Psychologists have tried to escape the dualistic conflict inherited from traditional philosophy. Dualism has split the world into bodies and souls, leaving bodies to scientific study and assigning souls to psychologists.

Several attempts have been made to revise this division of the subject matter of research. Dilthey and all who followed in his footsteps assigned to psychology all the *products* of human mind, the culture. They made psychology the queen of the humanities, which do not deal with objects or bodies but study the immense area of human culture.

The structuralists entrenched themselves in "consciousness." They recognized the supremacy of physiology and leaned heavily on studies in the nervous system in a perpetual search for a neurological interpretation for psychology. They discarded the immortal soul with its faculties and borrowed the empirical and experimental methods from the natural scientists. Psychology, they said, dealt with phenomena which could not be seen from the outside; hence introspection was the perfect and the only possible substitute for extrospection. Rigorous methods, resembling those of physical and physiological laboratories, were developed. Psychologists did not define their topic as nonmaterial. They drew a thin line between themselves and other natural scientists out of sheer necessity, because the phenomena they had to cover could be seen by inner observation only. No one could blame Titchener or Wundt for being a priori mentalistic. Even less blame could be put on the phenomenological school or the functionalists. The phenomenologists studied what was going on inasmuch as it was observable. James rejected the concept of soul and sought an integrating force instead.

The functionalists took an additional step in the direction of the natural sciences, especially biology. They refused to deal with consciousness or with phenomena given in introspection outside the context of biological processes. Psychological capacities, whether conscious or not,

530

are regarded by functionalists as important functions in the adjustment to the environment; they are no less needed, no less vital than the legs which carry the organism or the stomach which digests the food. Psychological capacities are, in Dewey's way of thinking an "instrument" in adjustment, and one of the most necessary functions of the organism.

The "objective" psychologists rejected mentalism and studied the *behavior* of men. Behavior does not prejudge the issue. Methodologically speaking, behaviorism is a naïve empiricism: you can easily see, compare, predict, and verify. No wonder behaviorism was received with so much enthusiasm and hope.

But too many problems remained unsolved. The so-called higher mental processes resisted the efforts of too simple an explanation. Is thinking really nothing but prevocal talking? Cannot deaf-mutes solve problems and reason without any talk whatsoever?

The neo-behaviorists could not avoid the soma-psyche issue. Tolman, Hull, Skinner, and others contributed immensely both to the methodology and to factual data in psychology, but they could not solve this problem.

Some solutions were offered by Lashley, Kantor, Hebb, and the gestaltists. Each of the proposed solutions has been discussed in the present volume. Each increased our knowledge of factual data but could not find the bridge between the somatic and the psychic.

The cautious Pavlov avoided psychological terms but left the door open for a "methodological dualism" in the spirit of a bridge-building philosophy. The Soviet psychologists kept working on various problems in neurology and psychology on the assumption that the psychological reflects the physical. This methodological dualism enabled Soviet psychology to overcome the arid and naïve reductionism of Bekhterev, but it does not solve the problem under consideration.

Freud was fully aware of this problem. When he started his work at the crossroads of the centuries the general atmosphere in psychiatry was unfavorable to a nonorganic theory of mental disturbances. Freud was accused of mentalism, but it was he who said: "The future may teach us how to exercise a direct influence, by means of particular chemical substances, upon the amounts of energy and their distribution in the apparatus of mind."[1]

Freud was a *theoretical reductionist* for he believed that mental energy originated from physical energy and assumed that all mental processes are processes of discharge of energy in accordance with Newton's laws.

But meanwhile Freud was a methodological non-reductionist. He doubted the usefulness of an unproved, glib, unempirical, and speculative reductionism. Instead he developed a series of logical constructs on a non-reductionistic level—the id, ego, superego, transference, etc.

[1] Sigmund Freud, *Outline of Psychoanalysis*, Norton, 1949, p. 79.

The Bridge Between Physical and Mental

Sometimes one wonders how true the soma-psyche dichotomy is and how much of it does relate to our inability to overcome primitive ways of reasoning in antinomies, such as good and bad, old and young, healthy and sick, asleep and awake. Each of these terms represents *degrees* of the same continuum and not genuine opposites.

The ancient Ionian philosophers insisted that there are four "elements": fire, water, air, and soil. Especially fire and water gave the impression of being irreconcilable opposites. The history of science shows that many of these pseudo opposites have been discarded. While the speculative philosopher Hegel believed that the development of the world is a dialectic struggle of opposites, the empirical scientist Darwin developed the theory of a gradual evolution.

Consider the division of all physical bodies into gas, fluids, and solid bodies. At certain points one cannot be certain whether mist is gas or fluid, or whether melting snow is still solid.

Crude as these examples may be, let us utilize them for a tentative exploration in the soma-psyche dichotomy. No doubt brain waves are soma and the feeling of pride is psyche; to say that these two are the same would violate the laws of both empirical perception and logical reasoning. But in certain areas of the functioning of the organism the gap between soma and psyche becomes so narrow that there seems to be promise in concentrating our scientific efforts there. The deep layers of unconscious attacked by psychoanalytic method represent one end of the gap, while the interoceptive functions of the inner organs represent the other.

Illuminating examples of the psyche-soma relationships have been offered by S. I. Franz in his studies in reeducation of patients whose brains had been injured by wounds or illness.[2] A fifty-seven-year-old aphasic patient paralyzed on his right side was capable of relearning names of colors, prayers, and a poem. A soldier paralyzed after being hit by an explosive was ordered by the power of suggestion to walk without a cane. Bykov and associates reported cases of conditioning with practically any inner organ; the frequency and amount of urination, for example, were changed and conditioned by external sensory stimuli which usually have nothing to do with urination. These and other (cf. Chap. 2, section 6) neurophysiological studies seem to have weakened the wall separating mental phenomena from neurological.

Two men who have contributed the most toward the solution of the problem went about their empirical research without building imaginary and unseen bridges. These men are Pavlov and Freud. Most of us believe

---

[2] Shepherd I. Franz, *Nervous and Mental Re-education*, Macmillan, 1923.

that there is a bridge between the physical and the mental phenomena. Nature crosses the bridge very often. Whenever alcohol or drugs change one's mood, or a tranquilizer calms down an upset individual, the bridge is crossed from its somatic-physical side. Whenever one develops a peptic ulcer, or a skin rash, or vomiting, the only reason being his emotional problems, the bridge is crossed from its psychological side.

The neurophysiological studies of Sherrington, Sechenov, Pavlov, Franz, Lashley, Bykov, Hebb, and others represent the somatic end of the gap. One may be as pessimistic as Sherrington or as optimistic as Pavlov and Lashley in regard to the final outcome of research on the gap between soma and psyche, but everyone must agree that the gap is today narrower than ever before owing to the indefatigable work of the above-mentioned and scores of others.

Thus the attitude of Freud and of Pavlov has been well justified. Freud took a stand on the psychological side and built his road toward the invisible bridge. The rocks he used were mental, such as wish, fear, love, hate—all of them derived from statements of individuals who were fully (consciously) or dimly (unconsciously) aware of something like wish, fear, love, or hate.

Pavlov stood on the other side of the bridge. He expressed the hope that the bridge would be crossed by scientific research and that a psychology based on physiology would come into being. But his job was digging and paving the road from the neurophysiological side of the bridge. The rocks he used were taken from the physiology of the higher mental processes irrespective of their mental counterparts or results.

Transitionism

The transition from physical to mental is an undeniable, daily observed fact. Our moods, feelings, and thoughts change with the intake of chemicals; our bodies change under the influence of mental factors. Nature crosses this bridge every day but scientists seek it in vain.

This daily experience strengthens our belief in the *unity* or at least *continuity* of the universe. Any other concept, such as pluralism, is less acceptable and leads unavoidably to unsolvable problems of "coexistence" between matter and spirit, body and mind. Any dualistic system breaks up the continuity of the world. This theoretical cleavage cannot be corroborated by any empirical research or accepted by any speculative study. It leaves us in confusion as to the nature of the world with no possible way out, be it that suggested by Plato or by Descartes.

Thus this writer proposes to postulate the concept of *transitionism*, which is an evolutionary interpretation of monism. The world is one world composed of things, but these things are different and cannot be reduced to their origins. Within the realm of organic nature all species have something in common; all are parts of the living matter, yet the higher species are not the same as the lower ones. Monkeys are not amoebas, mammals are not protozoa. There is a *transition* from one species to the other.

At a certain point of evolution the organism becomes capable of receiving stimuli; of responding to them. This ability, observed in lower species, undergoes changes. At a high level of evolution there is the undeniable fact of *awareness*, conscious or otherwise, which cannot be empirically found or logically inferred from observations of primitive organisms. The only way out is to assume a *continuum* of transformation or evolution. *Transitionism is the theory of a continuous transition of organic life from one stage to another.* Transitionism excludes any kind of unilateral simple reductionism. If the chain of transition is

$$A \to B \to C \to D \to$$

it does not mean that B = A, C = B, etc. It means only that B contains at least some parts of A or that A in its totality or some parts of A were included in the emergence of B. In other words, B emerged out of A, but B is not A. A scientific interpretation of B cannot lead to a reduction of B to A. B cannot be interpreted in terms of A, since B differs from A.

This assumption permits a search for some elements, stemming from A, that are incorporated in B. *Transitionism assumes continuity.* Some elements of the past are included in the present; some inorganic elements are included in any organism. The personality of an adult contains some elements of his infancy; the plant contains some elements of the seed from which it grew.

Transitionism applies the principle of evolution to the soma-psyche pseudo dichotomy. Higher species developed out of lower species, higher somatic structures out of lower ones, mental processes out of higher somatic structures. Although biologists assume that mammals developed from protozoa, no biologist would "reduce" the sexual procreation in mammals to the procreation by division in protozoa.

This is why, so this writer believes, any theoretical reductionism must fail. Men are not rats, and even less do they resemble magnetic fields or collections of electrons. There is no doubt that the basic elements of nature have been included in the development of the human organism, and they are still there. But, in the course of millennia, they have undergone so many and so radical changes that whoever hopes to be able to interpret human behavior in physicochemical terms is like a man who after twenty years comes to visit someone he remembers as a newborn baby, expecting to find the twenty-year-old man in a crib sucking a nipple. Or he is like the gardener who chopped down a tree in order to find the seed from which the tree developed.

Transitionism has to be postulated in psychology, just as determinism does. We do not have direct evidence for the transitionist hypothesis nor do we know how to find it. But indirect proof is given by psychosomatic medicine or perhaps by the total area of medicine, and by our daily experience, which bears witness to the continuity of the changing world.

It seems that the unconscious is closer to the organic than is the conscious part of personality. A. Adler called psychosomatic symptoms "the language of the organism." The deepest layers of the unconscious, such as the dim, yet definite feeling of oncoming danger found in animals and in many mentally disturbed individuals, are among the areas where mental processes must come pretty close to physical processes or at least indicate more clearly the points of transition.

2. LUST FOR LIFE

Loeb, Freud, Pavlov, Goldstein, and other keen observers of organisms noticed that all the actions of living matter are directed toward promotion of life and protection of it. This tendency, be it called drive or instinct, is obviously inherited, universal, and deeply embedded in the nature of living matter. According to Pavlov the food center is very important but the protection against the breaking of bones and immediate loss of life is stronger than hunger.

In Freud's system self-preservation and the preservation of species have been combined into one instinctual force, Eros, or the instinct of life. The mental energy put at the disposal of Eros, the libido, can be cathected (invested) in oneself or in others. In 1920 Freud postulated the instinct of death and destruction, Thanatos.

Psychologists found the idea of hate, aggression, and destruction a highly controversial one. In Freud's theory destruction of life means regression to inanimate nature in accordance with the principle of constancy. Thus Eros and Thanatos are two opposite poles, the instincts of life and death respectively.

This presentation met with serious objections from both psychoanalysts and opponents. The author of this volume suggests here some new ideas concerning Freud's hypothesis of Eros and Thanatos.

The Death Instinct

Instincts are forces which facilitate the discharge of energy in order to remove tension and to restore equilibrium. Instincts have a somatic source, aim, and object. It seems, however, impossible to trace the source of the instinct of death.

The life and death instincts could not possibly be two contradictory instinctual forces, each of them moving quantities of energy. The life instinct uses energies; it stimulates the discharge of physical energies for the protection of life. When these energies are low, life comes to an end. The decline of instinctual forces indicates a decline in vitality and the approaching of the point of zero energies. The absolute point of not-life is usually called death.

Whether organic matter moves in the direction of inorganic matter is a question not easily answered. It is the speculation of Herbert Spencer that evolution will be followed by dissolution. It is Hegel's idea that life and death follow each other. But neither Spencer nor Hegel brought any empirical evidence in support of their philosophical speculations.

Actually, the term "death" is inapplicable to inorganic matter. Inorganic nature is neither alive nor dead. Living bodies may stop living and then they are called dead, but stones, rivers, and clouds are neither dead nor alive. Men, animals, and plants can be alive or dead, but a wind, a rock, CO_2, HCl are neither alive nor dead. The Dead Sea is called Dead because it is full of living organisms which died. All other seas are neither dead nor alive. When an organism "dies" or ceases to live, other organisms start to live.

Life can be measured by the amount of energy in it. An organism may be full of life and blooming, or declining, starving, or decaying. The instinct of life serves to protect life and increase vitality. Can the supposed death instinct serve to increase or protect death? The decline of life brings one closer to death, but death itself cannot be measured. Death cannot be perceived, for death is the zero point, nothingness, "not-life." No action "serves" or "protects" death or dying; no living organism uses instinctual energy to die or to increase or to strengthen or to protect death. There are many causes of death, but it would be fanciful to assume that there is an inner, innate instinctual force which leads to death of the organism.

Life can be equilibrium and disequilibrium, action and rest, waking and sleeping, a dynamic homeostasis or tensions and reliefs. Death is neither action nor inaction, neither tension nor relief, neither equilibrium nor disequilibrium. Life is metabolism, sometimes balanced and sometimes disbalanced. In accordance with the principle of constancy, there is a tendency to restore the balance of life, the balance of the living organism. The principle of constancy is inapplicable to death, since constancy deals with the balance of energy. Death, containing no energy, cannot be a balance of energy.

Additional criticism of the idea of a death instinct can be invoked by a quotation of Freud's definition of instinct, and this is actually what Fenichel did: "A death instinct would not be compatible with the approved biological concept of instinct. . . . The thesis of an instinct source that makes the organism react to stimuli with drives toward 'instinct actions' which then change the source in an appropriate manner cannot be applied to a death instinct. The dissimulation in the cells, an objective destruction, cannot be a 'source' of a destructive instinct in the same way that the chemical sensitizing of the central nervous system in regard to stimulation of the erogenous zones is the source of the sexual instinct. According to the definition, the instinct attempts to remove the somatic changes at the source of the instinct. The death instinct does not attempt to remove the dissimulation."[3]

One may add to Fenichel's statements a few remarks. There is no deficiency or excitation or any other disturbance in a man hit by a bullet. Yet he will die. Death does not remove tension nor does it restore equilibrium. It is the end of everything, of tension and relief alike. There cannot be equilibrium or disequilibrium without life.

The Concept of Death

Semantically "death" is a misleading term, since no such thing as death ever existed. The name "death" does not contain any designates, nor does it represent any object, function, or state, or any category, class, or system of objects, functions, or states. Actually, one cannot make logical statements about death, because the only meaning of death is nonexistence, not-life. Life includes a variety of phenomena; death does not include any. Life means "is"; death means "is not."

Biology deals with life and life only, and with its various phenomena in the living cells, tissues, and organisms. No biologists ever transgressed these limits. In the ontogenetic development there is a starting point, growth, development, decline, and decay. From the phylogenetic point of view each life is a continuation of life. The individual life comes to an end, and some species may even disappear, but no biologist has ever analyzed, studied, or described death. There are descriptions of a dying organism, but the dying organism is still alive. A dead animal is no longer an animal. In a dead organism the vital processes of the organism, such as metabolism, digestion, respiration, circulation, and secretion, have come to an end.

Some religions tried to penetrate this "mystery," but whenever men talked about death they inevitably talked about life. Religions painted the picture of the eternal life after death, denying the fact that men die. The hereafter very often became the "hundred years" of the Sleeping Beauty with Prince Charming bringing the craved resurrection. What happened after death was pictured as some sort of quiet and peaceful life, resembling a useful sleep of a tired man and a dream of a pleasant reawakening. Men afraid of nothingness (they claim: *natura abhorret*

[3] Otto Fenichel, *The Psychoanalytic Theory of Neurosis*, Norton, 1945, p. 60.

vacuum) filled death with wishful thinking and believed in the continuation of life. Death is indeed unbelievable; it is even unperceivable.

Death is neither love nor hate, neither constructiveness nor destructiveness. Nor does a dead organism go back to inorganic matter. In fact, in the body of a dead man or animal organic processes continue. But these are no longer organic processes of the dead organism. The organism as a biological entity has ceased to exist.

Whenever men think about those who are dead, the dead appear in thoughts as if they were alive. The deceased love objects become incorporated and very much alive in the introjecting minds. Mythologies talk about the deceased as if they were alive, as ghosts, spirits, and friendly or unfriendly observers. Whenever one talks about a deceased person, he talks in terms of what he was or was believed to be before he died. Poets and philosophers describe the dead in terms of living, telling what the dead have lost, how they suffer, and what they wait for. Our language is a language of life and we have no separate words to describe death.

Thus death is unperceivable, undescribable, unexpressible; the term "death" is an empty word which erroneously suggests that something is included in its category. Actually, it is a word which does not denote anything. Linguistic purists should have used instead the term "not-life," in analogy to "no pain," "no dynamite," or "no trees." Nobody ever tried to describe how no trees, no pain, and no dynamite look.

Sleep and Death

One of the misleading analogies is the analogy drawn between death and sleep. Sleep is not death, nor does it relate to death. Pavlov believed that sleep is a "general inhibition" which enables the living organism to keep an equilibrium between the processes of cellular destruction and restoration (1928). Action destroys the living substance; sleep restores it. Sleep preserves energy, increases the energetic reserves, strengthens vitality, and serves life. Sleep serves to restore equilibrium in accordance with Pavlov's version of the principle of constancy.

Death is not equilibrium. The death of an organism represents the transition from somethingness into nothingness. Death is the zero point of energy of a living organism. Organisms die when their energy is exhausted as a result of old age, disease, excessive use of energy, or physical violence which destroys the vital centers.

Sleep and death represent two entirely different situations of the organism, the former serving its preservation and the latter representing its destruction. The only similarity of these two states lies in the overt passivity of the organism. This superficial similarity is no more enlightening than the similarity between eating and yawning; in both functions the mouth opens.

The fear of death makes men afraid of sleep. The Jewish morning prayer contains thanks to God for the restoration of the soul into the body. Children afraid of death are often afraid to fall asleep. The fear of death caused men to compare death to a sleep from which there is no awakening. It has been, indeed, a great consolation to allay the fear of death by representing death as a sort of deep and relaxing sleep with an expected pleasant awakening of resurrection. Greek mythology described the relaxing and peaceful hereafter in Elysium, where happy souls of deceased men wander aimlessly with no worries of the future and no memories of the past. The monotheistic religions believe in the hereafter and in resurrection perceived as a return of the soul to the body after a long and peaceful sleep which death was supposed to resemble. The "Requiem" prayer alludes to this "resting in peace" as if a dead organism were capable of "resting" peacefully.

The regressive wish to sleep is not necessarily a wish to die. The manic-depressive wish to unite with mother is actually a wish to sleep well, in the safest place—the womb. It is not a wish to die.

The Two Dimensions

The theory of Eros and Thanatos tries to present in one dimension something which is bidimensional. Life and death deal with *amounts* of energy. Life represents some energy; death none. Life is power; decline of life is decline of power, which comes to an end when all the energy is used up.

Once there is life, the energy can be used in two directions, either to promote life or to destroy it. The instinctual force which serves the promotion of life is *Eros*, love. Love can be directed to oneself or to others. Let us name the instinct of destruction *Ares*.[4] Ares too can be

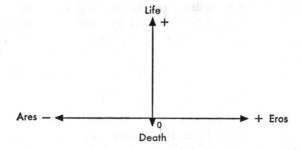

directed toward oneself or toward others. Life and death deal with amounts of energy, but the instincts of love and hostility deal with the direction and aim to which this energy is pushed by Eros and Ares. It can be represented graphically on the Cartesian coordinates as follows.

[4] The Greek god of war.

The vertical dimension represents life: energy is marked $+$ and no energy is marked 0. The horizontal dimension represents the direction in which the energy is used: the plus sign marks Eros or promotion of life and the minus sign marks Ares or destruction.

Libido Development

The actions of a living organism *in relation to objects* can be divided into two categories. Actions aimed at giving life, protecting life, or increasing the vitality of an object belong to the first category, to the realm of Eros, and the energy used in them is *libido*. Actions of the second type aim at destroying or hurting or impairing the chances for survival of an object. These belong to the realm of Ares and the energy used in them is *destrudo*.

Both kinds of actions are functions of the living organism, sometimes uniting and sometimes branching off. Freud's principle of constancy is applicable to both types and in both of them tension is followed by a discharge of energy and the attainment of relief.

Since both types of action are found in neonates—since even the youngest infants display love and hate—it seems logical to assume that both Eros and Ares are instinctual or innate drives. Love and hate are, as Freud postulated, innate forces. We are born to live, and life includes both love and hate.

Do both types of action, those of Eros and of Ares, serve the perpetuation of life of the acting individual? As a rule, Eros serves life. When the energy of Eros, the libido, is cathected in oneself, it serves the protection of one's own life. When it is object-cathected, it serves the life of the object.

As a rule, at the start of life the libido is cathected in one's own organism. This is the primary narcissism. Step by step, through the stages of libido development elaborated by Freud and Abraham, libido goes the long way toward the genital, adult type of object cathexis. The individual becomes gradually less and less selfish and more capable of sacrificing his own protection for the protection of his love objects. More and more libido becomes channeled into non-selfish, aim-inhibited, sublimated, and idealistic love. The infant's oral love is very selfish, destructive, and cannibalistic. Anal love is "tender," with a great deal of consideration for the love object. Phallic love is possessive, but it protects the love object. After the resolution of the Oedipus complex, individuals are more ready to aim-inhibit their love. Adult love contains all the elements of earlier stages subordinated to the desire for mutual happiness.

Interindividual Cathexis

For several years the writer tried to correlate the Freudian frame of reference with data obtained by the method of observation of overt behavior and experimental psychology. It cannot be expected that the results will be identical. Physics and chemistry are not identical either. Thus no wonder that the experimental studies (Sears, 1943) did not yield results identical with those of the psychoanalytical studies. What could be expected was that the experimental and psychoanalytical studies would not contradict each other but would support each other's findings. In the ideal situation psychoanalysis and experimental psychology would become mutually interdependent, analogous to the relationship between physics and chemistry.

Several empirical studies have led this writer to postulate a more general hypothesis of social relations based on power (ability to satisfy needs) and acceptance (willingness to do so). Power and acceptance seem to be the decisive factors in any kind of social relations, and their distribution may determine the nature of these relations and help to predict social behavior.[5] An individual may have certain needs which cannot be satisfied unless he is helped by others. He enters social relations in the hope of attaining his own goals. He may regard the other party as strong (able to satisfy his needs) and friendly (willing to do so). He may not intend to give anything unless compelled to; the only reason he joins this relationship is to get as much as possible out of it. Thus, this relationship is *instrumental* for him.

When people join social relations having in mind to *give* and to *get,* they form a *mutual acceptance* group. Friendliness, mutuality, and good will characterize this kind of relationship.

The third or vectorial type of social relationship, is characterized by willingness to *give* without taking. An individual offers his service to others or to an objective ideal without asking for reward. He is ready for self-sacrifice for others or for an ideal.

There are no pure types of groups; groups are what they are to their members. Yet some groups represent fairly well the three respective types. The child-mother relationship is *instrumental.* Most business associations are too. Most college classes are of the same nature since the student joins them in order to get some knowledge or points of credit. A close friendship represents a *mutual acceptance* type of group; marriage is often based on readiness for mutual help. The mother-child relationship is *vectorial;* most mothers are prepared for self-sacrifice irre-

[5] Benjamin B. Wolman, *Freedom and Discipline in Education* (Hebrew), Massada, 1949; "Leadership and Group Dynamics," *Journal of Social Psychology,* 1956, **43,** 11–25; "Instrumental, Mutual Acceptance and Vectorial Groups," *Acta Sociologica,* 1958, **3,** 19–27.

spective of the children's attitude to them. People who sacrifice their lives for the benefit of mankind or for great religious, social, or national ideals form vectorial groups.

These three types of relationship correspond roughly to the balance of interindividual libido cathexis. A narcissistic individual who expects to have his needs taken care by others relates to others in an instrumental way. An individual who is capable of object libido cathexis on a give-and-take level relates to others in a mutual acceptance way. An individual who is capable of giving love without asking anything in return relates to others in a vectorial way. Childhood is basically instrumental. Adulthood is mutual acceptance. Parenthood is vectorial, the readiness to give *without* taking and the readiness for responsibility and self-sacrifice.

The well-balanced adult is capable of all three types of relationships.

Hostile actions are undeniable facts in interindividual relations. Yet there is no room for hate in our developmental schedule from instrumentalism toward vectorialism. There is no room for hostility in any theory of development. Hostility, so we hypothesize, is (1) a protective function of the living organism, always related to self-love; (2) it is always primitive. There cannot be any "progress" in destrudo. Destrudo is the normal state in animals and in infants. In adults it is always a sign of regression.

Let us elaborate our hypothesis and bring in some supportive evidence.

Ares, the Guarding Instinct

Ares, like Eros, has impetus, source, object, and aim. Its impetus is the amount of destrudo energy at its disposal. Its source, we believe, is the *feeling of danger, of a threat to life.* Its object can be any living or inanimate thing (inclusive of one's own organism) which represents the threat. Ares' energy, destrudo, can be cathected in any object. Its aim can be complete or partial destruction depending upon the degree of fusion with the libido and upon the inhibiting actions of the ego and superego.

Ares, the instinct of hostility, fits well into the Freudian definition of instinct given by Fenichel. As quoted above, "the instinct attempts to remove the somatic changes at the source of the instinct." The somatic changes are increased heartbeat, perspiration, trembling, contraction of muscles, etc. The threat of annihilation lies at the roots of the somatic changes, at the source of Ares. The hostile action, a discharge of destrudo aiming at destruction of the threatening object, restores the balance in analogy to the actions of Eros. The threat may be related to an inner stimulus of hunger or an outer hostile stimulus that prevents satisfaction of hunger or prevents escape from hostility, or any other combination of stimuli.

Several studies, starting with Charles Darwin and continuing through Huxley, Schjelderup-Ebbe, and Konrad Lorentz, have pointed to violence and the use of physical force for self-defense as the general law of nature. The survival of the fittest is explained in that vein. Schjelderup-Ebbe found that social relations among birds are based on the pecking order or the right of the stronger. Lorentz believes that hate is a more general and more fundamental pattern than love. All animal psychologists emphasize hostility as the prevailing pattern in the animal kingdom.

Even the cautious I. P. Pavlov came to the conclusion that hostile behavior in dogs is primarily a *guarding reaction* against injury or a threat of it. The experimental studies on frustration in children by Dollard and others in 1939 stressed the fact that frustrated children became hostile. It seems as though adverse life conditions act as releasers of hostile actions, whether in the scapegoat mechanism, antisocial actions in new immigrants, or general hostility.

Pavlov appears to have found the guarding reflex the most powerful one. Moreover, it was always victorious in the case of conflicting motives. When men or animals are tired, they are in no mood for love and they can be easily provoked into violence. When they are hurt, hungry, thirsty, wounded, exhausted, sick, frustrated, or starved, whenever their energies are low, the available energy is predominantly destructive. It is as if the emergency situation were calling forth the emergency forces, and in emergency animals fly into a furious rage. Hate seems to be a more powerful, primary, and primitive incentive than love.

Ares, the Primary Instinct

Freud's theory of libido development describes in detail the way the child grows from the primary narcissism through the oral, anal, urethral, phallic, and latency stages toward the genital adulthood. Scores of workers confirmed Freud's findings and elaborated them in a more detailed manner.

No such work was ever done on *destrudo* (or, as Federn calls it, *mortido*). The existence of aggressive impulses in children and adults cannot be denied. How is it possible that no satisfactorily detailed theory of development of destrudo was ever presented? Our answer is simple. The Ares and destrudo have no developmental line. Ares is always archaic, primitive, and primordial. It is always indicative of aggression. Libido is love and there are many stages in love. Destrudo is hate; it is regression to aggression, to wilderness, to savagery, to bestiality. There is no progress in hate.

And this is how Freud himself explains the problem. "This aggressive cruelty usually lies in wait for some provocation, or else it steps into the service of some other purpose, the aim of which might as well have been achieved by milder measures. . . . It also manifests itself spontaneously and reveals men as savage beasts to whom the thought of sparing their own kind is alien. . . . The existence of this tendency for aggression . . . makes it necessary for culture to institute its high demands. Civilized society is perpetually menaced with disintegration through this primary hostility of men towards one another."[6]

This classic statement answers our question. Aggressive cruelty precedes cooperation. Mankind can never be rid of it, but no society can accept it. Ares is a threat and must be stopped.

Destrudo in Children

In the ontogenetic development our proposed modification of Freud's theory could be briefly outlined as follows: The neonate is endowed with two instinctual forces, Eros and Ares, both serving initially protection and preservation of the organism, both capable of cathexis of the mental energies at their disposal, the libido and destrudo respectively.

Human neonates start their life with narcissistic or self-cathected libido. They have no object relations, neither object love nor object hate. Gradually, all objects serving the child's survival foster the development of object cathexis of libido and all objects threatening the infant foster object cathexis of destrudo.

In normal development there is a gradual decline of overt hostile activity. The destructive forces become fused with libidinal forces and partially aim-inhibited and sublimated.

Small children are very destructive. Their oral love is a fusion of object libido with object destrudo, with obvious predominance of destrudo. At the anal stage, in "tenderness," the libido object cathexis becomes stronger. At the phallic stage, in possessive-protective love, we see an additional gain of libido over destrudo. In well-adjusted adults destrudo is partially sublimated, partially aim-inhibited, and partially sufficiently repressed. In short, the normal progress of libido development is accompanied by "binding and neutralizing" of the destrudo.

In regressive cases the opposite process takes place. Children who failed to make proper libidinal progress are aggressive. Psychotics, manic-depressives, and especially schizophrenics display excessive destructiveness. To quote Anna Freud, "the pathological aggressiveness stems not from the aggressive tendencies themselves but from the lack of fusion between them and libidinal (erotic) urges. The pathological factor is found in the realm of erotic, emotional development which has been held up through adverse external or internal conditions. . . . Owing to the defects on the emotional side, the aggressive urges are not brought into the fusion and thereby bound and partially neutralized, but remain free

---

[6] Sigmund Freud, *Beyond the Pleasure Principle*, Liveright, 1950, pp. 85–86.

and seek expression in the forms of pure, unadulterated, independent destructiveness."[7]

We are still lacking a well-developed theory of developmental stages in childhood which will do as much justice to destrudo as it does to libido. Possibly the energy of love, libido, and the energy of hostility, destrudo, can be transformed into each other. When a child's object love has been frustrated, part of the libido is turned back into narcissistic love (secondary narcissism) and part turns into destrudo. Reaction formation is another case in point.

Four Types of Hostility

It may be useful to distinguish four types of hostile actions, i.e., actions aiming at the annihilation of the object.[8] The first two categories aim directly at the enhancement of one's own protection. The first category follows the *wolf vs. sheep* pattern. The wolf acts in a hostile manner against the sheep with the aim of eating it up. No feeling of hate is involved in this case. The man who eats chicken does not hate the chicken, yet he destroys it. The instinctual source of this action is related to narcissistic self-love and hostility serves here as self-preservation. The second type of hostility is caused by frustration and is usually combined with hate. It is aimed at the destruction of a menace. It is the fight of the sheep against the wolf, the man against the snake, or the child against another child who took away his toy. It is hostility for survival, hostility aimed at destroying the force which jeopardizes survival.

The two other types of hostility do not serve directly the task of self-preservation, but they by no means interfere with self-preservation. The first type is related to a careless discharge of energy, to lack of consideration, lack of "tenderness" for the outer world. It is the child's play in the garden in which he damages flowers; damaging flowers is a taboo in the Indian culture. Another example of this kind of hostility is the careless bull in a china store or the elephant stepping on chicks without any deliberate intention of killing them, but at the same time without consideration for their life. This action is not related to hate but to the lack of object love. Nor does it contradict self-love. It may occasionally enhance self-love and the feeling of omnipotence.

The last type of hostile action is intentional hurting, but the hate has been displaced from the menacing object to some other object. It is displaced hate or scapegoatism. Destrudo turns not against the real cause of frustration but against someone else, the scapegoat.

---

[7] Anna Freud, "Aggression in Relation to Emotional Development, Normal and Pathological," *The Psychoanalytic Study of the Child*, 1949, Vol. III–IV, pp. 41–42.

[8] We avoid persistently the term "aggressiveness," which may mean both initiative and hostility.

3. BEYOND PLEASURE

The Problem of Pleasure

Pleasure and reduction of tension are not identical terms. Pleasure can increase glandular or muscular tension, and this is exactly what takes place in sexual foreplay or in the sight of food to a hungry man. Goldstein was critical for Fechner's and Freud's system of pleasure-relief vs. displeasure-tension. He suggested instead the pleasurable tension on an optimal level of functioning.

G. Murphy[8] distinguished between preparatory appetite and consummatory functions. Both are pleasure procuring. What Sherrington proposed on a physiological basis has been applied by Murphy to the interpretation of psychological processes.

In our discussion of learning processes (cf Chaps. 2, 3, and 4) the distinction between reward and reinforcement has been clarified. Reward is the concomitant of pleasure; reinforcement, as used by Pavlov, is not. Nor is it in Hull's theory.

The only way out is to assume that there are at least two different types of learning, one not related to pleasure and the other more or less related to pleasure. Skinner believed that Pavlov's classic conditioning depends on the autonomic responses and not on Thorndike's law of effect with its satisfiers and annoyers. Operant conditioning is a function of the skeletal muscles and depends on the law of effect.

Razran suggested three evolutionary levels of conditioning, the first related to Ukhtomski's prepotence or "sheer force," the second related to pleasure and reward, and the third related to cognitive factors.

It can be hypothesized that in the phylogenetic evolution the prehedonic stage antecedes the hedonic. Probably the lower organisms are incapable of pleasure-displeasure, yet they function, and even learn. No one could ascribe pleasure to plants, or to their vital functions of osmosis, assimilation of carbon, or tropism.

A great part of the functions of higher mammals is accompanied by pain or pleasure. Undoubtedly the greatest part of human functions is performed on the pleasure level, and Thorndike's annoyers and satisfiers stem from empirical observations of animals and men.

Freud introduced a useful distinction. Whenever the urge for pleasure is *immediate*, it is called the pleasure principle, which is the principle of immediate gratification. Whenever the satisfaction is postponed or modified in order to avoid displeasure, it is in accordance with the reality principle.

Apparently a crucial role in this controversy has to be assigned to the

---

[8] Gardner Murphy, *Personality: A Biosocial Approach,* Harper, 1947, pp. 102 ff.

recent experimentation in visceral conditioning conducted by Bykov and associates. These studies prove beyond doubt that some inner organs are responsive to stimuli but do not respond with the pain-pleasure reaction. The recent Yale studies on the pleasure-pain center are of great promise, and meanwhile there is sufficient evidence that pain and pleasure are not universal. They probably start on a certain evolutionary level.

Three Levels

This writer proposes to introduce three main levels of conditioning and other mental processes: the *pre-hedonic,* the *hedonic* and the *post-hedonic.* This does not mean that the classic conditioning is pre-hedonic and the operant conditioning hedonic. It is simply that some functions of the human organism are not accompanied by a feeling of pleasure while other functions are. For instance, the functions of division, growth, and decline of cells, the secretion of thyroxine and perspiration, the growth of hair and nails, of bones and muscles, and of tumors in their initial stage are usually not accompanied by pleasure or pain. They are pre-hedonic. On the other hand, the secretion of semen, sucking, eating and drinking, rhythmical movements, overcoming of obstacles, singing, hugging, and kissing are usually accompanied by pleasure. Deprivation of food is painful; deprivation of certain nutritional values may become in the long run dangerous for the organism, yet it is not painful, at least in its beginning. Thus pleasure applies to a certain part of human actions; some actions are guided by pre-pleasure, some by post-pleasure factors.

The Antigone Principle

In some human actions the pain-pleasure consideration seems to disappear, or at least to become weak. Bykov reported cases of wounded men who controlled their own pain. In the frame of reference of instrumental, mutual acceptance, and vectorial relations (cf. section 2), an analysis of vectorial attitudes shows that certain individuals are capable of suffering for the sake of others and sacrifice themselves to make others happy. The prototype of this attitude is parenthood, or the willingness to give without taking.

Let us call this attitude the *Antigone principle* after Antigone, the daughter of King Oedipus. After Oedipus left Thebes, his two sons started a fight and one was killed. The king forbade the body of the fratricidal brother to be buried. Refusal of burial meant, in accordance with the Greek religion, eternal suffering of the soul. Antigone decided to save her brother's soul and to bury him, even though Antigone knew that the King imposed capital punishment on violators of his order. This willingness to sacrifice one's own life for the beloved one, or for the ideal, is called the *post-hedonic* or Antigone principle. Whenever parents sacrifice their life for their child, whenever men give away life for their religious or political ideals, whenever men are willing to suffer to make others happy, it is no more a pleasure-pain motivation. It is the post-hedonic Antigone principle.

Experimental and clinical studies, some of them mentioned in the preceding section, made the author of this book believe that the vectorial attitude may lead to overcoming of pleasure-pain principle. It is a well-known fact that the pain sensation is greatly reduced in schizophrenics. Studies[9] have shown that schizophrenia is basically a too early and too extreme development of vectorialism (*vectoriasis praecox*) which starts whenever children are forced to become the "parents of their own parents" and to protect and sacrifice themselves for their parents. This is a pathological development. Normal individuals are capable of balanced interindividual relations and of functioning on all three levels, the pre-hedonic, the hedonic, and the post-hedonic.

4. PERSONALITY: A BIOSOCIAL APPROACH

Theory of personality represents an important testing ground for psychological theories. Psychological theories may deal with various aspects of human behavior, but they cannot overlook the doing of an individual as a unit, as a whole. Most psychological theories, as Murphy has shown, can apply their principles toward the understanding of the individual as (1) differentiated from others, (2) a structured whole, and (3) an organism-environment field.[10]

When we deal with such complexity, a great many problems must be considered: heredity and environment, organic and psychogenic factors, motivation and perception, conditioning and canalization, and the organization of the individual and his interaction with the environment.

There is more than one answer to a complex scientific problem, and various systems of hypotheses can be used—for example, the molecular and molar theories are applied in optics.

It is not to be concluded that the different sets of hypotheses represent various degrees of generalization in the development of a theory. Consider Adler's inferiority feeling and striving toward superiority. It seems to fit quite well the manic-depressive pattern of behavior, but it does not apply well to other types of human behavior. Jung's statement concerning the danger of mental breakdown in cases where the conscious gets too far out of touch with the unconscious is undoubtedly true, but it applies mainly to the schizoid type of behavior. No theory encompasses the totality of available empirical data or answers all questions.

[9] Benjamin B. Wolman, "Explorations in Latent Schizophrenia," *American Journal of Psychotherapy*, 1957, 11, 560–588.
[10] Murphy, *op. cit.*, pp. 6–9.

It seems that the best and strongest position belongs to Freud and Pavlov. Their systems are undoubtedly more general, more encompassing, than any other system. They have in common the principles of equilibrium, tension release, energetism, conservation, and transferability of energy.

The main difference lies in the point of observation. Freud looked on humans in stress, Pavlov on animals in harness. Freud observed symbolic productions; Pavlov used symbolic stimuli. Freud and his disciples tried to penetrate the mysteries of the first reactions of the living human organism; Pavlov and his disciples tested the reactions of the inner organs. Both were natural scientists, determinists, and monists. Both believed that some day a psychology would develop on physiological foundations. Meanwhile Pavlov built the physiological bridge ahead while Freud built the psychological one.

Gardner Murphy put a subtitle to his volume on personality: "A Biosocial Approach," which actually said all that could be said about this problem. Pavlov called his work the studies of the higher nervous processes; Freud's model of personality included the biological drives of the id and the social pressures of the superego, with the controlling and mediating functions of the ego, which were mostly conscious and observable. Murphy put all this together. He analyzed the role of biological and sociological factors, of heredity and environment, of conditioning and preferences in learning, of perception and creativity, the formation of self, and the environment.

Is that not the entire history of psychology? The early psychologists dealt with observable phenomena of our conscious. Some psychologists preferred to confine their studies to the biological and neurophysiological foundations of human nature. Some emphasized the social and cultural influences. Psychology must take all these aspects into consideration. In Murphy's words, "the task of the psychology of personality today is to apply ruthlessly, and to the limit, every promising suggestion of today, but always with the spice of a healthy skepticism which will know how infinite are nature the macrocosm and man the microcosm, how infinitesimal our knowledge of it and of him."[11]

5. CONVERGENCIES AND DIVERGENCIES

Progress

The history of science is a history of errors; criticism and discovery of mistakes are often no less fruitful than positive discoveries and hypotheses. Whether we have any chance to discover the entire and all-embracing truth cannot be predicted. Perhaps we approach truth asymp-

[11] *Ibid.*, p. 926.

totically, coming closer and closer to it but never being able to know the entire truth.

For there is progress in psychology. There is a conspicuous progress in methodology. Compare, for instance, Hull's precise system with Watson's theory, or Bykov's techniques to Bekhterev's, or Rorschach to graphology, or Binet to old examinations, or the contemporary psychological laboratories to Wundt's laboratory in Leipzig. There is more cautiousness, more self-criticism, more rigorous pursuance of truth.

"The history of psychology," says Smith, "does not reveal the same impressive and clear-cut, step-like progression which is apparent in physics, as one hypothesis is clearly displaced by another which is more defensible in the light of the available evidence. Phrenology and faculty psychology have receded, it is true; but the changes or steps in explanation in psychology have tended to be in the nature of changes of vogue. with no one mode of explanation entirely displacing those which preceded it. . . . The coexistence of so many different modes of reducing the provocation arising from observation suggests not only that there is a problem or core of provocation to be allayed, but also that the theoretical structure of psychology relevant to this problem is in a very fluid or uncertain state."[12]

Learning

There is something of a "social climate" in the attention given by psychologists to various issues. When psychology was under the influence of physiology, sensation and perception were the matters of primary concern in psychology. Fechner, Weber, Wundt, Titchener, and others studied perception and paid relatively less attention to other areas of psychology. When psychology became influenced by biology, the problems of adjustment and learning became focal. Thorndike, Dewey, Watson, Tolman, Hull, and others considered learning the main area of psychology.

Learning is a change in behavior, but learning is not the only factor that can cause change. Behavior changes with growth and development, with drug addiction and fatigue, and with motivation and emotional tension.

Learning can be best defined as a persistent change due to experience or training as distinguished from change caused by growth and maturation or temporary change caused by drugs, fatigue, or emotional upheaval. However, it is good to bear in mind that there is a close relationship between growth and learning (Gesell, Piaget, Freud) and that some emotionally induced changes may persist, i.e., they may be learned.

Contemporary theories in psychology pay less and less attention to

[12] F. V. Smith, *The Explanation of Human Behavior*, Constable, 1951, p. 5.

the traditional division into schools and systems. Actually, any systematic and consistent division into schools seems impossible today. Tolman started with behaviorism and developed a gestalt theory. Borrowing heavily from Watson and McDougall he introduced gestalt into behaviorism. Sullivan combined some psychoanalytic ideas with a far-fetched environmentalism and with some elements of field theory. Kardiner may consider himself a faithful psychoanalyst but his theories come quite close to Spranger's.

Three Methods

This disregard for "schools" and the present daring eclecticism are encouraging symptoms.

Psychology as a science can be studied by at least three independent methods, the physiological, the clinical, and the observational-experimental. Each of these methods collects and verifies empirical data and creates theories binding the data together in a system of natural laws. The collection and verification of facts is the descriptive part of science, the theory construction is the interpretative part. The three methods must not be mutually exclusive or contradictory.

As things stand now, psychologists make definite studies in all three directions. The physiological branch of psychology under the leadership of Pavlov has amassed a great number of cautiously observed data and developed the theoretical-physiological system of conditioned reflexes. Clinical psychology under the leadership of Freud has accumulated many carefully observed data on human behavior in normal and pathological conditions. Freud's psychoanalysis is a highly developed theory. The observational-experimental or "behavioral" part of psychology has probably collected the largest number of most carefully observed data. Hull, Tolman, Skinner, and Razran have developed theoretical systems with apparent emphasis on learning.

It is time to try to relate the three psychologies. An excellent effort to develop a biosocial system was made by G. Murphy. Mowrer, Miller, Dollard, and others tried to combine Hull with Freud. Razran, a faithful Pavlovian, believes that the future belongs to Pavlov and Freud combined. We believe this too. We believe in the necessity of a theory of behavior developed out of observational-experimental studies which will unite Freud's and Pavlov's theories and include all available data.

We believe that psychology is a branch of biology. Our point of view is that of *monistic transitionism* or a theory of a unity of living matter that includes neurological and psychological data in one continuum without being reductionistic. The somato-psychic organism has to be studied in interaction with its environment. Accordingly, *soma, psyche,* and *ecos* form the triple frame of reference for the study of human behavior.

SUMMARY OF PART IV

Chapters 14 and 15 form the last part of this book. Chapter 14 analyzes some problems related to the application of the scientific method in psychology, but it does not describe the research methods of psychology in detail.

The chapter starts with the distinction between research and the resulting system of propositions or statements. Nine principles are suggested, among them verifiability, generality, and objectivity. The position of maximalism in epistemology is suggested.

Scientific statements are statements about something which is a part of nature. Accordingly, all sciences, including psychology, are natural sciences, and their propositions are a result of (1) perception of things and what is happening to them and (2) interpretation of these perceptions.

A systematic and planned perception of things and events is called observation. All scientists, psychologists included, observe their subject matter. However, certain parts of human behavior, e.g., pain and pleasure, are directly perceivable to the organism in which they take place; some are not observable at all. This fact gave rise to the introspective method in psychology. Introspection is the least objective but still an indispensable method in psychology.

The usual principles of empiricism are applicable to psychology. Psychological theory has been influenced lately by operationism. Operationism can be interpreted as a radical empiricism which applies the rules and canons of F. Bacon, J. S. Mill, and others. Taken literally, as it was by its creator P. W. Bridgman, operationism leads to an overemphasis on the operations performed by the scientist himself and ultimately ends in an arid solipsism. S. S. Stevens tried to save operationism by the legitimate demand for "public" vs. "private" operations. Even the improved version of operationism is still open to criticism directed against the assumption that the perception of activities (operations) of the research worker is superior to observations of things and events.

The most precise research method in psychology is experimentation. Some caution is required in regard to the influence of the experimental design and apparatus upon the results. In addition, the unobservable parts of behavior, as well as the more emotional expressions of overt behavior, do not fit into a laboratory. The experimentalist deals with a part of behavior in a precise manner; the scope of the clinical research is broad, but its methods are not always exact. The application of both research methods for a mutual checking of results seems to be promising.

The third section of the chapter is devoted to the interpretation of data by formation of hypotheses and theory construction. Both inductive and deductive methods are legitimate ways of empirical research.

Some rules for hypothesis formation have been suggested; the most important are immanent truth and testability. Hypothetical statements can be made in a great variety of forms; some of them can be simply postulated as guiding principles which could never be fully proved but are accepted as long as they are not refuted by empirical data or modified by methodological convenience. Hypothetical statements can be introduced in the form of definitions, logical constructs, intervening variables, etc. The experimental psychologists favor intervening variables because this is the most convenient way of presenting their data.

Psychological hypotheses use constructs such as "instinct," "drive," "need," "ego"; interpretation in psychology can be psychogenic or by reduction to any other source, preferably physics, chemistry, biology, and physiology.

A system of hypotheses forms a theory. Theories deal with the relationship between bodies and events, and seek to discover "laws of nature." The relationship between bodies and events in psychology is permeated with causation. Determinism in psychology must be postulated as the first principle for interpretation of scientific data.

Laws of nature express the regularity of everything that happens in nature. Laws of nature have been discovered in all other natural sciences; they must be discovered in psychology too. Some of them, such as homeostasis or constancy, adjustment, and learning by experience, are generally recognized. Some, such as molar vs. molecular, gestalt vs. association, are highly controversial. Laws of nature in the realm of psychology must be formulated in such a way as to make possible prediction of behavior.

The last section of the chapter is devoted to some problems related to the use of language in psychology, both conventional and symbolic.

The fifteenth chapter of the book raises more questions than it answers. It is entitled "Some Crucial Questions and Tentative Answers." A hypothesis of a monistic *transitionism* is proposed as an answer to the problems of reductionism. A general theory of *lust for life* based on studies conducted by Pavlov, Freud, and Goldstein is suggested instead of Freud's life and death instincts. A theory of three levels of motivation, namely, the pre-hedonic, hedonic, and post-hedonic, is proposed as a way out in the questions of reward, reinforcement, and pleasure principle. Murphy's biosocial theory of personality is suggested as a solution in the theory of personality. Finally, several unsolved problems and the lack of an all-encompassing psychological theory are presented as a scientific task for the future.

Bibliography

General

Boring, E. G. *A history of experimental psychology*. (2nd ed.) New York: Appleton-Century-Crofts, 1950.

Brett, G. S. *History of psychology*. London: Allen & Unwin, 1912–21. 3 vols.

Dennis, W. *Readings in the history of psychology*. New York: Appleton-Century-Crofts, 1948.

Dessoir, M. *Outlines of the history of psychology*. New York: Macmillan, 1912.

Döring, W. *Die Hauptströmungen in der neueren Psychologie*. Leipzig: Engelmann, 1932.

Erdmann, J. E. *History of philosophy*. London: Allen & Unwin, 3 vols.

Flugel, J. C. *A hundred years of psychology*. (2nd ed.) London: Duckworth, 1951.

Garrett, H. E. *Great experiments in psychology*. (3rd ed.) New York: Appleton-Century-Crofts, 1951.

Heidbreder, E. *Seven psychologies*. New York: Century, 1933.

Helson, H. (Ed.) *Theoretical foundations of psychology*. New York: Van Nostrand, 1950.

Hilgard, E. R. *Theories of learning*. (2nd ed.) New York: Appleton-Century-Crofts, 1956.

Marx, M. H. *Psychological theory: Contemporary readings*. New York: Macmillan, 1951.

Murchison, C. (Ed.) *Psychologies of 1930*. Worcester, Mass.: Clark Univer. Press, 1930.

Murchison, C. (Ed.) *History of psychology in autobiography*. Worcester, Mass.: Clark Univer. Press, 1930–36. 3 vols.

Murphy, G. *Historical introduction to modern psychology*. (Rev. ed.) New York: Harcourt, Brace, 1949.

Peters, R. S. (Ed.) *Brett's history of psychology*. London: Allen & Unwin, 1953.

Roback, A. A. *History of American psychology*. New York: Library Publishers, 1952.

Smith, F. V. *The explanation of human behavior*. London: Constable: 1951.

Stevens, S. S. (Ed.) *Handbook of experimental psychology*. New York: Wiley, 1951.

Woodworth, R. S. *Contemporary schools of psychology*. (Rev. ed.) New York: Ronald, 1948.

Zilboorg, G., & Henry, G. W. *A history of medical psychology*. New York: Norton, 1941.

Chapter 1. Conditioning, Behaviorism, and Purposivism

1. *Psychophysical Parallelism and Introspectionism*

Bain, A. *Mental science: A compendium of psychology and the history of philosophy*. New York: Appleton, 1868.

Baldwin, J. M. *History of psychology: A sketch and an interpretation*. New York: Putnam, 1913.

Boring, E. G. *Sensation and perception in the history of experimental psychology.* New York: Appleton-Century, 1942.

Boring, E. G. A history of introspection. *Psychol. Bull.*, 1953, **50**, 169–189.

Ebbinghaus, H. *Memory.* New York: Teachers College, Columbia University, 1913.

Hall, G. St. *Founders of modern psychology.* New York: Appleton, 1912.

Helmholtz, H. L. F. *On the sensation of tone.* (4th ed.) New York: Longmans, Green, 1912.

Herbart, J. F. *Sämtliche Werke.* Langesalza: Kehrbach, 1891. 12 vols.

Ladd, G. T., & Woodworth, R. S. *Elements of physiological psychology.* New York: Scribner, 1911.

Locke, J. *An essay concerning human understanding.* London: Basset, 1690.

Müller, G. E. Experimentelle Beiträge zur Untersuchung des Gedächtnisses. *Z. Psychol.*, 1894, **6**, 81–190, 250–339.

Randall, J. H. *The making of the modern mind.* (Rev. ed.) Boston: Houghton Mifflin, 1940.

Ribot, T. A. *German psychology of today.* New York: Scribner, 1886.

Titchener, E. B. The postulates of a structural psychology. *Phil. Rev.*, 1898, **7**, 449–465.

Titchener, E. B. Structural and functional psychology. *Phil. Rev.*, 1899, **8**, 290–299.

Titchener, E. B. *Experimental psychology, a manual of laboratory practice.* New York: Macmillan, 1901–5. 2 vols.

Titchener, E. B. *Lectures on the experimental psychology of the thought processes.* New York: Macmillan, 1909.

Titchener, E. B. *A textbook of psychology.* New York: Macmillan, 1909–10.

Titchener, E. B. *Systematic psychology: Prolegomena.* New York: Macmillan, 1929.

Warren, H. C. *A history of the association psychology from Hartley to Lewes.* New York: Scribner, 1921.

Woodworth, R. S. *Experimental psychology.* New York: Holt, 1938.

Wundt, W. *Principles of physiological psychology.* London: Macmillan, 1874. 2 vols.

Wundt, W. *Lectures on human and animal psychology.* London: Allen, 1894.

Wundt, W. *Outlines of psychology.* New York: Stechert, 1907.

Wundt, W. *Elements of folk-psychology.* London: Macmillan, 1916.

2. *Functionalism*

Angell, J. R. *Psychology, an introductory study of the structure and function of human consciousness.* New York: Holt, 1904.

Angell, J. R. The province of functional psychology. *Psychol. Rev.* 1907, **14**, 61–91.

Angell, J. R. *An introduction to psychology.* New York: Holt, 1918.

Carr, H. A. *Psychology, a study of mental activity.* New York: Longmans, Green, 1925.

Carr, H. A. The laws of association. *Psychol. Rev.*, 1931, **38**, 212–228.

Carr, H. A. *An introduction to space perception.* New York: Longmans, Green, 1935.

Darwin, C. R. *The origin of species.* London: 1859.

Darwin, C. R. *The expression of the emotions in man and animals.* London: 1872.

Dewey, J. The reflex arc concept in psychology. *Psychol. Rev.,* 1896, **3,** 357–370,

Dewey, J. *How we think.* Boston: Heath, 1910.

Dewey, J. *Influence of Darwin on philosophy.* New York: Holt, 1920.

Dewey, J. *Human nature and conduct.* New York: Holt, 1922.

Dewey, J. *Logic, the theory of inquiry.* New York: Holt, 1938.

Dewey, J., & Bentley, A. F. *Knowing and the known.* Boston: Beacon, 1949.

Henderson, L. J. *The fitness of the environment.* New York: Macmillan, 1913.

Hobhouse, L. R. *Mind in evolution.* New York: Macmillan, 1901.

Hobhouse, L. R. *Development and purpose.* New York: Macmillan, 1913.

Hunter, W. S. *Human behavior.* Chicago: Univer. of Chicago Press, 1928.

Huxley, J. *The living thoughts of Darwin.* New York: Longmans, Green, 1939.

Huxley, J. *Evolution, the modern synthesis.* New York: Harper, 1942.

James, W. *Principles of psychology.* New York: Holt, 1890. 2 vols.

James, W. *Pragmatism.* New York: Longmans, Green, 1907.

James, W. *A pluralistic universe.* New York: Longmans, Green, 1909.

James, W. *Essays in radical empiricism.* New York: Longmans, Green, 1912.

Luh, C. W. The conditions of retention. *Psychol. Monogr.,* 1922, **31,** No. 142.

McGeoch, J. A. Forgetting and the law of disuse. *Psychol. Rev.,* 1932, **39,** 352–370.

McGeoch, J. A., & Irion, A. L. *The psychology of human learning.* (Rev. ed.) New York: Longmans, Green, 1942.

Mayhew, K. C., & Edwards, A. C. *The Dewey School: The laboratory school at the University of Chicago, 1896–1903.* New York: Appleton-Century, 1936.

Melton, A. W. Learning. In W. S. Monroe (Ed.), *Encyclopedia of educational research.* New York: Macmillan, 1941.

Ratner, J. *Intelligence in the modern world: John Dewey's philosophy.* New York: Modern Library, 1939.

Robinson, E. S. *Association theory today.* New York: Appleton-Century, 1932.

Robinson, E. S. *Man as psychology sees him.* New York: Macmillan, 1932.

Spencer, H. *Principles of psychology.* London: 1855.

Washburn, M. F. *The animal mind.* New York: Macmillan, 1908.

Weiss, A. P. *A theoretical basis of human behavior.* (2nd ed.) Columbus, Ohio: Adams, 1929.

Woodworth, R. S. *Dynamic psychology.* New York: Columbia Univer. Press, 1918.

Woodworth, R. S. Situation- and goal-set. *Amer. J. Psychol.,* 1937, **50,** 130–140.

3. *Edward L. Thorndike: Connectionism*

Gates, A. I. Connectionism: Present concepts and interpretations. In *41st Yearb. nat. Soc. Stud. Educ.,* 1942, Part 2.

Lorge, I. Irrelevant rewards in animal learning. *J. comp. Psychol.,* 1936, **21,** 105–128.

Meehl, P. E. On the circularity of the law of effect. *Psychol. Bull.*, 1950, **47**, 52–75.

Postman, L. The history and present status of the Law of Effect. *Psychol. Bull.*, 1947, **44**, 489–563.

Rock, R. T., Jr. The influence upon learning of the quantitative variation of after-effects. *Teach. Coll. Contr. Educ.*, 1935, No. 650.

Thorndike, E. L. Animal intelligence: an experimental study of the associative processes in animals. *Psychol. Rev. Monogr. Suppl.*, 1898, **2**, No. 8.

Thorndike, E. L. *Educational psychology.* New York: Lemcke & Buechner, 1903.

Thorndike, E. L. The effect of practice in the case of a purely intellectual function. *Amer. J. Psychol.*, 1908, **19**, 374–384.

Thorndike, E. L. *Animal intelligence.* New York: Macmillan, 1911.

Thorndike, E. L. *Educational psychology.* New York: Teachers College, 1913. 2 vols.

Thorndike, E. L. The influence of primacy. *J. exp. Psychol.*, 1927, **10**, 18–29.

Thorndike, E. L. *The fundamentals of learning.* New York: Teachers College, 1932.

Thorndike, E. L. Reward and punishment in animal learning. *Comp. Psychol. Monogr.*, 1932, **8**, No. 39.

Thorndike, E. L. A proof of the law of effect. *Science*, 1933, **77**, 173–175.

Thorndike, E. L. An experimental study of rewards. *Teach. Coll. Contr. Educ.*, 1933, No. 580.

Thorndike, E. L. *The psychology of wants, interests, and attitudes.* New York: Appleton-Century, 1935.

Thorndike, E. L. *Human nature and the social order.* New York: Macmillan, 1940.

Thorndike, E. L. *Selected writings from a connectionist's psychology.* New York: Appleton-Century-Crofts, 1949.

Thorndike, E. L., & Lorge, I. The influence of relevance and belonging. *J. exp. Psychol.*, 1935, **18**, 574–584.

Tilton, J. W. Gradients of effect. *J. genet. Psychol.*, 1945, **66**, 3–19.

4. *The Origins of the New Systems* [*]

Allport, F. H. *Theories of perception and the concept of structure.* New York: Wiley, 1955.

Dashiell, J. F. Some rapprochements in contemporary psychology. *Psychol. Bull.*, 1939, **36**, 1–24.

Dennis, W. (Ed.) *Current trends in psychological theory.* Pittsburgh: Univer. of Pittsburgh Press, 1951.

Hilgard, E. R., & Marquis, D. G. *Conditioning and learning.* New York: Appleton-Century, 1940.

Klüver, H. Contemporary German psychology as a "cultural science." In G. Murphy, *An historical introduction to modern psychology.* New York: Harcourt, Brace, 1929.

Miller, H. *An historical introduction to modern philosophy.* New York: Macmillan, 1947.

[*] A part of Section 1. Chap. 1.

Morgan, C. L. *An introduction to comparative psychology.* London: Scott, 1894.

Sachs, H. *Freud, master and friend.* Cambridge, Mass.: Harvard Univer. Press, 1944.

Chapter 2. Conditioned Reflexes

Anan'yev, B. G., et al. (Eds.) *Materials of the conference on psychology.* (Russian.) Moscow: Acad. Pedag. Nauk SSSR, 1957.

Anrep, G. V. The irradiation of conditioned reflexes. *Proc. Royal Soc.,* 1923, 94B, 404–426.

Asratian, E. A. *I. P. Pavlov: His life and work.* Moscow: Foreign Lang. Publ. House, 1953.

Ayrapetyants, E. Sh. *Higher nervous activity and the receptors of internal organs* (Russian). Moscow: Acad. Nauk SSSR, 1952.

Babkin, B. P. *Pavlov, a biography.* Chicago: Univer. of Chicago Press, 1949.

Bauer, R. *The new man in Soviet psychology.* Cambridge, Mass.: Harvard Univer. Press, 1952.

Bekhterev, V. M. *Objective psychology* (Russian). St. Petersburg: Soikin, 1907.

Bekhterev, V. M. *Psychology, reflexology, and Marxism* (Russian). Leningrad: Giz, 1925.

Bekhterev, V. M. *General principles of human reflexology.* New York: International Publishers, 1932.

Burns, E. (Ed.) *A handbook of Marxism.* New York: International Publishers, 1935.

Bykov, K. M. *The cerebral cortex and the internal organs.* New York: Chemical Publishing, 1957.

Delgado, J. M. R., Roberts, W. W., & Miller, N. E. Learning motivated by electrical stimulation of the brain. *Amer. J. Physiol.,* 1954, 179, 587–593.

Engels, F. *Ludwig Feuerbach and the outcome of German classical philosophy.* New York: International Publishers, 1927.

Frolov, I. P. *Pavlov and his school.* New York: Oxford Univer. Press, 1937.

Gantt, W. H. An experimental approach to psychiatry. *Amer. J. Psychiat.,* 1936, 92, 1007–1021.

Gantt, W. H. *Russian medicine.* New York: Hoeber, 1937.

Gantt, W. H. *Physiological bases of psychiatry.* Springfield, Ill.: Thomas, 1958.

Haldane, J. B. S. *The Marxist philosophy and the sciences.* New York: Random House, 1939.

Hilgard, E., & Marquis, D. G. *Conditioning and learning.* New York: Appleton-Century-Crofts, 1940.

Hook, S. *From Hegel to Marx.* New York: Reynal, 1936.

Kornilov, K. M., Smirnov, A. A., & Teplov, M. (Eds.) *Psychology* (Russian). Moscow: Uchpedgiz., 1948.

Lenin, N. *Materialism and empirico-criticism.* New York: International Publishers, 1934.

London, I. D. Research on sensory interaction in the Soviet Union. *Psychol. Bull.,* 1954, 51, 531–563.

Loucks, R. B. An appraisal of Pavlov's systematization of behavior from the experimental standpoint. *J. comp. Psychol.*, 1933, **15**, 1–47.

Luria, A. R. *The nature of human conflict.* New York: Liveright, 1932.

Marx, K. *Capital.* New York: Scribner, 1925.

Pavlov, I. P. *Conditioned reflexes.* London: Oxford Univer. Press, 1927.

Pavlov, I. P. *Lectures on conditioned reflexes.* New York: International Publishers, 1928.

Pavlov, I. P. *Pavlov's Wednesday seminars* (Russian). Moscow: Acad. Nauk SSSR, 1949. 3 vols.

Pavlov, I. P. *Complete works* (Russian). (2nd ed.) Moscow: Acad. Nauk SSSR, 1951. 5 vols.

Pavlov, I. P. *Selected Works.* Moscow: Foreign Lang. Publ. House, 1955.

Pavlov, I. P. *Experimental psychology and other essays.* New York: Philosophical Library, 1957.

Razran, G. Theory of conditioning and related phenomena. *Psychol. Rev.*, 1930, **37**, 25–43.

Razran, G. Conditioned responses: A classified bibliography. *Psychol. Bull.*, 1937, **34**, 191–256.

Razran, G. The nature of the extinctive process. *Psychol. Rev.*, 1939, **46**, 264–297.

Razran, G. The dominance-contiguity theory of the acquisition of classical conditioning. *Psychol. Bull.*, 1957, **54**, 1–46.

Razran, G. Soviet psychology since 1950. *Science*, 1957, **126**, 1100–1107.

Razran, G. Soviet psychology and psychophysiology. *Science*, 1958, **128**, 1187–1194.

Schlossberg, H. The relationship between success and the laws of conditioning. *Psychol. Rev.*, 1937, **44**, 379–394.

Scientific Session on the Physiological Teachings of I. P. Pavlov. Moscow: Foreign Language Publishing House, 1951.

Sechenov, I. M. *Reflexes of the brain.* Moscow: Uchpedgiz, 1942.

Simon, B. (Ed.) *Psychology in the Soviet Union.* Stanford, Calif.: Stanford Univer. Press, 1957.

Smirnov, A. A., Leont'yev, A. N., Rubinstein, S. L., & Teplov, B. M. (Eds.) *Psychology* (Russian). Moscow: Uchpedgiz, 1956.

Stagner, R. Conditioned reflex theories of learning. *Psychol. Rev.*, 1931, **38**, 42–59.

Wortis, J. *Soviet psychiatry.* Baltimore, Md.: Williams & Wilkins, 1950.

Zeliony, G. P. Effets de l'ablation des hémisphères cérébraux. *Rev. méd.*, 1924, **46**, 191–214.

Chapter 3. Behaviorism and Reductionism

Cannon, W. B. *Bodily changes in pain, hunger, fear, and rage.* (2nd ed.) New York: Appleton, 1929.

Cannon, W. B. *The wisdom of the body.* New York: Norton, 1932.

Coghill, G. E. *Anatomy and the problem of behavior.* London: Cambridge Univer. Press, 1929.

Franz, S. I. On the functions of the cerebrum: The frontal lobes. *Arch. Psychol.*, 1907, No. 2.

Franz, S. I. *Nervous and mental re-education.* New York: Macmillan, 1923.

Franz, S. I., & Lashley, K. S. The effects of cerebral destruction upon habit formation and retention in the albino rat. *Psychobiol.*, 1917. **1**, 71–139.

Hebb, D. O. Studies of the organization of behavior: I. Behavior of the rat in a field orientation. *J. comp. Psychol.*, 1938, **25**, 333–352.

Hebb, D. O. Studies of the organization of behavior: II. Changes in the field orientation of the rat after cortical destruction. *J. comp. Psychol.*, 1938, **26**, 427–444.

Hebb, D. O. *The organization of behavior: a neuropsychological theory.* New York: Wiley, 1949.

Hebb, D. O. *A textbook of psychology.* Philadelphia: Saunders, 1958.

Hebb, D. O., & Foord, E. N. Errors of visual recognition and the nature of the trace. *J. exp. Psychol.*, 1945, **35**, 335–348.

Holt, E. B. *The concept of consciousness.* New York: Macmillan, 1914.

Holt, E. B. *The Freudian wish and its place in ethics.* New York: Holt, 1915.

Holt, E. B. *Animal drives and the learning process.* New York: Holt, 1931.

Hunter, W. S. *Human behavior.* Chicago: Univer. of Chicago Press, 1928.

Hunter, W. S. The psychological study of behavior. *Psychol. Rev.*, 1932, **39**, 1–24.

Hunter, W. S. Basic phenomena in learning. *J. gen. Psychol.*, 1933, **8**, 299–317.

Hunter, W. S. Conditioning and extinction in the rat. *Brit. J. Psychol.*, 1935, **26**, 135–148.

Hunter, W. S. Conditioning and maze learning in the rat. *J. comp. Psychol.*, 1935, **19**, 417–424.

Hunter, W. S. Learning curves for conditioning and maze learning. *J. exp. Psychol.*, 1936, **19**, 121–128.

Lashley, K. S. The human salivary reflex and its use in psychology. *Psychol. Rev.*, 1916, **23**, 446–464.

Lashley, K. S. Reflex secretion of the human parotid gland. *J. exp. Psychol.*, 1916, **1**, 461–493.

Lashley, K. S. The behavioristic interpretation of consciousness. *Psychol. Rev.*, 1923, **30**, 237–272.

Lashley, K. S. *Brain mechanisms and intelligence.* Chicago: Univer. of Chicago Press, 1929.

Lashley, K. S. Basic neural mechanisms in behavior. *Psychol. Rev.*, 1930, **37**, 1–24.

Lashley, K. S. Cerebral control versus reflexology: A reply to Professor Hunter. *J. gen. Psychol.*, 1931, **5**, 3–20.

Lashley, K. S. Nervous mechanisms in learning. In C. Murchison (Ed.), *A handbook of general experimental psychology.* Worcester, Mass.: Clark Univer. Press, 1934.

Lashley, K. S. Experimental analysis of instinctive behavior. *Psychol. Rev.*, 1938, **45**, 445–472.

Lashley, K. S. Coalescence of neurology and psychology. *Proc. Amer. philos. Soc.*, 1941, **84**, 461–470.

Lashley, K. S. Structural variation in the nervous system in relation to behavior. *Psychol. Rev.*, 1947, **54**, 325–334.

Lashley, K. S., & Wade, M. The pavlovian theory of generalization. *Psychol. Rev.*, 1946, **53**, 72–87.

Liddell, H. S. The conditioned reflex. In F. A. Moss (Ed.), *Comparative psychology.* New York: Prentice-Hall, 1934.

Mateer, F. *Child behavior, a critical and experimental study of young children by the method of conditioned reflexes.* Boston: Badger, 1918.

Sherrington, C. S. *The integrative action of the nervous system.* (New ed.) New Haven: Yale Univer. Press, 1947.

Sherrington, C. S. *Man on his nature.* New York: Macmillan, 1941.

Smith, S., & Guthrie, E. R. *General psychology in terms of behavior.* New York: Appleton, 1921.

Washburn, M. F. *The animal mind.* New York: Macmillan, 1908.

Watson, J. B. Kinesthetic and organic sensations: Their role in the reaction of the white rat to the maze. *Psychol. Monogr.*, 1907, 8, No. 33.

Watson, J. B. Psychology as a behaviorist views it. *Psychol. Rev.*, 1913, **20**, 158–177.

Watson, J. B. *Behavior: An introduction to comparative psychology.* New York: Holt, 1914.

Watson, J. B. The place of the conditioned reflex in psychology. *Psychol. Rev.*, 1916, **23**, 89–117.

Watson, J. B. The effect of delayed feeding upon learning. *Psychobiol.*, 1917, **1**, 51–60.

Watson, J. B. *Psychology from the standpoint of a behaviorist.* Philadelphia: Lippincott, 1919.

Watson, J. B. Behaviorism: a psychology based on reflexes. *Arch. Neurol. Psychiat.*, 1926, **15**, 185–204.

Watson, J. B. *Behaviorism.* (Rev. ed.) New York: Norton, 1930.

Watson, J. B., & Morgan, J. J. B. Emotional reactions and psychological experimentation. *Amer. J. Psychol.*, 1917, **28**, 163–174.

Watson, J. B., & Raynor, R. Conditioned emotional reactions. *J. exp. Psychol.*, 1920, **3**, 1–14.

Weiss, A. P. *A theoretical basis of human behavior.* (2nd ed.) Columbus, Ohio: Adams, 1929.

Weiss, A. P. Feeling and emotion as forms of behavior. In M. L. Reymert (Ed.), *Feeling and emotions: The Wittenberg symposium.* Worcester, Mass.: Clark Univer. Press, 1930.

Chapter 4. Neo-Behaviorism and Learning Theory

1, 2, 3, 4, 5. Guthrie, Hull, Skinner, Tolman, Razran

Adams, O. K. Experimental studies of adaptive behavior in cats. *Comp. Psychol. Monogr.*, 1929, **6**, No. 27.

Arnold, W. J. Simple reaction chains and their integration. I. Homogeneous chaining with terminal reinforcement. *J. comp. physiol. Psychol.*, 1947, **40**, 349–363.

Baernstein, H. D., & Hull, C. L. A mechanical model of the conditioned reflex. *J. gen. Psychol.*, 1931, **5**, 99–106.

Bass, M. J., & Hull, C. L. The irradiation of a tactile conditioned reflex in man. *J. comp. Psychol.*, 1934, **17**, 46–65.

Bendig, A. W. Latent learning in a water maze. *J. exp. Psychol.*, 1953, **43**, 134–137.

Bergmann, G., & Spence, K. W. The logic of psychological measurement. *Psychol. Rev.*, 1944, **51**, 1–24.

Birch, H. G., & Bittermann, M. E. Reinforcement and learning: The process of sensory integration. *Psychol. Rev.*, 1949, **56**, 292–308.

Blodgett, H. C. The effect of the introduction of reward upon the maze performance of rats. *Univer. Calif. Publ. Psychol.*, 1929, **4**, 113–134.

Brown, J. S., & Farber, I. E. Emotions conceptualized as intervening variables—with suggestions toward a theory of frustration. *Psychol. Bull.*, 1951, **48**, 465–495.

Buxton, C. E. Latent learning and the goal gradient hypothesis. *Contr. psychol. Theor.*, 1940, **2**, No. 2.

Carlin, Jean E. Drive stimulus generalization. Unpublished M.A. thesis, Univer. of Minnesota, 1952.

Chisholm, R. M. Intentionality and the theory of signs. *Philos. Stud.*, 1952, **3**, 56–63.

Christie, R. Experimental naïveté and experiential naïveté. *Psychol. Bull.*, 1951, **48**, 327–339.

Christie, R. The role of drive discrimination in learning under irrelevant motivation. *J. exp. Psychol.*, 1951, **42**, 13–19.

Christie, R. The effect of some early experiences in the latent learning of adult rats. *J. comp. physiol. Psychol.*, 1952, **43**, 281–288.

Cook, S. W., & Skinner, B. F. Some factors influencing the distribution of associated words. *Psychol. Rec.*, 1939, **3**, 178–184.

Crespi, L. P. Quantitative variation of incentive and performance in the white rat. *Amer. J. Psychol.*, 1942, **55**, 467–517.

Crespi, L. P. Amount of reinforcement and level of reinforcement. *Psychol. Rev.*, 1944, **51**, 341–357.

Daub, C. T. The effect of doors on latent learning. *J. comp. Psychol.*, 1933, **15**, 49–58.

Denny, M. R. The role of secondary reinforcement in a partial reinforcement learning situation. *J. exp. Psychol.*, 1946, **36**, 373–389.

Denny, M. R., & David, R. H. A test of latent learning for a non-goal significate. *J. comp. physiol. Psychol.*, 1951, **44**, 590–595.

Elliott, M. H. The effect of appropriateness of rewards and of complex incentives on maze performance. *Univer. Calif. Publ. Psychol.*, 1929, **4**, 91–98.

Ellson, D. G. Quantitative studies of the interaction of simple habits. I. Recovery from specific and generalized effects of extinction. *J. exp. Psychol.*, 1938, **23**, 339–358.

Estes, W. K. An experimental study of punishment. *Psychol. Monogr.*, 1944, **57**, No. 3.

Estes, W. K. Effects of competing reactions on the conditioning curve for bar-pressing. *J. exp. Psychol.*, 1950, **40**, 200–205.

Estes, W. K., Koch, S., MacCorquodale, K., Meehl, P. E., Mueller, C. G., Jr., Schoenfeld, W. N., & Verplanck, W. S. *Modern Learning Theory*. New York: Appleton-Century-Crofts, 1954.

Estes, W. K., & Skinner, B. F. Some quantitative properties of anxiety. *J. exp. Psychol.*, 1941, **29**, 390–400.

Fehrer, Elizabeth. Latent learning in the sophisticated rat. *J. exp. Psychol.*, 1951, **42**, 409–416.

Felsinger, J. M., Gladstone, A. I. Yamaguchi, H. G., & Hull, C. L. Reaction latency ($_s t_R$) as a function of the number of reinforcements (N). *J. exp. Psychol.*, 1947, **37**, 214–228.

Finan, J. L. Quantitative studies in motivation. I. Strength of conditioning in rats under varying degrees of hunger. *J. comp. Psychol.*, 1940, **29**, 119–134.

Gibson, E. J. A systematic application of the concepts of generalization and differentiation to verbal learning. *Psychol. Rev.*, 1940, **47**, 196–229.

Gilchrist, J. C. Characteristics of latent and reinforcement learning as a function of time. *J. comp. physiol. Psychol.*, 1952, **45**, 198–203.

Gladstone, A. I., Yamaguchi, H. G., Hull, C. L., & Felsinger, J. M. Some functional relationships of reaction potential (sEr) and related phenomena. *J. exp. Psychol.*, 1947, **37**, 510–526.

Gleitman, H. Studies in motivation and learning: II. Thirsty rats trained in maze with food but not water; then run hungry. *J. exp. Psychol.*, 1950, **40**, 169–174.

Graham, C. H., & Gagné, R. M. The acquisition, extinction, and spontaneous recovery of a conditioned operant response. *J. exp. Psychol.*, 1940, **26**, 251–280.

Grice, G. R. An experimental test of the expectation theory of learning. *J. comp. physiol. Psychol.*, 1940, **41**, 137–143.

Grindley, G. C. Experiments on the influence of the amount of reward on learning in young chickens. *Brit. J. Psychol.*, 1929, **20**, 173–180.

Guthrie, E. R. Purpose and mechanism in psychology. *J. Phil.*, 1924, **21**, 673–682.

Guthrie, E. R. Measuring introversion and extraversion. *J. abnorm. soc. Psychol.*, 1927, **22**, 82–88.

Guthrie, E. R. Conditioning as a principle of learning. *Psychol. Rev.*, 1930, **37**, 412–428.

Guthrie, E. R. On the nature of psychological explanations. *Psychol. Rev.*, 1933, **40**, 124–137.

Guthrie, E. R. Association as a function of time interval. *Psychol. Rev.*, 1933, **40**, 355–367.

Guthrie, E. R. Reward and punishment. *Psychol. Rev.*, 1934, **41**, 450–460.

Guthrie, E. R. *The psychology of learning*. New York: Harper, 1935.

Guthrie, E. R. Psychological principles and scientific truth. *Proc. 25th Anniv. Celeb. Inaugur. grad. Stud.*, Univer. of Southern California, 1936.

Guthrie, E. R. *The psychology of human conflict*. New York: Harper, 1938.

Guthrie, E. R. The effect of outcome on learning. *Psychol. Rev.*, 1939, **46**, 480–485.

Guthrie, E. R. Association and the law of effect. *Psychol. Rev.*, 1940, **47**, 127–148.

Guthrie, E. R. Conditioning: a theory of learning in terms of stimulus, response and association. *Yearb. nat. Soc. Stud. Educ.*, 1942, **41**, 17–60.

Guthrie, E. R. The principle of associative learning. In F. P. Clarke, & M. C. Nahm, *Philosophical essays in honor of Edgar Arthur Singer, Jr.* Philadelphia: Univer. of Pennsylvania Press, 1942.

Guthrie, E. R. Psychological facts and psychological theory. *Psychol. Bull.*, 1946, **43**, 1–20.

Guthrie, E. R. The status of systematic psychology. *Amer. Psychologist*, 1950, **5**, 97–101.

Guthrie, E. R. *The psychology of learning.* (Rev. ed.) New York: Harper, 1952.

Guthrie, E. R., & Edwards, A. L. *Psychology: A first course in human behavior.* New York: Harper, 1949.

Guthrie, E. R., & Horton, G. P. *Cats in a puzzle box.* New York: Rinehart, 1946.

Guthrie, E. R. & Powers, F. F. *Educational psychology.* New York: Ronald, 1950.

Haney, G. W. The effect of familiarity on maze performance of albino rats. *Univer. Calif. Publ. Psychol.*, 1931, **4**, 319–333.

Hempel, C. G. The logical analysis of psychology. In H. Feigl & W. Sellars, *Readings in philosophical analysis.* New York: Appleton-Century-Crofts, 1949. Pp. 373–384.

Hempel, C. G. Problems and changes in the empiricist criterion of meaning. *Rev. int. de Phil.*, 1950, **4**, 41–63.

Herb, F. H. Latent learning—non-reward followed by food in blinds. *J. comp. Psychol.*, 1940, **29**, 247–255.

Heron, W. T. The rate of extinction in maze-bright and maze-dull rats. *Psychol. Rev.*, 1940, **4**, 11–18.

Heron, W. T., & Skinner, B. F. Changes in hunger during starvation. *Psychol. Rev.*, 1947, **1**, 51–60.

Heron, W. T. Internal stimuli and learning. *J. comp. physiol. Psychol.*, 1949, **42**, 486–492.

Hill, C. H. Goal gradient, anticipation, and perseveration in compound trial-and-error learning. *J. exp. Psychol.*, 1930, **25**, 566–585.

Hovland, C. I. The generalization of conditioned responses: I. The sensory generalization of conditioned responses with varying frequencies of tone. *J. gen. Psychol.*, 1937, **17**, 125–148.

Hovland, C. I. The generalization of conditioned responses: II. The sensory generalization of conditioned responses with varying intensities of tone. *J. genet. Psychol.*, 1937, **51**, 279–291.

Hovland, C. I. The generalization of conditioned responses. IV. The effects of varying amounts of reinforcement upon the degree of generalization of conditional responses. *J. exp. Psychol.*, 1937, **21**, 261–276.

Hull, C. L. A functional interpretation of the conditioned reflex. *Psychol. Rev.*, 1929, **36**, 498–511.

Hull, C. L. Simple trial-and-error learning: A study in psychological theory. *Psychol. Rev.*, 1930, **37**, 241–256.

Hull, C. L. Knowledge and purpose as habit mechanisms. *Psychol. Rev.*, 1930, **37**, 511–525.

Hull, C. L. Goal attraction and directing ideas conceived as habit phenomena. *Psychol. Rev.,* 1931, **38**, 487–506.

Hull, C. L. The goal gradient hypothesis and maze learning. *Psychol. Rev.,* 1932, **39**, 25–43.

Hull, C. L. Differential habituation to internal stimuli in the albino rat. *J. comp. Psychol.,* 1933, **16**, 255–274.

Hull, C. L. The concept of the habit-family hierarchy, and maze learning. Part I. *Psychol. Rev.,* 1934, **41**, 33–54.

Hull, C. L. The concept of the habit-family hierarchy, and maze learning. Part II. *Psychol. Rev.,* 1934, **41**, 134–152.

Hull, C. L. Learning: II. The factor of the conditioned reflex. In C. Murchison (Ed.), *A handbook of general experimental psychology.* Worcester, Mass.: Clark Univer. Press, 1934.

Hull, C. L. The rat's speed of locomotion gradient in the approach to food. *J. comp. Psychol.,* 1934, **17**, 393–422.

Hull, C. L. The mechanism of the assembly of behavior segments in novel combinations suitable for problem solution. *Psychol. Rev.,* 1935, **42**, 219–245.

Hull, C. L. The conflicting psychologies of learning—a way out. *Psychol. Rev.,* 1935, **42**, 491–516.

Hull, C. L. The influence of caffeine and other factors on certain phenomena of rote learning. *J. gen. Psychol.,* 1935, **13**, 249–274.

Hull, C. L. Special review: Thorndike's *Fundamentals of learning. Psychol. Bull.,* 1935, **32**, 807–823.

Hull, C. L. Mind, mechanism and adaptive behavior. *Psychol. Rev.,* 1937, **44**, 1–32.

Hull, C. L. A comment on Dr. Adams' note on method. *Psychol. Rev.,* 1937, **44**, 219–221.

Hull, C. L. The goal-gradient hypothesis applied to some "field-force" problems in the behavior of young children. *Psychol. Rev.,* 1938, **45**, 271–300.

Hull, C. L. The problem of stimulus equivalence in behavior theory. *Psychol. Rev.,* 1939, **46**, 9–30.

Hull, C. L. Modern behaviorism and psychoanalysis. *Trans. N.Y. Acad. Sci.,* 1939, **1**, Ser. II, 78–82.

Hull, C. L. Simple trial-and-error learning—an empirical investigation. *J. comp. Psychol.,* 1939, **27**, 233–258.

Hull, C. L. Explorations in the patterning of stimuli conditioned to the G.S.R. *J. exp. Psychol.,* 1940, **27**, 95–110.

Hull, C. L. *Psychological seminar memoranda, 1939–1940.* Bound mimeographed manuscript on file in the libraries of Yale Univer., Univer. of Iowa, & Oberlin Coll.

Hull, C. L. Conditioning: Outline of a systematic theory of learning. *Yearb. nat. Soc. Stud. Educ.,* 1942, **41**, Part 2, 61–95.

Hull, C. L. *Principles of behavior: An introduction to behavior theory.* New York: Appleton-Century-Crofts, 1943.

Hull, C. L. The problem of intervening variables in molar behavior theory. *Psychol. Rev.,* 1943, **50**, 273–291.

Hull, C. L. A postscript concerning intervening variables. *Psychol. Rev.,* 1943, **50**, 540.

Hull, C. L. *Psychological memoranda, 1940–1944.* Bound mimeographed manuscript on file in the libraries of Yale Univer., Univer. of Iowa, & Univer. of North Carolina.

Hull, C. L. Moral values, behaviorism, and the world crisis. *Trans. N.Y. Acad. Sci.,* 1945, **7,** 90–94.

Hull, C. L. The place of innate individual and species differences in a natural-science theory of behavior. *Psychol. Rev.,* 1945, **52,** 55–60.

Hull, C. L. The discrimination of stimulus configurations and the hypothesis of afferent neural interaction. *Psychol. Rev.,* 1945, **52,** 133–142.

Hull, C. L. Research memorandum concerning the quantitative empirical determination of certain basic behavioral constants and their functional relationships. May 29, 1945. (Mimeographed manuscript on file in Yale Library.)

Hull, C. L. The problem of primary stimulus generalization. *Psychol. Rev.,* 1947, **54,** 120–134.

Hull, C. L. Reactively heterogeneous compound trial-and-error learning with distributed trials and terminal reinforcement. *J. exp. Psychol.,* 1947, **37,** 118–135.

Hull, C. L. Reactively heterogeneous compound trial-and-error learning with distributed trials and serial reinforcement. *J. exp. Psychol.,* 1948, **38,** 17–28.

Hull, C. L. Memorandum on behavior theory. Oct. 4, 1949. (Mimeographed manuscript on file in Yale Library.)

Hull, C. L. Stimulus intensity dynamism (V) and stimulus generalization. *Psychol. Rev.,* 1949, **56,** 67–76.

Hull, C. L. Behavior postulates and corollaries—1949. *Psychol. Rev.,* 1950, **57,** 173–180.

Hull, C. L. Simple qualitative discrimination learning. *Psychol. Rev.,* 1950, **57,** 303–313.

Hull, C. L. A primary social science law. *Sci. Mon., N.Y.* 1950, **71,** 221–228.

Hull, C. L. Memorandum concerning behavior theory. Feb. 7, 1950. (Mimeographed manuscript on file in Yale Library.)

Hull, C. L. Memorandum concerning behavior theory. Mar. 6, 1950. (Mimeographed manuscript on file in Yale Library.)

Hull, C. L. *Essentials of behavior.* New Haven: Yale Univer. Press, 1951.

Hull, C. L. *A Behavior System.* New Haven: Yale Univer. Press, 1952.

Hull, C. L. Clark L. Hull. In E. G. Boring, H. S. Langfeld, H. Werner, & R. M. Yerkes (Eds.), *A history of psychology in autobiography—Volume IV.* Worcester, Mass.: Clark Univer. Press, 1952.

Hull, C. L., & Baernstein, H. D. A mechanical parallel to the conditioned reflex. *Science,* 1929, **70,** 14–15.

Hull, C. L., Felsinger, J. M., Gladstone, A. I., and Yamaguchi, H. G. A proposed quantification of habit strength. *Psychol. Rev.,* 1947, **54,** 237–254.

Hull, C. L., Hovland, C. I., Ross, R. T., Hall, M., Perkins, D. T., & Fitch, F. B. *Mathematico-deductive theory of rote learning: A study in scientific methodology.* New Haven: Yale Univer. Press, 1940.

Hull, C. L., Johnston, R. L., Rouse, R. O., & Barker, A. H. True, sham, and esophageal feeding as reinforcements. *J. comp. physiol. Psychol.,* 1951, **44,** 236–245.

Hull, C. L., & Krueger, R. C. An electro-chemical parallel to the conditioned reflex. *J. gen. Psychol.*, 1931, **5**, 262–269.

Hull, C. L., & Mowrer, O. H. *Hull's psychological seminars, 1936–38. Notices and abstracts of proceedings.* Bound mimeographed material on file in the libraries of the Univer. of Chicago, Univer. of North Carolina, & Yale Univer.

Hull, C. L. & Spence, K. W. "Correction" vs. "non-correction" method of trial-and-error learning in rats. *J. comp. Psychol.*, 1938, **25**, 127–145.

Humphreys, L. G. The effect of random alternation of reinforcement on the acquisition and extinction of conditioned eyelid reactions. *J. exp. Psychol.*, 1939, **25**, 141–158.

Humphreys, L. G. Generalization as a function of method of reinforcement. *J. exp. Psychol.*, 1939, **25**, 361–372.

Jenkins, W. O., & Stanley, J. C. Partial reinforcement: A review and critique. *Psychol. Bull.*, 1950, **47**, 193–234.

Kappauf, W. E., & Schlosberg, H. Conditioned responses in the white rat. III. Conditioning as a function of the length of the period of delay. *J. genet. Psychol.*, 1937, **50**, 27–45.

Karn, H. W., & Porter, H. M., Jr. The effects of certain pre-training procedures upon maze performance and their significance for the concept of latent learning. *J. exp. Psychol.*, 1946, **36**, 461–469.

Kendler, H. H. Drive interaction: II. Experimental analysis of the role of drive in learning theory. *J. exp. Psychol.*, 1945, **35**, 188–198.

Kendler, H. H. A comparison of learning under motivated and satiated conditions in the white rat. *J. exp. Psychol.*, 1947, **37**, 545–549.

Kendler, H. H. An investigation of latent learning in a T-maze. *J. comp. Psychol.*, 1947, **40**, 265–270.

Kendler, H. H. "What is learned?"—a theoretical blind alley. *Psychol. Rev.*, 1952, **59**, 269–277.

Kendler, H. H., & Ianner, J. H. A further test of the ability of rats to learn the location of food when motivated by thirst. *J. exp. Psychol.*, 1950, **40**, 762–765.

Kendler, H. H., & Mencher, H. C. The ability of rats to learn the location of food when motivated by thirst—an experimental reply to Leeper. *J. exp. Psychol.*, 1948, **38**, 82–88.

Kimble, G. A. Conditioning as a function of the time between conditioned and unconditioned stimuli. *J. exp. Psychol.*, 1947, **37**, 1–15.

Kimble, G. A. An experimental test of a two-factor theory of inhibition. *J. exp. Psychol.*, 1949, **39**, 15–23.

Koch, S. The logical character of the motivation concept. I. *Psychol. Rev.*, 1941, **48**, 15–38.

Koch, S. Review of Hull's Principles of Behavior. *Psychol. Bull.*, 1944, **41**, 269–286.

Koch, S. Form and content in hypothetico-deductive systems: A reply to Woodbury. *J. Psychol.*, 1947, **24**, 237–246.

Koch, S. & Clark L. Hull. In W. K. Estes, & others, *Modern learning theory.* New York: Appleton-Century-Crofts, 1954.

Koch, S., & Daniel, W. J. The effect of satiation on the behavior mediated by a habit of maximum strength. *J. exp. Psychol.*, 1945, **35**, 167–187.

Krechevsky, I. "Hypotheses" versus "chance" in the presolution period in sensory discrimination-learning. *Univer. Calif. Publ. Psychol.*, 1932, 6, 27–44.

Leeper, R. The role of motivation in learning: A study of the phenomenon of differential motivational control of the utilization of habits. *J. genet. Psychol.*, 1935, 46, 3–40.

Leeper, R. Dr. Hull's Principles of Behavior. *J. genet. Psychol.*, 1944, 65, 3–52.

Leeper, R. The experiments by Spence and Lippitt and by Kendler on the sign-gestalt theory of learning. *J. exp. Psychol.*, 1948, 38, 102–106.

Littman, R. A. Latent learning in a T-maze after two degrees of training. *J. comp. physiol. Psychol.*, 1950, 43, 135–147.

Littman, R. A., & Rosen, E. Molar and molecular. *Psychol. Rev.*, 1950, 57, 58–65.

MacCorquodale, K. Preliminary suggestions as to a formalization of expectancy theory. *Psychol. Rev.*, 1953, 60, 55–63.

MacCorquodale, K., & Meehl, P. E. "Cognitive" learning in the absence of competition of incentives. *J. comp. physiol. Psychol.*, 1949, 42, 383–390.

MacDuff, Mary A. The effect on retention of varying degrees of motivation during learning in rats. *J. comp. physiol. Psychol.*, 1943, 33, 369–386.

Maltzman, I. M. An experimental study of learning under an irrelevant need. *J. exp. Psychol.*, 1950, 40, 788–793.

Meehl, P. E. An examination of the treatment of stimulus patterning in Professor Hull's Principles of Behavior. *Psychol. Rev.*, 1945, 52, 324–332.

Meehl, P. E. On the circularity of the law of effect. *Psychol. Bull.*, 1950, 47, 52–75.

Meehl, P. E. A failure to find the Blodgett effect, and some secondary observations on drive conditioning. *J. comp. physiol. Psychol.*, 1951, 44, 178–183.

Meehl, P. E. Some methological comments concerning expectancy theory. *Psychol. Rev.*, 1951, 58, 230–233.

Meehl, P. E. Drive conditioning as a factor in latent learning. *J. exp. Psychol.*, 1953, 43, 20–24.

Meehl, P. E., & MacCorquodale, K. A. A further study of latent learning in the T-maze. *J. comp. physiol. Psychol.*, 1948, 41, 372–396.

Miller, N. E. Studies of fear as an acquirable drive: I. Fear as motivation and fear-reduction as reinforcement in the learning of new responses. *J. exp. Psychol.*, 1948, 38, 89–101.

Miller, N. E. Learnable drives and rewards. In S. S. Stevens (Ed.), *Handbook of experimental psychology.* New York: Wiley, 1951.

Montgomery, K. C. "Spontaneous alternation" as a function of time between trials and amount of work. *J. exp. Psychol.*, 1951, 42, 82–93.

Montgomery, K. C. Exploratory behavior and its relation to spontaneous alternation in a series of maze exposures. *J. comp. physiol. Psychol.*, 1952, 45, 50–57.

Mowrer, O. H., & Jones, H. M. Extinction and behavior variability as functions of effortfulness of task. *J. exp. Psychol.*, 1943, 33, 369–386.

Muenzinger, K. F. Plasticity and mechanization of the problem box habit in guinea pigs. *J. comp. Psychol.*, 1928, 8, 45–69.

Muenzinger, K. F., Koerner, L., & Irey, E. Variability of an habitual movement in guinea pigs. *J. comp. Psychol.*, 1929, **9**, 425–436.

Nissen, H. W. Description of the learned response in discrimination behavior. *Psychol. Rev.*, 1950, **57**, 121–131.

Notterman, J. M. A study of some relations among aperiodic reinforcement, discrimination training, and secondary reinforcement. *J. exp. Psychol.*, 1951, **41**, 161–169.

Perin, C. T. Behavior potentiality as a joint function of the amount of training and the degree of hunger at the time of extinction. *J. exp. Psychol.*, 1942, **30**, 93–113.

Perin, C. T. A quantitative investigation of the delay-of-reinforcement gradient. *J. exp. Psychol.*, 1943, **32**, 37–51.

Postman, L. The history and present status of the law of effect. *Psychol. Bull.*, 1947, **44**, 489–563.

Prentice, W. C. H. Continuity in human learning. *J. exp. Psychol.*, 1949, **39**, 187–194.

Razran, G. Sensory capacities of the dog as studied by the conditioned reflex method (with C. J. Warden). *Psychol. Bull.*, 1929, **26**, 202–222.

Razran, G. Theory of conditioning and of related phenomena. *Psychol. Rev.*, 1930, **37**, 225–243.

Razran, G. The summation method in statistics (with M. E. Wagner). *J. exp. Psychol.*, 1931, **21**, 270–283.

Razran, G. Conditioned responses in animals other than dogs. *Psychol. Bull.*, 1933, **30**, 261–324.

Razran, G. Conditioned responses in children. *Arch. Psychol.*, 1933, **23**, No. 148.

Razran, G. Conditioned withdrawal responses in adult human subjects. *Psychol. Bull.*, 1934, **31**, 111–143.

Razran, G. Salivary conditioning in adult human subjects. *Psychol. Bull.*, 1934, **31**, 634–635.

Razran, G. Conditioned responses: An experimental study and a theoretical analysis. *Arch. Psychol.*, 1935, **28**, No. 191.

Razran, G. Psychology in the U.S.S.R. *J. Phil.*, 1935, **32**, 19–25.

Razran, G. Salivary conditioning in adult human subjects. *Psychol. Bull.*, 1935, **32**, 561–562.

Razran, G. The conditioning of voluntary reactions. *J. exp. Psychol.*, 1936, **19**, 653–655.

Razran, G. Salivating and thinking in different languages. *J. Psychol.*, 1936, **2**, 145–152.

Razran, G. Attitudinal control of human conditioning. *J. Psychol.*, 1936, **2**, 327–337.

Razran, G. Conditioned responses: A classified bibliography. *Psychol. Bull.*, 1937, **34**, 191–256.

Razran, G. Configural and colligated conditioning. *Psychol. Bull.*, 1937, **34**, 515–516.

Razran, G. The number of articles of psychological interest published in the Russian language. *Amer. J. Psychol.*, 1937, **50**, 316.

Razran, G. Music, art, and the conditioned response. *Psychol. Bull.*, 1938, **35**, 532.

Razran, G. Conditioning away social bias by the luncheon technique. *Psychol. Bull.*, 1938, **35**, 693.

Razran, G. Ratios and elements in salivary conditioning to various musical intervals. *Psychol. Rec.*, 1938, **2**, 370–376.

Razran, G. Transposition of relational responses and generalization of conditioned responses. *Psychol. Rev.*, 1938, **45**, 532–538.

Razran, G. Conditioning and attitudes. *J. exp. Psychol.*, 1939, **24**, 215–226.

Razran, G. Decremental and incremental effects of distracting stimuli upon the salivary Crs of 24 adult human subjects. *J. exp. Psychol.*, 1939, **24**, 647–652.

Razran, G. Extinction, spontaneous recovery, and forgetting. *Amer. J. Psychol.*, 1939, **52**, 100–103.

Razran, G. The nature of the extinctive process. *Psychol. Rev.*, 1939, **46**, 264–297.

Razran, G. The law of effect or the law of qualitative conditioning. *Psychol. Rev.*, 1939, **46**, 445–463.

Razran, G. A simple technique for controlling subjective attitudes in salivary conditioning of adult human subjects. *Science*, 1939, **89**, 160–162.

Razran, G. A quantitative study of meaning by a conditioned salivary technique: (semantic conditioning). *Science*, 1939, **90**, 89–91.

Razran, G. Semantic, syntactic, and phonetographic conditioning. *Psychol. Bull.*, 1939, **36**, 578.

Razran, G. Reflexive or attitudinal—or quantitative and qualitative—conditioning. *Psychol. Bull.*, 1939, **36**, 660.

Razran, G. Studies in configural conditioning. I. Historical and preliminary experimentation. *J. gen. Psychol.*, 1939, **21**, 307–330.

Razran, G. Studies in configural conditioning. II. The effects of subjects' attitudes and tasks sets upon configural conditioning. *J. exp. Psychol.*, 1939, **24**, 95–105.

Razran, G. Studies in configural conditioning. III. The factors of similarity, proximity, and continuity in configural conditioning. *J. exp. Psychol.*, 1939, **24**, 202–210.

Razran, G. Studies in configural conditioning. IV. Gestalt organization and configural conditioning. *J. Psychol.*, 1939, **7**, 3–16.

Razran, G. Studies in configural conditioning. V. Generalization and transposition. *J. genet. Psychol.*, 1940, 3–11.

Razran, G. Studies in configural conditioning. VI. Comparative extinction and forgetting of pattern and single-stimulus conditioning. *J. exp. Psychol.*, 1939, **24**, 432–439.

Razran, G. Conditioned response changes in rating and appraising sociopolitical slogans. *Psychol. Bull.*, 1940, **37**, 481.

Razran, G. Determinants of the consolidation (memorial generalization-differential) or "Praegnanz" of conditioned preferences. *Psychol. Bull.*, 1940, **37**, 564.

Razran, G. Current psychological theory in the U.S.S.R. *Psychol. Bull.*, 1942, **39**, 445–446.

Razran, G. Schools of psychology. In H. N. Rivlin & H. Schueler (Eds.) *The Encyclopedia of modern education.* New York: Philosophical Library, 1943, 624–637.

Razran, G. Semantic and phonetographic generalizations of salivary conditioning to verbal stimuli. *J. exp. Psychol.,* 1949, **39,** 642–652.

Razran, G. Attitudinal determinants of conditioning and of generalization of conditioning. *J. exp. Psychol.,* 1949, **39,** 820–829.

Razran, G. Sentential and propositional generalizations of salivary conditioning to verbal stimuli. *Science,* 1949, **109,** 447–448.

Razran, G. Some psychological factors in the generalization of salivary conditioning to verbal stimuli. *Amer. J. Psychol.,* 1949, **62,** 247–256.

Razran, G. Stimulus generalization of conditioned responses. *Psychol. Bull.,* 1949, **46,** 337–365.

Razran, G. Ethnic dislikes and stereotypes: A laboratory study. *J. abnorm. soc. Psychol.,* 1950, **45,** 7–27.

Razran, G. A note on London's historical survey of psychology in the U.S.S.R. *Psychol. Bull.,* 1950, **47,** 146–149.

Razran, G. Unpublished confidential report to OSS. The effects of arctic conditions upon the physiology and psychology of human behavior. 36 pp.

Razran, G. "A reply to: *Grice's Comments on Razran's Discussion of Stimulus Generalization.*" *Psychol. Bull.,* 1951, **48,** No. 2.

Razran, G. Experimental semantics. *N.Y. Acad. Sci.,* 1952, **14,** 171–177.

Razran, G. The conditioned evocation of attitudes (cognitive conditioning). *J. exp. Psychol.,* 1954, **48,** 278–282.

Razran, G. Conditioning and perception. *Psychol. Rev.,* 1955, **62,** 83–95.

Razran, G. Backward conditioning. *Psychol. Bull.,* 1956, **53,** 55–69.

Razran, G. Extinction re-examined and re-analyzed: A new theory. *Psychol. Rev.,* 1956, **63,** 39–52.

Razran, G. The dominance-contiguity theory of the acquisition of classical conditioning. *Psychol. Bull.,* 1957, **54,** 1–46.

Razran, G. Pavlov and Lamarck. *Science,* 1958, **128,** 758–760.

Reynolds, B. A. The acquisition of a trace conditioned response as a function of the magnitude of the stimulus trace. *J. exp. Psychol.,* 1945, **35,** 15–30.

Reynolds, B. A. A repetition of the Blodgett experiment on "latent learning." *J. exp. Psychol.,* 1945, **35,** 504–516.

Reynolds, B. A. The relationship between the strength of a habit and the degree of drive present during acquisition. *J. exp. Psychol.,* 1949, **39,** 296–305.

Ritchie, B. F. Hull's treatment of learning. *Psychol. Bull.,* 1944, **41,** 640–652.

Ritchie, B. F. Studies in spatial learning. III. Two paths to the same location and two paths to two different locations. *J. exp. Psychol.,* 1947, **37,** 25–38.

Ritchie, B. F. Studies in spatial learning. VI. Place orientation and direction orientation. *J. exp. Psychol.,* 1948, **38,** 659–669.

Ritchie, B. F., Aeschliman, B., & Pierce, P. Studies in spatial learning. VIII. Place performance and the acquisition of place dispositions. *J. comp. physiol. Psychol.,* 1950, **43,** 73–85.

Ritchie, B. F., Hay, Alice, & Hare, Rachel. Studies in spatial learning. IX. A dispositional analysis of response performance. *J. comp. physiol. Psychol.,* 1951, **44,** 442–449.

Saltzman, I., & Koch, S. The effect of low intensities of hunger on the behavior mediated by a habit of maximum strength. *J. exp. Psychol.*, 1948, **38**, 347–370.

Schiller, P. S. Analysis of detour behavior. I. Learning of round-about pathways in fish. *J. comp. physiol. Psychol.*, 1949, **42**, 463–475.

Schoenfeld, W. N. An experimental approach to anxiety, escape and avoidance behavior. Chap. 5 in P. Hoch & J. Zubin (Eds.), *Anxiety*. New York: Grune & Stratton, 1950.

Sellars, W. S. Concepts as involving laws and inconceivable without them. *Phil. Sci.*, 1948, **15**, 287–315.

Sellars, W. Mind, meaning, and behavior. *Philos. Stud.*, 1952, **3**, 83–95.

Seward, J. P. A theoretical derivation of latent learning. *Psychol. Rev.*, 1947, **54**, 83–98.

Seward, J. P. An experimental analysis of latent learning. *J. exp. Psychol.*, 1949, **39**, 177–186.

Seward, J. P. Secondary reinforcement as tertiary motivation: A revision of Hull's revision. *Psychol. Rev.*, 1950, **57**, 362–374.

Seward, J. P., Levy, N., & Handlon, J. P., Jr. Incidental learning in the rat. *J. comp. physiol. Psychol.*, 1950, **43**, 240–251.

Shaw, M. E., & Waters, R. H. An experimental test of latent learning in a relatively free-choice situation. *J. genet. Psychol.*, 1950, **77**, 283–292.

Sheffield, F. D. Avoidance training and the contiguity principle. *J. comp. physiol. Psychol.*, 1948, **41**, 165–177.

Sheffield, F. D., & Roby, T. B. Reward value of a non-nutritive sweet taste. *J. comp. physiol. Psychol.*, 1950, **43**, 471–481.

Simley, O. A. The relation of subliminal to supraliminal learning. *Arch. Psychol.*, 1933, No. 146.

Simmons, Rietta. The relative effectiveness of certain incentives in animal learning. *Comp. psychol. Monogr.*, 1924, **2**, 1–79.

Skinner, B. F. On the conditions of elicitation of certain eating reflexes. *Proc. nat. Acad. Sci.*, 1930, **16**, 433–438.

Skinner, B. F. The concept of the reflex in the description of behavior. *J. gen. Psychol.*, 1931, **5**, 427–458.

Skinner, B. F. Drive and reflex strength. *J. gen. Psychol.*, 1932, **6**, 22–37.

Skinner, B. F. Drive and reflex strength: II. *J. gen. Psychol.*, 1932, **6**, 38–48.

Skinner, B. F. On the rate of formation of a conditioned reflex. *J. gen. Psychol.*, 1932, **7**, 274–286.

Skinner, B. F. On the rate of extinction of a conditioned reflex. *J. gen. Psychol.*, 1933, **8**, 114–129.

Skinner, B. F. The measurement of "spontaneous activity." *J. gen. Psychol.*, 1933, **9**, 3–23.

Skinner, B. F. The rate of establishment of a discrimination. *J. gen. Psychol.*, 1933, **9**, 302–350.

Skinner, B. F. "Resistance to extinction" in the process of conditioning. *J. gen. Psychol.*, 1933, **9**, 420–429.

Skinner, B. F. The abolishment of a discrimination. *Proc. nat. Acad. Sci.*, 1933, **19**, 825–828.

Skinner, B. F. The extinction of chained reflexes. *Proc. nat. Acad. Sci.*, 1934, **20**, 234–237.

Skinner, B. F. A discrimination without previous conditioning. *Proc. nat. Acad. Sci.*, 1934, **20**, 532–536.

Skinner, B. F. The generic nature of the concepts of stimulus and response. *J. gen. Psychol.*, 1935, **12**, 40–65.

Skinner, B. F. Two types of conditioned reflex and a pseudotype. *J. gen. Psychol.*, 1935, **12**, 66–77.

Skinner, B. F. A discrimination based upon a change in the properties of a stimulus. *J. gen. Psychol.*, 1935, **12**, 313–336.

Skinner, B. F. The extinction ratio and its modification by a temporal discrimination. *Psychol. Bull.*, 1936, **33**, 784. (Abstr.)

Skinner, B. F. A failure to obtain "disinhibition." *J. gen. Psychol.*, 1936, **14**, 127–135.

Skinner, B. F. The reinforcing effect of a differentiating stimulus. *J. gen. Psychol.*, 1936, **14**, 263–278.

Skinner, B. F. The effect of the amount of conditioning of an interval of time before reinforcement. *J. gen. Psychol.*, 1936, **14**, 279–295.

Skinner, B. F. Conditioning and extinction and their relation to drive. *J. gen. Psychol.*, 1936, **14**, 296–317.

Skinner, B. F. Thirst as an arbitrary drive. *J. gen. Psychol.*, 1936, **15**, 205–210.

Skinner, B. F. The verbal summator and a method for the study of latent speech. *J. Psychol.*, 1936, **2**, 71–107.

Skinner, B. F., & Heron, W. T. Effects of caffeine and benzedrine upon conditioning and extinction. *Psychol. Rec.*, 1937, **1**, 340–346.

Skinner, B. F. The distribution of associated words. *Psychol. Rec.*, 1937, **1**, 71–76.

Skinner, B. F. Two types of conditioned reflex: A reply to Konorski and Miller. *J. gen. Psychol.*, 1937, **16**, 272–279.

Skinner, B. F. *The behavior of organisms: An experimental analysis.* New York: Appleton-Century-Crofts, 1938.

Skinner, B. F. The frequencies of occurrences of associated words. *Psychol. Bull.*, 1938, **35**, 675. (Abstr.)

Skinner, B. F. The alliteration in Shakespeare's sonnets: A study of literary behavior. *Psychol. Rec.*, 1939, **3**, 186–192.

Skinner, B. F. A method of maintaining an arbitrary degree of hunger. *J. comp. Psychol.*, 1940, **30**, 139–145.

Skinner, B. F. The nature of the operant reserve. *Psychol. Bull.*, 1940, **37**, 423. (Abstr.)

Skinner, B. F. A quantitative estimate of certain types of sound patterning in poetry. *Amer. J. Psychol.*, 1941, **54**, 64–79.

Skinner, B. F. Some quantitative properties of anxiety. *Psychol. Bull.*, 1941, **38**, 539. (Abstr.)

Skinner, B. F. The processes involved in the repeated guessing of alternatives. *J. exp. Psychol.*, 1942, **30**, 495–503.

Skinner, B. F. Reply to Dr. Yacorzynsky. *J. exp. Psychol.*, 1943, **32**, 93–94.

Skinner, B. F. Review of Hull's Principles of Behavior. *Amer. J. Psychol.*, 1944, **57**, 276–281.

Skinner, B. F. The operational analysis of psychological terms. *Psychol. Rev.*, 1945, **52**, 270–277.

Skinner, B. F. Differential reinforcement with respect to time. *Amer. Psychologist,* 1946, **1**, 274–275. (Abstr.)

Skinner, B. F. The effect of the difficulty of a response upon its rate of emission. *Amer. Psychologist,* 1946, **1**, 462. (Abstr.)

Skinner, B. F. Experimental psychology. In W. Dennis (Ed.), *Current trends in psychology.* Pittsburgh: Univer. of Pittsburgh Press, 1947.

Skinner, B. F. "Superstition" in the pigeon. *Amer. Psychologist,* 1947, **2**, 426. (Abstr.)

Skinner, B. F. "Superstition" in the pigeon. *J. exp. Psychol.,* 1948, **38**, 168–172.

Skinner, B. F. Are theories of learning necessary? *Psychol. Rev.,* 1950, **57**, 193–216.

Skinner, B. F. *Cumulative record.* New York: Appleton-Century-Crofts, 1959.

Spence, K. W. The nature of discrimination learning in animals. *Psychol. Rev.,* 1936, **43**, 427–449.

Spence, K. W. Analysis of the formation of visual discrimination habits in the chimpanzee. *J. comp. Psychol.,* 1937, **23**, 77–100.

Spence, K. W. The differential response in animals to stimuli varying within a single dimension. *Psychol. Rev.,* 1937, **44**, 430–444.

Spence, K. W. Continuous versus non-continuous interpretations of discrimination learning. *Psychol. Rev.,* 1940, **47**, 271–288.

Spence, K. W. Failure of transposition in size discrimination of chimpanzees. *Amer. J. Psychol.,* 1941, **54**, 223–229.

Spence, K. W. The basis of solution by chimpanzees of the intermediate size problem. *J. exp. Psychol.,* 1942, **31**, 257–271.

Spence, K. W. Theories of learning. In F. A. Moss (Ed.), *Comparative psychology.* (Rev. ed.) New York: Prentice-Hall, 1942.

Spence, K. W. An experimental test of the continuity and non-continuity theories of discrimination learning. *J. exp. Psychol.,* 1945, **35**, 253–266.

Spence, K. W. The role of secondary reinforcement in delayed reward learning. *Psychol. Rev.,* 1947, **54**, 1–8.

Spence, K. W. The postulates and methods of "behaviorism." *Psychol. Rev.,* 1948, **55**, 67–78.

Spence, K. W. Cognitive versus stimulus-response theories of learning. *Psychol. Rev.,* 1950, **57**, 159–172.

Spence, K. W. Theoretical interpretations of learning. In C. P. Stone (Ed.), *Comparative psychology.* (3rd ed.) New York: Prentice-Hall, 1951.

Spence, K. W. Theoretical interpretations of learning. In S. S. Stevens (Ed.), *Handbook of experimental psychology.* New York: Wiley, 1951.

Spence, K. W., Bergmann, G., & Lippitt, R. O. A study of simple learning under irrelevant motivational-reward conditions. *J. exp. Psychol.,* 1950, **40**, 539–551.

Spence, K. W., & Kendler, H. H. The speculations of Leeper with respect to the Iowa tests of the sign-gestalt theory of learning. *J. exp. Psychol.,* 1948, **38**, 106–109.

Spence, K. W., & Lippitt, R. O. An experimental test of the sign-gestalt theory of trial and error learning. *J. exp. Psychol.,* 1946, **36**, 491–502.

Spence, K. W., & Lippitt, R. O. "Latent" learning of a simple maze problem with relevant needs satiated. *Psychol. Bull.,* 1940, **37**, 429.

Sprow, A. J. Reactively homogenous compound trial-and-error learning with distributed trials and terminal reinforcement. *J. exp. Psychol.*, 1947, **37**, 197–213.

Strange, J. R. Latent learning under conditions of high motivation. *J. comp. physiol. Psychol.*, 1950, **43**, 194–197.

Thistlethwaite, D. L. A critical review of latent learning and related experiments. *Psychol. Bull.*, 1951, **48**, 97–129.

Thistlethwaite, D. L. An experimental test of a reinforcement interpretation of latent learning. *J. comp. physiol. Psychol.*, 1951, **44**, 431–441.

Thistlethwaite, D. L. Conditions of irrelevant incentive learning. *J. comp. physiol. Psychol.*, 1952, **45**, 517–525.

Tinbergen, N. The hierarchical organization of nervous mechanisms underlying instinctive behavior. In *Physiological mechanisms in animal behavior.* New York: Academic Press, 1950.

Tinklepaugh, O. L. An experimental study of representative factors in monkeys. *J. comp. Psychol.*, 1928, **8**, 197–236.

Tolman, E. C. More concerning the temporal relations of meaning and imagery. *Psychol. Rev.*, 1917, **24**, 114–138.

Tolman, E. C. Nerve process and cognition. *Psychol. Rev.*, 1918, **25**, 423–442.

Tolman, E. C. Retroactive inhibition as affected by conditions of learning. *Psychol. Monogr.*, 1918, **25**, No. 107.

Tolman, E. C. Instinct and purpose. *Psychol. Rev.*, 1920, **27**, 217–233.

Tolman, E. C. Can instincts be given up in psychology? *J. abnorm. soc. Psychol.*, 1922, **17**, 139–152.

Tolman, E. C. A new formula for behaviorism. *Psychol. Rev.*, 1922, **29**, 44–53.

Tolman, E. C. A behavioristic account of the emotions. *Psychol. Rev.*, 1923, **30**, 217–227.

Tolman, E. C. The effects of underlearning upon long- and short-time retentions. *J. exp. Psychol.*, 1923, **6**, 466–474.

Tolman, E. C. The nature of instinct. *Psychol. Bull.*, 1923, **20**, 200–216.

Tolman, E. C. The inheritance of maze-learning ability in rats. *J. comp. Psychol.*, 1924, **4**, 1–18.

Tolman, E. C. Behaviorism and purpose. *J. Phil.*, 1925, **22**, 36–41.

Tolman, E. C. Purpose and cognition: The determiners of animal learning. *Psychol. Rev.*, 1925, **32**, 285–297.

Tolman, E. C. A behavioristic theory of ideas. *Psychol. Rev.*, 1926, **33**, 352–369.

Tolman, E. C. The nature of the fundamental drives. *J. abnorm. soc. Psychol.*, 1926, **20**, 349–358.

Tolman, E. C. A behaviorist's definition of consciousness. *Psychol. Rev.*, 1927, **34**, 433–439.

Tolman, E. C. Habit formation and higher mental processes in animals. *Psychol. Bull.*, 1927, **24**, 1–35; 1928, **25**, 24–53.

Tolman, E. C. Purposive behavior. *Psychol. Rev.*, 1928, **35**, 524–530.

Tolman, E. C. "Insight" in rats. *Univer. Calif. Publ. Psychol.*, 1930, **4**, 215–232.

Tolman, E. C. Maze performance a function of motivation and of reward as well as of knowledge of the maze paths. *J. gen. Psychol.*, 1930, **4**, 338–342.

Tolman, E. C. Lewin's concept of vectors. *J. gen. Psychol.*, 1932, **7**, 3–15.

Tolman, E. C. *Purposive behavior in animals and men.* New York: Appleton-Century, 1932.

Tolman, E. C. The law of effect. A reply to Dr. Goodenough. *J. exp. Psychol.*, 1933, **16**, 463–470.

Tolman, E. C. Sign-gestalt or conditioned reflex? *Psychol. Rev.*, 1933, **40**, 246–255.

Tolman, E. C. Backward elimination of errors in two successive discrimination habits. *Univer. Calif. Publ. Psychol.*, 1934, **5**, 145–152.

Tolman, E. C. Theories of learning. In F. A. Moss (Ed.), *Comparative psychology.* New York: Prentice-Hall, 1934. Pp. 367–408.

Tolman, E. C. Psychology versus immediate experience. *Philos. Sci.*, 1935, **2**, 356–380.

Tolman, E. C. Connectionism: Wants, interests, and attitudes. *Charact. & Pers.*, 1936, **4**, 245–253.

Tolman, E. C. Operational behaviorism and current trends in psychology. *Proc. 25th Anniv. Celeb. Inaugur. grad. Stud.* Los Angeles: Univer. of Southern California Press, 1936.

Tolman, E. C. The perception of spatial relations by the rat: A type of response not easily explained by conditioning. *J. comp. Psychol.*, 1936, **22**, 287–318.

Tolman, E. C. Demands and conflicts. *Psychol. Rev.*, 1937, **44**, 158–169.

Tolman, E. C. The acquisition of string-pulling by rats—conditioned response or sign-gestalt? *Psychol. Rev.*, 1937, **44**, 195–211.

Tolman, E. C. An operational analysis of "demands." *Erkenntnis*, 1937, **6**, 383–392.

Tolman, E. C. The action of punishment in acceleration learning. *J. comp. Psychol.*, 1938, **26**, 187–200.

Tolman, E. C. The determiners of behavior at a choice point. *Psychol. Rev.*, 1938, **45**, 1–41.

Tolman, E. C. A reply to Professor Guthrie. *Psychol. Rev.*, 1938, **45**, 163–164.

Tolman, E. C. The law of effect. *Psychol. Rev.*, 1938, **45**, 200–203.

Tolman, E. C. Prediction of vicarious trial and error by means of the schematic sowbug. *Psychol. Rev.*, 1939, **46**, 318–336.

Tolman, E. C. Spatial angle and vicarious trial and error. *J. comp. Psychol.*, 1940, **30**, 129–135.

Tolman, E. C. Discrimination vs. learning and the schematic sowbug. *Psychol. Rev.*, 1941, **48**, 367–382.

Tolman, E. C. Motivation, learning and adjustment. *Proc. Amer. philos. soc.*, 1941, **84**, 543–563.

Tolman, E. C. A drive-conversion diagram. *Psychol. Rev.*, 1943, **50**, 503–513.

Tolman, E. C. A stimulus-expectancy need-cathexis psychology. *Science*, 1945, **101**, 160–166.

Tolman, E. C., & Kalish, D. Studies in spatial learning. I. Orientation and the short-cut. *J. exp. Psychol.*, 1946, **36**, 13–24.

Tolman, E. C. Studies in spatial learning. II. Place learning vs. response learning. *J. exp. Psychol.*, 1946, **36**, 221–229.

Tolman, E. C. Studies in spatial learning. IV. The transfer of place learning to other starting paths. *J. exp. Psychol.*, 1947, **37**, 39–47.

Tolman, E. C., Ritchie, B. F., & Kalish, D. Studies in spatial learning. V. Response learning vs. place learning by the non-correction method. *J. exp. Psychol.*, 1947, **37**, 285–292.

Tolman, E. C. Studies in spatial learning: VII. Place and response learning under different degrees of motivation. *J. exp. Psychol.*, 1949, **39**, 653–659.

Tolman, E. C. Discussion: Interrelationships between perception and personality. *J. Pers.*, 1949, **18**, 48–50.

Tolman, E. C. The nature and functioning of wants. *Psychol. Rev.*, 1949, **56**, 357–369.

Tolman, E. C. The psychology of social learning. *J. soc. Issues*, 1949, **5**, Suppl. No. 3, 5–18.

Tolman, E. C., & Brunswik, E. The organism and the causal texture of the environment. *Psychol. Rev.*, 1935, **42**, 43–77.

Tolman, E. C., & Davis, F. C. A note on the correlations between two mazes. *J. comp. Psychol.*, 1924, **4**, 125–135.

Tolman, E. C., & Geier, F. M. Goal distance and restless activity. I. The goal gradient of restless activity. *J. comp. Psychol.*, 1943, **35**, 197–204.

Tolman, E. C., & Gleitman, H. Studies in learning and motivation: I. Equal reinforcements in both end-boxes, followed by shock in one end-box. *J. exp. Psychol.*, 1949, **39**, 810–819.

Tolman, E. C., Hall, C. S., & Bretnall, E. P. A disproof of the law of effect and a substitution of the laws of emphasis, motivation, and disruption. *J. exp. Psychol.*, 1932, **15**, 601–614.

Tolman, E. C., & Honzik, C. H. Degrees of hunger, reward and non-reward, and maze learning in rats. *Univer. Calif. Publ. Psychol.*, 1930, **4**, 241–257.

Tolman, E. C., & Honzik, C. H. Introduction and removal of reward and maze performance of rats. *Univer. Calif. Publ. Psychol.*, 1930, **4**, 257–275.

Tolman, E. C., & Horowitz, J. A. A reply to Mr. Koffka. *Psychol. Bull.*, 1933, **30**, 459–465.

Tolman, E. C., & Krechevsky, I. Means-end-readiness and hypothesis. A contribution to comparative psychology. *Psychol. Rev.*, 1933, **40**, 60–70.

Tolman, E. C., & Levin, M. Individual differences in emotionality, hypothesis formation, vicarious trial and error, and visual discrimination learning in rats. *Comp. Psychol. Monogr.*, 1941, **17**, No. 3.

Tolman, E. C., & Minium, E. VTE in rats: Overlearning and difficulty of discrimination. *J. comp. Psychol.*, 1942, **34**, 301–306.

Tolman, E. C., & Ritchie, B. F. Correlation between VTE's on a maze and on a visual discrimination apparatus. *J. comp. Psychol.*, 1943, **36**, 91–98.

Tolman, E. C., & Robinson, E. W. The effect of degrees of hunger upon the order of elimination of long and short blinds. *Univer. Calif. Publ. Psychol.*, 1930, **4**, 189–202.

Tolman, E. C., & Sams, C. F. Time discrimination in white rats. *J. comp. Psychol.*, 1925, **5**, 255–263.

Tolman, E. C., & White, A. E. A note on the elimination of short and long blind alleys. *J. comp. Psychol.*, 1923, **3**, 327–332.

Voeks, V. W. Formalization and clarification of a theory of learning. *J. Psychol.*, 1950, **30**, 341–362.

Walker, E. L. The acquisition of a response to food under conditions of food satiation. *Amer. Psychologist,* 1948, **3,** 239. (Reported by title only.)

Walker, E. L. Drive specificity and learning. *J. exp. Psychol.,* 1948, **38,** 39–49.

Walker, E. L. Drive specificity and learning: Demonstration of a response tendency acquired under a strong irrelevant drive. *J. comp. physiol. Psychol.,* 1951, **44,** 596–603.

Walker, E. L., Knotter, M. C., & DeValois, R. L. Drive specificity and learning: The acquisition of a spatial response to food under conditions of water deprivation and food satiation. *J. exp. Psychol.,* 1950, **40,** 161–168.

Webb, W. B., & Nolan, C. Y. Cues for discrimination as secondary reinforcing agents: A confirmation. *J. comp. physiol. Psychol.,* 1953, **46,** 180–181.

White, R. K. The case for the Tolman-Lewin interpretation of learning. *Psychol. Rev.,* 1943, **50,** 157–186.

Wilcoxen, H. C., Hays, R., & Jull, C. L. A preliminary determination of the functional relationship of effective reaction potential (sEr) to the ordinal number of Vincentized extinction reactions (n). *J. exp. Psychol.,* 1950, **40,** 194–199.

Williams, K. A. The reward value of a conditioned stimulus. *Univer. Calif. Publ. Psychol.,* 1929, **4,** 31–55.

Williams, S. B. Resistance to extinction as a function of the number of reinforcements. *J. exp. Psychol.,* 1938, **23,** 506–522.

Wingfield, R. C., & Dennis, W. The dependence of the white rat's choice of pathways upon the length of the daily trial series. *J. comp. Psychol.,* 1934, **18,** 135–148.

Wolfle, H. M. Time factors in conditioning finger-withdrawal. *J. gen. Psychol.,* 1930, **4,** 372–378.

Woodbury, C. B. The learning of stimulus patterns by dogs. *J. comp. Psychol.,* 1943, **35,** 29–40.

Yamaguchi, H. G. Superthreshold reaction potential (sEr) as a function of experimental extinction (n). *J. exp. Psychol.,* 1951, **41,** 391–400.

Yamaguchi, H. G. Drive (D) as a function of hours of hunger (h). *J. exp. Psychol.,* 1951, **42,** 108–117.

Yamaguchi, H. G., Hull, C. L., Felsinger, J. M., & Gladstone, A. I. Characteristics of dispersions based on the pooled momentary reaction potentials (sEr) of a group. *Psychol. Rev.,* 1948, **55,** 216–238.

Youtz, R. E. P. The weakening of one Thorndikian response following the extinction of another. *J. exp. Psychol.,* 1939, **24,** 294–304.

6. *Learning Theory Influenced by Psychoanalysis*

Dollard, J., Doob, L. W., Miller, N. E., Mowrer, O. H., Sears, R. R., Ford, C. S., Hovland, C. I. & Sollenberger R. T. *Frustration and aggression.* New Haven: Yale Univer. Press, 1939.

Dollard, J., & Miller, N. E. *Personality and psychotherapy.* New York: McGraw-Hill, 1950.

Eriksen, C. W. Defense against ego-threat in memory and perception. *J. abnorm. soc. Psychol.,* 1942, **47,** 230–235.

Friedman, S. M. An empirical study of the castration and oedipus complexes. *Genet. Psychol. Monogr.,* 1952, **46,** 61–130.

Hilgard, E. R. *Theories of learning.* (Rev. ed.) New York: Appleton-Century-Crofts, 1956.

Hilgard, E. R., Kubie, L. S., & Pumpian-Mindlin, E. *Psychoanalysis and science.* Stanford, Calif.: Stanford Univer. Press, 1952.

Hull, C. L. Modern behaviorism and psychoanalysis. *Trans. N.Y. Acad. Sci.,* 1939, **1**, 78–82.

Maier, N. R. F. *Frustration, the study of behavior without a goal.* New York: McGraw-Hill, 1949.

Miller, N. E. Experiments relating Freudian displacement to generalization of conditioning. *Psychol. Bull.,* 1939, **36**, 516–517.

Miller, N. E. The frustration-aggression hypothesis. *Psychol. Rev.,* 1941, **48**, 337–342.

Miller, N. E. Experimental studies in conflict. In J. McV. Hunt (Ed.), *Personality and the behavior disorders.* New York: Ronald, 1944.

Miller, N. E. Theory and experiment relating psychoanalytic displacement to stimulus-response generalization. *J. abnorm. soc. Psych.,* 1948, **43**, 155–178.

Miller, N. E., & Dollard, J. *Social learning and imitation.* New Haven: Yale Univer. Press. 1941.

Misbach, L. Psychoanalysis and theories of learning. *Psychol. Rev.,* 1948, **55**, 143–156.

Mowrer, O. H. Anxiety reduction and learning. *J. exp. Psychol.,* 1940, **27**, 497–516 .

Mowrer, O. H. An experimental analogue of "repression" with incidental observations on "reaction formation." *J. abnorm. soc. Psychol.,* 1940, **35**, 56–87.

Mowrer, O. H. On the dual nature of learning: a re-interpretation of "conditioning" and "problem-solving." *Harvard educ. Rev.,* 1947, **17**, 102–148.

Mowrer, O. H. Learning theory and the neurotic paradox. *Amer. J. Orthopsychiat.,* 1948, **18**, 577–610.

Mowrer, O. H. *Learning theory and personality dynamics.* New York: Ronald, 1950.

Mowrer, O. H. Two-factor learning theory: Summary and comment. *Psychol. Rev.,* 1951, **58**, 350–354.

Mowrer, O. H. *Psychotherapy: Theory and research.* New York: Ronald, 1953.

Mowrer, O. H. Learning theory: historical review and re-interpretation. *Harvard educ. Rev.,* 1954, **24**, 37–58.

Murray, E. J., & Berkum, M. M. Displacement as a function of conflict. *J. abnorm. soc. Psychol.,* 1955, **51**, 47–56.

Sarbin, T. R. Metal age changes in experimental regression. *J. Pers.,* 1950, **19**, 221–228.

Sears, R. R. Experimental studies of projection: I. Attribution of traits. *J. soc. Psychol.,* 1936, **7**, 151–163.

Sears, R. R. Experimental studies of projection: II. Ideas of reference. *J. soc. Psychol.,* 1937, **8**, 389–400.

Sears, R. R. *Survey of objective studies of psychoanalytic concepts.* Soc. Sci. Res. Counc., 1943.

Sears, R. R. Effects of frustration and anxiety on fantasy aggression. *Amer. J. Orthopsychiat.,* 1951, **21**, 498–505.

Sears, R. R. Social behavior and personality development. In T. Parsons and E. A. Shils (Eds.), *Toward a general theory of action.* Cambridge, Mass.: Harvard Univer. Press, 1951.

Sears, R. R. A theoretical framework for personality and social behavior. *Amer. Psychologist,* 1951, **6**, 476–482.

Sears, R. R., & Wise, G. W. The relation of cup feeding in infancy to thumb-sucking and the oral drive. *Amer. J. Orthopsychiat.,* 1950, **20**, 123–138.

7. *Some Problems in the Theory of Learning*

Estes, W. K., Koch, S., MacCorquodale, K., Meehl, P. E., Mueller, C. G., Jr., Schoenfeld, W. N., & Verplanck, W. S. *Modern learning theory.* New York: Appleton-Century-Crofts, 1954.

Hilgard, E. R. *Theories of learning.* (2nd ed.) New York: Appleton-Century-Crofts, 1956.

Kentucky Symposium. *Learning theory, personality theory, and clinical research.* New York: Wiley, 1954.

Melton, A. W. Learning. In W. S. Monroe (Ed.), *Encyclopedia of educational research.* (Rev. ed.) New York: Macmillan, 1950.

Newman, E. B. Learning. In H. Helson (Ed.), *Theoretical foundations of psychology.* New York: Van Nostrand, 1951.

Spence, K. W. Theoretical interpretations of learning. In S. S. Stevens (Ed.), *Handbook of experimental psychology.* New York: Wiley, 1951.

Spence, K. W. *Behavior theory and conditioning.* Silliman Lectures. New Haven: Yale Univer. Press, 1956.

Chapter 5. Hormic and Holistic Theories

Bernard, L. L. *Instinct, a study of social psychology.* New York: Holt, 1924.

Bugnion, E. The origins of instinct. *Psyche,* 1925, **5**, 6–41.

Dunlap, K. Are there any instincts? *J. abnorm. Psychol.,* 1919, **14**, 307–311.

Freiman, J. S. Kurt Goldstein—an appreciation. *Amer. J. Psychother.,* 1954, **8**, 1–10.

Goldstein, K. Das Wesen der amnestischen Aphasie. *Dtsch. Ztschr. Nervenheilkunde,* 1924, **82**, 324–339.

Goldstein, K. Das psychophysische Problem in seiner Bedeutung für ärztliches Handeln. *Therapie der Gegenwart,* 1931, **72**, 1–11.

Goldstein, K. Clinical and theoretical aspects of lesions of the frontal lobes. *Arch. Neurol. Psychiat.* 1939, **41**, 856–867.

Goldstein, K. *The organism, a holistic approach to biology derived from pathological data in man.* New York: American Book, 1939.

Goldstein, K. *Human nature in the light of psychopathology.* Cambridge, Mass.: Harvard Univer. Press, 1940.

Goldstein, K. Organismic approach to the problem of motivation. *Trans. N.Y. Acad. Sci.,* 1947, **9**, 218–230.

Goldstein, K. *Language and language disturbances.* New York: Grune & Stratton, 1948.

Goldstein, K. Frontal lobotomy and impairment of abstraction. *J. nerv. ment. Dis.,* 1949, **110**, No. 2.

Goldstein, K. On emotions: considerations from the organismic point of view. *J. Psychol.*, 1951, **31**, 37–49.

Goldstein, K. The effect of brain damage on personality. *Psychiatry*, 1952, **15**, 245–260.

Goldstein, K. New ideas on mental health. In J. Fairchild (Ed.), *Personal problems and psychological frontiers.* New York: Sheridan, 1957.

Goldstein, K., & Gelb, A. Über Farbennamenaphasie. *Psychol. Forsch.*, 1924, **6**, 127–186.

Goldstein, K., and Scherer, M. Abstract and concrete behavior: An experimental study with special tests. *Psychol. Monogr.*, 1941, **53**, No. 2.

Journal of individual Psychology. Kurt Goldstein 80th Anniversary Issue, 1959, 15.

Kantor, J. R. *Principles of psychology.* New York: Knopf, 1924–26. 2 vols.

Kantor, J. R. *An outline of social psychology.* Chicago: Follett, 1929.

Kantor, J. R. *A survey of the science of psychology.* Bloomington, Ind.: Principia Press, 1933.

Kantor, J. R. *Problems of physiological psychology.* Bloomington, Ind.: Principia Press, 1947.

Kuo, Z. Y. The fundamental error of the concept of purpose and the trial and error fallacy. *Psychol. Rev.*, 1928, **35**, 414–433.

McDougall, W. *Physiological psychology.* London: Dent, 1905.

McDougall, W. *Introduction to social psychology.* London: Methuen, 1908.

McDougall, W. *Psychology, the study of behavior.* London: Williams & Norgate, 1912.

McDougall, W. *Outline of psychology.* New York: Scribner, 1923.

McDougall, W. Fundamentals of psychology. *Psyche*, 1924, **5**, 13–32.

McDougall, W. *Outline of abnormal psychology.* New York: Scribner, 1926.

McDougall, W. An experiment for the testing of the hypothesis of Lamarck. *Brit. J. Psychol.*, 1927, **17**, 267–304.

McDougall, W. *Modern materialism and emergent evolution.* London: Methuen, 1929.

McDougall, W. *The energies of men, a study of the fundamentals of dynamic psychology.* London: Methuen, 1932.

McDougall, W. Experimental psychology and psychological experiment. *Charact. & Pers.*, 1932–33, **1**, 195–213.

McDougall, W. *Psychoanalysis and social psychology.* London: Methuen, 1936.

Meiers, J., & Mintz, N. L. Kurt Goldstein bibliography: 1936–1959. *J. indiv. Psychol.*, 1959, **15**, 15–19.

Meyer, A. The role of the mental factors in psychiatry. *Amer. J. Insan.*, 1908, **65**, 39–56.

Meyer, A. *Common sense psychiatry.* (New ed.) New York: McGraw-Hill, 1948.

Morgan, C. T., & Stellar, E. *Physiological psychology.* (2nd ed.) New York: McGraw-Hill, 1950.

Pratt, K. C., Nelson, A. K., & Sun, K. H. The behavior of the newborn infant. *Iowa Univer. Contrib. Psychol.*, 1934, No. 10.

Rennie, T. A. C. Adolf Meyer and psychobiology: The man, his methodology, and its relation to therapy. *Pap. Amer. Congr. gen. Semant.*, 1943, **2**, 156–165.

Richards, E. L. *Introduction to psychobiology and psychiatry.* St. Louis: Mosby, 1941.

Robinson, A. L. *William McDougall, a bibliography together with a brief outline of his life.* Durham, N.C.: Duke Univer. Press, 1943.

Rosenblueth, A., Wiener, N., & Bigelow J. Behavior, purpose, and teleology. *Phil. Sci.*, 1943, **10**, 18–24.

Smuts, J. C. *Holism and evolution.* New York: Macmillan, 1926.

Swindle, P. F. An analysis of nesting activities. *Amer. J. Psychol.*, 1919, **30**, 173–186.

Tead, O. *Instincts in industry.* Boston: Houghton Mifflin, 1918.

Tolman, E. C. Instinct and purpose. *Psychol. Rev.*, 1920, **27**, 217–233.

Werner, H. *Comparative study of mental development.* (Rev. ed.) Chicago: Follett, 1948.

Wheeler, R. H. *The science of psychology.* (2nd ed.) New York: Crowell, 1940.

Chapter 6. Psychoanalysis

Abraham, K. *Selected papers on psychoanalysis.* London: Hogarth, 1927.

Alexander, F., Freud, A., Levine, M., & De Saussure, M. *Evolution et tendence actuelle de la psychanalyse.* Paris: Hermann, 1950.

Bernfeld, S. *The psychology of the infant.* New York: Brentano, 1929.

Blum, G. *Psychoanalytic theories of personality.* New York: McGraw-Hill, 1953.

Brill, A. A. *Fundamental conceptions of psychoanalysis.* New York: Harcourt, Brace, 1921.

Charcot, J. M. *Lectures on the diseases of the nervous system.* London: New Sydenham Soc., 1877.

Eissler, R. S., & others. (Eds.) *The psychoanalytic study of the child.* New York: International Universities Press, 1945–59. 13 vols.

Ellis, A. An introduction to the principles of scientific psychoanalysis. *Genet. Psychol. Monogr.*, 1950, **41**, 147–212.

Fenichel, O. *The psychoanalytic theory of neurosis.* New York: Norton, 1945.

Freud, Anna. *The ego and the mechanisms of defense.* New York: International Universities Press, 1946.

Freud, S. *Gesammelte Werke chronologisch geordnet.* London: Imago, 1940–48. 17 vols.

Freud, S. *Collected papers.* London: Hogarth, 1924–50. 5 vols.

Freud, S. *General selection from his works.* (New ed.) London: Hogarth, 1953.

Freud, S. *The standard edition of the complete work of . . .* London: Hogarth, 1953.

Freud, S. *The origins of psychoanalysis, letters to Wilhelm Fliess, drafts and notes.* 1887–1902. New York: Basic Books, 1954.

Frosch, J., & Ross, N. (Eds.) *The annual survey of psychoanalysis.* New York: International Universities Press, 1950–59. 5 vols.

Galdston, I. (Ed.) *Freud and contemporary culture.* New York: International Universities Press, 1956.

Glover, E. *Psychoanalysis.* London: Bole Medical Publishers, 1939.

Grinstein, A. *The index of psychoanalytic writings.* New York: International Universities Press, 1952–59. 5 vols.

Groddeck, G. *The book of It.* Washington: Nervous & Mental Disease Publishing Co., 1928.

Hall, C. S. *A primer of Freudian psychology.* Cleveland: World, 1954.

Hartman, H. *Die Grundlagen der Psychoanalyse.* Leipzig: Thieme, 1927.

Healy, W., Bronner, A. F., & Bowers, A. M. *The structure and meaning of psychoanalysis.* New York: Knopf, 1930.

Hendrick, I. *Facts and theories of psychoanalysis.* New York: Knopf, 1939.

Hook, S. (Ed.) *Psychoanalysis, scientific method and philosophy.* New York: New York Univer. Press, 1959.

Janet, P. *L'automatisme psychologique.* Paris: Alcan, 1889.

Jekels, L. *Selected papers.* New York: International Universities Press, 1952.

Jones, E. *Papers on psychoanalysis.* New York: Wood, 1913.

Jones, E. *The life and work of Sigmund Freud.* New York: Basic Books, 1953–57. 3 vols.

Kubie, L. S. *Practical and theoretical aspects of psychoanalysis.* New York: International Universities Press, 1950.

Lorand, S. (Ed.) *Psychoanalysis today, its scope and function.* New York: International Universities Press, 1944.

Lorand, S. (Ed.) *The yearbook of psychoanalysis.* New York: International Universities Press, 1945–59. 10 vols.

Munroe, Ruth L. *Schools of psychoanalytic thought.* New York: Dryden, 1955.

Münsterberg, W., & Axelrod, S. *Psychoanalysis and the Social Sciences.* New York: International Universities Press, 1949–59. 5 vols.

Murphy, G. The current impact of Freud upon psychology. *Amer. Psychologist,* 1956, **11**, 663–672.

Nunberg, H. *Principles of psychoanalysis.* (Rev. ed.) New York: International Universities Press, 1955.

Pumpian-Mindlin, E. (Ed.) *Psychoanalysis as science.* Stanford, Calif.: Stanford Univer. Press, 1952.

Puner, H. W. *Freud, his life and his mind.* New York: Howell, Soskin, 1947.

Rapaport, D. *Emotions and memory.* (2nd ed.) New York: International Universities Press, 1950.

Rapaport, D. On the psychoanalytic theory of thinking. *Int. J. Psychoanal.,* 1950, **31**, 1–10.

Rapaport, D. The conceptual model of psychoanalysis. *J. Pers.,* 1951, **20**, 56–81.

Rapaport, D. (Ed.) *Organization and pathology of thought.* New York: Columbia Univer. Press, 1951.

Reik, T. *From thirty years with Freud.* New York: Farrar & Rinehart, 1940.

Sachs, H. *Freud, master and friend.* Cambridge, Mass.: Harvard Univer. Press, 1944.

Sears, R. R. *Survey of objective studies of psychoanalytic concepts.* New York: Soc. Sci. Res. Counc., 1943.

Sterba, R. *Introduction to the psychoanalytic theory of the libido.* Nerv. & ment. Dis. Monogr., No. 68, 1947.

Symonds, P. M. *The dynamics of human adjustment.* New York: Appleton-Century-Crofts, 1946.

Thompson, Clara. *Psychoanalysis: Evolution and development.* New York: Hermitage, 1950.

Zilboorg, G. *Sigmund Freud, his exploration of the mind of man.* New York: Norton, 1941.

Zilboorg, G., & Henry, G. W. *A history of medical psychology.* New York: Norton, 1941.

Chapter 7. Individual and Analytic Psychologies

1. *Alfred Adler: Individual Psychology*

Adler, A. *The neurotic constitution.* New York: Moffat, 1917.

Adler, A. *A study of organ inferiority and its psychical compensation.* Nerv. & ment. Dis. Monogr., No. 24, 1917.

Adler, A. *The practice and theory of individual psychology.* New York: Harcourt, Brace, 1927.

Adler, A. *Understanding human nature.* New York: Greenberg, 1927.

Adler, A. *The science of living.* New York: Greenberg, 1929.

Adler, A. *The pattern of life.* New York: Rinehart, 1930.

Adler, A. *What life should mean to you.* Boston: Little, Brown, 1931.

Adler, A. Persönlichkeit als geschlossene Einheit. *Int. Z. indiv. Psychol.,* 1932, **10**, 81–89.

Adler, A. *Social interest: a challenge to mankind.* London: Faber, 1938.

Adler, A. Physical manifestations of psychic disturbances. *Ind. Psychol. Bull.,* 1944, **4**, 3–8.

Adler, A., & Furtmüller, C. (Eds.) *Heilen und Bilden.* Münich: Reinhardt, 1914.

Ansbacher, H. L. Causality and indeterminism according to Alfred Adler and some current American personality theories. *Ind. Psychol. Bull.,* 1951, **9**, 96–107.

Ansbacher, H. L., & Ansbacher, R. R. *The individual psychology of Alfred Adler.* New York: Basic Books, 1956.

Bottome, Phyllis. *Alfred Adler, a biography.* New York: Putnam, 1939.

Colby, K. M. On the disagreement between Freud and Adler. *Amer. Images,* 1951, **8**, 229–238.

Dreikurs, R. *Fundamentals of Adlerian psychology.* New York: Greenberg, 1950.

Ganz, Madeleine. *La psychologie d'Alfred Adler et le développement de l'enfant.* Geneva, 1935.

Orgler, Hertha. *Alfred Adler, the man and his work.* London: Daniel, 1939.

Sperber, M. *Alfred Adler: der Mensch und Seine Lehre.* Münich: Bergmann, 1926.

Vaihinger, H. *The philosophy of "as if"; a system of the theoretical, practical and religious fictions of mankind.* New York: Harcourt, Brace, 1925.

Way, L. *Adler's place in psychology.* New York: Macmillan, 1950.

Wexberg, E. *Individual psychology.* New York: Cosmopolitan Book, 1929.

2. Carl Gustav Jung: Analytic Psychology

Adler, G. *Studies in analytical psychology.* New York: Norton, 1948.

Campbell, J. *The hero with a thousand faces.* New York: Pantheon, 1949.

Fordham, Frieda. *An introduction to Jung's psychology.* London: Penguin, 1953.

Fordham, M. Professor C. G. Jung. *Brit. J. med. Psychol.,* 1945, **20,** 221–235.

Glover, E. *Freud or Jung.* New York: Norton, 1950.

Gray, H. Freud and Jung: Their contrasting psychological types. *Psychoanal. Rev.,* 1949, **36,** 22–44.

Harding, Mary E. *Psychic energy, its course and goal.* New York: Pantheon, 1947.

Jacobi, J. *The psychology of Jung.* (Rev. ed.) New Haven: Yale Univer. Press, 1951.

Jung, C. G. *Collected papers on analytical psychology.* New York: Moffat, 1917.

Jung, C. G. *Contributions to analytical psychology.* New York: Harcourt, Brace, 1928.

Jung, C. G. *Psychological types.* New York: Harcourt, Brace, 1933.

Jung, C. G. *The integration of personality.* New York: Farrar and Rinehart, 1939.

Jung, C. G. *Über psychische Energetik und des Wesen der Träume.* Zürich: Rascher, 1948.

Jung, C. G. *Collected works.* New York: Pantheon, Bollingen Series, 1953—. 18 vols.

Jung, C. G. *Psychological reflections, anthology of writings.* Ed. by J. Jacobi. New York: Pantheon, 1953.

Jung, C. G. *Von den Wurzeln des Bewusstseins.* Zürich: Rascher, 1954.

Jung, C. G. *The undiscovered self.* Boston: Little, Brown, 1959.

Jung, C. G., & Pauli, W. *The interpretation of nature and the psyche.* New York: Pantheon, 1955.

Jung, C. G., & Kerenyi, C. *Essays on a science of mythology.* New York: Pantheon, 1949.

Neumann, E. *The origins and history of consciousness.* New York: Pantheon, 1954.

Neumann, E. *The great mother.* London: Routledge & Kegan Paul, 1955.

Progoff, I. *Jung's psychology and its social meaning.* New York: Julian, 1953.

Thompson, Clara. *Psychoanalysis: Evolution and development.* New York: Hermitage, 1950.

Wickes, Frances G. *The inner world of man.* New York: Holt, 1948.

Wilhelm, R., & Jung, C. G. *The secret of the golden flower.* New York: Harcourt, Brace, 1931.

Chapter 8. New Theories in Psychoanalysis

Alexander, F. *Fundamentals of psychoanalysis.* New York: Norton, 1949.

Alexander, F. *Psychosomatic medicine: Its principles and applications.* New York: Norton, 1950.

Alexander, F. *Our age of unreason*. Philadelphia: Lippincott, 1951.

Alexander, F., & Ross, H. (Eds.) *Twenty years of psychoanalysis*. New York: Norton, 1953.

Bergler, E. *Superego, unconscious conscience*. New York: Grune & Stratton, 1952.

Bergmann, G. Psychoanalysis and experimental psychology: A review from the standpoint of scientific empiricism. *Mind*, 1943, **52**, 122–140.

Brierley, M. *Trends in psychoanalysis*. London: Hogarth, 1951.

Daim, W. *Umwertung der Psychoanalyse*. Wien: Herold, 1951.

Deutsch, F. *On the mysterious leap from the mind to the body*. New York: International Universities Press, 1959.

Erikson, E. K. *Childhood and society*. New York: Norton, 1950.

Fairbairn, W. R. D. *Psychoanalytic studies of personality*. London: Routledge, 1952.

Fairbairn, W. R. D. *An object-relations theory of personality*. New York: Basic Books, 1954.

Federn, P. *Ego psychology and the psychoses*. New York: Basic Books, 1953.

Fenichel, O. *Collected papers*. New York: Norton, 1953–54. 2 vols.

Ferenczi, S. *Contributions to psychoanalysis*. Boston: Badger, 1916.

Ferenczi, S. *Further contributions to the theory and technique of psychoanalysis*. London: Hogarth, 1926.

Ferenczi, S. *Sex in psychoanalysis*. New York: Basic Books & Brunner, 1950.

Ferenczi, S. *First contributions to psychoanalysis*. London: Hogarth, 1953.

Flowerman, S. H. Psychoanalytic theory and science. *Amer. J. Psychother.*, 1954, **8**, 415–441.

Fodor, N. *The search for the beloved*. New York: Hermitage, 1949.

Fodor, N. *New approaches to dream interpretation*. New York: Citadel, 1951.

French, T. M. *The integration of behavior*. Vol. I. *Basic postulates*. Chicago: Univer. of Chicago Press, 1952.

Frosch, J., & Ross, V. (Eds.) *The annual survey of psychoanalysis*. New York: International Universities Press, 1950–59. 5 vols.

Glover, E. Examination of the Klein system of child psychology. *Psychoanal. Study of the Child*, 1945, **1**.

Hartmann, H. Comments on the psychoanalytic theory of the ego. *Psychoanal. Study of the Child*, 1950, **5**.

Hartmann, H. *Ego psychology and the problem of adaptation*. New York: International Universities Press, 1959.

Hartmann, H., Kris, E., & Loewenstein, R. M. Comments on the formation of psychic structure. *Psychoanal. Study of the Child*, 1947, **2**.

Isaacs, Suzanne. *Social development in young children*. New York: Humanities, 1954.

Kardiner, A. *The individual and his society*. New York: Columbia Univer. Press, 1939.

Kardiner, A. *The psychological frontiers of society*. New York: Columbia Univer. Press, 1945.

Karpf, M. *Psychology and psychotherapy of Otto Rank*. New York: Philosophical Library, 1953.

Klein, M. *The psychoanalysis of children.* London: Hogarth, 1932.

Klein, M. *Contributions to psychoanalysis, 1921–1948.* London: Hogarth, 1948.

Klein, M., Heimann, P., Isaacs, S., & Riviere, J. *Developments in psychoanalysis.* London: Hogarth, 1952.

Klein, M., & Riviere, J. *Love, hate, and reparation.* London: Hogarth, 1938.

Kris, E. The nature of psychoanalytic propositions and their validation. In S. Hook and R. Konvitz (Eds.), *Freedom and experience.* Ithaca, N.Y.: Cornell Univer. Press, 1947.

Kris, E. *Psychoanalytic explorations in art.* New York: International Universities Press, 1952.

Lorand, S. (Ed.) *Psychoanalysis today.* New York: International Universities Press, 1944.

Lowenstein, R. M. (Ed.) *Drives, affects, behavior: Contributions to the theory and practice of psychoanalysis and its applications.* New York: International Universities Press, 1953.

Miller, N. E., & Dollard, J. *Social learning and imitation.* New Haven: Yale Univer. Press, 1941.

Misbach, L. Psychoanalysis and theories of learning. *Psychol. Rev.,* 1948, **55,** 143–156.

Mowrer, O. H. *Learning theory and personality dynamics.* New York: Ronald, 1950.

Mullahy, P. *Oedipus myth and complex.* New York: Hermitage, 1948.

Nuttin, J. *Psychoanalysis and personality.* New York: Sheed & Ward, 1953.

Oberndorf, C. P. *History of psychoanalysis in America.* New York: Grune & Stratton, 1953.

Rank, O. *Art and artist.* New York: Knopf, 1932.

Rank, O. *Modern education.* New York: Knopf, 1932.

Rank, O. *Beyond psychology.* New York: Haddon, 1941.

Rank, O. *Will therapy and truth and reality.* New York: Knopf, 1945.

Rank, O. *Psychology and the soul.* Philadelphia: Univer. of Pennsylvania Press, 1950.

Rank, O. *The myth of the birth of the hero.* New York: Brunner, 1952.

Rank, O. *Trauma of birth.* New York: Brunner, 1952.

Rank, O., & Ferenczi, S. *The development of psychoanalysis.* New York: Nervous & Mental Disease Publishing Co., 1925.

Rapaport, D. On the psychoanalytic theory of thinking. *Int. J. Psychoanal.,* 1950, **31,** 1–10.

Rapaport, D. On the psychoanalytic theory of affects. *Int. J. Psychoanal.,* 1953, **34,** 177–198.

Reich, W. *Character analysis.* New York: Orgone Institute, 1945.

Reik, T. *Listening with the third ear.* New York: Harcourt, Brace, 1949.

Roheim, G. *Psychoanalysis and anthropology; culture, personality, and the unconscious.* New York: International Universities Press, 1950.

Roheim, G. *The gates of the dream.* New York: International Universities Press, 1952.

Sachs, H. *The creative unconscious: Studies in the psychoanalysis of art.* (2nd ed.) Boston: Sci-Art, 1951.

Sartre, J. P. *Existential psychoanalysis.* New York: Philosophical Library, 1953.

Scheidlinger, S. *Psychoanalysis and group behavior: A study of Freudian group psychology.* New York: Norton, 1952.

Schilder, P. *Mind: Perception and thoughts in their constructive aspects.* New York: Columbia Univer. Press, 1945.

Schilder, P. *Psychoanalysis, man and society.* New York: Norton, 1951.

Stekel, W. *Autobiography: The life story of a pioneer psychoanalyst.* New York: Liveright, 1950.

Weiss, E. Regression and projection in the superego. *Int. J. Psychoanal.,* 1932, **13,** 449–478.

Wisdom, J. *Philosophy and psychoanalysis.* New York: Philosophical Library, 1953.

Chapter 9. Away from Freud: The Sociological School

Beaglehole, E. Notes on interpersonal theory. *Psychiatry,* 1940, **3,** 511–526.

Fromm, E. *Die Entstehung des Christusdogma.* Wien: Psychoanal. Verlag, 1930.

Fromm, E. *Escape from freedom.* New York: Farrar & Rinehart, 1941.

Fromm, E. *Man for himself.* New York: Rinehart, 1947.

Fromm, E. The Oedipus complex and the Oedipus myth. In Ruth N. Anshen (Ed.), *The family: its function and destiny.* New York: Harper, 1948.

Fromm, E. *Psychoanalysis and religion.* New Haven: Yale Univer. Press, 1950.

Fromm, E. *The forgotten language: An introduction to the understanding of dreams, fairy tales, and myths.* New York: Rinehart, 1951.

Fromm, E. *Sane society.* New York: Rinehart, 1955.

Horney, K. *The neurotic personality of our time.* New York: Norton, 1937.

Horney, K. *New ways in psychoanalysis.* New York: Norton, 1939.

Horney, K. *Our inner conflicts.* New York: Norton, 1945.

Horney, K. *Neurosis and human growth.* New York: Norton, 1950.

James, W. T. Karen Horney and Erich Fromm in relation to Alfred Adler. *Indiv. Psychol. Bull.,* 1947, **6,** 105–116.

Mullahy, P. A theory of interpersonal relations and the evolution of personality. *Psychiatry,* 1945, **8,** 177–206.

Mullahy, P. *Oedipus—myth and complex.* New York: Hermitage, 1948.

Mullahy, P. (Ed.) *A study of interpersonal relations.* New York: Hermitage, 1949.

Mullahy, P. (Ed.) *The contributions of Harry Stack Sullivan.* New York: Hermitage, 1952.

Sullivan, H. S. Introduction to the study of interpersonal relations. *Psychiatry,* 1938, **1,** 121–134.

Sullivan, H. S. *Conceptions of modern psychiatry.* Washington: W. A. White Foundation, 1947.

Sullivan, H. S. *The interpersonal theory of psychiatry.* New York: Norton, 1953.

Sullivan, H. S. *Psychiatric interview.* New York: Norton, 1954.

Thompson, Clara. *Psychoanalysis: Evolution and development.* New York: Hermitage, 1950.

Wolman, B. B. Psychoanalysis without libido: K. Horney's contribution to psychological theory. *Amer. J. Psychother.,* 1954, **8,** 21–31.

Chapter 10. Phenomenology and Understanding Psychology

Brett, G. S. *History of psychology*. Ed. R. S. Peters. London: Allen & Unwin, 1951.

Dilthey, W. *Gesammelte Schriften*. Leipzig: Teubner, 1924.

Ebbinghaus, H. *Memory*. New York: Teachers College, Columbia Univer., 1913.

Hodges, H. A. *Wilhelm Dilthey, an introduction*. London: Routledge & Kegan Paul, 1949.

Hodges, H. A. *The philosophy of Wilhelm Dilthey*. London: Routledge & Kegan Paul, 1952.

Husserl, E. Phenomenology. In *Encyclopaedia Britannica*. (14th ed.) New York: 1929.

Husserl, E. *Ideas: General introduction to pure phenomenology*. Trans. W. R. Boyce Gibson. London: Allen & Unwin, 1931.

Kant, I. *Prolegomena to metaphysics*. Ed. P. Cerus. La Salle, Ill.: Open Court, 1902.

Kant, I. *The critique of pure reason*. New York: Macmillan, 1914.

Kaufmann, F. In memoriam Edmund Husserl. *Soc. Res.*, 1940, 61–91.

Kaufmann, F. Cassirer, Neo-Kantianism, and phenomenology. In P. A. Schilpp (Ed.), *The philosophy of Ernst Cassirer*. Evanston, Ill.: Living Philosophies, 1949.

Klüver, H. Contemporary German psychology as a "cultural science." In G. Murphy, *An historical introduction to modern psychology*. New York: Harcourt, Brace, 1929.

Laird, J. *Recent philosophy*. London: Butterworth, 1936.

Mach, E. *The analysis of sensation*. La Salle, Ill.: Open Court, 1914.

MacLeod, R. B. The phenomenological approach to social psychology. *Psychol. Rev.*, 1947, **54**, 193–210.

Mead, G. H. *Movements of thought in the nineteenth century*. Chicago: Univer. of Chicago Press, 1936.

Miller, H. *An historical introduction to modern philosophy*. New York: Macmillan, 1947.

Puglisi, M. Franz Brentano: A biographical sketch. *Amer. J. Psychol.*, 1924, **35**, 414–419.

Randall, J. H. *The making of the modern mind*. Boston: Houghton Mifflin, 1926.

Russell, B. *The history of Western philosophy*. New York: Simon & Schuster, 1945.

Soucek, R. Alfred Binet et l'école de Brentano. *J. Psychol. norm. path.*, 1924, **21**, 883–888.

Windelband, W. *An introduction to philosophy*. London: Allen & Unwin, 1921.

Chapter 11. Personalistic Psychology

Allport, G. W. The functional autonomy of motives. *Amer. J. Psychol.*, 1937, **50**, 141–156.

Allport, G. W. The personalistic psychology of William Stern. *Charact. and Pers.*, 1937, **5**, 231–246.

Allport, G. W. *Personality: A psychological interpretation.* New York: Holt, 1937.

Allport, G. W. Effect: A secondary principle of learning. *Psychol. Rev.*, 1946, **53**, 335–347.

Allport, G. W. *The individual and his religion.* New York: Macmillan, 1950.

Allport, G. W. *The nature of personality: Selected papers.* Cambridge, Mass.: Addison-Wesley, 1950.

Allport, G. W. The psychological nature of personality. *Personalist,* 1953, **34**, 347–357.

Allport, G. W. *The nature of prejudice.* Cambridge, Mass.: Addison-Wesley, 1954.

Allport, G. W. *Becoming: Basic considerations for a psychology of personality.* New Haven: Yale Univer. Press, 1955.

Allport, G. W., & Vernon, P. E. *A study of values.* Boston: Houghton Mifflin, 1931.

Allport, G. W., & Vernon, P. E. *Studies in expressive movement.* New York: Macmillan, 1933.

Bertocci, P. A. A critique of G. W. Allport's theory of motivation. *Psychol. Rev.*, 1940, **47**, 501–532.

Casper, S. *Die personalistische Weltanschauung W. Stern's.* Leipzig: Barth, 1933.

Coutu, W. *Emergent human nature.* New York: Knopf, 1949.

Spranger, E. *Psychologie des Jugendalters.* Leipzig: Quelle & Meyer, 1925.

Spranger, E. *Types of men.* Trans. P. J. W. Pigors. Halle: Niemyer, 1928.

Spranger, E. Der Sinn der Voraussetzungslosigkeit in den Geisteswissenschaften. *Preuss. Akad. d. Wissenschaften,* 1929.

Stern, W. *Über Psychologie der individuellen Differenzen.* Leipzig: Barth, 1900.

Stern, W. *Person und Sache: System der philosophischen Weltanschauung.* Leipzig: Barth, 1906–24.

Stern, W. *Psychology of early childhood up to the sixth year of age.* (3rd ed.) New York: Holt, 1930.

Stern, W. *Studien zur Personwissenschaft.* Leipzig: Barth, 1930.

Stern, W. *General psychology from the personalistic standpoint.* Trans. H. D. Spoerl. New York: Macmillan, 1938.

Chapter 12. The Gestalt Psychology

1. Opposition to Associationism

Ach, N. *Über den Willensakt und das Temperament: Eine experimentelle Untersuchung.* Leipzig: Quelle & Meyer, 1910.

Binet, A. Étude expérimentale de l'intelligence. Paris: Schleicher, 1910.

Boring, E. G. *A history of experimental psychology.* (2nd ed.) New York: Appleton-Century-Crofts, 1950.

Bühler, K. Tatsachen und probleme zu einer Psychologie der Denkvorgänge. I.

Über Gedanken. II Über Gedanken Zusammenhänge. III Über Gedanken erinnerungen. *Arch. Psychol.*, 1907, **9**, 297–305; 1908, **12**, 1–23; 1908, **12**, 24–92.

Bühler, K. *Gestalt Perzeption.* Stuttgart: Speeman, 1913.

Bühler, K. *Die Theorie der Perzeption.* Jena: Fischer, 1922.

Claparède, E. La genèse de l'hypothèse, étude expérimentale. *Arch. Psychol.*, 1933, **24**, 1–154.

Humphrey, G. *Thinking: An introduction to its experimental psychology.* London: Methuen, 1951.

Janet, P. *L'automatisme psychologique.* Paris: Alcan, 1889.

Külpe, O. Aussichten der experimentellen Psychologie. *Philos. Monatshefte*, 1894, **30**, 281–294.

Külpe, O. Über die Objektivierung und Subjektivierung von Sinnesausdrücken. *Philos. Stud.*, 1902, **19**, 508–556.

Kälpe, O. Pour la psychologie du sentiment. *J. Psychol. norm. path.*, 1910, **7**, 1–13.

Külpe, O. *Vorlesungen über die Psychologie.* (2nd ed., ed. K. Bühler.) Leipzig: Hirzel, 1922.

Messer, A. Experimentell-psychologische Untersuchungen über das Denken. *Arch. gen. Psychol.*, 1906, **8**, 1–224.

Michotte, A. *La perception de la causalité.* Louvain: Inst. Supérieur Philos., 1946.

Müller, G. E. Experimentelle Beiträge zur Untersuchung des Gedächtnisses. *Z. Psychol.*, 1894, **6**, 81–190, 257–339.

Müller, G. E. *Komplextheorie und Gestalttheorie.* Göttingen: Vanderhoeck, 1923.

Murphy, G. *Historical introduction to modern psychology.* (Rev. ed.) New York: Harcourt, Brace, 1949.

Stout, G. F. *Analytic psychology.* London: Allen & Unwin, 1902. 2 vols.

Ward, J. Psychology. In *Encyclopaedia Britannica.* (9th ed.) London: 1886.

Watt, H. J. Experimentelle Beiträge zu einer Theorie des Denkeus. *Arch ges. Psychol.*, 1905, **4**, 289–436.

2, 3. Gestalt

Adamson, R. E., & Taylor, D. W. Functional fixedness as related to elapsed time and set. *J. exp. Psychol.*, 1954, **47**, 122–126.

Allport, H. *Theories of perception and the concept of structure.* New York: Wiley, 1955.

Asch, S. Max Wertheimer's contribution to modern psychology. *Soc. Res.*, 1946, **13**, 81–102.

Birch, H. G. The role of motivational factors in insightful problem-solving. *J. comp. Psychol.*, 1945, **38**, 295–317.

Boring, E. G. The gestalt psychology and the gestalt movement. *Amer. J. Psychol.*, 1930, **42**, 308–315.

Duncker, K. On problem solving. *Psychol. Monogr.*, 1945, **58**, No. 270.

Ehrenfels, C. V. On gestalt qualities. *Psychol. Rev.*, 1937, **44**, 521–524.

Ellis, W. D. *A source book of gestalt psychology.* New York: Harcourt, Brace, 1938.

Hartmann, G. W. *Gestalt psychology, a survey of facts and principles.* New York: Ronald, 1935.

Helson, H. The fundamental propositions of gestalt psychology. *Psychol. Rev.,* 1933, **40,** 13–32.

Henle, M. An experimental investigation of past experience as a determinant of visual form of perception. *J. exp. Psychol.,* 1942, **30,** 1–22.

Hilgard, E. R. *Theories of learning.* (2nd ed.) New York: Appleton-Century-Crofts, 1956.

Humphrey, G. *Thinking.* London: Methuen, 1951.

Katona, G. *Organizing and memorizing: Studies in the psychology of learning and teaching.* New York: Columbia Univer. Press, 1940.

Katz, G. *Gestalt psychology, its nature and significance.* New York: Ronald, 1950.

Koffka, K. *The growth of the mind.* London: Kegan Paul, 1924.

Koffka, K. *Principles of gestalt psychology.* New York: Harcourt, Brace, 1935.

Köhler, W. *Die physikalischen Gestalten in Ruhe und in stationären Zustand.* Erlangen: Weltkreis, 1920.

Köhler, W. *The mentality of apes.* New York: Harcourt, Brace, 1925.

Köhler, W. *Psychologische Probleme.* Berlin: Springer, 1933.

Köhler, W. Zur Psychophysik des Vergleichs und des Raumes. *Psychol. Forsch.,* 1933, **18,** 343–360.

Köhler, W. *The place of value in a world of facts.* New York: Liveright, 1938.

Köhler, W. *Dynamics in psychology.* New York: Liveright, 1940.

Köhler, W. On the nature of associations. *Proc. Amer. Philos. Soc.,* 1941, **84,** 489–502.

Köhler, W. *Gestalt psychology.* New York: Liveright, 1947.

Köhler, W., & Restorff, H. Analyse von Vorgängen im Spurenfeld. *Psychol. Forsch.,* 1935, **21,** 56–112.

Köhler, W., & Wallach, H. Figural after-effects: an investigation of visual processes. *Proc. Amer. Philos. Soc.,* 1944, **88,** 269–357.

Kruger, F. E. Über psychische Ganzheit. *Neue psychol. Stud.,* 1926, **1,** 1–123.

Newman, E. B. Forgetting of meaningful material during sleep and waking. *Amer. J. Psychol.,* 1939, **52,** 65–71.

Pechstein, L. A., & Brown, F. D. An experimental analysis of the alleged criteria of insight learning. *J. educ. Psychol.,* 1939, **30,** 38–52.

Petermann, B. *The gestalt theory and the problem of configuration.* New York: Harcourt, Brace, 1932.

Spence, K. W. Cognitive versus stimulus-response theories of learning. *Psychol. Rev.,* 1950, **57,** 159–172.

Spitz, H. The present status of the Köhler-Wallach theory of satiation. *Psychol. Bull.,* 1958, **55,** 1–28.

Stolurov, L. M. (Ed.) *Readings in learning.* New York: Prentice-Hall, 1953.

Wertheimer, M. Experimentelle Studien über das Sehen von Bewegung. *Z. Psychol.,* 1912, **61,** 161–265.

Wertheimer, M. Untersuchung zur Lehre von der Gestalt. *Psychol. Forsch.,* 1922, **1,** 47–65; 1923, **4,** 301–350.

Wertheimer, M. *Drei Abhandlungen zur Gestalttheorie.* Berlin: Erlangen, 1935.

Wertheimer, M. *Productive thinking.* New York: Harper, 1945.

Yerkes, R. M. The mind of a gorilla. *Genet. Psychol. Monogr.,* 1927, **2.**

Chapter 13. The Field Theory

Barker, R. G., Dembo, T., & Lewin, K. Frustration and regression: An experiment with young children. *Univer. Iowa Stud. Child Welf.,* 1941, **18,** 1–314.

Brown, J. F. On the use of mathematics in psychological theory. *Psychometrika,* 1936, **1,** 7–15, 77–90.

Cassirer, E. *Substanzbegriff und Funktionsbegriff.* Berlin: Cassirer, 1910.

Cohen, M. R. *Reason and nature.* New York: Harcourt, Brace, 1931.

Dembo, T. Der Ärger als dynamisches Problem. *Psychol. Forsch.,* 1931, **15,** 1–144.

Deutsch, M. Field theory in social psychology. In G. Lindzey (Ed.), *Handbook of social psychology.* Cambridge, Mass.: Addison-Wesley, 1954.

Estes, W. K., & others. *Modern learning theory.* New York: Appleton-Century-Crofts, 1954.

Fajans, S. Erfolg, Ausdauer und Aktivität beim Säugling und Kleinkind. *Psychol. Forsch.,* 1933, **17,** 268–305.

Feigl, H. Principles and problems of theory construction in psychology. In W. Dennis (Ed.), *Current trends in psychological theory.* Pittsburgh: Univer. of Pittsburgh Press, 1951.

Garrett, H. E. Lewin's "topological" psychology: An evaluation. *Psychol. Rev.,* 1939, **46,** 517–524.

Hilgard, E. R. *Theories of learning.* (2nd ed.) New York: Appleton-Century-Crofts, 1956.

Hodges, H. A. *Wilhelm Dilthey: An introduction.* London: Routledge and Kegan Paul, 1949.

Hoppe, F. Erfolg und Misserfolg. *Psychol. Forsch.,* 1930, **14,** 1–62.

Keredjarto, von B. *Vorlesungen über Topologie.* Berlin: Springer, 1923.

Leeper, R. W. *Lewin's topological and vector psychology.* Eugene, Ore.: Univer. of Oregon Press, 1943.

Lewin, K. Die psychische Tätigkeit bei der Hemmung von Willensvorgängen und das Grundgesetz der Assoziation. *Z. Psychol.,* 1917, **77,** 212–247.

Lewin, K. Das Problem der Willensmessung und das Grundgesetz der Assoziation. *Psychol. Forsch.,* 1921, **1,** 191–302; 1922, **2,** 65–140.

Lewin, K. *Der Begriff der Genese in Physik, Biologie, und Entwicklungsgeschichte.* Berlin: Bornträger, 1922.

Lewin, K. *Forsatz, Wille, und Bedürfnis.* Berlin: Springer, 1926.

Lewin, K. Gesetz und Experiment in der Psychologie. *Symposium.,* 1927, **1,** 375–421.

Lewin, K. *Die Entwicklung der experimentellen Willenspsychologie und die Psychotherapie.* Leipzig: Hirzel, 1929.

Lewin, K. Vectors, cognitive processes, and Mr. Tolman's criticism. *J. gen. Psychol.,* 1933, **8,** 318–345.

Lewin, K. Environmental forces. In C. Murchison (Ed.), *Handbook of child psychology.* Worcester, Mass.: Clark Univer. Press, 1934.

Lewin, K. *A dynamic theory of personality.* New York: McGraw-Hill, 1935.

Lewin, K. *Principles of topological psychology.* New York: McGraw-Hill, 1936.

Lewin, K. The conceptual representation and measurement of psychological forces. *Univer. Iowa Contr. psychol. Theory,* 1938, **1**, No. 4, 1–247.

Lewin, K. Formalization and progress in psychology. *Univer. Iowa Contr. psychol. Theory,* 1940, **3**, 7–42.

Lewin, K. Field theory of learning. *Yearb. nat. Soc. Stud. Educ.,* 1942, **41**, Part II, 215–242.

Lewin, K. Defining the "field at a given time." *Psychol. Rev.,* 1943, **50**, 292–310.

Lewin, K. Constructs in psychology and psychological ecology. *Univer. Iowa Stud. Child Welf.,* 1944, **20**, 1–29.

Lewin, K. Behavior and development as a function of the total situation. In L. Carmichael (Ed.), *Manual of child psychology.* New York: Wiley, 1946.

Lewin, K. Cassirer's philosophy of science and the social sciences. In P. A. Schilpp (Ed.), *The philosophy of Ernst Cassirer.* Evanston, Ill.: Living Philosophies, 1949.

Lewin, K. *Field theory in social science.* New York: Harper, 1951.

Lippitt, R. An experimental study of the effect of democratic and authoritarian group atmospheres. *Univer. Iowa Stud. Child Welf.,* 1940, **16**, 3, 44–195.

London, I. O. Psychologists' misuse of the auxiliary concepts of physics and mathematics. *Psychol. Rev.,* 1944, **51**, 266–291.

MacCall, S. H. A comparative study of the systems of Lewin and Koffka with specific reference to memory phenomena. *Contr. psychol. Theory,* Duke Univer. Press, 1939, **2**, No. 1.

Marrow, A. J. Goal tension and recall. *J. gen. Psychol.,* 1938, **19**, 3–35, 37–64.

Ovsiankina, M. Die Wiederaufnahme von unterbrochener Handlungen. *Psychol. Forsch.,* 1928, **11**, 302–389.

Sierpinski, W. *Introduction to general topology.* Toronto: Univer. of Toronto Press, 1934.

Spence, K. W. The nature of theory construction in contemporary psychology. *Psychol. Rev.,* 1944, **51**, 47–68.

Spence, K. W. Theoretical interpretations of learning. In S. S. Stevens (Ed.), *Handbook of experimental psychology.* New York: Wiley, 1951.

White, R. K. The case for the Tolman-Lewin interpretation of learning. *Psychol. Rev.,* 1943, **50**, 157–186.

Wolman, B. Chance: A philosophical study. *Tarbitz, Hebrew Univer. Quart.* (Hebrew), 1938, **10**, 56–80.

Wolman, B. Historical laws—do they exist? *Proceedings of the Tenth International Congress of Philosophy,* Amsterdam, 1948. (Abstr.)

Zeigarnik, B. Über das Behalten erledigter und unerledigter Handlungen. *Psychol. Forsch.,* 1927, **9**, 1–85.

Chapter 14. The Scientific Method

d'Abro, A. *The evolution of scientific thought from Newton to Einstein.* (2nd ed.) New York: Dover, 1950.

Andrews, T. G. (Ed.) *Methods of psychology.* New York: Wiley, 1948.

Bergmann, G. The logic of psychological concepts. *Phil. Sci.,* 1951, **18**, 93–110.

Bergmann, G., & Spence, K. Operationism and theory in psychology. *Psychol. Rev.*, 1941, **48**, 1–14.

Bertalanffy, L. von. Theoretical models in biology and psychology. *J. Pers.*, 1951, **20**, 24–38.

Boring, E. The role of theory in experimental psychology. *Amer. J. Psychol.*, 1953, **66**, 169–184.

Bridgman, P. W. *The logic of modern physics.* New York: Macmillan, 1927.

Bridgman, P. Some general principles of operational analysis. *Psychol. Rev.*, 1945, **52**, 246–249.

Brunswik, E. *The conceptual framework of psychology.* Chicago: Univer. of Chicago Press, 1952.

Cohen, M. *Reason and nature.* New York: Harcourt, Brace, 1931.

Cohen, M. R., & Nagel, E. *An introduction to logic and scientific method.* New York: Harcourt, Brace, 1934.

Dallenbach, K. M. The place of theory in science. *Psychol. Rev.*, 1953, **60**, 33–39.

Einstein, A., & Infeld, L. *The evolution of physics.* New York: Simon & Schuster, 1942.

Feigl, H., & Scriven, M. *Minnesota studies in the philosophy of science.* Minneapolis: Univer. of Minnesota Press, 1956–58. 2 vols.

Ferm, V. (Ed.) *A history of philosophical systems.* New York: Philosophical Library, 1950.

Höffding, H. *Modern philosophers.* New York: Macmillan, 1915.

Kotarbinski, T. *Elements of logic, epistemology, and methodology of science.* (Polish.) Warsaw: Atlas, 1929.

Laird, J. *Recent philosophy.* London: Methuen, 1936.

MacCorquodale, K., & Meehl, P. E. On a distinction between hypothetical constructs and intervening variables. *Psychol. Rev.*, 1948, **55**, 95–107.

Marx, M. (Ed.) *Psychological theory.* New York: Macmillan, 1951.

Nagel, E. *Logic without metaphysics.* Glencoe, Ill.: Free Press, 1956.

Peters, R. S. (Ed.) *Brett's history of psychology.* London: Allen & Unwin, 1951.

Poincaré, H. *The foundations of science.* New York: Science Press, 1913.

Pratt, C. C. *The logic of modern psychology.* New York: Macmillan, 1939.

Reichenbach, H. *Experience and prediction.* Chicago: Univer. of Chicago Press, 1938.

Russell, B. *Human knowledge, its scope and limits.* New York: Norton, 1948.

Russell, B., & Whitehead, A. N. *Principia Mathematica.* (2nd Ed.) Cambridge: Oxford Univer. Press, 1925–27. 2 vols.

Spence, K. W. The nature of theory construction in contemporary psychology. *Psychol. Rev.*, 1944, **51**, 47–68.

Stevens, S. S. Psychology and the science. *Psychol. Bull.*, 1939, **36**, 221–263.

Tarski, A. *Introduction to logic.* New York: Oxford Univer. Press, 1941.

Tolman, E. C. Operational behaviorism and current trends in psychology. *Proc. 25th Anniv. Celeb. Inaug. grad. Stud.* Los Angeles: Univer. of Southern California Press, 1936.

Whitehead, A. N. *Science and the modern world.* New York: Macmillan, 1925.

Wolman, B. B. Chance, a philosophical study. *Tarbitz, Hebrew Univer. Quart.* (Hebrew), 1938, **10**, 56–80.

Wolman, B. B. *Prolegomena to sociology.* (Hebrew.) Jerusalem: Kiryat Sefer, 1948.

Wolman, B. B. Scientific study of educational aims. *Teachers Coll. Rec.,* 1949, **50,** 471–481.

Wolman, B. B. The theory of history. *J. Phil.,* 1949, **46,** 342–351.

Woodworth, R. S., & Schlosberg, H. *Experimental psychology.* (Rev. ed.) New York: Holt, 1954.

Chapter 15. Some Crucial Questions and Tentative Answers

Andrews, T. G. *Methods of psychology.* New York: Wiley, 1948.

Baumgarten, F. *Les forces régulatrices de l'âme et la structure psychique.* Paris: Synthèse, 1958.

Cohen, M. *Reason and nature.* New York: Harcourt, Brace, 1931.

Dashiell, J. F. Some rapprochements in contemporary psychology. *Psychol. Bull.,* 1939, **36,** 1–24.

Dennis, E. (Ed.) *Current trends in psychological theory.* Pittsburgh: Univer. of Pittsburgh Press, 1951.

Deutsch, F. *On the mysterious leap from the mind to the body.* New York: International Universities Press, 1959.

Feigl, H., & Scriven, M. *Minnesota studies in the philosophy of science.* Minneapolis: Univer. of Minnesota Press, 1956–58. 2 vols.

French, T. M. Interrelations between psychoanalysis and the experimental work of Pavlov. *Amer. J. Psychiat.,* 1933, **89,** 1165–1203.

Frenkel-Brunswik, E. Psychoanalysis and the unity of science. *Proc. Amer. Acad. Arts and Sciences,* 1954, **80,** 271–347.

Harlow, H. F., & Woolsey, C. N. Biological and biochemical bases of behavior. Madison: Univer. of Wisconsin Press, 1958.

Helson, H. (Ed.) *Theoretical foundations of psychology.* New York: Van Nostrand, 1951.

Jones, M. R. (Ed.) *Current theory and research in motivation.* Lincoln, Neb.: Univer. of Nebraska Symposium on Motivation, 1954–59. 5 vols.

Kantor, J. R. Current trends in psychological theory. *Psychol. Rev.,* 1941, **38,** 29–65.

Koch, S. (Ed.) *Psychology, a study of science.* New York: McGraw-Hill, 1958.

Krech, D. Notes toward a psychological theory. *J. Pers.,* 1949, **18,** 66–87.

Krech, D., & Klein, G. S. *Theoretical models and personality theory.* Durham, N. C.: Duke Univer. Press, 1952.

Marx, M. H. (Ed.) *Psychological theory: A source book.* New York: Macmillan, 1951.

Murphy, G. *Personality: A biosocial approach.* New York: Harper, 1947.

Reeves, J. W. *Body and mind in western thought.* Baltimore, Md.: Penguin, 1958.

Rosenzweig, S. Schools of psychology: A complementary pattern. *Phil. Sci.,* 1937, **4,** 96–106.

Smith, F. V. *The explanation of human behavior.* London: Constable, 1951.

Viand, G. *Les instincts.* Paris: Press Universitaire, 1959.

Wolman, B. B. Leadership and group dynamics. *J. soc. Psychol.*, 1956, **43**, 11–25.

Wolman, B. B. Exploration in latent schizophrenia. *Amer. J. Psychother.*, 1957, **11**, 560–588.

Wolman, B. B. Instrumental, mutual acceptance, and vectorial groups. *Acta Sociologica*, 1958, **3**, 19–27.

Wolman, B. B. Group psychotherapy in latent schizophrenia. *Int. J. Group Psychother.*, 1960 (in press).

Wolman, B. B. The impact of failure on group cohesiveness. *J. soc. Psychol.*, 1960, **51**, 409–418.

Zilboorg, H., & Henry, G. W. *History of medical psychology.* New York: Norton, 1941.

Index of Names

Abraham, K., 232, 234, 263, 264, 266, 330, 383, 541
Ach, N., 406, 426, 427
Adams, K. D., 97, 140
Adler, A., 3, 20, 64, 82, 279, 283–298, 299, 300, 301, 318, 325, 329, 337, 351, 352, 364, 369, 379, 386, 410, 490, 535
Agar, W. E., 180
Alexander, F., 328, 329–330, 386
Allport, F. H., 441, 442, 492
Allport, G. W., 184, 406, 410, 417–421, 508, 519
Angell, J. R., 28–29, 32, 194
Ansbacher, H. L. and Rowena R., 284, 286
Arieti, S., 189
Aristotle, 32, 448, 449, 461, 482, 493, 502
Arnold, W. J., 122

Bacon, F., 126, 201, 505, 552
Bain, A., 6, 33, 391, 399, 422
Balakschina, V. L., 73
Barker, R. G., 341, 474
Bateson, G., 331
Beaunis, H., 424
Bekhterev, V. M., 62, 63, 64–67, 68, 69, 76, 78, 82, 84, 88, 89, 174, 195, 531, 550
Bell, C., 8
Benedict, Ruth, 345
Bergmann, H., 526
Bergson, H., 300
Bernheim, H., 213, 214
Bertocci, P., 420
Betlheim, 338
Binet, A., 17, 40, 410, 424–425, 427, 492, 506, 550
Blodgett, H. C., 147
Boring, E. C., 4
Braid, J., 213
Brand, H., 341
Brentano, F., 12, 397, 398, 404, 407, 415, 424, 428, 431, 491
Brett, G. S., 68, 395

Breuer, J., 18, 201, 214, 215
Brian, S., 74
Bridgman, P. W., 381, 504, 505, 507, 552
Brill, A. A., 222
Brown, J. F., 464, 483, 512
Brown, J. S., 125
Brunswik, E., 153
Büchner, L., 65, 70
Bühler, Charlotte, 503
Bühler, K., 165, 280, 414, 427–428, 492, 503
Burns, E., 69
Burt, C., 17, 410, 424
Bykov, K. M., 73–75, 89, 103, 157, 175, 195, 532, 533, 547, 550

Cannon, W. B., 43, 185, 370, 460, 472, 526
Carmichael, L., 469
Carnap, R., 106
Cartwright, D., 454
Cassirer, E., 396, 493
Charcot, J. M., 18, 201, 205, 213, 214, 391, 424, 425
Chernakov, E. T., 70, 71, 72
Claparède, E., 425
Cohen, H., 396
Cohen, M. R., 482, 510
Comte, A., 126, 399, 493, 498, 499, 524, 525
Copernicus, N., 405, 406, 506
Cowles, J. T., 153
Craig, W., 144
Culler, E., 51

Darwin, C., 8, 17, 21, 22, 33, 65, 178, 201, 240, 268, 284, 290, 391, 399, 500, 531, 543
Dembo, Tamara, 341, 434, 466, 467, 472, 474
Dennis, W., 447
Derner, G. F., 189
Descartes, R., 16, 83, 174, 368, 533

Dewey, J., 26–28, 30, 31, 34, 35, 76, 194, 196, 531, 550
Diderot, D., 65
Dilthey, W., 20, 42, 70, 174, 262, 284, 385, 391, 395, 399–406, 407, 408, 410, 411, 412, 447, 491, 492, 493, 499, 522, 530
Dingle, W., 525
Dollard, J., 125, 140, 165–170, 172, 173, 196, 340, 376, 543, 551
Doob, L. W., 168, 340
Driesch, H., 21, 22, 177
Duncker, K., 440
Dunlap, K., 145
Durkheim, E., 308
Dürr, E., 427

Ebbinghaus, H., 33, 396, 397, 407, 423, 503
Ehrenfels, C. von, 414, 428, 435
Einstein, A., 6, 138, 439, 499, 504, 525
Engels, F., 67, 69, 70, 72
Erikson, E. H., 345
Estes, W. K., 123, 137, 140
Euclid, 121, 451, 457, 483, 485, 500, 501

Fajans, Sara, 466, 467
Farrell, B. A., 341
Fechner, G. T., 10, 211, 430, 503, 546, 550
Federn, P., 228, 319
Feigl, H., 139, 447, 505, 516, 517, 519, 520
Fenichel, O., 200, 207, 245, 262, 281, 319, 383, 508, 536, 537, 542
Ferenczi, S., 327–329, 330, 386
Flourens, P., 9, 391
Flugel, J. C., 4
Ford, C. S., 168
Frank, T. D., 467
Franz, S. I., 89, 90, 532, 533
French, J. R. P., 477
French, T., 328
Freud, Anna, 293, 319, 327, 341, 383, 544
Freud, S., 3, 4, 18, 19, 20, 21, 22, 27, 33, 42, 43, 62, 64, 84, 87, 137, 139, 140, 145, 155, 156, 157, 165, 168, 169, 171, 173, 174, 181, 185, 186, 190, 199–282, 283, 285, 286, 287, 288, 289, 290, 291, 293, 294, 296, 297, 298, 299, 300, 301, 302, 306, 311, 317, 318, 319, 320, 321, 323, 324, 325, 326, 327, 328, 329, 330, 331, 332, 336, 337, 338, 339, 340, 341, 342, 343, 344, 345, 346, 347, 348, 349, 350, 351, 352, 354, 355, 356, 357, 358, 361, 362, 363, 365, 366, 367, 368, 369, 370, 372, 374, 376, 377, 379, 382, 383,

384, 385, 386, 387, 391, 399, 414, 424, 465, 471, 481, 490, 506, 508, 517, 519, 520, 521, 522, 525, 526, 527, 531, 532, 533, 535, 536, 541, 542, 543, 544, 546, 549, 550, 551, 553
Fritsch, G., 52
Fromm, E., 298, 329, 332, 337, 344, 345, 346, 355–368, 383, 387, 410
Fromm-Reichmann, Frieda, 381

Galileo, G., 448, 449, 458, 490, 493
Galton, F., 21, 22, 178
Gantt, W. H., 73
Gesell, A., 240, 348, 503, 527, 550
Girden, E., 63, 157
Glover, E., 319, 383
Goldstein, K., 3, 93, 95, 177, 184–190, 193, 196, 199, 279, 285, 370, 414, 428, 460, 503, 506, 517, 520, 521, 522, 524, 525, 526, 535, 546, 553
Gould, R., 467
Gottschaldt, K., 438, 439
Guthrie, E. R., 19, 35, 62, 98–104, 113, 140, 156, 160, 170, 175, 195, 280, 504, 513

Haeckel, E., 225, 226, 240, 242
Hall, S., 503
Halverson, H. M., 341
Hamilton, J. A., 339
Harrower, M. R., 440
Hartley, D., 6, 33, 391, 399
Hartley, E. L., 478
Hartmann, H., 319, 338
Hebb, D. O., 93–97, 175, 190, 195, 503, 531, 533
Hegel, G. W. F., 70, 275, 276, 301, 356, 532, 536
Heidbreder, Edna, 3, 516
Helmholtz, H. von, 11
Helvetius, C. A., 65
Hempel, C. G., 499
Henry, G. W., 213
Heraclitus, 490
Herbart, J. F., 6–7, 13, 33, 65, 282, 395, 529
Herodotus, 301
Hesse, Mary, 507
Hilgard, E. R., 91, 103, 140, 165, 343
Hippocrates, 61, 295, 296
Hitzig, E., 52
Hodges, H. A., 396, 399, 401, 402, 404
Holbach, P. d', 65
Holt, E. B., 86, 87, 195
Honzik, C. M., 153
Hook, S., 68
Hoppe, F., 467
Horney, Karen, 4, 20, 62, 279, 290, 294,

298, 329, 332, 337, 344, 345, 346–355, 367, 368, 383, 387, 410
Horton, G. P., 100
Hovland, C. I., 123, 125, 168
Hull, C. L., 3, 4, 19, 28, 34, 54, 62, 87, 91, 105–125, 140, 154, 155, 156, 157, 158, 161, 166, 167, 171, 173, 175, 176, 184, 190, 195, 196, 279, 280, 282, 481, 511, 516, 519, 522, 531, 550, 551
Hume, D., 6, 83, 104, 106, 392, 399, 400, 403, 404, 411, 487, 502, 505, 524
Humphrey, G., 427, 440
Hunt, J. McV., 100, 339
Hunter, W. S., 87–88, 195
Husserl, E., 20, 397–398, 399, 400, 404, 405, 406, 408, 411, 414, 415, 429, 491
Huxley, T., 21, 22, 573

Isaacs, Suzanne, 342, 503

Jaensch, E. R., 376
James, W., 10, 23–25, 26, 30, 31, 34, 35, 76, 194, 196, 499, 508, 509, 530
Janet, P., 18, 87, 213, 391, 424, 425
Jones, E., 200, 319, 383
Jung, C. G., 3, 20, 283, 298–317, 318, 325, 329, 337, 386, 508, 518, 548

Kant, I., 13, 20, 70, 86, 88, 273, 275, 300, 380, 391–395, 396, 397, 398, 399, 400, 401, 404, 405, 406, 408, 412, 423, 429, 491, 493, 499, 502, 505, 507
Kantor, J. R., 191–193, 196, 531
Kardiner, A., 20, 332–336, 337, 344, 345, 348, 357, 386, 387, 551
Karsten, Anitra, 466, 470, 472
Katz, D., 436
Keller, F. S., 133
Kelson, H., 524
Kempf, E. J., 145, 146
Kempthorne, O., 512
Kepler, J., 506
Kerékjártó, B. von, 451
Kerenyi, K., 304, 308, 309
Kessen, M. L., 168, 176
Kimble, G. A., 112, 125
Klein, G. S., 515
Klein, Melanie, 326–327, 329, 386
Klineberg, O., xii
Koch, H. L., 342
Koch, S., 123, 124, 140
Koffka, K., 140, 433–442, 471, 492
Köhler, W., 3, 91, 93, 94, 140, 149, 151, 429–442, 492, 503, 512, 521, 522, 526
Konradi, G. P., 73
Kornilov, K. N., 68 ·
Korsakoff, S. S., 338
Kotarbinski, T., 501

Krasnogorski, N. I., 78
Krechevsky, I., 91, 339
Kretschmer, E., 508
Kris, E., 319
Krueger, F. E., 414
Kuhlmann, F., 17
Külpe, O., 20, 415, 426, 427, 492
Kuo, Z. Y., 77, 180

La Mettrie, J. O., 65, 83
Lamarck, J. B. P. A. de, 21, 22, 179
Lange, C. G., 25
Lange, F. A., 65
Laplace, P. S. de, 506
Lashley, K. S., 88–93, 164, 195, 414, 503, 522, 525, 531, 533
Le Bon, G., 269
Leeper, R. W., 155
Lenin, W. I., 67, 68–70, 72
Leontyev, A. N., 70
Levy, D. M., 341
Lévy-Bruhl, L., 308
Lewin, K., 3, 4, 21, 59, 64, 97, 105, 124, 140, 143, 154, 155, 156, 193, 207, 279, 282, 293, 294, 296, 341, 345, 368, 374, 378, 379, 380, 387, 391, 396, 406, 410, 415, 417, 420, 433, 434, 443–490, 491, 493, 503, 512, 516, 519, 520, 529
Liebault, A., 18, 213
Linton, R., 332, 335, 344, 345
Lippitt, R., 477, 514
Lissner, K., 465, 466
Locke, J., 6, 392, 399
Loeb, J., 17, 535
Loewenstein, R., 319
London, I. D., 67, 68
Lorand, S., 200
Lorentz, K., 543
Luria, A. R., 70, 75, 195

MacCall, Sylvia H., 468
MacCorquodale, K., 123, 140, 519
McDougall, W., 4, 19, 31, 32, 35, 118, 140, 144, 155, 177–184, 187, 285, 418, 421, 428, 450, 509, 519, 551
McGeoch, J. A., 29
Mach, E., 126, 158, 396, 429, 431, 505, 520
Magendie, F., 8
Maier, N. R. F., 440
Malinowski, B., 330
Marx, K., 43, 62, 67, 68–70, 72, 73, 74, 195, 275, 331, 356
Marx, M., 107, 141
Mateer, Florence, 78
Mayer, A., 426
Mead, G. H., 307, 346, 368, 378
Mead, Margaret, 331, 345

Meehl, P. E., 123, 140, 519
Meinong, A., 397
Melton, A. W., 29
Mendel, G., 519
Mendelyeev, D. I., 138
Mesmer, A., 212, 213
Mettler, F. A., 51
Meumann, E., 17, 396
Meyer, A., 191, 368
Michotte, A., 425
Mill, J., 6, 422
Mill, J. S., 6, 126, 201, 399, 400, 422, 487, 505, 552
Miller, N. E., 125, 140, 165–170, 172, 173, 176, 196, 340, 551
Moleschott, J., 65, 70
Moreno, J. L., 307
Morgan, C. L., 18
Mowrer, O. H., 125, 166, 168, 170–172, 173, 196, 342, 343, 551
Mueller, C. G., Jr., 123, 140
Mullahy, P., 366, 378
Müller, G. E., 425, 426, 436
Müller, J., 8, 9
Murchison, C., 3, 88, 241, 284, 298, 425
Murphy, G., 4, 87, 200, 212, 319, 346, 427, 443, 444, 472, 485, 546, 548, 549, 551, 553
Murphy, Lois, 346

Nagel, E., 516
Natorp, P., 396
Newcomb, T., 346, 478
Newton, I., 6, 458, 499, 506, 525, 531
Nissen, H. W., 153

O'Kelly, L. I., 339
Orth, J., 426
Ostwald, W., 520
Ovsiankina, Maria, 465

Parsons, T., 172
Pauli, W., 300
Pavlov, I. P., 3, 4, 19, 21, 33, 34, 37, 42–64, 66, 69, 70, 71, 72, 73, 75, 76, 78, 86, 87, 89, 91, 92, 93, 94, 98, 99, 101, 103, 104, 108, 113, 118, 121, 124, 131, 132, 140, 143, 147, 155, 156, 157, 159, 160, 162, 164, 171, 173, 174, 175, 176, 185, 190, 194, 195, 196, 199, 279, 280, 296, 342, 385, 391, 395, 399, 414, 423, 437, 503, 506, 519, 521, 522, 525, 526, 531, 532, 533, 535, 538, 543, 546, 549, 551, 553
Peters, R. S., 68
Piaget, J., 240, 248, 274, 348, 373, 425, 503, 506, 527, 550
Pierce, C. S., 26, 505

Pieri, M., 123, 124
Pieron, H., 425
Piotrowski, Z., 189, 338
Planck, M., 526
Plato, 209, 502, 533
Poincaré, H., 106, 502, 510, 516
Pratt, Carrol, 521
Pshonik, A. T., 74

Rank, O., 319–325, 386, 518
Rapaport, D., 200
Razran, G., 19, 63, 67, 72, 91, 156–165, 171, 175, 176, 196, 441, 509, 546, 551
Reich, W., 263, 319, 331–332, 386
Reichenbach, H., 524
Ribot, T., 424, 425
Rickert, H., 396
Riemann, G. F. B., 457, 485
Roback, A. A., 30
Robinson, E. S., 29–30
Roby, T. B., 103, 176
Roheim, G., 334
Rorschach, H., 84, 506, 550
Rubin, E., 436
Rubinstein, S. L., 71–72
Runes, D. D., 395
Russell, B., 394, 395, 450, 501

Sargent, S. S., 344, 356
Schjelderup-Ebbe, T., 543
Schlick, M., 106, 500
Schoenfeld, W. N., 123, 133, 140
Schopenhauer, A., 13, 229, 394, 395, 505
Schrötter, K., 338
Scriven, M., 139
Sears, R. R., 168, 172–173, 196, 339, 340, 341, 346, 387, 541
Sechenov, I. M., 71, 194, 391, 533
Seward, J. P., 41, 103, 166
Sheffield, F. D., 103, 166, 176
Sheldon, W. H., 508
Sherrington, C. S., 45, 90, 92, 102, 533, 546
Shils, E. A., 172
Simon, T., 17, 424, 425
Skinner, B. F., 3, 4, 19, 34, 54, 91, 118, 122, 125–139, 143, 155, 156, 157, 158, 162, 171, 175, 176, 196, 199, 280, 381, 504, 513, 531, 546, 551
Smirnov, K. M., 195
Smith, F. V., 32, 180, 184, 550
Smith, M., 344, 356
Sollenberger, R. T., 168
Spearman, C. E., 17
Spence, K. W., 125, 140, 167, 469, 490, 526
Spencer, H., 22, 33, 35, 201, 229, 399, 536

Spinoza, B., 190, 487
Spranger, E., 70, 174, 195, 262, 293, 391, 395, 406, 407–410, 414, 491, 492, 493, 508, 551
Stern, W., 4, 17, 20, 21, 40, 71, 280, 355, 368, 391, 395, 406, 410–417, 419, 424, 428, 448, 471, 491, 492, 493, 503
Stevens, S. S., 140, 156, 505, 506, 512, 552
Stout, G. F., 423–424
Strachey, J., 224
Sullivan, H. S., 4, 20, 172, 278, 290, 292, 298, 321, 337, 344, 346, 351, 363, 368–383, 387, 475, 505, 508, 519, 551
Sully, J., 16

Taine, H., 424
Terman, L. M., 17, 410
Thompson, Clara, 278, 298, 315, 345
Thorndike, E. L., 4, 17, 21, 27, 32–41, 53, 54, 64, 78, 79, 81, 89, 90, 99, 100, 101, 103, 112, 118, 119, 122, 132, 140, 143, 147, 149, 155, 156, 157, 162, 168, 174, 176, 280, 423, 437, 513, 546, 550
Titchener, E. B., 14–16, 17, 18, 20, 24, 30, 31, 32, 194, 423, 441, 522, 530, 550
Tolman, E. C., 3, 19, 28, 32, 34, 40, 54, 91, 123, 140–156, 157, 164, 175, 184, 196, 279, 280, 285, 428, 444, 504, 518, 519, 531, 550, 551
Tschachotine, S., 157
Tschernigowski, W. N., 73

Ukhtomski, A. A., 160, 546

Vaihinger, H., 286
Vernon, P. E., 421, 508
Verplanck, W. S., 123, 140
Voeks, V. W., 104
Vogt, K. C., 65, 70
Voltaire, F., 399

Voskresensky, L. N., 57
Vygotskii, L. S., 70

Wallace, A. R., 178
Ward, J., 423, 493
Warden, C. J., 141
Watson, J. B., 19, 27, 32, 34, 35, 62, 63, 66, 76–85, 86, 87, 88, 89, 91, 92, 93, 94, 96, 97, 118, 135, 139, 140, 155, 173, 174, 178, 190, 195, 196, 199, 280, 368, 380, 423, 490, 517, 518, 519, 550, 551
Watt, H. J., 426, 427
Weber, E. H., 8, 9, 10, 503, 550
Weiss, A. P., 85–86, 93, 195
Weissmann, A., 22
Wertheimer, M., 4, 345, 391, 406, 428, 435–442, 493, 519
White, R. K., 514
Windelband, W., 20, 21, 284, 295, 386, 396, 397, 400, 417, 447, 483, 493, 509
Wittgenstein, R., 106
Wolman, B. B., 6, 62, 65, 189, 203, 205, 228, 259, 275, 281, 410, 477, 487, 497–551
Woodworth, R. S., 3, 30–32, 53, 140, 194, 200, 427, 441, 518
Wortis, J., 60, 63
Wulf, F., 438
Wundt, W., 11–14, 15, 16, 17, 18, 20, 24, 194, 396, 397, 407, 414, 423, 428, 441, 503, 530, 550

Yamaguchi, H. G., 125
Yenchman, 67, 82
Yerkes, R. M., 17, 76, 437
Youtz, R. P., 339

Zeigarnik, Bluma, 341, 464, 465, 468
Zeller, A. F., 340, 341
Zener, K. E., 140
Zilboorg, G., 213

Index of Subjects

Abstract and concrete behavior (Goldstein), 187, 188
Act and content in psychology, 12, 397, 404, 405, 415, 424
Adjustment, Angell, 28
  Carr, 29
  Darwin, 23
  Dewey, 26
  James, 23
  Spencer, 22
Affect, affection, see Emotion
Aggression, Adler, 268, 287
  Dollard and Miller, 167, 168, 340
  Doob and Sears, 340
  Freud, 228–233, 268–271, 276, 277, 281, 543, 544
  Klein, 326
  Pavlov, 58, 543
  Wolman, 542–545
Alchemy (Jung), 309, 310
Analytic psychology, 298–317
  archetypes, 308, 309
  complexes, 306–308
  conscious, unconscious, 303–315
  dream interpretation, 304–308
  libido, 300–303
  method of research, 298–300, 315–317
  personality types, 311–314
  religion, 315
  self, 309–311
Analyzers (Pavlov), 44, 45, 74
Anthroponomy (Hunter), 87
Antigone principle (Wolman), 547, 548
Anxiety, Freud, 252–254
  Horney, 350
  Skinner, 136
  Sullivan, 370–372
Apperception, Herbart, 7
  Titchener, 14
  Wundt, 13
Archetypes and complexes (Jung), 306–309
Assembly of neurons (Hebb), 94

Associationism, Aristotle, 32
  Bain, 6, 33, 422
  Guthrie, 100
  Hartley, 6, 33
  Herbart, 7, 33
  James, 25, 422
  Mill, J. S., 6
  Pavlov, 64
  Spencer, 22
  Wundt, 13
Attention (Titchener), 14

Behaviorism, background, 19, 20
  criticism of, 83–85
  Holt, 86, 87
  Hunter, 87, 88
  Lashley, 88–93
  methodological, 84
  principles, 76
  Skinner, 125–139
  Tolman, 140–155
  Watson, 76–84
  Weiss, 85–86
Biology in relation to psychology, 21, 22, 23, 28, 85, 86, 107, 108, 129, 200, 201, 348
Biosocial approach, Murphy, 548, 549
  Weiss, 86
Birth trauma (Rank), 319, 320
Body-soul dichotomy, see Soma-psyche

Causation, Adler, 285, 286, 297
  Freud, 204, 205
  Guthrie, 104
  Jung, 300
  Lewin, 461, 462, 487, 488, 489
  Pavlov, 43
  Skinner, 126, 127
  Wolman, 523–526
Character, theory of (Reich), 331, 332
Character types, see Typology
Child development, Adler, 290–293
  Freud, 230–241
  Fromm, 361–362

Child development (*Continued*)
  Jung, 311
  Klein, 326, 327
  Lewin, 473, 474
  Rank, 320, 321
  Sullivan, 375–377
Classification as a scientific method, Aristotle, 448, 449
  Galileo, 448–450
  Lewin, 448–450, 481–483
  Wolman, 507–509
Classification of sciences, 498, 499
Clinical method, 337, 338, 515
Conditioning, association, 55
  background, 19
  Bekhterev, 65, 66
  Bykov, 73, 74
  concentration, 45, 46
  and connectionism, 64
  contiguity, 98, 100–102
  configural, 163, 164
  and decortication, 51
  delayed, 51, 101, 105
  discrimination, 52, 65, 89
  drive reduction, 108, 112–114, 122
  excitation, 45, 46, 48, 53, 54, 65
  extinction, 55, 101, 105, 120
  evolutionary levels of, 159–165
  generalization, 52, 65, 89, 117, 118, 168
  Guthrie, 98–104
  higher order, 51
  Hull, 111–124
  induction, 45, 54
  inhibition, 45–48, 53–56, 65, 101, 113, 116, 118
  inner organs of, 73, 74
  irradiation, 45
  Lashley, 89, 92
  Pavlov, 50–57
  pleasure and pain, 54, 73, 74, 176
  principles of, 41–43
  and psychoanalysis, 165–173
  Razran, 159–165
  reinforcement, 53, 101–104, 108, 112–119, 132–134, 162, 168
  reflex, conditioned, definition of, 50
  reward, 53, 102, 103, 162
  Skinner, 131–137
  symbolic, 66
  Tolman, 147, 148, 149, 151
  Watson, 78, 79
        See also Learning theory; Reflex
Connectionism (Thorndike), 32–41
Consciousness (conscious), Adler, 291–292, 298
  Bekhterev, 66
  Freud, 216, 217
  Jung, 300, 303, 304

James, 24
Marx and Engels, 68, 69
Pavlov, 59
Rubinstein, 71, 72
Sullivan, 374
Titchener, 15
Watson, 76, 77, 80
Wundt, 13
Contiguity, Guthrie, 100–104
  James, 25
  Mill, J. S., 6
  Razran, 160, 161
Conventionalism (Poincaré), 106
Cultural sciences, Adler, 284
  Dilthey, 401, 405
  Freud, 266–277, 278
  Fromm, 355–361, 365–368
  Jung, 308–310, 314–317
  Kardiner and Linton, 332–336
  Malinowski, 330
  Marxism, 70–72
  Rank, 322, 324
  Spranger, 21
  Stern, 21
  Windelband, 20, 390, 400
  Wundt, 12

Death instinct, Freud, 228–230, 270, 271, 276, 281
  Wolman, 535–540
        See also Aggression
Deductive method, Hull, 105, 106
  Razran, 158
  Wolman, 516, 517, 518
Descriptive method, Dilthey, 20, 401–404, 408
  Skinner, 126
  Titchener, 14
  Wolman, 499
Determining tendency (Ach), 426, 427
Dream interpretation, Freud, 217–221
  Jung, 304–308
Drives, Freud (instinctual drives), 222–230
  Hull, 113, 114
  Skinner, 134, 135
  Stern, 415
  Watson, 78
  Woodworth, 31
  Wolman (instinctual drives), 535–545
        See also Instincts
Dynamic psychology (Woodworth), 30–32

Ego, Freud, 244–257
  Jung, 304, 311
Emotion, Adler, 294
  Darwin, 17, 23

Hebb, 96
James-Lange, 25
McDougall, 182, 183
Rank, 320
Skinner, 135–137
Stern, 416
Titchener, 14
Watson, 80, 81
Wundt, 13
Empathy (Sullivan), 370, 371
Empiricism, Freud, 200, 201, 274, 275
Guthrie, 98, 99
Hull, 105
James, 23
Razran, 157, 158
Skinner, 127, 138
Wolman, 501–507
Energy (energetism), Bekhterev, 65–67
Freud, 207–211
Jung, 301–303
Pavlov, 43
Entelechy, 177
Entropy (Jung), 302
Epistemology, Dilthey, 400
Freud, 202
Holt, 86
James, 23
Kant, 392–395
Wolman, 499–501
Equilibrium, constancy (Freud), 209, 210
equilibration (Goldstein), 185, 186
equilibrium (Lewin), 462–464
equilibrium (Pavlov), 43–44
homeostasis (Cannon), 43
Equipotentiality (Lashley), 90
Ethics, Dewey, 26
Freud, 259, 260, 273, 274, 276
Fromm, 365, 366
Evolution theory, 8, 21, 22, 24, 28
Experience as subject matter of psychology, Dilthey, 399, 402, 403
Husserl, 397, 398, 406
Rubinstein, 71, 72
Spranger, 408
Stern, 413, 414
Sully, 16
Titchener, 14
Wundt, 12
Experimental method, Dilthey, 401, 402
Fechner, 10
Helmholtz, 11
Hull, 122, 123
and psychoanalysis, 337–343
Skinner, 127
Stern, 412
Titchener, 15
Wolman, 512–516

Wundt, 11–14, 20
Explanation and explanatory method, Dilthey, 401–404
Skinner, 126
Spranger, 408
Titchener, 14

Feeling, *see* Emotion
Field theory, 443–490
causation, 461, 462, 487
force, 458–460
genotype, 449
hodological space, 456, 457
idiophenomena, 447–450
learning, 468–470
level of aspiration, 467
mathematics, 445, 450–456, 485–487
personality, 470–475
psychological field, 453–456
social psychology, 475–480
theory construction, 444–447, 481–490
topology, 451–456
Figure and ground, Goldstein, 188, 189
Hebb, 94
Köhler, 436
Rubin, 436
Stern, 414
Force, Herbart, 7
Lewin, 458–461, 462–466
Functionalism, Angell, 28, 29
background, 19, 21–23
Binet, 424, 425
Bühler, 427, 428
Carr, 29, 30
Dewey, 26–28
James, 23–25
Robinson, 29, 30
Stout, 423, 424
Ward, 423

Gestalt, vs. associationism, 425–429
field, 433, 434
isomorphism, 433
laws of, 429, 431, 435, 436
learning, 436–439
mathematics, 430
perception, 435, 436, 437, 441
thinking, 439, 440
Group dynamics, Freud, 268–270
Lewin, 475–480
Wolman, 541, 542

Habit, Dewey, 27
Hull, 109, 112–115
James, 25
Watson, 78
Heredity, 21, 22, 23, 146, 179, 180, 308

History and psychology, Dilthey, 400, 401, 405
    Freud, 268–271, 275, 276
    Fromm, 355–357, 359–361, 367, 368
    Jung, 314, 315
    Wolman, 500, 509
    Wundt, 13, 20
History of psychology, 4–33, 391–406, 422–428, 549, 550
Horme (McDougall), 179
Hypnotism, 18, 213, 214
Hypotheses in theory formation, Dewey, 28
    Freud, 203
    Skinner, 126
    Stevens, 506
    Wolman, 517–520
Hypothetico-deductive method (Hull), 105–107
Hysteria, 61, 253

Idiophenomena, 20, 21, 284, 396, 417, 447, 448, 509, 510, 511
Individual differences, Hull, 121
    Stern, 412, 416
Individual psychology, 283–298
    aggression, 286, 287
    causation, 285, 286
    inferiority, 287
    purposivism, 285, 286
    sociability, 289
    style of life, 292–295
    typology, 295–296
Inductive method, Pavlov, 45, 46
    Razran, 157, 158
    Skinner, 126
    Wolman, 516, 517
Inhibitory potential (Hull), 116
Insight, 436–439
Instincts, Dewey, 27
    Ferenczi, 327–329
    Freud, 222–230
    James, 25
    McDougall, 180–183
    Pavlov, 48, 49, 57, 58
    Spencer, 22
    Wolman, 535–545
    Woodworth, 31
Instrumental, mutual acceptance, and vectorial groups (Wolman), 541, 542
Instrumentalism (Dewey), 26
Intelligence, Binet and Simon, 17
    Dewey, 27
    Stern, 414
    Thorndike, 39–40
Intelligence tests, *see* Mental tests
Interoceptors, 74

Introspection, Angell, 28
    criticism of, 15–20
    Titchener, 14, 15
    Wolman, 503
    Wundt, 12, 15
Introversion and extraversion (Jung), 312–314
Irrationality as a method, 298, 299, 300

Kant's influence upon psychology, 392–395, 396, 397, 398, 399, 400, 404, 405, 406, 412

Laws of behavior (Skinner), 129–131
Laws of nature, Windelband, 447
    Wolman, 526
Laws of science, Freud, 204, 207
    Guthrie, 98, 99
    Lewin, 448–450
    Wolman, 497–499
Leadership, Freud, 269, 270
    Lewin, 477, 478
Learning theory, criticism of, 173–176
    Dewey, 27
    Dollard and Miller, 166–170
    Gestalt, 436–439
    Guthrie, 99–102
    Hebb, 95
    Holt, 87
    Hull, 108–125
    Lashley, 90–91
    Lewin, 468–470
    Mowrer, 170
    Pavlov, 50–57
    Razran, 159–164
    Robinson, 30
    Skinner, 131–137
    Thorndike, 34–39
    Tolman, 146–155
    Watson, 78, 79
Libido, Freud, 207, 208, 224–228
    Jung, 300–303
Life instinct, Freud, 222–228
    Goldstein, 185–188
    Pavlov, 57, 58, 63, 64
    Wolman, 535, 540
Logical positivism, 106, 202

Manic-depressive (cyclic, affective) psychosis, 61, 259
Marxism, 67–72
Mass-action (Lashley), 89, 90
Materialism, dialectic, 67–70
    metaphysical, 6
    naïve, 64–67
    Pavlov, 42, 43
Mathematics, Gestalt, 430
    Hull, 105–107, 124

Kant, 393
Lewin, 445, 450–456, 485–487
Russell, 394
Stevens, 511, 512
Wolman, 511, 512, 528, 529
Mental faculties, 5
Mental philosophy, 5, 11
Mental tests, 17, 23, 40
Metaphysics, 5, 6, 7, 11
Metapsychology, 260–262
Modalities of life (Stern), 413, 414
Molar vs. molecular, Binet, 424
Dewey, 28
Hull, 109, 110, 124, 125
Kantor, 191
Spranger, 407
Stern, 411
Thorndike, 38
Tolman, 142
Watson, 83
Wolman, 520
Motivation, Allport, 418, 419
Carr, 29
Guthrie, 102
Hebb, 95, 96
Hull, 112–118
Tolman, 144–146, 154
Wolman, 176, 535–548
Woodworth, 31, 32

Neo-Kantians, 394–398
Nervous system, analyzers, 44, 45
conduction, 8–11
Gestalt theory on, 431–433
Hebb, 94, 95
Hull, 109, 111
Lashley, 89–91
localization theory, 9, 48, 89, 90, 189
Pavlov, 44–48, 62, 63
Thorndike, 33, 34, 38
Watson, 78, 79
Neurasthenia, 61
Neurosis, 59, 60, 171, 222, 253, 270, 322, 352, 353

Omnipotence (Ferenczi), 327
Operant and respondent behavior, 131, 132
Operationism, Bridgman, 504, 505, 507
Dewey, 28
Skinner, 125–127
Stevens, 505, 506
Tolman, 140, 141
Wolman, 504–507

Perception, Dilthey, 399
Freud, 247–249, 278
Gestalt, 438, 439

Herbart, 6, 7
Hunter, 88
Müller, J., 8
Rubinstein, 71, 72
Watson, 79
Personality theories, Adler, 292–296
Allport, 419–421
Freud, 241–265
Fromm, 362–365
Horney, 351, 352
James, 24, 25
Jung, 309–314
Kardiner, 332–334
Lewin, 470–475
Murphy, 548, 549
Pavlov, 57–61
Stern, 416, 417
Watson, 81, 82
Phenomenology, 397, 398, 400, 429
Physics, Hebb, 96, 97
Lewin, 443, 449
Physiology in relation to psychology, Hull, 109, 110, 124
Kantor, 193
Pavlov, 42–44, 62–64
Titchener, 14
Watson, 82–85
Pleasure and pain, Freud, 210–212, 243, 244, 279, 280
Hebb, 96
Horney, 349, 350
James, 25
Mowrer, 171
Pshonik, 74
Thorndike, 35
Wolman, 546–548
Pleasure principle, 171, 226, 243, 342, 343
Postulates, Freud, 204–212
Hull, 111–121
Pragmatism, 23, 25
Problem solving, Carr, 29
Dewey, 28
Skinner, 138
Wertheimer, 439, 440
Psychoanalysis, 199–282
anxiety, 252–254
catharsis, 214
cathexis, 223, 227
causation, 204, 205
conscious, preconscious, unconscious, 214–222
constancy principle, 209, 279
defense mechanisms, 254–256
dream interpretation, 217–221
education, 276, 277
and experimental studies, 338–343
fixation, 240

Psychoanalysis (*Continued*)
 instincts, 222–230; death, 228–230,
  268–271, 277, 281; life, 227, 228;
  self-preservation, 226, 227; sexual,
  224–226
 interpretation of history and culture,
  266–276
 metapsychology, 260–262
 methods of research, 199–212, 274,
  275, 281, 282
 narcissism, 227, 228
 perception, 247–249
 personality, 241–265; character types,
  262–265; ego, 244–257; id, 243, 244;
  superego, 257–260
 pleasure, displeasure, 210, 211, 212,
  224–226, 279, 280
 pleasure principle, 171, 226, 243
 reality principle, 226, 246, 247
 religion, 271, 272, 273
 social psychology, 266–272
 stages of development, 230–241; anal,
  233, 234; latency, 238, 239; neonate, 230; oral, 230–233; phallic and
  Oedipus complex, 235–238; puberty,
  239, 240; urethral, 235
Psychological field, Koffka, 433, 434
 Lewin, 453–456
Psychophysical parallelism, 9–11
Purposivism, Adler, 285, 286
 Goldstein, 184–188
 McDougall, 177–184

Reactology (Kornilov), 68
Reale, das (Herbart), 6
Reality principle (Freud), 171, 246, 247
Reductionism, Alexander, 329, 330
 Bekhterev, 66, 67
 Flourens, 9
 Freud, 205–208
 Gestalt, 431–433
 Guthrie, 99
 Hebb, 97
 Herbart, 7
 Hull, 110, 124, 125
 James, 23
 Kantor, 191, 192
 Lashley, 92, 93
 Lewin, 447
 Marxism, 67–71
 McDougall, 178
 Morgan, 18
 Pavlov, 62, 63
 Razran, 159
 Skinner, 127, 128
 Spranger, 408
 Stern, 412, 413
 Sullivan, 369

Thorndike, 33
Titchener, 15
Tolman, 140
Watson, 80, 82, 83
Weiss, 85
Wolman, 520–523
Reflex, arc (Dewey), 8
 Bell, 8
 breath catching, 65
 food, 49
 guarding, 49, 58
 life, 49
 Skinner, 128–131
 Spencer, 22
 thermic, 50
 unconditioned (Pavlov), 47, 48, 49, 50
Religion, Freud, 271–273
 Fromm, 359, 360
 Jung, 303, 309, 310, 311, 315
 Rank, 323, 324

Safety and satisfaction (Horney), 349
Satisfaction and security (Sullivan), 360,
 370–372
Schizophrenia, 61, 259
Science and scientific method (Wolman),
 497–529
 causation, 523–526
 classification, 507–509
 deductive and inductive method, 516,
  517
 definition of, 497–499
 empiricism, observation, and operationism, 501–507
 experimental method, 512–516
 hypotheses, constructs, and variables,
  517–520
 language of, 527–529
 laws of nature, 526, 527
 mathematics, 511, 512, 528, 529
 reductionism, 520–523
 truth, scientific, 504–507
Self, James, 24
 Jung, 309
 Skinner, 137
 Sullivan, 378, 379
Self-actualization (Goldstein), 186, 187
Self-observation, *see* Introspection
Sign-gestalt (Tolman), 142–147, 149–155
Sleep, Freud, 217, 218, 230
 Hebb, 96
 Pavlov, 56, 57
 Wolman, 538, 539
Social psychology, Adler, 285–291
 Dollard and Miller, 167–170
 Freud, 266–272
 Fromm, 355–361, 366
 Jung, 308–309, 312–314

Kardiner and Linton, 332–336
Lewin, 475–480
Sears, 172, 173
Sullivan, 378–381
Wolman, 541–542
Soma-psyche dichotomy, Bekhterev, 65, 67
Descartes, 16
Holt, 88
James, 23
Jung, 301–303, 308
Lashley, 92, 93
Marxism, 69, 70, 71, 75
Pavlov, 42, 43, 63, 64
Razran, 159
Sherrington, 92
Stern, 412, 413
Sullivan, 379, 380
Wolman, 530–535
Wundt, 12
Speech, Bekhterev, 65
Freud, 249
Holt, 86
Pavlov, 59
Sullivan, 373
Watson, 80
Style of life (Adler), 291, 292
Structuralism, 14–15
Sublimation, Dewey, 27
Freud, 223

t factor (Hebb), 94
Temperaments, Adler, 295, 296
Hippocrates, 61, 295
Pavlov, 60, 61
Temporal maze (Hunter), 88
Theory formation, Adler, 297, 298
Bekhterev, 66, 67
Dilthey, 399, 401–404, 406
Freud, 199–212, 274, 275, 281, 282
Goldstein, 185, 190
Guthrie, 99, 103, 104
Hull, 105–107, 123–125
Jung, 298–300, 315–317
Lewin, 443–461, 481–490
McDougall, 177, 178, 183, 184
Rank, 324, 325
Razran, 156–158, 165
Skinner, 125–127, 138, 139
Sullivan, 368, 369, 381, 382
Tolman, 140–144, 155–156
Watson, 76, 77, 83–85
Wolman, 516–529
Thinking (thought), Binet, 425
Bühler, 427, 428
Dewey, 27, 28
Freud, 249
Skinner, 138

Watson, 80
Wertheimer, 439–441
Würzburg School, 425–427
Threshold initial and differential, 10
Transitionism (Wolman), 530–535
Trial and error, Pavlov, 64
Thorndike, 34, 39
Tropism, 17
Truth, immanent, 106, 500
Kant, 392, 393, 499
transcendent, 106, 500
Russell, 501
Wolman, 499–501
Typology (types of personality), Adler, 295, 296
Allport-Vernon, 421
Freud, 262–265
Fromm, 364, 365
Jung, 311–314
Lewin, 473, 474, 480
Pavlov, 60, 61
Rank, 321, 322
Spranger, 409, 410

Unconditioned reflex, *see* Reflex; Conditioning
Unconscious and preconscious, Adler, 291, 292
Freud, 215–222
Jung, 299, 303–309
Rubinstein, 71, 72
Sullivan, 374
"Understanding" psychology, 20, 21, 402–408

Valence, Lewin, 459, 460, 464, 466, 467
Tolman, 143, 145
Variables, dependent, 123, 127, 142, 518, 519
independent, 123, 127, 141, 142, 518, 519
intervening, 123, 143, 144, 518, 519, 520
Vector theory (Alexander), 329
Verbal report (Watson), 79
Viennese circle of logical positivists, 106, 500
See also Logical positivism
Vitalism (Driesch), 21, 22
Volition and will, Freud (ego), 250, 251
Rank (will), 319
Skinner (decision-making), 137
Wundt (volition), 13

Warsaw School of logicians, 500
Weber's law, 10
Will, *see* Volition and will
Würzburg School, 425–427